KT-483-060

PREFACE

This volume, devoted to the county of Hampshire and the Isle of Wight, lists existing brasses, indents and lost brasses, with illustrations of all figure brasses pre-dating 1700. In addition, selected inscriptions, later brasses, indents and lost brasses are also illustrated.

The format, alphabetical sequence and numbering established by Rev. Herbert Haines and Mill Stephenson in their respective lists of 1861 and 1926 have been followed. Entries for each church comprise (a) existing brasses listed by Mill Stephenson, numbered with his Roman 'M.S.' numbers'; (b) existing brasses not originally listed and reordered brasses, numbered with italicised Roman numerals; and (c) indents, lost brasses and lost indents, numbered with arabic numerals.

The starting point for each entry has been Mill Stephenson's description and in many cases this has not been altered. References in italics denote published illustrations which have been updated to include the many works produced since Stephenson's *List* appeared in 1926. The final section provides measurements, attribution of style and conservation details. Measurements taken from metal or from rubbings are given to the nearest millimetre. Where this has not been possible dimensions have been scaled from microfiche prints of rubbings in the collection of the Society of Antiquaries of London or converted from imperial measurements obtained from published sources and these are given to the nearest five millimetres. The entry for each church concludes with a list of source material. Several standard works on workshop attribution are included in the bibliography.

The ancient (pre-1832) county and parochial boundaries have been adopted as published by the Institute of Heraldic and Genealogical Studies. As in previous volumes, these boundaries substantially correspond to those prevailing at the time when Mill Stephenson compiled his *List*.

Grateful thanks are due to Patrick Farman, Peter Hacker, Jane Houghton and Janet Whitham who have visited innumerable churches and undertaken the arduous task of proof reading. Patrick Farman and Janet Whitham have also produced the majority of rubbings for illustration. Gratitude is also due to Sally Badham for the workshop attribution of many brasses and indents; to Jerome Bertram for the translation of numerous Latin inscriptions; and to Nancy Briggs for reviewing and contributing greatly to the introduction and bibliography.

Invaluable assistance has also been received from the following members of the Monumental Brass Society: David Barrick, Chris Byrom, Derrick Chivers, Peter Heseltine, Melvyn Paige-Hagg, David Parrott, Nicholas Rogers and John Titterton. Special thanks must also go to Suzanne Foster, Archivist at Winchester College.

Acknowledgement is also made to the Society of Antiquaries of London for permission to reproduce rubbings of brasses in their collection.

A work of this nature can never be totally accurate or complete and accordingly all corrections and additions are warmly welcomed.

March 2007

INTRODUCTION

Hampshire, surveyed from 2005 to 2007, is the fourteenth volume in the *County Series*. Stephenson's *List* records 210 brasses, of which seven were not found during the survey, with four additions dated prior to 1700. Those brasses not found were Alton 29, Bramshott 20 and 21, Colemore 2, Oakley Church 19, Southampton, Holy Rood 4 and Farleigh Wallop 7.

The county contains a number of brasses of national importance. The earliest are the fine and unusual, London A, half effigies commemorating Raulin Brocas and his sister, Margaret, c.1360, at Sherborne St. John I, while at King's Somborne I is a brass, probably to the memory of two brothers, c.1380. The brass at Ringwood I to John Prophete, 1416, is now considerably mutilated, but the figure shows an ecclesiastic in cope with saints on the orphreys. Series B brasses can be found at Crondall I, to the memory of Nicholas Kaerwent, rector, 1381, while Winchester, St. Cross I shows John de Campeden, 1382, in cope, as does the brass at Havant I, to Thomas Aileward, 1413. A fine London D brass at Thruxton I, engraved c.1425, commemorates Sir John Lysle, d.1407, in armour under triple canopy. Two distinctive series F brasses survive at Brown Candover I and Weeke I. The former is a unique plate showing a civilian and wife arm in arm, c.1490. At Weeke, the brass to William Complyn, d.1498, comprises a lengthy inscription and a fine figure of St. Christopher.

Other notable brasses include Eversley I, a cross of unique design, perhaps indicating the perpetual nature of life by the series of interlocking rings that form the cross. Colemore 2, dated 1541, imitates the marble architectural frames so often found on contemporary wall monuments. Crondall III shows a skeleton lying on a rolled mattress. The plate attributed to Francis Grigs, of London, was probably sent to Crondall where the name, John Eager, and date of death, 1641, appear to have been added. Fordingbridge I, engraved 1568, is similar in design to Cople VII, Bedfordshire, 1556; both to members of the Bulkeley family. The elaborate and intriguing brass formerly at Netley Abbey is supposed to have been found in a "poor man's house, where it served as a back to a grate, from which it was obtained for a moderate gratuity". The brass was presented in 1861 to the Surrey Archaeological Society by Rev. H. Burnaby Greene, of Longparish. It purports to commemorate members of the Compton family, on account of the fire beacons and scrolls that form the background to the plate, but opinion about which family it actually commemorates is divided. Headbourne Worthy I shows John Kent, [1434], a scholar of Winchester College. Nether Wallop I depicts Dame Mary Gore, prioress of Amesbury, 1436, which was probably rescued when the priory was suppressed. South Warnborough I shows Robert Whyte, engraved c.1490, in armour kneeling on one knee. Winchester, St. Cross IV depicts Richard Harward, 1493, in cap and almuce, whilst VI shows Thomas Lawne, 1518, in mass vestments. Children are portrayed in swaddling clothes at Winchester, St. Swithun-upon-Kingsgate *I*, 1612, and Odiham *IX*, 1636.

A small number of brasses have proved to be palimpsest. The earliest, found on the reverse of Odiham *VIII*, shows part of either an abbot or bishop holding the shaft of a crosier, c.1320, together with parts of a chasuble of another abbot or bishop, c.1520. At Southwick I, the effigies forming the memorial, 1548, to John White, have been appropriated and date from c.1520. The chamfer inscription is also palimpsest comprising a number of fragments. The reverse of Winchester College *XIV*, engraved c.1548, reveals a portion of a widow, c.1420. Winchester, St. Cross VII, 1551, contains two lines of drapery on the reverse. Yateley IV, 1578, has part of a civilian, c.1500, and worn fragments of a 14th/15th century Flemish border on the reverse.

Aldershot II, 1583, reveals part of a c.1405 macaronic inscription from the London D workshop. Dummer V, 1591, yields an earlier inscription to Robert Clerk, sometime chaplain of the chantry of Peter Fabiller, c.1470.

A small number of brasses show unique or unusual features. Alton IV, the brass to Christopher Walaston, 1563, combines the letter 'W' with a tun in the corners forming a rebus on his name. He is also described as a 'yostregere', a keeper of the goshawks or falconer. Crawley I, 1609, contains an engraver's error in the third line of the Latin inscription; the letters 'vt' in the word 'putantur' have been let into the plate on a separate piece of brass. Heckfield II, 1518, has a rebus on the deceased's name. Hinton Ampner II, 1601, contains an error, since St. Decumans is in the county of Somerset, not Devonshire, as stated on the brass. Kimpton I, 1522, incorporates a small cross showing the wounds of Christ. At Nursling I, the capital letters of lines 14 and 15 reveal the date of Andrew Munday's death, 1632. A lozenge-shaped plate above the inscription contains an arrangement of seven stars similar to the constellation of the Great Bear, but in this case, upside down, possibly an engraver's error; in the lower half of the lozenge is a terrestrial globe on which are delineated the meridians, the polar circles, the tropics and the equator. Odiham *VI*, 1522, includes a crossbow. Rowner *II*, 1778, incorporates a relief figure of Father Time, a setting sun and cherub's heads in its design. Two 19th century brasses at Southampton, or Portswood *III* and *IV* both contain the canting arms of Crabbe. South Warnborough I includes a large pointing finger or pilchrow. Winchester, St. Cross I has two shields, one with a verbal Trinity, the other showing instruments of the Passion. An interesting and complete series of plates at Baughurst I, Monk Sherborne II, Pamber I, Sherborne St. John VI, Tadley I and Wootton St. Lawrence I commemorate the benefactions of Thomas Sympson, 1674. Although non-monumental, Bournemouth, St. Peter *XXXII* records the fact that William Gladstone took communion in this church in March 1898 before leaving for Hawarden, where he died a short time afterwards.

A number of brasses were produced by Messrs. Waller, the most important of which commemorates Harriet, wife of Col. Eyre John Crabbe, d.1848, but engraved 1878, at Southampton, or Portswood *IV*. She is shown standing on a bracket surrounded by a marginal inscription; much original colouring survives. The brass to her husband, Southampton, or Portswood *III*, is probably a Waller product. Southampton, or Portswood *I* is an elaborate cross to Joshua Arthur Brandon (1822-47), the architect of the church with his brother, Raphael Brandon (1817-77), in 1846-7. They were the authors of *Analysis of Gothic Architecture* (1847) and *Open Timber Roofs of the Middle Ages* (1847). Other important cross brasses by the firm can be seen at Hartley Wespall *III*, Heckfield *V* and Hursley *III* (to a design by William Butterfield). Christchurch Priory *V*, a Hardman brass to Anne, first wife of A.W.N. Pugin, 1814-32, was designed by her husband in 1850; the inscription gives his full names, Augustus Welby Northmore and also the French prefix of 'de' to his surname. Bursledon *VII*, 1903, is an effigial brass by John Hardman & Co. of Birmingham. Yateley *XII*, a Jones & Willis brass, depicts a plain cross, around which are entwined two lilies.

A number of modern inscriptions were produced by local engravers including: Garrett & Haysom of Southampton; J. Seargent of Winton (Winchester); G.T. Young of Southampton; Foster of Southsea; and Mannell & Co. of Bournemouth. Surprisingly, Nately Scures *III* was engraved by R.H. Green & Son, of St. John, New Brunswick, Canada. The list could be extended and the county, like many other counties, had firms that could turn their hand to producing simple inscriptions when required.

Many other firms of national importance, who manufactured modern brasses, are represented by numerous examples in the county. Among them are A. & N. Aux. C.S.L.; Benham & Froud; Messrs. Gawthorp; Jones and Willis; T. Pratt & Sons; and J. Wippell & Co. Two brasses, Powett *IV* and South Hayling *IV*, dated 1911, were produced by Omar Ramsden and Alwyn Carr. Both men were silversmiths of high repute; Carr provided the financial backing, while Ramsden was responsible for producing the finished product. At the height of his fame Ramsden had twenty assistants working for him; they produced many ornate pieces and were patronised by church bodies for their superbly wrought, large-scale ecclesiastical ornaments. Farnborough, St. Mark *XI*, a large and impressive World War I military composition, was designed by Byam Shaw (1872-1919), a painter and illustrator.

Many important indents can be found in the county. Beaulieu Abbey 1 is attributed to Isabel Marshall, 1st wife of Richard, Earl of Cornwall, who died c.1315. It shows the indent of a lady beneath a single canopy, surrounded by a marginal inscription in Lombardics and has been attributed to the Camoys series. Michelmersh 7, c.1375, shows an equal armed cross with fleur-de-lis terminals; on either side of the upper arm are the letters 'I N' and below an indent for an inscription. Nether Wallop 27, c.1400, depicts either an abbot or bishop standing beneath a single and super-canopy. The two niches and the super-canopy on the dexter side of the slab suggest that half of the monument is lost. At Christchurch Priory are a number of indents with incised inscriptions which may have been originally filled with a coloured composition. Romsey Abbey 59, c.1510, commemorates an abbess, in mantle with crosier. North Baddesley 11 comprises an inscription over a heart. Winchester Cathedral 64 commemorates a prior under an elaborate triple canopy of 15th century date. Winchester Cathedral 66 commemorates Thomas Langton, Bishop of Winchester, 1501, represented in pontificals under a triple canopy and super-canopy with saints in the side shafts; four gartered shields complete the composition.

Ringwood I commemorates John Prophete (c.1350-1416), Dean of York and administrator, who was Welsh by birth. He became Keeper of the Privy Seal under Henry IV, but resigned in June 1415, as Henry V was leaving for France. Prophete was buried at Ringwood, in accordance with the directions in his will. Church Oakley I commemorates the parents of William Warham, Archbishop of Canterbury (1503-32); he is shown in academicals among his brothers. Winchester Cathedral *IV* and the facsimile at Alton *XIII* commemorate Richard Boles, a Royalist army colonel, about whom little is known. He was a Lincolnshire man, who displayed much valour at the Battle of Edgehill, thus attracting Charles I's attention. In 1643 at Alton, Col. Boles and about 500 infantrymen were surprised by General Waller, initially holding off a far superior force, before being forced to withdraw from Alton House to higher ground around the church. By the afternoon Boles and his, by now exhausted, troops were forced to take cover inside the church, which was immediately surrounded by two regiments of Parliamentary soldiers. The barricaded door was broken down the soldiers, who now numbered in the region of eighty men, made a last heroic stand in the nave and chancel. Boles himself was killed in the pulpit. Bullet holes, some still containing shot from the battle, survive in the south door.

Two brasses commemorate the novelist, Jane Austen (1775-1817), who was born in the rectory at Steventon, the seventh child and youngest daughter of George Austen and his wife Cassandra. She is best known for the novels *Sense and Sensibility* (1811) and *Pride and Prejudice* (1813). Jane was taken ill in 1816, complaining of a number of symptoms, which suggest that her death may have been caused by tuberculosis, cancer or Addison's disease. She died at College Street, Winchester on 18 July the following year and was buried in the Cathedral five days later beneath a black marble slab in the north aisle; Winchester Cathedral *VI* was placed above the grave by her nephew in 1872. Steventon *II* was placed in the church in 1936 by a great-grandniece.

Hartley Wespall *III* commemorates John Keate (1773-1852) who was born at Wells, Somerset, where his father was a canon of the Cathedral. Keate was educated at Eton and King's College, Cambridge, becoming a classical scholar and brilliant writer of Latin verse. He graduated B.A. in 1796, M.A. in 1799 and obtained his D.D. in 1810. Keate was appointed assistant master at Eton about 1797. He married Frances, daughter of Charles Brown, M.D. the following year. In 1809 he was elected headmaster of the school; under him he had seven assistants for five hundred boys. Keate had to control about 170 boys in a single room; because of this discipline was bad and he was often subjected to rough behaviour, having, on one occasion, his desk smashed. His answer to the lack of discipline was frequent beating; in June 1832 he flogged more than eighty boys to suppress what he thought was going to be a rebellion. W.E. Gladstone was a pupil at Eton at this period. Keate retired from Eton in 1834 and moved to Hartley Wespall, where he had been rector since 1824 and was eventually buried.

Hursley *III* is to the memory of John Keble (1792-1866) who was born at Fairford, Gloucestershire. Failing to obtain a demyship at Magdalen College, Oxford, he was admitted as a Gloucester scholar at Corpus Christi College, where his father had been both scholar and fellow. In 1811, he gained double first-class honours and was elected to an open fellowship at Oriel College the following year, being appointed a college tutor in 1817. He was ordained a deacon on Trinity Sunday 1815, and priested one year later, taking temporary charge of the parishes of Eastleach and Burthorp, Gloucestershire. In about 1823 he accepted the curacy of Southrop near his father's living at Coln St. Aldwyn in Gloucestershire. After the death of his father in 1835 he married Charlotte Clarke; she was fourteen years his junior and of delicate constitution. The following year Keble was appointed vicar of Hursley, where he remained for the rest of his life living at the rectory with his invalid sister, Elizabeth, d.1860. He was devoted to them both, often referring to them, without any hint of embarrassment as his 'two wives'. Keble was active in the Oxford Movement, publishing tracts and letters on doctrinal issues, some written jointly with either Newman or Pusey. He died at Bournemouth where he had gone for the sake of his wife's health; Charlotte died shortly afterwards. Both are buried at Hursley. At a meeting held at Lambeth Palace in May 1866 it was resolved to build a college at Oxford to Keble's memory, which would offer education at a moderate cost in line with the teaching of the Church of England. Keble College was opened in 1870.

The Royal Garrison Church at Portsmouth contains a number of brasses to distinguished Army and Navy officers. Sir John Moore (1761-1809) (*XV*) was born at Glasgow and served with the army in Europe and the West Indies. He is best remembered for his command at the Battle of Corunna where he defeated the French, but was mortally wounded. Sir Thomas Foley d.1833, (*I*) served in the American Station during the War of Independence. He was a great friend of Nelson and led the attack against at the Battle of the Nile. Foley was promoted rear-admiral in 1808 and commanded the Downs station at Deal three years later. In 1830 he was appointed commander-in-chief at Portsmouth and died at Government House. Arthur Wellesley, 1st Duke of Wellington (1769-1852) (*XX*) had a long career which only burgeoned after 1796 when his regiment went to India. Wellesley was appointed Governor of Seringapatam and commander of the forces in Mysore. He was given the task of extending British influence in the area and in 1803 captured Poona. On his return to Britain he was knighted. Sir Arthur fought in the Peninsular War, remaining undefeated, although often outnumbered. After his victory at Waterloo in 1815, he returned to England and immersed himself in politics, becoming Prime Minister in 1828. He was buried in St. Paul's Cathedral. Sir Henry Barnard (1798-1857) (*XXXVIII*) died during the Indian Mutiny leading a relief column to raise the Siege of Delhi. He died of cholera and was buried at Rajpur cemetery.

Odiham *XXI* commemorates Philip Lutley Sclater (1829-1913), well known to the world of zoological science. He was born at Tangier Park, the second son of William Lutley Sclater and his wife, Anna Maria. Sclater was educated at Winchester College and then at Corpus Christi where he received a first in mathematics in 1849. He remained at Oxford for a further two years studying natural history and modern languages and became an accomplished ornithologist, publishing a number of articles in the journals of the Linnean and Zoological societies. However, his most important paper, "On the general geographic distribution of the members of the class *aves*", sought to identify six geographic regions of the world according to its bird life. Sclater's hypothesis is still in current use in a modified form. He was elected a fellow of the Zoological Society of London in 1850, served on its council for a number of years and became secretary in 1859, before retiring in 1902. Sclater died as a result of a carriage accident at his home, Odiham Priory. Eversley *V* commemorates the restoration of the church in 1875 in memory of Charles Kingsley (1819-75), the author, while Eversley *IX* commemorates Mary Kingsley (1862-1900), his niece. Mary is best known for her travels in West Africa in the 1890s, at a time when Victorian women were supposed to stay at home; she published two books on her travels. Mary caught enteric fever while nursing Boer War prisoners at Simons Town, South Africa and was buried at sea with full naval honours. Winchester Cathedral *LV* commemorates William Walker (1869-1918), the diver, who, between 1906-11, worked in almost nil visibility to replace the raft of beech logs on which the retrochoir had originally been built, with sacks of concrete, to form a solid foundation. Eventually the majority of the cathedral was underpinned in this way. Walker was awarded the M.V.O. by King George V for "saving the cathedral". A statue, with accompanying inscription, was placed in the Cathedral in October 2001. Major Robert Mayo (1891-1957) is commemorated by Winchester Cathedral *LIII*. Major Mayo invented the Short Mayo Composite; a piggyback long-range seaplane/flying boat combination produced by Short Brothers to provide a reliable long-range air transport service to the United States and the far reaches of the British Empire and the Commonwealth. Richard Meinertzhagen (1878-1967), the soldier and ornithologist, is commemorated by Mottisfont *VII*. He spent much of his childhood in the village where he began his lifelong interest in the study of birds. Meinertzhagen served in the army before leaving in 1925 to devote his time to ornithology which became a cover to enable him to observe international politics, mostly in western and central Asia. He was awarded the Godman Salvin medal of the British Ornithologists' Union in 1951. Six years later he was appointed a C.B.E. for services to ornithology. Bramshott *XVII* commemorates the rehanging of the church bells in memory of the 'horror' actor, Boris Karloff (1887-1969) "who lived & died within the sound of the bells". Chawton *XXVII* commemorates Caroline Glyn (1948-81), who was the author of seven novels between 1963 and 1977; probably the best known of these was *In Him was Life* (1975), a novelistic rendering of the Gospel story. She became a member of the Poor Clares at the Convent of St. Mary, Stroud, New South Wales, Australia. Christchurch Priory *L* commemorates Sir Donald Bailey (1901-85), a civil servant in the War Office. At the Experimental Bridging Establishment at Christchurch, in the early 1940s, he developed a method of building bridges which could be quickly assembled using unskilled labour.

Two holders of the Victoria Cross are included on brass memorials. Winchester Cathedral *XXVIII* commemorates Lt. Frederick Roberts, only surviving son of Field-Marshal Lord Roberts, of the

King's Royal Rifle Corps, who was decorated with the highest award for gallantry for the action he took on 15th December 1899, at the Battle of Colenso, during the second Boer War. The detachments that had been manning the 14th and 66th batteries of guns had all been either killed, wounded or driven from their posts by enemy fire. Sheltering in a donga, or watercourse, approximately 500 yards behind the lines, were some of the drivers and horses responsible for pulling the limbers. Together with a Captain Congreve, of the Rifle Brigade, they managed to hook up a team of horses and rode out to limber up one of the guns. Congreve was wounded and took shelter but saw that Roberts was badly wounded; he managed to bring him back to the safety of the donga before returning to retrieve the gun. Roberts died of his wounds two days later at Chiveley, Natal. His Victoria Cross is now in the National Army Museum, London. Petersfield *XXII* and *XXIII* commemorate Commander Loftus Jones (1879-1916), the captain of H.M.S. Shark, who led a division of destroyers to attack the German battle cruiser squadron at the Battle of Jutland. H.M.S. Shark was disabled by shell fire during the engagement and lay helpless between the two fleets. The midships gun was kept in action by three surviving seamen until a further hit resulted in Commander Jones losing a leg. He continued to give orders to the crew until the ship was sunk by a torpedo. Jones was awarded a posthumous Victoria Cross.

Three surviving wills made requests for engraved monuments, almost certainly brasses. John Bowyer of Basingstoke, whose will was proved at Winchester in 1536, directs that his executors are "to ordeyne a ston of ij yards long and a yarde of bredyth w(i)t(h) a picture of a man and ij women and under the same stone a man childe and iij maydyns and scrypture consarnyng the same." Basingstoke, St. Michael 25, although almost effaced, may possibly be identified with this bequest. The will of Thomas Fasshon, c.1554/5, requests that, should he be buried in the church of Southampton, St. Michael, then his executors were to "make over me a toumbe as yt is one the other side wher the sepulker ys And that ther be written upon yt my name what I was and of what place and my picture to be made in the fourme of A merchaunte and of my two wyves and all my children behind them and me. That is to say v sonnes and vii daughters. . .". Elizabeth Martyn, last Prioress of Wyntney, died in 1584 leaving instructions in her will that a stone "should be layde over my graue w(i)th a picture made of a plate of a woman in a longe garment w(i)th wyde sleves her handes joined together. . .". She was probably buried in the church of Hartley Wintney.

There is one Hampshire contract for the erection of a monument, which included brasses. In March 1536, William, Lord Sandys, K.G. (d.1542) contracted with 'Arnoult Hermaszone, natif dAusterdamme en Hollande, a present demourant a Aire en Artois' to make two tombs of 'pierre dAntoing'. Each tomb was to have a cross of copper and a marginal inscription on the coverstone. The tombs were placed in the Holy Trinity chapel at Basingstoke, founded by Lord Sandys next to the Holy Ghost chapel. Stone fragments of the tomb survive, but the coverstones have been lost.

Authenticated losses of brasses are rare in the county. The brasses in Winchester Cathedral are supposed to have been removed in 1644 according to Mercurius Rusticus, a Royalist pamphleteer, whose statement should perhaps be viewed with caution. Brown Candover 6 and 7 disappeared shortly after 1845, following exhibition at the Winchester Congress of the Archaeological Institute. A number of brasses in Winchester College were stolen in 1875 during the restoration of the chapel. The brasses were replaced by facsimiles paid for by Dr. Edwin Freshfield, F.S.A., who exhibited them at a meeting of the Society of Antiquaries in December 1881. F.J. Baigent (1830-1918) in his manuscript collections makes frequent mention of brasses lost during Victorian restorations.

A number of lost brasses or indents are recorded by William Pavey, one of the founders of the Society of Antiquaries in 1717, but beyond this virtually nothing is known about him. His manuscripts are now in the British Library (Add. 14296 and Stowe 845) and the majority of the entries are dated. He visited a small number of churches, both in Hampshire and the Isle of Wight. Portsmouth Cathedral 56 is only known because Pavey recorded it; the inscription commemorating members of the Cook family had only been placed in the churchyard a few years before Pavey's visit.

Hampshire, unlike many English counties, never had an antiquary who compiled a complete county history. A number of writers produced volumes about individual parts of the county. Richard Warner (1763-1857) was born at Marylebone, the only son of Richard Warner, a successful businessman, who retired to Lymington. Richard was sent to Christchurch Grammar School and soon familiarised himself with the New Forest and its surrounding antiquities. He had intended to enter the church, but his chosen route, via Winchester College, New College, Oxford, and a fellowship, was barred to him. However, after a period in an attorney's office, he entered St. Mary's Hall, Oxford, but left after eight terms without a degree. Warner took up the curacy of Boldre, serving under the Rev. William Gilpin, who became his mentor. The Bishop of Winchester would not ordain a non-graduate; Warner was eventually ordained by Archbishop Markham of York, where he served three months as a curate of Wales, near Doncaster, before returning to Boldre. In 1793 he became curate of Fawley. Warner who wanted, not only fame, but also money, wrote a number of books about the county including *A Companion in a Tour Round Lymington* (1789) which resulted in a loss of £22 5s; his translation of the Hampshire Domesday, also appeared in the same year. However, his *Southampton Guide* (1790) made a profit of £5. In 1793 his two volume work, *South-Western Parts of Hampshire*, appeared, followed two years later by *A History of the Isle of Wight*. He drew up a proposal for a full-scale three volume history of Hampshire and, although enough subscribers were obtained by 1793, he abandoned the project on account of the expense involved. Warner's *History of Hampshire* (1795) is attributed to him, but is in reality a compilation by an anonymous author. In 1794 his association with the county ceased when he became the first minister of All Saints, Bath. At his death he was buried at Chelwood, Somerset, where he had been rector. The books published by Warner were written for commercial gain and cannot be considered scholarly; furthermore, they are often inaccurate. F.J. Baigent (1830-1918) is the nearest the county has to a true historian. He was born and died in Winchester. His manuscript collections, formed with the idea of producing a parochial history of Hampshire, are now in the British Library (Add. MSS. 39959-72). Baigent published little during his lifetime and his death did not even warrant an obituary notice in the *Hampshire Antiquary and Naturalist*. C.J.P. Cave (1871-1950) contributed an important series of articles relating to the county's brasses to volumes V and VI of the *Transactions of the Monumental Brass Society*. Cave was elected a Vice-President when the Society was revived in 1934, publishing a photograph of an episcopal indent in Winchester Cathedral shortly before his death.

Winchester, as might be expected, had a large number of books written about both the Cathedral and the town. Samuel Gale (1782-54) was the author of one of the earliest. He had been born in London, the youngest surviving son of Thomas Gale (1635/6-1702), Dean of York, an antiquary, and his wife Barbara Pepys. Gale was educated at St. Paul's School, London, where his father was high master. In 1702 he obtained a position in the Customs House, London, where he soon became "searcher of the books and curiosities imported into this Kingdom". He was a keen antiquarian with a particular interest in ecclesiastical history. The only work published in his lifetime was *A History of Winchester Cathedral* (1715). Gale was a founder member of the revived Society of Antiquaries and served as its first treasurer up to 1739-40. He was a great friend of Dr. William Stukeley and Dr. Andrew Coltee Ducarel and assisted many other antiquaries. John Milner (1752-1826) wrote two books about Winchester. He was born in London, the son of Joseph Miller and his wife, Helen Marsland, both of whom were Roman Catholics from Lancashire. At the age of seven Miller was sent to the Franciscan school at Edgbaston and from there, at the age of thirteen, to the school at Sedgley Park, Wolverhampton. By about 1765 it appears that the family name had been changed to Milner. In about 1776 he was sent to the English College at Douai for clerical training, returning to England in 1777. Two years later he was placed in the mission at Winchester, whilst there, Milner published two books, *The History, Civil and Ecclesiastical, and Survey of the Antiquities of Winchester* (1798-1801) and *The History and Survey of the Antiquities of Winchester* (1839). The former work gained Milner fellowship of the Society of Antiquaries. A year after the Relief Act of 1791, he built St. Peter's (R.C.) chapel (now Milner Hall). This building, designed by John Carter, was one of the first in England to revive the Gothic style and greatly influenced A.W.N. Pugin. Milner left Winchester in 1803, on his appointment as Vicar Apostolic of the Midland District, thereby severing his connection with the county. However, Pugin later designed a memorial brass, which was placed in the chapel at Oscott College Chapel, Birmingham, in 1842.

In conclusion, Hampshire is a county of contrasts. The brasses to be found in country churches predominantly commemorate minor landed gentry, while the brasses in Winchester Cathedral, the College Chapel and Cloisters and St. Cross commemorate numerous clergy. Many Victorian and modern brasses reflect the county's association with the Army and Navy. Not since the survey by C.J.P. Cave, published in 1908-13, has any attempt been made to list or illustrate the many and varied brasses of the county.

Isle of Wight
Surprisingly, the Island contains rather more brasses than might be expected. Freshwater, All Saints I, is a series A knight of the Compton family. Other notable brasses include Arreton I, a London B brass of c.1430 and Shorwell I, a London F variant brass, shows a former vicar, Richard Bethell, 1518, in surplice and scarf. Shorwell II contains 17th century allegorical representations.

Two brasses have been found to be palimpsest. Ryde, Isle of Wight Museum Service *I*, formerly Kingston I, the reverse of the inscription to Richard Mewys, 1535, reveals another to the same person and is probably wasted work. The second, at Newport, St. Thomas *I*, commemorating Elizabeth, second daughter of Charles I, who died in 1650 at the age of 14, but retrospectively engraved in 1793, contains a very lightly engraved inscription to George Shergold, minister of Newport, 1707; it must be presumed to have been produced locally.

A number of brasses show unusual features. Shorwell II, 1619, shows the two wives of Barnabas Leigh, Elizabeth and Gartrude. Elizabeth, shown with her fifteen children, is described in Latin as "frugifera", while Gartrude is described as "sterilis". Calbourne III, 1652, shows the figures of Time and Death, together with an anagram of the deceased's name, Daniel Evance, spelling out the line 'I can deal even'.

Two Victorian brasses are of interest. Ryde, St. Mary (R.C.) *I* commemorating Charlotte Elliot, 1861, is a product of the Hardman workshop. Ryde, or Swanmore *III* shows Samuel Wilberforce, Bishop of Oxford (1845-69) and Bishop of Winchester (1869-73), in his surplice carrying his crosier; it is not known who the engraver was.

Few indents remain on the island. At Freshwater, All Saints 21 is the indent of a man in armour and and wife, c.1385, under a double canopy with foot inscription, two scrolls and two shields. In the same church are indents for a lady under a single canopy with a large scroll encircling the head, dated c.1390. Godshill 7-10 are worn indents, while Arreton 16 is a civilian and wife of about 1500.

Carisbrooke, St. Mary I commemorates William Keeling (1578-1620), the first European to see the islands, which were subsequently named after him, in 1609; he became captain of Cowes, c.1617. Brading, St. Mary *XII* commemorates Legh Richmond (1772-1827), who was curate here and at Yaverland, before being ordained a priest in February 1798. While at Brading he collected material for his three tales of village life, "The Dairyman's Daughter", "The Young Cottager" and "The Negro Servant". All these stories were, however, written under the pseudonym of 'Simplex' in 1809 after he left the island. Following publication they achieved instant popularity, being reprinted by the Religious Tract Society in 1814 under the title of *The Annals of the Poor.* They were translated into a number of European languages and also had a wide circulation in America. During the lifetime of the author it was calculated that two million copies of the English language edition were printed. Richmond left the island in 1805 to become assistant chaplain to the Lock Hospital in London and was subsequently inducted as rector of Turvey, Bedfordshire. He was a great supporter of both the British and Foreign Bible Society and the Church Missionary Society. He died at Turvey; the brass commemorating him was placed in Brading church in 1898. West Cowes, St. Mary the Virgin *XVI* is to the memory of Thomas Arnold (1795-1842), who was born in West Cowes. He was ordained into the Church of England in 1818 and was headmaster of Rugby School from 1828-42, where he had a profound influence on public school education. Arnold was buried in the school chapel; the brass was placed in Cowes church about 1900. Samuel Wilberforce (1805-1873), who is shown on Ryde, or Swanmore *III,* was for a time rector of Brighstone before becoming Bishop of Oxford and later Bishop of Winchester. As Bishop of Oxford he attacked Darwin's book *Origin of the Species* (1859), in a debate at the University against Thomas Huxley. However, Huxley won the day with his arguments. Ryde, or Swanmore *XIII*, is to the memory of Arthur John White (1890-1913), who died in Belgium while saving the lives of two boy scouts; the composition includes the Scout badge on a shield. East Cowes, St. James *XV* commemorates Uffa Fox (1898-1972), who was born on the island and grew up on the Cowes waterfront. He was apprenticed to a firm of boat builders, S.E. Saunders, for seven years, during which time he learnt boat building, shipbuilding and design. At the age of twenty-one he started his own business and was responsible for designing and building many types of dinghy. During Cowes Week he often crewed for H.R.H. the Duke of Edinburgh.

At Brading, in the chancel are the tombs to members of the Oglander family, to which are attached small brass inscriptions (I-IV). The will, dated 10 November 1640, of Sir John Oglander (1585-1655), author of the well known Oglander manuscript, refers to these inscriptions thus "I further give towards the erectinge of a toombe for my ffather, Sir William Oglander and myself. My father to be placed on the south side of my chancel to the east of Mr John Oglander's toombe, and my inscription of brass in my studdie to be set on it, and the statue in my house to be placed thereon, and my own toombe to be set at the east end of my grate grandfather Oliver Oglander, with the statue already in my chancel to be placed thereon, and an inscription of brass to be set on the tombe shewing when myself and Wife died, and the commands I have made. And my son George's statue, who died at Caen in Normandie, to be placed in the arch I made over the place I intended to be buried in, with the frame in my studdie (to be new written) I made in memory of him, with an inscription in brass to be set over it shewing who he was, the adge, time and place he died in, &c." This most interesting will extract shows that, not only did Oglander not trust his executors to be responsible for the erecting of any form of monument, but the plates were in his study, ready for erection after his death.

Few antiquaries have devoted time and energy to the brasses on the island for obvious reasons. Charles Tomkins published *A Tour to the Isle of Wight* (1796); it included a few illustrations of brasses, but he was mainly interested in views and landscapes. Sir John Oglander, although not an antiquary in the more usual sense of the word, kept a diary of noteworthy events. The diary also includes a description of the island mentioning a number of brasses and a few indents which have since been lost; for example Arreton 18 and several at Godshill. Oglander's diary was not published until 1888. Percy Goddard Stone in *The Architectural Antiquities of the Isle of Wight* (1891) gives a few illustrations of brasses and several of the more interesting indents. In 1892, R.W.M. Lewis (1866-1954) published a survey of the island's brasses in *Transactions of the Cambridge University Association of Brass Collectors* (later the *Monumental Brass Society Transactions*); he served as President of the Society from 1934-54. In 1972, E.N. Staines published *A Guide to the Monumental Brasses & Incised Slabs on the Isle of Wight*; although illustrated, it was not by no mean exhaustive.

Although the Isle of Wight contains few brasses they form an interesting series of monuments reflecting the history of the island.

LIST OF SUBSCRIBERS
IN ALPHABETICAL ORDER

Ali, J.Z., B.A.(Oxon.), Bramley Fold Farm, Hawkshaw, Bury, Lancashire BL8 4LG

Arthur, Mrs. J.M., Candelmas, 6C Leafield Road, Biggar, Lanarkshire ML12 6AY

Badham, Miss S.F., F.S.A., Dawn Cottage, Purrants Lane, Leafield, Oxfordshire OX29 9PN

Baker, Prof. Sir John H., Q.C., LL.B., Ph.D., M.A., LL.D., F.B.A., St. Catharine's College,
   Cambridge CB2 1RL

Bayliss, J.C., B.A., 31 Churchfields, Hethersett, Norwich, Norfolk NR9 3AF

Bell, A.G., B.Sc., 3 Grange Drive, Park Lane, Cottingham, North Humberside HU16 5RE

Bertram, Rev. Fr. J.F.A., M.A., F.S.A., The Oratory, 25 Woodstock Road, Oxford OX2 6HA

Blair, Dr. C., C.V.O., O.B.E., M.A., Litt.D., F.S.A., 90 Links Road, Ashtead, Surrey KT21 2HW

Blair, Prof. W.J., M.A., D.Phil., F.S.A., The Queen's College, Oxford OX1 4AW

Bradbury, G.G., A.K.C., Wayside, Brook Street, Shipton Gorge, Bridport, Dorset DT6 4NA

Brownridge, Dr. D.S., M.B., B.S., M.R.C.S., L.R.C.P., Vern House,
   Old Worcester Road, Hartlebury, Kidderminster, Worcestershire DY11 7XQ

Burge, Prof. P.S., M.B., B.S., M.R.C.P., 56 Broad Oaks Road, Solihull, West Midlands B91 1HZ

Burton, B., B.A., C.Eng., M.I.E.E., 56 Daiglen Drive, South Ockendon, Essex RM15 5RW

Busby, R.J., F.C.I.L.I.P., F.S.A., 1 Palmerston Close, Welwyn Garden City,
   Hertfordshire AL8 7DL

Butler-Stoney, M.C., Burwood Hall, Mileham, King's Lynn, Norfolk PE32 2RA

Dyrom, C.M., B.A., C.Biol., M.I.Biol., Grad.I.C.S.A., 11 Sarum Court, 2 St. Osmunds Road,
   Poole, Dorset BH14 9JN

Careless, G.C., Flat 5, 43 Cambridge Road, Aldershot, Hampshire GU11 3LF

Catling, Dr. H.W., C.B.E., M.A., D.Phil., F.S.A., Dunford House, Langford,
   Lechlade, Gloucestershire GL7 3LN

Chaddock, M.J., 63 St. John's Avenue, Bridlington, East Yorkshire YO16 4ND

Chambers, C.J.P., M.B.E., B.Sc.(Eng.), 6 May Pole Knap, Somerton, Somerset TA11 6HR

Cherry, J., M.A., F.S.A., F.R.Hist.S., 58 Lancaster Road, London N4 4PT

Chivers, D.A., B.A.(Hons.), F.S.A., Flat 2, 28 Lofting Road, Islington, London N1 1ET

Coales, J., O.B.E., F.S.A., The Mount, Parsonage Hill, Somerton, Somerset TA11 7PF

Cockerham, Dr. P.D., M.A., Ph.D., Vet.M.B., F.S.A., M.R.C.V.S., Sharwood, Lezerea,
   Wendron, Helston, Cornwall TR13 0ED

Coker, Miss B.A., B.Ed., 46 St. Bartholomew's Road, East Ham, London E6 3AG

Cook, B.R., 13 The Weavers, Denstone, Uttoxeter, Staffordshire ST14 5DP

Cook, D.B., 59 Loxwood Close, Feltham, Middlesex TW14 8SQ

Coss, Prof. P.R., B.A., Ph.D., F.S.A., F.R.Hist.S., 5 Allen Close, Old St. Mellons,
   Cardiff CF3 5DH

Creed, Dr. C.D., B.Sc., Ph.D., 28 Victoria Grove, Southsea, Portsmouth, Hampshire PO5 1NF

Day, Mrs. I., 86D High Street, Stony Stratford, Milton Keynes, Buckinghamshire MK11 1AH

Dennison, Dr. L.E., M.A., Ph.D., F.S.A., Manor Farm, 79 High Street, Watchfield, Swindon,
   Wiltshire SN6 8TL

Desler, Miss R., Flat 3, 120 Barrowgate Road, Chiswick, London W4 4QP

Dickens, Dr. T.K., B.Sc., Ph.D., 14A East Hatley, Hatley St. George, Sandy,
   Bedfordshire SG19 3JA

Dobson, J., "Cephas", 311 Rayleigh Road, Thundersley, Benfleet, Essex SS7 3XA

Dormagen, H.G., Goltsteinstr. 51a, D 50968, Köln, Germany

Dowden, Mrs. A., B.A., 17 St. Mark Drive, Colchester, Essex CO4 4LP

Downing, R.M., Dip.Arch., R.I.B.A., 105 Pixmore Way, Letchworth, Hertfordshire SG6 3TR

Draffin, Mrs. M., B.A., 3 Hornedale Avenue, Barrow-in-Furness, Cumbria LA13 9AS

Driscoll, Lieut. Commander M.J., U.S.N.(Ret.), 301 Driver Avenue, Corey Woods, Summerville
South Carolina 29483, U.S.A.

Edwards, Mrs. N.R., M.A., F.S.A., 43 Maltese Road, Chelmsford, Essex CM1 2PB

Egan, B.S.H., 110 Clarence Road, Stony Stratford, Milton Keynes, Buckinghamshire MK11 1JG

Elson, Prof. D.M., J.P., C.Text., F.T.I., Lic.I.Q.A., F.R.S.A., 5 Sunningdale Drive, Woodborough,
Nottingham NG14 6EQ

Farman, P.D., and Hacker, P.F., 4 Hollins Crescent, Harrogate, North Yorkshire HG1 2JG

Freeth S.G.H., B.A., 83 College Road, Epsom, Surrey KT17 4HH

Fry, D.J., B.Ed., Cert.Ed., M.I.I.T.T., Stocks, Lyth Bank, Shrewsbury, Shropshire SY3 0BE

Gilhespy, B.P., B.Sc., C.Phys., M.Inst.P., 51 Leafield Rise, Two Mile Ash, Milton Keynes,
Buckinghamshire MK8 8BX

Gittos, Mr. and Mrs. B.C., 4 Linden Road, Yeovil, Somerset BA20 2BH

Glogg, J.J.T., 95 Park Crescent, Erith, Kent DA8 3EA

Griffith, Dr. D.M., c/o Department of English, Univesity of Birmingham, Edgbaston,
Birmingham B15 2TT

Guilford, Dr. H., B.Sc., D.Phil., 14 Green Park, Prestwood, Great Missenden,
Buckinghamshire HP16 0PZ

Harris, C.C., M.A., 55 Macfarlane Road, Shepherds Bush, London W12 7JY

Harris, Rear-Admiral M.G.T., J.P., B.A., King's Lodge, Church Street, Whitchurch,
Hampshire RG28 7AS

Harris, S.J., Edmonstone Mains Farmhouse, Stewart Grove, Danderhall, Scotland EH22 1QY

Harrod, Mrs. J.E., 54 Lansdowne Road, Littlehampton, West Sussex BN17 6JG

Hawes, E.M., B.Sc., M.A., Westbrook Lodge, Hollow Lane, Kingsley, Frodsham,
Cheshire WA6 8EF

Herring, K.H.W., LL.B., Dip.T.P., "Clemridge", The Street, Shalford, Braintree,
Essex CM7 5HN

Heseltine, P.J., 3 Earning Street, Godmanchester, Huntingdon, Cambridgeshire PE18 8JD

Hopkins, J.C., 26 Bridgend Road, Aberkenfig, Bridgend CF32 9BG

Hopkinson, D.S., 3 The Squirrels, Hertford, Hertfordshire SG13 7UT

Houghton, Ms J.E.M., M.C.I.L.I.P., 9 Enstone Road, Lowestoft, Suffolk NR33 0NE

Howell, I.P., 58 Elder Close, Badger Farm, Winchester, Hampshire SO22 4LH

Hutchinson, D.R., F.S.A., Barton Cottage, Church Street, Amberley, Arundel,
West Sussex BN18 9NE

Jarrold, Mrs. E.A., The Acorn, Longland Cross, East Cornworthy, Devon TQ9 7HF

Jenkins, Mr. and Mrs. R.P., Fugitives Drift, 31A Victoria Street, Fleckney, Leicester LE8 8AZ

Kibbey, S.S., 3 Cleveland Court, Kent Avenue, Ealing, London W13 8BJ

Lack, G.J., M.A.(Cantab.), The Smithy and Forge, Gilbert's End, Hanley Castle, Malvern, Worcestershire WR8 0AS

Lack, W.G., B.Sc., Two, Three and Four, The Radleth, Plealey, Pontesbury, Shrewsbury, Shropshire SY5 0XF

Lamp, R., Feddersenstr. 15a, D-22607 Hamburg, Germany

Lankester, P.J., B.Sc., M.A., A.M.A., F.S.A., F.S.A.Scot., 29 Stanley Street, York YO31 8NW

Larimore, T.J., 43 Reginald Road South, Chaddesden, Derbyshire DE21 6NG

Lillistone, D.C., B.A., 75 Quarry Lane, Ecclesall, Sheffield, South Yorkshire S11 9EA

McCreanor, Mrs. J.M., 3 South Grange Road, Ripon, North Yorkshire HG4 2NH

McEune, Rev. P.J., 82 Danvers Way, Westbury, Wiltshire BA13 3UF

Meara, Rev. Canon D.G., M.A., F.S.A., St. Bride's Rectory, Fleet Street, London EC4Y 8AU

Moir-Shepherd, J.B., M.A., F.R.C.S., Goxhill Lodge, 90 Thorne Road, Doncaster, South Yorkshire DN2 5BJ

Moor, J.L.H., LL.B.(Hons.), B.A.(Hons.), Applegarth, Temeside, Ludlow, Shropshire SY8 1JW

Morgan, Prof. N.J., M.A., Ph.D., F.S.A., 32 Thornton Court, Girton, Cambridge, Cambridgeshire CB3 0NS

Morton, J., Forest Way, Mill Lane, Burley, Ringwood, Hampshire BH24 4HR

Newsome, J.D., 3 Palmers Road, Wootton Bridge, Ryde, Isle of Wight PO33 4NA

Oakley, R.G., 9 Capstan Square, Stewart Street, London E14 3EU

Oosterwijk, Dr. S., M.A., Ph.D., F.S.A., 34 Bridge Street, Shepshed, Leicestershire LE12 9AD

Osborne, Mrs. J.A., 36 College Road, Ringwood, Hampshire BH24 1NX

Paige-Hagg, M.A., B.Tech., M.Sc., 37 Saxon Way, Old Windsor, Berkshire SL4 2PU

Parrott, D.M., 110 Hillside Avenue, Bitterne Park, Southampton, Hampshire SO2 4JY

Pettman, I.S., F.R.S.A., 21 Cleaver Square, Kennington, London SE11 4DW

Pither, J.E., I.Eng., A.M.R.Aes., 9 Cypress Way, Darby Green, Blackwater, Camberley, Surrey GU17 0EG

Pugh-Thomas, A., Glebe Court, West Monkton, Taunton, Somerset TA2 8QT

Rogers, N.J., M.A., M.Litt., F.S.A., c/o Muniment Room, Sidney Sussex College, Cambridge CB2 3HU

Rumble, Miss E.M., Garden Cottage, Westhope, Craven Arms, Shropshire SY7 9JN

Salmon, Dr. J.R., 11 Old Park Ridings, London N21 2EX

Saul, Prof. N.E., M.A., D.Phil., F.S.A., F.R.Hist.S., Gresham House, Egham Hill, Egham, Surrey TW20 0ER

Saunders, M.W.B., 48 Testlands Avenue, Nursling, Southampton, Hampshire SO16 0XG

Simpson, Miss M.M., 5 Beech House, Station Road, Marlow, Buckinghamshire SL7 1NN

Smith, L.A., 68 Charles Street, Herne Bay, Kent CT6 5HW

Smith, Rev. W.J.T., 7 Trelawn, Church Road, Boreham, Chelmsford, Essex CM3 3EF

Sneddon, Dr. J.M., B.Sc., Ph.D., Chetwynd House, 144 Northwood Lane, Clayton, Newcastle-under-Lyme, Staffordshire S75 4BZ

Steer, C.O., M.A., c/o Department of History, Royal Holloway, University of London, Egham, Surrey TW20 0EX

Stuchfield, H.M., J.P., F.S.A., Lowe Hill House, Stratford St. Mary, Suffolk CO7 6JX

Surman, K.R., B.Sc.(Econ.), 13 Green Crescent, Flackwell Heath, High Wycombe, Buckinghamshire HP10 9JQ

Taylor, Prof. G.I., A.O., M.D., F.R.A.C.S., F.R.C.S.(Eng.), F.R.C.S.(Ed.), 7th Floor,
766 Elizabeth Street, Melbourne, Victoria, Australia 3000
Thompson, N.J., M.A., Dip.Lib., A.L.A., Cert.F.E., Ash House, 2 Breinton Lee,
King's Acre Road, Hereford, HR11 0SZ
Tryon, P.M., Sisland, Green Close, Drinkstone, Bury St. Edmunds, Suffolk IP30 9TE
Tsushima, Mrs. J.E., F.S.A., Malmaison, Church Street, Great Bedwyn, Wiltshire SN8 3PE

Voice, Mr. and Mrs. A.J., 11 Thatchers Close, Horsham, West Sussex RH12 5TL

Waddell, J.A., 1 The Close, Broadstone, Dorset BH18 9JE
Wheaton, F.D.P., 3 Ashwood Gardens, Hayes, Middlesex UB3 4LT
Whittemore, P.J., Lynton House, 16 Colne Road, Winchmore Hill, London N21 2JD
Willatts, Miss R.M., M.A., Barlows Cottage, 2 Barlows Lane, Wilbarston,
Market Harborough, Leicestershire LE16 8QB
Wood, G.D., M.A.(Oxon.), Lansdown Cottage, Lansdown Road, Canterbury, Kent CT1 3JR
Wright, Miss J.M., 7 Wood Glen Road, Scarborough, Ontario, Canada M1N 2V6

Council for the Care of Churches, Church House, Great Smith Street, London SW1P 3NZ
Genealogists, The Society of, 14 Charterhouse Buildings, London EC1M 7BA
Lambeth Palace Library, Lambeth Palace Road, London SE1 7JU
London Library, 14 St. James's Square, London SW1Y 4LG

BIBLIOGRAPHY

Alcuin Club Colls., The Ornaments of the Ministers as shown on English Monumental
    Brasses, XXII, 1919.
Antiquary. The Antiquary, 1880-1915.
Arch. Jour. Journal of the Royal Archaeological Institute, 159 vols., 1845-.
Archaeologia. Archaeologia or Miscellaneous Tracts relating to Antiquity published by the
    Society of Antiquaries of London, 109 vols., 1770-.
Ashdown, Armour. British and Foreign Arms and Armour, by Mrs. C.H. Ashdown, 1909.

B.A.A. Jour. Journal of the British Archaeological Association, 159 vols., 1845-.
Beaumont. Ancient Memorial Brasses, by E.T. Beaumont, 1913.
Berks. The Monumental Brasses of Berkshire, by William Lack, H. Martin Stuchfield
    and Philip Whittemore, 1993.
Bertram, Brasses. Brasses and Brass Rubbing in England, by Jerome Bertram, 1971.
Bertram, Rare Brass Rubbings. Rare Brass Rubbing from the Ashmolean Collection,
    by Jerome Bertram, 1977.
Bouquet, Church Brasses. Church Brasses, by A.C. Bouquet, 1956.
Boutell, Br. and Slabs. Monumental Brasses and Slabs, by C. Boutell, 1847.
Boutell, Series. The Monumental Brasses of England, a series of engravings on wood,
    by C. Boutell, 1849.
Bracken, Noble Order of the Garter. The Most Noble Order of the Garter as depicted on
    Church Monumental Brasses, by Jim Bracken, 1991.
Brasses as Art and Hist. Monumental Brasses as Art and History, ed. by Jerome Bertram, 1996.
Brettell. Handbook to the Isle of Wight, by T. Brettell, 1st edn., 1840, 2nd edn., 1844.
Burke's Peerage and Baronetage. Burke's Peerage and Baronetage, 105th edn., 4th imp., 1980.
Busby, Companion Guide. A Companion Guide to Brasses and Brass Rubbing,
    by R.J. Busby, 1973.

Church Monuments Jour. Journal of the Church Monuments Society, 20 vols., 1985-.
Clinch, Churches. Old English Churches, by G. Clinch, 1900.
Clinch, Costume. English Costume, by G. Clinch, 1909.

Death in Towns. Death in Towns: Urban Responses to the Dying and the Dead, 100-1600,
    ed. S. Bassett, 1992
D.N.B. Dictionary of National Biography, 22 vols., 1885-1901.
Duthy. Sketches of Hampshire, by John Duthy, 1839.

Earliest English Brasses. The Earliest English Brasses, ed. by J. Coales, 1987.
E. & S. The Repair of Monumental Brasses, by B.S.H. Egan and H.M. Stuchfield, 1981.

Franklyn. Brasses, by Julian Franklyn, 1964, 2nd edn., 1969.

Gawthorp. The Brasses of our Homeland Churches, by W.E. Gawthorp, 1923.
Gent. Mag. The Gentleman's Magazine, 1731-1868.
Gent. Mag. Lib. Eng. Topog. Topographical History of Hampshire, Herefordshire, Hertfordshire
    and Huntingdonshire: a classified collection from the Gentleman's Magazine, 1731-1868,
    ed. G.L. Gomme, 1894.
Gittings. Brasses and Brass Rubbing, by Clare Gittings, 1970.
Gough. Sepulchral Monuments of Great Britain, by Richard Gough, 2 vols., 1786-96
    (frequently bound in 5 parts).

Haines. A Manual of Monumental Brasses, by H. Haines, 2 vols., 1861, reprinted 1970.

Hampshire Antiquary. The Hampshire Antiquary and Naturalist, [being N. and Q. reports of meetings of the Hampshire Field Club etc. reprinted from The Hampshire Independent], 2 vols., 1891.

Hampshire History. A General History of Hampshire, by B.B. Woodward, Rev. Theodore C. Willis and Charles Lockhart, 3 vols., 1858-69.

Hampshire N. and Q. Hampshire Notes and Queries, 6 vols., 1883-92.

Hampton. Memorials of the Wars of the Roses, by W.E. Hampton, 1979.

Hants Proc. Papers and Proceedings of the Hampshire Field Club, 58 vols., 1885-.

Heseltine, Heraldry. Heraldry on Brass: Mill Stephenson Collection of Arms on British Brasses at the Society of Antiquaries, by Peter Heseltine, 1994.

Hewitt, Armour. Ancient Armour and Weapons in Europe, by J. Hewitt, 3 vols., 1855-60.

Historical Metallurgy. Journal of the Historical Metallurgy Society, 40 vols., 1962-

Jeans. A Handbook for Travellers in the Isle of Wight, by Rev. G.E. Jeans, 1898.

Lack and Whittemore. A Series of Monumental Brasses, Indents and Incised Slabs from the 13th to the 20th Century, by William Lack and Philip Whittemore, 2 vols., 2000-.

Lamp and Herring. "Das Antlitz im Boden": Abriebe norddeutscher und englischer Metallgrabplatten des Mittelalters (exhibition catalogue), by Reinhard Lamp and Kevin Herring, 2006.

Leach. A History of Winchester College, by Arthur F. Leach, 1899.

Lewis. Through England on my knees, by Betsy Lewis, 1977.

Long. The Oglander Memoirs: extracts from the MSS. of Sir John Oglander, Knt., ed. by W.H. Long, 1888.

Macklin, Br. of Eng. The Brasses of England, by H.W. Macklin, 1907.

Mann. Monumental Brasses, by Sir James Mann, 1957.

Manning. A List of the Monumental Brasses remaining in England, by Rev. C.R. Manning, 1846.

M.B.S. Bulletin. Monumental Brass Society Bulletin, 1972-.

M.B.S. Portfolio. Monumental Brass Society Portfolio, 8 vols., 1894-1984.

M.B.S. Trans. Monumental Brass Society Transactions, 17 vols., 1887-.

Meara, Pugin. A.W.N. Pugin and the Revival of Memorial Brasses, by David Meara, 1991.

Meara, Victorian Brasses. Victorian Memorial Brasses, by David Meara, 1983.

Mee, Hampshire. The King's England: Hampshire with the Isle of Wight, by A. Mee, 1939.

Milner, History. The History, Civil and Ecclesiastical and Survey of the Antiquities of Winchester, by Rev. John Milner, 2 vols., 1801.

Milner, Survey. The History and Survey of the Antiquities of Winchester, by Rev. John Milner, 2 vols., 1839.

Misc. Gen. et Her. Miscellanea Genealogica et Heraldica, 1868-1938.

Moody. Antiquarian and Topographical Sketches of Hampshire, by Henry Moody, 1846.

M.S. A List of Monumental Brasses in the British Isles, by Mill Stephenson, 1926, with appendix, 1938.

Newcastle Soc. Antiq. Proc. Proceedings of the Society of Antiquaries of Newcastle-upon-Tyne, 1st series, 1 vol., 1855-8; 2nd series, 10 vols., 1882-1902; 3rd series, 10 vols., 1903-22; 4th series, 11 vols., 1923-50; 5th series, 1 vol., 1951-6.

Norris, Craft. Monumental Brasses: The Craft, by M.W. Norris, 1978.
Norris, Memorials. Monumental Brasses: The Memorials, by M.W. Norris, 2 vols., 1977.

Oxford Man. A Manual for the study of Monumental Brasses, ed. H. Haines, 1847.

Page-Phillips, Macklin. Macklin's Monumental Brasses, by J.C. Page-Phillips, 1969.
Page-Phillips, Children. Children on Brasses, by J.C. Page-Phillips, 1970.
Palimpsests. The Palimpsests, by J.C. Page-Phillips, 2 vols., 1980, and appendices 1-7, published
    in *M.B.S. Bulletin*, 1982-97 (page nos. in appendices are lower case Roman numerals).
Pevsner, Hampshire. Buildings of England: Hampshire and the Isle of Wight,
    by Nikolaus Pevsner and David Lloyd, 1st edn., 1967.
Portfolio Book. Monumental Brasses, the Portfolio Plates of the Monumental Brass Society
    1894-1984, 1988.

Sadler, Dorset and Hampshire. The Indents of Lost Monumental Brasses in Dorset and
    Hampshire, by A.G. Sadler, 1975, Appendix I, pt.2, 1979.
Sadler, Southern England. The Indents of Lost Monumental Brasses in Southern England,
    by A.G. Sadler, 1976, appx. I, intro., 1980, appx. II, 1985, appx. III, 1986,
    appx. IV, 1990.
Simpson. A List of the Sepulchral Brasses of England, by Justin Simpson, 1857.
Soc. Antiq. Lond. Proc. Proceedings of the Society of Antiquaries of London, 1st series, 1843-59;
    2nd series, 1859-1920.
Specimens of Lettering. Specimens of Lettering from English Monumental Brasses,
    by Sally Badham, W.J. Blair and R.C. Emmerson, 1976.
Squibb. The Visitation of Hampshire and the Isle of Wight, 1686. Transcribed and ed.
    by G.D. Squibb, 1991.
Staines. A Guide to the Monumental Brasses and Incised Slabs on the Isle of Wight,
    by Rev. E.N. Staines, 1972.
Stone. Architectural Antiquities of the Isle of Wight from the eleventh to the
    seventeenth centuries inclusive, by Percy G. Stone, 4 pts. in 2 vols., 1891.
Suffling. English Church Brasses, by E.R. Suffling, 1910, reprinted 1970.
Surrey Arch. Colls. Surrey Archaeological Collections, 92 vols., 1858-.

Tomkins. A Tour to the Isle of Wight, by C. Tomkins, 2 vols., 1796.
Trivick, Craft. The Craft and Design of Monumental Brasses, by H. Trivick, 1969.
Trivick, Picture Book. The Picture Book of Brasses in Gilt, by H. Trivick, 1971.

V. and A. Mus. List. List of Rubbings of Brasses in the Victoria and Albert Museum,
    classified and arranged in chronological order, 1915, 2nd edn., 1929.
V.C.H., Hampshire. Victoria County History, Hampshire and the Isle of Wight, 5 vols., 1900-73.

Warner. Collections for the History of Hampshire and the Bishopric of Winchester,
    by Rev. Richard Warner, I, 1795.
Warton. The History and Antiquities of Winchester, by Thomas Warton, 2 vols., 1773.
Winchester, Description. A Description of the City, College and Cathedral of Winchester, 1763.
Worsley. The History of the Isle of Wight, [by Richard Worsley], 1781.

Additional relevant reading on styles of engraving:
Badham, Sally, An interim study of the stones used for the slabs of English Monumental Brasses, *M.B.S. Trans.*, XIII (1985), pp.475-83.
Badham, Sally, Monumental Brasses and the Black Death - A Reappraisal, *Antiq. Jour.*, LXXX (2000), pp.207-47.
Emmerson, R.C., Monumental Brasses: London Design c.1420-85, *B.A.A. Jour.*, CXXXI (1978), pp.50-78.
Esdaile, Mrs. A.J.K., The Sculptor and the Brass, *M.B.S. Trans.*, VII (1935), pp.49-64.
Esdaile, Mrs. A.J.K., and D'Elboux, R.H., An Alphabetical Lost of post-Reformation Brasses of known Authorship, *M.B.S. Trans.*, VIII (1944), pp.37-56, (1946), pp.140-4.
Kent, J.P.C., Monumental Brasses - A new classification of Military Effigies, *B.A.A. Jour.*, XII (1949), pp.70-97.
Page-Phillips, J.C., Future Palimpsest Discoveries, 1979 (unpublished typescript).

Collections of brass rubbings:
Camb. coll. Cambridge Antiquarian Society coll. (1847-),
    now in the University Library, Cambridge.
Soc. Antiq. coll. Society of Antiquaries of London coll. (early 19th cent.-).

Manuscript Sources:
Bodleian Library:
Bod. Lib. MS. Ashmole 1107. MS. collections of Elias Ashmole, late 17th cent.
Bod. Lib. Gough Gen. Top. 33. MS. collections of Richard Gough, late 18th cent.
Bod. Lib. Gough Maps 223-4, 226, 228. Drgs. and engr. proofs in Gough MS., c.1780-1800.
Bod. Lib. MS. Gough Misc. Antiq. 15. Collections of Richard Gough, c.1780-1800.
Bod. Lib. MS. Rubbings Phillips/Robinson 485, 493. Collection of rubbings by
    Henry Hinton and James Hunt, c.1790-1815.
Bod. Lib. MS. Wood D.4. MS. collections of Anthony Wood, 1632-95.

British Library:
Brit. Lib. Add. MS. 5836. MS. Notes, by William Cole, 1740-60.
Brit. Lib. Add. MS. 14296. Topographical Notes, 1719.
Brit. Lib. Add MS. 18478. Antique and Armorial Collections consisting of notices of
    various Architectural and Monumental Antiquities in various counties of England,
    by Rev. Alfred Inigo Suckling, rector of Barsham, Suff. 1821-39, 1832.
Brit. Lib. Add MS. 32478. Impressions made by Sir John Cullum and Craven Ord, 1779-86.
Brit. Lib. Add. MS. 39959, 39962-8, 39970-2, 39987, 39993. Baigent Collection. Antiquarian and
    Genealogical Collections relating to Hampshire by Francis Joseph Baigent, d.1918.
Brit. Lib. Harl. MS. 4944. Arms and Pedigrees of Essex Families (with addition of
    Hampshire notes), early-mid 17th cent.
Brit. Lib. Maps K. Top. 14. Miscellaneous Hampshire material, undated.
Brit. Lib. Stowe MS. 845. MS. notes by William Pavey, 1702-6.

Society of Antiquaries of London:
Soc. Antiq. MS. 875/6. Monumental Brasses of Hampshire, by H.G. Field.
    [Notes mostly based on the series of articles published by C.J.P. Cave in
    M.B.S. Trans., V, pp.247-91, pp.295-325, pp.343-71, VI, pp.1-39, pp.121-57].
Soc. Antiq. MS. 943/1. Correspondence and notes on Hampshire Brasses by C.J.P. Cave.
Soc. Antiq. MS. 1014/12. Conservation Reports by Bryan S.H. Egan, 1966-99.

ABBREVIATIONS, ETC.

acad.	academical dress	mar.	married
ach.	achievement	marg.	marginal
A.D.C.	Aide-de Camp	mcht.	merchant
approp.	appropriated	M.S.R.	Mill Stephenson Revision
arm.	armour	mur.	mural, against wall
attd.	attached	mutil.	mutilated
A.T.	altar tomb	N.	nave, north
Bart.	Baronet	N.A.	north aisle
Battn.	Battalion	N.C.	north chapel
Brig.	Brigadier	N.C.A.	north choir aisle
Brit. Mus.	British Museum	n.d.	not dated
B.S.H.E.	B.S.H. Egan	N.Tr.	north transept
C.	choir, chancel	obv.	obverse
c.	circa, about	orig.	original, originally
Capt.	Captain	palimp.	palimpsest
ch.	church	par.	parish
Co.	Company	P.C.C.	Parochial Church Council
coh.	coheir	pl.	plate
Col.	Colonel	pos.	posuit, placed
Coll.	College	Pte.	Private
coll.	collection	rect. pl.	rectangular plate
Cmdr.	Commander	Regt.	Regiment
C.-in-C.	Commander-in-Chief	rel.	relaid
Cpl.	Corporal	rep.	repaired
commem.	commemorating	rev.	reverse
dau.	daughter	Rev.	Reverend
dec.	deceased	R.H.P.	R.H. Pearson
dext.	dexter	S.	south
drg.	drawing	S.A.	south aisle
eff.	effigy	S.C.	south chapel
Eng.	English	S.C.A.	south choir aisle
engr.	engraved	Sgt.	Sergeant
esq.	esquire	Sqdn.	Squadron
Evang. symbols	evangelistic symbols	S.Tr.	south transept
fig.	figure	sh.	shield
Fr.	French	sin.	sinister
frag.	fragment	sm.	small
Gen.	General	Soc. Antiq.	Society of Antiquaries
h.	heir	temp.	temporary
hf.	half	U.R.C.	United Reformed Church
H.F.O.E.	H.F. Owen Evans	V. and A. Mus.	Victoria and Albert Museum
H.K.C.	H.K. Cameron	Ven.	Venerable
hon.	honorary	vests.	vestments
H.Q.	Headquarters	vv.	verses
inscr.	inscription	w.	wife
kng.	kneeling	yst.	youngest
Knt.	knight	W.E.G.	W.E. Gawthorp
Lat.	Latin	W.G.L.	W.G. Lack
Lt.-Col.	Lieutenant Colonel		

Hampshire

ABBOT'S ANN, St. Mary the Virgin (new church).

I. Inscr. Elizabeth, dau. of Richard Monday of Derbyshire, esq., w. of John Johnson, D.D., rector, archdeacon of Worcester, treasurer of St. David's, **1613**, C. Inscr. 161 x 548 mm, non-Purbeck slab 1150 x 865 mm.

II. Inscr. in Lat. recording installation of organ in **1888** in the 51st year of the reign of Queen Victoria, on organ, C. *III.* Inscr. with verse. Mary, w. of Stephen H. Allen, of Eastover, 1829-**1902**, mur., N. *IV.* Inscr. recording lectern light pos. in mem. of Montagu William Dance, organist and headmaster, and w. Julia Gertrude, engr. c.1910, on lectern, N. *V.* Inscr. in Lat. Keddey Ray Fletcher, **1913**, on cross, C. *VI.* Inscr. John Purver Dance, chorister for 74 years, **1931**, aged 87, on pulpit, N. *VII.* Inscr. recording gift of electric [organ] blower in **1949** by Mabel M. Hammans in mem. of parents, Stephen Henry Allen and w. Mary, copper, on organ blower, C. *VIII.* Inscr. recording renovation of ch. clock and installation of new winding gear in mem. of Charles George Precious, husband, father and grandfather, 1890-**1966**, mur., N. *IX & X.* Two inscrs. [Elizabeth] Annie Whatley, [**1974**, aged 81], and Rhoda Ponting, on flowerstands, C. *XI.* Inscr. Jesse Doust Threadgill, M.B.E., churchwarden, councillor, "Lifelong servant of church and community", 1888-**1978**, and w. Marion, 1891-1977, copper, mur., on panelling, C.

Ref: *M.B.S. Trans.*, V, p.247; *M.S.,* p.157; *Soc. Antiq. MS. 875/6*, p.1.

Ch. built, 1726.

ALDERSHOT, St. Michael the Archangel.

I. Inscr. with ach. and 2 shs. Sir John Whyte, alderman, citizen and grocer of London, died 15[73] (date not filled in), engr. c.**1570**, mur., in marble frame, old C., now S.C. *Branson, J.W., The Old Parish Church of St. Michael the Archangel, Aldershot,* 1966, p.12; *Gawthorp,* pl.51, opp. p.96; *M.B.S. Portfolio,* III, pl.10; *Portfolio Book,* pl.358; *Trivick, Picture Book,* pl.131; *Winchester Diocesan Chronicle,* Nov., 1906. Rect. pl. 680 x 550 mm. Style: London G (script 9).

II. Inscr. Mary, w. of Robert White, esq., **1583**, had 2 sons, Robert and Robert, and 2 daus., Helen, Marye; palimp., on rev. another inscr. in Lat., Fr. and Eng. Richard Spage and 2 ws. Emily and Alice, c.1405; mur., old., C., now S.C. *M.B.S. Trans.*, X, p.24 (obv. and rev.); *Palimpsests,* pl.121 (rev.). Inscr. 126 x 522 mm. Style: London G (script 10, obv.), London D (rev.).

III. Inscr. [recording gift of credence table] in mem. of Mary Ellen Branson, **1889**, on credence table, C. *IV.* Inscr. in raised letters recording gift of chalice and tablet pos. by parishioners in mem. of Annie Chalwin, **1906**, served par. for 40 years, copper, mur., on board, old N., now S.A. *V.* Inscr. in raised letters recording gift of tenor bell by friends in mem. of William Fludder, verger 1858[-1910], par. clerk 1873[-1910], "A LIFE LONG SERVANT OF THIS CHURCH", **1910**, bronze, mur., on board, Tower. *VI.* Inscr. recording dedication of "FOUR ANGEL FIGURES ROUND THE ALTAR" in mem. of Eric Barnes, 13th Hussars, "MADE HIS LAST COMMUNION IN THIS CHAPEL", **1911**, maker's name E. FINCH & SONS. ALDERSHOT, mur., on panelling, old C., now S.C. *VII.* Inscr. Stephen Newcome, **1911**, copper, on altar rail, old C., now S.C. *VIII.* Inscr. Lt.-Col. Simpson Powell, M.D., Royal Army Medical Corps, son of Christopher Bolland Powell, of Southborough, Kent, stationed at Aldershot 1904-1908, died at Rangoon, [Burma], **1911**, on

HERE LYETH THE BODY OF ELIZABETH LATE WIFE OF IOHNS
IOHNSON DOCTOR OF DIVINITY RECTOR OF THIS CHVRCH
ARCHDECON OF WORCESTER & TREASVRER OF ST DAVIDS SHE DEPTED
THIS LIFE IN CHRISTIAN FAITH Y 4 DAY OF SEPT 1613 SHE WAS Y ONLY
CHILD OF RICHARD MONDAY OF DARBISHERE ESQ & BY HER MOTHER
WAS OF THE ANCIENT FAMILY OF THE STEWKELYES OF STEWKLYE IN
THE COVNTY OF HVNT KNIGHTS & ESQVIERS FOR MANY DISCENTS

Abbot's Ann I

MORIRE·MVDO   VIVAS·DEO

Aldershot I

2

Here vnder lyeth the bodye of Marie whit late wife to
Robert whit of Aldershot in the Countye of Southe
hampton Esquier who departed this lyfe the xxi of Julie
m D lxxxm by whom he had Issue ii sonnes and ii daughters
vp : Robert and Robert he reu and Marye :

Aldershot II

Pries pur l'alme de Richer Spaine qui gist ici :
Et pur les almes de Emeline ꞇ Alice ses femes aussi
De profundis clamaui : dites pater noster ꞇ Aue mari /
Jhesu Merci . ladii helpe Jhesu Merci . Amen :

Aldershot II   palimpsest reverse

Alton I

3

stall, old C., now S.C. *IX.* Inscr. recording dedication of reredos in **1912** by friends in mem. of Anna Camilla Hoyle, on reredos, C. *X.* Inscr. James Oliver and Alice Salter, [pos. by] B.A.R., J.A. S[alter], S.C. S[alter], L.R. S[alter], E.D.L. and L.E. S[alter], engr. c.**1930**, ?brass, on cross, C. *XI.* Inscr. recording that a peal of Kent Treble Bob Major 5,024 changes was rung in **1931** in 3 hours 2 minutes by the Guildford Diocesan Guild; C.W. Denyer, treble; Miss Nancie Denyer, 2nd; A.H. Pulling, 3rd; W.H. Viggers, 4th; W. Denyer, 5th; L[ance-]Sgt. E.J. Bragg, 6th; R. Overy, 7th; C.E. Smith, tenor; conducted by A.H. Pulling, mur., on board, Tower. *XII.* Inscr. recording gift of [north] chapel furnishings by friends in mem. of Mary [Emily Ann] Bragg, **1966**, aged 19, copper, on board, on bench front, N.C./N.A. *XIII.* Inscr. recording that bell tower lamp is in mem. of Adelaide Fisher, [bell]ringer for many years, 1897-**1971**, bronze, on jamb of west door outside Tower. *XIV.* Inscr. Frederick John Brockman, [**1976**], on display case, old N., now S.A. *XV.* Inscr. Roy Pavey, 1924-**1996**, on cupboard, Parish Meeting Room. *XVI.* Inscr. Betty Truss, 1924-**1996**, on gate, Churchyard. *XVII.* Inscr. Reginald Frank Haskell, 1926-**2000**, on cupboard, N. *XVIII.* Inscr. David Michael Howells, 1933-**2002**, on statue plinth, old C., now S.C.

INDENTS & LOST BRASSES. 19. Indent, eff. and 2 shs. Robert White, 1599, in gown, left w. Mary, only dau. and h. of William Forster, citizen of London, and 2 daus. and coh., Ellen, w. of Sir Richard Tichborne, son and h. of Sir Benjamin Tichborne, Knt., of Tichborne, and Mary, w. of Sir Walter Tichborne, 2nd son of Sir Benjamin Tichborne, Knt.; with incised inscr.; formerly on A.T., ?C.; in 2006 covered by fitted carpet, old C., now S.C. Recorded (incised inscr. with eff. lost and 2 shs. "which being loose were carried home by White Tichbourne, Esq") by Pavey (1706). *Sadler, Dorset and Hampshire*, appx. I, pt.2, p.12 (drg. of lower pt. of eff.). Eff. c.610 mm, shs. 135 x 120 mm, slab 2360 x 1120 mm. 20. Lost brass, inscr., C. Recorded (inscr. mutil.) by Pavey (1706). 21. Lost brass, inscr., C. Recorded (lost) by Pavey (1706).

Ref: *Brit. Lib. Stowe MS. 845,* ff.32-3; *Gawthorp*, p.96; *Haines*, II, p.76; *Heseltine, Heraldry*, p.36; *M.B.S. Trans.*, V, pp.247-9, VIII, p.367, X, pp.23-4; *M.S.*, p.157; *Norris, Memorials*, p.97, p.237; *Palimpsests*, 286L1-2, p.71; *Sadler, Dorset and Hampshire,* appx. I, pt.2, pp.12-5; *Soc. Antiq. MS. 875/6*, pp.1-3.

Ch. originally chancel with a nave rebuilt in 1865; in 1910-11 a new chancel, nave and north aisle were added to the north of the old ch. with the old chancel and nave becoming a south chapel and south aisle.

ALRESFORD, NEW, St. John the Baptist.

I. Inscr. Rev. Henry Collins, chaplain at Trieste, Italy, **1859**, [aged 38], buried at Bishops Sutton, pos. by "Contributions of his hearers during his temporary ministrations in this Church", mur., N.A. *II.* Cross with inscr. and verse on circlet. Christopher Cooke, 1833, aged 74, engr. c.**1880**, mur., on marble, N.A. *III.* Inscr. recording gift of reredos by w. in mem. of Capt. George Francis Marx, J.P., D[urham] L[ight] I[nfantry], of Arlebury, **1883**, aged 34, on reredos, N.C. *IV.* Inscr. with verse. John Herbert Hall, **1887**, aged 16, pos. by "Schoolfellows" 1880-1887, maker's name JONES & WILLIS, mur., N.A. *V.* Inscr. Edward Blackmore, 1879, aged 79, and w. Mary, **1890**, aged 87, [residents] in the par. for many years, both [buried] at Torquay, [Devon]; also eld. son, Edward [Blackmore], 1890, aged 57, [buried] at Beauworth, maker's name HART, SON, PEARD & Cº, LONDON, mur., N.C. *VI.* Inscr. recording rehanging of bells in **1897** by public subscription to commem. diamond jubilee of Queen Victoria; [Rev.] A[lexander] A[rthur] Headley, rector [1889-1915]; J. Hall and J.G. Gladstones, churchwardens, mur., W.Porch/Tower. *VII.* Inscr. with Lat. verse. Midshipman Edward Thomas Hodgson, R.N., H.M.S. Invincible, [son of Harold Hodgson, M.B., J.P., and w. Jessie], killed at the Battle of Jutland, **1916**, aged 17, pos. by friends, mur., S.A. *VIII.* Inscr. with Lat. verse. Lt. John Solomon Riddell Hodgson, 2nd Battn. Dorsetshire Regt., [son of Harold Hodgson, M.B., J.P., and w. Jessie], killed in action leading his platoon at Jebel Hamrin, Mesopotamia, **1917**, aged 20, mur., S.A. *IX.* Inscr. with verse and regt. insignia. [Pte.] Hugh Frederick Denys Pring, [767371, C Co. London Regt. (Artists' Rifles), son of Engineer-Capt. Frederick Pring, R.N., and w. Agnes Mabel, of The Old House, killed] in action near Aveluy Wood, France, **1918**, aged 18 years and 9 months, buried at Varennes [Military Cemetery], mur., S.A. *X.* Inscr. with enamelled ach. in relief. Herbert Henry Walford, "TO WHOM THE RESTORATION AND REBUILDING OF THIS CHURCH IN 1898 WAS PRINCIPALLY DUE", 1835-**1928**, mur., in stone frame, sedilia, C. *XI.* Inscr. with verse. Charles Dysart and [w.] Edyth Dysart; Charles William Galwey Dysart; C. Hugh Galwey Dysart; and Lt.-Col. John Scot Graham, I[ndian] A[rmy], engr. c.**1930**, on reredos with no.*III*, N.C. *XII.* Inscr. recording rehanging of bells ("IN AN IRON FRAME") in **1936** by public subscription to commem. silver jubilee of George V; [Rev.] Canon A[ndrew] J[ohn] Robertson, [M.A.], rector [1925-1942], r[ural] d[ean]; E.O. Barker, M.W. Loveridge and J.A. Monck, churchwardens, bronze, mur., W.Porch/Tower. *XIII.* Inscr. recording gift [of ship's plaque] in **1942** by capt. and ship's company of H.M.S. Alresford to "THE TOWN OF ALRESFORD", copper, on ship's plaque, S.A. *XIV.* Inscr. recording gift of electrical mechanism for ch. clock in **1949** by Elizabeth Frances Culley, 1952, in mem. of 2 sons, bronze, on screen, N. *XV.* Inscr. Digby Grist, "WHO LOVED AND WORKED FOR ALRESFORD", engr. c.**1950**, on display case, S.A. *XVI.* Inscr. [Rev.] Arthur John Pearson, M.C., rector 1949-**1970**, bronze, mur., sedilia, C. *XVII.* Inscr. recording that Royal Arms [of Queen Elizabeth II] pos. in mem. of Rev. Arthur John Pearson, M.C., rector 1949-**1970**, bronze, on screen with no.*XIV*, N. *XVIII.* Inscr. recording completion of tower restoration in **1991** by public subscription; [Rev.] G[raham] C[harles] G[eorge] Trasler, [M.A.], rector [1984-2002]; Mrs. D. Thornton and D[avid M.] Griffiths, churchwardens, mur., W.Porch/Tower. *XIX.* Inscr. Frank May Lunn, "HE LOVED TO WORSHIP HERE", 1894-**1993**, on prie-dieu, C. *XX.* Inscr. Ron Read, 1913-**1998**, bronze, on bench, Churchyard.

Ch. essentially, 1898.

ALRESFORD, OLD, St. Mary (new church).

I. Inscr. recording dedication [of pulpit] by son and dau., George Henry [Heywood] and Mary Elizabeth Sumner, in mem. of Thomas Heywood, **1866**, on pulpit, N. *II.* Inscr. Mary E. Heywood, **1870**, on lectern, N. *III.* Inscr. with verse. Guildford James Hillier Mainwaring Ellerker Onslow, **1882**, [buried] in the churchyard, mur., on marble, N. *IV.* Inscr. with verse. Harriet Charlotte Matilda Onslow, 1885, [aged 59]; also sister, S.A. Arabella Onslow, **1899**, aged 82, maker's name *J. WIPPELL & COMP^Y EXETER & LONDON*, mur., on marble, N. *V.* Inscr. Rear-Admiral John S. Hallifax, churchwarden, **1904**, aged 58, maker's name *J. WIPPELL & C^O L^TD EXETER & LONDON*, mur., N. *VI.* [Rev.] Frederick Mathews Middleton, [M.A.], rector 1894-1904, **1904**, aged 73, pos. by parishioners, rect. pl., inscr. on base of stepped cross and marg. inscr. with verse and roundels at corners, maker's name T. PRATT & SONS, LONDON, mur., Organ Chamber. *VII.* Inscr. recording gift of electric organ blower in **1950** by parents, rector and Mrs. Selwyn, in mem. of Robert Jasper Selwyn, pos. by P.C.C., mur., Organ Chamber.

VIII. Inscr. Rosina Kate Rogers, **1967**, aged 95, bronze, on wooden cross, Churchyard. *IX.* Inscr. recording restoration [of lychgate] in **1972** in mem. of Florence Maud Richardson, 1890-1971, on lychgate, Churchyard. *X.* Inscr. recording refurbishment of ch. clock in **1982** in mem. of Susan Augusta Mary Isaac, of Fobdown, 1891-1980, mur., on board, W.Porch/Tower. *XI.* Inscr. "Forever thinking of Our little princess Gemma" [Jeanette Smith, 1982-**1997**], bronze, on bench, Churchyard. *XII.* Inscr. "Our dear little boy Josh ❤", engr. c.**1997**, bronze, on bench with no.*XI*, Churchyard. *XIII.* Inscr. on oval-shaped pl. Leslie Charles Ings, 1912-**2000**, on paschal candleholder, N. *XIV.* Inscr. recording "MILLENNIUM PROJECT" in **2000** (reordering front and rear of the nave to create more space, improving access to the font and extending the wall panelling to incorporate notice boards), mur., on panelling, N. *XV.* Inscr. Peggy Burchett, 1920-**2001**, on bench, Churchyard.

INDENTS & LOST BRASSES. 16. Lost brass, inscr. Henry Cryvin, canon of Wells, rector, 1485, C. Recorded by Pavey (1706).

Ref: *Brit. Lib. Add. MS. 14296*, f.94, *Add. MS. 39959,* f.39r, *Stowe MS. 845*, f.94; *M.B.S. Trans.*, V, p.249; *Soc. Antiq. MS. 875/6*, p.3.

Ch. built, 1753 and 1769.

ALTON, St. Lawrence.

I. Lady, c.**1510**; inscr. lost; formerly N., now mur., on pillar, N.; orig. slab, Churchyard. Probably Joan, w. of John Fylder, 1518. Eff. 492 x 169 mm, slab 1410 x 705 mm. Style: London F.

II. Three daus., c.**1510**; formerly N., now mur., on pillar with no.I, N. Daus. 109 x 91 mm. Style: London ?F.

III. Inscr. Richard Clarke, 1485, and dau. Margery, w. of Richard Fylder, **1534**; formerly C., now mur., on pillar with nos.I & II, N. Inscr. 143 x 353 mm. Style: London F.

IV. Inscr. with rebus. Christopher Walaston, groom of the chamber and "on of ye yostregere (keeper of the goshawks) unto ye late kynges & quenes of famous memorye", **1563** (date added), mur., on pillar with nos.I, II & III, N. *Couper*, p.12; *M.B.S. Trans.*, V, p.251. Inscr. 252 x 317 mm. Style: London G (script 9).

V. (Formerly M.S.VI). Inscr. with 2 Eng. and 2 Lat. vv. Elizabeth Geale, **1638**; formerly S.A., now mur., on pillar with nos.I, II, III & IV, N. Inscr 160 x 414 mm.

VI. (Formerly M.S.VII). Inscr. Robert Lamport, **1667**, worn; formerly S.A., now mur., Vestry. Inscr. 414 x 313 mm.

VII. Inscr. Thomas Pinke, senior, 1713, and w. Ann, 1726; also son, Thomas Pinke, **1765**, w. Elizabeth, 1753, and 3 children, buried in family vault near pillar, maker's name *Wm Roe Alton Sculp*, copper, mur., on pillar, C. Inscr. 215 x 315 mm. *VIII.* Inscr. on oval-shaped pl. John Pinke, **1772**, aged 65; now mur., Vestry; orig. slab, Churchyard. Inscr. 405 x 358 mm, slab 1860-1930 x 970 mm. *IX.* Inscr. Thomas Clement, 1826, aged 71, and w. Jane, dau. of

6

Alton II

Of yo[u]r charite pray for the soul of rychard
clarke whyche decesid [the] xi day of aprill in [the] yere
of o[u]r lord god M wᶜ lxxxv and for the soule of
margery his dowghter late the wyfe of wyl
fylder [the] whyche decesid xxv day of aprill
in [the] yere of o[u]r lord god Mᵒ vᶜ xxvij on
whos soul ihu have mercy AMEN

Alton III

Here under lyeth xpofor wallsi-
to who sumtyme was grome of [the]
chamber & on of [the] postregere unto
[the] late kynges & quenes of famous
memorye henry the viij edwarde
[the] sixte phillype and marye and to
our Soueraigne ladye Elizabethe [the]
Quenes maiestie that now is wᶜ
xpofor Departid thys miserable
worlde the xvi daye of [the] monght
of Anuarie An dm M vᶜ lxvij

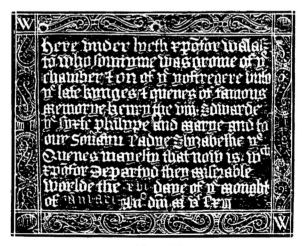

Alton IV

7

MEMENTO MORI

HERE LYETH. THE BODY OF ELIZABETH GEALE WHO
DEPARTED THIS LIFE THE XXV. DAY OF MAIE
ANNO DOMINI 1638.
Her defire or her Parents was as followeth
DEARE PARENTS WEEPE NOT. I LIVE. & HAVE ABODE
IN BLISSE: ENIOYING HEAVEN. POSTERITY. & GOD
VIVO. FRVOR TANDEM VERIS: NE FLETE PARENTES.)
DELICIIS. CŒLO. POSTERITATE. DEO.

Alton *V*

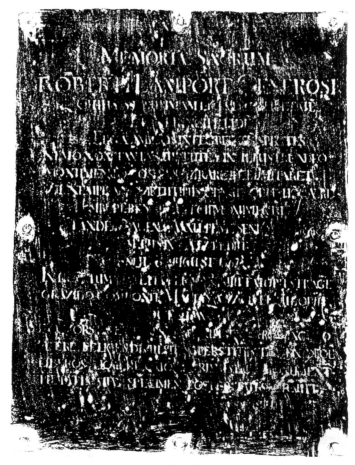

Alton *VI*

IN the FAMILY VAULT near this PILLAR.
Lyeth the Body of THOMAS PINKE, Sen.
Who died Oct: the 22, 1715.
ALSO of ANN, his Wife Who died Feb: the 1, 1720.
ALSO of THOMAS PINKE, his SON, who died
MAY the 10, 1765.
ALSO of ELIZABETH, his Wife who died
JUNE the 24 1755.
With 5 Small Children of THO. and ELIZ.

Alton *VII*

In Humble HOPE
of a
BLESSED RESURECTION
HERE
are Deposited the Remains
of
Mr IOHN PINKE,
of this Town.
He Departed this Life
the 17th September 1772
Aged 65 Years.

Alton *VIII*

HERE LYETH Y BODY OF ROBERT FRY (LATE
HEDD BAILLIFFE OF THIS TOWNE) WHO DIED Y
TWELVETH DAY OF NOVEMB. AND WAS BVRIED
Y FIVETEENTH DAY OF Y SAME AN. DNI 1620.
VILLICATIONIS RATIONEM REDDIDI

Alton 29

Benjamin White, of South Lambeth, **1831**, aged 75, [buried] in vault on south side of pillar, mur., on pillar with nos.I, II, IV & *V*, N. *X.* Inscr. in Lat. [Ven. Dr.] Thomas Balguy, D.D., archdeacon of Winchester, vicar 1771-1795, and [Very Rev. Dr.] Thomas Rennell, D.D., Dean [of Winchester], vicar 1795-1814, pos. in 1846 by [Rev.] Edward James, M.A., vicar [1832-**1854**], mur., on pillar with no.*VII*, C. *XI.* Inscr. in Lat. recording east window pos. by widow, children and friends in mem. of [Rev.] Edward James, M.A., vicar for 22 years [1832-1854], **1854**, mur., on pillar with nos.*VII & X*, C. *XII.* Inscr. in Lat. recording gift [of lectern] in **1868** by [Rev.] A.W. Deey, M.A., [F.R.A.S., curate], bronze, on lectern, N. *XIII.* Inscr. Richard Boles, killed at Alton, 1641, maker's name J SEARGENT, FECIT WINTON. **1871**; a facsimile, mur., on pillar, N. Inscr. 342-368 x 240 mm. See Winchester Cathedral no.*IV*. *XIV.* Inscr. Joseph and Emma Thompson; also children, Annette, Emma, William and Margaret Katherine Thompson, pos. in **1876** by only surviving child, Elizabeth Mary Thompson, mur., on pillar with no.*XIII*, N. Inscr. 360 x 270 mm. *XV.* Inscr. in raised letters recording insertion of glass in [east south chapel] window in **1884** by public subscription in mem. of Louis Leslie, M.D., of Amery House, physician in the town and neighbourhood for nearly 40 years, 1822-1883 bronze, mur., below window, S.C. *XVI.* Inscr. with regt. insignia within border of oak leaves, acorns and thistles. Major William Bruce Brand, 93[rd (Sutherland] Highlanders[) Regt. of Foot], died at Aldershot, **1890**, aged 40, pos. by brother officers, maker's name HART SON PEARD & CO LONDON, mur., N. *XVII.* Inscr. in Lat. John Atkinson Plow, master of Alton Grammar School (founded in 1643) for 35 years and in charge of ecclesiastical matters for 28 years, 1896, aged 90, pos. in **1897** by pupils, mur., S.C. *XVIII.* Inscr. Arthur Curtis, of Exmouth, died at Alton, **1898**, and w. Maria Emily, died at Davos, Switzerland, 1896, mur., on pillar, N. *XIX.* Inscr. with verse. Cpl. Percy Hetherington, Thorneycroft's Mounted Infantry, killed at Spion Kop, South Africa, **1900**, [aged 22], maker's name HART · SON · PEARD · & · C⁰ · L^D. LONDON, mur., S.C. *XX.* Inscr. with Lat. verse and 4 regt. insignia recording erection of tablet and choir gas standards by public subscription in mem. of Farrier-Cpl. W. Goddard, Army Service Corps; Pte. S. Pitt, 3rd [Battn.] Hampshire Regt.; Pte. T. Youde, Volunteer Co. 1st [Battn.] Hampshire Regt.; and Cpl. P[ercy] Hetherington, Thorneycroft's Mounted Infantry, [killed] in the South African War 1899-**1902**, maker's name HART SON PEARD & C⁰ L^D LONDON, mur., S.A. *XXI.* Inscr. with verse in raised letters. John Lowis, government advocate and member of the Legislative Council of Burma, **1905**; also Katherine Harriet, w. of R.A. D'O. Bignell, 1900, son and dau. of John Mangles Lowis and [w.] Ellen, of Amery House, mur., S.C. *XXII.* Inscr. Lt. John Rollo Lowis, Hants Yeomanry attd. 15th Battn. Hampshire Regt., [son of Hon. John Lowis and w. Monica, of The White House, Fawkham, Kent, **1918**], aged 24, [buried at Voormezeele Enclosure No. 3, Ieper, West Vlaanderen, Belgium]; Temporary-Major Tom Lowis Bourdillon, [M.C.], 8th [Battn.] King's Royal Rifle Corps, [son of Sir James and Lady Bourdillon, of Westlands, Liphook, 1917], aged 29, [buried at Tyne Cot Cemetery, Zonnebeke, West Vlaanderen, Belgium]; and Lt. Robin Lowis Campbell Brown, 8th Trench Mortar Battery, [Royal Field Artillery, son of Colin Campbell Brown and w. Louise, of Vernon, British Columbia, Canada, 1917], aged 22, [buried at Lijssentheok Military Cemetery, Poperinge, West Vlaanderen, Belgium]; grandsons of John M[angles] Lowis and [w.] Ellen, of Amery House, maker's name A. & N. AUX. C.S.L. LONDON, mur., S.C. *XXIII.* Inscr. recording gift of chair in **1920** for use in the "War Memorial Chapel of S. Michael and S. George" in mem. of a priest, on chair, S.C. *XXIV.* Inscr. with verse and regt. insignia. Major Godfrey Percy Burrell, M.C., 4th Battn. Hampshire Regt., served with regt. in [World War I] and twice mentioned in despatches, **1931**, aged 50, maker's name MAILE LTD. ENGRAVERS. 367 EUSTON R^D LONDON, copper, mur., on pillar, S.C. *XXV.* Inscr. Dorothy Burke, **1963**, bronze, mur., S.C. *XXVI.* Inscr. recording [south] chapel pews in mem. of William Hugh Curtis, churchwarden, and w. Avesia, engr. **1966**, bronze; on pew, S.C., now S.A. *XXVII.* Inscr.

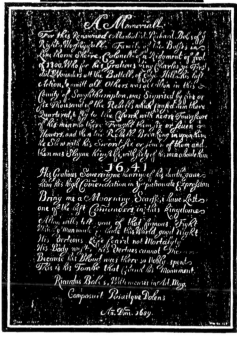

A FAC-SIMILE OF THE BRASS TABLET IN
Winchester Cathedral.

A Memoriall.

For this Renowned Martialist Richard Boles of ye Right Worshipfull Family of the Boles in Lincolne Shire, Colonell of a Regiment of foot of 1200, Who for his Gratious King Charles ye First did Wonders att the Battell of Edge Hill. His last Action, to omitt all Others was at Alton in this County of Southampton, was Surprised by five or Six Thousand of the Rebells which caused him there Quarter'd, he fly to the Church with neare fourscore of his men who there Fought them six or seaven Howers, and then the Rebell Breaking in upon him he Slew with his Sword six or seaven of them and then was Slayne himselfe, with sixty of his men aboute him

16,41

His Gratious Soveraigne hearing of his death gave him his high Commendation in ye pathionate Expression

Bring me a Mourning Scarffe, i have Lost one of the best Commanders in this Kingdome

Alun will; tell you of that famous Fight Which y man made & bade this World good Night His Verteous Life feard not Mortality His Body must, his Vertues cannot Die Because his Blood was there so Nobly spent This is his Tombe that Church his Monument.

Ricardus Boles, Withimensis in Art. Mgg.

Composuit Posuitque Dolens

An. Dni. 1689.

Alton *XIII*

To the Glory of GOD and in loving memory of Joseph and Emma Thompson and of their children Annette Emma William and Margaret Katherine Thompson
The remains of Emma Thompson are laid in a vault near this spot
This Tablet is placed here by Elizabeth Mary Thompson only surviving child of the above named Joseph and Emma Thompson
AD 1876

Alton *XIV*

recording gift [of piano] in **1969** by Constance Kerridge in mem. of husband, Leonard Cecil Kerridge, and father, Robert Charles Hayward, organist, on piano, S.C. *XXVIII*. Inscr. recording presentation [of bench] in **2002** by Alton Townswomen's Guild, on bench, Churchyard.

INDENTS & LOST BRASSES. 29. *(Formerly M.S.V)*. Lost brass, inscr. Robert Fry "LATE HEDD BAILLIFFE OF THIS TOWNE", 1620; formerly S.A., Churchyard, mur., Vestry; orig. slab, Churchyard. Recorded by Cave (1908) but not found (2006). Illustration from rubbing in Soc. Antiq. coll. Rubbing in Soc. Antiq. coll. (n.d.). Inscr. 148 x 449 mm, freestone slab 1850 x 790 mm.

Ref: *Bod. Lib. Gough Gen. Top. 33*, f.187, *MS. Gough Misc. Antiq. 15*, f.5; *Brit. Lib. Add. MS. 39959*, ff.167-8; *Couper, D.L., The Story of the Parish Church of St. Lawrence, Alton*, 8th edn., 2002, p.13, p.16, p.31, p.37, p.43; *Gawthorp*, p.103; *Gough*, II, pt.2, p.295; *Haines*, II, pp.71-2; *Hampshire History*, III, p.314; *M.B.S. Bulletin*, 23, p.15; *M.B.S. Trans.*, V, pp.250-3, VI, p.122, VIII, p.215; *Mee, Hampshire*, p.24; *M.S.*, pp.157-8; *Sadler, Dorset and Hampshire*, appx. I, pt.2, p.41; *Soc. Antiq. MS. 875/6*, pp.4-7; *Squibb*, p.223; *V.C.H., Hampshire*, II, p.482.

ALVERSTOKE, St. Mary (new church).

I. Inscr. Elizabeth, dau. of William Cotten, w. of Daniel Bradly, **1664**, aged 26, N.A. Inscr. 252 x 850 mm, black marble slab 1210 x 730 mm.

II. Inscr. Richard New, **1760**, aged 82, mur., Baptistry/S.A. Inscr. 424 x 269 mm. *III.* Inscr. with verse. Robert Cruickshank, founder of ch., **1853**, [aged 68, buried] in vault beneath, maker's name WALLER FECIT LONDON (and monogram), mur., N.A.; from Anglesey (q.v.). *IV.* Inscr. in Lat. Amelia Francesca, [dau. of Samuel Bamfyde] Windser [and w. Blanche Marianne], died on a sea voyage, 1854, engr. c.1865, mur., below window, S.C. *V.* Inscr. [Rev.] Joseph W. Barlow, 1859, engr. c.1865, mur., sedilia, C. *VI.* Inscr. Richard Hallilay, R.N., died at Bath, [Somerset], 1860, and w. Sarah, died [at Alverstoke], 1847, pos. by 3 surviving children, engr. c.1865, mur., below window, S.C. *VII.* Inscr. with verse in mem. of Thomas Potter, 1862, and w. Georgina Eliza, 1857, engr. c.1865, mur., below window, S.C. *VIII.* Inscr. recording erection of east window in mem. of [Rt. Rev. Dr.] Samuel Wilberforce, D.D., rector 1840-1845, Bishop of Oxford 1845-1869, Bishop of Winchester 1869-1873, [1805-1873], and gift of mural painting surrounding east window by [Wilberforce] family in mem. of [Rev.] Edward Barnard, M.A., rector 1825-1840, engr. c.1875, mur., sedilia, C. See also Alverstoke, or Gosport, Fort Brockhurst no.*XXXIII*, Hinton Ampner no.*IX*, Newport, St. Thomas the Apostle no.*IX*, Petersfield no.*VI*, Ryde, or Swanmore, St. Michael and All Angels no.*III* and Winchester Cathedral no.*X*. *IX.* Inscr. recording erection of nave and aisles in mem. of [Rev. Canon] Thomas Walpole, M.A., hon. canon of Winchester Cathedral, rector for 35 years [1846-1881, 1805-]**1881**, mur., S.A. *X.* Inscr. with verse recording lectern pos. by w. and brother officers in mem. of Major Henry Harford Strong, Royal Marine L[igh]t Infantry, killed at the Battle of Tel-el-Kebir, Egypt, "WHILE GALLANTLY LEADING THE FIGHTING LINE OF HIS BATTALION", **1882**, on lectern, N. *XI.* Marg. inscr. with 4 angels at corners. Harriet Susanna, widow of Robert Cruickshank, 1799-**1885**, maker's name COX & BUCKLEY LONDON, mur., N.A.; from Anglesey (q.v.). *XII.* Inscr. with verse on lozenge-shaped pl. Mary Louisa, dau. of Robert Cruickshank [and w. Harriet Susanna], 1814-**1885**, maker's name COX & BUCKLEY LONDON, mur., N.A.; from Anglesey (q.v.). *XIII.* Inscr. Frances Charles Lane, chorister, **1886**, mur., on board, Choir

HERE LYETH INTERRED THE BODY OF =
E⬜ZABETH BRADLY WIFE OF DANIEL BRADLY
DAVGHTER OF WILLIAM COtten OF ALDERSTOCK
WHOE DEPARTED THIS LIFE THE 25TH OF =
NOVEMBER 1664 BEING 26 YEARES OF HER AGE

Alverstoke I

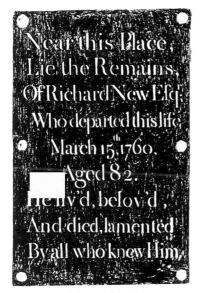

Near this Place,
Lie the Remains,
Of Richard New Efq:
Who departed this life
March 15, 1760.
Aged 82.
He liv'd, belov'd,
And died, lamented
By all who knew Him,

Alverstoke *II*

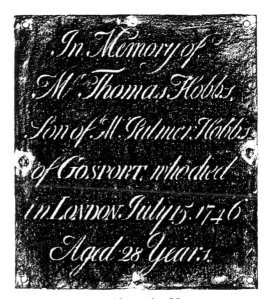

In Memory of
M[r] Thomas Hobbs,
Son of M[r] Palmer Hobbs,
of Gosport, who died
in London, July 15, 1746
Aged 28 Year:1.

Alverstoke 35

ALSO
In Memory Of
M[r] PALMER HOBBS
of Gosport who Departed this Life
the 25 Day of August 1740
AGED 67 YEARS

Alverstoke 36

Vestry. *XIV.* Inscr. Mary Anne Paffard Larcom, w. of Lt.-Gen. M[ontagu] Burrows, 1832; Capt. Joseph Paffard Dickson Larcom, R.N., [1795-]1850; Rt. Hon. Major-Gen. Sir Thomas Aiskew Larcom, [1st] Bart., [P.C.], K.C.B., [LL.D., F.R.S.], R[oyal] E[ngineers, 1801-]1879; Elizabeth Larcom, 1866; and Harriet Georgina Larcom, **1886**, children of Capt. Joseph Larcom, [R.N., 1818, aged 54] and w. Ann, [dau. of William Hollis, 1843, aged 82], mur., below window, S.A. *XV.* Inscr. Thomas John Ursell, chorister, **1887**, mur., on board, Choir Vestry. *XVI.* Inscr. with verse on lozenge-shaped pl. Ellen Haldane, dau. of Robert Cruickshank [and w. Harriet Susanna], 1819-**1892**, maker's name COX & BUCKLEY LONDON, mur., N.A.; from Anglesey (q.v.). *XVII.* Inscr. in Lat. with ach. [Rev.] John Charles Dawkins, [M.A.], vicar of Elson [Gosport] for 21 years, [died after baptising a child suffering from diphtheria], **1894**, aged 53, mur., on marble, N.A. *XVIII.* Inscr. Rev. Purefoy Collis, M.A., curate for 50 years, 1779, aged 77; also Emily Sarah Langtry, "THE LAST OF HER GENERATION", **1894**, aged 87, mur., below window, N.A. *XIX.* Inscr. with verse. Inspector-Gen. Benjamin William Marlow, M.D., C.B., "SERVED THROUGHOUT THE CRIMEAN CAMPAIGN 1854-1856, AND WAS PRESENT AT THE BATTLES OF THE ALMA AND INKERMAN, AND WAS PRESENT AT THE SIEGE AND FALL OF SEVASTOPOL FOR WHICH WAR SERVICE HE RECEIVED THE CRIMEAN MEDAL WITH THREE CLASPS, THE ORDER OF THE LEGION OF HONOUR, AND THE TURKISH MEDAL. HE ALSO SERVED IN INDIA FOR MANY YEARS AND WAS MADE A COMPANION OF THE BATH IN 1873", **1894**, aged 74, maker's name JONES & WILLIS, mur., N. *XX.* Inscr. in raised letters. Mary Kane, 1798-**1895**, on lychgate, Churchyard. *XXI.* Inscr. with verse on lozenge-shaped pl. Eliza, dau. of Robert Cruickshank [and w. Harriet Susanna], 1813-**1898**, [maker's name COX & BUCKLEY LONDON], mur., N.A.; from Anglesey (q.v.). *XXII.* Inscr. recording removal of nos.*III, XI, XII, XVI & XXI* from orig. position over family vault following demolition of Anglesey ch. in **1911**, mur., below nos.*III, XI, XII, XVI & XXI*, N.A. *XXIII.* Inscr. within border of 4 anchors and chains. Vice-Admiral Frank Hannam Henderson, C.M.G., D.S.O., J.P., [son of John Hannam Henderson and w. Laura Catherine, of Worth, Kent], died "WHILE NOBLY SERVING HIS COUNTRY IN COMMAND OF CONVOYS", **1918**, aged 68, [buried at Haslar Royal Naval Cemetery], and w. [Agnes Jane] (Nesta), maker's name A&N AUX C.S.L LONDON, mur., S.A. *XXIV.* Inscr. with verse. Col. Robert Alexander Wauchope, C.B., C.I.E., C.M.G., Royal Engineers, died at Morgins, Switzerland, 1855-1921, [buried] at Lausanne, [Switzerland], and w. Catherine Mary, died at Simla, India, 1861-1896, maker's name A&N. AUX C.S.L. LONDON, engr. **1928**, copper, mur., S.A. *XXV & XXVI.* Two inscrs. Charles Woollven Greening, D.S.O., D.S.C., R.N., **1958**, on vases, N.A. *XXVII.* Inscr. Ernest Douglas, F.R.C.O., choirmaster and organist 1899-**1959**, pos. by [choristers], on organ, N.A. *XXVIII.* Inscr. H.R. and D.W. Haggis, engr. c.**1975**, on flowerstand, N. *XXIX.* Inscr. recording gift of [display] case and book in mem. of George Scurlock Bowen Evans, 1927-1984, on display case, N.A. *XXX.* Inscr. Herbert Hayward Edridge, 1911-**1985**, bronze, on bench, Churchyard. *XXXI.* Inscr. commem. the ch. parade led by H/Capt. R.C. Creelman for the Canadian troops prior to embarkation for Normandy on 50th anniversary of D-Day in **1994**, mur., on board, S.Porch. *XXXII.* Inscr. "IN MEMORIAM Donations to St. Mary's Organ Fund have been given in memory of those whose names appear within this book", engr. c.**1995**, on display case on organ, N.A. *XXXIV.* Inscr. with heart on separate pl. Phyllis May Lane, 1923-**1998**, bronze, on gravestone, Churchyard.

INDENTS & LOST BRASSES. 35. Lost brass, inscr. Thomas Hobbs, son of Palmer Hobbs, of Gosport, died in London, 1746, aged 28. Recorded by Stephenson (1938) but not found (2006). Illustration from rubbing in Soc. Antiq. coll. Rubbing in Soc. Antiq. coll. (1909). Inscr. 279 x 252 mm. 36. Lost brass, inscr. Palmer Hobbs, of Gosport, 1749, aged 67. Recorded by Stephenson (1938) but not found (2006). Illustration from rubbing in Soc. Antiq. coll. Rubbing

Alverstoke 37

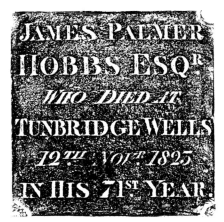

Alverstoke 38

Alverstoke 39

in Soc. Antiq. coll. (1909). Inscr. 145 x 251 mm. 37. Lost brass, inscr. Ann, w. of Capt. James Hobbs, 1766, aged 54. Recorded by Stephenson (1938) but not found (2006). Illustration from rubbing in Soc. Antiq. coll. Rubbing in Soc. Antiq. coll. (1909). Inscr. 203 x 152 mm. 38. Lost brass, inscr. James Palmer Hobbs, died at Tunbridge Wells, [Kent], 1825, [aged 70]. Recorded by Stephenson (1938) but not found (2006). Illustration from rubbing in Soc. Antiq. coll. Rubbing in Soc. Antiq. coll. (1909). Inscr. 254 x 252 mm. 39. Lost brass, inscr. Elizabeth Hobbs, 1830, aged 79. Recorded by Stephenson (1938) but not found (2006). Illustration from rubbing in Soc. Antiq. coll. Rubbing in Soc. Antiq. coll. (1909). Inscr. 145 x 329 mm.

Ref: *Burke's Peerage and Baronetage*, p.1541, p.2742; *M.B.S. Trans.*, V, p.253; *M.S.*, p.158, p.753; *Soc. Antiq. MS. 875/6*, p.7.

Ch. built, 1865, 1885 and 1906.

ALVERSTOKE, or ANGLESEY, St. Mark (now demolished).

Inscr. with verse. Robert Cruickshank, founder of ch., **1853**, [aged 68, buried] in vault beneath, maker's name WALLER FECIT LONDON (and monogram); moved to Alverstoke (q.v.) (1911). Marg. inscr. with 4 angels at corners. Harriet Susanna, widow of Robert Cruickshank, 1799-**1885**, maker's name COX & BUCKLEY LONDON; moved to Alverstoke (q.v.) (1911). Inscr. with verse on lozenge-shaped pl. Mary Louisa, dau. of Robert Cruickshank [and w. Harriet Susanna], 1814-**1885**, maker's name COX & BUCKLEY LONDON; moved to Alverstoke (q.v.) (1911). Inscr. with verse on lozenge-shaped pl. Ellen Haldane, dau. of Robert Cruickshank [and w. Harriet Susanna], 1819-**1892**, maker's name COX & BUCKLEY LONDON; moved to Alverstoke (q.v.) (1911). Inscr. with verse on lozenge-shaped pl. Eliza, dau. of Robert Cruickshank [and w. Harriet Susanna], 1813-**1898**, [maker's name COX & BUCKLEY LONDON]; moved to Alverstoke (q.v.) (1911).

Ch. built, 1844; demolished, 1911.

ALVERSTOKE, or GOSPORT, Fort Brockhurst (English Heritage store).

I. Inscr. Capt. William Simpson, R.N., [buried] in the ch., 1790-**1838**; from Portsmouth, Royal Garrison Church (q.v.). Accession no. EH: 87900142. *II.* Inscr. recording erection of pulpit by shipmates stationed in the Baltic, Cape of Good Hope and East Indies in mem. of seamen and marines of H.M.S. Penelope killed at Bomarsund [in the Baltic Sea] or "DIED IN THE SERVICE OF THEIR COUNTRY", **1858**; from Portsmouth, Royal Garrison Church (q.v.). Accession no. EH: 87900117. *III.* Inscr. recording gift of [west nave] window by widow, Maria Wilhemia, in mem. of Gen. Sir Charles Menzies, K.C.B., K.H., knt. of Charles III [of Spain], Col. of Royal Marine Artillery, A.D.C. to Queen [Victoria, 1783-]**1866**; from Portsmouth, Royal Garrison Church (q.v.). Accession no. EH: 87900136. *IV.* Inscr. recording erection of [west] window in mem. of Lt.-Col. H.J.P. Booth; Capt. G.R. Mure; Capt. R.F.T. Hamilton; Capt. F. Utterton; Capt. A.R. Close; Lt. F.G.E. Glove; Ensign G.I. Langland; Sgt.-Major J. Vance; Sgt. M. Clifford; Cpl. J. Wheeler; Bugler J. Blackwall; Pte. J. Audley; Pte. G. Bradbrook; Pte. S. Bolton; Pte. P. Fitzgerald; Pte. H. Goff; Pte. J. Holbrook; Pte. J. Holohan; Pte. S. Hornsby; Pte. R. Johnson; Pte. I. Lane; Pte. T. Madden; Pte.J. Maher; Pte. J. Mcguire; Pte. R. Phelan; Pte. F. Pratt; Pte.

G. Robbins; Pte. F. Trann; Pte. W.H. Varlow; and Pte. H. Wilkinson, of the 43rd Monmouthshire Light Infantry killed in action or died of wounds during the New Zealand War 1863-**1866**; from Portsmouth, Royal Garrison Church (q.v.). Accession no. EH: 87900141. *V.* Inscr. recording gift of [south nave] window by [brother] officers, NCO's and [men] in mem. of comrades of 46th (South Devon) Regt. [of Foot, killed] in the Crimea, Corfu and the 3 presidencies of Bengal, Madras and Bombay 1854-**1868**; from Portsmouth, Royal Garrison Church (q.v.). Accession no. EH: 87900134. *VI.* Inscr. recording gift of [west nave] window by friends in mem. Major-Gen. Sir John William Gordon, K.C.B., Royal Engineers, **1870**, aged 55; from Portsmouth, Royal Garrison Church (q.v.). Accession no. EH: 87900135. *VII.* Inscr. recording dedication of [north] nave window by widow, [Catherine, only dau. of Capt. John Street, Royal Artillery] in mem. of Col. Edwin Wodehouse, C.B., [Royal Artillery], A.D.C. to Queen [Victoria], eld. son of Vice-Admiral the Hon. Philip Wodehouse, died at Portsmouth, [1817-]**1870**; from Portsmouth, Royal Garrison Church (q.v.). Accession no. EH: 87900121. *VIII.* Inscr. Town-Major Henry White, 74th (Highlanders) [Regt. of Foot], "AFTER MUCH ACTIVE SERVICE IN THE WARS OF HOLLAND AND THE PENINSULA WHERE HE WAS FOUR TIMES SEVERELY WOUNDED. HE WAS 25 YEARS TOWN MAJOR OF THIS GARRISON", 1849, aged 69, and w. Jean, died at Durham, **1870**, aged 90, pos. by son, Lt.-Col. George Francis White, 31st Regt. [of Foot]; from Portsmouth, Royal Garrison Church (q.v.). Accession no. EH: 87900143. *IX.* Inscr. on 2 pls. recording erection of [north nave] window in **1872** by [brother] officers in mem. of officers (18 names), 250 NCO's and [men] of 82nd Regt. Prince of Wales Volunteers killed in action or died since the regt. embarked for the Crimea in 1855; from Portsmouth, Royal Garrison Church (q.v.). Accession nos. EH: 87900129 & EH: 87900139. *X.* Inscr. recording erection of [north nave] window in **1872** by [brother] officers in mem. of Col. R.J. Straton, C.B.; Major H.A. Macdonald; [Major] R.H. Willington; [Major] W.N.M. Orpen; Capt. W. Gair; [Capt.] H.S. Weighall; Lt.-Adjutant G. Cook; Lt. A.T. Butts; [Lt.] A. Bishop; Ensign A.L. Heming; [Ensign] C.J. Arnold; [Ensign] F.P. Ferguson; [Ensign] H.N. Moore; and 515 NCO's and [men] of 77th (East Middlesex) Regt. [of Foot, killed] 1856-1872; from Portsmouth, Royal Garrison Church (q.v.). Accession no. EH: 87900137. *XI.* Inscr. recording dedication of [south nave] window in **1873** by widow, Augusta, [dau. of George Boyle, 4th Earl of Glasgow, G.C.H., F.R.S.], in mem. of Lt.-Gen. Lord Frederick FitzClarence, G.C.H., A.D.C. to William IV and Queen Victoria, son of William IV, entered the Coldstream Guards 1814, Lt.-Col. 1824, commanded the 11th Regt. of Infantry and 7th (Royal Fusiliers) Regt. of Foot, Lt.-Governor of Portsmouth 1847-1851, Col. 36th Regt., C.-in-C. of H.M. Forces and Honourable East India Companies Army in Bombay 1852, died at Poorundhur, India, 1799-1854; from Portsmouth, Royal Garrison Church (q.v.). Accession no. EH: 87900132. *XII.* Inscr. Capt. D[aniel] G[reen] Clery, [1869]; Capt. E[dward] M[ontagu] Kemp; Lt. and Adjutant H[enry] A[rthur] G[rey] Todd; Surgeon J. B[enjamin] Lane; and Sub-Lt. G.A. Monroe, 1st Battn. 4th (King's Own Royal) Regt. [of Foot], pos. in **1874** by brother officers; from Portsmouth, Royal Garrison Church (q.v.). Accession no. EH: 87900116. *XIII.* Inscr. in mem. of officers, NCOs and men killed or died of disease during the Ashanti Expedition, [West Africa], 1873-**1874**, pos. by Rt. Hon. Gathorne-Hardy, M.P.; from Portsmouth, Royal Garrison Church (q.v.). Accession no. EH: 87900106. *XIV.* Inscr. Major Thomas Oldfield, Royal Marines, killed at the defence of Acre, [Syria], 1799, aged 43, engr. c.**1875**; from Portsmouth, Royal Garrison Church (q.v.). Accession no. EH: 87900133. *XV.* Inscr. with verse. F.M.F.M., 1831 and M.F.F.M., 1835, engr. c.**1875**; from Portsmouth, Royal Garrison Church (q.v.). Accession no. EH: 87900123. *XVI.* Inscr. Gen. Lord [Robert] Edward H[enry] Somerset, G.C.B., [3rd] son of Henry [Somerset], 5th Duke of Beaufort, [K.G., D.C.L.], knt. of the Tower and Sword of the Order of Maria Theresa and St. Vladimir of Russia, 1776-1842; pos. by [only] son, Major-Gen. E[dward] A[rthur] Somerset, C.B., and [grand-]dau., engr. c.**1875**; from Portsmouth, Royal Garrison Church (q.v.). Accession no. EH: 87900102. *XVII.* Inscr. Capt. the Hon. [Granville] Charles Cornwallis Eliot, 1st Battn. Coldstream Guards, killed while Acting-Adjutant at the Battle of Inkerman, [1828-]1854; pos. by father, [Edward Granville Cornwallis Eliot, 3rd] Earl of St. Germans, G.C.B., [P.C., LL.D.], engr. c.**1875**; from Portsmouth, Royal Garrison Church (q.v.). Accession no. EH: 87900107. *XVIII.* Inscr. Lt.-Col. F.J. Elliot, [killed] while commanding the 79th Cameron Highlanders at Varana, 1854, pos. by M.E., engr. c.**1875**; from Portsmouth, Royal Garrison Church (q.v.). Accession no. EH: 87900105. *XIX.* Inscr. Major-Gen. Bucknell Escourt, Adjutant-Gen., died "FROM ILLNESS BROUGHT ON BY OVER EXERTION" before [the Siege of] Sevastopol, [1802-]1855, pos. by widow, [Caroline Carew], engr. c.**1875**; from Portsmouth, Royal Garrison Church (q.v.). Accession no. EH: 87900103. *XX.* Inscr. in mem. of 12 chaplains [killed] during the Crimean War [1854-1856], pos. by Chaplain's Dept., engr. c.**1875**; from Portsmouth, Royal Garrison Church (q.v.). Accession no. EH: 87900138. See also Portsmouth, Royal Garrison Church no.*XXXIII.* *XXI.* Inscr. in mem. of officers, NCOs and [men] of Coldstream Guards killed or died of disease during the Crimean War [1854-1856], pos. by regt., engr. c.**1875**; from Portsmouth, Royal Garrison Church (q.v.). Accession no. EH: 87900084. *XXII.* Inscr. in mem. of 8 officers, 7 NCOs and 233 [men] of 34th (Cumberland) Regt. [of Foot] killed or died of disease during the Crimean War [1854-1856], pos. by regt., engr. c.**1875**; from Portsmouth, Royal Garrison Church (q.v.). Accession no. EH: 87900104. *XXIII.* Inscr. in mem. of officers, NCOs and [men] of 95th (Derbyshire) Regt. [of Foot] killed or died of disease during the Crimean War [1854-1856], pos. by regt., engr. c.**1875**; from Portsmouth, Royal Garrison Church (q.v.). Accession no. EH: 87900110. *XXIV.* Inscr. in mem. of officers, NCOs and [men] of 68th (Durham Light Infantry) [Regt. of Foot] killed or died of disease during the Crimean War [1854-1856], pos. by regt., engr. c.**1875**; from Portsmouth, Royal Garrison Church (q.v.). Accession no. EH: 87900100. *XXV.* Inscr. in mem. of officers, NCOs and [men] of 77th (East Middlesex) Regt. [of Foot] killed or died of disease during the Crimean War [1854-1856], pos. by regt., engr. c.**1875**; from Portsmouth, Royal Garrison Church (q.v.). Accession no. EH: 87900114. *XXVI.* Inscr. in mem. of officers, NCOs and [men] of 9th (East Norfolk) Regt. [of Foot] killed or died of disease during the Crimean War [1854-1856], pos. by regt., engr. c.**1875**; from Portsmouth, Royal Garrison Church (q.v.). Accession no. EH: 87900113. *XXVII.* Inscr. in mem. of officers, NCOs and [men] of Grenadier Guards killed or died of disease during the Crimean War [1854-1856], pos. by regt., engr. c.**1875**; from Portsmouth, Royal Garrison Church (q.v.). Accession no. EH: 87900083. *XXVIII.* Inscr. in mem. of officers, NCOs and [men] of 47th (Lancashire) Regt. [of Foot] killed or died of disease during the Crimean War [1854-1856], pos. by regt., engr. c.**1875**; from Portsmouth, Royal Garrison Church (q.v.). Accession no. EH: 87900101. *XXIX.* Inscr. in mem. of officers, NCOs and [men] of Royal Engineers killed or died of disease during the Crimean War [1854-1856], pos. by regt., engr. c.**1875**; from Portsmouth, Royal Garrison Church (q.v.). Accession no. EH: 87900106. *XXX.* Inscr. in mem. of officers, NCOs and [men] of Scots Fusilier Guards killed or died of disease during the Crimean War [1854-1856], pos. by regt., engr. c.**1875**; from Portsmouth, Royal Garrison Church (q.v.). Accession no. EH: 87900082. *XXXI.* Inscr. in mem. of Rugbeians killed or died of disease during the Indian Mutiny [1857-1858], pos. by Rugby [school]masters, engr. c.**1875**; from Portsmouth, Royal Garrison Church (q.v.). Accession no. EH: 87900081. *XXXII.* Inscr. in mem. of officers, NCOs and [men] of 64th (2nd Staffordshire) Regt. [of Foot] killed or died of disease during the Indian Mutiny [1857-1858], pos. by regt., engr. c.**1875**; from Portsmouth, Royal Garrison Church (q.v.). Accession no. EH: 87900085. *XXXIII.* Inscr. [Rt. Rev. Dr.] Samuel Wilberforce, D.D., [Bishop of Oxford 1845-1869], Bishop of Winchester [1869-1873, 1805-1873], engr. c.**1875**; from Portsmouth, Royal Garrison Church (q.v.). Accession no.

EH: 87900118. See also Alverstoke no.*VIII*, Hinton Ampner no.*IX*, Newport, St. Thomas the Apostle no.*IX*, Petersfield no.*VI*, Ryde, or Swanmore, St. Michael and All Angels no.*III* and Winchester Cathedral no.*X*. *XXXIV.* Inscr. Lt. Charles Rufus Robson, R.N., only son of Rev. J. Stuart Robson, only brother of Ensign William James Stuart Robson, 17th Regt., engr. c.**1875**; from Portsmouth, Royal Garrison Church (q.v.). Accession no. EH: 87900140. *XXXV.* Inscr. recording dedication of nave gas standards in mem. of Major-Gen. Charles Richard Sackville-West, 6th Earl De La Warr, K.C.B., Viscount Cantelupe and Baron West, 2nd son of George John [Sackville-West], 5th Earl De La Warr, [officer] of the Legion of Honour, received the Crimea medal and 4 clasps, [knt. of the] Medjidie (3rd class), Sardinian and Turkish medals; entered the army in 1833 as ensign in the 43rd (Light Infantry) [Regt. of Foot] and in 1864 became Major-Gen., A.D.C. to Sir Hugh Gough in the Sikh War 1845, fought at Moodkee, Ferozshah and Sobraon (wounded) and received [Crimea] medal and 3 clasps and C.B., present at the Battles of Alma [1854], Balaclava [1854] and Inkerman [1854] and "SHARED IN THE ATTACKS" of the Redan [at the Siege of Sevastopol 1855], commanded a brigade in the expedition against Kinburn [1855], 1815-1873, pos. in **1876** by kinswomen by mar., Theresa Cornwallis West; from Portsmouth, Royal Garrison Church (q.v.). Accession no. EH: 87900131. *XXXVI.* Inscr. Major Charles Covey, 68th (Durham Light Infantry) [Regt. of Foot], died at Mejah, near Allahabad, India, **1881**; from Portsmouth, Royal Garrison Church (q.v.). Accession no. EH: 87900127. *XXXVII.* Inscr. Capt. Henry Humphries, commanded mounted infantry, Sgt.-Major 2nd Battn. Royal Inniskillen Fusiliers (108th Regt. [of Foot]) for 10 years, promoted to Lt. 2nd Battn. Welsh Regt. (69th [(South Lincolnshire Regt. of Foot)] 1881, "PROCEEDING TO EGYPT IN 1882 HE WAS APPOINTED PROVOST MARSHAL AND AFTERWARDS TO THE MOUNTED INFANTRY, WHICH CORPS HE COMMANDED WITH GREAT DISTINCTION IN THE CAMPAIGN IN THE SUDAN IN 1884", died at Cairo, Egypt, **1884**, aged 35, pos. by brother officers of Military Police and Mounted Infantry Corps; from Portsmouth, Royal Garrison Church (q.v.). Accession no. EH: 87900126. *XXXVIII.* Inscr. Major James Anderson Morice, Royal Marines, [killed] in the 1st Battle of El Teb, **1884**, pos. by brother officers and friends; from Portsmouth, Royal Garrison Church (q.v.). Accession no. EH: 87900144. *XXXIX.* Inscr. with verse. Admiral Robert FitzGerald Gambier, R.N., of Anglesey Terrace, chairman of the Sailors Home at Portsea for many years, 1803-**1885**; from Portsmouth, Royal Garrison Church (q.v.). Accession no. EH: 87900128. *XL.* Inscr. with regt. insignia and colours. Pte. J. Wakefield, Pte. T. Kay, Pte. W. Gatley, Pte. H. Spiers and Pte. T. Wilks "LOST THEIR LIVES THROUGH INJURIES RECEIVED AT AN EXPLOSION OF GAS" at Cambridge Barracks, **1887**, pos. by NCOs and [men] of 2nd Battn. Worcestershire Regt.; from Portsmouth, Royal Garrison Church (q.v.). Accession no. EH: 87900130. *XLI.* Inscr. Constance Adelaide Newton, pos. by M. St. Quintin, engr. c.**1900**; from Portsmouth, Royal Garrison Church (q.v.). Accession no. EH: 87900099. *XLII.* Inscr. Richard William Ford, clerk of the peace, [1822-]1900, and [w.] Emma, [1832-]1892, pos. in **1902** by [son,] Archibald [Ford, 1846-1930]; from Portsmouth, Royal Garrison Church (q.v.). Accession no. EH: 87900124 See also Wymering nos.*II, VIII & IX*. *XLIII.* Inscr. recording gift of bench by children and sister in mem. of Helen Wolseley Cox, president of Guild of St. Helena, 1840-**1905**; from Portsmouth, Royal Garrison Church (q.v.). Accession no. EH: 87900097. *XLIV.* Inscr. Rev. Joseph Barnaby Charles Murphy, M.A., chaplain to [H.M.] Forces [at Aldershot 1887-1890, Portsmouth 1890-1895 and Colchester 1899-1903], pos. in **1908** by friends; from Portsmouth, Royal Garrison Church (q.v.). Accession no. EH: 87900092. *XLV.* Inscr. recording restoration of chapel in **1908** by friends in mem. of [Rev.] Joseph Barnaby Charles Murphy, M.A., chaplain to [H.M.] Forces [at Aldershot 1887-1890, Portsmouth 1890-1895 and Colchester 1899-1903]; from Portsmouth, Royal Garrison Church (q.v.). Accession no. EH: 87900109. *XLVI.* Inscr. William and Ellen French, **1909**; from

Portsmouth, Royal Garrison Church (q.v.). Accession no. EH: 87900089. *XLVII*. Inscr. Capt. Henry Hann, **1909**, pos. by dau., Bertha Morley; from Portsmouth, Royal Garrison Church (q.v.). Accession no. EH: 87900087. *XLVIII*. Inscr. George Long, 1823-**1909**, pos. by dau. Jane Long; from Portsmouth, Royal Garrison Church (q.v.). Accession no. EH: 87900096. *XLIX*. Inscr. "A THANKOFFERING FOR THE DAILY EUCHARIST LENT", **1910**; from Portsmouth, Royal Garrison Church (q.v.). Accession no. EH: 87900095. *L*. Inscr. Lysander Maybury, M.D., **1911**; from Portsmouth, Royal Garrison Church (q.v.). Accession no. EH: 87900091. *LI*. Inscr. pos. by sisters of Guild of St. Helena, **1911**; from Portsmouth, Royal Garrison Church (q.v.). Accession no. EH: 87900093. *LII*. Inscr. "A THANKOFFERING FOR THE DAILY EUCHARIST LENT", **1911**; from Portsmouth, Royal Garrison Church (q.v.). Accession no. EH: 87900098. *LIII*. Inscr. Josephine Price Heap, only dau. of William Price, M.D., of Cincinatti, Ohio, [America]; also eld. grandson, Lt. R[obert] C[unynghame] Slade-Baker, M.C., 1st Battn. Royal Berkshire Regt., [son of Brig.-Gen. Arthur Slade-Baker and w. Caroline Fisher], **1917**, [aged 21, buried at Beuvry Communal Cemetery extension, France]; from Portsmouth, Royal Garrison Church (q.v.). Accession no. EH: 87900111. *LIV*. Inscr. Jessie P.A.L., w. of Col. W.F. Graham, R[oyal] A[rtillery], **1918**, aged 58, pos. by husband and daus., Ethel D. Sargeaunt and Dorothy Harrison-Baker; from Portsmouth, Royal Garrison Church (q.v.). Accession no. EH: 87900115. *LV*. Inscr. Lt.-Col. and Battn.-Col. F[rederick] J[ohn] Evelegh, Oxfordshire Light Infantry and Royal Garrison Regt.; also [sons], Major C.N. Evelegh, Duke of Cornwall's Light Infantry; Lt.-Col. E[dmund] G[eorge] Evelegh, Royal Marine Light Infantry and Nelson Battn. R.N. Division, [1915, buried at Skew Bridge Cemetery, Turkey]; and Capt. R[osslyn] C[urzon] Evelegh, [2nd Battn.] Oxford and Bucks. Light Infantry, [1914, aged 29, buried in Soupir Churchyard, France, pos. in] **1921**; from Portsmouth, Royal Garrison Church (q.v.). Accession no. EH: 87900112. *LVI*. Inscr. Rose Mills, lifelong ch.worshipper, **1922**; from Portsmouth, Royal Garrison Church (q.v.). Accession no. EH: 87900090. *LVII*. Inscr. E[dith] M. C[larkson, 1922], pos. in **1924**; from Portsmouth, Royal Garrison Church (q.v.). Accession no. EH: 87900086. *LVIII*. Inscr. Edith [M.] Clarkson, 1922, pos. in **1924** by family; from Portsmouth, Royal Garrison Church (q.v.). Accession no. EH: 87900094.

Ref: *Burke's Peerage and Baronetage*, p.211-2, p.755, p.1104, p.1492, p.2351.

AMPORT, St. Mary.

I. Inscr. recording presentation [of font] in **1865** by [William Ward, 1st] Earl of Dudley, [1817-1885], to [Mary], Marchioness of Winchester, [dau. of Gen. Sir Henry Montagu, 6th Baron Rokeby, w. of John Paulet, 14th Marquess of Winchester], "whilst on a visit to Amport St Marys'", on font plinth, N. *II*. Inscr. recording presentation of R.A.F. ensign in **1955** by Air Officer C.-in-C. Maintenance ground on behalf of H.Q. Maintenance Command at Amport House, mur., N. *III*. Inscr. Claude A.P. Truman, 1864-**1958**, bronze, on wooden cross, Churchyard. *IV*. Inscr. recording extension of communion rails in **1964** by children, Guy Richmond and Ray Winifred Parry, in mem. of Frederick Charles Richmond-Parry and [w.] Kate Julia, on stool, C. *V*. Inscr. Doris, w. [of Claude A.P.] Truman, 1894-**1976**, bronze, on wooden cross with no.*III*, Churchyard. *VI*. Inscr. recording restoration in mem. of Charles William Richardson, churchwarden 1961-**1980**, par. council chairman 1959-1979, copper, mur., on board, Crossing. *VII*. Inscr. with dog recording replacement of bell ropes in **2003** by family in mem. of Wing-Cmdr. William Arthur James Iles, R.A.F.V.R., 1913-2002, mur., on board, Crossing. *VIII*. Inscr. recording gift of tower flagpole in **2004** by family in mem. of Brig. Charles [Harold Arthur] Olivier, C.B.E., [Royal Artillery, 1912-1992], mur., on board, Crossing.

Ref: *Burke's Peerage and Baronetage*, pp.843-4, p.2854.

ANDOVER, St. Mary (new church).

I. Inscr. and ach. Nicholas Venables, gent., **1602**, aged 73, father of 2 sons and 3 daus.; his son Richard pos.; mur., on board, C. Inscr. 211 x 524 mm, ach. 299 x 264 mm.

II. Inscr. recording [gift] of [book stand] in **1871** by C.C.B., on book stand, C. *III.* Inscr. recording [south-east south aisle] window pos. in mem. of Caroline Pressly, **1876**, aged 78, maker's name HART, SON, PEARD & C°, LONDON, mur., below window, S.A. *IV.* Inscr. Anne, w. of Giles Westbury, 1878, aged 65; also dau., Elizabeth, w. of A.P. Southey, **1881**, aged 42, maker's name MAYER & C° 149. NEW BOND Sᵀ·, mur., below window, N.A. *V.* Inscr. recording [south aisle] window above [south] porch pos. in **1883** by widow in mem. of W[illia]m Gradidge, [chemist], 1869, mur., S.A. *VI.* Inscr. recording 4 lights of the upper [east] chancel window pos. in **1883** by John Moore, mayor, in mem. of parents, brothers and sister, mur., C. *VII.* Inscr. recording centre light of the upper [east] chancel window pos. in **1883** by Rev. [Sir] E[van] Y[orke] Nepean, [4th Bart., M.A., 1825-1903] in mem. of [w.] Maria Theresa, [dau. of Rev. Frederick Morgan Payler, 1875], mur., C. *VIII.* Inscr. Cmdr. John Poore, R.N., 1875, aged 80, and w. Martha Sone, **1885**, aged 81; also dau., Anne, 1844; son, William [Poore], 1875; and eld. son, Lt.-Col. John Poore, Royal Marine Artillery, died at Eastney Barracks, [Portsmouth], 1880, mur., below window, N.A. *IX.* Inscr. recording erection of [south-east chancel] window by Robert Dowling, 1884, aged 72, and w. Susanna, **1886**, aged 64, mur., below window, C. *X.* Inscr. Giles Westbury, [land agent and surveyor], **1894**, aged 88; also eld. son, Edward Harris [Westbury], 1890, aged 54, mur., below no.*IV*, N.A. *XI.* Inscr. with verse in raised letters on 2 pls. recording dedication of organ in **1904** by subscribers; [Rev. Dr.] Frederic [Walker] Joy, D.D., F.S.A., vicar; F.C. Ellen and J. Compton Reeks, churchwardens, copper, on organ, C. *XII.* Inscr. recording screen figures pos. by nieces, Annie Loxley and Ellen Pressly, in mem. of Henry Thompson, engr. c.**1905**, on choir stall, C. *XIII.* Inscr. with crest and motto. Lt.-Col. Reginald Norton Knatchbull, D.S.O., 2nd Battn. Leicestershire Regt., [son of Col. Norton Knatchbull], educated at Haileybury and R.M.C. Sandhurst, served in the [South African] War 1899-1900 under Sir George White and took part in the defence of Ladysmith, mentioned in despatches and awarded the Queen's Medal with 5 clasps, "ACCOMPANIED THE INDIAN EXPEDITIONARY FORCE TO FRANCE IN 1914 WHEN HE WAS SEVERELY WOUNDED & AGAIN RECEIVED A SERIOUS WOUND AT THE ATTEMPTED RELIEF OF KUT IN 1916", "GAVE HIS LIFE FOR HIS COUNTRY WHEN IN COMMAND OF HIS REGᵀ IN MESOPOTAMIA", [1872-]**1917**, [buried] North British Cemetery, Bagdad, maker's name A&N AUX C.S.L LONDON, mur., below window, S.A. *XIV.* Inscr. George Henry Westbury, **1922**, aged 73, maker's name *JONES & WILLIS Lᵀᴰ*, mur., below window, N.A. *XV.* Inscr. with Lat. verse. Horace Arthur Rose, I[ndian] C[ivil] S[ervice], Sessions Judge, Punjab, commandant of the Indian Labour Corps in France 1917, press censor 1918, "A LOVER OF EQUITY. A LIFELONG STUDENT AND WRITER ON ETHNOLOGY. HE EVER STROVE TO INFLUENCE THE CASTES TO IMPROVE THE STATUS OF WOMEN IN THE PUNJAB", 1867-**1933**, maker's name MAILE LTD. ENGRAVERS. 367. EUSTON Rᴰ LONDON, mur., S.Tr. *XVI.* Inscr. Ernest Augustus Farr, **1935**, on processional cross, C. *XVII.* Inscr. Oscar James Smart, [bell]ringer for 50 years, **1947**, [pos. by] Winchester & Portsmouth

Diocesan Guild of Church Bell Ringers, maker's name F. OSBORNE & CO · LTD · LONDON. W.C.1., mur., on board, Tower. *XVIII*. Inscr. with Lat. verse recording rehanging of peal of 8 bells; 3rd recast and rededicated in **1947** by Rt. Rev. E[dmund] R[obert] Morgan, M.A., Bishop of Southampton [1943-1951]; cost was raised by public subscription; Alderman R. Charlton, mayor; [Rev.] Alfred C[arlos] Fletcher, M.A., vicar [1940-1951], r[ural] d[ean]; R.J. Ackerman and A.E.C. Macey, churchwardens, maker's name F. OSBORNE & CO · LTD · LONDON. W.C.1., mur., on board, Tower. *XIX*. Inscr. recording [gift] of [north transept] window by Adeline Vida Temblett, **1950**, in mem. of Agnes Bennett, Augusta Bennett and Arthur Charles Bennett, organist 1924-1940, mur., on board below window, N.Tr. *XX*. Inscr. recording presentation [of prie-dieu] by Mrs. Bentham in mem. of [Rev.] Walter Reid Bentham, [M.A.], curate [1907-1912], rector of Upper Clatford, engr. c.**1950**, on prie-dieu, N.Tr. *XXI*. Inscr recording gift of aumbry by Friends of St. Mary and sanctuary redecorated under the will of Mrs. Leah Lawrence in **1959**; [Rev. Canon Dr.] Ivor [William John] Machin, vicar [1952-1967]; A.E.C. Macey and T.W. Redman, churchwardens, mur., on board, C. *XXII*. Inscr. recording that [pew] was made and presented in **1961** by Enham Industries Ltd.; Brenda Machin, mayor, on pew, N. *XXIII*. Inscr. recording rebuilding of organ (stops given in mem. of E. Austin, G. Cook, Elsie Cook, R. and D. Dangerfield, Mrs. Fry, Mrs. C. March, Mrs. Stevens and others; also by Dr. Blyth, Mr. and Mrs. Cornwell, T. King & Sons, Mr. A. Macey, Mrs. Machin, Mr. L. Ponting, Mr. L. Rimmer and Mr. and Mrs. Shaw-Potter, C.E.M.S., C[hurch] of E[ngland] School, Friends of St. Mary, Mothers' Union and local organisations; individual pipes were given by "those recorded in the Book of Gratitude; the organ loft "was also an In Memorial Gift") in **1965**; Rev. Canon Dr. [Ivor] Machin, vicar [1952-1967]; T.W. Redman and F. Giles, churchwardens; Lloyd Ponting, [A.R.C.O., L.R.A.M.], organist [1940-1977], on organ with no.*XI*, C. *XXIV*. Inscr. recording list of organists [1772-1940] (15 names) engr. c.**1965**, on organ with nos.*XI & XXIII*, C. *XXV*. Inscr. Edgar and Helen Goodyear; also Gertrude, engr. **1966**, on pew, N.Tr. *XXVI*. Inscr. Florence Emily Jeffery, engr. **1966**, on pew, N.Tr. *XXVII*. Inscr. [Rev. Canon Dr.] Ivor [William John] Machin, [vicar 1952-1967], engr. **1966**, on pew with no.*XXVI*, N.Tr. *XXVIII*. Inscr. Frederick Arthur Sansom, engr. **1966**, on pew, N.Tr. *XXIX*. Inscr. Isabel Schwabe, engr. **1966**, on pew, N.Tr. *XXX*. Inscr. Eric Sheldon Shrimpton, engr. **1966**, on pew, N.Tr. *XXXI*. Inscr. recording installation of memorial pews in **1966**, on pew, N.Tr. *XXXII*. Inscr. recording gift of sanctuary lamp in **1967** in mem. of John Alfred Judge, mur., below sanctuary lamp, C. *XXXIII*. Inscr. Flight-Lt. William Edgerton Taylor, "SERVED HIS COUNTRY IN TWO WORLD WARS", 1894-1964; mar. in the ch.; "THROUGH HER MUNIFICENT GENEROSITY THAT WORK BEGAN IN **1983** TO RESTORE AND REORDER THIS BUILDING FOR THE WORSHIP OF GOD", pos. by w. Millicent Noyce, mur., N. *XXXIV*. Inscr. recording gift [of stall] in mem. of Dora Chant, ch. member and worshipper for 74 years, 1889-**1988**, on stall, C. *XXXV*. Inscr. with Lat. verse. (Skip) Charles A. Harris, B.E.M., founder and capt. 2nd Andover Co., Boy's Brigade, **1990**, aged 91, mur., S.A. *XXXVI*. Inscr. Fred Musson, engr. c.**1995**, on chair, S.A. *XXXVII*. Inscr. recording presentation [of paschal candleholder] in **1996** by Hazel Beauchamp, [1940-1999], and Peter Hull, churchwardens, on paschal candleholder, C. *XXXVIII*. Inscr. Wendy Scott, 1951-**1996**, on grave marker, Churchyard. *XXXIX*. Inscr. Hazel Beauchamp, 1940-**1999**, on grave marker, Churchyard. *XL*. Inscr. Violet Ursula Gregory, 1918-1991, whose [legacy] made a major contribution to the ch. refurbishment, [pos. in] **1999**, mur., N. *XLI*. Inscr. recording list of organists [1977-2002] (6 names) engr. c.**2000**, on organ below no.*XXIV*, C. *XLII*. Inscr. with verse. Milly Wilson, 2005-**2005**, on grave marker, Churchyard.

INDENTS & LOST BRASSES. 43. Lost indent, civilian and w., 2 children, 4 shs. and marg. inscr. Recorded by George (1686).

HIC IACET NICHOLAVS VENABLES GENEROS' REVE
RENDVS SENEX FILVS DVORVM FILIORVM TRIVMQ
FILIARVM PATER ANNOS SPIRAVIT 73 HONESTE
VIXIT PATIENTER OBIJT 3 DIE IANVARIJ 1602. IN
CVIVS VITÆ ET MORTIS MEMORIAM, RICHARDVS
VENABLES FILIORV IVNIOR HOC MARMOR POSVIT.
DVM VIXIT VERVS CVM MORTVVS INCOLA CŒLI
SIMPLICITER FÆLIX PIETATE & PROLE & AMICIS.
PROSPICE FINEM

Andover I

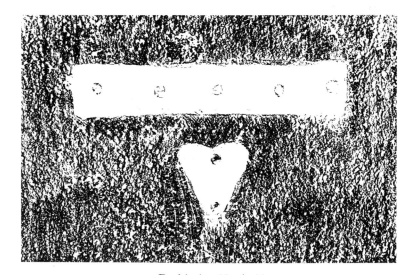

Baddesley, North 11

23

Ref: *Brit. Lib. Add. MS. 14296*, f.65, *Add. MS. 39959*, f.275; *Burke's Peerage and Baronetage*, p.332, p.1953; *Heseltine, Heraldry*, p.36; *M.B.S. Trans.*, V, pp.253-4; *M.S.*, p.158; *Soc. Antiq. MS. 875/6*, pp.7-8; *Squibb*, p.211; *V.C.H., Hampshire*, IV, p.355.

Ch. built, 1840-6.

ANGLESEY, (see ALVERSTOKE).

ASHE, Holy Trinity and St. Andrew (old church).

INDENTS & LOST BRASSES. 1. Lost indents, "here also have been some brass fixed upon flat gravestones but none of them remain". Recorded by Pavey (1702).

Ref: *Brit. Lib. Stowe MS. 845*, f.77; *M.B.S. Trans.*, V, p.254; *Soc. Antiq. MS. 875/6*, p.8.

ASHE, Holy Trinity and St. Andrew (new church).

I. Inscr. Rev. Charles [Richard] Pettat, [B.A.], rector of Ashe and Deane for 27 years, [rural dean], died suddenly, **1873**, aged 59, maker's name HART SON PEARD & C^O LONDON, mur., on marble, N. *II.* Inscr. recording presentation of centre light of east window in **1878** by Newman Barfoot Thoyts in mem. of father, Mortimer George Thoyts, of Sulhamstead, Berks., 1875, maker's name T. PRATT & SONS. TAVISTOCK S^T LONDON, mur., Organ Chamber. *III.* Inscr. recording presentation of organ in **1878** by Rosa M. Thoyts, maker's name T. PRATT & SONS. TAVISTOCK S^T LONDON, on organ, Organ Chamber. *IV.* Inscr. recording presentation of font in **1878** by [Rev.] Richard Pole, M.A., rector of Wolverton [1844-1879], maker's name T. PRATT & SONS. TAVISTOCK S^T LONDON, on font plinth, N. *V.* Inscr. recording presentation [of boards listing patrons 1309-1873 (26 names) and rectors 1308-1906 (37 names)] in **1889** by Wyndham Spencer Portal, of Malshanger, maker's name T. PRATT & SONS. TAVISTOCK S^T LONDON, mur., on list of patrons board, C. *VI.* Inscr. recording presentation [of prie-dieu] by sailors and soldiers who served in World War I, on prie-dieu, C. *VII.* Inscr. recording gift [of board listing rectors 1935-1992 (4 names)] in **1970** in mem. of Arthur Terry, w. Martha and son Henry, mur., on list of incumbents board, C. *VIII.* Inscr. recording installation of gate in south wall by parishioners to commem. silver jubilee of Queen Elizabeth II, **1977**, mur., N. *IX.* Inscr. William Frederick Humphrey, organist 1954-**1978**, mur., N. *X.* Inscr. recording installation of electric [organ] blower in **1979** in mem. of Nelly Terry, on organ with no.*III*, Organ Chamber. *XI.* Inscr. on scroll-shaped pl. Patrick Spencer Boyle, churchwarden, 1905-1978, engr. **1985**, ?brass, on churchwardens' wand, N. *XII.* Inscr. on scroll-shaped pl. recording gift [of churchwardens' wand] by W.P. Serocold, churchwarden, 1971-**1985**, in mem. of Monica, ?brass, on churchwardens' wand, N. *XIII.* Inscr. Brig. Charles Walter Philipps Richardson, D.S.O., King's Own Scottish Borderers, churchwarden 1964-1993, 1905-**1993**, copper, mur., N. *XIV.* Inscr. Bert Holmes, ch. worshipper 1946-1994, 1920-**1994**, on bench, N.

Ref: *Who's Who*, 1967, p.2571.

Ch. built, 1877-9.

ASHLEY, St. Mary (redundant, now vested in The Churches Conservation Trust).

I. Inscr. with verse. Rev. James Hannay, M.A., fellow of Worcester Coll., Oxford, rector for 49 years [1843-1892], 1813-**1892**, mur., C. *II.* World War I memorial in raised letters (6 names), pos. by parishioners, bronze, mur., in wooden frame, N.

Ch. declared redundant, 1976; vested, 1980.

AVINGTON, St. Mary the Virgin (old church).

INDENTS & LOST BRASSES. 1. Lost brass, lady, inscr., B.V. Mary and Child and scroll. Elizabeth Wisham, 1514, mur., N. Recorded (complete) by Pavey (1703). 2. Lost brass, inscr. and 5 shs. John Unwyn, of Yabington, 1685, N. Recorded (complete) by Pavey (1703).

Ref: *Brit. Lib. Stowe MS. 845*, f.90; *Heseltine, Heraldry*, p.36; *M.B.S. Trans.*, V, pp.254-5; *Soc. Antiq. MS. 875/6*, pp.8-9.

AVINGTON, St. Mary the Virgin (new church).

I. Inscr. recording side-lights of east window filled with glass in mem. of [Rev.] William Edward Green, [M.A.], rector 18/2-**1896**, maker's name *I WIPPELL & C⁰ Lᵀᴰ*, on window splay.

Ch. built, 1768-71.

BADDESLEY, NORTH, St. John the Baptist.

I. Inscr. with verse. Pilot-Officer Richard Bowyer, [72981], R.A.F., only son of Alderman and Mrs. Percy Vincent Bowyer, killed on active service, 1912-**1939**, mur., N. *II.* Inscr. [Rev.] Vernon A[shby] Busbridge, vicar 1923-1936, **1939**, aged 77, bronze, on wooden cross, Churchyard. *III.* Inscr. with verse. Paul Llewellyn Owen, **1964**, aged 9 months, "PAUL'S ASHES NOURISH THIS ALMOND TREE", bronze, on tree post, Churchyard. *IV.* Inscr. recording dedication of organ in **1987** by [Rt. Rev.] Colin [Clement Walter James], Bishop of Winchester [1985-1995], in mem. of Tom Rogers, reader in the benefice for many years, on Gallery/N. *V.* Inscr. Gordon F. Westlake, [husband, father and grandfather, **1988**, aged 59], bronze, on bench, Churchyard. *VI.* Inscr. Ernest and Irene Lashmar, engr. c.**1990**, bronze, on bench, Churchyard. *VII.* Inscr. John Frampton, 1934-**1997**, on bench, Churchyard. *VIII.* Inscr. recording donation of seat by work colleagues in mem. of Glenn David Munns, 1960-**1998**, on bench, Churchyard. *IX.* Inscr. Jim McKay, 1934-**2001**, on wooden cross, Churchyard. *X.* Inscr. Terence (Terry) Spencer, 1945-**2004**, on bench, Churchyard.

INDENTS & LOST BRASSES. 11. Indent, inscr. and heart, N. *Sadler, Dorset and Hampshire*, appx. I, pt.2, p.16 (drg.). Inscr. 80 x 455 mm, heart 120 x 100 mm, slab 2580 x 1170 mm.

Ref: *M.B.S. Trans.*, V, p.255; *Sadler, Dorset and Hampshire*, appx. I, pt.2, p.16; *Soc. Antiq. MS. 875/6*, p.9; *V.C.H., Hampshire*, III, p.465.

BARTON STACEY, All Saints.

I. Inscr. recording gift of altar cross in **1895** by 3 surviving children in mem. of Rev. James Jolliffe, M.A., of Exeter Coll., Oxford, curate "WITH SOLE CHARGE" of Barton Stacey 1818-1836, [and Stoke Charity 1836-1847, 1794-1864], on cross, Vestry/N.Tr.   See also Whippingham nos.IV & *XI*.   *II*. Inscr. Rev. Abraham Horwill Stogdon, [M.A.], vicar 1872-1892, died at Exeter, [Devon], **1895**, aged 80, maker's name *J. WIPPELL & COMPY. EXETER & LONDON*, mur., C.   *III*. Inscr. recording dedication of panelling in **1916** by F. K[irkman] H[odgson], P. K[irkman] H[odgson], D. K[irkman] H[odgson] and C.E.N. in mem. of brothers, [Capt.] Michael [Reginald Kirkman Hodgson, 2nd Battn. attd. 4th Battn. Royal Fusiliers, killed in action near Ypres, Belgium, 1915, aged 35], and [Capt.] Maurice [Kirkman] Hodgson, [1st Battn. Sherwood Foresters], killed in action [near Neuve Chapelle, France], 1915, [aged 34, buried at Estaires Communal Cemetery, France, sons of Robert Kirkman Hodgson, J.P., D.L., of Gravelacre, and w. Norah Janet], bronze, mur., on panelling, C.   *IV*. Inscr. with verse. Robert Kirkman Hodgson, [J.P., D.L.], of Gravelacre, 1850-**1924**, pos. by widow, [Norah Janet] and children, P. K[irkman] H[odgson], D. K[irkman] H[odgson] and C.E.N., mur., in stone frame, N.A.   *V*. Inscr. recording presentation [of regt. plaque] by 25th Field Regt. Royal Artillery, "MANY OF WHOM WORSHIPPED AT THIS CHURCH WHILE THE REGIMENT WAS STATIONED AT BARTON STACEY" 1959-**1961**, on regt. plaque, N.   *VI*. Inscr. recording restoration work carried out in **1971** by 12th Engineer Brigade under the supervision of Capt. D.J. O'Regan, R[oyal] E[ngineers]; "THIS PLAQUE IS SITED ABOVE A LARGE VAULT DISCOVERED DURING THE WORK"; [Rev.] J[ohn] H[umphrey] N[orman] Llewelyn, [T.D., M.A.], vicar [1969-1985], mur., on board, N.A.   *VII*. Inscr. Frank Smith, husband and father, 1919-**1973**, on wooden cross, Churchyard.   *VIII*. Inscr. Reginald Riggs, 1909-**1976**, on bookcase, S.A.   *IX*. Inscr. with verse. Eric Greensmith, 1923-**1996**, on wooden cross, Churchyard.   *X*. Inscr. with verse. Pat Greensmith, 1926-**2001**, on wooden cross with no.*IX*, Churchyard.

INDENTS & LOST BRASSES.   11. Lost brass, civilian and w., c.1500.   Recorded by Haines (1861).

Ref: *Haines*, II, p.72; *M.B.S. Trans.*, I, pt.8, p.24; *M.S.*, p.170.

BASING, St. Mary.

I. Inscr. Francis Russell Apletree, 1845-**1849**, mur., N.A.   *II*. Inscr. Frances Louisa, [last surviving child of William] Apletree, 1805-**1850**, mur., N.A.   *III*. Inscr. Margaret, Countess of Wiltshire, 1682; Lord Thomas Paulet, 1690; Amelie Willemine, Marchioness of Monpouillon, 1695, aged 49; Louise Harmeline of Caumont, Lady William Pawlett, 1696, aged 32; Frances, Marchioness of Winchester, 1696, aged 35; Charles Pawlet, Duke of Bolton, K.G., 1699, aged 69; Hon. Jane Pawlet, 1717; Mary, Countess of Ross, 1718; Charles [Pawlet], Duke of Bolton, K.G., 1722; Henrietta, Duchess Dowager of Bolton, 1729, aged 47; Lord William Paulet, 1729, aged 63; Major-Gen. the Hon. James Crofts, 1731, aged 54; Hon. William Egerton, 1732, aged 48; Lady Ann Powlett, 1737; Hon. Nassau Paulett, 1741, aged 7; Lord Nassau Powlett, K.B., 1741, aged 44; Hon. Francis Powlet, 1741, aged 8; Hon. Charles Powlett, 1747, aged 61; Major-Gen. the Hon. Sir Charles Armand Powlett, K.B., 1751, aged 56; Charles Powlett, Duke of Bolton, K.G., 1754, aged 68; Hon. William Powlett, 1757, aged 66; Henry Powlett, Duke of Bolton, 1759, aged 68; Charles [Powlett, 5th] Duke of Bolton, K.B., 1765, aged 46; Hon.

Ann Marie Egerton, 1768, aged 60; Lady Ann Powlett, 1769, aged 71; Harry [Powlett, 6th] Duke of Bolton, 1794, aged 74; Hon. Ann Powlett, 1804, aged 20; Thomas [Orde-Powlett 1st], Lord Bolton, 1807, aged 60; Katherine, Duchess of Bolton, 1809, aged 73; Jean Mary, Baroness Bolton, [dau. of Charles Powlett, 5th Duke of Bolton, K.B., w. of Thomas Orde-Powlett, 1st Baron Bolton], 1814, aged 63; Lady Amelia Powlett, 1816, aged 48; William Powlett, [2nd] Lord Bolton, [1782-]1850; and Maria, Baroness Bolton, [eld. dau. of Gen. Sir Guy Carleton, 1st Baron Dorchester, K.B., w. of William Powlett, 2nd Baron Bolton], 1863, aged 86, [buried] in vault beneath south chapel, maker's name A. & N. AUX C.S.L. LONDON, engr. c.**1905**, mur., S.C. See also Carisbrooke Castle no.*II*. *IV*. Inscr. Amelia Booth, died at Old Basing, 1816-1892, and Admiral Augustus St. Clair Booth, died at Leatherhead, Surrey, 1810-**1906**, maker's name A. & N. AUX. C.S.L. LONDON, mur., N.A. *V*. Inscr. George James Randall, chorister 1887, churchwarden 1922, 1865-**1928**, on choir stall, Crossing. *VI*. Inscr. Richard Hall, chorister for 70 years, 1879-**1957**, on choir stall with no.*V*, Crossing. *VII*. Inscr. Florence May Goodall, chorister and sacristan for many years, 1889-**1958**, on pew, S.C. *VIII*. Inscr. Win Marlow, **1970**, pos. by sister, Edie, on choir stall with nos.*V & VI*, Crossing. *IX*. Inscr. Rose Ann Catchpole, chorister for many years, 1910-**1977**, on choir stall, Crossing. *X*. Inscr. Herbert John Payne, [chorister] and verger, 1891-**1978**, on choir stall with no.*IX*, Crossing. *XI*. Inscr. with verse on 2 pls. Margaret Mary Pickett, 1931-**1987**, bronze, on bench, Churchyard. *XII*. Inscr. Ernest Pyle, 1886-1950, engr. **1993**, bronze, on bench, Churchyard. *XIII*. Inscr. George William Pyle, 1931-**1993**, bronze, on bench, Churchyard. *XIV*. Inscr. Mabel Payne, chorister and verger, 1909-**1994**, on choir stall with no.*IX & X*, Crossing. *XV*. Inscr. Heather Stewart, engr. c.**1995**, on bench, Churchyard. *XVI*. Inscr. Fred Westo, engr. c.**1995**, bronze, on bench, Churchyard.

Ref: *Burke's Peerage and Baronetage*, p.299.

BASINGSTOKE, St. Michael.

I. Inscr. with 6 Eng. vv. Roger Ryve, [**1587**]; formerly N.A., mur., N., rel., C. Inscr. 148 x 486-492 mm. Style: London G (script 10).

II. Robert Stocker, yeoman, **1606**, aged 67, in civil dress, and w. Ursula, with 9 sons and 2 daus., inscr.; formerly N., mur., N., rel., C. Male eff. 579 x 223 mm, female eff. 533 x 235 mm, inscr. 113 x 647 mm, sons 160-171 x 392-416 mm, daus. 150-171 x 148-158 mm. Style: Johnson.

III. John, son of Thomas Hilliard, gent., **1621**, a child, inscr.; formerly mur., C. (eff.), mur., N. (inscr.), rel., C. Eff. 303 x 115 mm, inscr. 82 x 368 mm. Style: Johnson.

IV. [Rev. Canon Dr.] James Elwin Millard, M.A., D.D., fellow of Magdalen Coll., Oxford, hon. canon of Winchester Cathedral, vicar for 26 years [1864-1890], 1823-**1894**, in mass vests., hands folded, chalice on breast, head on cushion under canopy, inscr. in Lat., rect. pl., mur., N. Rect. pl. 814 x 452 mm. *V*. Inscr. with Lat. verse in raised letters and regt. insignia in relief. Pte. Richard Edward Sutton, 1st Volunteer Co. 2nd [Battn.] Hampshire Regt., "A NATIVE OF THIS TOWN WHO VOLUNTEERED FOR ACTIVE SERVICE IN THE SOUTH AFRICAN WAR AND GAVE HIS LIFE FOR HIS QUEEN AND COUNTRY", died at Pretoria, **1900**, aged 25, bronze, mur., Tower. *VI*. Inscr. in Lat. recording gift of altar in mem. of Clare Frances Lefroy, **1907**, mur., S.C. *VII*. Inscr. Henry White, sexton and tower capt. 1885-1918, "LABOURED WITH UNTIRING ZEAL FOR THE IMPROVEMENT OF BELLRINGING AND THE CULTIVATION OF THE ART OF

Here lyeth Roger Gage who dyed the xi daye of Novembr
farewell, strengthe, wealthe, with worldlye lybertie.
And welcome, soules healthe, by the grace of the almytie
Thynke well of thy brother, that lyethe here dede
Thoughe death under cleye, hath closed hys heade
The poore speakethe well, and layethe no blame
his dedes in his lyfe, honor deserved the same

Basingstoke I

HEERE LYETH THE BODY OF IOHN HILLIARD
SONNE OF THOMAS HILLIARD GENT. WHO
WAS BVERYED THE 25 OF OCTOBER 1621

Basingstoke III

HERE LYETH BVRYED THE BODIE OF ROBERT STOCKER YEO
MAN, WHO HAD ISSVE BY VRSVLA HIS WIFE, 9 SONNES AND 2
DAVGHT. HE DEPTED THIS LIFE Y 20 OF MARCIE 1606 BEINGE
67 YEARES OF AGE: HE LEDD A VERTVOVS LIFE & MADE A GODLY

Basingstoke II

CHANGERINGING", **1918**, aged 61; [Rev. Dr.] H[arry] W[ilson] Boustead, D.D., vicar [1905-1936], mur., on board, Tower. *VIII.* Inscr. Mrs. Bessie Gledhill, engr. c.**1950**, on chair, C. *IX.* Inscr. [Rev.] Rolf Gledhill, [M.A.], engr. c.**1950**, on chair, C. *X.* Inscr. Frederick George Wilson and [w.] Mary Emma, engr. c.**1955**, bronze, on altar rail, N.C. *XI.* Inscr. in raised letters recording presentation of "FESTAL ALTAR FRONTAL WITH AN INDUSTRIAL THEME" by friends of Lansing Bagnall Ltd. in mem. of John Reginald Sharp, C.B.E., 1912-**1965**, bronze, mur., on board, C. *XII.* Inscr. recording award of Royal Arms of Queen Elizabeth II in **1991** by Cookson PLC, mur., on framed arms, N.C. *XIII.* Inscr. Alfred James Saunders, chorister c.1900, and John Saunders, chorister 1935, engr. c.**2000**, on choir stall/chair, N. *XIV.* Inscr. [Capt.] Victor Robert Bull, [171711, Royal Artillery, son of Henry James Bull and w. Lilian Agnes], 1915-1945, [buried at Cologne Southern Cemetery, Germany], engr. c.**2000**, on choir stall/chair, N. *XV.* Inscr. Dorothy Simmonds (née Harmsworth), mother, 1889-1951, engr. c.**2000**, on choir stall/chair, N. *XVI.* Inscr. Peter Jeffrey Godden, chorister 1970-1975, and Christopher Michael Godden, chorister 1970-1978, engr. c.**2000**, on choir stall/chair, N. *XVII.* Inscr. Bertha (Ciss) Bull, 1914-1988, engr. c.**2000**, on choir stall/chair, N. *XVIII.* Inscr. Marjorie S. Jones, 1902-1992, engr. c.**2000**, on choir stall/chair, N. *XIX.* Inscr. Brian L. Soane, 1922-1992, engr. c.**2000**, on choir stall/chair, N. *XX.* Inscr. Sheila Hazzard, 1930-1997, engr. c.**2000**, on choir stall/chair, N. *XXI.* Inscr. Geoffrey Bull, 1927-1998, engr. c.**2000**, on choir stall/chair, N. *XXII.* Inscr. Grace Marshall, 1910-1998, engr. c.**2000**, on choir stall/chair, N. *XXIII.* Inscr. Ivy and John Mayer, engr. c.**2000**, on choir stall/chair, N. *XXIV.* Inscr. with verse. Anne and Peter, 35th wedding anniversary, engr. c.**2000**, on choir stall/chair, N.

INDENTS & LOST BRASSES. 25. Indent, 3 effs. and inscr., 3 rivets only, effaced, S.Porch. Purbeck slab 2435 x 905 mm. 26. Lost brass, sh., Henchman, 1768. Recorded by Baigent and Millard (1889). 27. Lost ?brass, civilian and 2 ws., inscr., 1 son and 3 daus. John Bowyer, 1536. Possibly no.25.

Ref: *Baigent, F.J., and Millard, J.E., A history of the ancient town and manor of Basingstoke in the county of Southampton: with a brief account of the siege of Basing House, A.D. 1643-1645,* 1889, pp.96-8; *Brit. Lib. Stowe MS. 845,* ff.120-1; *Haines,* II, p.72; *Heseltine, Heraldry,* p.36; *M.B.S. Trans.,* V, pp.255-6, VI, p.252; *Mee, Hampshire,* p.47; *M.S.,* p.158; *Soc. Antiq. MS. 875/6,* pp.9-10; *Squibb,* pp.223-4; *V.C.H., Hampshire,* IV, p.138.

BAUGHURST, St. Stephen (new church).

I. Benefaction of Thomas Sympson, **1674**, mur., in wooden frame, N. Inscr. 288 x 416 mm.

II. Capt. Cranstoun George Ridout, 11th Light Dragoons and 2nd Life Guards, 2nd son of John Christopher Ridout and [w.] Caroline, of Baughurst House, joined the Army in 1801, served throughout the Peninsula War at El Bodon, Badajoz and Ciudad Rodrigo and was with the army of occupation in Paris in 1815, [died] at Brighton, [Sussex], **1881**, aged 93, pos. by surviving child and grandchildren, maker's name GAWTHORP Sᶜ LONDON, mur., C. *III.* Inscr. with verse. Sarah, widow of George Follett, of Hillside Farm, **1889**, aged 83, maker's name GILKES & SON READING, mur., N. *IV.* Inscr. Walter [Hunter], 1910, aged 68, Francis [Hunter], 1890, aged 41, and Leonard [Hunter], 1910, aged 61, sons of Walter John Hunter, H[onourable] E[ast] I[ndia] C[ompany] S[ervice], of Baughurst House, pos. in **1911** by 2 surviving brothers, mur., N. *V.* Inscr. Cecil Hunter, of Pamber Place, yst. son of Walter John Hunter, H[onourable] E[ast]

Basingstoke *IV*

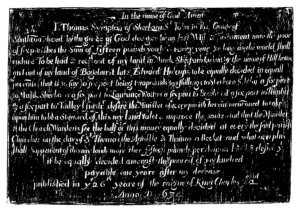

Baughurst I

I[ndia] C[ompany] S[ervice], of Baughurst House, died at Bath, [Somerset], 1917, aged 63, pos. in **1919** by surviving brother and sister, mur., N. *VI*. Inscr. Beryl Florence Smyth, 1901-**1968**, bronze, on screen, Vestry/N. *VII*. Inscr. recording erection of organ from Patcham Methodist Church by voluntary helpers led by Derrick Carrington, Philip J. Wells and Clifford Bolton, organist; dedicated in **1969** by [Rt. Rev. Dr. Kenneth Edward Norman Lamplugh, D.D.], Bishop of Southampton [1951-1972], bronze, on organ, N. *VIII*. Inscr. Clifford Bolton, choirmaster and organist 1966-**1984**, on organ with no.*VII*, N. *IX*. Inscr. recording repair of Norman arch built in the west wall of the ch. in mem. of Susan Mary Macphail, engr. c.**1990**; in 2006 loose on board in N. Inscr. 102 x 153 mm.

Ref: *M.B.S. Trans.*, V, p.257; *M.S.*, p.158; *Soc. Antiq. MS. 875/6*, p.11; *V.C.H., Hampshire*, IV, p.276.

Ch. built, 1845.

BEAULIEU, Abbey Church of St. Mary.

INDENTS & LOST BRASSES. 1. Indent, lady, canopy, 2 shs. and marg. inscr. in Lombardics; in 2006 loose against wall, lay brothers' frater. Possibly Isabel Marshall, 1st w. of Richard, Earl of Cornwall, c.1315. *Bod. Lib. Gough Maps 224*, f.305; *Sadler, Dorset and Hampshire*, pt. II, p.5 (drg.). Eff. 1850 x 520 mm, canopy 2120 x 650 mm, shs. 150 x 115 mm, Purbeck slab 2310 x 865 mm. Style: London (Camoys). 2. Indent, inscr., effaced, at entrance to Refectory, now the par. ch. Inscr. 150 x 460 mm. 3. Lost brass, inscr. Edward Kemp, gent., 6th son of Sir William Kemp, Knt., 1605, left w. Elizabeth, and sons, Thomas, Edward, Francis and Robert, C. Recorded by Warner (1795).

The monument to a lady, vase-like bracket and canopy inlaid in white marble, 2 shs. and marg. inscr. in Lombardics, attributed to Princess Eleanor, dau. of Edward I, 1311, aged 5, recorded by Gough and Sadler as an indent, is an incised slab.

Ref: *Bod. Lib. Gough Maps 224*, f.30; *Earliest English Brasses*, p.189; *Gent. Mag.*, 1820, II, pp.489-90; *Gent. Mag. Lib. Eng. Topog.*, p.45; *Gough*, I, pt.1, p.42; *Hampshire, Antiquary*, II, p.103; *M.B.S. Bulletin*, 23, p.16, 27, p.15, 36, p.95, 71, p.220, 72, p.236; *M.B.S. Trans.*, V, pp.257-8, XV, p.426, XV, p.235; *Sadler, Dorset and Hampshire*, pt. II, p.4, p.6, appx. I, pt.2, p.17; *Soc. Antiq. MS. 875/6*, pp.11-2; *V.C.H., Hampshire*, IV, p.654; *Warner*, I, p.53.

BEDHAMPTON, St. Thomas à Becket.

I. Inscr. recording restoration of chancel in **1869** by Thomas Castle, of Liverpool, with ch. restored and vestry built by voluntary contributions; [Rev.] Edmund Thomas Daubeny, B.A., rector [1865-1884]; W.P. Snell and B.W. Gibbins, churchwardens, maker's name HART, SON, PEARD & Cº, LONDON, mur., C. *II*. Inscr. recording addition of [north] aisle and vestry enlarged in **1878**; [Rev.] Edmund Thomas Daubeny, B.A., rector [1865-1884]; Spencer Giffin and George Lane, churchwardens, maker's name T. PRATT & SONS ENGRAVERS, TAVISTOCK Sᵀ LONDON, on window splay, N.A. *III*. Inscr. with verse, crest and motto. [Sub-]Lt. Edward Wilder, R.N.R., [H.M. Yacht Oriana], "DIED IN THE SERVICE OF HIS COUNTRY", 1915, aged 28; also brother, 2nd-Lt. Frank [Wilder], Q Battery, R[oyal] H[orse] A[rtillery], killed in action at Arras, **1916**,

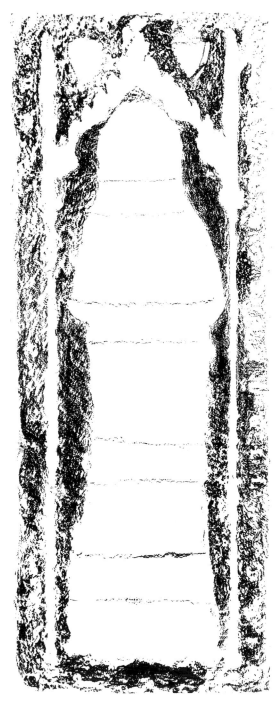

Beaulieu, Abbey 1

aged 35, [buried at Faubourg d'Amiens Cemetery, Arras, France, sons of George Wilder and w. Mary], maker's name MANNELL & C⁰ BOURNEMOUTH, mur., on marble, N.A. *IV*. World War I memorial (28 names), maker's name FOSTER SOUTHSEA, mur., in wooden frame, N. *V*. Inscr. recording presentation [of board listing rectors 1303-1990 (42 names)] by parishioners in mem. of Rev. H[enry] Pelham Stokes, M.A., rector 1911-**1928**, mur., on board below list of incumbents, N. *VI*. Inscr. in raised letters. Rear-Admiral Peyton Hoskyns, C.M.G., M.V.O., R.N., died at Brookside, 1919, and w. Grace Macduff, died at Salisbury, South Rhodesia, **1935**, bronze, mur., on marble, N.A. *VII*. World War II memorial (22 names), mur., in wooden frame with no.*IV*, N. *VIII*. Inscr. Arthur Frank Weeks, M.B.E., [of the] N[ational] S[ociety for the] P[revention of] C[ruelty to] C[hildren], **1958**, aged 67, on paschal candleholder, C. *IX*. Inscr. with verse recording gift of sound system in mem. of David W.H. Hampshire, reader 1965-1976, 1997-**2001**, mur., N.A.

BENTLEY, St. Mary.

I. Inscr. with verse. Arthur Jackson, died at Mercara Coorg, [India], **1882**, aged 29; also Frederick Dorville Jackson, died at Mercara Coorg, [India], 1878, aged 19, maker's name *J. WIPPELL & C⁰. L*ᵀᴰ*. EXETER & LONDON*, mur., N. *II*. Inscr. recording restoration of font in **1889** by "THE GIFTS OF THE POOR" in mem. of Isabella Schroder, of Northbrook, 1863, mur., N. *III*. Inscr. recording dedication of east window in **1889** by cousin and successor, Frederick Thresher Giles, [1908, aged 75], in mem. of Frederick Richard Thresher, J.P., of Marsh House, [only son of Richard Thresher and w. Ann Augusta], judicial chairman of the Court of Quarter Sessions for 10 years [1850-1860, 1799-1867], mur., C. *IV*. Inscr. recording erection of pulpit by children in **1890** in mem. of father, Rev. Charles Jackson, [B.A.], maker's name T. PRATT & SONS. TAVISTOCK Sᵀ LONDON, mur., N. *V*. Inscr. with verse recording enlargement of the National School in **1892** by family in mem. of Mary Cooper, 1808-1890; Ann Cooper, 1811-1891; Eliza Cooper, 1821-1866; and Sarah Williams Cooper, 1823-1880; daus. of William Cooper and [w.] Mary, of The Grove, Kentish Town, London, grand-daus. of John Eggar and [w.] Ann, of East Worldham, formerly of the par., mur., S.C. See also East Worldham no.*I*. *VI*. Inscr. dedication of east chancel aisle [south chapel] window by husband and children in mem. of w. Mary Janet, 1899; also husband, Rev. Owen Charles Seymour Lang, [M.A.], rector [1885-1908], **1908**, maker's name John Hardman & C⁰· Birmᵐ·, mur., S.C. *VII*. Inscr. Frederick Faichen, par. clerk for 47 years, **1910**, maker's name *J. WIPPELL & C⁰· L*ᵀᴰ*. EXETER & LONDON*, mur., N. *VIII*. Inscr. John Henderson Petrie, 1905, and w. Emily Jane Eggar, **1910**, maker's name John Hardman & C⁰· Birmᵐ·, mur., S.C. *IX*. Inscr. W.H. Moody, 1908-**1916**, on crucifix, N. *X*. Inscr. Major John Campbell Petrie, I.A.R.O., O.B.E., civil engineer, yst. son of John Henderson Petrie, grandson of James Eggar, of Jenkyn Place, born at Crox, Bentley, died in Bombay, India, 1884-**1921**, mur., S.C. *XI*. Inscr. Lucy Jane Raggett, served ch. 1903-**1948**, copper, mur., on board, S.A. *XII*. Inscr. recording improvement and extension of organ in **1993** in mem. of Fred Brooker, chorister and server for 77 years, on organ, Organ Chamber. *XIII*. Inscr. with verse. Harvey Bonner, 1924-**2003**, bronze, on bench, Churchyard.

Ref: *M.B.S. Bulletin*, 23, p.13.

BIGHTON, All Saints.

I. Inscr. with verse. Ensign Richard Grenville Deane, 30th Regt., yst. son of Rev. George Deane, rector, [killed] at [the Siege of] Sevastopol, **1855**, aged 18, maker's name WALLER . FECIT . LONDON (and monogram), mur., C. *II*. Inscr. in Lat. recording gift of window in **1856** by John Wilder in mem. of w. Maria; Rev. George Deane, [M.A.], rector, mur., C. *III*. Inscr. with verse. Col. Bonar Millett Deane, 2nd son of Rev. George Deane, [M.A.], rector, [killed] leading a column under Gen. Sir George Colley at the Battle of Lang's Nek, South Africa, **1881**, aged 46, mur., on marble, C. *IV*. Inscr. Nathaniel Wedd Cooke, died at Sydney, N[ew] S[outh] W[ales, Australia], **1890**, aged 53, mur., C. *V*. Inscr. recording dedication of chancel beam and aisle ceilings in **1904** by w. [Sarah Mary, 1917, aged 81], in mem. of George Christian, worshipped in the ch. for 33 years, mur., S.A. *VI*. Inscr. George Philip Christian, 1860-1925, and Admiral Arthur Henry Christian, C.B., M.V.O., served in [World War I], 1863-**1926**, 2nd and 4th sons of George Christian, and [w.] Mary, mur., S.A. *VII*. Inscr. Hazel, dau. of Col. Edward Hanning-Lee, w. of Bishop Palmer, 1877-**1931**, pos. by brothers and sister, on chair, C. *VIII*. Inscr. George Hart, **1936**, aged 67, on wooden cross, Churchyard. *IX*. Inscr. Francis Barton, lay reader, **1955**, and w. Florence Sophia, 1954, on pulpit, N. *X*. Inscr. with R.A.F. insignia. Walter Thomas Jeffrey and [w.] Mary Ellen, residents in the par. 1954-**1977**, bronze, on bench, Churchyard. *XI*. Inscr. recording restoration [of organ] in **2003** in mem. of Theo Barton and Frank Sargent, organists for many years, on organ, N.A. *XII*. Inscr. Jessica Frances Love, 2000-**2004**, on tree post, Churchyard.

Ref: *Haines*, II, p.238.

BINSTED, Holy Cross.

I. Inscr. Henry, son of Richard Heighes, gent., **1595**, aged 45; mar. Thomasina, dau. of Wilfred Upton, had 9 sons and 6 daus.; formerly mur., Vestry, now mur., on board, C. Inscr. 160 x 520 mm. Style: Johnson.

II. Inscr. Susanna, dau. of William, Lord Maynard, w. of Nicholas Bowell, esq., **1644**, S.C. Inscr. 186 x 519 mm, black marble slab 1680 x 810 mm.

III. Inscr. Richard Cheyney, left £100 to the poor, **1701**, [aged 65], C. Inscr. 464 x 688 mm, grey marble slab 1840 x 850 mm. *IV*. Inscr. "TO THE GLORY OF GOD IN MEMORIAM FEAST OF PENTECOST **1893**"; [Rev.] W[illiam] G.G. T[hompson], on processional cross, Vestry. *V*. Inscr. recording gift [of missal stand] in **1895** by members of the Guild of St. Mary, Lyndhurst, "AS A TOKEN OF LOVE AND RESPECT FOR THEIR WARDEN", [Rev.] William G.G. Thompson, on missal stand, Vestry. *VI*. Inscr. recording gift of lectern by friends and parishioners in mem. of George Langrish, churchwarden for 37 years, **1896**, on lectern, N. *VII*. Inscr. with verse recording restoration of lady chapel by Charles Arthur Richard Hoare, **1908**, pos. by parishioners, mur., on board, S.C. *VIII*. Inscr. with verse recording dedication of altar rails by parishioners in mem. of Edward VII, [1841-]**1910**, maker's name *JONES & WILLIS L*ᵀᴰ, mur., on board, C. *IX*. Inscr. recording gift of electric organ blower in **1938** by George G. Chalcraft in mem. of Beatrice M[ary] Chalcraft, [1922, aged 52], and Kathleen R[uth] Chalcraft, [1938, aged 50], bronze, on organ, N.C. *X*. Inscr. in raised letters recording that ch. was "NEWLY LIGHTED" in **1938** by N. C[halcraft] in mem. of Herbert Chalcraft, of West Court, bronze, mur., on board, S.A. *XI*. Inscr. recording restoration of organ in **1962** through generosity of Charlotte [Helen] Bonham Carter, [dau. of Col. Lewis Ogilvy, C.B., widow of Sir Edgar Bonham Carter, K.C.M.G., C.I.E.], of Binsted Wick, [1893-1989], bronze, on organ with no.*IX*, N.C.

Ref: *Haines*, II, p.76; *M.B.S. Trans.*, V, p.259; *M.S.*, p.158; *Soc. Antiq. MS. 875/6*, p.13; *V.C.H., Hampshire*, II, p.489.

BISHOPSTOKE, St. Mary (new church).

I. Inscr. Benefaction of Henry Twynham, of Quobleigh, and brother, George Twynham, of Whitchurch, **1851**, mur., W.Porch/Tower. *II.* Inscr. [Very Rev.] Thomas Garnier, [D.C.L.], Dean of Winchester [1840-1872], rector for more than 60 years [1807-1869, 1776-]**1873**, and w. Mary, 1849, aged 68, pos. by dau., maker's name COX & SONS, LONDON, mur., N. See Winchester Cathedral no.*XI.* *III.* Inscr. in raised letters recording dedication of chancel screen by children in mem. of George Postlethwaite, of Oakleigh, East Grinstead, [Sussex], 1881, and w. Elizabeth Davies, died at Chislehurst, [Kent], **1901**; also brother, John Guy Postlethwaite, died at Colorado Springs, [America], 1890, mur., C. *IV.* Inscr. recording dedication of ch. tower in 1909 by Rt. Rev. Herbert [Edward] Ryle, Bishop of Winchester [1903-1911]; the peal of 5 bells consists of 3 bells (removed from old ch. and inscribed: "IN GOD IS MY HOPE. 1589"; "GIVE THANKS TO GOD. 1598"; and "SEEK THE LORD. 1600") and the gift of 2 bells "TOGETHER WITH THIS BRASS" by Henry White; the full peal was 1st rung in **1910**; [Rev.] S[idney] N[ewman] Sedgwick, [M.A.], rector [1905-1922]; Henry White and W.G. Maffey, churchwardens, maker's name ROSE & Co. SOUTHAMPTON, mur., on board, W.Porch/Tower. *V.* Inscr. with verse. Harvey Collyer, [verger and par. clerk, lost with the S.S. Titanic], "WHO FELL ASLEEP IN THE DEEP", [1880-]**1912**, on notice board, N. *VI.* Inscr. with verse. Anne Webb, **1912**, on lectern, N. *VII.* Inscr. with verse recording clock pos. by mother in mem. of 2nd-Lt. Edwin Newland Finney, 6th Cycle Corps, [Leinster Regt., son of Edwin Finney and w. Ann Elizabeth, school[master and Sunday schoolmaster, [killed on active service] **1917**, aged 22, [buried at Point-du-Jour Military Cemetery, Athies, France], on clock, W.Porch/Tower. *VIII.* Inscr. recording gift [of churchwardens' wand] in **1951** by Mr. [Henry Ivill, 1886-1977] and Mrs. [Ella] Ivill, [1886-1969], on churchwardens' wand, N. *IX.* Inscr. Carolyn Vibert, ch. [servant], **1965**, on cross, C. *X.* Inscr. [Rev.] Reginald John Allen, [B.A.], rector 1949-1955, [1974], engr. c.**1975**, on lectern, C. *XI.* Inscr. Henry Ivill, 1886-**1977**, and [w.] Ella, 1886-1969, on altar, S.C./S.A. *XII.* Inscr. Bertram Cheater, **1978**, aged 92, pos. by family and friends, on portable font, S.C./S.A. *XIII.* Inscr. Ronald Norman Apps, churchwarden 1957-1960, 1898-1976, and w. Dorothy Olive, 1900-**1985**, ?brass, on flowerstand, C. *XIV.* Inscr. Richard Henry Griffiths, 1877-1955, and [w.] Mabel Rose, 1897-**1989**, [buried] in the churchyard, bronze, on bench, Churchyard.

Ref: *Brit. Lib. Add. MS. 39962*, f.102, f.104.

Ch. built, 1890-1 and 1909.

BISHOPSTOKE, St. Mary (old church, now demolished).

INDENTS & LOST BRASSES. 1. Lost brass, William Button, esq., **1590**; mar. Mary, dau. of Sir William Kellwey, had 8 children, Ambrose, John, Frances, Edward, Henry, Dorothy, Cecile.

Ref: *Haines*, I, p.218, II, p.76; *M.S.*, p.170.

Ch. demolished, 1965.

BOSCOMBE, (see BOURNEMOUTH).

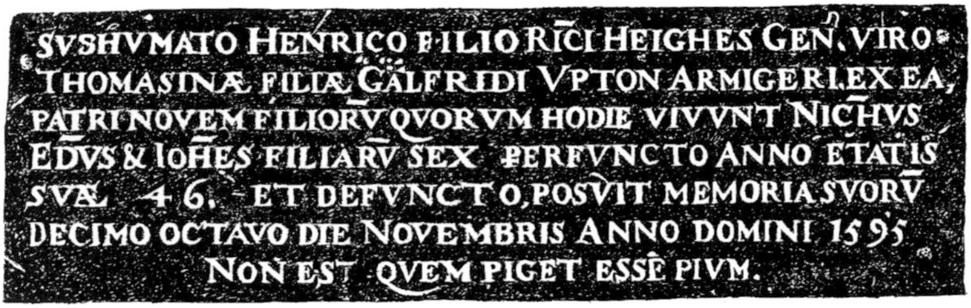

SVSHVMATO HENRICO FILIO RICI HEIGHES GEN, VIRO
THOMASINÆ FILIÆ GALFRIDI VPTON ARMIGER LEX EA,
PATRI NOVEM FILIORV QVORVM HODIE VIVVNT NICHVS
EDVS & IOHES FILIARV SEX PERFVNCTO ANNO ETATIS
SVÆ 46. ET DEFVNCTO POSVIT MEMORIA SVORV
DECIMO OCTAVO DIE NOVEMBRIS ANNO DOMINI 1595
NON EST QVEM PIGET ESSE PIVM.

Binsted I

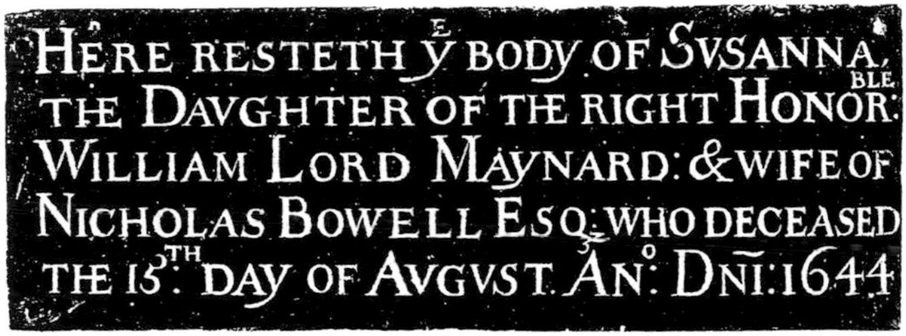

HERE RESTETH ȳ BODY OF SVSANNA,
THE DAVGHTER OF THE RIGHT HONOR:BLE
WILLIAM LORD MAYNARD: & WIFE OF
NICHOLAS BOWELL ESQ: WHO DECEASED
THE 15TH DAY OF AVGVST AN: DNI: 1644

Binsted II

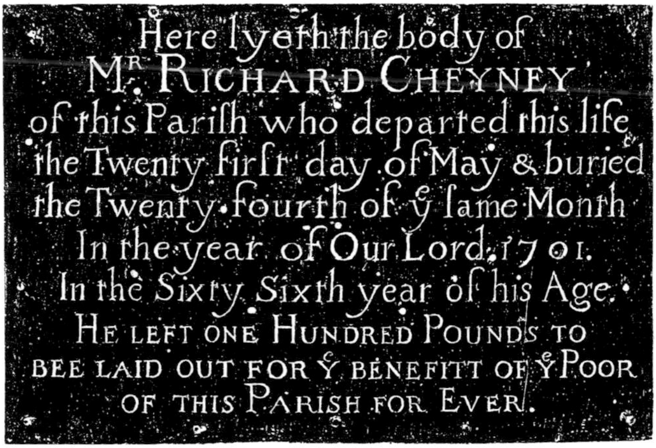

Here lyeth the body of
MR RICHARD CHEYNEY
of this Parish who departed this life
the Twenty firft day of May & buried
the Twenty fourth of ȳ fame Month
In the year of Our Lord 1701.
In the Sixty Sixth year of his Age.
HE LEFT ONE HUNDRED POUNDS TO
BEE LAID OUT FOR Ȳ BENEFITT OF Ȳ POOR
OF THIS PARISH FOR EVER.

Binsted *III*

FROM THIS STALL GLADSTONE MADE
HIS LAST COMMVNION IN CHVRCH
ON THVRSDAY MARCH 3RD A:D:1898

Bournemouth, St. Peter *XXXII*

37

BOURNEMOUTH, or BOSCOMBE, Corpus Christi (R.C.) (now in Dorset).

I. "This Church, under the title of Corpus Christi, was built by The Baroness Pauline von Hugel, Who spent her life in the service of the poor and in all good works. It was solemnly opened, Septr. 8th, 1896, by the Rt. Rev. John Vertue, 1st Bishop of Portsmouth, And given with the Presbytery and other Endowment, to the Fathers of the Society of Jesus. This Tablet was erected by the Fathers and Congregation of the Church in Grateful Memory of the Foundress who died March 29th, 1901, of her faithful friend, Mary Ellen Redmayne, who died February 7th, **1902**, And of others who assisted her in the establishment of the Mission In order that they who worship in this beautiful house Of God, may ever remember them in prayer", rect. pl, inscr. beneath ogee arch, lozenge and 2 monogrammed roundels, maker's name John Hardman & C⁰· Birmᵐ·, mur., on board on pillar, S.A. *II.* Inscr. recording enlargement of ch. with addition of tower and belfry in 1932-1933 through numerous gifts especially that of Margaret Coakly Cundy, 1934, in mem. of [Rev.] Charles de la Pasture, [Society of Jesus], "who laboured for twenty five years among the Faithful of this parish", [1st par. priest 1897-1904, 1923, aged 84]; opened in **1934** by Rt. Rev. [Dr.] William Timothy Cotter, D.D., Bishop of Portsmouth [1910-1940], mur., on board on pillar, N.A. *III.* Inscr. recording gift of [south chapel] altar by Elizabeth Mary Turner, **1938**, mur., on board, S.C. *IV.* Inscr. James W. Murphy, builder, **1978**, aged 62 years; modernised the ch. in 1962, pos. by w. and sons, mur., on board on pillar, S.A. of C. *V.* "The "Mary" organ December **1985**", on organ, S.A. of C.

Ch. built, 1895-6 and 1932-4.

Transferred from Hampshire to Dorset in 1974.

BOURNEMOUTH, or BOSCOMBE, St. Andrew (now in Dorset).

I. Inscr. recording dedication of lectern in **1893** by w. Frances Sanford in mem. of Rev. William Andrew Crawford, M.A., rector of Shalden for 32 years, on lectern, N. *II.* Inscr. recording gift of pulpit in **1908** by Frances Sanford Crawford, w. of no.*I*, 1908, on pulpit, N. *III.* Inscr. recording presentation of organ in **1908** by Alfred Trapnell, on organ, S.C. *IV.* Inscr. with verse. Harry Hugben, chorister, 1916-**1954**, on choir stall, C. *V.* Inscr. recording renovation of organ, restoration of west window and other improvements and repairs carried out in **1958** through [legacy] of Mrs. Eva Gladys Gwynn, 1958, mur., on board, N.Porch. *VI.* Inscr. Frank Victor Hale, verger 1930-**1960**, on credence table, C. *VII.* Inscr. Albert Frank Parsons, churchwarden and benefactor, 1934-**1960**, mur., C. *VIII.* Inscr. recording rewiring of ch. in **1961** through legacy of Albert Frank Parsons, churchwarden 1936-1960, mur., on board, N.Porch. *IX.* Inscr. Marjorie Gainsborough Gardiner, worshipped in the ch. for 40 years, 1964, whose [legacy] paid for the restoration of the exterior stonework of the ch. in **1964**, mur., on board, N.Porch. *X.* Inscr. Olive Morley, 1894-**1964**, on table, S.A. *XI.* Inscr. J.M. Footner, 1906-**1980**, on candelholder, N.

Ch. built, 1907-8.

Transferred from Hampshire to Dorset in 1974.

BOURNEMOUTH, or BOSCOMBE, St. Clement (now in Dorset).

I. Inscr. in raised letters. [Rev.] George Douglas Tinling, [B.A.], 1st vicar, **1880**, aged 36, buried at Pau, [France], mur., wall outside N.A. *II.* Inscr. in Lat. recording erection of [south chancel] windows by friends and parishioners in mem. of [Rev.] William Purton, [M.A.], vicar for 11 years [1889-1891], **1891**, mur., below window, C. *III.* Inscr. in raised letters recording dedication of window by parents in mem. of Maud Mary Aiden Cannon, 1865-**1898**, mur., below window, Baptistry. *IV.* Inscr. Brevet-Major George Edward Begbie, D.S.O., Highland Light Infantry, died at Netley Hospital, **1907**, aged 38, pos. by brother officers, maker's name John Hardman & C°· Birm^m·, mur., on marble, N. *V.* Inscr. Eliza Leake Broun, **1923**, mur., N. *VI.* Inscr. recording gift of rails and furniture in mem. of Winifred Kate Wilson, Sunday School teacher and superintendent at St. Mary's for over 25 years, **1942**, on rail, N.A. *VII.* Inscr. H[enr]y H. Hancock, F.R.C.O., **1949**, on notice board, N. *VIII.* Inscr. recording erection of [north aisle] window in mem. of Thomas Oldham and [w.] Leonie; also dau., Sydney Louise Oldham, **n.d.**, mur., below window, N.A. *IX.* Inscr. Pascoe Phelan, [pos. by] friends, **n.d.**, on bench, Churchyard.

Ch. built, 1871-3 and 1890-3.

Transferred from Hampshire to Dorset in 1974.

BOURNEMOUTH, or BOSCOMBE, St. John the Evangelist (now in Dorset).

I. Inscr. with verse recording reredos pos. by w. Charlotte in mem. of [Rev.] Henry Francis Udny Hall, [M.A.], , rector of Kings Worthy, **1880**, aged 59, mur., on board, C. *II.* Inscr. in Lat. Mary Nixon, 1801-**1894**, on lectern, N. *III.* Inscr. recording gift [of pulpit] by parents and relatives of Rev. E[rnest] A[ugustus] Causton, [M.A.], 1st curate 1891-**1895**, on pulpit, N. *IV.* Inscr. with verse. Flora Moore, headmistress of St. John's National Girls' School for 17 years, **1910**, pos. by parishioners, maker's name, J. STREET & SONS, mur., on board, S.A. *V.* Inscr. recording erection of [north and south chancel] windows in **1912** by John Henry Crompton and w. Selina, mur., on board below window, C. *VI.* Inscr. in raised letters. Walter John Street, churchwarden for 22 years, 1930; Charles Thomas Miles, F.R.I.B.A., joint architect of the ch. and sidesman for 30 years, 1930; and Lt.-Col. Arthur Heygate Vernon, T.D., J.P., F.R.C.S., churchwarden for 8 years, P.C.C. vice-chairman, **1931**, pos. by congregation, mur., on board, Counselling Room. *VII.* Inscr. Brother and sister, **1932**; formerly on pew; in 2006 loose in ch. safe, Clergy Vestry. *VIII.* Inscr. Mary Tryon, **1939**, on offertory box stand, Churchwardens' Vestry. *IX.* Inscr. [Leading-Aircraftsman] Robert Gunstone Mitchell, [1319691], R.A.F.[V.R.], Staff-Sgt. 2nd Bournemouth Co., Boy's Brigade, ch. worshipper, died while serving at Canora, Saskatchewan, Canada, **1942**, [aged 20, buried at Yorkton Cemetery, Canada]; in 2006 loose in N.C. *X.* Inscr. recording gift of organ console by friends in mem. of [Rev.] Canon Albert William Parsons, vicar 1936-**1951**, mur., on pillar, N.C. *XI.* Inscr. Alice Jane Guscott, 1951, and Eli Guscott, **1956**, pos. children; in 2006 loose in N.C. *XII.* Inscr. recording gift of [altar] rail in **1960** in mem. of Norah and Noel Pragley and other family members who worshipped in the ch. for many years; in 2006 loose in N.C. *XIII.* Inscr. Emil Springman, **1981**, [pos. by] w. and family, on flowerstand, C. *XIV.* Inscr. recording gift [of flowerstand] by friends in mem. of Emil Springman, [**1981**], on flowerstand, C. *XV.* Inscr. Alfred Henry Child, 1906-**1983**, worn, on pulpit, N. *XVI.* Inscr. Jill Marris, 1937-**1991**, on table, C.

Ch. built, 1893-5.

Transferred from Hampshire to Dorset in 1974.

BOURNEMOUTH, Sacred Heart (R.C.) (now in Dorset).

I. Inscr. in Lat. on 3 pls. recording gift of altar by Helen Stuart and Ethel Bennett in mem. of Michael Bruce, 1883, and Frances Bruce, **1885**, on altar, S.C. *II.* Inscr. in Lat., sh. and crest recording erection of [south] chapel by widow in mem. of Demetrio Maria Lapizburu Y. O'Daly, **1892**, mur., S.C. *III.* Inscr. recording erection of lady chapel in mem. of [Rev.] Henry Schomberg Kerr, S[ociety of] J[esus], superior of the mission and director of the Sodality 1888-1891, died at Grahamstown, South Africa, 1895; carving added by William Cassell Maude in mem. of mother, Martha Matilda Maude, **1899**, aged 77, maker's name John Hardman & C⁰· Birmᵐ·, mur., N.C. *IV.* Inscr. Carmen Lapizburu, **1900**, on chair, C. *V.* Inscr. recording presentation [of icon of B.V. Mary and Child] in **1903** by children, M.Y. and J.C., mur., on framed icon, N. *VI.* Inscr. recording erection of [north chapel] windows in **1904** by sister, Frances Mary Remington, in mem. of Frederic Hardy Remington, died at Paignton, [Devon], 1899, mur., below windows, N.C. *VII.* Inscr. on 2 pls. Demetrio Larizburu Y. O'Daly; Maria del Carmen Lapizburu Y. Hill; and relatives, engr. c.**1905**, on altar, S.Tr. *VIII.* Inscr. recording transformation of chapel and erection of altar in 1921-**1922** through [legacy] of Ethel Maude Mary Bennett, 1921, mur., with no.*I*, N.C. *IX.* Inscr. [recording gift of statue of B.V. Mary by Lt.-Col.] Sir Dodington [George Richard Sherston] Sherston-Baker, [5th] Bart., [eld. son of Sir George Sherston Baker, 4th Bart., J.P. 1877-1944] and family, engr. c.**1950**, mur., below statue, N.

Ref: *Burke's Peerage and Baronetage*, p.161.

Ch. built, 1872-4 and 1896-8.

Transferred from Hampshire to Dorset in 1974.

BOURNEMOUTH, St. Andrew (now in Dorset).

I. Inscr. recording erection of apse in mem. of Barbara, w. of Rev. Canon [William] Eliot, [M.A.], vicar of Holy Trinity, Bournemouth [1891-1906], **1894**, pos. by husband, children and relatives, maker's name BACON & CURTIS Lᴰ BOURNEMOUTH, mur., Baptistry. *II.* Inscr recording foundation of ch. [in 1891] in mem. of Willoughby Marshall Burslem, M.D., physician in the town for many years, [1818-1889]; "with the help of many friends, the parish of Holy Trinity Bournemouth was constituted in the year of our Lord 1867", maker's name BACON & CURTIS Lᴰ BOURNEMOUTH, engr. c.**1895**, mur., C. *III.* Inscr. with verse recording erection of organ by mother in mem. of Francis Wyndham, son of Rev. [George] Crespigny La Motte, [and w. Caroline Jennetta], grandson of Vice-Admiral J[oseph] Digby, 1887, engr. **1897**, maker's name T. THOMASON & C⁰ BIRMINGHAM, mur., C. *IV.* Inscr. with verse recording erection of reredos by mother in mem. of Gertrude Daisy, dau. of Rev. [George] Crespigny La Motte [and w. Caroline Jennetta], grand-dau. of Vice-Admiral J[oseph] Digby, **1897**, mur., with no.*III*, C. *V.* Inscr. recording erection of a large portion of the nave in **1900** by widow, Eleanor, in mem. of [Rev.] Joseph Clarke, M.A., vicar of Eling [1885-1897], 1897, maker's name BACON & CURTIS Lᴰ BOURNEMOUTH; formerly mur., N.; in 2006 loose in Baptistry. See also Eling no.*II*. *VI.* Inscr. recording gift of stained glass windows in baptistry in **1907** by Mrs. Clarke, of Salway Lodge, and dedication in mem. of Rev. [Canon] Claude [Henry] Eliot, [M.A.], vicar of Christ Church, Hoxton, [Middx.], maker's name BACON & CURTIS Lᴰ BOURNEMOUTH, Baptistry.

VII. Inscr. Harriet Adey, Florence Adey, Lydia Toop, Walter E. Toop, **1918**, mur., N.A. *VIII.* Inscr. recording gift of £500 towards the cost of the organ by niece, Caroline Beatrice Hooper, in mem. of Mariane Parker, ch. worshipper for many years, **1923**, on organ, C. *IX.* Inscr. recording erection of chancel railing in **1933** in mem. of w. Harriet by Major F[rank] J[oseph] Ruddle, churchwarden, mur., on board with no.*VII,* N.A. *X.* Inscr. [Major] Frank Joseph Ruddle, **1942**, pos. by P.C.C., mur., on board with nos.*VII & IX,* N.A. *XI.* Inscr. William Adey, **1944**, mur., on board with nos.*VII, IX & X,* N.A. *XII.* Inscr. recording erection of [churchyard] gates in mem. of Dora May Caslake, kindergarten Sunday school superintendent for 5 years, **1944**, aged 33, on gate, Churchyard. *XIII.* Inscr. recording erection of [churchyard] wall and dedication in **1949** in "thanksgiving for our deliverance and in memory of all those in this parish who served in our country's forces in the fight for freedom 1939-1945", on gatepost, Churchyard. *XIV.* Inscr. Amy Katherine Lloyd, worshipped in the ch. for 50 years, **1954**, mur., on board with nos.*VII, IX, X & XI,* N.A. *XV.* Inscr. recording installation of oil-fired heating system in **1963** in mem. of Doris Grace Buckingham, 1898-1961, Sunday school teacher and worshipped in the ch. for many years, mur., on board with nos.*VII, IX, X, XI & XIV,* N.A. *XVI.* Inscr. recording gift of chest [of drawers] by family and friends in mem. of Edwin James Hickman, 1911-**1982**, on chest of drawers, S.A. *XVII.* Inscr. recording refurbishment of vestries in **1982** by friends in mem. of Leonard James Smith, verger for many years, 1906-1981, mur., on board with nos.*VII, IX, X, XI, XIV & XV,* N.A. *XVIII.* Inscr. Winefred Mary Baker, 1902-**1983**, on bookstall, S.A. *XIX.* Inscr. recording gift [of prie-dieu] by family and friends in mem. of Winifred Ellen Hickman, 1906-**1984**, on prie-dieu, S.A. *XX.* Inscr. recording gift of aumbry lamp in the memorial chapel in **1992** by family and friends in mem. of James Edward Claydon, ch. worshipper, 1920-1982, mur., on board with nos.*VII, IX, X, XI, XIV, XV & XVII,* N.A. *XXI.* Inscr. recording consecration of altar in **1992** by [Rt. Rev.] Colin [Clement Walter James], Bishop of Winchester [1985-1995], in mem. of Ernest Mesher and [w.] Norah, "who loved this church and served it faithfully", on altar, N.; from Bournemouth, or Springbourne, St. Mary the Virgin (q.v.). *XXII.* Inscr. Eve Moor, 1930-**1994**, on portable font cover, S.A. *XXIII.* Inscr. recording that "This altar was originally made for St. Anne's Chapel of the Parish Church of St. Mary the Virgin, Holdenhurst Road, Bournemouth. The Church was closed in **1995**. The Altar has been transferred to the Parish church of St. Andrew, Bennett Road, with the permission of Mrs. Hazel Osborne who donated it in 1992 in memory of her parents, Mr. & Mrs. Mesher for many years faithful members of St. Mary's", on altar with no.*XXI,* N. *XXIV.* Inscr. Feltham family, **1995**, on chair, N. *XXV.* Inscr. Allan Whitcombe, 1941-**1995**, on chair, N. *XXVI.* Inscr. Lily and Harold Whitcombe, 1921-1979, engr. c.**1995**, on chair, N. *XXVII.* Inscr. Lillian Baker, engr c.**1995**, on chair, N. *XXVIII.* Inscr. Mr. and Mrs. Benz, engr. c.**1995**, on chair, N. *XXIX.* Inscr. Robert William and Florence Mary Boniface, engr. c.**1995**, on chair, S.A. *XXX.* Inscr. Chris and Jill Bright, engr. c.**1995**, on chair, N. *XXXI.* Inscr. Maurice and Beryl Bright, engr. c.**1995**, on chair, N. *XXXII.* Inscr. Margaret Brumell, engr. c.**1995**, on chair, N. *XXXIII.* Inscr. Ernest and Beatrice Chambers, engr. c.**1995**, on chair, N. *XXXIV.* Inscr. Cowling family, engr. c.**1995**, on chair, N. *XXXV.* Inscr. Christopher and Joan Day, engr. c.**1995**, on chair, N.A. *XXXVI.* Inscr. Harold and Mabel Drysdale, engr. c.**1995**, on chair, N. *XXXVII.* Inscr. Elizabeth, w. of Geoffrey Duffall, engr. c.**1995**, on chair, N. *XXXVIII.* Inscr. Gage family, engr. c.**1995**, on chair, N. *XXXIX.* Inscr. Ella Greenwood, engr. c.**1995**, on chair, N. *XL.* Inscr. Leon and Doris Hiscock, engr. c.**1995**, on chair, N. *XLI.* Inscr. Hilda and Albert Dorries and Olive and Arthur Hopson, engr. c.**1995**, on chair, N. *XLII.* Inscr. recording donation [of chair] by Angela and Bryer Howard in mem. of Ray and Mary Howard, engr. c.**1995**, on chair, N. *XLIII.* Inscr. Lily and Harold Lambeth, engr. c.**1995**, on chair, N. *XLIV.* Inscr. Doris Martin, engr. c.**1995**, on chair, N. *XLV.* Inscr. recording donation [of chair] by John and Elizabeth in mem. of

I.A. Richenda Rham, engr. c.**1995**, on chair, N. *XLVI.* Inscr. Rev. Canon R[obert] C[lifford] Rham, [B.D., A.K.C.], vicar 1946-1954, engr. c.**1995**, on chair, N.A. *XLVII.* Inscr. Rita Twinn, engr. c.**1995**, on chair, N. *XLVIII.* Inscr. Rev. [Canon Michael Vonberg, B.A., curate 1959-1961, hon. canon of Southwark Cathedral] and Mrs. Vonberg, engr. c.**1995**, on chair, N. *XLIX.* Inscr. Claude Williams, engr. c.**1995**, on chair, N. *L.* Inscr. Arthur and Gertrude Woolford, engr. c.**1995**, on chair, N. *LI.* Inscr. John, husband and father, engr. c.**1995**, on chair, N. *LII.* Inscr. Mary, pos. by Kelson, engr. c.**1995**, on chair, N. *LIII.* Inscr. Arthur John Brown, sidesman for 30 years, **n.d.**, mur., on board with nos.*VII, IX, X, XI, XIV, XV, XVII & XX*, N.A. *LIV.* Inscr. recording gift [of flag stand] by Miss E. Stevenson, a friend of the group, **n.d.**, on stand, Baptistry.

Ch. built, 1891-1900.

Transferred from Hampshire to Dorset in 1974.

BOURNEMOUTH, St. Augustin (now in Dorset).

I. Inscr. with verse. [Rev. Canon] Henry Twells, [M.A.], hon. canon of Peterborough Cathedral, founder of ch. [and 1st priest-in-charge 1892-]**1900**, pos. by organist and choristers, maker's name JONES & WILLIS, on organ, C. *II.* Inscr. [Rev.] Canon Henry Twells, [M.A.], founder [of ch.] and 1st priest-in-charge 1892-**1900**, mur., on framed photo., N. *III.* Inscr. Rev. S[omerset] C[orry] Lowry, M.A., 1st vicar 1900-**1911**, mur., on framed photo., N. *IV.* Inscr Capt. Edward Claude Whiteley, [22nd Field Co.] Royal Engineers, [son of John J. Whiteley and w. Gertrude], born at Madra, [India], killed in action at Shaiba, Mesopotamia, 1889-**1915**, [buried at Basra War Cemetery, Iraq], on perspex., N. A. *V.* Inscr. recording gift of organ by w. in mem. of Capt. Alfred Sinclair Leatham, 75th Foot Gordon Highlanders, **1917**, on organ, C. *VI.* World War I memorial in raised letters on 2 pls. (66 names); "Their memorial St. Augustin's Cottage Enham Village Centre", bronze, mur., S.A. *VII.* Inscr. Rev. G[eorge] A[lexander] Johnstone, [M.A.], 2nd vicar 1911-**1927**, mur., on framed photo., N. *VIII.* Inscr. [Rev.] Canon A[lexander] P[ercy] Annand, [M.A., hon. canon of Winchester Cathedral], 3rd vicar 1927-**1929**, r[ural] d[ean], mur., on framed photo., N. *IX.* Inscr. recording presentation [of lectern] to Wychwood School by Michael John Spink, 1941-1947, and brother, Richard Nigel Spink, 1945-**1951**, on lectern, S.C. *X.* Inscr. recording presentation of screen by w. and family in mem. of William Kenyon Moss, **1961**, on screen, C. *XI.* Inscr. commem. centenary of ch. 1892-**1992**, on paschal candleholder, C. *XII.* Inscr. Philip Manners, husband, **n.d.**, on bench, Churchyard.

Ch. built, 1891-2.

Transferred from Hampshire to Dorset in 1974.

BOURNEMOUTH, St. John the Evangelist (now in Dorset).

I. Inscr. recording presentation [of prie-dieu] "IN AFFECTIONATE REMEMBRANCE OF HAPPY ASSOCIATION IN WORK 1883-**1896**" by Eaton Square, St. Peter, to Rev. Charles Stewart Miller, M.A., on appointment as vicar [1896]; A. Fairbanks, T. Hill, G.R. Holden, A. Thornton, Trevor B. Woodd, C.C. Wilkinson, A. Devonshire, K.W. Drake and C.C. Richardson, on prie-dieu, N.

II. Inscr. with verse recording presentation [of lectern] in **1898** by Helen Wells in mem. of eld. son, Thomas Wells, drowned while bathing 1880-1897, on lectern, N. *III.* Inscr. with sh., crest and motto in mem. of 2nd-Lt. Colin Landseer Mackenzie, [2nd Battn.] Highland Light Infantry, only son [of Landseer Mackenzie and w. Laura, killed] in action at the Battle of the Aisne, **1914**, aged 22, buried "ON THE RIDGE ABOVE VERNEUIL" [at Vendresse British Cemetery, France], maker's name CULN, mur., on marble, N. *IV.* Inscr. 2nd-Lt. Sidney Herbert White, [C Co.] 1st [Battn.] Wilts[hire] Regt., [son of Benjamin White and w. Annie], chorister for 15 years, died of wounds received in action, **1917**, [aged 25, buried at Bethune Town Cemetery, France], on choir stall, C. *V.* Inscr. Cpl. Sidney John Adams, [27400, Northern Aeroplane Repair Depot.], R.A.F., chorister for 25 years, **1918**, aged 34, [buried at Bournemouth (Wimborne Road) Cemetery], on choir stall, C. *VI.* Inscr. William Stagg, **1928**, chorister for 39 years, on choir stall, C. *VII.* Inscr. Benjamin Revell White, **1930**, chorister for 32 years, on choir stall, C. *VIII.* Inscr. Walter Evanson, **1931**, chorister for 32 years, on choir stall, C. *IX.* Inscr. John William Bryan, **1938**, chorister for 24 years, on choir stall, C. *X.* Inscr. Michael Kirkpatrick, **1944**, on choir stall, C. *XI.* Inscr. Herbert Charles Strugnell, **1950**, chorister for 40 years, on choir stall, C. *XII.* Inscr. Charles Barnes Ford, **1951**, chorister for 47 years, on choir stall, C. *XIII.* Inscr. Kenneth John Durrant, **1952**, chorister for 10 years, on choir stall, C. *XIV.* Inscr. Frank Charles Park, **1952**, chorister for 42 years, on choir stall, C. *XV.* Inscr. George Cutts, **1958**, chorister for 16 years, on choir stall, C. *XVI.* Inscr. Arthur Jordan, **1958**, chorister for 14 years, C. *XVII.* Inscr. J. Hedley Bryan, chorister, choirmaster and organist for 62 years 1902-**1964**, on organ, C. *XVIII.* Inscr. Edward Adams, **1971**, chorister for 40 years, C. *XIX.* Inscr. Ellen Rose Long, 1895-**1971**, on pew, N. *XX.* Inscr. with verse recording erection of screen glazing in **1983** in mem. of Douglas and Irene Newton Seth-Smith, mur., S.C. *XXI.* Inscr. Henry Webb, verger 1960-**1983**, on bench, Churchyard. *XXII.* Inscr. recording renovation of organ [1980-]**1984**; funded by parishioners "and other well-wishers among whom the following are remembered" (32 names), on organ, C. *XXIII.* Inscr. Louise Victoria Gilbert, 1897-**1986**, on candleholder, N. *XXIV.* Inscr. recording [burial] of time capsule (beneath pulpit) in **1989** to commem. centenary of the ch., on pulpit, N.

Ch. built, 1889, 1898 and 1906.

Transferred from Hampshire to Dorset in 1974.

BOURNEMOUTH, St. Michael and All Angels (now in Dorset).

I. Inscr. [Rev.] Thomas Pearce, M.A., vicar of Morden [1853-1885], 1820-**1885**, mur., N.A. *II.* Inscr. with verse. Louisa Andrews, 1890; Irene Louisa Andrews, 1891; Harriet Andrews, 1892; and John Simpson Andrews, **1892**, on lectern, N. *III.* Inscr. with verse recording dedication of font by A.F. Andrews in mem. of father, James Richards Andrews, paymaster-in-chief R.N., 1901; also sister, Louisa Andrews, **1901**, maker's name BLUNT & WRAY, on font plinth, N. *IV.* Inscr. Phebe Edmunds, **1901**, aged 63, pos. "by children now scattered abroad, and by some of her fellow workers, in grateful remembrance of happy schooldays and of 34 years devoted work in Salisbury and Bournemouth", mur., S.A. *V.* Inscr. with verse. Annie Eliza Toyne, 1841-**1915**, pos by Mothers' Union members, mur., on marble, C. *VI.* Inscr. Sgt. H.E. Haynes, M.M., R[oyal] G[arrison] A[rtillery], chorister for many years, killed in action **1918**, on table, S.C. *VII.* Inscr. John Caldwell Uhthoff, M.D., F.R.C.S., K.St.J., 1856-1927, reader of ch. lessons 1923-**1926**, maker's name *JONES & WILLIS L*ᵀᴰ, mur., N. *VIII.* Inscr. in raised letters with verse. Mary Fenn, pos. in **1929** by children, maker's name CULN GAWTHORP & SONS Lᵀᴰ,

43

LONDON, mur., S.A. *IX.* Inscr. Ann Decima Edmunds, sister and school-partner (Salisbury, 1871-1883; and St. Margaret's Hall, Bournemouth, 1883-1911) of Phebe Edmunds, 1849-**1935**, mur., below no.*IV*, S.A. *X.* Inscr. Christopher Pearce, churchwarden 1909-1939, 1856-**1939**, mur., N.A. *XI.* Inscr. Wilfred and Hilary Griffith, **1944**, on offertory bowl stand, N. *XII.* Inscr. with verse. Reginald Frank Vivian, chorister, 1897-1956, pos. by w. and son, on choir stall, C. *XIII.* Inscr. recording rededication of organ (on [centenary] of installation) in **1993** by Rev. Kelvin [John] Randall, [J.P., B.D., A.K.C.], vicar; funds raised by Bournemouth people over 4 years; D.P. Thompson, of Bridport, organ builder; Christian Knighton and Robert Whetton, assistants; David Portsmouth and Ian Smith, organists, on organ, C. *XIV.* Inscr. David Lewis, chorister for 43 years, **1996**, on choir stall, C.

Ref: *Busby, Companion Guide,* p.201.

Ch. built, 1873-6 and 1900-1.

Transferred from Hampshire to Dorset in 1974.

BOURNEMOUTH, St. Peter (now in Dorset).

I. Inscr. Lewis Dymoke Grosvenor Tregonwell, [J.P., D.L.], of Anderson and Cranborne Lodge, Dorset, [in 1810 erected the 1st house in Bournemouth on the site of what is now the Royal Exeter Hotel, 1758-]1832; also son, Grosvenor Portman Tregonwell, died an infant, 1837, "Their remains were removed from Anderson to this spot on the 26th of February, **1846**. Bournemouth, which Mr Tregonwell was the first to bring into notice as a watering place, by erecting a Mansion for his own occupation, having been his favourite retreat for many years before his death", maker's name LEVI Sct PORTSEA, on tomb, Churchyard. *II.* Inscr. Henrietta, dau. of Henry William Portman, of Bryanstone House, and w. Ann, widow of L[ewis] D[ymoke] G[rosvenor] Tregonwell, of Anderson and Cranborne Lodge, Dorset, died at Bournemouth, **1846**, aged 76, maker's name LEVI Sct PORTSEA, on tomb with no.*I*, Churchyard. *III.* Inscr. recording presentation of 2 [south aisle] windows in **1852** by congregation in mem. of Marianne Elizabeth, w. of [Rev.] Alexander Morden Bennett, [M.A., vicar]; also only dau., Elizabeth Ann Bennett, mur., on board below windows, S.A. *IV.* Inscr. recording presentation of [south aisle] window by elder brother's widow, Henrietta Lewina Monro, in mem. of Capt. Edmund Augustus Monro, H[onourable] E[ast] I[ndia] C[ompany] S[ervice], 2nd son of Lt.-Gen. William Hector Monro, died suddenly at Bath, [Somerset], **1852**, mur., on board below window, S.A. *V.* Inscr. Percival Sellon, died in India 1848, and Frederick Sellon, **1853**, mur., on board below window, N.A. *VI.* Inscr. Cecilia Tuck, **1853**, aged 8 years and 7 months, mur., on board below window, N.A. *VII.* Inscr. John Fletcher and w. Elizabeth, both died at Leamington, **1854**, mur., on board below window, N.A. *VIII.* Inscr. recording presentation [of south aisle window] by mother in mem. of James Meyrick, **1854**, mur., on board below window, S.A. *IX.* Inscr. George Martin Barnard, died at Nice-Piedmont, [France], **1859**, mur., on board below window, N.A. *X.* Inscr. recording presentation [of 2 north aisle windows] in **1859** by only sister in mem. of Harriet Elizabeth Hornby, died in London, 1857, mur., on board below windows, N.A. *XI.* Inscr. recording the presentation of [north aisle] window in **1859** by only dau., Henrietta Maria Stephens, in mem. of Lt.-Gen. the Rt. Hon. Sir Henry [Eldred Curwen] Pottinger, [1st] Bart., G.C.B., [1st Governor of Hong Kong], died at Malta, [1789-]1856, mur., on board below window, N.A. *XII.* Inscr. Sarah Prince Swallow, **1859**, mur., on board below window, N.A. *XIII.* Inscr. St. Barbe Tregonwell, eld. son of Lewis D[ymoke] G[rosvenor] Tregonwell, of Anderson and Cranborne [Lodge, Dorset], born at Clyst St. George [Devon], died at Bournemouth, 1782-**1859**, [buried] in vault, on tomb with nos.*I & II*, Churchyard. *XIV.* Inscr. Richard Addison, infant son of Rev. Frederick Bankes, B.D., and w. Eliza Jane, died at East Parley, **1860**, mur., on board below window, N.A. *XV.* Inscr. recording presentation of [north aisle] window by uncle, John Hibidage, in mem. of Angelina Elizabeth Butler, died at Ford House, Newport, Isle of Wight, **1860**, aged 14, mur., on board below window, N.A. *XVI.* Inscr. William Richard Baker Sellon, **1860**, mur., on board below window, N.A. *XVII.* Inscr. recording presentation of [north aisle] window by children in mem. of Major-Gen. William Daniel Jones, R[oyal] A[rtillery], and w. Eliza Margaret, engr. c.**1860**, mur., on board below window, N.A. *XVIII.* Inscr. Henrietta Lewina, dau. of Lewis D[ymoke] G[rosvenor] Tregonwell, widow of Hector W. Monro, of Edmondsham, Dorset, and Ewell Castle, died at Bournemouth, **1864**, aged 62, [buried] in vault, on tomb with nos.*I, II & XIII*, Churchyard. *XIX.* Inscr. [Rev.] Matthew McCobb, curate of Corfe Mullen, [Dorset], for 18 years, 1857, and w. Elizabeth, died at Salisbury, [Wilts.], **1867**; also dau., Elizabeth, died at Bournemouth, 1861, mur., on board below window, N.A. *XX.* Inscr. recording that 6 bells were rung in **1871** "AS A MARK OF ESTEEM AND RESPECT" for Rev. Alexander Morden Bennett, M.A., vicar, maker's name HART, SON, PEARD & C[o], LONDON, mur., Tower. *XXI.* Inscr. recording presentation of [south aisle] window by Florence Iacomb in mem. of brother, Ernest Iacomb, **1876**, buried in the churchyard, mur., on board below window, S.A. *XXII.* Inscr. recording presentation of [north aisle] window by congregation and friends in mem. of Rev. Alexander Morden Bennett, M.A., vicar for 34 years, by whose exertions this church was built, 1808-**1880**, mur., below window, Vestry/N.A. *XXIII.* Inscr. recording erection of [tower] window by 2 sons in mem. of Rev. Alexander Morden Bennett, [M.A.], founder and 1st vicar, [1808-]**1880**, mur., on board, Tower. *XXIV.* Inscr. recording erection of [tower] window in **1880** by Benjamin Lancaster in mem. of [w.] Rosamira, foundress of St. Peter's Community, Kilburn, mur., on board, Tower. *XXV.* Inscr. recording gift of fresco (on south spandrel of sanctuary) by sister in mem. of Edward Boucher Baker, **1881**, mur., C. *XXVI.* Inscr. recording gift of fresco (on south spandrel of sacrarium) by Dr. and Mrs. Horace Dobell in mem. of 2nd dau., Violet Fordham, w. of Dr. Charles Meymott Tidy, died after a protracted and painful illness in London, **1881**, maker's name GAWTHORP S[c] LONDON, mur., C. *XXVII.* Inscr. John Tregonwell, son of L[ewis] D[ymoke] G[rosvenor] Tregonwell and w. Henrietta, of Anderson and Cranborne Lodge, Dorset, [1811-]**1885**, on tomb with nos.*I, II, XIII & XVIII*, Churchyard. See also Cranborne, Dorset no.*II.* *XXVIII.* Inscr. recording [gift] of frescoes (St. Agnes and St. Etheldreda) by daus., Augusta Langton and Mary Dawkins, in mem. of Ann Dawkins, **1886**, mur., C. *XXIX.* Inscr. recording the gift of fresco (St. Margaret on the north wall of the sanctuary) by brothers and sisters in mem. of Florence Iacomb, **1889**, [buried] with no.*XXI*, mur., on board below no.*XXI*, S.A. *XXX.* Inscr. recording gift of frescoes (on sanctuary roof) by friends and dedication in **1891** in mem. of [Rev.] George Stopford Ram, M.A., vicar 1881-1889, [1838-1889], maker's name GAWTHORP, S[c], mur., C. See also Bournemouth, St. Swithun no.*VI.* *XXXI.* Inscr. recording gift of [south aisle] window by Edward Wise Rebbeck, of Stafford Lodge, and dedication in **1896** in mem. of w. Susannah, 1893; also [parents], William Edward Rebbeck and [w.] Jane Irwin; sister, Harriet Rachel Rebbeck; and foster parents of w., Robert and Georgina Crowther Kerley, [buried] in the churchyard, mur., below window, S.A. *XXXII.* Inscr. "FROM THIS STALL GLADSTONE MADE HIS LAST COMMVNION IN CHVRCH ON THVRSDAY MARCH 3RD A:D: **1898**", [Rt. Hon. William Ewart Gladstone, Prime Minister 1868-1874, 1880-1885, 1886 and 1892-1894, 1809-1898], on choir stall, C. Inscr. 62 x 312 mm. *XXXIII.* Inscr. recording dedication of mosaic panels (on north sanctuary wall) in **1899** in mem. of Charles J. Nixon, churchwarden and sidesman 1873-1893, 1895, mur., C. *XXXIV.* Inscr. Rachael, dau. of

Rev. Robert Lowth, widow of John Tregonwell, of Anderson and Cranborne Lodge, Dorset, **1901**, aged 85, on tomb with nos.*I, II, XIII, XVIII & XXVII*, Churchyard. See also Cranborne, Dorset no.*V. XXXV.* Inscr. with insignia. "TO THE MEMORY OF OUR COMRADES WHO MADE THE SUPREME SACRIFICE", 1899-**1902**, pos. by South Africa Veterans' Association, mur., on board, S.A. *XXXVI.* Inscr. recording erection of reredos in mem. of Julia, [eld. dau. of Henry John Conyers, of Copt Hall, Essex], widow of Hon. (Anthony) John Ashley[-Cooper, Q.C., 4th son of Cropley Ashley-Cooper, 6th Earl of Shaftesbury], **1907**, mur., on pillar, C. *XXXVII.* Inscr. with verse. Sir Dan Godfrey, Knt., director of music to Bournemouth Corporation for 45 years, [1868-]**1939**, on gravestone, Churchyard. *XXXVIII.* Inscr. with verse. Ellen Stevens, w. of Malcolm Leggett, **1946**, mur., on board, S.A. *XXXIX.* Inscr. with verse. Charles James Edwards, O.B.E., **1947**, aged 81, mur., on board, S.A. *XL.* Inscr. with verse. Lucy Heath, widow of Charles James Edwards, O.B.E., **1949**, aged 77, mur., on board, S.A. *XLI.* Inscr. [Rev.] Arthur Treeve Stephens, engr. c.**1965**, on bench, Churchyard. *XLII.* Inscr. recording gift of music desks in **1970** by Ethel Dilke Rowley in memory of parents, John Scott and [w.] Sarah, mar. in the ch. 1878, on choir stall, C. *XLIII.* Inscr. with insignia recording that the Bournemouth and District Branch of the Old Contemptibles Association Standard, dedicated in 1928, was [laid up] in **1972**, mur., on board on pillar, N.A. *XLIV.* Inscr. Cyril Maynard, chorister 1908-**1978**, on choir stall, C. *XLV.* Inscr. Leslie G.W. Mallows, 1906-**1981**, on portable font, N.C. *XLVI.* Inscr. recording gift of choir stall lights in **1983** by William Rowley in mem. of w. Ethel, on choir stall, C. *XLVII.* Inscr. on 2 pls. "IN HONOURED MEMORY OF THOSE MEN AND WOMEN OF THE ARMED SERVICES WHO FOUGHT, DIED OR WERE WOUNDED IN THE DUNKIRK AREA IN THE SUMMER OF 1940 AND WHO BY THEIR HEROIC EFFORTS IN COMPANY WITH CIVILIAN VOLUNTEERS MADE POSSIBLE THE SUCCESSFUL EVACUATION OF THE BRITISH EXPEDITIONARY FORCE TO THE HAVEN OF ENGLISH SHORES". pos. by Bournemouth, Poole and District Branch of the 1940 Dunkirk Veterans' Association to commem. 25th anniversary of branch 1958-**1983**, mur., on board, S.A. *XLVIII.* Inscr. recording installation of [altar] rail (previously in Bournemouth, St. Paul [demolished in 1984]) by family in mem. of Reginald Sylvester Morris, mayor 1965-1966, engr. c.**1985**, mur., on board, C. *XLIX.* Inscr. recording gift of table in mem. of Tip Pearmain, ch. member and servant for many years, **1986**, on table, N.Tr. *L.* Inscr. with verse recording restoration of screen in **2003** in mem. of Edna Marjorie Ashton and Judith Helen Miles, mur., C. *LI.* Inscr. recording refurbishment and gilding of font cover in **2005** in mem. of Albert Dykes, [ch.] servant for 70 years, and [w.] Doreen, bellringer for 52 years, mur., on board, S.A.

Ref: *Burke's Peerage and Baronetage*, p.2412; *M.B.S. Bulletin*, 61, p.11.

Ch. built, 1841-3, 1851, 1854-9, 1869 and 1879.

Transferred from Hampshire to Dorset in 1974.

BOURNEMOUTH, St. Stephen (now in Dorset).

I. Inscr. Louisa Susan Anne Moore, 1864, and Isabella Sophia Ann Moore, **1884**, mur., below window, N.A. *II.* Inscr. recording [erection] of ch. in mem. of [Rev.] Alexander Morden Bennett, [M.A., founder and] 1st vicar of Bournemouth, St. Peter, [1808-]1880, maker's name AISH, engr. c.**1885**, mur., on marble, N.Porch. *III.* Inscr. [Rev.] John Haviland, **1887**, mur., below window, N.A. *IV.* Inscr. Peter Ellis, 1884, and [w.] Mary Helen, **1888**, mur., below window, N.A. *V.* Inscr. recording gift of triptych altar rails, screens, choir stalls and 2 apse windows in **1899** by Thomas Holt Briscoe and w. Anne, mur., below window, C. *VI.* Inscr. recording dedication of [north aisle] window by congregation and friends to commem. 30 years ministry of Rev. Alexander Sykes Bennett, M.A., [eld. son of no.*II*], 1st vicar 1881-**1911**, [1837-1912], mur., on marble, N.C./N.Tr. *VII.* Inscr. Anne Sophia, widow of Hon. Robert Campbell, M.L.C., born at Sydney, N[ew] S[outh] Wales, [Australia], died in London, 1816-1881; also 2nd dau., Fanny Campbell, died in London 1840-**1911**, mur., below window, N.A. *VIII.* Inscr. recording insertion of window by children in mem. of Rev. A[lexander] S[ykes] Bennett, [M.A.], 1st vicar [1881-1911], 1837-**1912**, mur., below window, C. *IX.* Inscr. with verse, crest and motto within border of oak leaves and acorns. Capt. Cyril Oswald Denman-Jubb, B.A., of Oriel Coll., Oxford, [son of Rev. Henry Denman-Jubb], Adjutant 76th Duke of Wellington's [(West Riding)] Regt., mentioned in despatches, [killed] in action at Mons, Belgium, 1876-**1914**, [buried at Hautrage Military Cemetery, Belgium], maker's name CULN. GAWTHORP & SONS · LONDON, mur., N.C. *X.* Inscr. with verse and insignia within border of thistles. Lt. Ronald Mosse MacDonald, 79th Regt. Queen's Own Cameron Highlanders, wounded at the Battle of the Aisne, [killed] in action near Ypres, 1890-**1914**, mur., N.C. *XI.* Inscr. Elizabeth Brackenbury, engr c.1915, mur., below window, N.A. *XII.* Inscr. recording installation of [north chapel] window and others under the will of Ellen Pressly, engr. c.1915, mur., N.C./N.Tr. *XIII.* Inscr. recording gift of statue (B.V. Mary cast by Christopher Burnett) from sculptress, Diane Gorvin, and dedication in **1986** in mem. of Donald Nelson Willoughby, churchwarden of [Bournemouth], Holy Trinity 1958-1973, par. warden and churchwarden of [Bournemouth], St. Swithun-cum-Holy Trinity 1974-1981, mur., below statue, S.A

Ch. built, 1881-98 and 1907-8.

Transferred from Hampshire to Dorset in 1974.

BOURNEMOUTH, St. Swithun (Bournemouth Family Church) (now in Dorset).

I. Inscr. Amelia Caroline Hyde, **1881**, mur., below window, C. *II.* Inscr. Henry Wyatt-Smith, **1883**, aged 14, mur., below window, C. *III.* Inscr. Rev. Henry James Cotton, [B.A.], **1884**, mur., below window, C. *IV.* Inscr. Anne Helen Erskine, **1887**, mur., below window, C. *V.* Inscr. Alice Ellen Patton, **1887**, mur., below window, C. *VI.* Inscr. recording [chancel] window pos. by friends and parishioners in mem. of [Rev.] George Stopford Ram, M.A., vicar 1881-**1889**, [1838-1889], mur., below window, C. See also Bournemouth, St. Peter no.*XXX.* *VII.* Inscr. John [Jardine], son of Manfred Jardine and [w.] Jane, died at Boscombe **1891**, mur., below window, N. *VIII.* Inscr. Queen Victoria, reigned 1837-**1901**, [1819-1901], mur., below window, N. *IX.* Inscr. Walter Charles Parker, **1902**, mur., below window, N.C. *X.* Inscr. Elizabeth Onslow, **1904**, mur., below window, N. *XI.* Inscr. "to the glory of God, March 29th **1906**", mur., below window, N. *XII.* Inscr. with sh. and lozenge. Margaret Anne Tottenham, 1908; also sister, Sarah de Cliffe Tottenham, **1930**, maker's name W.A. HOARE, BOSCOMBE, mur., below window, N. *XIII.* Inscr. Henry Gerald Willis, chorister and crossbearer, 1894-**1947**, mur., on board below window, N.

Ch. built, 1876; declared redundant, 1996; reopened as (Evangelical Charismatic) ch., 1998.

Transferred from Hampshire to Dorset in 1974.

BOURNEMOUTH, or CHARMINSTER, St. Francis of Assisi (now in Dorset).

I. Inscr. F.S., mother, 1844, engr. c.**1930**, on chair, organ gallery, N. *II.* Inscr. R.M.L., 1883, engr. c.**1930**, on chair, N. *III.* Inscr. E. Dean, 1897, engr. c.**1930**, on chair, N. *IV.* Inscr. E.W. Hocking, 1900, engr. c.**1930**, on chair, N. *V.* Inscr. S.S.P., 1902, engr. c.**1930**, on chair, N. *VI.* Inscr. E.R.W., 1904, engr. c.**1930**, on chair, N. *VII.* Inscr. K.A., 1905, engr. c.**1930**, on chair, N. *VIII.* Inscr. [Rev.] Robert White, 1905, engr. c.**1930**, on chair, N. *IX.* Inscr. M.W., 1907, engr. c.**1930**, on chair, N. *X.* Inscr. May Price, 1908, engr. c.**1930**, on chair, N. *XI.* Inscr. J.P., 1909, engr. c.**1930**, on chair, N. *XII & XIII.* Two inscrs. T.J., 1910, engr. c.**1930**, on chairs, organ gallery and N. *XIV & XV.* Two inscrs. F.J.C., 1912, engr. c.**1930**, on chairs, N. *XVI.* Inscr. R. Hocking, 1913, engr. c.**1930**, on chair, N. *XVII.* Inscr. M.R., 1913, engr. c.**1930**, on chair, N. *XVIII.* Inscr. S.A. Walker, mother, 1913, engr. c.**1930**, on chair, N. *XIX.* Inscr. Benjamin Nelson, 1915, engr. c.**1930**, on chair, N. *XX.* Inscr. [Rev.] Richard Francis Herring, [M.A., A.K.C.], 1916, engr. c.**1930**, on chair, N. *XXI.* Inscr. L.J., 1916, engr. c.**1930**, on chair, N. *XXII.* Inscr. A.P., 1916, engr. c.**1930**, on chair, N. *XXIII.* Inscr. M.P., 1916, engr. c.**1930**, on chair, N. *XXIV.* Inscr. J.S., 1916, engr. c.**1930**, on chair, N. *XXV.* Inscr. R.G.W., [World] War [I], 1916, engr. c.**1930**, on chair, N. *XXVI.* Inscr. Ninian, 1916, engr. c.**1930**, on chair, N. *XXVII, XXVIII, XXIX, XXX, XXXI, XXXII & XXXIII.* Seven inscrs. R[oyal] Sussex Regt., [World War I], engr c.**1930**, on chairs, N. *XXXIV.* Inscr. G.B.D., 1918, engr. c.**1930**, on chair, N. *XXXV.* Inscr. A.A., 1919, engr. c.**1930**, on chair, N. *XXXVI.* Inscr. A.M., 1920, engr. c.**1930**, on chair, N. *XXXVII.* Inscr. M.H.T.M., 1923, engr. c.**1930**, on chair, N. *XXXVIII.* Inscr. E.M.W., 1923, engr. c.**1930**, on chair, N. *XXXIX.* Inscr. H.P.M.C., 1924, engr. c.**1930**, on chair, organ gallery, N. *XL.* Inscr. L. Davies, 1924, engr. c.**1930**, on chair, N. *XLI.* Inscr. S. Hocking, 1924, engr. c.**1930**, on chair, N. *XLII.* Inscr. F.Z. (BP) 1924, engr. c.**1930**, on chair, N. *XLIII.* Inscr. F.S.D., 1926, engr. c.**1930**, on chair, N. *XLIV.* Inscr. R.C. Hocking, 1926, engr. c.**1930**, on chair, N. *XLV.* Inscr. B. LeRoy, 1926, engr. c.**1930**, on chair, N. *XLVI.* Inscr. E.M.C. and L.E.B., 1927, engr. c.**1930**, on chair, N. *XLVII.* Inscr. G.T.C., 1927, engr. c.**1930**, on chair, N. *XLVIII.* Inscr. A.R., 1927, engr. c.**1930**, on chair, N. *XLIX.* Inscr. [Rev.] G[ilbert] A[dolphus] Rideout, [M.A.], 1927, engr. c.**1930**, on chair, N. *L.* Inscr. R.M.C., 1928, engr. c.**1930**, on chair, N. *LI.* Inscr. Ellen LeRoy Davis, 1928, engr. c.**1930**, on chair, N. *LII.* Inscr. F.B.D., 1928, engr. c.**1930**, on chair, N. *LIII.* Inscr. H. Hall, 1928, engr. c.**1930**, on chair, N. *LIV.* Inscr. Tessie, 1928, engr. c.**1930**, on chair, N. *LV.* Inscr. M.A., 1929, engr. c.**1930**, on chair, N. *LVI.* Inscr. J.W.C., 1929, engr. c.**1930**, on chair, N. *LVII.* Inscr. [Rev.] Samuel Frederick Leighton Green, [M.C. and bar], 1929, engr. c.**1930**, on chair, N. *LVIII.* Inscr. A.J.K., 1929, engr. c.**1930**, on chair, N. *LIX.* Inscr. C.E.N., 1929, engr. c.**1930**, on chair, N. *LX.* Inscr. L.A.R., 1929, engr. c.**1930**, on chair, N. *LXI.* Inscr. [Rev.] O.A.S., 1929, engr c.**1930**, on chair, N. *LXII.* Inscr. C.A., **1930**, on chair, N. *LXIII.* Inscr. A.E.C., **1930**, on chair, N. *LXIV.* Inscr. F.J.C., **1930**, on chair, N. *LXV.* Inscr. Margaret Carola, **1930**, on chair, N. *LXVI.* Inscr. G.R.D., **1930**, on chair, N. *LXVII.* Inscr. F.T.E., **1930**, on chair, N. *LXVIII.* Inscr. F.H., **1930**, on chair, N. *LXIX.* Inscr. I.M.H., **1930**, on chair, N. *LXX.* Inscr. R.H., **1930**, on chair, N. *LXXI.* Inscr. G.M., **1930**, on chair, N. *LXXII.* Inscr. G.E.M., **1930**, on chair, N. *LXXIII.* Inscr. H.E.O., **1930**, on chair, N. *LXXIV.* Inscr. Jane Shirley-Price, **1930**, on chair, N. *LXXV.* Inscr. N.K.P., churchwarden, 1930, on chair, N. *LXXVI.* Inscr. O.P., **1930**, on chair, N. *LXXVII.* Inscr. J.R., **1930**, on chair, N. *LXXVIII.* Inscr. I.W.S., **1930**, on chair, N. *LXXIX.* Inscr. H.A. Thompson, **1930**, on chair, N. *LXXX.* Inscr. Christine Ness Walton, **1930**, on chair, N. *LXXXI.* Inscr. Mary Ness Walton, **1930**, on chair, N. *LXXXII.* Inscr. Mollie White, **1930**, on chair, N. *LXXXIII.* Inscr. A.B.W.W., **1930**, on chair, N. *LXXXIV.* Inscr. A.M.W., **1930**, on chair, organ gallery, N. *LXXXV.* Inscr. [Grandmother], **1930**, on chair, N. *LXXXVI.* Inscr. "Two Sisters", **1930**, on chair, N. *LXXXVII.* Inscr. St. Chad, 672, eng. c.**1930**, on chair, N. *LXXXVIII.* Inscr. Padre Serafico, 1226, engr. c.**1930**, on chair, N. *LXXXIX.* Inscr. Santa Chiara, 1253, engr. c.**1930**, on chair, N. *XC.* Inscr. Charles 1st K[ing] and M[artyr, 1649], engr. c.**1930**, on chair, N. *XCI.* Inscr. M.A. and Mrs. Bartlett, engr. c.**1930**, on chair, N. *XCII.* Inscr. A. Butler, engr. c.**1930**, on chair, N. *XCIII.* Inscr. F.A. Butler, engr. c.**1930**, on chair, N. *XCIV.* Inscr. K.C. Butler, engr. c.**1930**, on chair, N. *XCV.* Inscr. E.M.B., engr. c.**1930**, on chair, N. *XCVI.* Inscr. recording gift [of chair] by H.F.B., engr. c.**1930**, on chair, N. *XCVII.* Inscr. recording gift [of chair] by W.B., engr. c.**1930**, on chair, N. *XCVIII.* Inscr. Ida Helen Crabb, engr. c.**1930**, on chair, N. *XCIX.* Inscr. Jessie Florence Crabb, engr. c.**1930**, on chair, N. *C.* Inscr. E.C., engr. c.**1930**, on chair, N. *CI.* Inscr. I.F.D., engr. c.**1930**, on chair, N. *CII.* Inscr. recording thank offering by J.D., engr. c.**1930**, on chair, N. *CIII.* Inscr. Father, [pos. by] E.M.E., engr. c.**1930**, on chair, N. *CIV.* Inscr. Mother, [pos. by] E.M.E., engr. c.**1930**, on chair, N. *CV.* Inscr. E.D.F., engr. c.**1930**, on chair, N. *CVI.* Inscr. S.F., engr. c.**1930**, on chair, N. *CVII.* Inscr. [Rev.] E.C. Greenwood, engr. c.**1930**, on chair, N. *CVIII.* Inscr. F.W.T. Greenwood, engr. c.**1930**, on chair, N. *CIX.* Inscr. S.J.S. and D.A.H., engr. c.**1930**, on chair, N. *CX.* Inscr. E.G.H. and F.J.H., engr. c.**1930**, on chair, N. *CXI.* Inscr. J.O.H., engr. c.**1930**, on chair, N. *CXII, CXIII, CXIV, CXV, CXVI, CXVII, CXVIII, CXIX & CXX.* Nine inscrs. recording gift [of chairs] by Holdenhurst Village Church, engr. c.**1930**, on chairs, N. *CXXI.* Inscr. A.H.J., engr. c.**1930**, on chair, N. *CXXII.* Inscr. M.E.J., engr. c.**1930**, on chair, N. *CXXIII.* Inscr. P.L.J., engr. c.**1930**, on chair, N. *CXXIV.* Inscr. M.E.K., engr. c.**1930**, on chair, N. *CXXV.* Inscr. A.F. Maidment, engr. c.**1930**, on chair, N. *CXXVI.* Inscr. G.M., engr. c.**1930**, on chair, N. *CXXVII.* Inscr. E.A.O., engr. c.**1930**, on chair, N. *CXXVIII.* Inscr. [Rev.] Henry [Charles] Percival, engr. c.**1930**, on chair, organ gallery, N. *CXXIX.* Inscr. Parents, [pos. by] A.E.P., engr. c.**1930**, on chair, organ gallery, N. *CXXX.* Inscr. recording [thank] offering by child, J.N.P., engr. c.**1930**, on chair, N. *CXXXI.* Inscr. recording [thank] offering by baby, M.M.P., engr. c.**1930**, on chair, N. *CXXXII.* Inscr. Sister Benedicta Ruth, S.S.M., engr. c.**1930**, on chair, N. *CXXXIII.* Inscr. J.M.R., engr. c.**1930**, on chair, N. *CXXXIV.* Inscr. Rosemary, engr. c.**1930**, on chair, N. *CXXXV.* Inscr. recording gift [of chair] by St. Clement's Church, engr. c.**1930**, on chair, N. *CXXXVI.* Inscr. [recording gift of chair by] New Southgate, St. Paul, engr. c.**1930**, on chair, N. *CXXXVII.* Inscr. F.G.F.T., engr. c.**1930**, on chair, N. *CXXXVIII.* Inscr. recording a thank offering by E.W.W., engr. c.**1930**, on chair, N. *CXXXIX.* Inscr. recording a thank offering by J.W.W., engr. c.**1930**, on chair, N. *CXL.* Inscr. "A Very Grateful Little Boy", engr c.**1930**, on chair, N. *CXLI.* Inscr. Edith Collis, **1931**, on chair, N. *CXLII.* Inscr. G.F.A.C., **1931**, on chair, N. *CXLIII.* Inscr. H.A.R., **1931**, on chair, N. *CXLIV.* Inscr. V.W., **1931**, on chair, N. *CXLV.* Inscr. W.E. Johnson, **1932**, on chair, N. *CXLVI.* Inscr. B.C.F., **1933**, on chair, N. *CXLVII.* Inscr. St. Mary Magdalene, **1933**, on chair, N. *CXLVIII.* Inscr. Marjorie Ethel Foote, **1972**, on lectern, C. *CXLIX.* Inscr. recording restoration of organ in **1985** in mem. of Harold Whitburn and [w.] Irene, on organ, organ gallery, N. *CL.* Inscr. recording installation of sound system in mem. of Isabel Cooper, **1990**, on door, N.C. *CLI.* Inscr. John Windebank, 1911-1986, and [w.] Doreen, 1910-**1998**, on piano, N.C. *CLII.* Inscr. recording refurbishment of lady chapel in **2004** in mem. of Peter Foote, 1929-2002; chairs in mem. of Fred Read, 1912-2002, mur., N.C.

Ch. built, 1929-30.

Transferred from Hampshire to Dorset in 1974.

BOURNEMOUTH, or HENGISTBURY HEAD, St. Nicholas (now in Dorset).

I. Inscr. recording presentation [of book stand] by Janet Young in mem. of mother, Rosemary Goodchild, **1965**, on book stand, Sacristy.

Ch. built, 1961.

Transferred from Hampshire to Dorset in 1974.

BOURNEMOUTH, or ILFORD, St. Saviour (now in Dorset).

I. Inscr. recording consecration of ch. in 1936 by [Rt. Rev. Cyril Forster Garbett], Bishop of Winchester [1932-1942]; Rev. C[hetwode] W[illiam] Caulfeild-Browne, 1st vicar 1934-**1939**; Frederic Lawrence, F.R.I.B.A., architect; F.A. Grigg & Sons, contractor, mur., S.Porch. *II.* Inscr. Lucy Lilian Edwards, ch. worker 1936[-1956], 1956, aged 78; also Arthur Samuel Edwards, chorister and ch. worker 1936-1957, **1958**, aged 80, on lectern, S.C. *III.* Inscr. Frank Richard Packman, **1965**, on prie-dieu, C. *IV.* Inscr. recording presentation of east window in **1968** by H.W. Widdup in mem. of w., Elsie May, and sister, Margaret Victoria Sparrow, mur., on board, N.C. *V.* Inscr. Mrs. Olive Gandy, **1982**, on table, N.A. *VI.* Inscr. Mary B. Hale, founder member of ch., teacher, 1903-**1999**, on bench Churchyard.

Ch. built, 1934-5.

Transferred from Hampshire to Dorset in 1974.

BOURNEMOUTH, or ILFORD, St. Thomas More (R.C.) (now in Dorset).

I. Inscr. recording erection of ch. chiefly through the gift of Margaret Coakley Cundy, [1934], in mem. of [Rev.] Charles de la Pasture, S[ociety of] J[esus], "who laboured for twenty five years among the Faithful of this parish", [1923, aged 84]; opened in **1939** by Rt. Rev. [Dr.] William Timothy Cotter, D.D., Bishop of Portsmouth [1910-1940], mur., on pillar, N. *II.* Inscr. recording dedication of plaque by parishioners in recognition of donations for the provision of a new forecourt, expanded narthex, resiting of the font, creation of the Theresa Connolly Resource Room and the repair and refurbishment of the Gallery; blessed in **2005** by Rt. Rev. [Roger Francis] Crispian Hollis, [M.A.], Bishop of Portsmouth [1988-], mur., Narthex.

Ch. built, 1939.

Transferred from Hampshire to Dorset in 1974.

BOURNEMOUTH, or MOORDOWN St. John the Baptist (now in Dorset).

I. Inscr. recording erection of [south aisle] window in mem. of Cpl. Robert Thomas Dale, 2nd [Battn.] Hampshire Regt.; M.I. G[unne]r Ernest George Gollop, R[oyal] G[arrison] A[rtillery]; Pte. Hector Eli Bursey, 2nd [Battn.] RI. West Surrey Regt.; and Pte. Joseph James Burt, 2nd [Battn.]

Dorsetshire Regt., killed in the South African War 1899-**1902**, maker's name *JONES & WILLIS L*[TD], mur., S.A. *II.* Inscr. Emily Kidner, **1916**, on pulpit, N. *III.* Inscr. recording dedication of [pulpit] panel in **1919** in mem. of Pte. Cecil Frank Ivamy, [4583, 1st Battn.] Oxford and Bucks. L[ight] I[nfantry, son of Edward Ivamy and w. Elizabeth], server, chorister at [Bournemouth], St. Luke, killed in action at Thiepval, France, 1916, [aged 26] on pulpit with no.*II*, N. *IV.* Inscr. recording dedication of [2 pulpit] panels in **1919** in mem. of Emily Kidner, headmistress of C[hurch] of E[ngland] Infants' Day School 1892-1916, on pulpit with nos.*II & III*, N. *V.* Inscr. Priscilla Seare, ch. worker and organist 1854-1877, **1923**, aged 84, on pulpit with nos.*II, III & IV*, N. *VI.* Inscr. in raised letters recording dedication of tower in 1923 by Ven. Alfred E Daldy, archdeacon of Winchester, and dedication of clock in **1924** by Rev. Frank C[rosland] Learoyd, [M.A.], vicar of [Bournemouth], St. Luke [1917-1944], in mem. of those [killed] in World War I; [Rev.] Herbert Bloomfield, [M.A.], vicar [1905-1924], bronze, mur., S.Porch. *VII.* Inscr. recording gift of table in mem. of Boaz Bloomer, **1926**, on table, N. *VIII.* Inscr. on semi-circular-shaped pl. William James Snell, verger for 22 years, 1911, aged 39, and w. Eliza, verger for 15 years, **1926**, aged 54, on chair, C. *IX.* Inscr. recording gift of seat in **1927** by Mothers' Union [members], on bench, S.Porch. *X.* John Richard Jackson, vicar's [church]warden, **1936**, mur., S.C. *XI.* Inscr. recording erection of screen ornamentation by St. John's Comforts Fund in mem. of those [killed] in World War II, mur., S.A. *XII.* Inscr. [Rev.] Canon Percy Luker, [A.K.C.], vicar 1937-1953, **1964**, on wooden cross, Churchyard. *XIII.* Inscr. G.H. and K.E. Merrick, **n.d.**, on flowerstand, C.

Ch. built, 1873-4 and 1886-7.

Transferred from Hampshire to Dorset in 1974.

BOURNEMOUTH, or POKESDOWN St. James the Greater (now in Dorset).

I. Inscr. recording dedication of [nave] window by John Edward Walcott in mem. of w. Charlotte Anne, **1863**, aged 66, mur., below window, N. *II.* Inscr. Anne Anderson, **1868**, aged 64, mur., below window, N. *III.* Inscr. recording dedication [of nave window] by children, Agatha [Catherine] and Constance, in mem. of Admiral John Edward Walcott, M.P., **1868**, aged 77, maker's name BARR ENG[R] LONDON, mur., below window, N. *IV.* Inscr. [Rev.] William Battersby, M.A., 1st incumbent, **1875**, aged 66, mur., below window, N. *V.* Inscr. Rev. Michael Ward Blagg, curate, **1875**, aged 44, mur., below window, N. *VI.* Inscr. recording erection of [north aisle] window by Constance Butler in mem. of sister, Agatha Liddell, **1884**, mur., below window, N.A. *VII.* Inscr. with 3 shs. crests and mottoes recording the erection of [west nave] window in mem. of Admiral William Charnock Popham, of Stourfield, 1864, aged 73, and widow, Clara, died at Stourfield, **1884**, aged 68; also Ensign Bernard Brunswick Home Popham, 2nd Queen's Royal Regt., died at Bermuda, 1864, aged 21; Lt. Harcourt Frances Pauncefote Popham, J.P., R.N., died at Jersey, 1879, aged 34; and widow, Anne Kate, died at Jersey, 1879, aged 34, maker's name MAYER & C[O] LONDON & MUNICH, mur., below window, N. *VIII.* Inscr. Cecil Harcourt Wingfield Popham, died at Harcourt, Southbourne, **1923**, aged 54, mur., below no.*VII*, N. *IX.* Inscr. Thomas Partridge, vicar's [church]warden 1910-**1924**, on choir stall, N. *X.* Inscr. recording dedication of clergy stalls in memory of [Rev.] Cecil Vincent Goddard, M.A., voluntary assistant priest, 1923-**1933**, on stall, N. *XI.* Inscr. recording erection of choir stalls in **1933** by friends and parishioners in mem. of Alice Parwell, par. worker for many years, on choir stall, N. *XII.* Inscr. Edith Emily Marsterman, 1901-**1979**, on hymn board, N. *XIII.* Inscr. with verse. [Rev.] Canon Douglas Noble, [hon. canon of Rochester Cathedral], 1924-**1989**, on prie-dieu, N. *XIV.* Inscr. with verse. Robert Starks, par.

clerk and verger for 30 years, **1992**, maker's name W.A. HOARE, mur., N. *XV.* Inscr. with verse. Leonard Jarvis, par. clerk and verger for 39 years, **1996**, mur., N. *XVI.* Inscr. Dorothy Tedder, 1920-**2002**, on bench, Churchyard. *XVII.* Inscr. June Stebbings, **n.d.**, on bench, Churchyard.

Ch. built, 1857-8, 1870 and 1931.

Transferred from Hampshire to Dorset in 1974.

BOURNEMOUTH, or SOUTHBOURNE, All Saints (now in Dorset).

I. Inscr. recording dedication of lectern by w. in mem. of Rev. Richard Hosgood, M.A., **1902**, on lectern, N. *II.* Inscr with verse in mem. of mother, **1912**, on font plinth, N.A. *III.* Inscr. recording presentation of pulpit canopy in **1928** by family and friends in mem. of Francis Frederick Smith, churchwarden 1907-1917, and w. Myra Ellis, mur., on board, N. *IV.* Inscr. Lily Marsh Ray, **1931**, mur., on framed picture, N.A. *V.* Inscr. Frederick Sidney Green, husband, **1952**, on bench, Churchyard. *VI.* Inscr. recording erection of [north] porch through legacy of Miss Clara M. Fletcher; dedicated in **1956** by [Rt. Rev. Alwyn Terrell Petre Williams], Bishop of Winchester [1952-1961], mur., on board, N.Porch. *VII.* Inscr. Samuel Dawson and Victoria Gertrude Caws, **1969**, on prie-dieu, C. *VIII.* Inscr. recording erection of annex in 1973-**1974** to replace ch. hall (served from 1902-1915 until dedication of ch.); Rev. Canon R[eginald] J[ohn] Allen, B.A., vicar, r[ural] d[ean]; H.C. Croucher, and R.G.C. Turpin, churchwardens; Max Cross, architect; Peter Rathbone, quantity surveyor; J. Carter & Sons Ltd., contractors, mur., Annex. *IX.* Inscr. Lorna Penelope Durling, 1921-**1984**, on door, S.C. *X.* Inscr. Harold Glaister, 1899-1978, and [w.] Lily, 1900-**1984**, on handrail, Churchyard. *XI.* Inscr. Martha Eleanor Nesbitt, 1909-**1984**, on handrail, Churchyard. *XII.* Inscr. Sidney Day, churchwarden and sidesman, engr. c.**1985**, on handrail, Churchyard. *XIII.* Inscr. Arthur William King, Bournemouth Male Voice Choir member, 1909-**1986**, on lectern, Basement. *XIV.* Inscr. Austin Silvester White, chorister and librarian, 1912-**1988**, on lectern with no.*XIII*, Basement. *XV.* Inscr. recording gift of handrails in mem. of Rev. David Harwood Hughes, B.A., hon. assistant priest 1975-**1992**, mur., outside Hall, Churchyard. *XVI.* Inscr. Winifred Mary Miller, 1905-**1994**, on candleholder, N.A. *XVII & XVIII.* Two inscrs. Rev. W[illiam] R[alph] Nesbitt, [hon.] curate 1976-**1994**, on bookcase, N. *XIX & XX.* Two inscrs. Frank R. Metcalf, organist, engr. c.**1995**, on bookcase, N. *XXI.* Inscr. recording gift of window (designed by Andrew Taylor of Devizes, Wilts.) in **2000** in mem. of Dorothy Bailey, ch. worshipper 1982-1995, and parents and grandparents who cared for their children, Billie, Jonathan, Laura, and Abigail Clark, mur., below window, N.A. *XXII.* Inscr. recording "ALL SAINTS MILLENNIUM GARDEN PROJECT" made possible in **2000** through the help of Rev. [Brian Gerald Apps, M.A., vicar], and Mrs. Apps; contributions from congregation at coffee mornings; Mrs. K. Parker, Cox family; Richardson family; Boyes family; Mrs. J. Downs; Mrs. Croucher; Simonis family, Mrs. Crocker; Youth Club members; Mr. and Mrs. K. Andrews; Miss Emery, Homebase (Christchurch); Golden Acres Nurseries; B. & Q. (Christchurch); Bournemouth Daily Echo; Woodman Timber Supplies; Eco Composting; and Dorset Nature Trust, on bench, S.Porch. *XXIII.* Inscr. Louisa Emery, mother, 1906-**2004**, on prie-dieu, S.A. *XXIV.* Inscr. with verse recording the presentation [of portable font] in **2006** by Douglas and Nina Eyre, on portable font, N.

Ch. built, 1913-4.

Transferred from Hampshire to Dorset in 1974.

BOURNEMOUTH, or SOUTHBOURNE,
Our Lady Queen of Peace and Blessed Margaret Pole (R.C.) (now in Dorset).

I. Inscr. Reginald Cecil Lybbe-Powys-Lybbe, gave the site for the ch., "A mass is said annually on Low Sunday for the repose of his soul", [1881-**1930**], mur., on board, N.A. *II.* Inscr. recording presentation [of a painting of The Annunciation] in **1942** by Isabel Kann, par. member on opening of ch. in 1938, mur., S.C. *III.* World War II memorial (11 names), mur., on board, N.

Ch. built, 1938.

Transferred from Hampshire to Dorset in 1974.

BOURNEMOUTH, or SOUTHBOURNE, St. Christopher (now in Dorset).

I. Inscr. with verse recording dedication of golden jubilee window in **1983** by Rt. Rev. [Dr.] John Vernon Taylor, D.D., Bishop of Winchester [1974-1985; Rev.] F[rank] H[enry] Vear, vicar [1975-1986]; N.F. Chandler and R.D. Tanner, churchwardens, mur., on board, C. *II.* Inscr. with verse. Kathleen Nicholls, ch. worshipper and Sunday school superintendent 1975-**1985**, on board on flag-stand, N. *III.* Inscr. recording dedication of [south chapel] window in mem. of donor, Percy Charles Haydon Bacon, **n.d.**, mur., below window, S.C. *IV.* Inscr. Patrol-Leader Nicholas Staines, "who always did his best", **n.d.**, on flag-stand, N.

Ch. built, 1933.

Transferred from Hampshire to Dorset in 1974.

BOURNEMOUTH, or SOUTHBOURNE, St. Katharine (now in Dorset).

I. Inscr. Arthur Robert Parsons, Natal Mounted Police, [2nd son of Major-Gen. James E.B. Parsons, I.S.C. and 2nd w. Tempé Susan, killed] in the Battle of Isandhlwana, [South Africa], **1879**, aged 19, mur., on window splay, S.A. *II.* Inscr. Charles Needham Parsons, [6th son of Major-Gen. James E.B. Parsons, I.S.C. and 2nd w. Tempé Susan], died at Broxbourne, Herts., **1899**, aged 33, mur., on window splay with no.*I*, S.A. *III.* Inscr. recording gift centre east light window by dau. in mem. of parents, Tom A. Bevis, 1896, and [w.] Katharine, **1901**, mur., S.A. *IV.* Inscr. Edward Aubrey James (Bobbie) [Branson], eld. son of Col. C.E.D. Branson and [w.] Mabel, born in the par., baptised in the ch., 1894-**1901**, buried at Christchurch, maker's name A. & N. AUX. C.S.L. LONDON, mur., C. *V.* Inscr. Jemima, widow of Joseph Gace, **1901**, aged 85, mur., below window, N.A. *VI.* Inscr. recording gift of [south aisle] window by Major-Gen. James E.B. Parsons, I.S.C. and 2nd w. Tempé Susan, in mem. of eld. son, Major James Henry Parsons, I.S.C., Burma Commission, died at Minbu, [Burma], **1901**, aged 43, mur., on window splay with nos.*I & II*, S.A. *VII.* Inscr. recording gift [of pulpit] by parishioners on departure for the par. of Holy Trinity, [West Cowes], Isle of Wight, to [Rev.] Lawrence R[obert] Whigham, M.A., [LL.B.], 1st vicar 1885-**1902**, and w. Amelia Wingham, on pulpit step, N. *VIII.* Inscr. recording gift of font in **1905** by dau., J.B. Adams, in mem. of Mary Ann Adams, 1898, aged 82, on font plinth, N. *IX.* Inscr. Major-Gen. James Edmund Bacon Parsons, Indian Army, died at The Gables, **1905**, aged 75, mur., on window splay with nos.*I, II & VI*, S.A. *X.* Inscr. in Lat. in raised letters. William Salisbury Boyle, **1906**, bronze, on reredos, Sanctuary. *XI.* Inscr. in Lat. in raised letters. Edward Burrard Boyle, **1907**, bronze, on reredos with no.*X*, Sanctuary. *XII.* Inscr. Cicely Margaret Gwyn Elger, Grassendale Guild member, died at Clayton Court Hospital, **1910**, mur., on board, N.A. *XIII.* Inscr. Hon. Lt.-Col. Clement George Parsons, 3rd son [of Major-Gen. James E.B. Parsons, I.S.C. and 2nd w. Tempé Susan], commissioner of Lahore and member of the Legislative Council, Punjab, India, died and buried in the Red Sea, **1912**, aged 51, on window splay with nos.*I, II, VI & IX*, S.A. *XIV.* Inscr. Octavius Sydney Parsons, Indian Civil Service, 7th son [of Major-Gen. James E.B. Parsons, I.S.C. and 2nd w. Tempé Susan], died at Bournemouth, **1912**, aged 42, mur., on window splay with nos.*I, II, VI, IX & XIII*, S.A. *XV.* Inscr. [2nd-]Lt. Douglas Montgomery Parsons, 5th Field Co. R[oyal] E[ngineers], 2nd son of Major J.H. Parsons, Indian Cavalry, [and w. Ellen C.H.], killed at the Battle of Neuve Chapelle, France, **1915**, aged 20, on window splay with nos.*I, II, VI, IX, XIII & XIV*, S.A. *XVI.* Inscr. in raised letters. Mary Buxton, matron of Pembroke Lodge for 15 years, **1916**, pos. by boys of the school, bronze, [designed by Harold Stabler], mur., N.A. *XVII.* Inscr. Enid Margaret Kentish, Grassendale [Girls' School] 1908-1911, died while nursing the wounded at Cornelia Hospital, Poole, [Dorset], **1916**, mur., on board with no.*XII*, N.A. *XVIII.* Inscr. [Nurse] Hermione Angela Rogers, 14th V[oluntary] A[id] D[etachment], British Red Cross Society, dau. of Francis Edward Newman Rogers and w. Louisa Annie], Grassendale Girl[s' School], "GAVE HER LIFE IN THE SERVICE OF KING AND COUNTRY", **1917**, [aged 22, buried at Alexandria (Hadra) War Memorial Cemetery, Egypt], mur., on board with nos.*XII & XVII*, N.A. *XIX.* Inscr. Beatrice Caroline, eld. dau. [of Major-Gen. James E.B. Parsons, I.S.C. and 2nd w. Tempé Susan], w. of Lt.-Col. A.G.B. Lang, I[ndian] A[rmy], died at Church Crookham, **1918**, aged 49, mur.,on window splay with nos.*I, II, VI, IX, XIII, XIV & XV*, S.A. *XX.* World War I memorial in raised letters (19 names); old boys and masters of Pembroke Lodge, bronze, mur., N.A. *XXI.* Inscr. Col. Charles Edward Douglas Branson, Indian Army, people's churchwarden for 15 years, **1920**, aged 78 years, pos. by parishioners, maker's name CULN GAWTHORP & SONS. LONDON, mur., C. *XXII.* Inscr. Tempé Susan, [2nd w. of Major-Gen. James E.B.] Parsons, died at The Croft, **1921**, aged 82, on window splay with nos.*I, II, VI, IX, XIII, XIV, XV & XIX*, S.A. *XXIII.* Inscr. Yelerton Dawson, M.D., vicar's churchwarden for 15 years and warden emeritus until death, **1922**, aged 77, maker's name CULN GAWTHORP & SONS L[TD], LONDON, mur., C. *XXIV.* Inscr. Amelia Agnes Ann, widow [Dr. Robert] Spencer, 1854-**1940**, mur., below window, S.A. *XXV.* Inscr. Thomas Henry Withers, **1953**, on book stand, N. *XXVI.* Inscr. John Kill, 1946-**1960**, on prie-dieu, N.C. *XXVII.* Inscr. Dulcie Louisa Morris, **1962**, on bench, Churchyard. *XXVIII.* Inscr. Frederick Arthur Scadding, 1916-**1970**, on lectern, C. *XXIX.* Inscr. Len Clay, **1972**, pos. by the Cubs and Scouts, on bench, Churchyard. *XXX.* Inscr. Elizabeth Sait, w., mother and grandmother, 1919-**1996**, on bench, Churchyard. *XXXI.* Inscr. recording replacement of vestry windows in **2002** through generosity of parishioners to commem. the golden jubilee of Queen Elizabeth II; Rev. J[ohn] C[ooper] White, [B.Ed.]; M. Fraser and W. Rushworth, churchwardens, mur., Vestry. *XXXII.* Inscr. Arthur Bridge, **n.d.**, on bench, Churchyard.

Ref: *Pevsner, Hampshire*, p.600.

Ch. built, 1881-2 and 1899-1900.

Transferred from Hampshire to Dorset in 1974.

BOURNEMOUTH, or SPRINGBOURNE, St. Mary the Virgin (redundant) (now in Dorset).

I. Inscr. in Lat. [Rev.] Arthur Sharp, **1932**, mur., N.C. *II.* Inscr. recording gift of [north chapel] window in **1947** by relatives, friends and congregation in mem. of

[Rev. Horace Charles] Caswall, [M.A.], ch. built while priest-in-charge and vicar [1922-1947], mur., below window, N.C. Inscr. [recording presentation of frontal chest] in mem. of Elizabeth Agnes Vernon, ch. benefactress, 1866-**1951**, on frontal chest, N.A.; moved to Bournemouth, or Winton, St. Alban (q.v.) (1997). *III.* Inscr. [Rev.] Harry Bushell, vicar 1947-**1960**, mur., N.C. Inscr. recording consecration of altar in **1992** by [Rt. Rev.] Colin [Clement Walter James], Bishop of Winchester [1985-1995], in mem. of Ernest Mesher and [w.] Norah, "who loved this church and served it faithfully", on altar; moved to Bournemouth, St. Andrew (q.v.).

Ch. built, 1926-34; closed, 1995; declared redundant, 1996.

Transferred from Hampshire to Dorset in 1974.

BOURNEMOUTH, or STROUDEN PARK, St. Edmund Campion (R.C.) (now in Dorset).

I. Inscr. on 2 pls. recording presentation [of chair] by sister, Mary Ellen Brosnan and family in mem. of [Rev.] John B. Murphy, par. priest 1981-**1982**, on chair, C. *II.* Inscr. on oval-shaped pl., Keith Elks, **1986**, pos. by w. Bernadette, mur., below crucifix, S.C. *III.* Inscr. with verse. John Vincent Murphy, 1940-**1994**, mur., below window, N. *IV.* Inscr. Ethel Mary Elmes, w. and mother, 1913-**1997**, mur., below window, N. *V.* Inscr. Alice Mary Bosley Jones, 1905-**1999**, mur., below window, N. *VI.* Inscr. Michael Theocleous, husband and father, 1935-**2003**, mur., on board, N.

Ch. built, 1981.

BOURNEMOUTH, or THROOP, St. Paul (now in Dorset).

I. Inscr. recording consecration of ch. in **1984** by Rt. Rev. [Dr.] John Vernon Taylor, [D.D.], Bishop of Winchester [1974-1985]; ch. paid for with payments received from the compulsory purchase of [Bournemouth], St. Paul 1881-1984, on board, Lounge. *II.* Inscr. recording purchase of piano in **2002** through legacy of Muriel Davies, [ch.] member, on piano, N. *III.* Inscr. Frank White, [ch.] member, **n.d.**, on chest of drawers, Vestry.

Ch. built, 1984.

BOURNEMOUTH, or WESTBOURNE, Christ Church (now in Dorset).

I. Inscr. recording dedication of [east north chapel] window in mem. of Charles Curteis Philpott, **1915**, mur., below, N.C. *II.* Inscr. recording dedication of organ case by mother in mem. of Lt. Ernest Reginald Aston, R.N.V.R., [Howe Battn. R.N. Division, killed] in action at Beaumont-Hamel, **1916**, aged 22, [son of David Aston and w. Fanny M., buried at Ancre British Cemetery, Beaumont-Hamel, France], on organ, C. *III.* Inscr. Henry George Holliday, **1960**, on organ with no.*II*, C. *IV.* Inscr. Francis Harry Ford, D.C.M., 1970, and w. Elizabeth Zilpah, **1977**, on pew, N. *V.* Inscr. recording presentation [of bookcase] in mem. of George Tuson, M.B.E., 1925-**1997**, on bookcase, N. *VI.* Inscr. recording donation of equipment by Brigitte Gregory, 1937-**2002**, and friends, mur., in wooden frame on pillar, N.

Ch. built, 1913.

Transferred from Hampshire to Dorset in 1974.

BOURNEMOUTH, or WESTBOURNE, Our Lady Immaculate (R.C.) (now in Dorset).

I, II, III, IV, V, VI & VII. Seven inscrs. Gwendolyn Louisa Nunes, **n.d.**, on pews, N.

Transferred from Hampshire to Dorset in 1974.

BOURNEMOUTH, or WESTBOURNE, St. Ambrose (now in Dorset).

I. Inscr. recording erection of panelling (north and south sides of sanctuary) and sedilia in **1918** in mem. of [Rev.] William Ward Goddard, [M.A.], mur., sedilia, C. *II.* Inscr. recording presentation [of a credence table] as a thank offering to Rev. J[ohn] I[rwin] Patterson, [M.A.], pos. by C.F., engr. c.**1945**, on credence table, S.C. *III.* Inscr. with verse recording gift and dedication of 2 sanctuary lamps in **1948** in mem. of Arthur Edmund Pottle, served ch. as chorister, churchwarden and server for 60 years, 1878-1945, on choir stall, C. *IV.* Inscr. Edith Anstice Condry, **1964**, on hymn board, N. *V.* Inscr. recording dedication of "St Ambrose Church Memorial Corner" in mem. of congregation members who have died since **1970**, mur., S.A. *VI.* Inscr. Charles Skinner, ch. servant for 55 years, **1979**, mur., S.A. *VII.* Inscr. Stanley A. Dobbins, 1907-**1983**, on crucifix, mur., S.C. *VIII.* Inscr. on 2 pls. Aidan Baker, **n.d.**, on cross, S.A.

Ch. built, 1898-1900 and 1907.

Transferred from Hampshire to Dorset in 1974.

BOURNEMOUTH, or WINTON, Annunciation (R.C.) (now in Dorset).

I. Inscr. in raised letters recording erection of ch. in **1907** by dau., Edith, [w. of Capt. Lionel Henry St. Croix] Coxon, in mem. of Lt.-Gen. Augustus [William Henry] Meyrick, Scots Guards, copper, mur., on pillar, N. *II.* Inscr. Harold Wrangel Clarke, [M.D.], **1945**, N. *III.* Inscr. Jane Teresa (Sissy) Allen, pos. by mother and [grandmother], **n.d.**, mur., on board on pillar, N.

Ch. built, 1905-6.

Transferred from Hampshire to Dorset in 1974.

BOURNEMOUTH, or WINTON, St. Alban (now in Dorset).

I. Inscr. Arthur George Tollemache, eld. son of Murray Tollemache and w. Mardic, capt. of S.S. Umsinga, died at Bombay, [India], 1878-**1912**, maker's name *JONES & WILLIS L*^*TD*, mur., N.C.

II. Inscr. in raised letters recording erection of east window in mem. of those [killed in World War I], maker's name W^{M.} MORRIS & C^{O.} (WESTMINSTER) L^{TD}, bronze, mur., on board, N. *III.* Inscr. William Robert Akers, friend of the ch. for 16 years, engr c.**1930**, on lectern, N. *IV.* Inscr. in raised letters. [Rev.] Somerset Corry Lowry, [M.A.], poet, ch. built while vicar 1900-1911, 1885-**1932**, pos. by friends, maker's name F. OSBORNE & CO LTD London, mur., on wooden board, N. *V.* Inscr. recording gift [of clock] in mem. of the Tattam family, 1909-**1939**, mur., below clock, N. *VI.* Inscr. Thomas William Brumby, churchwarden 1940-**1945**, and w. Clara, ch. workers, on screen, N. *VII.* Inscr. in mem. of those [killed in World War II], on screen, N. *VIII.* Inscr. recording the erection [of wooden panelling] by brother, George Insley, in mem. of Evelyn Marguerite Crockford, 1912-**1947**, mur., on panelling, C. *IX.* Inscr. [recording presentation of frontal chest] in mem. of Elizabeth Agnes Vernon, ch. benefactress, 1866-**1951**, on frontal chest, N.A.; from Bournemouth, or Springbourne, St. Mary the Virgin (q.v.). *X.* Inscr. Richmond Lewis Watts, chorister, **1979**, on choir stall, C. *XI.* Inscr. recording that "This Frontal Chest was made for the Parish Church of St. Mary the Virgin in Holdenhurst Road, Bournemouth. The Church was closed in June 1985, and the Parish ceased to exist in January 1997. The Chest was moved to St. Alban's Church in Charminster Road, Bournemouth in November **1997**", on frontal chest with no.*IX*, N.A.

Ch. built, 1907-9.

Transferred from Hampshire to Dorset in 1974.

BOURNEMOUTH, or WINTON, St. Luke (now in Dorset).

I. Inscr. with verse recording dedication [of cross] in mem. Arthur George Whichelo, **1913**, on cross, S.A. *II.* Inscr. Michael David Chapman, hon. verger and sacristan, 1922-**2000**, on lectern, N. *III.* Inscr. recording erection of flood lamps in mem. of Florence and George Oakes; Margaret and Edgar Jury; Lucy and William Kilford; and George Arthur Cooper, **n.d.**, on board below floodlighting, Churchyard.

Ch. built, 1898 and 1913.

Transferred from Hampshire to Dorset in 1974.

BRAMDEAN, SS. Simon and Jude.

I. Inscr. Mary, w. of Thomas Travers, **1639**, mur., in wooden frame on panelling, C. Inscr. 144 x 356 mm.

II. Inscr. recording dedication of chancel windows in **1863** by relative, Gen. Sir William Maynard Gomm, G.C.B., in mem. of Rev. William Gomm, rector for 38 years, and family members, mur., in wooden frame on panelling, C. *III.* Inscr. on 2 pls. recording [south aisle] window pos. in **1867** by widow in mem. of William Cooper Coles, mur., below window, S.A. *IV.* Inscr. on 2 pls. recording [gift] of reredos in **1889** by widow in mem. of [Rev.] Alfred Caesar Bishop, M.A., [rector of Martyr Worthy 1851-1866], 1885, mur., on board, C. *V.* Inscr. on 2 pls.

recording [altar rails] pos. in **1894** by sister, Louisa K. Bishop, on altar rails, C. *VI.* Inscr. recording dedication [of pulpit desk] in **1898** by sons and grandchildren of brother, Henry Legge, in mem. of Honora Augusta Cowper Coles, on pulpit desk, N. *VII.* Inscr. James Belstone Hawkins, chorister, 1890-**1902**, on hymn board, N. *VIII.* Inscr. recording erection of choir stalls in **1911** by Hubert Garle in mem. of mother, mur., on panelling, C. *IX.* Inscr. recording gift of organ in **1911** by M.A. Garle, on organ, S.A. *X.* Inscr. with verse. Mary Ann Eugenie, w. of Richard Webb, **1918**, aged 61, maker's name *JONES & WILLIS L*TD, mur., S.A. *XI.* Inscr. Edward William Grazebrook, **1962**, [aged 69], on door, N.Porch. *XII.* Inscr. recording gift [of pulpit] in **1972** by parishioners from the redundant ch. of Silvertown, St. Barnabas, on pulpit, N. *XIII.* Inscr. Mrs. O.C.L. Feilden, of Bramdean House, engr. c.**1975**, on chair, N. *XIV.* Inscr. Brig. E[dward] S[tephen] B[ruce] Williams, C.B.E., Rifle Brigade, of The Old Rectory, 1892-**1977**, pos. by family, on table, S.Tr. *XV.* Inscr. Margaret Llewelyn, 1934-**1988**, on lectern, N. *XVI.* Inscr. T.B. Newsom, **1988**, on hymn board, N. *XVII.* Inscr. Henry James Hawes, [1998, aged 95], and [w.] Dorothy Kathleen, [**1998**, aged 95, mother and father], bronze, on bench, Churchyard.

Ref: *M.B.S. Trans.*, V, p.260; *M.S.*, p.158; *Soc. Antiq. MS. 875/6*, p.14; *Who's Who,* 1967, p.3299.

BRAMLEY, St. James.

I. William Joye, yeoman, **1452**, in civil dress, with 6 sons standing by his side, inscr., very worn, Tower. Eff. 473 x 132 mm, inscr. 61 x 427 mm, dext. sons 128-138 x 102 mm, sin. sons 126-135 x 107 mm, Purbeck slab 1415 x c.600 mm. Style: London D.

II. Gwen More, dau. of John Shelford, "of ye cite of Harford", esq., "modyr to dame Elizabeth Shelforde abbes of the monastery of Shaftysbury", 1504, (mutil.), inscr. and 1 sh. (3 others lost) engr. c.**1520**, S.C. Recorded (2 shs.) by Cave (1908). *M.B.S. Trans.*, V, p.262; *Mee, Hampshire*, p.115 (drg. of eff.); *Somerset and Dorset N. and Q.*, X, p.31; *V. and A. Mus. List*, pl.45, no.1 (eff.). Eff. orig. 738 x c.225 mm, now 738 x 215 mm, inscr. 130 x 652 mm, upper dext. sh. 158 x 131 mm, upper sin. sh. indent 160 x 135 mm, lower dext. sh. indent effaced, lower sin. sh. indent effaced, Purbeck slab 2065 remains x 975 mm. Style: London F debased. Rep. by B.S.H.E. (1979).

III. Richard Carter, **1529**, in civil dress, and w. Alys, inscr., S.C. *Page-Phillips' Macklin*, fig.2, p.77 (drg. of head of female eff.); *Page-Phillips, 16th Cent. Workshop*, p.16 (inscr.); *Williams*, opp. p.xiii. Male eff. 396 x 137 mm, female eff. 395 x 136 mm, inscr. 78 x 489 mm, Purbeck slab 1460 x 780 mm. Rep. by B.S.H.E. (1979). Style: London G (Gyfford, script 1).

IV. Inscr. Alfred B. Welch Thornton, **1900**, aged 75, on lectern, N. *V.* Inscr. with sh. recording gift [of chair] in **1970** by Court "Pride of Bramley Street" of the Ancient Order of Foresters to commem. centenary, on chair, N. *VI.* Inscr. Rosemary Ann Head, **1974**, bronze, on grave marker, Churchyard. *VII.* Inscr. in raised letters recording planting by par. council in mem. of Donald Faircloth, Rosemary [Ann] Head and Phyllis Millar, [killed in] rail accident, **1974**, bronze, on tree post, Churchyard. *VIII.* Inscr. recording gift [of hymn board] in **1975** by dau., Mollie, in mem. of Joseph F. Jibb and [w.] Florence, on hymn board, N. *IX.* Inscr. in raised letters. Zoe Phyllis Jane Forbes, 1921-**1977**, bronze, on grave marker, Churchyard. *X.* Inscr.

Hic Iacet Maria Trauers
vxor Thomæ Trauers que
obijt 27 Maij Anno 1639

Bramdean I

Bramley I

Of yo charite may tye yⁱ soule of Gwen ꝯ ore sum tyme yᵉ wyf of John
the lord of yᵉ cite of harford elqⁱner ⁊ moder to dame Elizabeth Shelforde
Abbes of the monastery of Shaftesbury the which Gwen dyed the vⁱⁱⁱ
day of august yᵉ yere of our lord ꝳ cccccⁱⁱⁱ on whose soule ihu haue mcy

Bramley II

60

Of yo charite pray for the foules of Richard Tarter and
Alis his wyff whiche Richard decesse d the xxt day of februari
in y yere of o lord god m b⁺ xxix on whose foules Jhu have mci

Bramley III

Bramley 12

C. Osler, [tower] capt., and w. Jenny, [P.C.C.] secretary, engr. c.**1985**, on clock, Tower. *XI.* Inscr. in raised letters. Frederick William (Bill) Davies, 1925-**1995**, bronze, on grave marker, Churchyard.

INDENTS & LOST BRASSES. 12. Indent, lady with 6 daus. standing by her side, inscr., c.1450, Tower. Eff. 465 x c.160 mm, inscr. 60 x 470 mm, dext. daus. 135-140 x 100 mm, sin. daus. 135-140 x 100 mm, Purbeck slab 1460 x 590 mm. Possibly w. of no.I. Style: London D. 13. Lost indent, 1 rivet only, Tower. Recorded by Cave (1908) but not found (2006).

Ref: *E. & S.*, p.29; *Haines*, II, p.72; *Heseltine, Heraldry,* p.36; *Manning*, p.31; *M.B.S. Bulletin*, 93, p.676; *M.B.S. Trans.*, V, pp.260-1, p.263; *Mee, Hampshire*, p.89; *M.S.*, p.158; *Norris, Memorials*, p.165; *Pevsner, Hampshire*, p.137; *Simpson*, p.28; *Soc. Antiq. MS. 875/6*, pp.14-7, *MS. 1014/12*; *V.C.H., Hampshire*, IV, p.144; *Williams, J.F., The Early Churchwardens' Account of Hampshire*, 1913, p.xiii.

BRAMSHOTT, St. Mary the Virgin.

I. John Weston "de Chyltellee", esq., in civil dress, and w. Elizabeth, c.**1430**, inscr. and 6 scrolls; son, 2 groups of children and 1 scroll lost; formerly N.A., mur., C., now N.Tr. *M.B.S. Trans.*, V, p.264; *Mee, Hampshire*, p.115 (drg. of effs.). Male eff. 448 x 140 mm, male eff. scroll orig. 395 x 70 x 27 mm, now 382 x 70 x 27 mm, female eff. 422 x 164 mm, female eff. scroll 370 x 87 x 27 mm, inscr. 80 x 565 mm, dext. children indent 170 x 150 mm, son indent 265 x 75 mm, sin. children indent 175 x 140-150 mm, upper dext. scroll orig. 75 x 128 x 33 mm, now 67 x 128 x 33 mm, upper sin. scroll orig. 72 x 127 x 32 mm, now 59 x 127 x 32 mm, centre scroll orig. 84 x 582 x 28 mm, now 84 x 345 x 28 mm, lower dext. scroll indent 70 x 130 x 35 mm, lower sin. scroll 74 x 128 x 33 mm, Petworth marble slab 1955 x 910 mm. Style: London D. Rep. (1933).

II. Inscr. (sh. lost). John Hooke of Bramshott, esq., **1613**; formerly mur., C., now N.Tr. Recorded (complete) by Cave (1908). *M.B.S. Trans.*, V, p.265 (with lost sh.). Illustration (sh.) from rubbing in Soc. Antiq. coll. Rubbing (sh.) in Soc. Antiq. coll. (1909). Inscr. 161 x 596 mm, sh. indent 175 x 150 mm, slab 1900 x c.900 mm.

III. Inscr. Anne, w. of [Rev.] Robert Briscoe, rector of Whitbourne, Herefs. [1833-1870], **1895**, aged 89, maker's name John Hardman & C[o.] Birm[m.], mur., below window, C. *IV.* Inscr. Henry Charles Butler, M.A. of Queen's Coll., Oxford, barrister-at-law of the Inner Temple; mar. 1877 at Holy Trinity, Marylebone, 1825-**1895**, pos. by son and heir, Robert Charles Walter Henry Butler, of Downlands Park, lord of the manor, born 1878, maker's name J. WIPPELL & C[o] L[TD] EXETER & LONDON, mur., C. *V.* Inscr. recording dedication of [north-east-centre north aisle] window in mem. of William Chalcraft, of Hewshott, 1814-1884, engr. c.**1895**, on window splay, N.A. *VI.* Inscr. recording dedication of [north-west-centre north aisle] window by neighbours in mem. of Rt. Hon. Sir William Erie, [judge of the common pleas], engr. c.**1895**, on window splay, N.A. *VII.* Inscr. recording dedication of [north-east north aisle] window in mem. of John Whitehill Stevens, of Chitley, 1891, and w. Fanny Amelia, 1890, engr. c.**1895**, on window splay, N.A. *VIII.* Inscr. John Fulleck, 1777-1858, and w. Henrietta, 1778-1848, both buried beneath the ch.; also [children], John Fulleck, 1807-1879, buried in the churchyard; Harriet Mitchell, 1802-1894, buried at Petersfield; Helen Lacy, 1803-1884, buried at Froxfield; Emily Binstead, 1805-1833, buried at Wakefield; Hannah Henrietta Butler, 1811-1892, buried in the churchyard;

Bramshott I

and Elizabeth Bloxham, 1814-**1897**, buried at Heston, [Middx.], mur., W.Porch. *IX.* Inscr. recording [chancel] window pos. in **1906** by children in mem. of James and Annett Fowler, mur., below window, C. *X.* Inscr. in raised letters. Capt. George Henry Jackson, Indian Army, 1842-**1910**, on cross plinth, Churchyard. *XI.* Inscr. recording dedication of [south-west-centre south aisle] window in mem. of William Barrington Tristram, of Fowley, 1822-1877, and w. Eliza Eleanor, 1831-**1920**, on window splay, S.A. *XII.* Inscr. recording paved terrace was laid in mem. of Air Vice-Marshal Frederick Crosby Halahan, C.M.G., C.B.E., D.S.O., M.V.O., (formerly R.N. 1900-1917), of The Glebe House, and w. Muriel, engr. c.**1930**, bronze, mur., W.Porch. *XIII.* Inscr. Arthur Harry Taylor, assistant curate 1923-1933, **1934**, on pulpit, N. *XIV.* Inscr. recording dedication of [south-west south aisle] window in mem. of Anna Gertrude Titherington, 1865-**1938**, copper, mur., below window, S.A. *XV.* Inscr Helena Joanna Elizabeth Jackson, widow of no.*X*, 1861-**1939**; also widow of [Lt.-]Col. T[homas] Mowbray [Martin] Berkeley, [Black Watch (Royal Highlanders)], killed in action in France, 1916, [aged 56, buried at Warloy-Baillon Communal Cemetery], on cross plinth with no.*X*, Churchyard. *XVI.* Inscr. Christian Lewis, 1972, and [w.] Marion Carlotta, **1972**, on stoup, N.Tr. *XVII.* Inscr. recording rehanging and rededication of bells in **1989** in mem. of Boris Karloff, actor, "who lived & died within the sound of the bells", [1887-1969], mur., S.Tr. Inscr. 230 x 305 mm. *XVIII.* Inscr. John and Muriel Caesar, pos. by friends, engr. c.**1990**, bronze, on gate post, Churchyard. *XIX.* Inscr. Anne and Harry Haskell, **1996**, bronze, on bench, Churchyard.

INDENTS & LOST BRASSES. 20. (Formerly M.S.III). Lost brass, lozenge with arms of Hooke, 17th cent.; discovered in 1913 under flooring in C. Illustration from rubbing in Soc. Antiq. coll. Rubbing in Soc. Antiq. coll. (n.d.). Lozenge 190 x 190 mm. 21. (Formerly M.S.IV). Lost brass, frag. of inscr. (mutil.), "HOOKE THE DAUGHTER OF /HOOKE OF BRAMSHOTT IN", 17th cent.; in 1934 loose in chest. Illustration from rubbing in Soc. Antiq. coll. Rubbing in Soc. Antiq. coll. (1934). Inscr. 45 x 321 mm remained. 22. Lost brass, inscr. "Countie", esq., 1668, S.A.

Ref: *Gent. Mag.*, 1795, I, p.40; *Gent. Mag. Lib. Eng. Topog.*, p.49, p.51; *Heseltine, Heraldry*, p.36; *M.B.S. Trans.*, V, pp.263-5; *Mee, Hampshire*, p.93; *M.S.*, p.158, p.753; *Pevsner, Hampshire*, p.141; *Simpson*, p.28; *Soc. Antiq. MS. 875/6*, pp.17-9; *V.C.H., Hampshire*, II, p.495.

BREAMORE, St. Mary.

I. Inscr. recording restoration of ch. in **1897** by Dame Katharine [Jane] Hulse, [only child of Very Rev. Henry Parr Hamilton, F.R.S., Dean of Salisbury, w. of Sir Edward Hulse, 5th Bart., M.A., D.L., High Sheriff 1868] and restoration of chancel in 1874 by Rev. E[dward] P[arker] Dew, [M.A., rector 1868-1903], mur., N. *II.* Inscr. with regt. insignia. 2nd-Lt. Harry Wilfrid Cuming, 1st Battn. Devonshire Regt., son of Vice-Admiral William Henry Cuming, and [w.] Mary, of The Rookery, killed at Kruger's Post in the [South African] War, **1900**, [aged 23], buried at Lydenburg Cemetery, South Africa, maker's name A & N. AUX C.S.L. LONDON, mur., Crossing. *III.* Inscr. recording erection of [south-east nave] window by brother officers in mem. of Charles Westrow Hulse, [J.P.], 4th Battn. Imperial Yeomanry, [2nd son of Sir Edward Hulse, 5th Bart.], killed in action at Braklaagte, South Africa, [1860-]**1901**, mur., N. *IV.* Inscr. recording gift [of lectern] by ?K[atharine] C[harlotte] M[aitland-Makgill-]Crichton, ?M[aria] E[leanor] Pleydell-Bouverie, Westrow and Hamilton Hulse, [children of Sir Edward Hulse, 5th Bart.], engr. c.**1905**, very worn, on lectern, N. *V.* Inscr. William Dymott, served ch. 1916-**1964**, on flowerstand, N. *VI.* Inscr. Rose May, [w. of Harold Sidney] Witt, 1892-**1976**, bronze, on gravestone, Churchyard.

HERE LYETH INTERRED THE BODY OF IOHN HOOKE OF BRAMSHOTT IN THE CONTY OF SOVTH ESQVIRE WHO DEPARTED THIS LIFE THE 29TH OF IVNE A° DNI: 1613·

Iob the 19, Chap: the 25. & 26 Ver: { Iknow that my redeemer liueth and that he shall stand at the latter day vpon the earth, And though after my skinne wormes destroy this body, yett in my flesh shall I see God,

Bramshott II

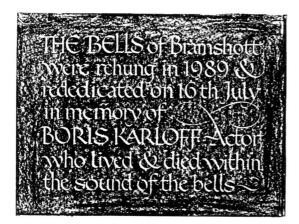

Bramshott *XVII*

Bramshott 20

HOOKE THE DAVGHTER OF HOOKE OF BRAMSHOTT IN

Bramshott 21

VII. Inscr. Sir Stephen Elliot Vyvyan Luke, K.C.M.G., 1905-**1988**, bronze, on seat, Churchyard. *VIII.* Inscr. Jack Mussell, bellringer 1925-**1995**, tower capt. "FOR MANY OF THOSE YEARS", mur., on board, Crossing. *IX.* Inscr. Geoffrey Harold Witt, 1953, aged 37, and Vera Grace Witt, **1999**, aged 77, "WHOSE ASHES LIE UPON THE MARSH", bronze, on wooden cross, Churchyard.

Ref: *Burke's Peerage and Baronetage*, p.1393; *Who's Who*, 1967, p.1881.

BURGHCLERE, All Saints (old church, redundant).

I. Inscr. Thomas Hilman, **1615**, N. Inscr. 111 x 445 mm, Petworth marble slab 1525 x 740 mm.

II. Inscr. John Brownejohn, gent., **1633**, N.Tr. Inscr. 171 x 602 mm, black marble slab 2000 x 980 mm.

III. Inscr. Mary, w. of no.II, **1637**, N.Tr. Inscr. 142 x 350 mm, black marble slab 1570 x 785 mm.

IV. Inscr. (mutil.). Katharine, dau. of John and Mary Brownejohn, w. of John Hunt of Ham., gent., **1638**; since 1905 covered by organ, N.Tr. Illustration from rubbing in Soc. Antiq. coll. Rubbing in Soc. Antiq. coll. (1908). Inscr. orig. 118 x 460 mm, now 118 x 445 mm, black marble slab 640 visible x 860 mm.

V & VI. Two inscrs. [Rev.] G[eorge] R[aymond] P[ortal, M.A.], rector [1871-1889], **1874**, on candlesticks, C. *VII.* World War I memorial (11 names), mur., on board, N. *VIII.* World War II memorial (2 names), maker's name F. OSBORNE & CO LTD · LONDON W.C.1., mur., on board, N. *IX & X.* Two inscrs. John Fowles, pos. in **2004** by Sandy, Ashley, Martyn and families, on wooden crosses, Churchyard.

Ref: *M.B.S. Trans.*, V, pp.265-6; *M.S.*, p.158; *Soc. Antiq. MS. 875/6*, pp.19-20; *V.C.H., Hampshire*, IV, p.280.

Ch. declared redundant, 1980.

BURGHCLERE, Ascension (new church).

I. Inscr. [Rev.] William Brudenell Barter, M.A., rector for 33 years [1825-1859], pos. in **1859** by parishioners, mur., N.C./N.Tr. *II.* Inscr. with verse recording gift [of lectern] in 1875 by John Lamb, of Worting, on lectern, N. *III.* Inscr. with verse in raised letters recording pulpit pos. in **1890** by friends and tenants in mem. of Henry Howard Molyneux, 4th Earl of Carnarvon, [P.C., D.C.L., LL.D., 1831-1890], on pulpit, N. *IV.* Inscr. recording litany desk pos. in **1905** by friends and parishioners in mem. of Helen Mary Charlotte[, w. of Rev. Canon George Raymond] Portal, [1904], on prie-dieu, N. *V.* Inscr. recording erection of screen in **1914** by son, Francis Bacon, in mem. of [Rev.] John Bacon, [M.A.], 1st incumbent of Woodlands St. Mary, Berks. [1837-1863], rector of Wymondham, Leics., and [w.] Mary, on screen, C. See also Woodlands St. Mary, Berks. no.*II.* *VI.* Inscr. recording enrichment of screen with light tracery by Francis Bacon and [w.] Mary as a thank offering for the safe return of son, Alban Francis Langley Bacon, after

HERE LYETH BVRIED Y^E BODY OF THOMAS
HILMAN WHO DIED THE XXIX DAY OF
SEPTEMBER ANNO DÑI 1615·

Burghclere, All Saints I

HERE LYES BVRIED THE BODY OF
Iohn BrowneIohn GENT;
WHO DIED THE 17TH OF 8^{BR} 1633·

Burghclere, All Saints II

HERE LYETH BVRIED THE BODY
OF MARY BROWNEIOHN WIFE
TO IOHN BROWNEIOHN GENT
(DECEASED) WHO DIED THE 14TH
OF DECEMBER ANNO DÑI 1637·

Burghclere, All Saints III

HERE LYETH BVRIED THE BODY OF KATHARINE
HVNT WIFE TO IOHN HVNT OF HAM GENT·
ONE OF THE DAVGHTERS OF IOHN AND MARY
BROWNEIOHN (DECEASED) WHO DYED MARCH THE
FIRST 1638·

Burghclere, All Saints IV

4 years and 4 months service in World War I, on screen, C. *VII.* Inscr. recording gift of desk in **1926** by Lt.-Col. [John Ford Elkington, D.S.O., 1866-1944] and Mrs. Elkington, on desk, N.C./N.Tr. *VIII.* Inscr. Capt. William Herbert Fox, [6026, 2nd Battn.] Seaforth Highlanders, of Adbury, [son of Edward Herbert Fox and w. Alice Marion, killed] in France, **1940**, aged 38, [pos. by] C.M. F[ox and] E.M.A., on pedestal, N. *IX.* Inscr. recording presentation of electric [organ] blower by "THOSE WHO FOUND REFUGE HERE DURING THE WORLD WAR 1939-**1945**", on organ, Organ Chamber. *X.* Inscr. recording that altar furniture was designed and made in **1963** by Leonard Parry who was blinded in World War I, on altar rail, N.C./N.Tr. *XI.* Inscr. commem. the centenary in **1968** of the National Deposit Friendly Society founded by [Rev. Canon] George Raymond Portal, M.A., hon. canon of Winchester Cathedral, rector, [1871-1889], on bookcase, N. *XII.* Inscr. Niel Morison, churchwarden 1975-**1978**, and w. Peggy, on cupboard, Organ Chamber. *XIII.* Inscr. recording gift [of vestment chest] by family and friends in mem. of Frank Hayward, chorister for 69 years, 1902-**1979**, on vestment chest, Vestry.

Ref: *Burke's Peerage and Baronetage*, p.486.

Ch. built, 1838 and 1875.

BURITON, St. Mary.

I. Inscr. Emme, dau. of Robert Bowyer of Chichester, mcht., w. of Thomas Hanbury, esq., lord of the manor of Mapledurham and one of the 7 auditors of the exchequer, **1595**; formerly mur., C., now mur., Vestry/S.A. *Locke, A., Hanbury Family*, p.314. Inscr. 136 x 676 mm. Style: Johnson (script 12).

II. (Formerly M.S.VIII). Inscr. Anne, dau. of Sir Thomas Bilson, **1644**; dredged in c.1929 from the village pond; now mur., Vestry/S.A. Inscr. 88 x 160 mm.

III. (Formerly M.S.II). Inscr. Susanna, w. of Thomas Hanbury, esq., **1661**; formerly mur., C., now mur., Vestry/S.A. *Locke*, p.314. Inscr. 111 x 404 mm.

IV. (Formerly M.S.III). Inscr. Thomas, son of Thomas Hanbury, esq., "Great Grandchild to Auditour Hanbury", **1668**; formerly mur., C., now mur., Vestry/S.A. *Bod. Lib. Gough Maps 228*, f.329; *Locke*, p.314. Inscr. 127 x 288 mm.

V. (Formerly M.S.IV). Inscr. with lozenge. Katherine, dau. of Sir John Jefferys, widow of Thomas Hanbury, esq., **1678**, aged 71; formerly mur., C., now mur., Vestry/S.A. *Locke*, p.314, p.318. Inscr. 213 x 204 mm.

VI. (Formerly M.S.V). Inscr. with ach. Thomas Hanbury, esq., son of Thomas and Susanna Hanbury, **1686**, aged 28; formerly mur., C., now mur., Vestry/S.A. *Locke*, p.314. Inscr. 275 x 436 mm.

VII. (Formerly M.S.VI). Inscr. with ach. William Warne, citizen and scrivener of London, **1697**, aged 72, mur., Vestry/S.A. Inscr. 436 x 349 mm.

VIII. (Formerly M.S.VII). Plate bearing the word "RESVRGAM", mur., Vestry/S.A. Probably belonging to no. *V.* Pl. 48 x 206 mm.

Here lieth buried the bodye of Anne the Daughter of Robert Bowyer of the Cytie of Chichester Marchant and was the wife of Thomas Hanbury Esquier lorde of this mannor of Mapledurham & one of y⁶ seaven Auditors of the Queenes Ma⁶ Courte of Exchequier at Westmr who died the xxviij daye of Februarie Anno Domini 1595

Buriton I

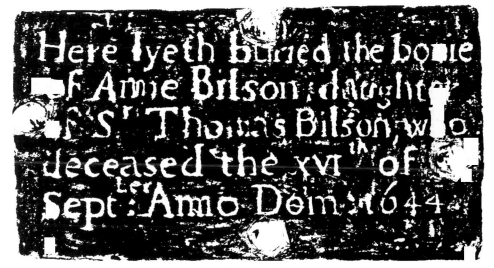

Here lyeth buried the bodie
of Amie Bilson, daughter
of S⁶ Thomas Bilson, who
deceased the xvi^th of
Sept:^ter Anno Dom: 1644

Buriton *II*

HERE LYETH THE BODY OF M^R
SVSANNA HANBVRY WIFE TO
THOMAS HANBVRY ESQ DECEMB^R 3^D
1661

Buriton *III*

69

Here Lyeth the Body of Thomas Hanbury
Efquire Sonne of Thomas Hanbury Efquire.
Great Grandchild to Auditour Hanbury.
Who Departed this Life: March the 20th:
I.668.

Buriton *IV*

Here lyeth interred the Body of
KATHERINE HANBVRY
Relict of Thomas Hanbury Efq: &
Daughter of Sr Iohn Iefferys
of Southton who lived a widow
27 yeares carefully educating
many children and after a tedi
ous ficknes, vndergon with
an exemplary patience devout
ly refigned her soule to God
23° Martii {Anno Dñi 1678
{Ætatis suæ 71

Buriton *V*

70

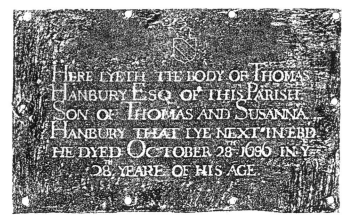

HERE LYETH THE BODY OF THOMAS
HANBURY ESQ OF THIS PARISH
SON OF THOMAS AND SUSANNA
HANBURY THAT LYE NEXT INTERD
HE DYED OCTOBER 28 1696 IN Y
28 YEARE OF HIS AGE

Buriton *VI*

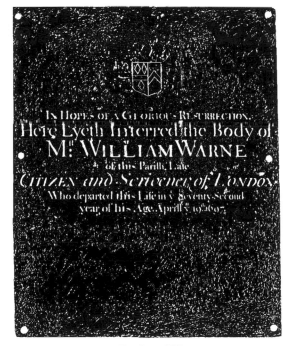

IN HOPES OF A GLORIOUS RESURRECTION.
Here Lyeth Interred the Body of
Mr WILLIAM WARNE
of this Parish, Late
CITIZEN and Scrivener of LONDON
Who departed this Life in y seventy second
year of his Age, April y 10 1697.

Buriton *VII*

RESVRGAM

Buriton *VIII*

71

IX. Inscr. Capt. Francis James Hugonin, 39th Regt., of Nursted, son of Lt.-Col. Hugonin, 4th Light Dragoons, died at Torquay, [Devon], 1818-**1875**, mur., C. *X*. Inscr. recording dedication of [chancel] window by parishioners in mem. of Mary, w. of [Rev.] J[ohn] M[aunoir] Sumner, [M.A.], rector [1845-1890], **1875**, on window splay, C. *XI*. Inscr. recording gift of [east] window by children in mem. of John Bonham-Carter, **1884**, aged 67, on window splay, C. *XII*. Inscr. in Lat. recording installation of heating in **1896** by I.R. Bennion, on window splay, N.A. *XIII*. Inscr. recording gift of tower clock in **1906** by John Rowe and Harriet Bennion in mem. of daus., Alice and Mary Mabel, mur., W.Porch/Tower. *XIV*. Inscr. Maria Elizabeth [Hugonin], w. of no.*IX*, died at Bournemouth, 1827-**1911**, maker's name *J. WIPPELL & Cᴼ Lᵀᴰ EXETER & LONDON*, mur., below no.*IX*, C. *XV*. Inscr. in raised letters within border of laurel leaves in relief with verse on scroll, 2 shs. and regt. insignia in relief. Capt. Guy Bonham Carter, 19th [(Queen Alexandra's Own)] Royal Hussars and Adjutant Oxfordshire Yeomanry, 3rd son of Alfred Bonham Carter, C.B. and [w.] Mary [Henrietta], killed in action near Ypres, **1915**, aged 30, buried at Vlamertinghe [Military Cemetery], bronze, mur., on marble, C. *XVI*. Inscr. recording erection of [south aisle] window by husband, children, brothers and sisters in mem. of E. Maude Bonham-Carter, 1857-**1915**, mur., below window, S.A. *XVII*. Inscr. with verse in raised letters with 4 shs. and regt. insignia within border of laurel leaves all in relief. Capt. Arthur Thomas Bonham Carter, [3rd Battn. attd. 1st Battn.] Hampshire Regt., 1st Pusine Judge British East Africa, killed in action at Beaumont-Hamel, **1916**, aged 47, buried [at Serre Road No.2 Cemetery], bronze, mur., C. *XVIII*. Inscr. in raised letters within border of laurel leaves in relief with verse on scroll and 2 shs. in relief. [2nd-Lt.] Norman Bonham Carter, Indian Civil Service, Household Battn., [killed] at the Battle of Arras, **1917**, pos. by w., brothers and sisters, mur., on marble, C. *XIX*. World War I memorial (41 names), **1919**, maker's name HERBERT WAUTHIER del · F. OSBORNE & CO LTD · London, mur., W.Porch/Tower. *XX*. Inscr. recording creation of vestry in **1957** through [legacy] of Olive Geraldine Seward in mem. of husband, Percy William Seward, churchwarden 1895-1941, bronze, on door, W.Porch/Tower. *XXI*. Inscr. Amy Isabel Bone, organist for 63 years, 1887-**1976**, on organ, C. *XXII*. Inscr. Helen Mary Gibson, **1989**, on flowerstand, C. *XXIII*. Inscr. recording gift of piano by Helen Mary Piggott, 1911-**1998**, on piano, N.

INDENTS & LOST BRASSES. 24. Indent, inscr. and 4 shs., nearly effaced, Churchyard. Inscr. c.140 x c.690 mm, shs. c.170 x 140 mm, Petworth marble slab 1755 x 830 mm remains.

Ref: *Bod. Lib. Gough Maps 228*, f.329; *Heseltine, Heraldry*, p.36; *M.B.S. Trans.*, V, pp.266-8, XIV, p.490; *M.S.*, pp.158-9; *Soc. Antiq. MS. 875/6,* pp.20-2; *V.C.H., Hampshire*, III, p.92.

BURLEY, St. John the Baptist.

I. Inscr. Edwin R.J. Wigram, resident in the par. for 10 years, **1892**, aged 37, maker's name GAWTHORP, Sᶜ LONDON (and monogram), mur., on board, N. *II*. Inscr. with sh. Ruth, only dau., **1896**, [aged 14], mur., below window, C. *III*. Inscr. Rev. the Hon. Arthur Charles Baillie Hamilton, [M.A.], churchwarden for 10 years, 1838-**1910**, pos. by congregation, maker's name GARRET & HAYSOM. SOUTHAMPTON, mur., on board, N. *IV*. Inscr. with verse, crest and motto within border of laurel leaves. Lt. George Masterman Thompson, [1st Battn.] Royal Scots, son of Col. G[eorge] W[illiam] Thompson, of Beechwood, born at Eshowe, Zululand, "KILLED WHILE SERVING WITH THE WEST AFRICAN FRONTIER FORCE GALLANTLY LEADING AN ATTACK ON A STRONGLY ENTRENCHED POSITION OF THE ENEMY AT CHRA, TOGOLAND", [1st British officer killed in action during World War I], 1890-**1914**, [buried at Wahala Cemetery, Togo]; also "SERGEANT ASURI MOSHI AND A PRIVATE OF THE GOLD COAST REGIMENT, A SERGEANT, 2 CORPORALS AND 9 TIRAILLEURS (SENEGALESE) WHO BRAVELY FOLLOWED THEIR YOUNG LEADER AND LAID DOWN THEIR LIVES IN DEFENCE OF HIS BODY", maker's name A&N. AUX C.S.L. LONDON, mur., on board, N. *V.* Inscr. in raised letters. Capt. Abdy Fellowes Anderson, 3rd Battn. The Cameronians (Scottish Rifles), Lt. 13th Hussars, [son of Col. J. Anderson], killed near Ypres, **1915**, aged 43, copper, mur., N. *VI.* Inscr. with Lat. verse. Capt. Herbert Charles Bruce Cummins, 9th [(Pioneer) Battn.] Seaforth Highlanders, [son of Rev. William Henry Cummins, M.A. and w. Jeanie Douglas], killed near Armentières, **1916**, aged 39, [buried at Nieppe Communal Cemetery, France], maker's name HART SON PEARD & Cº Lᴰ, mur., on board, N. *VII.* Inscr. with verse. Ethel Mary Wakeling, [1903-]**1917**, maker's name HART SON PEARD & Cº Lᴰ, mur., on board, N. *VIII.* Inscr. James Welch, actor, "WHOSE ART OF COMEDY HUMOUR AND PITY WERE RARELY BLENDED, AS THEY WERE ALSO IN THE HARMONY OF HIS OWN GENTLE AND GENEROUS SPIRIT", 1869-**1917**, buried in the churchyard, pos. by friends "IN WHOSE HEARTS HIS LAUGHTER AND TENDERNESS STILL LIVE ON", maker's name CULN GAWTHORP, & SONS Lᵀᴰ LONDON, mur., on board, N. *IX.* Inscr. [Gunner] Sidney Arthur Stride, [75767, 132nd Heavy Battery, Royal Garrison Artillery, son of Philip Stride and w. Fanny], died of wounds received in action, **1918**, aged 27, [buried] at [St. Sever Cemetery Extension], Rouen, mur., on board, N. *X.* Inscr. with R.A.F. insignia. John Bourchier Wimbush, 1905, aged 37; also only child, Lt. Ewart Austin Bourchier Wimbush, D.F.C., [C Sqdn.] R.A.F., [killed] in action at Gallipoli, [Turkey], **1918**, "ON HIS 21ˢᵀ BIRTHDAY", mur., on board, N. *XI.* Inscr. [recording World War I memorial] made from timber removed from H.M.S. Britannia (cadet training ship at Dartmouth 1869-1905), engr. c.**1920**, mur., on triptych, N. *XII.* Inscr. James Easterbrook, M.A., of Whitemoor, died at Mentone, **1923**, aged 71, maker's name A&N. C.S.L. LONDON, mur., on board, N. *XIII.* Inscr. with crest and motto. William Morris Fletcher, J.P. for Hants and Dominica, B[ritish] W[est] I[ndies], served in the revenue survey dept. of the Bombay Government for 28 years and afterwards lived at Burley Beacon for many years, died at Fiesole, Italy, **1925**, aged 79, maker's name A&N. C.S.L. LONDON, mur., on board, N. *XIV.* Inscr. with verse, sh., crest and motto. John Keith Murray, died at Selangor, F[ederated] M[alay] S[tates], **1927**, aged 21, mur., on board, N. *XV.* Inscr. Florence Ferguson, 1880-**1932**, mur., on board, N. *XVI.* Inscr. in raised letters. Admiral Arthur William Edward Prothero, J.P., died at Burley Croft, 1931, [aged 80], and w. Helen Lucy, **1932**, maker's name F. OSBORNE & CO LTD London, copper, mur., N. *XVII.* Inscr. Ethel Maud Hughes, of Lavender Cottage, died at Buxton, **1934**, maker's name A&N C.S.L. LONDON, mur., on board, N. *XVIII.* Inscr. with verse and R.A.F. insignia in relief. Flight-Lt. John Frank Hough Andrews, [72017, pilot, 58th Sqdn.], R.A.F.[V.R.], Coastal Command, killed on active service, 1912-**1943**, [buried in the churchyard], mur., on board, N. *XIX.* Inscr. [Rev.] Peter Aldwin Munby, R.N.V.R., chaplain to H.M.S. Penelope, [son of Lt.-Col. Aldwin Montgomery Munby and w. Evelyn Muriel (née Webb)], vicar of Wribbenhall, Worcs., killed in action in the Mediterranean, **1944**, aged 33, bronze, on wooden cross, Churchyard. *XX.* Inscr. George Henry Wakeling, 1859-1936, died at Forest Corner, and [w.] Katharine St. George, 1876-**1948**, parents of Ethel Mary Wakeling, 1903-1917, mur., on board, N. *XXI.* Inscr. in raised letters. Pamela Tennyson D'Eyncourt, **1962**, bronze, on step. C. *XXII.* Inscr. in raised letters. Lt.-Col. Sir Dudley Baines Forwood, Bart., C.M.G., [1875-]1961, and w. Norah Isabella, [eld.] dau. of Richard Robertson Lockett, **1962**, [aged 86], bronze, on step, C. *XXIII.* Inscr. in raised letters. Walter Maxwell Henderson-Scott, 1885-1959, and [w.] Marjorie, 1890-**1962**, bronze, Churchyard. *XXIV.* Inscr. Jennie Peirce, **1966**, aged 51, bronze, on wooden cross, Churchyard. *XXV.* Inscr. William Rigg Hargreaves, organist 1964-**1971**, mur., Organ Chamber. *XXVI.* Inscr. Rosemary, 1950-**1972**, bronze, on bench, Churchyard.

XXVII. Inscr. Charles Evemy, churchwarden 1888-1918, engr. c.**1980**, bronze, on notice board, N.Porch. *XXVIII.* Inscr. with "FUN, FITNESS, FRIENDSHIP" on scroll superimposed on globe recording gift [of north-east nave window in **1984**] by "HOCKEY FRIENDS THROUGHOUT THE WORLD" [in mem. of Constance Mary Katherine Applebee, 1873-1981], copper, on window splay, N. *XXIX.* Inscr. Margaret Rycroft Shail, engr. c.**1985**, on bookstall, N. *XXX.* Inscr. recording planting in mem. of Bill Rae, 1924-**1990**, on tree post, Churchyard. *XXXI.* Inscr. Simon Dixon, 1951-**1993**, on bench, Churchyard. *XXXII.* Inscr. Maureen Elizabeth Parker, [w., mother and grandmother, 1939-**2004**], bronze, on bench, Churchyard. *XXXIII.* Inscr. with verse and R.A.F. insignia. [Sqdn.-Leader] Vernon Churchill Simmonds, of Manor Farm, "ONE OF THE FEW · And of all his fellow pilots who helped save this country in the summer of 1940", [1920-2005], engr. **2006**, mur., on board, N.

Ref: *Burke's Peerage and Baronetage*, p.1042.

Ch. built, 1839 and 1886-7.

BURSLEDON, St. Leonard.

I. Inscr. with plan (showing ch. before alterations) recording restoration and partly rebuilding of ch. (new altar, choir seats, pavement in the chancel; new transepts, vestry and organ chamber; heating chamber and apparatus, nave lengthened westwards, new porch, bell turret and 2nd bell, entirely new flooring and the whole seated with chairs) in 1888 by subscription at a cost of more than £2,000; re-opened in **1889** by [Rt. Rev. Edward Harold Browne], Bishop of Winchester [1873-1890; Rev. Canon] Loraine Estridge, [M.A.], vicar [1885-1896]; J.D. Sedding, architect; Thomas W. Oliver and Edward Gurney, churchwardens, mur., on board, N. *II.* Inscr. Louisa Selina Turner, schoolmistress in the par. for 44 years, **1890**, pos. by parishioners, maker's name JONES & WILLIS, mur., N.Tr. *III.* Inscr. recording gift of pulpit in **1892** by [Rev. Canon] Loraine Estridge, [M.A.], vicar; carved by George Voisey, George Annett, Samuel Dubb, Charles Fisher, Thomas Freeman, Frederick French, John Hibberd, Edwin Skilton, Edward H. Smith, John Waterman, and H. Edwin Willsher, on pulpit, N. *IV.* Inscr. recording gift [of font cover] in **1893** by the "BOYS AND GIRLS OF BURSLEDON"; carved by William A. Fisher, William H. Randall, Albert J. Kent and Joseph Dubb, on font cover, N. *V.* Inscr. in raised letters with 4 anchors and rope. Cmdr. Thomas William Oliver, R.N., of Oak Hill, churchwarden for 12 years, died at Bedford, 1832-**1901**, and w. Elizabeth, 1837-1880, mur., on board, N. *VI.* Inscr. Louisa Seymour, of Ploverfield, **1902**, maker's name John Hardman & C⁰· Birmᵐ·, mur., below window, N.Tr. *VII.* [Rev. Canon] Loraine Estridge, M.A., [hon.] canon of Truro [Cathedral], vicar for 11 years [1885-1896], **1903**, [aged 62], pos. by parishioners, rect. pl., eff. and inscr., maker's name John Hardman & C⁰· Birmᵐ·, mur., on marble, C. Rect. pl. 759 x 327 mm. *VIII.* Inscr. in raised letters recording dedication of [north chancel] window in mem. of Charles James Matthews, 1824-**1905**, maker's name BENHAM & FROUD Lᴰ LONDON, mur., on board below window, C. *IX.* Inscr. in raised letters. Matthew Blakiston, of Free Hills, 1821-**1907**, maker's name GAWTHORP, Sᶜ LONDON (and monogram), mur., N.Tr. *X.* Inscr. Edith Anne, w. of Col. A.F. Perkins, of Evysley, 1900, aged 50; also yst. son, Hugh Donald Perkins, died suddenly, **1907**, aged 30, on screen, C. *XI.* Inscr. John Sparshott, churchwarden for 35 years, **1910**, aged 91, mur., on board, N. *XII.* Inscr. Edward Gurney, churchwarden for 38 years, **1920**, aged 80, maker's name G.T. YOUNG, ENGRAVER, SOUTHAMPTON, mur., N.

Ref: *Mee, Hampshire*, p.107.

To the Glory of GOD and in loving memory of
LORAINE ESTRIDGE, M.A. Canon of Truro,
and eleven years Vicar of this Parish.
Died May 11. 1903.
This memorial is erected by his late Parishioners.

Bursledon *VII*

CANDOVER, BROWN, St. Peter (new church).

I. Civilian and lady, arm in arm, c.**1490**; inscr. lost; lost for some years but discovered in 1889 at Chilton Candover Rectory and returned; formerly mur., C., now mur., on stone, N. *Brit. Lib. Add. MS. 39987*, f.53r; *Franklyn*, p.78, 2nd edn., p.86; *Hants Proc.*, III, p.276 (drg.); *M.B.S. Portfolio*, II, pl.46; *Mee, Hampshire*, p.347 (drg.); *Pevsner, Hampshire*, p.148; *Portfolio Book*, pl.236; *Soc. Antiq. Lond. Proc.*, 2 S. XII, p.335; *Trivick, Craft*, pl.67, opp. p.49; *Trivick, Picture Book*, pl.64; *Warren*, p.42. Pl. 478 x 274 mm. Style: London F.

II. Inscr. "THIS BRASS WAS FORMERLY IN BROWN CANDOVER OLD CHURCH PLACED HERE FOR PRESERVATION ON ACCOUNT OF ITS EXTREME INTEREST. A.D. **1889**. THE FIGURES ARE ARM IN ARM", mur., on stone below no.I, N. *III*. Combined World War I (4 names) and II (1 name) memorials, bronze, on crucifix plinth, Churchyard. *IV*. Inscr. Arch[ibald] Gandy, [1910-]**1989**, and [w. Beatrice] May, [1910-1985], bronze, on flowerstand, N. *V*. Inscr. John Harkness, 1924-**2003**, and [w.] Joan, 1922-1994, on bench, Churchyard.

INDENTS & LOST BRASSES. 6. Lost brass, John Latihall, priest, c.1520, in mass vests. without stole; exhibited in 1845 by Rev. W. Gunner at the Winchester Congress of the Archaeological Institute. Recorded by Duthy (1839) and (in poss. of ?Lord Ashburton) by Haines (1861). *Brit. Lib. Add. MS. 39987*, f.44r; *Lack and Whittemore*, II, pl.XIIIb. Eff. 195 x 50 mm. Style: London G. 7. Lost brass, inscr. Margery Wylson, 1559; exhibited in 1845 by Rev. W. Gunner at the Winchester Congress of the Archaeological Institute. Recorded by Duthy (1839) and (in poss. of ?Lord Ashburton) by Haines (1861).

Ref: *Antiquary*, XIX, p.231; *Archaeological Institute Proc.*, 1845, p.51; *Brit. Lib. Add. MS. 39987*, f.44, f.53; Duthy, p.140, *Haines*, II, p.72; *Hampshire, Antiquary*, I, p.71; *Hampshire N. and Q.*, IV, pp.51-2; *Hants Proc.*, III, pp.277-9; *Lack and Whittemore*, II, pt.2, 2006, pp.10-11; *M.B.S. Trans.*, I, pt.7, p.28, pt.8, p.16, III, p.244, V, pp.268-9; *Mee, Hampshire*, p.99; *M.S.*, p.159; *Norris, Memorials*, p.171; *Pevsner, Hampshire*, p.147; *Soc. Antiq. Lond. Proc.*, 2 S. XII, pp.334-8; *Soc. Antiq. MS. 875/6*, pp.22-3; *V.C.H., Hampshire*, IV, p.184; *Warren, W.T., Historic Sketches round Winchester*, 1902, pp.41-2.

Ch. built, 1845.

CANDOVER, PRESTON, St. Mary
(old church, redundant, now vested in The Churches Conservation Trust).

I. Katherine, dau. of Thomas Leggat of Dagnehams, Essex, esq., w. of Thomas Dabrigecourt of Preston Candover, gent., **1607**, inscr. and 1 sh. (another lost), C. *Brit. Lib. Add. MS. 39987*, f.58r; *M.B.S. Trans.*, V, p.271, XV, p.56. Eff. 597 x 225 mm, inscr. 167 x 544 mm, upper dext. sh. indent effaced, upper sin. sh. 157 x 131 mm, slab 1520 x 650 mm. Style: Johnson. Rep. by W.G.L. (1991).

II. Inscr. Dorothy, w. of Edmund Marshe, gent., **1610**, C. Inscr. 79 x 439 mm, slab 1175 x 615 mm. Rep. by W.G.L. (1991).

III. Inscr. on elliptical-topped pl. [Rev.] John Waterman, [vicar of Preston Candover] and Nutley for 59 years, "HIS FATHER AND UNCLE WAS MINISTERS OF THE SAID CHURCH'S BEFORE",

Candover, Brown I

Candover, Brown 6

77

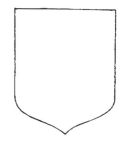

HERE LYETH THE BODYE OF KATHARINE DABRIGECORT
DAVGHTER VNTO THOMAS LEGGATT OF DAGNEHAMS IN
THE COVNTIE OF ESSEX ESQVIRE & LATE WIFE VNTO
THOMAS DABRIGECORT OF PRESTONE CANDIVER
GENTELMAN WHO DYED THE VITH
DAYE OF IVNE 1607:

Candover, Preston I

HERE LYETH DOROTHY MARSHE WIFE OF EDMVND
MARSHE GENT: WHO DIED IN Y FAITH OF CHRIST:
THE XXTH OF MAY 1610:

Candover, Preston II

HERE LYETH
THE BODY OF THE REVEREND
MR JOHN WATERMAN, WHO WAS
MINISTER OF THIS CHURCH AND
TLEY 59 YEARS: AND HIS FATHER
AND UNCLE WAS MINISTERS OF THE
SAID CHURCH'S BEFORE, HE DIED IN THE
FAITH OF CHRIST, IN THE YEAR
1726

Candover, Preston III

Hic Iacent
Venerabilis Vir Georgius Gillingham S.T.P.
Nuper Rector Huius Ecclesiæ et Isabella
Gillingham Vxor Eius Dilectissima
Quorum
Hic obiit Dec: 16
Illa Ianuarii 15 1668

Chalton I

79

1726, on same slab as no.II, C. Inscr. 210 x 418 mm. Rep. by W.G.L. (1991). *IV.* Inscr. George Gardiner and Sophia Allen, pos. in **1930** by children, on bier, C.

Ref: *Brit. Lib. Add. MS. 39987,* f.58; *Duthy,* p.137; *Haines*, II, p.73; *Hampshire N. and Q.*, V, p.91; *Heseltine, Heraldry*, p.36; *M.B.S. Trans.*, V, p.270, p.272, XV, p.57; *Mee, Hampshire*, p.285; *M.S.*, p.159, p.753; *Soc. Antiq. MS. 875/6*, pp.24-6; *V.C.H., Hampshire*, III, p.376.

Ch. declared redundant, 1989; vested, 1989.

CANDOVER, PRESTON, St. Mary (new church).

I. Inscr. recording erection of pulpit by nephews and nieces in mem. of Harriet Blunt, of Preston Cottage, died at Odiham, 1867, aged 82, engr. c.**1885**, on pulpit, N. *II.* Inscr. recording gift of reredos by children in mem. of [Rev.] Edward Wickham, M.A., vicar 1853-1862, engr. c.**1885**, mur., C. *III.* Inscr. Emily Mary Anderson, engr. c.**1930**, on altar rail, C. *IV.* Inscr. William James Mansbridge and w. Marie; also dau., Nellie, engr. c.**1930**, mur., N.A. *V.* Inscr. Reginald Ernest Whitworth, 1903-**1981**, on processional cross, C. *VI.* Inscr. with enamelled [Royal] British Legion insignia in relief recording planting of trees in mem. of Capt. Geoffrey Cooper, **1984**, Churchyard. *VII.* Inscr. in raised letters. Gwen Coakes, of Thorp's, organist for 30 years, ch. and community servant, 1906-**1985,** bronze, mur., C. *VIII.* Inscr. [Kathleen] Mary French, 1929-**1992**, bronze, on bench, Churchyard.

Ch. built, 1884-5.

CHALTON, St. Michael and All Angels.

I. Inscr. George Gillingham, S.T.P., rector, and w. Isabel, both died **1668**, mur., N. Inscr. 166 x 285 mm.

II. Inscr. with verse. Elizabeth, w. of Rev. J[ohn] W[olvey] Astley, [M.A.], rector, **1872**, maker's name COX & SONS LONDON, mur., C. *III.* Inscr. Rev. John Wolvey Astley, M.A., fellow of King's Coll., Camb., rector of Chalton, Clanfield and Idsworth for 27 years [1848-1875], **1875**, aged 60, maker's name COX & SONS LONDON, mur., C. *IV.* Inscr. on lozenge-shaped pl. Rich[ar]d Yaldwyn, 1739, aged 30, engr. **1892**, C. Inscr. 150 x 150 mm. *V.* Inscr. on lozenge-shaped pl. [Rev. Dr.] W[illia]m Denison, D.D., rector [1756-1786], 1786, engr. **1892**, C. Inscr. 150 x 150 mm. *VI.* Inscr. recording presentation and dedication of organ in **1896** by Harry Clarke Jervoise in mem. of parents, Samuel Clarke Jervoise, [1890], and [w.] Emily Ann, [dau. of General Sir Henry John Cumming], on organ, N. *VII.* World War I memorial (8 names), on lychgate, Churchyard.

Nos. *IV & V* mark the sites of stone slabs which were covered/lost during the restoration of ch. completed in 1892.

Ref: *M.B.S. Trans.*, V, p.272; *M.S.,* p.159; *Soc. Antiq. MS. 875/6*, p.26.

CHARMINSTER, (see BOURNEMOUTH).

Chalton *IV*

Chalton *V*

We pray you remember
in the Lord
Montagu Edward
Bradford
Eldest son of Col:
Sir Edward Ridley
Colborne Bradford K C B. K C S I
and of Elizabeth Adela his wife, who died at
Calcutta Aug. 22. 1890 aged 23 in loving
recollection of whom this screen is dedicated
Grant him O Lord, Eternal Rest
& let light perpetual shine upon him.

HVMANI NIHIL ALIENVM

Chawton *VII*

CHAWTON, St. Nicholas.

I. Inscr. Robert Fripp, son of Francis Fripp and [w.] Grizelda, of Witchampton, Dorset, **1865**, pos. by sons, John Trude Fripp, of Broughton, and Samuel Fripp, of Melbourne, Australia, mur., N. *II.* Inscr. Capt. Benjamin Clement, R.N., [1785-]1835, and w. Ann Mary, yst. dau. of William Prowting, [1787-]1858; also sons, William Thomas [Clement], 1864, aged 43, and [Rev. Canon] Benjamin Prowting, M.A., of Exeter Coll., Oxford, minor canon of Winchester Cathedral for 34 years, **1873**, aged 60, mur., C. *III.* Inscr. William Prowting, J.P., D.L., 1821, aged 67, and w. Elizabeth, 1832, aged 80; also sons, William, 1799, aged 14, and John Rowland, 1800, aged 9, [buried in] family vault in the churchyard, engr c.1875, mur., C. *IV.* Inscr. with verse and enamelled sh. Capt. Brook John Knight, 6th Dragoon Guards (Carabiniers), yst. son of Edward Knight, of Godmersham Park, Kent, and Chawton House, **1878**, aged 69, maker's name HART, SON, PEARD & Cº, LONDON, mur., on marble, C. *V.* Inscr. recording gift [of west window] by children in mem. of Edward Knight, 1794-**1879**, on window splay, N. *VI.* Inscr. in raised letters recording erection of 2 bells and dedication of 4 new bells in mem. of Isabella Barbara Shaw Stewart, died at Chawton House, **1888**, bronze, mur., N. *VII.* Inscr. with verse and ach. recording dedication of screen in mem. of Montagu Edward Bradford, eld. son of Col. Sir Edward Ridley Colborne Bradford, [1st Bart.], K.C.B., K.C.S.I. and w. Elizabeth Adela, died at Calcutta, [1867-]**1890**, on screen, C. Inscr. 209 x 171 mm. *VIII.* Inscr. George Wolfe, 1883, aged 49, and w. Anne Mary, only dau. of Capt. Benjamin Clement, R.N., **1893**, aged 69, pos. by niece, Lilias Edith Clement, mur., N. *IX.* Inscr. William Thomas Clement, yst. son of Capt. Benjamin Clement, R.N., 1864, aged 43; also only dau., Lilias Edith Clement, **1895**, aged 35, mur., N. *X.* Inscr. with verse and ach. Lt.-Col. Henry John Knight, 1st [Battn.] Seaforth Highlanders, yst. son of Edward Knight and w. Adela, died at Grasse, 1848-**1896**, on organ screen, C. Inscr. 209 x 171 mm. *XI.* Inscr. with verse and ach. Capt. William Brodnax Knight, 2nd Dragoon Guards [(The Queen's Bays)], 5th son of Edward Knight and w. Mary Dorothea, died at Winchester, 1838-**1896**; mar. 1863, Louisa Octavia Charlotte, dau. of Courtney Stacey, of Sandling Place, Maidstone, [Kent], on organ screen with no.*X*, C. Inscr. 210 x 173 mm. See also Pamber no.*III.* *XII.* Inscr. Francis Triggs, verger for 33 years, **1906**, maker's name *CULN J. WIPPELL & Cº LᵀᴰD*, copper, mur., N. *XIII.* Inscr. recording presentation of 9 candelabra in 1900-**1912** by members of the Chawton Carving Class, maker's name *CULN J. WIPPELL & Cº LᵀᴰD*, copper, mur., N. *XIV.* Inscr. with verse in raised letters with ach. and regt. insignia in relief recording dedication of [west north aisle] window in mem. of Lt.-Col. [Sir] Evelyn Ridley Bradford, [2nd] Bart., 2nd [Battn.] Seaforth Highlanders, [son of Col. Sir Edward Ridley Colborne Bradford, 1st Bart., G.C.B., G.C.V.O., K.C.S.I., and Lady Elizabeth Adela Bradford, 3rd dau. of Edward Knight, D.L., killed] while commanding regt. in the Battle of the Aisne, France, [1869]-**1914**, buried at Bucy-le-Long, mur., on board below window, N.A. *XV.* Inscr. in raised letters with Lat. verse on scroll, enamelled ach. and regt. insignia. Lt.-Col. Donald Wood, 1st [Battn.] Rifle Brigade, yst. son of Arthur Hardy Wood and w. Annis Matilda, served at the defence of Ladysmith in the South African War 1899, [killed] at the Battle of the Somme, 1878-**1916**; mar. Irene Madeleine, dau. of Henry Thornton Ross, mur., on marble, N. *XVI.* Inscr. with verse in raised letters recording erection of churchyard extension lychgate in mem. of Capt. Richard Brodnax Knight, [3rd Battn. attd. 4th Battn.] Bedfordshire Regt., yst. son of Rev. C[harles] E[dward] Knight, [rector 1876-1912, and w. Emma G.], died of wounds at Rouen, 1880-**1918**, [buried at St. Sever Cemetery, Rouen, France], mur., N.A. *XVII.* Inscr. in raised letters with verse on scroll, ach. and 2 regt. insignia in relief. Lt.-Gen. Sir Alfred Robert Martin, K.C.B., Col. 5th Royal Gurkhas Frontier Force, retired in 1912 "AFTER LONG AND DISTINGUISHED SERVICE IN THE INDIAN ARMY", died at St. Peters, Faringdon, 1926, [aged 73], and w. Bessie Charlotte St. George, dau. of Sir Annesley Castriot DeRenzy, K.C.B., Surgeon-Gen. Indian Army, 1862-**1929**; also yst.

Ur pray you remember in the Lord ⚬ Henry John Knight Lt Col. 1st Seaforth Highlanders youngest son of Edward Knight Esq of this place and of Adela his wife ⚬ born Mar 6 1848 ⚬⚬⚬⚬ died at Grasse Feb 27 1896 ⚬⚬⚬⚬⚬

Lord all pitying Jesu Blest ⚬⚬⚬ grant him Shine Eternal Rest

Chawton *X*

⚬⚬ We pray you remember in the Lord ⚬⚬ William Brodnax Knight ⚬ Captain 2nd Dragoon Guards 5th son of Edward Knight Esq ⚬⚬ of this place and of Mary Dorothea his wife born Feb 3rd 1835 died at Winchester Nov. 4th 1896 ⚬ He married in 1863 Louisa Octavia Charlotte daughter of Courtney Stacey Esq of Sandling Place Maidstone ⚬⚬ Grant him O Lord Eternal Rest and let light perpetual shine upon him ⚬⚬

Chawton *XI*

son, 2nd-Lt. Douglas Francis DeRenzy Martin, Temporary-Capt. 5th [Battn.] Northumberland Fusiliers, killed in action "WHILE LEADING HIS MEN", near Arras, France, 1917, aged 19, bronze, mur., on marble, N. *XVIII.* Inscr. Adela Louisa Cassandra Hardy, dau. of Edward Knight, of Chawton House, "WHO WITH HER HUSBAND HERBERT CARBY HARDY GAVE MANY GIFTS TO THIS CHURCH", 1849-**1931**, on reredos, C. *XIX.* Inscr. D. W[ood], engr. c.**1960**, bronze, on pew, N. *XX & XXI.* Two inscrs. H.C. W[ood] and J.H. W[ood], engr. c.**1960**, bronze, on pews, N. *XXII.* Inscr. recording gift and dedication of vestry extension in **1961** by Robert and Nita McAndrew, on screen, Vestry/N.A. *XXIII.* Inscr. John [T.] Beaty-Pownall, [**1961**, aged 86], on pew, N. *XXIV.* Inscr. Benefaction of Henry Winton Donisthorpe, who left £100 towards modernising the heating system, **1968**, mur., N. *XXV.* Inscr. Helen Theodora, 1967, aged 84, w. of J[ohn] T. B[eaty]-P[ownall], 1961, aged 86, ashes buried in the churchyard in **1968**, copper, on pew with no.*XXIII*, N. *XXVI.* Inscr. Orby Cox, verger for 37 years, **1971**, mur., N. *XXVII.* Inscr. Caroline Glyn, novelist, "Lived and Wrote in this Village", member of Poor Clares at the Convent of St. Mary, Stroud, New South Wales, Australia, [1948-]**1981**, mur., N.A. *XXVIII.* Inscr. Ernest Skates, chorister for 59 years, **1988**, mur., N. *XXIX.* Inscr. with ach. recording installation of organ in 1989 and dedication in **1990** in mem. of Patrick [de Laszlo], 1909-1980, and [w.] Deborah, 1917-1980, parents of Damon, Stephanie, Meriel, Grania and Charmian de Laszlo, on organ screen with nos.*X & XI*, C. *XXX.* Inscr. with Lat. verse. David John Haddock, ch. servant, churchwarden 1982-**1995**, mur., N. *XXXI.* Inscr. recording gift [of kitchenette] in mem. of Dian Kirby, 1939-**2003**, on kitchenette, N.A.

Ref: *Burke's Peerage and Baronetage*, p.337.

Ch. built, 1871.

CHILBOLTON, St. Mary-the-Less.

I. Inscr. and ach. Thomas Tutt, c.**1610**, mur., in stone frame, N. Inscr. 102 x 407 mm, ach. 255 x 207 mm.

II. Inscr. recording dedication of [east south aisle] window by friends in mem. of Rev. Charles Collier, M.A., F.S.A., hon. canon of Winchester [Cathedral], rector, principal of the Diocesan Training Coll. for 19 years [1859-1878], vicar of Andover for 11 years [1878-1889], **1890**, aged 71, mur., below window, S.A. *III.* Inscr. recording gift [of south-west south aisle window] by Children in **1892** in mem. of Gertrude Adela de Courcy Pereira, mur., below window, S.A. *IV.* Inscr. in raised letters. Edward Silva, of Testcombe and Cadogan Gardens, London, "THE WELFARE OF THIS CHURCH AND THE VILLAGE OF CHILBOLTON WAS TO HIM AN EVER PRESENT CARE", 1841-**1899**, [buried] in the churchyard, copper, mur., N.A. *V.* Inscr. recording erection of clock in **1905** by Marian Silva in mem. of husband, [no.*IV*], and sister, Rosa Pearman, maker's name A. & N. AUX C.S.L. LONDON, mur., S.A. *VI.* Inscr. Major-Gen. William Lambert, C.B., 88th Foot, 1907, son of Rev. A[nthony] L[ewis] Lambert, M.A., rector 1848-1869, and w. Margaret, **1909**, both buried at St. Faith's, Winchester, bronze, on lychgate, Churchyard. *VII.* Inscr. [Rev.] Augustus Newton Obbard, [M.A.], rector 1895-**1909**, mur., C. *VIII.* World War II memorial (8 names), mur., on board, N.A. *IX.* Inscr. Michael A.S. Riley, 1938-**1982**, bronze, on bench, Churchyard. *X.* Inscr. Peter John Richardson, 1933-**1984**, bronze, on wooden cross, Churchyard.

Ref: *Heseltine, Heraldry*, p.36; *M.B.S. Trans.*, V, p.272; *M.S.*, p.159; *Soc. Antiq. MS. 875/6*, p.26.

Thomas Iutt obijt   die   Anno dñi

CHRIST IS TO ME LIFE, AND DEATHE
IS TO ME AN ADVANTAGE, FOR I
KNOWE THAT MY REDEME LYVETH

Chilbolton I

Here lieth the Body of Anne, the first and beloved wife of Augustus Welby Northmore de Pugin, Architect: who departed this life at London, on the XXVII day of May in the year of our Lord, MDCCCXLIIII. R.I.P. Amen.

Christchurch, Priory V

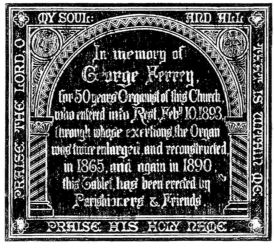

Christchurch, Priory XXVIII

CHRISTCHURCH, Priory Church of the Holy Trinity (now in Dorset).

I. (Formerly H.D.1). Inscr. on 2 pls. Maria Morgan, **1796**, aged 46, pos. by [Mary Eleanor], Countess of Strathmore, [w. of John Bowes, 9th Earl of Strathmore, 1749-1800], worn; in 2006 covered by fitted carpet, Lady Chapel. *II. (Formerly H.D.5).* Inscr. Harriet Susan, Viscountess FitzHarris, [dau. of Francis Bateman Dashwood, of Well Vale, Lincoln], w. of James [Edward Harris], 2nd Earl of Malmesbury, 1815, aged 31, engr. c.*1820*, mur., Sacrarium/Crypt. *III. (Formerly H.D.4).* Inscr. James Edward [Harris], 2nd Earl of Malmesbury, [eld. son of Rt. Hon. Sir James Harris, 1st Earl of Malmesbury, K.B.], 1778-**1841**, mur., Sacrarium/Crypt. *IV. (Formerly H.D.25).* Inscr. Elizabeth Bartlett, mistress of the Christchurch National and Sunday Girls' School for 25 years, **1845**, aged 66, mur., on board on pillar, S.A. of N. *V. (Formerly H.D.3).* Inscr. Anne [Garnet], 1st w. of Augustus Welby Northmore de Pugin, architect, died in London, [1814-]1832, engr. **1850**, [designed by Pugin, engr. by John Hardman & Cᵒ· Birmᵐ·], N.A. of C. *Meara, Pugin,* fig.66, p.174. Inscr. 225 x 458 mm. *VI. (Formerly H.D.1).* Inscr. Ann Goodchild, dau. of Maria Morgan, 1846, aged 72; also dau., Florentia Goodchild, died at Lymington, **1854**, aged 53; in 2006 covered by fitted carpet below no.*I*, Lady Chapel. *VII. (Formerly H.D.18).* Inscr. Mary Lady Matthews, 1723, engr. c.**1855**, S.Tr./Crypt. Recorded by Druitt (1907). *VIII. (Formerly H.D.19).* Inscr. Sir Peter Mews, Knt., of Hinton Admiral, [M.P. for Christchurch] 1722, 1725, engr. c.**1855**, S.Tr./Crypt. Recorded by Druitt (1907). *IX. (Formerly H.D.12).* Inscr. Constantia Jane Jarvis, dau. of Sir George Ivison Tapps, [1st Bart.], of Hinton Admiral, and [w.] Sarah, [dau. of Barrington Buggin], 1808, aged 15, engr. c.**1855**, S.Tr./Crypt. Recorded by Druitt (1907). *X. (Formerly H.D.13).* Inscr. Jane, [dau. of J. Ivison, of Carlisle], widow of George Jarvis Tapps, of Northchurch, Herts. 1808, aged 86; palimp. on rev. inscr. for no.*IX*, Waster; engr. c.**1855**, S.Tr./Crypt. Recorded (loose) by Druitt (1907). *XI. (Formerly H.D.16).* Inscr. Sarah, [dau. of Barrington Buggin], w. of Sir George Ivison Tapps [1st Bart.], of Hinton Admiral, 1813, aged 51, S.Tr./Crypt. engr. c.**1855**, Recorded by Druitt (1907). *XII. (Formerly H.D.14).* Inscr. Clara, [eld. dau. of Augustus Elliott Fuller, of Rosehill and Ashdown House, Sussex], w. of Sir George William Tapps[-]Gervis, [2nd] Bart., of Hinton Admiral, M.P. for [Christchurch], 1831, [aged 29], engr. c.**1855**; removed in 1835 from St. Marylebone New Church, London, S.Tr./Crypt. Recorded by Druitt (1907). *XIII. (Formerly H.D.17).* Inscr. Sir George Ivison Tapps, [1st] Bart., of Hinton Admiral, [1753-]1835, engr. c.**1855**, S.Tr./Crypt. Recorded by Druitt (1907). *XIV. (Formerly H.D.15).* Inscr. Sir George William Tapps[-]Gervis, [2nd] Bart., of Hinton Admiral, [only son of Sir George Ivison Tapps, 1st Bart., 1795-]1842, engr. c.**1855**, S.Tr./Crypt. Recorded by Druitt (1907). *XV. (Formerly H.D.11).* Inscr. Anne, [eld. dau. of Simon Yorke, of Erddig, Denbighshire], w. of C.T.S. Birch Reynardson, [of Holywell, Lincs., died at] Hinton Admiral, 1853, aged 43, engr. c.**1855**, S.Tr./Crypt. Recorded by Druitt (1907). *XVI. (Formerly H.D.6).* Inscr. Corisande Emma, Countess of Malmesbury, [only dau. of Charles Augustus Bennet, 5th Earl of Tankerville, 1st w. of James Howard Harris, 3rd Earl of Malmesbury, P.C., G.C.B., D.C.L.], 1807-**1876**, mur., Sacrarium/Crypt. *XVII. (Formerly H.D.21).* Inscr. with verse. Alfred George Drake [Pocock], yst. son of Sir George Edward Pocock, [2nd] Bart., of The Priory, 1838-**1879**, pos. by widow, maker's name HART, SON, PEARD & Cᵒ·, LONDON, mur., S.A. of N. *XVIII. (Formerly H.D.23).* Inscr. with verse. Shoeing Smith W. Kemsley, 1878; Driver W. Hobbs, died at Hay, Brecon, 1878; Cpl. Rough Rider C. Cook, killed by a fall from his horse, 1878; Driver William Fowler, died at Christchurch, 1879; and Gunner John Davis, died at Christchurch, 1881, died while battery was quartered at Christchurch 1878-**1881**, pos. by officers, NCOs and men of Major W.S. Curzon's G Battery, C Brigade, Royal Horse Artillery, mur., on marble, S.A. of N. *XIX. (Formerly H.D.28).* Inscr. Rev. Zachary Nash, [M.A.], curate [1857-1871] and vicar for 26 years [1871-1883], **1883**, on lectern, N. *XX.* Inscr. with verse on quadrilobe-shaped pl.

Annie, dau. of Charles Reeks and [w.] Elizabeth, w. of George William Wiltshire, of Frome Selwood, **1883**, aged 25, [buried] in the churchyard at Frome Selwood, [Somerset], mur., N.A. of N. *XXI. (Formerly H.D.2).* Inscr. with verse. Sir William Rose, K.C.B., 4th son of Sir George and Lady Rose, 1808-**1885**, mur., on marble, N.A. of C. *XXII. (Formerly H.D.22).* Inscr. recording [south aisle] window pos. in mem. of John Kemp-Welch, of Sopley Park, [1810-1885], and [w.] Marion Ransford, 1885; also James Kemp-Welch, **1887**, maker's name MAYER & C⁰ LONDON & MUNICH, mur., below window, S.A. of N. *XXIII. (Formerly H.D.8).* Inscr. Admiral the Hon. Sir Edward A[lfred] J[ohn] Harris, K.C.B., [2nd son of James Edward Harris, 2nd Earl of Malmesbury], 1808-**1888**, mur., Sacrarium/Crypt. *XXIV. (Formerly H.D.7).* Inscr. James Howard [Harris], 3rd Earl of Malmesbury, [P.C.], G.C.B., [D.C.L., 1807-]**1889**, mur., Sacrarium/Crypt. *XXV. (Formerly H.D.26).* Inscr. Sir Percy Florence Shelley, [3rd] Bart., [J.P., D.L.], son of Percy Bysshe Shelley, poet, and w. Mary Wollstonecraft, [High Sheriff 1865, 1819-]**1889**, maker's name COX & BUCKLEY LONDON, mur., on marble, Baptistry/Tower. *XXVI. (Formerly H.D.29).* Inscr. George Druitt and [w.] Sarah Neyle Chapman, **1890**, on cross, Salisbury Chapel/N.A. of C. *XXVII. (Formerly H.D.20).* Inscr. with verse on lozenge-shaped pl. Robert William, eld. son of William Watmough and w. Catherine, died at Runnymede, [Kansas, America], 1868-**1890**, buried at Harper Cemetery, Kansas, [America], maker's name MATTHEWS, 19 CASTLE Sᵀ EAST OXFORD Sᵀ LONDON W., mur., on marble, N.A. of N. *XXVIII. (Formerly H.D.24).* Inscr. with verse. George Ferrey, organist for 50 years, "through whose exertions the Organ was twice enlarged and reconstructed in 1865 and again in 1890", **1893**, pos. by friends and parishioners, maker's name SINGER & SONS FROME & LONDON, mur., on marble, S.A. of N. Inscr. 457 x 511 mm. *XXIX. (Formerly H.D.27).* Inscr. with verse. Midshipman Lawrence James Peter Scarlett, "WENT · DOWN · WITH · SOME · 400 · SHIPMATES · IN H·M·S · VICTORIA AFTER · COLLISION · WITH H·M·S · CAMPERDOWN", 1877-**1893**, maker's name COX & BUCKLEY LONDON, mur., in marble frame, Baptistry/Tower. *XXX. (Formerly H.D.9).* Inscr. Emma Wylly, [yst. dau. of Capt. Samuel Chambers, R.N.], w. of Admiral the Hon. Sir Edward [Alfred] J[ohn] Harris, K.C.B., 1812-**1896**, mur., Sacrarium/Crypt. *XXXI. (Formerly H.D.30).* Inscr. recording presentation [of ewer] in **1903** by Sunday school boys, on ewer, Baptistry/Tower. *XXXII.* Inscr. in raised letters with ach., regt. insignia and effs. of soldier with head bowed and left hand on reversed rifle in relief. Gen. Sir Charles Cameron Shute, K.C.B., Inniskilling Dragoons, son of T[homas] D[eane] Shute, [J.P., D.L.], of Burton and Bramshaw Hill, served in the Kurnool Expedition 1839, the Crimean Campaign (including the Battles of Balaklava and Inkerman, the Siege of Sevastopol and the Battle of Tchernaya), 1854-1856, 1816-**1904**, copper, mur., on board, S.A. of C. *XXXIII.* Inscr. with verse and enamelled insignia of Order of St. John of Jerusalem. Agnes Charlotte Burne, L.G.St.J., dau. of George Sholto Douglas, 19th Earl of Morton, and w. Frances Theodora [(née Rose), 2nd] w. of Major-Gen. Sir Owen Tudor Burne, [G.C.I.E., K.C.S.I.], born at Dalmahoy, [Scotland], died at Christchurch, 1842-[**1907**], buried in the churchyard next to uncle, Field-Marshal [Hugh Henry Rose, 1st Baron] Strathnairn, [G.C.B., G.C.S.I., 1801-1885], maker's name T. PRATT & SONS, LONDON, mur., on marble, N.A. of C. *XXXIV.* Inscr. with verse within border of oak leaves and acorns. Major George Ewen Eyre Gordon Cameron, Gordon Highlanders, 2nd son of Gen. Sir William Gordon Cameron, G.C.B., [V.D.], of Nea House, 1871-**1908**, mur., on marble, S.A. of C. *XXXV.* Inscr. with verse on lozenge-shaped pl. Rev. Thomas Henry Bush, M.A., vicar for 25 years [1884-1909], **1909**, aged 76, mur., on marble, S.A. of N. *XXXVI.* Inscr. in Lat. Fanny Kinch, **1911**, copper, mur., on board, S.A. of N. *XXXVII.* Inscr. Arthur Mears, 1847-**1912**, on prie-dieu, Lady Chapel. *XXXVIII.* Inscr. with verse within border of oak leaves and acorns. Capt. Napier Charles Gordon Cameron, 1st Battn. The Queen's Own Cameron Highlanders, yst. son of Gen. Sir William Gordon Cameron, G.C.B., [V.D.], of Nea House, killed in action during the Battle of the Aisne, France, 1876-**1914**, [buried at Bourg-et-Comin Communal Cemetery, France], mur., on marble,

S.A. of C. *XXXIX*. Inscr. with facsimile stall pl. recording erection of banner, [helm, mantling] and crest (consecrated in 1913 at the re-inauguration of the Henry VII Chapel in Westminster Abbey for the Order of the Bath where the orig. stall pl. remains) in **1914** of Gen. Sir William Gordon Cameron, G.C.B., V.D., of Nea House, 1827-1913, mur., S.A. of C. *XL & XLI*. Two inscrs. Choristers [killed in World War I], on chairs, N. *XLII*. Inscr. James Edward [Harris], 5th Earl of Malmesbury, [J.P., D.L., son of Lt.-Col. Edward James Harris, 4th Earl of Malmesbury, D.L.], 1872-**1950**, on door, Sacrarium/Crypt. *XLIII*. Inscr. Frederick Charles Cutler Vincent, chorister 1908-1959, **1960**, aged 70, on choir stall, N. *XLIV*. Inscr. Dorothy, Countess of Malmesbury, w. of [James Edward Harris], 5th Earl [of Malmesbury, J.P., D.L., yst. dau. and coh. of Augustus Cholmondeley Gough-Calthorpe, 6th Baron Calthorpe, J.P., D.L.], 1885-**1972**, on door with no.*XLII*, Sacrarium/Crypt. *XLV*. Inscr. recording mosaic panel made by Edward Thomas Higgs and given in **1973** by family in mem., mur., Harys Chapel/S.A. of C. *XLVI*. Inscr. [Rev. Dr.] John Robert Towers, M.A., D.D. (for Oriental languages), stipendiary priest 1909-1955, hon. assistant priest 1955-**1979**, bronze, on chest, Retrochoir. *XLVII*. Inscr. recording restoration of great quire windows and ceiling bosses from 1978-**1981** by Christchurch Priory Repairs Committee at a cost of £57,502; R.A. Newbury, chairman; Rev. Basil H[enry] T[revor] Trevor-Morgan, B.A., vicar; I.C.M. Beckwith and E.H. Fryer, churchwardens; D.J. Hewitt and J.S. Jones, churchwardens; I.J. Jessop, A.R.I.B.A., architect, mur., C. *XLVIII*. Inscr. Lance-Cpl. B[rett] P[atrick] Giffin, Royal Marines, killed in action in the Falklands War, **1982**, on flowerstand, War Memorial Chapel, S.A. of N. *XLIX*. Inscr. Lady Elizabeth Berwick, only dau. of [James Edward Harris], 5th Earl of Malmesbury, [J.P., D.L.], 1906-**1983**, on door with nos.*XLII & XLIV*, Sacrarium/Crypt. *L*. Sir Donald Coleman Bailey, Knt., O.B.E., inventor of the World War II Bailey bridge at the Experimental Bridging Establishment, 1901-**1985**, pos. by "Comrades of the Corps of Royal Engineers", rect. pl., inscr., regt. insignia and scene in relief depicting the launching of a Bailey Bridge by Royal Engineers of the 4th Division across the Rapido River at Cassino, [Italy], on the night of 12th/13th May 1944 based on a painting by the war artist Terence Cuneo, bronze, mur., on board on pillar, S.A. of N. *LI*. Inscr. [Rev.] Keith James Gerrard, [B.Sc., curate 1986-1988, 1928-]**1988**, on pulpit rail, N. *LII*. Inscr. Audrey Vincent, "Mistress of the Choir Robes" for more than 30 years, 1900-**1990**, on chair, N.Tr. *LIII*. Inscr. Col. Edward [Walter Hall] Berwick, Royal Canadian Dragoons, [son of Walter Mark Berwick, of Toronto, 2nd] husband of Lady Elizabeth Berwick (née Harris), 1908-**1993**, on door with nos.*XLII, XLIV & XLIX*, Sacrarium/Crypt. *LIV*. Inscr. *"This stained glass window marks 900 years of continuous worship in this priory church. Designed and made by Jane Gray it shows a starry night in which the Cross of Christianity dominates the design. The cross is surrounded by circles, symbols of both Eternity and Perfection, arranged to create the feeling of space and time. Shafts of light representing the Christian faith issue from the centres of the circles, which are on the rim of a halo enclosing the Cross. The white shafts overlap and weave over, under and through the remaining circles of the Cross, suggesting another dimension to the design. At the centre of the largest circle is the Chi-Ro, or Monogram of Christ, demonstrating and reaffirming nine hundred years of Christian worship within this ancient building"*, engr. **1994**, mur., below window, N.Tr. *LV*. Inscr. commem. the visit in **1995** of the N[ew] Z[ealand] Canterbury Plainsmen [Barbershop Chorus], on candlestick, Vergers' Vestry. *LVI*. Inscr. recording presentation [of display case] in mem. of Martin John Wilkinson, engr. c.**1995**, on display case, St. Stephen's Chapel, S.A. of N. *LVII*. Inscr. "In 1981 the opening of the Prior's door led to the building of the Cloister Way connecting the church to the Priory House. The installation of the stained glass windows, with the 49 roundels depicting episodes in the history of the Priory Church, was completed in **1999**", mur., on board, corridor between S.Tr. and Priory House. *LVIII*. Inscr. [William James Harris], 6th Earl of Malmesbury, [T.D., J.P.], Lord-Lt. 1973-1982, official verderer of the New Forest 1966-1974, 1907-**2000**, and [3rd] w.

Bridget [Hawkings], Countess of Malmesbury, 1927-1999, on door with nos.*XLII, XLIV, XLIX &* *LIII*, Sacrarium/Crypt. *LIX.* Inscr. on 2 pls. [recording gift of bench to] commem. the Millennium by Christchurch Townswomen's Guild, 1930-**2000**, on bench, Churchyard.

INDENTS & LOST BRASSES. 60. *(Formerly H.D.I)*. Indent, priest, hf. eff. in ?cope. John Wodenham, 18th prior, 1397; with incised marg. inscr. in Lombardics; nearly effaced, N.A. of N. Blue Bit slab 2630 x 1245 mm. 61. Indent, man in arm. and w., inscr. and double canopy, c.1405, nearly effaced; discovered in 1919 in S.A. of N., now mur., St. Michael's Loft Museum. Probably Sir Thomas West, 3rd Lord West, constable of Christchurch Castle, 1405, and w. Joan de la Warre, 1404. Male eff. c.1260 x 360 mm, female eff. ? x c.325 mm, canopy c.2085 x 880 mm, inscr. c.75 x c.710 mm, Purbeck slab 560-1120 x 1030 mm and 735-1040 x 1030 mm. Style: London A. 62. *(Formerly H.D.XVIII)*. Indent, priest, hf. eff. in cope and almuce, inscr., John Borard, 19th prior, c.1410; with incised marg. inscr. in Lombardics; Retrochoir. *Church Monuments Jour.*, XIX, fig.11, p.32; *Sadler, Dorset and Hampshire*, pt.II, p.11 (drg.). Eff. 470 x 310 mm, inscr. 190 x 470 mm, Blue Bit slab 2790 x 1160 mm. Style: London B. 63. *(Formerly H.D.XII)*. Indent, priest, hf. eff. in mass vests. and inscr. Thomas Talbot, 20th prior, 1420; with incised marg. inscr. nearly effaced; N.A. of C. Recorded (lost) by Warner (1795). *Sadler, Dorset and Hampshire*, pt.II, p.10 (drg.). Eff. 355 x 215 mm, inscr. 115 x 400 mm, Purbeck slab 2390 x 840 mm. Style: London B. 64. *(Formerly H.D.VII)*. Indent, lady in kirtle and mantle, 2 shs. and marg. inscr., c.1420; in 2006 covered by carpet, C. *Sadler, Dorset and Hampshire*, pt.II, p.13 (drg.). Eff. 1385 x 420 mm, dext. sh. 285 x 210 mm, sin. sh. 285 x 210 mm, marg. inscr. 2075 x 1040 x 55 mm, Purbeck slab 2450 x 1245 mm. 65. *(Formerly H.D.XIII)*. Indent, priest, hf. eff. in mass vests. and inscr., c.1430, N.A. of C. *Sadler, Dorset and Hampshire*, pt.II, p.9 (drg.). Possibly John Wimborne, prior, or William Norton, prior. Eff. 345 x 230 mm, inscr. 70 x 465 mm, Blue Bit slab 2175 x 1140, approp. for John Savage, 1773, aged 11 weeks and John Savage, of Burton, 1791. Style: London ?D. 66. *(Formerly H.D.XVI)*. Indent, inscr. (chamfer). Sir John Chidiock, 1449, and w. Catherine, 1461; formerly A.T., N.Tr., now A.T., N.A. of C.; 3 shs., mur., in stone panels of A.T. Inscr. (chamfer) 2640 x 1180 x 40 mm, Purbeck coverstone 2700 x 1240 mm, shs. mur. 140 x 115 mm. 67. *(Formerly H.D.XI)*. Indent, civilian, inscr. and scroll, c.1480, nearly effaced, N.A. of C. *Sadler, Dorset and Hampshire*, pt.II, p.12 (drg.). Eff. 240 x 180 mm, inscr. 40 x 350 mm, scroll 90 x 170 x 25 mm, Purbeck slab 965 remains x 460 mm remains. Style: London ?D. 68. *(Formerly H.D.V)*. Indent, ?man in arm. and 4 shs., ?late 15th cent., nearly effaced, N.A. of N. Eff. effaced, shs. c.165 x 125 mm, Purbeck slab 2730 x 1335 mm. 69. *(Formerly H.D.XV)*. Indent, lady. Joan Cokrell, mother of no.74, early 16th cent.; with incised marg. inscr.; N.A. of C. *Sadler, Dorset and Hampshire*, pt.II, p.8 (drg.). Eff. 450 x 170 mm, Purbeck slab 2180 x 935 mm. Style: London G. 70. *(Formerly H.D.X)*. Indent, inscr. and ?inscr. (chamfer), early 16th cent., A.T., N.A. of C. Possibly a member of the White family. Inscr. 45 x 355 mm, inscr. (chamfer) 1825 x 435 x 30 mm, Purbeck coverstone 1795 x 560 mm. 71. *(Formerly H.D.XVII)*. Indent, ?priest, hf. eff. in mass vests., inscr. and 2 shs., early 16th cent., N.A. of C. *Sadler, Dorset and Hampshire*, pt.II, p.6 (drg.). Eff. 295 x 135 mm, inscr. 110 x 310 mm, dext. sh. 140 x 115 mm, sin. sh. 140 x 115 mm, Purbeck slab 13700 x 690 mm, approp. for Rev. William Dale, 1771, aged 67. Style: London. 72. *(Formerly H.D.XIX)*. ?Indent, inscr. (chamfer), early 16th cent., A.T., Lady Chapel. Possibly a member of the West family. 73. *(Formerly H.D.XX)*. ?Indent, inscr. (chamfer), early 16th cent., A.T., Lady Chapel. Inscr. (chamfer) 2270 x 980 x 40 mm. 74. *(Formerly H.D.XIV)*. Indent, priest in ?cassock, surplice and almuce, inscr. William Eyre, 25th prior, 1520; with incised marg. inscr.; N.A. of C. Recorded (lost) by Warner (1795). *Sadler, Dorset and Hampshire*, pt.II, p.7 (drg.). Eff. 685 x 285 mm, inscr. 60 x 435 mm, Purbeck slab 2480 x 1295 mm, approp. for members of the Mouatt family, 1801-36. Style: London F debased. 75. *(Formerly H.D.VIII)*. Indent, lady in

Christchurch, Priory 61

Christchurch, Priory 62

Christchurch, Priory 63

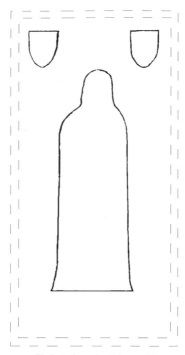

Christchurch, Priory 64

Christchurch, Priory 75

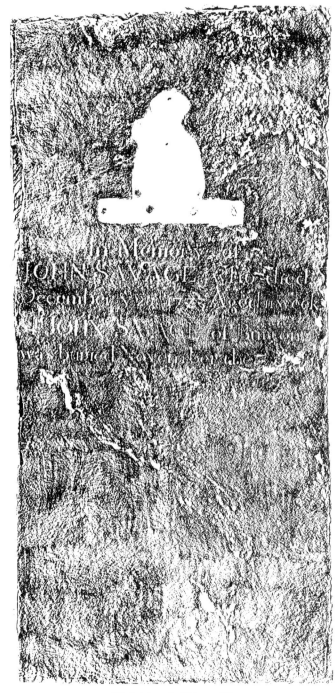

In Memory of
JOHN SAVAGE who died
December ye 17 Aged
of JOHN SAVAGE of
was buried

Christchurch, Priory 65

Christchurch, Priory 67

Christchurch, Priory 69

96

Christchurch, Priory 71

Christchurch, Priory 74

mantle, inscr., c.1520-30, C. Eff. 345 x c.120 mm, inscr. 150 x 390 mm, Purbeck slab 1620 x 760 mm. 76. *(Formerly H.D.IV)*. Indent, ?priest and marg. inscr., effaced, N.A. of N. Eff. effaced, marg. inscr. 1740 x 820 x 35 mm, Purbeck slab 1970 x 920 mm. 77. *(Formerly H.D.II)*. Indent, inscr., N.A. of N. Inscr. 65 x 430 mm, slab 1790 x 915 mm. 78. *(Formerly H.D.III)*. Indent, inscr., effaced, N.A. of N. Inscr. eff., Purbeck slab 1800 x 780 mm. 79. *(Formerly H.D.VI)*. Indent, inscr., N.A. of N. Inscr. 50 x 355 mm, Purbeck slab 2275 x 1195 mm, approp. for Rev. Luke Imber, 1773, aged 76. 80. *(Formerly H.D.IX)*. Indent, inscr., C. Inscr. 255 x 590 mm, Purbeck slab 1450 x 625 mm. 81. *(Formerly H.D.10)*. Lost brass, inscr. recording enlargement of organ (given by Gustavus Brander and built in 1788 by Alex[ande]r Cumming) by Henry Willis in 1865 by subscription, on organ, S.Tr. Recorded by Druitt (1907). 82. Lost indent, ?inscr. Robert Say; with incised marg. inscr.; S.A. of C. Recorded (lost) by Warner (1795).

Ref: *Brayley, E., and Britton, J., The Beauties of England and Wales*, VI, 1805, p.216; *Burke's Peerage and Baronetage*, pp.452-3, p.757, pp.1735-6, p.1804, p.1891, p.2560, p.2612; *Busby, Companion Guide*, p.187; *Ferrey, B., The Antiquities of The Priory of Christ Church, Hants*, 1834, p.46, p.64, p.68; *M.B.S. Bulletin*, 2, p.6, 67, p.136; *M.B.S. Trans.*, V, pp.191-204 ('H.D.' nos. are those used by Herbert Druitt), pp.273-5; *Meara, Pugin*, p.175; *Moody*, p.258; *M.S.*, p.170; *Sadler, Dorset and Hampshire*, pt.II, pp.6-15, p.38, appx. I, pt. 2, pp.5-6, p.8; *Soc. Antiq. MS. 875/6*, pp.27-9; *Warner*, I, p.199.

Transferred from Hampshire to Dorset in 1974.

COLEMORE, St. Peter ad Vincula (redundant, now vested in The Churches Conservation Trust).

I. Inscr. Richard Pocock, LL.B., rector for 59 years, **1718**, aged 83, and w. Constance, 1674, aged 34, C. Inscr. 300 x 304 mm, slab 2210 x 1130 mm, approp. with illegible inscr.

INDENTS & LOST BRASSES. 2. *(Formerly M.S.I)*. Lost brass, inscr. John and Sara Greaves, their sons pos., 1640; formerly mur., C., in 1906 loose in Vestry. *Bertram, Brasses*, fig.81, p.129. Illustration from rubbing in Soc. Antiq. coll. Rubbing in Soc. Antiq. coll. (1908). Inscr. 945 x 786 mm.

Ref: *Bertram, Brasses*, p.128; *M.B.S. Trans.*, V, pp.278-9; *Mee, Hampshire*, p.128; *M.S.*, p.159; *Soc. Antiq. MS. 875/6*, pp.32-3.

Ch. declared redundant, 1972; vested, 1974.

CORHAMPTON, dedication unknown.

I. Inscr. recording gift of organ in **1857** by Mr. [John Henry Campbell Wyndham, 1868, aged 70], and Mrs. Campbell Wyndham, on organ, Gallery/N. *II.* Inscr. with verse recording presentation of trestles with embroidered coverings in **1913** by Rev. H[arloe] R[obert] Fleming, [M.A.], vicar 1874-1897, in mem. of w. Jane, 1835-1913, "WHOSE BODY RESTED ON THEM", buried in "GOD'S ACRE"; Rev. Henry Churton, vicar [1897-1919], on trestle, Gallery/N. *III.* Inscr. Peter William Lewis Ward, churchwarden, husband, father and grandfather, 1919-**2000**, on bench, Churchyard.

PATRI SVO CHARISSIMO
ET MATRI DVLCISSIMAE
IOHANNI ET SARAE GREAVES

PARENTIBVS OPTIMIS
PIISSIMIS MERITISSIMIS
IOANNES NICOLAVS THOMAS
EDOVARDO GREAVES

FILII POSVERVNT
ANNO DOM CIƆ IƆC XLI

PRO MAGNIS MERITIS ET DVLCI MVNERE VITÆ
VOBIS CVM LACRYMIS SOLA SEPVLCRA DAMVS

Colemore 2

HERE LYES THE BODY OF
RICHARD POCOCK LL.B. WHO
WAS 59 YEARS RECTOR OF THIS
PARISH A MAN OF SINGULAR
PROBITY EMINENT PIETY
AND GREAT CHARITY
OB MAR 20 1718 AN ÆTAT 83
HERE LYES ALSO THE BODY OF
CONSTANCE HIS WIFE WHO
DIED NOV ... 1674 AN ÆTAT 34

Colemore *I*

ANNO DNI 1609 XXVI DIE AVGVSTI
HEERE LYETH BVRIED THE BODYES OF MICHAELL
RENIGER, DOCTOR OF DVINITYE, ARCHDEACON
OF WINCHESTER AND PARSON OF CRAWLYE &
OF IOHN HIS SONE: WHICH MICHAELL RENIGER
DEPARED THIS LIFE Y DAY & Y EARE ABOVE
WRITTEN ANNO · ÆTATIS SVÆ LXXIX ·

MICHAELL RENIGER EPITAPHIVM

VIR PLVS AC DOCTVS, VERÆ QVI REELIGIONIS
STRENVVS ASSERTOR (SPRETIS QVÆ CHARA PVTANTVR
ET PATRIA, ATQ OPIBVS, DVLCI QVOQ CONIVGE) PVLSVS
EXVL IN HELVETIAM MIGRAVIT, ET INDE REVERSVS
REGINÆ A SACRIS, RECTOR FVIT ISTIVS ÆDIS:
ATQ DECEM LVSTRIS, ANNO ET PLVS, PRÆFVIT ILLI
ATQ DIV VIGILANS, VERBO, EXEMPLOQ REFECIT
PASTOR OVES CHRISTI: SERA IAM MORTE SOLVTVS
SPIRITVS ALTA PETIT: REGITVRQ HOC MARMORE CORPVS

Crawley I

101

CRAWLEY, St. Mary.

I. Inscr. and 9 Lat. vv. Michael Reniger, D.D., rector, archdeacon of Winchester, **1609**, aged 79, and son John, mur., on marble, C. Inscr. 231 x 632 mm, vv. 292 x 771 mm.

II. Inscr. with verse. Grace Ellen, w. of Adam Kennard, of Crawley Court, 1840-**1880**, on window splay, N.A. *III.* Inscr. on scroll-shaped pl. recording gift of [east] window in **1887** in mem. of [Ven.] Philip Jacob, archdeacon and canon of Winchester [Cathedral], rector of Crawley and Honton for 53 years [1831-1884], mur., below window, C. *IV.* Inscr. with sh. recording rebuilding of chancel and addition of adjoining organ chamber in **1887** by sons and daus.-in-law, John Henry Mee, Alice Ann Mee, Edward Melford Mee and Emily Mary Mee, in mem. of Very Rev. John Mee, M.A., Dean of Grahamstown, South Africa [1861-1864], rector of Westbourne, Sussex [1871-1884], mur., in recess, C. *V.* Inscr. recording partial rebuilding of tower and rehanging of bells in **1901** by public subscription; [Rev.] W[illiam] J[ames] Smith, M.A., rector [1896-1917]; T. Eastman and G. Ferguson, churchwardens, mur., Tower. *VI.* Inscr. recording gift of 4 flowering trees by Rev. D[ennis] E[dward] J[oseph] Earle, rector 1955-**1961**, in mem. of [w.] Fenella, mur., S.Porch. *VII.* Inscr. recording dedication of [west] window designed by w. Pat in mem. of Edward Asa Thomas, T.D., churchwarden 1961-**1983**, mur., below window, Tower.

Ref: *M.B.S. Trans.*, V, p.279; *Mee, Hampshire*, p.131; *M.S.*, p.159; *Soc. Antiq. MS. 875/6*, p.33; *V.C.H., Hampshire*, III, p.412.

CRONDALL, All Saints.

I. [Nicholas Kaerwent, rector [1361-1381, **1381**], in mass vests.; canopy and marg. inscr. lost; rel., C. Recorded (eff., canopy and marg. inscr. mutil.) by Pavey (1706) and (eff. with canopy and marg. inscr. lost) by Baigent (c.1850). *Bertram, Brasses*, fig.40, p.91; *Brit. Lib. Add. MS. 39987*, f.19; *Haines*, p.67 (drg.); *Lamp and Herring*, p.132; *M.B.S. Portfolio*, I, pt.3, pl.2; *Oxford Man.*, p.26; *Portfolio Book*, pl.59. Eff. 1474 x 427 mm. Style: London B.

II. John Gyfford, esq., heir apparent to Sir William Gyfford, **1563**, in arm., kng., and w. Elizabeth (eff. lost), dau. of Sir George Throkmarton, with 5 sons (lost) and 8 daus., inscr. and ach., mur., A.T., C.; 3 shs., mur., in stone panels of A.T., lost. Recorded (complete) by Pavey (1706). *M.B.S. Trans.*, XV, p.165 (detail). Male eff. 325 x 228 mm, female eff. indent 325 x 210 mm, inscr. 145-180 x 175 mm, sons indent 145-180 x 175 mm, daus. 120-172 x 222 mm, ach. 240 x 177 mm, slab 760 x 1370 mm, coverstone 1805 x 580 mm, sh. mur. indents 145 x 115 mm. Style: London G (Lytkott, script 9).

III. John Eager, **1641**, a skeleton, rect. pl. with 4 Eng. vv., mur., S.C. *Bertram, Brasses*, fig.2, p.20; *M.B.S. Trans.*, V, p.282. Rect. pl.145 x 382 mm. Style: Francis Grigs.

IV. Cross and inscr. Charles Edward Lefroy, of Itchel Manor, 1810-**1861**, mur., S.C. *V.* Inscr. Midshipman Fraser Sumner Stooks, of H.M.S. Victoria "went down with his vessel in the Mediterranean, off Tripoli", **1893**, aged 16, pos. by friends and neighbours, mur., N.A. *VI.* Inscr. with verse. Sophia Anna, 3rd dau. of J.H.G. Lefroy, of Itchel [Manor], widow of [Rev. Canon] Ernest Hawkins, canon of Westminster for 23 years, secretary of the S.P.G., 1814-**1897**, mur., S.C. *VII.* Inscr. with verse, 2 shs. and fyflot cross. Charles James Maxwell Lefroy, of

Crondall I

Here under lieth the body of John Guffard Squyer beinge Apparant of Sir Willm Guffard knight who had to wive Elzabeth one of the Daughteres of Sir George Throkmarton knight & had by her fower sonnys and viii Daughteres and in theund this mortall lyff the XVII Day of May in the yere of our lord god 1563 on whose Sawle Jesu have mci

Crondall II

Crondall II

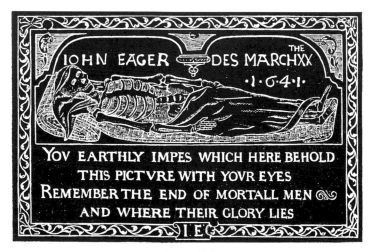

Crondall III

105

Itchel Manor, son of no.*IV*, "AN IDEAL LANDLORD SQUIRE" of the par. for 47 years, lord of the manors of Ewshott and Itchell, "HEAD OF THE ENGLISH BRANCH OF THE HUGENOT FAMILY OF LOFFROY OF CAMBRAY WHO PREFERRING TO GIVE UP THEIR COUNTRY & POSSESSIONS RATHER THAN THEIR RELIGION LEFT FRANCE FOR CANTERBURY A.D. 1587. EVENTUALLY SETTLING IN HAMPSHIRE", [died] suddenly, 1848-**1908**, mur., S.C. *VIII*. Inscr. recording dedication of [south-west south aisle] window in mem. of Capt. the Hon. Archibald Rodney Hewitt, D.S.O., 2nd Battn. East Surrey Regt., yst. son of [Capt. Archibald Robert Hewitt, R.N.], 6th Viscount Lifford, [of Hill House, Lyndhurst], killed at the 2nd Battle of Ypres, [1883-]**1915**, mur., below window, S.A. *IX*. Inscr. with verse, fyflot cross and R.N. insignia. Lt. Patrick Egerton [Lefroy], R.N., 6th son of Charles James Maxwell Lefroy, of Itchel Manor, and w. Elizabeth Caroline, killed in action in the Dardanelles on board H.M.S. Mosquito, 1888-**1915**, [pos. by] mother, mur., S.C. *X*. Inscr. on arch-shaped pl. Lt. John Horsley Mitchell, [305th Siege Battery], R[oyal] G[arrison] A[rtillery], son of Alfred Mitchell and w. Catherine], killed in action at Ploegsteert, **1917**, [aged 35, buried at Maple Leaf Cemetery, Belgium, pos. by w., Winifred], mur., on marble, S.A. *XI*. Inscr. with verse. Dorothy Kate, eld. dau. of [Arthur John] Brandon [and w. Kate Alethea], 1882-**1967**, bronze, on gravestone, Churchyard. *XII*. Inscr. recording dedication of organ (installed "AS A TOKEN OF THE AFFECTION OF THE BRANDON FAMILY. PAST AND PRESENT FOR THE PARISH OF CRONDALL") in **1971**, copper, on organ console, N. *XIII*. Inscr. Geoffrey Thomas Stanley Clarke, 1879-**1971**, and Gladys Helen Stanley Clarke, 1886-1964, bronze, on memorial wall, Churchyard. *XIV*. Inscr. with verse. Brig. Ronald Patrick George Anderson, Royal Engineers, husband of Enid [Marjorie] (née Brandon) for 52 years, 1900-**1981**, bronze, on gravestone with no.*XI,* Churchyard. *XV*. Inscr. Noel, w. of Capt. E.G. Jukes-Hughes, C.B.E., R.N., 1896-**1982**, copper, on memorial wall, Churchyard. *XVI*. Inscr. William John Raby Noble, 1957-**1982**, bronze, on memorial wall, Churchyard. *XVII*. Inscr. Sheila Witt, 1902-**1982**, bronze, on memorial wall, Churchyard. *XVIII*. Inscr. Lt.-Cmdr. Edward Copson (Peter) Peake, R.N., 1908-1982, and w. Nicola Katharine Margaret Murray (Peggy), 1910-**1983**, bronze, on memorial wall, Churchyard. *XIX*. Inscr. Brian Witt, 1899-**1983**, bronze, on memorial wall, Churchyard. *XX*. Inscr. with verse recording donation [of bench] by relatives and friends in mem. of Shaun Lockwood Croft, [killed] "IN THE "MARCHIONESS" RIVER THAMES DISASTER", **1989**, aged 26, bronze, on bench, Churchyard. *XXI*. Inscr. Ian Bide, J.P., 1940-**1990**, bronze, on memorial wall, Churchyard. *XXII*. Inscr. Elsa Crawshaw (née Newman), 1909-**1990**, bronze, on memorial wall, Churchyard. *XXIII*. Inscr. George Richard Goddard, **1990**, aged 74, pos. by w. Olive, and sons, Peter and Robert, bronze, on memorial wall, Churchyard. *XXIV*. Inscr. Sybil Brambley, **1993**, aged 65, bronze, on memorial wall, Churchyard. *XXV*. Inscr. Barbara Anne Hodson, 1933-**1993**, bronze, on memorial wall, Churchyard. *XXVI*. Inscr. with verse. Enid Marjorie Anderson (née Brandon), w. of no.*XIV*, 1903-**1994**, bronze, on gravestone with nos.*XI & XIV*, Churchyard. *XXVII*. Inscr. with verse. Mary, w. [of Michael O'Gorman], 1924-**1994**, bronze, on memorial wall, Churchyard. *XXVIII*. Inscr. Frederick Cane, husband and father, 1894-1982; also Lilly Kathleen, w., mother and grandmother, 1898-**1995**, bronze, on memorial wall, Churchyard. *XXIX*. Inscr. with verse. John Ernest Heathcote Sorby, 1908-**1995**, bronze, on memorial wall, Churchyard. *XXX*. Inscr. Morrie W.H. Phillips, engr. c.**1995**, bronze, on bench, Churchyard. *XXXI*. Inscr. Robin Buchanan Cowan, 1927-**1996**, bronze, on memorial wall, Churchyard. *XXXII*. Inscr. Henrietta Louise Hook, 1925-**1996**, on window splay, S.A. *XXXIII*. Inscr. with verse. Donald Brambley, **1997**, aged 70, bronze, on memorial wall, Churchyard. *XXXIV*. Inscr. Pauline Ann Rich, 1936-1995, engr. **2002**, on window splay, N.A. *XXXV*. Inscr. Jitka Perceval Judge, 1946-1999, engr. **2002**, on window splay with no.*XXXIV*, N.A. *XXXVI*. Inscr. Arthur John Percy Puddephatt, 1907-1983, and [w.] Frances Grace, 1909-1999, engr. **2002**, on window splay with nos.*XXXIV & XXXV*, N.A. *XXXVII*. Inscr. recording donation [of south-east south aisle window] by Patrick Lloyd and [w.] Elisabeth, engr.

2002, on window splay, S.A. *XXXVIII*. Inscr. recording presentation [of bench] by the Crondall Society in gratitude to Rev. Paul [Michael] Rich, O.B.E., vicar 1991-**2005**, bronze, on bench, Churchyard.

INDENTS & LOST BRASSES. 39. Indent, ?2 effs. and inscr., 9 plugs only, effaced, S.A. Purbeck slab 790 remains x 575 mm. 40. Lost brass, lady, inscr. and 4 shs. Mary, w. of John Gyfard, 1470. Recorded by Pavey (1706). 41. Lost brass, lady, inscr. and 4 shs. Dame Elynor, w. of Sir William Gyfford, Knt., 1563. Recorded by Pavey (1706).

Ref: *Brit. Lib. Add. MS. 39964*, f.49, *Add. MS. 39987*, f.19, *Stowe MS. 845*, f.45; *Burke's Peerage and Baronetage*, p.1608; *Gawthorp*, p.103; *Haines*, I, p.142, II, p.72; *Heseltine, Heraldry*, p.36; *Lamp and Herring*, p.131; *Manning*, p.92; *M.B.S. Bulletin*, 61, p.11; *M.B.S. Trans.*, I, pt.10, p.7, V, pp.280-3, VIII, p.367, X, p.9, XV, p.183; *Mee, Hampshire*, p.132; *M.S.*, p.159; *Norris, Memorials*, p.63, p.247; *Pevsner, Hampshire*, p.188; *Simpson*, p.28; *Soc. Antiq. MS. 875/6*, pp.34-7; *V.C.H., Hampshire*, IV, pp.12-3.

DAMERHAM, St. George (formerly in Wiltshire).

I. Inscr. with verse. [Pte.] Gilbert Sidney Britten, [60302], 15th [Battn.] Cheshire [Regt.], only child of Sidney Britten and [w.] Bessie, [killed] in France, **1918**, aged 22, pos. by [parents, buried at Bagneux British Cemetery, Gezaincourt, France], mur., on board, N.A. *II.* Inscr. recording repair of tower (at a cost of £282 raised by voluntary subscription and a grant of £70 from the Diocesan Building Committee) and tuning and rehanging of bells in **1937** in mem. of Major and Mrs. Hugh Custance, mur., Tower. *III.* Inscr. recording presentation of treble bell (inscribed "I TELL ALLENFORD'S GRATITUDE") in **1937** by Mr. and Mrs. E.T. Hibberd, of Allenford, mur., Tower. *IV.* Inscr. Leslie G. Tiller, 1912-**1982**, on notice board, S.Porch. *V.* Inscr. Alan Brown, 1894-**1986**, and [w.] Margaret (née Nasmyth), 1898-1983, mur., on board below framed baptismal roll, S.A. *VI.* Inscr. Betty Waterman, engr. c.**1995**, bronze, on bench, Churchyard. *VII.* Inscr. on cross-shaped pl. Kirsty Macildowie, 1981-**1999**, on wooden cross, Churchyard.

Transferred from Wiltshire to Hampshire in 1895.

DEANE, All Saints (old church).

INDENTS & LOST BRASSES. 1. Lost brass, civilian and w., inscr., 3 sons and 3 daus. Nicholas Ayliff, of Halle, farmer, 1493, and w. Jane, N. Recorded (complete) by Pavey (1702).

Ref: *Brit. Lib. Stowe MS. 845*, f.73; *Haines*, II, p.72; *M.B.S. Trans.*, V, p.283; *M.S.*, p.170; *Soc. Antiq. MS. 875/6*, p.37.

DEANE, All Saints (new church).

I. Inscr. with verse. Alice Palmer, **1909**, maker's name A. & N. AUX C.S.L. LONDON, mur., C. *II.* World War I memorial (9 names), maker's name CULN GAWTHORP & SONS LONDON, mur., on marble, N. *III.* Inscr. [Rev.] Frederick Spencer Howard Marle, [B.A.], rector of Ashe and Deane for over 30 years [1935-1968], **1968**, mur., C. *IV.* Inscr. recording dedication of [east south porch] window in mem. of Rev. W[illiam] Basil Norris, [M.A.], rector 1968-**1976**, mur., on board, S.Porch. *V.* Inscr. [Rev.] Geoffrey [Raymond] Turner, rector 1976-**1992**, mur., C.

Ch. built, 1818.

DEAN, PRIOR'S, dedication unknown.

I. John Compton, gent., **1605**, in civil dress (mutil.), and w. Joan Michelborne, 1586, inscr., 1 Lat. line and ach., C. *Hervey, T., Hist. of Colmer and Prior's Dean*, p.155, and *Par. Registers of Colmer, etc.*, p.43; *M.B.S. Trans.*, V, p.366. Male eff. orig. c.610 x 221 mm, now 585 x 221 mm, female eff. 581 x 208 mm, inscrs. 55 x 245 mm and 201 x 590 mm, ach. 217 x 188 mm, Petworth marble slab 1945 x 950 mm. Style: Johnson.

Ref: *Brit. Lib. Add. MS. 39963*, f.315; *Heseltine, Heraldry*, p.36; *M.B.S. Bulletin*, 26, p.9; *M.B.S. Trans.*, II, pp.62-3, V, pp.365-7; *Mee, Hampshire*, p.285; *M.S.*, p.159; *Soc. Antiq. MS. 875/6*, p.97, p.99.

DOGMERSFIELD, All Saints (new church).

I. Anne, eld. dau. of John Poulett of Herriard, esq., w. of Nicholas Sutton, died in childbed, **1590**, aged 28, kng., with 3 daus. also kng., and an infant in swaddling clothes, rect. pl. with lozenge and inscr.; 8 Eng. vv. incised in stone below; formerly mur., C., now mur., N. *M.B.S. Trans.*, V, p.285; *Mee, Hampshire*, p.115 (drg. of effs.). Rect. pl. 377 x 438 mm, inscr. 145 x 398 mm. Style: Johnson (script 13).

II. Cross and inscr. Post-Capt. George William St. John Mildmay, R.N., 3rd son of Sir Henry Paulet St. John Mildmay, [3rd] Bart., and w. Jane, [1792-]**1851**, mur., on marble, N. *III.* Inscr. recording [south-west nave] window in mem. of Frances Lucy Penelope, dau. of Edward Lockwood Percival, of Dews Hall, Essex, [2nd] w. of Edw[ar]d St. John Mildmay, **1862**, aged 61; also dau., Fanny Percival, 1845, aged 7, mur., N. *IV.* Inscr. recording dedication of [centre and south-east nave] windows in **1863** by friends, parishioners and neighbours in mem. of Rev. Charles Dyson, M.A., fellow of Corpus Christi Coll., Oxford, rector [1836-1860], mur., below window, N. *V.* Paulet St. John Mildmay, of Hazelgrove, Somerset, 2nd son of Sir Henry Paulet St. John Mildmay, [3rd] Bart., of Dogmersfield Park, served in the Peninsular War under the Duke of Wellington, M.P. for City and Borough of Winchester for more than 20 years, died at Dogmersfield, [1791-]1845, buried in vault beneath chancel; mar. [1813], Wyndham Anna Maria, 3rd [and yst.] dau. of Hon. Bartholomew Bouverie, [M.P.], by whom 4 sons and 3 daus., rect. pl., double canopy, inscr., sh., motto, lozenge and Alpha-Omega symbols in roundels, engr. **1864**, mur., in stone frame, N. *VI.* Wyndham Anna Maria, [3rd and yst.] dau. of Hon. Bartholomew Bouverie, [M.P.] and w. Mary Wyndham, widow of no.*V*, died at Torquay, Devon, **1864**, aged 72, buried in vault [beneath chancel]; "On this tablet erected by herself her surviving children record her name in a space which had been left by her own desire for that purpose", rect. pl., double canopy, inscr., lozenge and Codex Alexandrinus-Codex Claromontanus symbols in roundels, mur., in stone frame with no.*V*, N. *VII.* Inscr. Edward St. John Mildmay, [6th] son of Sir Henry Paulet St. John Mildmay, [3rd Bart.], of Dogmersfield Park and Moulsham Hall, Essex, 1797-**1868**; also eld. son, Edward Wheatley St. John Mildmay, [1822-]1840, mur., N. *VIII.* Inscr. on triangular-shaped pl. recording erection of granite cross in the churchyard in mem. of [Rev.] Charles [Dyson, M.A., rector 1836-1860], Elizabeth and Mary Anne Dyson "ON

MORS NOBIS LVCRV VITÆ

IOHANNI COMPTON GENEROSO∞SEXTO APRILIS∘ANNO DOMINI
1605 AC ETIAM IOAÑÆ MICHELBORNE VXORI EIVS
CHARISSIMÆ, SECVNDO OCTOBRIS AÑO DÑI
1586. PIE DEFVNCTIS. TETRASTICHON.

MORS TVMVLO, ET CÆLO, FÆLIX. CONIVNXIT EODEM,
QVOS THALAMVS VITA, QVOS ITA IVNXIT AMOR
HÆC TIBI QVI LEGIS HÆC DOCVMENTA. CAPESSE VIATOR.
QVOD SATIS IS VITÆ, QVI BENE VIXIT HABET.

Dean, Prior's I

THE DEATH OF THE LAST IN **1878**", mur., below no.*IV*, N. *IX*. Inscr. Mary, dau. of Peter Baillie, jun[io]r, of Dochfour, [Inverness, Scotland], 1802-**1892**; [w.] (1) John Morritt, jun[io]r, of Rokeby [Park], (2) Capt. Geo[rge] W[illia]m St. John Mildmay, R.N., [4th son of Sir Henry Paulet St. John Mildmay, 3rd Bart., 1792-1851], mur., N. *X*. Inscr. in raised letters with regt. insignia in relief. 2nd-Lt. Nigel Hugh Wallington, [1st Battn.] Somerset Light Infantry, [son of T.A.B. Wallington and w. Constance], accidentally killed in France, **1917**, aged 19, [buried at Mindel Trench British Cemetery, St. Laurent-Blangy, France], maker's name CULN GAWTHORP & SONS, LONDON, mur., N. *XI*. Inscr. with verse. Walter Charles Trimmer, churchwarden for 21 years, engr. c.**1950**, bronze, on board on gate post, Churchyard. *XII*. Inscr. Eric Almond, churchwarden 1955-**1991**, on board on gate post, Churchyard.

INDENTS & LOST BRASSES. 13. Lost brass, inscr. "The above Brass was found in Dogmersfield House in 1904. It is supposed that it was taken from the old Church of this parish, pulled down in 1806. It was placed here in January 1905", mur., below no.I, N. Recorded by Cave (1908) but not found (2006).

Ref: *Brit. Lib. Stowe MS. 845*, f.113; *Burke's Peerage and Baronetage*, p.420, pp.1815-6, p.2200; *Heseltine, Heraldry*, p.36; *M.B.S. Trans.*, V, pp.283-4, p.286; *Mee, Hampshire*, p.135; *M.S.*, p.160; *Pevsner, Hampshire*, p.191; *Soc. Antiq. MS. 875/6*, pp.37-40; *V.C.H., Hampshire*, IV, pp.73-4.

Ch. built, 1843.

DRAYTON, (see FARLINGTON).

DROXFORD, St. Mary and All Saints.

I. Inscr. Edward Searle, farmer of Droxford, **1617**, aged 72, N.C. Inscr. 134 x 414 mm, black marble slab 1720 x 720 mm.

II. Inscr. with verse, crest and motto. [Rev.] James Adair Griffith Colpoys, M.A., son of Vice-Admiral Sir Edward Griffith Colpoys, K.C.B., rector 1831-1868, died at St. Leonards, **1868**, aged 67, maker's name BARR ENG^R LONDON, mur., on board, C. *III*. Inscr. [Rev.] Stephen Bridge, M.A., rector 1868-1886, born at Colchester, [Essex], died at Clifton, 1811-**1895**, [buried] in the churchyard, pos. by an old friend, mur., S.C. *IV*. Inscr. Alfred Douglas-Hamilton, J.P., D.L. for Essex, [of Gidea Hall, Essex, barrister-at-law], 1818-**1895**, and w. Adelaide, [2nd dau. and coh. of Alexander Black, of Gidea Hall], 1818-1870; also daus., Marie Adelaide Blanch, 1846-1872, Gertrude Eleanor, 1848-1872; also father, [Lt.] Augustus B[arrington] P[rice] P[owell] Hamilton, [R.N.], grandson of Lord Anne Hamilton, 1781-1849, and mother, Maria Catherine, [dau. and coh. of Very Rev. [Dr.] John Hyde, D.D., Dean of Wells, canon of Windsor, chaplain in ordinary to George III], grand-dau. of Lord Francis Seymour, 1783-1865; also grandfather, Admiral Charles P[owell] Hamilton, 1760-1825; and brother, Rev. Adolphus Douglas-Hamilton, [M.A., 1816-]1893, [buried] in churchyard vault, mur., on board, N.A. *V*. Inscr. recording gift [of pulpit desk] in **1902** by dau. in mem. of Samuel King, M.A., on pulpit desk, N. *VI*. Inscr. with crest and motto. Lt.-Col. John Bower, J.P., Madras Army, of Studwell Lodge, **1910**, aged 101, and w. Mary, 1901, aged 74; also infant son, John Richard Graham, maker's name A & N AUX C.S.L. LONDON, mur., S.C. *VII*. Inscr. on scroll shaped-pl. Lt.-Cmdr. Arthur Leyborne-Popham, R.N.,

Here lieth Anne the eldelt daughter of
Iohn Poulett of Herryard Efquyer, and
wyfe to Nicholas Sutton who died in
childbed the viij.th of Maye 1590. be=
ing of the age of xxviij yeres. on
whofe foule God haue mercye .

Dogmersfield I

HERE LYETH MrEDWARD SEARLE FARMER OF
DROXFORD WHO DEPARTED THIS LIFE Ye 8: DAY
OF MAY IN THE 15 YEARE OF Ye RAIGNE OF KING
IAMES OF ENGLAND & OF SCOTLAND Y 50 BEING 72
YEARES OLD WHEN HE DIED, & IN Ye YEARE OF OVR
LORD GOD 1617:

Droxford I

111

[son of Rev. Edward Leyborne-Popham, of Hemyock, Devon, killed] on active service while serving in H.M.S. Clan MacNaughton, 1878-**1915**, mur., on board, N.A. *VIII*. Inscr. Capt. Lancelot Napier Turton, R.N., [H.M.S. Venus], died at Aden, **1918**, mur., below window, N.A. *IX*. Inscr. recording gift of vases in mem. of Sapper Joseph Percy Manuel, [287th Field Co.] R[oyal] E[ngineers, son of Joseph Manuel and w. Bertha Mabel], died as a prisoner of war in Malaya, **1943**, aged 25, [buried at Thanbyuzayat War Cemetery, Myanmar], on shelf, N.A. *X*. Inscr. Stephen Frederick, 1840-1905, Margaret Emily, 1841-1931, Helena Marian, 1843-1937, Henry Hamilton, 1844-1935, Maude Maria, 1846-1944, Frances Julia, 1849-1895, Eliza Lucy, 1851-1945, Stewart, 1853-**1946**, and Ada Mary, 1857-1934, children [of Rev. Stephen Bridge, M.A., rector 1868-1886, 1811-1895, and w. Margaret, 1817-1901], bronze, mur., S.C. *XI*. Inscr. recording dedication of [west north aisle] window in mem. of Henry Peter Douglas Wigg, 1948, and [w.] Alice Kate, **1963**; also son, Major Robert John Wigg, mur., on board below window, N.A. *XII*. Inscr. Kate Dreyer, 1961-**1980**, on window splay, S.A. *XIII*. Inscr. Cmdr. E.N. Haines, D.S.C., R.N., brother of J.R.S. H[aines], 1902-**1983**, on bench, Churchyard.

INDENTS & LOST BRASSES. 14. Indent, inscr., N.C. Inscr. 90 x 405 mm, slab 1685 x 715 mm.

Ref: *Brit. Lib. Stowe MS. 845*, f.68; *Burke's Peerage and Baronetage*, pp.1215-6; *M.B.S. Trans.*, V, p.286; *M.S.*, p.160; *Sadler, Dorset and Hampshire*, appx. I, pt.2, p.41; *Soc. Antiq. MS. 875/6*, p.40.

DUMMER, All Saints.

I. Inscr. in 6 Lat. vv. William Dommer and w. Elen, **1427**; now mur., in wooden frame, N. Inscr. 177 x 383 mm.

II. Inscr. Roger Gollde, clerk, rector, **1564**; formerly C., now N. *Baigent, F.J., Hist. of Wyke Church*, 1865, p.8. Inscr. 105 x 277 mm, slab 315 x 310 mm. Style: London G (script 10).

III. William at Moore *alias* Dommer, esq., born 13 Feb. 1508, a clerk of the lord mayor's court, comptroller of the chamber of London for above 50 years, [died 1595], date not filled in, in civil dress, with 1 son (head gone) who died in his infancy, and w. Kinborowe (eff. lost), dau. of Edmund Brydges of London, draper, engr. c.**1580**, all kng., inscr., ach. and 2 shs., mur., in Purbeck frame, C. *M.B.S. Trans.*, V, p.288. Male eff. and son 260 x 258 mm, female eff. indent 255 x 320 mm, inscr. 145 x 527 mm, ach. 183 x 157 mm, dext. sh. 126 x 109 mm, sin. sh. 129 x 109 mm, frame 715 x 685 mm. Style: Johnson (script 12).

IV. Inscr. in 8 Eng. vv., ach. and 2 shs. (1 mutil.) marking burial place of William at Moore and stating he was lord of the manor and patron of the ch., engr. c.**1580**, C. *M.B.S. Trans.*, V, p.289. Inscr. 169 x 549 mm, ach. 185 x 153 mm, dext. sh. 125 x 108 mm, sin. sh. 125 x 106 mm, Unio Purbeck slab 1800 x 860 mm.

V. Inscr. Allys Magewik "of Dumer wedow". **1591**; palimp., on rev. another inscr. to Robert Clerk, "quondam capellanus cantaris petri ffabiller in presenti ecclesia fundat", c.**1470**; discovered in 1889 under pews; formerly N., now mur., in reversible frame, Baptistry/N. *Palimpsests*, pl.132 (rev.). Inscr. 64 x 239 mm. Style: London G (script 12, obv.), London D (rev.).

Dummer I

Dummer III

Here lyeth the buryed Roger Gollde
Clarke and parson of Dumer who
Deceassed y e xlv day of November
in the yere of o r Lorde God. 1564.

Dummer II

I William at Moore Dommer calde, doe here intoumbed lye
And Lordshp this and of thys Churche, the patronage had I.
Myne Auncestors me longe before, wesre owners of the same
obtayned by matche w th Dommers heire. Wherof theye tooke y e name
w th name and livinge here on earthe as from them I possesse
Soe nowe in earthe like them I am, for wormes becomme a gueste
Thus (reader) deathe on me hath wrought that to mankynd is due
And like of thee by natures course, is sure for to ensue.

Dummer IV

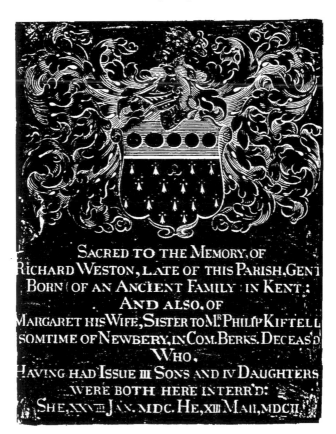

Here lyeth the body of Alice
Marmyon of Dimmer Widow
who dyed the xxij daye of
January Anno Dni 1591

Dummer V obverse

Hic iacet dns Robertus Clerk quondam
Capellanus Cantens pciii ffabnlle ?
pleoti eccia fundat cui aie pyciet ? ?

Dummer V palimpsest reverse

SACRED TO THE MEMORY, OF
RICHARD WESTON, LATE OF THIS PARISH, GENT
BORN OF AN ANCIENT FAMILY IN KENT;
AND ALSO, OF
MARGARET HIS WIFE, SISTER TO Mr. PHILIP KIFTELL
SOMTIME OF NEWBERY, IN COM. BERKS. DECEAS'D
WHO,
HAVING HAD ISSUE III SONS AND IV DAUGHTERS
WERE BOTH HERE INTERR'D:
SHE, XXVIII JAN. MDC. HE, XIII MAII, MDCII.

Dummer *VII*

115

VI. Inscr. Dennis, dau. of Henry Clarke of Goring, w. of Walter Pinke of Kempshot, **1621**, aged 38, had 3 sons and 5 daus., C. Inscr. 156 x 384 mm, slab 685 visible x 505 mm.

VII. Inscr. with ach. Richard Weston, gent., born in Kent, 1602, and w. Margaret, sister to Mr. Philip Kistell of Newbury, Berks., 1600, had 3 sons and 4 daus., mur., in stone frame, C., a modern restoration. Pl. 356 x 260 mm.

VIII. Inscr. with sh. and crest. Thomas [Terry], son of Michael Terry, grandson of [Rev.] Michael Terry, rector [for 38 years], **1829**, aged 88, and w. Elizabeth, only dau. of Robert Harding, of Upcott, Devon, 1811, aged 60, buried in family vault, pos. by 5 sons and 6 daus., mur., in stone frame, C. *IX.* Inscr. with verse on scroll-shaped pl. Edward Walter Blunt, of Kempshott Park, 1779-**1860**, mur., on marble, C. *X.* Inscr. with verse on scroll-shaped pl. Henry Blunt, 1823-**1862**, mur., on marble, C. *XI.* Inscr. Mary Elizabeth, eld. child of Rev. John Jenkins, chaplain to R.N., and w. Elizabeth Harding, died at Weymouth, [Dorset], **1868**, mur., C. *XII.* Inscr. Col. Robert Terry, 25th Regt., 3rd son of Thomas Terry, died at Winchester, **1869**, aged 87, maker's name COX & SON, LONDON, mur., on marble, C. *XIII.* Inscr. recording gift of lectern in **1890** by children in mem. of Rev. Sir William Dunbar, [6th] Bart., rector 1875-1881, [1804-1881], on lectern, N. *XIV.* Inscr. recording rebuilding of east end of the chancel in **1893** by family in mem. of Edward Walter Blunt, of Kempshott Park, and w. Janet Shirley, mur., C. *XV.* Inscr. recording east window pos. by w. Juliana, [eld. dau. of Sir John Ogilvy, 9th Bart.] in mem. of [Sir] Nelson Rycroft, 4th Bart., [D.L., High Sheriff 1881, 1831-]**1894**, copper, mur., C. *XVI.* Inscr. Capt. Llewellyn James Jones, [West India Regt. attd.] 7th [Battn.] East Surrey Regt., yst. son of Rev. George Jones, [M.A.], rector [1882-1926], and w. Rosamond Alice], died of wounds received in France, **1916**, [aged 34], buried at Bethune [Town] Cemetery, [France], mur., C. *XVII.* World War I memorial in raised letters on 2 pls. (13 names), bronze, on lychgate, Churchyard. *XVIII.* Inscr. E.R.C., **1921**, mur., on panelling, N. *XIX.* Inscr. Henry Roe and w. Julia Ann, **1925**, mur., on panelling, N. *XX.* Inscr. with sh., crest and motto recording completion of seating and wainscoting in mem. of [Sir] Richard Nelson Rycroft, 5th Bart., [D.L., High Sheriff 1899, patron], 1859-**1925**, on pew, N. Inscr. 345 x 210 mm. *XXI.* World War II memorial in raised letters (5 names), bronze, on lychgate with no.*XVII*, Churchyard. *XXII.* Inscr. recording that seating and panelling were made and completed in **1957** by Frederick Smith, mur., on panelling, Baptistry/N. *XXIII.* Inscr. S.R. Bailey, **1962**, on churchwardens' wand, N. *XXIV.* Inscr. I.G. Mitchell-Innes, **1978**, bronze, on bench, Churchyard. *XXV.* Inscr. Henry Archibald Taylor, churchwarden, 1892-**1980**, on prie-dieu, N. *XXVI.* Inscr. Marion Mitchell-Innes, engr. c.**1990**, on cupboard, Baptistry/N. *XXVII.* Inscr. "For the little people of Dummer Church from Pearl Kent **1998**", on lectern foot stand, N. *XXVIII.* Inscr. recording planting of "MILLENNIUM YEW" in **2001** by Sunday school children, bronze, on tree post, Churchyard. *XXIX.* Inscr. recording donation [of paschal candle] in **2003** by Clare Wilmot-Sitwell, copper, on paschal candle, C.

Ref: *Brit. Lib. Add. MS. 39964*, f.457; *Burke's Peerage and Baronetage*, p.853, p.2018, p.2331; *Haines*, II, p.72; *Heseltine, Heraldry*, p.36; *M.B.S. Trans.*, I, pt.9, p.27, IV, p.119, p.121, p.333, V, pp.286-91; *Mee, Hampshire*, p.138; *Moody*, pp.150-1; *M.S.*, p.160; *Palimpsests*, 308L1, p.74; *Soc. Antiq. MS. 875/6*, pp.40-5; *V.C.H., Hampshire*, III, p.359; *Warner*, I, p.207.

EASTON, St. Mary.

I. Inscr. on 2 pls. Agatha Barlow, [**1595**, aged about 90, dau. of Humphrey Welsborne, w. of William Barlow, Bishop of Chichester 1559-1568, by whom 2 sons, William and John and 5 daus., Margaret, Anne, Elizabeth, Frances, Antonine]; now mur., C. Inscrs. 90 x 585 mm and 135 x 585 mm.

*HERE LYETH Y BODY OF DENNIS PINKE WIFE OF
WALTER PINKE OF KEMPSHOT WHO HAD ISSVE
BY HIM 8 CHILDREN VIZ 3 SONNES AND V DAV
GHTERS SHE WAS THE DAVGHTER OF HENRY
CLARKE OF GORINGE AND DIED Y 27 OF NOV
1621 AT THE AGE OF 38 YEARES*

Dummer VI

This
seating and wainscoting
were completed to the
Glory of God
and in loving memory of
RICHARD NELSON RYCROFT
5th Baronet
Born December 12th 1859
Died October 25th 1925
C·A·P·D

FAYTHE HATHE NO FEAR

Dummer *XX*

HIC AGATHÆ TVMVLVS BARLOI, PRÆSVLIS INDE
EXVLIS, INDE HERVM PRÆSVLIS VXOR ERAT

PROLE BEATA FVIT, PLENA ANNIS, QVINQ SVARVM
PRÆSVLIBVS VIDIT, PRÆSVLIS IPSA DATAS.

Easton I

Easton V

118

In piam memoriam Algernon Wodehouse Ecclesiæ Rectoris ab anno Dm̄ Jesu Christi MDCCCLVIII ad MDCCCLXXXII ejus operâ Ædes hæc sacrosancta ad majorem Dei gloriam reparata et ornata est posuerunt amici.

Easton *IV*

II. Inscr. recording [south-east chancel] window and 3 apse windows filled with glass in mem. of Martha Ann Stocker, 1809-**1860**, on window splay, C. *III*. Inscr. Minnie Du Boulay, **1868**, on lectern, N. *IV*. [Rev.] Algernon Wodehouse, [M.A.], rector 1858-1882, [1814-]**1882**, hf. eff. in mass vests. and inscr. in Lat., mur., on marble, C. Eff. 324 x 187 mm, inscr. 178 x 385 mm. *V*. Angel holding inscr. on scroll. Rev. Benjamin Pidcock, [B.A., 1st vicar of St. Luke's, Leek, Staffs. 1845-1882], rector for 17 years [1882-1899], **1899**, aged 81, pos. by parishioners, maker's name JONES & WILLIS, mur., on marble in wooden frame, N. Pl. 445 x 447 mm. *VI*. Inscr. Harriet Emma Dawson, ch. worshipper for 41 years, **1915**, aged 89, mur., on picture frame, N. *VII*. World War I memorial (9 names) and who served (49 names) on 2 pls., on lychgate, Churchyard. *VIII*. Inscr. [Rev.] John Minet Freshfield, [M.A.], rector [1899-1919, 1835-1924], and w. Harriet Louisa, [1839-**1926**], mur., in stone frame, C. See also Martyr Worthy no.*XI*. *IX*. Inscr. [Miss] Anne Seaber Harris, "A MUSICIAN WHO LIVED HER WHOLE LIFE AT GRASMERE EASTON", 1903-**1977**, on organ console, C. *X*. Inscr. recording purchase of organ (replacing a pipe organ orig. built for the Preparatory School of Eastbourne Coll. to commem. the coronation of Queen Elizabeth II in 1953 and purchased by parishioners in 1997 through a [legacy] in mem. of no.*IX*) in **2003** by generosity of Rev. Jenni, Lady Napier on departure as asst. clergy of the Itchen Valley Benefice in 2001, on organ console with no.*IX*, C.

Ref: *Duthy*, p.207; *M.B.S. Trans.*, V, p.295; *Mee, Hampshire*, pp.143-4; *M.S.*, p.160; *Soc. Antiq. MS. 875/6*, p.46.

ELING, St. Mary the Virgin.

I. Inscr. and 3 shs. William, son of Sir Chidiock Pawlet of the noble and illustrious house of Pawlet of Basing, **1596**; mar. Dulcebel, dau. of James Paget of Powlton, had 5 sons and 3 daus.; missing for many years, said to have been found in the builder's yard of Messrs. Crook and returned in 1902; formerly mur., in wooden frame, N.C.; in 2007 in wooden frame loose in N.C. Inscr. 307 x 510 mm, dext. sh. 193 x 175 mm, centre. sh. 200 x 171 mm, sin. sh. 199 x 172 mm.

II. Inscr. Edward Coxwell, clerk [of the New Forest Union at Lyndhurst Road] for 46 years, 1805-**1880**, pos. by Board of Guardians of the New Forest Union, "HIS MANY FRIENDS IN THE COUNTY, AND NEIGHBOURHOOD OF SOUTHAMPTON, HAVE JOINED IN THIS TOKEN OF RESPECT FOR HIS MEMORY", mur., S.A. *III*. Inscr. recording presentation of [east north chapel] window in **1889** by w. to Rev. Joseph Clarke, M.A., of Corpus Christi Coll., Camb., "The last Vicar of the Entire Civil Parish of Eling", [vicar 1885-1897], maker's name G.T. YOUNG, ENGRAVER, SOUTHAMPTON, mur., below window, N.C. See also Bournemouth, St. Andrew no.*V*. *IV*. Inscr. recording [north-west north aisle] window filled with glass in **1898** by children and Charles Jupp, brother of Elizabeth Ashby, in mem. of Francis Stedman Ashby and [w.] Elizabeth Rebecca, on window splay, N.A. *V*. Inscr. recording glass in [west south aisle] window pos. in **1898** by friends and parishioners in mem. of Rev. Joseph Clarke, M.A., vicar 1885-1897, mur., on marble, S.A. *VI & VII*. Two inscrs. "For the Altar of Eling St. Mary E.G.T. **1899**", on candlesticks, C. *VIII*. Inscr. with Lat. verse. Trooper John Godden, C.-in-C.'s Body Guard, killed in action near Lindley, S[outh] Africa, **1901**, aged 24, maker's name J. WIPPELL & COMPᵞ EXETER & LONDON, mur., S.A. *IX*. Inscr. recording gift [of font cover] in **1905** by Bertha Alice Ashby, on font cover, S.A. *X*. Inscr. with Lat. verse. John Player, churchwarden for 24 years, **1906**, aged 66, mur., S.A. *XI*. Inscr. with verse. Percy Waldron, only son of Mrs. Eva Waldron, widow, "WITH THE CAPTAIN AND FOURTEEN OTHERS OF THE CREW, PERISHED IN THE SHIPWRECK OF THE

GVLIELMO PAWLET
DOMINI CHIDIOCH. PAWLET FILIO NOBILI ET
ILLVSTRI PAWLETTORVM DE BASING FAMILIA ORIVNDO
VIRO SVMMÆ HVMANITATIS ET CONSTANTIÆ IN AMICOS
AMORIS ET FIDELIN CONIVGEM PIETATIS IN DEV LAVDE
ORNATO CVM EX DVLCE BELLA PAGET FILIA IACOBI
PAGET DE POWLTON FOEMINA VT CONIVGII VINCVLO
SIC CONIVGALIVM VIRTVTVM LAVDE SIBI CONIVNCTIS
SIMA QVINQVE FILIOS ET TRES FILIAS SVSCEPISSET
IN ANNO ÆTATIS SVÆ XLII MORTE IMMATVRA PERCVS=
SO CHARISSIMA CONIVX LVGENS MOERENSQVE POSVIT
OBIIT IN DOMINO ANNO TEMPORIS NOVISSIMI
CIƆ IƆ XCVI VII DIE IANVARII

Eling I

Ellingham I

"SWANHILDA", OFF STATEN ISLAND, TERRA DEL FUEGO", **1910**, aged 18, maker's name H. ROSE & SON. SOUTHAMPTON, mur., S.A. *XII.* Inscr. William Taylor, master of the New Forest Union at Lyndhurst Road for 26 years, died at Shirley, **1912**, [aged 79], mur., S.A. *XIII.* Inscr. with verse. Frederick Walter Godwin, aged 34; William Thomas Fox, aged 27; and Tom Warwick, aged 25, of the par.; also Boysie Richard Russell, of Redbridge, aged 17½, and William Edward Hine, of Lyndhurst, aged 36, "LOST IN THE FOUNDERING OF THE S.S. "TITANIC", AFTER COLLISION WITH AN ICEBERG IN THE NORTH ATLANTIC AT MIDNIGHT, APRIL 14TH **1912**, WHEN MORE THAN FIFTEEN HUNDRED OF THE PASSENGERS & CREW WERE DROWNED", maker's name ROSE & Co. SOUTHAMPTON, mur., S.A. *XIV.* Inscr. George Duell, died on S.S. Kildonan Castle, **1913**, aged 38, buried at sea, maker's name ROSE & Co., mur., S.A. *XV.* Inscr. Lt.-Col. Courtenay Bruce, 6th Dragoon Guards (Carabiniers), of Testwood and Brooke House, Winchfield, **1914**, pos. by son, C.M.A. B[ruce], and dau., M.M.H., bronze, mur., on pillar, N./S.A. *XVI.* Inscr. "To the Glory of God and the Honour & Fame of the men of this Parish who fell in the war, 1914-**1918**", on screen C. *XVII.* World War I memorial (59 names), mur., N./S.A. *XVIII.* Inscr. with verse. Ethel Julia Goddard (Mrs. Wilson), Sunday school teacher for many years, ch. member, died at Cromwell, Otago, N[ew] Z[ealand], **1920**, aged 28, mur., S.A. *XIX.* Inscr. recording gift of [south-west south aisle] window in mem. of Dr. John Forbes Campbell, physician in the district for 25 years, **1945**, maker's name F. OSBORNE & CO LTD London, on window splay, S.A. *XX.* Inscr. with Lat. verse recording installation and dedication of lighting in mem. of [Rev.] Robert Jack Hitchcock, M.A., vicar 1936-**1951**, and w. Hilda Caroline, maker's name F OSBORNE & CO · LTD · London W.C.1, mur., on board, S.A. *XXI & XXII.* Two inscrs. [recording pedestals were] made by Jack Lawrence, **1961**, on pedestals, S.A. *XXIII.* Inscr. with verse. Sydney Walter Gurr, **1970**, aged 74, bronze, on grave marker, Churchyard. *XXIV.* Inscr. David Munday, 1940-**1971**, copper, on flowerstand, S.C. *XXV.* Inscr. recording gift [of piano] in **1986** by son, John [Lightfoot], and dau., Rosalind, in mem. of Nora A. Lightfoot, on piano, S.A. *XXVI.* Inscr. Rose Ireland, 1900-**1989**, bronze, on gravestone, Churchyard. *XXVII.* Inscr. William Edward Ireland, 1900-**1990**, bronze, on gravestone with no.*XXVI*, Churchyard. *XXVIII.* Inscr. Alice and Leslie Benson, engr. c.**2005**, bronze, on bench, Churchyard.

Ref: *Bullar, J., A Companion in a Tour round Southampton*, 1809, p.142; *Heseltine, Heraldry*, pp.36-7; *M.B.S. Trans.*, V, pp.295-6; *M.S.*, p.160; *Soc. Antiq. MS. 875/6*, pp.46-7; *Squibb*, p.214; *V.C.H., Hampshire*, IV, p.557.

ELLINGHAM, St. Mary and All Saints.

I. Inscr. Richard Puncherd, c.**1465**, C. Inscr. 47 x 190 mm, slab 1480 x 690 mm. Style: London D.

II. Inscr. with verse recording gift of [east] window by Caroline [Susan Augusta], Countess of Normanton, [w. of James Charles Herbert Welbore Ellis Agar, 3rd Earl of Normanton, M.A., D.L.], in mem. of mother, Jane Eliz[abe]th, Viscountess Barrington, [4th dau. of Sir Thomas Henry Liddell, 1st Baron Ravensworth, w. of William Keppel Barrington, 6th Viscount Barrington], ch. benefactress, **1883**, [aged 78], maker's name HART, SON, PEARD & CO LONDON, on window splay, C. *III.* Inscr. recording gift [of chandelier] by dau., Violet, in mem. of Frederic Fane, of Moyle's Court, and [w.] Fanny Eliza, worshipped in the ch. for many years, engr. c.**1885**, on chandelier, N. *IV.* Inscr. Rev. F[rederick Stephan] Trevor-Garrick, M.A., vicar 1892-**1898**, pos. by friends and parishioners; in 2006 loose in N. Inscr. 280 x 584 mm. *V.* Inscr. with Eng. and Lat. verse. Henry William John [Byng], 4th Earl of Strafford, K.C.V.O., C.B.,

1831-**1899**, pos. by dau., Amy [Frederica Alice], Countess of Normanton, [w. of Sidney James Agar, 4th Earl of Normanton, D.L.], mur., C. *VI.* Inscr. Laura Maria Marshall Wallis, of Blashford House, **1954**, bronze, on wooden cross, Churchyard. *VII.* Inscr. recording restoration of lamp in **1988** in mem. of Richard Hooper Archer, 1904-1983, and [w.] Margaret Evelyn (Peggy), 1907-1988, worshipped in the par., bronze, on gate post, Churchyard. *VIII.* Inscr. Bernard Caleb Wells, 1912-**1992**, on wooden cross, Churchyard. *IX.* Inscr. recording restoration of organ in **1994** in mem. of Clementia Raikes, soloist, benefactress, 1914-1994, on organ, C. *X.* Inscr. recording affiliation of ch. choir in **2003** to the Royal School of Church Music; Paul Wilkins, choirmaster and organist, on organ with no.*IX*, C.

Ref: *Brit. Lib. Add. MS. 39965,* f.120; *Burke's Peerage and Baronetage*, p.188, p.1985, p.226, p.2548.

EVERSLEY, St. Mary the Virgin.

I. Large cross and inscr. Richard Pendilton, servant to Giles, Lord Dawbney, chamberlain to Henry VII, **1502**, curious; in 2006 partly covered by foot pace of altar, C. *Fuller*, p.25 (photo.); *M.B.S. Portfolio*, II, pl.33; *Norris, Craft*, fig.238; *Portfolio Book*, pl.262. Cross 1915 x 670 mm, inscr. 87 x 564 mm, Purbeck slab 2180 visible x 925 mm. Style: London G.

II. Inscr. in Lat. Thomas Walker, **1859**, aged 59, mur., below window, N. *III.* Inscr. Charlotte Maria Froude, 1860, and John Ashley Warre, 1860, [pos.] in **1865** by C. W[arrc], mur., below window, N.C. *IV.* Inscr. on 3 pls. Rt. Hon. Thomas Erskine, [3rd son of Thomas Erskine, 1st Baron Erskine, 1788-1864], and w. Henrietta Eliza, [only dau. of Henry Trail, 1865]; also eld. son, Henry Trail [Erskine, 1815-1865, pos. in] **1867**, on font plinth, N.A. *V.* Inscr. in Lat. recording restoration of church in **1875** by friends and parishioners in mem. of [Rev. Canon] Charles Kingsley, [M.A., hon.] canon of St. Peter, Westminster, [hon. canon of Chester Cathedral, chaplain-in-ordinary to Queen Victoria], rector for 31 years [1844-1875, author of *Westward Ho!* (1855) and *The Water-Babies* (1863), 1819-1875]; formerly mur., Tower, now mur., on marble, N.A. *Fuller*, p.17 (photo.). *VI.* Inscr. Henry Neville Oldfield, drowned near Henley-on-Thames, **1877**, aged 24, mur., below window, N. *VII.* Inscr. with 2 shs., 2 crests and 2 mottos. [Rev. Canon] Charles Kingsley, [M.A.], eld. son of [Rev.] Charles Kingsley, M.A., rector of Chelsea, and w. Mary Lucas, [hon.] canon of [St. Peter], Westminster, rector [1844-1875], born at Holne, Devon, died at Eversley, 1819-1875, and w. Frances Eliza, dau. of Pascoe Grenfell, of Taplow, Bucks., and w. Hon. Georgina St. Leger, born at Taplow, died at Tachbrook, Warks., 1814-**1891**, pos. by dau., Rose Georgiana Kingsley, maker's name FRANK SMITH & CO. LONDON, mur., on marble, N. *VIII.* Cross and inscr. Rev. Sir William Henry Cope, [12th] Bart., [M.A.], of Bramshill, [only son of Lt.-Gen. Edmund Reilly Cope and w. Maria, dau. of James Furber, rector of Easton], 1811-**1892**, pos. by widow, [Harriet Margaret, 2nd dau. of Robert Jaffray Hautenville], maker's name John Hardman & C[o] Birm[m], mur., on marble, N.C. *IX.* Inscr. with Koranic verse. Mary Henrietta, dau. of George Kingsley, M.D. and w. Mary, niece of [Rev. Canon] Charles Kingsley, rector [1844-1875], traveller and author, born at Islington, [Middx.], died at Simon's Town, Cape Colony "WHERE SHE WAS MINISTERING TO THE NEEDS OF THE FEVER-STRICKEN PRISONERS TAKEN IN THE BOER WAR, AND BURIED AT SEA WITH NAVAL HONOURS", 1862-**1900**, pos. by brother, Charles George Kingsley; uncle, William Bailey; and cousins, Maurice Kingsley, Rose Kingsley and Mary St. Leger Harrison, maker's name FRANK SMITH & C[O.] LONDON, mur., on marble, N.A. Inscr. 681 x 958 mm. *X.* Inscr. in raised letters. George Lillie Craik, of Kitscroft, **1905**, aged 68, mur., below window,

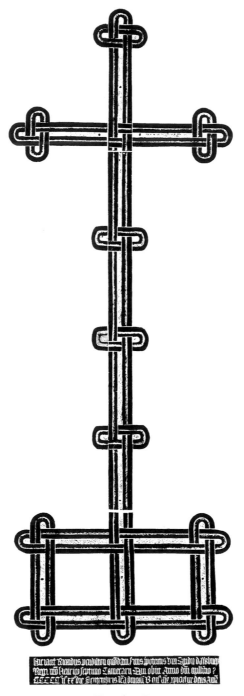

Eversley I

124

To the Glory of God
and to the Beloved Memory of
MARY HENRIETTA KINGSLEY
TRAVELLER AND AUTHOR
Daughter of George Kingsley M.D. and Mary his wife,
and Niece of Charles Kingsley sometime Rector of this Parish
Born 13th of October 1862 in the Parish of Islington
Died 3rd of June 1900 at Simon's Town, Cape Colony,
where she was ministering to the needs of the fever-stricken
prisoners taken in the Boer War, and buried at sea with naval honours.

"Talent de bien faire."

This Brass was erected by her brother Charles George Kingsley, her uncle William Bailey,
and her cousins Maurice Kingsley, Rose Kingsley, and Mary St. Leger Harrison.

Eversley *IX*

HERE LYETH INCLOSED THE BODY OF M ALICE
READE WIFE VNTO ROBERT READE OF LINKEN
HOLT GENT: BEINGE DAVGHTER & SOLE HEYRE
VNTO FRAVNCES POOLY ESQVIRE SHE DEPARTED
THIS LIFE THE 12. DAY OF OCTOBER A° DÑI 1598.

TERRA TENET TERRA, CONSVMVNT TEMPORA CORPVS,
SED TVA STAT VIRTVS SPIRITVS ASTRA TENET.

Faccombe I

N.A. *XI*. Inscr. recording presentation [of lectern] in **1905** by Lady Glass, maker's name JONES & WILLIS, on lectern, N. *XII*. Inscr. Lady Glass, of Warbrook, benefactress for 40 years, **1915**, pos. by friends "near her sitting in Church", maker's name A.& N. AUX C.S.L. LONDON, mur., N. *XIII*. Inscr. with verse and regt. insignia. 2nd-Lt. Archibald Arthur Tindal, [177th Brigade], R[oyal] F[ield] A[rtillery], of Gunyan, Queensland, son of C[harles] F[rederick] Tindal, of Ramornie, [Clarence River, Armidale], N[ew] S[outh] W[ales, Australia], grandson of C.G. Tindal, killed in action near Guillemont, France, 1888-**1916**, [buried at Guillemont Road Cemetery, Guillemont, France], mur., N. *XIV*. Inscr. with Lat. verse and regt. insignia. Gunner John Humphrey Tindal, B.A.(Camb.), [158, 134th Heavy Battery], R[oyal] G[arrison] A[rtillery], son of J[ohn] T. Tindal [and w. Mary I.], of Tatiara, Glen Innes, N[ew] S[outh] W[ales, Australia], grandson of C.G. Tindal, died of fever while on active service at Morogoro, [Tanzania], East Africa, 1889-**1917**, [buried at Morogoro Cemetery, Tanzania, East Africa], mur., N. *XV*. Inscr. with verse, sh., crest, motto and regt. insignia. Capt. Louis Nicolas Lindsay Tindal, M.C., 2nd Battn. Devonshire Regt., born at Ramornie, Clarence River, [Armidale], N[ew] S[outh] W[ales, Australia], killed in action] at Bois des Buttes, [France], 1895-**1918**, mur., N. *XVI*. Inscr. Rev. Henry Mosley, M.A., rector 1901-1917, pos. in **1923** by w., maker's name HERBERT WAUTHER del · F. OSBORNE & CO LTD London, mur., N. *XVII*. Inscr. with verse and regt. insignia. Lt. Charles Henry Tindal, M.C., R[oyal] F[ield] A[rtillery], eld. son of C[harles] F[rederick] Tindal, of Ramornie, [Clarence River, Armidale], New South Wales, [Australia], grandson of C.G. Tindal, "DIED OF SHELL SHOCK CONTRACTED IN THE WAR", 1887-**1926**, mur., N. *XVIII*. Inscr. recording presentation of communion rails in **1929** by Eversley Branch of the [Royal] British Legion, on altar rail, N.C. *XIX*. Inscr. Annie Boyde, engr. c.**1930**, on banner stand, N.C. *XX*. Inscr. Ven. Richard Cuthbert Rudgard, O.B.E., rector 1946-1960, [archdeacon of Basingstoke, 1901-]**1985**, pos. by members of the Young People's Fellowship "of which he was the founder", mur., N. *XXI*. Inscr. Ianthe Kershaw, [resident] 1929-1984, 1890-**1986**, on stall, N. *XXII*. Inscr. recording presentation [of bench] in **2001** by Eversley [Branch of the] Royal British Legion, on bench, Churchyard. *XXIII*. Inscr. recording presentation in **2004** by Eversley [Branch of the Royal] British Legion, on altar rail with no.*XVIII*, N.C.

Ref: *Brit. Lib. Add. MS. 39965*, f.186; *Burke's Peerage and Baronetage*, p.398, p.640; *Fuller, G. and R., The Story of Eversley Church*, 2004, pp.16-7, pp.19-20; *Gawthorp*, p.89; *Haines*, I, p.96, p.222, II, p.72; *M.B.S. Trans.*, V, p.296, XII, p.120; *Mee, Hampshire*, p.156; *M.S.*, p.160; *Norris, Memorials*, p.197; *Simpson*, p.28; *Soc. Antiq. MS. 875/6*, p.47; *V.C.H., Hampshire*, IV, p.40.

EWHURST, St. Mary the Virgin (redundant).

Inscr. Winifred, w. (1) of John Beconshaw, by whom John and Amy, (2) of Richard Ailif, **1570**, mur., C.; now deposited with Hampshire County Museum Service, Winchester (q.v.). *Bod. Lib. MS. Rubbings Phillips/Robinson* 485; *M.B.S. Bulletin*, 33, p.42.

I. Inscr. Rob[er]t Arthur, **1761**, aged 56, and w. Mary Eliz[abe]th, 1752, aged 30; also dau. Caroline, 1761, aged 12, [buried] in [churchyard] vault, mur., in stone frame, north wall outside C. *II*. Inscr. with verse. Mary Elizabeth, dau. of Robert Arthur and w. Mary Elizabeth, [buried] in a vault in St. James's ch., Westminster, Middx., w. of Robert Mackreth, **1784**, aged 39, mur., in marble frame, N.Tr. *III*. Inscr. with verse. Mary Eliz[abe]th, [dau. of Robert Arthur and w. Mary Elizabeth], w. of Rob[er]t Mackreth, **1784**, aged 39, [buried] in [churchyard] vault, mur., in stone frame, north wall outside C. *IV*. Inscr. "REMOVD by a FACULTY, from a VAULT in the *PARISH CHURCH* of S^T *JAMES WESTMINSTER*, and INTERRED in a VAULT UNDERNEATH, June y^e

2ᴅ *1786*"; in 2006 loose against north wall outside C. Inscr. 128 x 470 mm. *V.* Inscr. "The Ayliffe Vault", engr. c.**1875**, on step, C.

Ref: *Bod. Lib. MS. Rubbings Phillips/Robinson* 485; *Historical Metallurgy*, XVIII, pp.44-9; *M.B.S. Bulletin*, 33, pp.42-3.

Ch. built, 1873-4; declared redundant, 1971.

EXTON, SS. Peter and Paul.

I. Inscr. on lozenge-shaped pl. Francis Herbert Biddulph, died at Colon, Panama, **1883**, on lectern, N. *II & III.* Two inscrs. on sh.-shaped pls. recording [light brackets] pos. in **1910** by congregation in mem. of R.A.P. Bouverie Campbell-Wyndham, on light brackets, N.

FACCOMBE, St. Barnabas (new church).

I. Inscr. and 2 Lat. vv. Alice, dau. and h. of Frances Pooly, esq., w. of Robert Reade of Linkenholt, gent., **1598**, mur., N. Inscr. 145 x 533 mm, vv. 67 x 533 mm.

II. Inscr. recording restoration and completion of tower in **1897** by Mrs. [Ann Jane, w. of Rev.] C[harles] H[enry] Everett, [B.A., rector 1858-1896], maker's name *J. WIPPELL & COMPᵧ EXETER & LONDON*, mur., Tower. *III.* Inscr. recording presentation and dedication of organ in **1928** by H.J. Horn, of Faccombe Manor; [Rev.] J[ohn] Morris, [M.A.], rector [1911-1945]; J. Froome and H.B. Briant, churchwardens, mur., on board, N. *IV.* Inscr. recording installation of electric light in **1938** by parishioners subscription as "A THANK OFFERING FOR THE PRESERVATION OF PEACE", mur., Tower. *V.* Inscr. recording gift of chancel panelling and pulpit by S[ophia] I[sabelle (Zoe), 2nd dau. of Lionel Edward Massey, 5th Baron Clarina, 1888-1977], in mem. of husband, Hon. Eric B[rand] Butler Henderson, [6th son of Sir Alexander Henderson, 1st Bart., 1st Baron Faringdon, C.H., J.P., High Sheriff of Northants. 1929, 1884-]**1953**, copper, on pulpit, C. *VI.* Inscr. recording erection [of lychgate] by S[ophia] I[sabelle (Zoe), 2nd dau. of Lionel Edward Massey, 5th Baron Clarina, 1888-1977], in mem. of husband, Hon. Eric B[rand] Butler Henderson, [6th son of Sir Alexander Henderson, 1st Bart., 1st Baron Faringdon, C.H., J.P., High Sheriff of Northants. 1929, 1884-]**1953**, copper, on lychgate, Churchyard.

Ref: *Burke's Peerage and Baronetage*, p.986; *M.B.S. Trans.*, V, pp.296-7; *M.S.*, p.160, p.753; *Soc. Antiq. MS. 875/6*, pp.47-8; *V.C.H., Hampshire*, IV, p.318.

Ch. built, 1866.

FAREHAM, SS. Peter and Paul.

I. Inscr. with sh. Constance, dau. of Richard Hooke, gent., w. of Thomas Riggs, gent., **1653**, aged 33, mur., in wooden frame, old C., now N.C. Inscr. 314 x 261 mm.

II. Inscr. Eleanor Douglas, **1877**, aged 87, pos. by dau., Ann, widow of John Edward Paddon, mur., S.Tr. *III.* Inscr. Rear-Admiral Richard Carter, 4th son of Joseph and Caroline Carter, of

Forton House, Alverstoke, died at Fareham, **1887**, on window splay, N.C. *IV.* Inscr. recording dedication of [south-west chancel] window in **1897** by family and friends in mem. of William Kelsall, choirmaster 1855-1893, mur., below window, C. *V.* Inscr. with verse. Frances Harriet Gittens, chorister "FOR A LONG PERIOD", acting secretary of the Industrial Home for Girls "FOR UPWARDS OF 20 YEARS", **1909**, mur., S.Tr. *VI.* Inscr. Edgar Goble, vicar's [church]warden for 23 years, "BY HIS UNFAILING CHEERFULNESS HE BRIGHTENED THE LIVES OF ALL WHO KNEW HIM", **1909**, aged 71, mur., N.C. *VII.* Inscr. Mary Prideaux-Brune, 1870-**1957**, copper, on prie-dieu, N.A.

Ref: *Brit. Lib. Add. MS. 39965,* ff.280-3, *Stowe MS. 845*, f.141; *Heseltine, Heraldry*, p.37; *M.B.S. Trans.*, V, p.297; *M.S.*, p.160; *Soc. Antiq. MS. 875/6*, p.48.

FARLEY CHAMBERLAYNE, St. John.

I. Inscr. recording presentation [of pulpit] in **1910** by parishioners on restoration of ch., on pulpit, N. *II.* Inscr. Arthur Davis, churchwarden for many years, **1917**, aged 72, pos. by w. and family, mur., N. *III.* Inscr. recording dedication of [north-east chancel] window in mem. of mother, Jane, w. of [Rev.] William Henry Woodham, [B.A., curate 1862-1908], **1918**; also brothers, Capt. Charles Burnett Woodham, D.S.O., [1st Battn.] Duke of Cornwall's Light Infantry, [1915, aged 40, buried at First D.C.L.I. Cemetery, The Bluff, Ieper, West Vlaanderen, Belgium], and [Pte.] Ernest Woodham, [2755, 32nd Battn.] Australian Imp[eria]l Force, [1917, aged 35, buried at Bernafay Wood British Cemetery, Montauban, France], on window splay, C. *IV.* Inscr. Lucy Chapman, organist for 54 years, **1971**, pos. by parishioners, mur., on board, C.

FARLINGTON, or DRAYTON, Church of the Resurrection.

I. Inscr. recording gift of organ and sanctuary furniture in **1930** by Sir Heath and Lady Harrison, bronze, mur., C. *II.* Inscr. in raised letters recording presentation of font and cover in **1931** in mem. of John Edmund Bevis and Walter Louis Rogers, husband and nephew of Emma Duncan Bevis, bronze, on font plinth, N. *III.* Inscr. Richard James Dannan, 1951, aged 74, and [w.] Louisa Mary, **1966**, aged 85, mur., on board, S.A. *IV.* Inscr. with verse recording resiting of font in **1977** by Bella Offord in mem. of husband, Granville Offord; also parents, John Thomas and [w.] Isabella and godparents, on font plinth with no.*II*, N.

Ch. built, 1930.

FARLINGTON, St. Andrew.

I. Inscr. and sh. Antony Pounde of Drayton, esq., **1547**, mur., C. Inscr. 129 x 613 mm, sh. 183 x 155 mm. Style: London G (script 3).

II. Inscr. Gen. Sir Thomas Holloway, K.C.B., R.M.A., 1810-**1875**, mur., below window, N.A. *III.* Inscr. in Lat. J.S. Taylor, **1892**, worn, on ewer, N. *IV.* Inscr. with Lat. verse in raised letters with sh. in relief. Capt. Christopher Anthony Rowlandson Hodgson, 3rd Battn. Royal Warwickshire Regt., [son of Arthur Pemberton Hodgson], killed in action at Fleurbaix, France, **1914**, aged 41, pos. by w., brother and sisters, maker's name SAWIER DUBLIN, mur., N. *V.* Inscr.

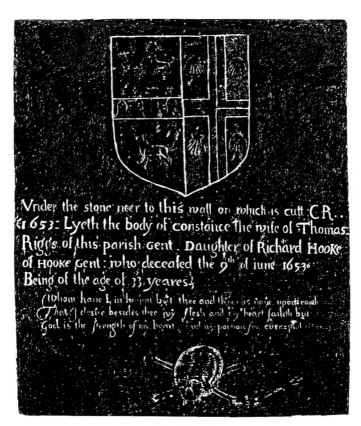

Vnder the stone neer to this wall on which is cutt :C.R.
1653: Lyeth the body of constonce the wife of Thomas
Riggs of this parish Gent. Daughter of Richard Hooke
of Hooke Gent: who deceased the 9th of iune 1653.
Being of the age of 33, yeares.

Whom haue I in heauen but thee and there is none vpon earth
That I desire besides thee my flesh and my heart faileth but
God is the strength of my heart and my portion for euer=psal

Fareham I

Of yo' charite pray for the Soule of Antony Pownde
of Drayton in the Countie of Suht Esquyer whiche
deceassd the xix day of february in the yere of our
lorde God M cccc xlviij on whose soule Iht haue mercy

Farlington I

129

with verse and 3 regt. insignia. Capt. Herbert Vesey Scott, [3rd Battn.] Rifle Brigade, Brigade-Major 17th Infantry Brigade, [son of Rev. Francis Montgomery Scott, M.A. and w. Anna Matilda], died at Wimereux, [France], **1915**, [aged 34], maker's name SAWIER *DUBLIN*, [buried at Wimereux Communal Cemetery, France], mur., on marble, N. *VI*. Inscr. with verse. [Pte.] John William Tidnam, [81888, 2nd Battn. Canadian Infantry (East Ontario Regt.)], Canadian Expeditionary Force, only son [of Mr. and Mrs. W.S. Tidman], killed at Ploegsteert, Belgium, **1915**, aged 26, [buried at Strand Military Cemetery], maker's name FOSTER SOUTHSEA, mur., N. *VII*. Inscr. recording gift of electric organ blower in **1949** by organist, Phyllis White, bronze, on organ, Organ Chamber. *VIII*. Inscr. recording fitting of electric [organ] blower by subscriptions from members, friends and residents in the district of St. Patrick's, [Milton], to commem. the coronation of Queen Elizabeth II [in **1953**]; Rev. R[onald] H[erbert] Wills, priest-in-charge; E.E.H. Day, organist, on organ with no.*VII*, Organ Chamber. *IX*. Inscr. recording dedication of electric organ blower in **1953** by Ven. J.K. Roberts, archdeacon of Portsmouth, on organ with nos.*VII* & *VIIII*, Organ Chamber. *X*. Inscr. Ben and Theo Pearson, 1907-**1995**, bronze, on bench, Churchyard. *XI*. Inscr. recording donation of organ by congregation of St. Patrick's, Milton, and installation in **1995** through legacy of Leonard Weir, on organ with nos.*VII, VIII & IX*, Organ Chamber. *XII*. Inscr. James Day, 1933-**1999**, bronze, on bench, Churchyard. *XIII*. Inscr. recording donation of Robina Frisia by Farlington and District Garden Club in mem. of Eric W. Baker, 1925-**2002**, bronze, on tree post, Churchyard.

Ref: *Heseltine, Heraldry*, p.37; *M.B.S. Trans.*, V, pp.297-8; *M.S.*, p.161; *Simpson*, p.28; *Soc. Antiq. MS. 875/6*, pp.48-9; *V.C.H., Hampshire*, III, p.151.

FARNBOROUGH, St. Mark.

I. Inscr. recording erection of pulpit by A.M. Harrison in mem. of [Rev. Canon Dr.] John Griffith, D.D., [hon.] canon of Rochester Cathedral 1827-1872, 1789-**1879**, on pulpit, N. *II*. Inscr. recording presentation [of font] in **1881** by Rev. I.H. Clayton, M.A., rector, on font plinth, Baptistry/N. *III*. Inscr. recording thank offering in **1891** by Edward Chatfield, on lectern, N. *IV*. Inscr. recording erection of [north-east north aisle] window in mem. of Arthur Farrant, 1884-**1891**, mur., N.A. *V*. Jessie Margaret, w. of Rev. Arthur S[utton] Valpy, M.A., [hon.] canon of Winchester Cathedral, rector of Farnborough when ch. was built and consecrated [1878-1882], **1897**, pos. by friends, rect. pl., canopy and inscr. partly on base of stepped cross, maker's name BARKENTIN & KRALL LONDON, mur., N. *VI*. Inscr. recording dedication of west window by Edward Chatfield, benefactor, **1899**, aged 84, in mem. of w. Ann, 1897, aged 84, maker's name HART · SON · PEARD · & · Cᴼ · Lᴰ · LONDON, mur., on board, Baptistry/N. *VII*. Inscr. Frances Horatia Grimston, **1906**, on lectern, N.C. *VIII*. Inscr. Arthur Michael Leaney, chorister and server, **1911**, aged 16, mur., on board, C. *IX*. Inscr. with verse in raised letters and regt. insignia in relief. Brig.-Gen. Neil Douglas Findlay, [C.B.], Royal Artillery, [son of Thomas Dunlop Findlay, of Easterhill, Lanarkshire], served in the Hazara Expedition 1888 and South Africa 1899-1900, killed in action in France while commanding the artillery of the 1st Division, **1914**, [aged 55, pos. by w. Alma], bronze, mur., on panelling, N.C. *X*. Inscr. with Lat. verse in raised letters and enamelled regt. insignia in relief. Col. John Gerald Panton, C.M.G., Royal Sussex Regt., **1915**, aged 54, mur., on marble, S.A. *XI*. Lt.-Col. Geoffrey Charles Shakerley, D.S.O., 1st Battn. King's Royal Rifle Corps, killed in action at Richebourg L'Avoue, France, 1869-1915; also brother, Capt. Eric Piers, [6th Battn. attd. 1st Battn. King's Royal Rifle Corps], killed in action at Givenchy, France, 1885-**1915**, [sons of Geoffrey Joseph Shakerley and w. Emma], pos. by Marjory, w. of Geoffrey Charles Shakerley, eff. of army officer in uniform, canopy, inscr., 2 verses, 2 enamelled shs. and marg. inscr., [designed by

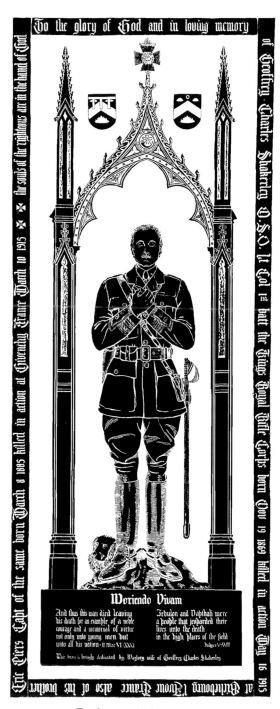

John Byam Shaw], N.C. Eff. 1073 x 379 mm, canopy 1617 x 554 mm, inscr. 222 x 591 mm, dext. sh. 108 x 88 mm, sin. sh. 108 x 88 mm, marg. inscr. 1982 x 764 x 51 mm, slab 2130 x 915 mm. *XII.* Inscr. with verse in raised letters and regt. insignia. Major George Nicholson Saunders, 3rd [Regt. of] Punjab Infantry, 1833-1875, and w. Frances Rachel, 1836-**1917**, bronze, mur., on panelling, N.C. *XIII.* Inscr. Frances Gwendoline Hughes, pos. in **1930** by friend, N.K.N., on prie-dieu, N.C. *XIV.* Inscr. recording gift of clock by dau. in mem. of George John Wallis, 1898, and [w.] Susan Elizabeth, **1940**, mur., on pillar, N. *XV.* Inscr. Annette Gertrude Godfrey-Faussett, 1873-**1949**, on altar plinth, C. *XVI.* Inscr. recording presentation [of bench front] in **1965** by nieces in mem. of Nita and Agnes Scudamore Smith, on bench front, N. *XVII.* Inscr. recording presentation [of bench front] in **1970** by Mr. and Mrs. F.W. Kent in mem. of parents, brothers and sisters, on bench front, N. *XVIII.* Inscr. recording presentation [of altar rail] in **1975** by family in mem. of Rose Burton, on altar rail, S.C./S.A. *XIX.* Inscr. Arthur E[dwin] Lloyd, [1968, aged 83], pos. by son, Glen A[rthur] Lloyd, vicar's [church]warden [for 22 years, 1914-1982]; M.R. Evans, 1960-1967; W.T. Kirkby, 1967-1972; L.R.H. Griffiths, 1972-1977; and M.E. Nicholas, 1977, engr. c.**1970**, ?brass, on churchwardens' wand, N. *XX.* Inscr. Madeline T[rude] Lloyd, [1968, aged 92], pos. by son, Glen A[rthur] Lloyd, people's [church]warden [for 22 years, 1914-1982]; G.A. Lloyd, 1960-1982; and C.J. Podger, 1982-1985, engr. c.**1970**, ?brass, on churchwardens' wand, N.

Ref: *M.B.S. Bulletin*, 38, p.128.

Ch. built, 1880.

FARRINGDON, All Saints.

Trinity, c.**1500**; said to have come from here, now in Winchester, Museums Service (q.v.). *M.B.S. Trans.*, X, p.91.

Two sons, c.**1515**; said to have come from here, are from brass to man in arm. and 2 ws., c.1515, at Blewbury, Berks. (q.v.)., now in Winchester, Museums Service (q.v.).

I. Inscr. Caroline Edith, [w. of Edward Briggs] Kennedy, **1935**, on processional cross, C. *II.* Inscr. Dawn Holt, 1910-**1975**, on bookcase, N.

Ref: *M.B.S. Bulletin*, 68, p.159; *M.B.S. Trans.*, X, p.90; *M.S.*, p.828.

FORDINGBRIDGE, St. Mary the Virgin.

I. William Bulkeley, esq., in arm., with 3 sons, Charles, William, John, and w. Jane, dau. of Baron Luke "of ye Quenes highnes exchequier", with 5 daus., Ann, Joyce, Judyth, Susan, Cisseley, all kng., engr. **1568**, rect. pl. with inscr., scrolls, ach. and 2 shs., mur., in orig. wooden frame, N. *M.B.S. Trans.*, V, p.299; *Page-Phillips, 16th Cent. Workshop*, p.26. Rect. pl. 530 x 476 mm. Style: London G (Lytkott, script 9).

II. Inscr. John Coventry, J.P., 2nd son of Hon. John Coventry, of Burgate House, **1871**, aged 73, mur., N. *III.* Inscr. with verse in raised letters. Stephen Tiller, **1879**, aged 75, and [w.] Rebecca, 1879, aged 75, [resident] in the par. for many years, pos. by son-in-law, William Sheppard, [of] Dublin, bronze, mur., N.C. *IV.* Inscr. with verse and regt. insignia. Trooper Harry Witt, 10th Royal Hussars, died of enteric fever at Winburg, Orange River Colony, South Africa, **1900**,

Fordingbridge I

[aged 20], mur., on board, N.A. *V.* Inscr. with enamelled ach. in relief recording gift of £500 "TOWARDS THE COST OF KEEPING THIS CHURCH IN REPAIR" in **1912** by descendant, Frederick William Harris, mcht. and shipowner of London, to commem. the baptism in 1664 of 8 children of Samuel Harris, bronze, mur., on board, S.A. *VI.* Inscr. with verse, crest and motto. Major Charles John Venables, D.S.O., [7th Battn.] Gloucestershire Regt., eld. son of [Rt. Rev.] Addington R[obert] P[eel] Venables, Bishop of Nassau [1864-1876], killed in action on Chanak Bair, Gallipoli, [Turkey], 1865-**1915**, mur., Tower. *VII.* Inscr. with verse. Gunner William Robert Hewitt, [141829, 30th Battery, 39th Brigade], R[oyal] F[ield] A[rtillery], killed in action at Mametz, France, **1916**, aged 19, maker's name *FRANK HIGHMAN & SON L*ᵀᴰ *SALISBURY*, [pos. by parents], mur., on board, N.A. *VIII.* Inscr. Alfred Hugh Hood, organist 1918-**1951**, bronze, on organ, S.A. *IX.* Inscr. recording erection [of aumbry] in **1951** by Reginald Albert Munday in mem. of w. Elsie Naomi, copper, on aumbry, C. *X.* Inscr. George Frederick Britton, choirmaster 1911-**1957**, bronze, on choir stall, C. *XI.* Inscr. David Arthur Maybury, chorister 1954-**1957**, [1957], aged 11, bronze, on choir stall, C. *XII.* Inscr. recording that vase was made and presented by Maurice Crossman, 1888-**1970**, bronze, on vase, N.C. *XIII.* Inscr. recording restoration of ch. during the incumbency of Rev. Canon John [Frederick Olney] Bown, T.D., M.A., [rector] 1971-**1979**, [hon. canon of Nairobi Cathedral, hon. chaplain to Queen Elizabeth II, rural dean of Christchurch 1974-1979], copper, mur., on board, N.

INDENTS & LOST BRASSES. 14. Indent, cross and marg. inscr. in Lombardics, early 14th cent., nearly effaced; in 2006 almost completely covered by organ; S.A. Purbeck slab c.1965 remains x c.1025 mm remains.

Ref: *Earliest English Brasses*, p.189; *Heseltine, Heraldry*, p.37; *M.B.S. Trans.*, V, pp.298-301, VIII, p.367, XII, pp.147-8; *Mee, Hampshire*, p.167; *M.S.*, p.161; *Norris, Memorials*, p.234, p.237; *Sadler, Dorset and Hampshire*, appx. I, pt.2, pp.21-2; *Soc. Antiq. MS. 875/6*, pp.49-52; *V.C.H., Hampshire*, IV, p.575.

FREEFOLK, St. Nicholas (redundant, now vested in The Churches Conservation Trust).

I. Inscr. (coffin pl.). Tho[ma]s Pearse, **1743**, aged 65, mur., on slate. *II.* Cross and marg. inscr. with verse. Clara, w. of Rev. J.S. Percival, chaplain, died at Pau, [France], **1863**, aged 25, mur., on marble.

Ch. declared redundant, 1974; vested, 1976.

FROYLE, St. Mary of the Assumption.

I. John Lighe, esq., **1575**, in civil dress, inscr., and ach.; eff. of w. Margaret, dau. of Thomas Saunders of Uxbridge, and 1 child lost during repairs in 1848; C. *M.B.S. Trans.*, V, p.302; *Page-Phillips, 16th Cent. Workshop*, p.27 (male eff. and inscr.). Illustration (female eff.) from rubbing in Soc. Antiq. coll. Rubbing (female eff.) in Soc. Antiq. coll. (n.d.). Male eff. 434 x 153 mm, lost female eff. 414 x 174 mm, inscr. 70 x 367 mm, child indent 190 x 65 mm., ach. 192 x 162 mm, Purbeck slab 1900 x 845 mm. Style: London G (Daston, script 9).

II. Inscr. Stanier Thomas, son of Thomas Burningham and [w.] Mary Juliana, **1837**, aged 1, N. Inscr. 154 x 356 mm. *III.* Inscr. Juliana Tryphena, dau. of Henry Burningham, w. of Sir Walter Henry Medhurst, of H.B.M. Consul at Shanghae, China, **1881**, aged 45, buried in the

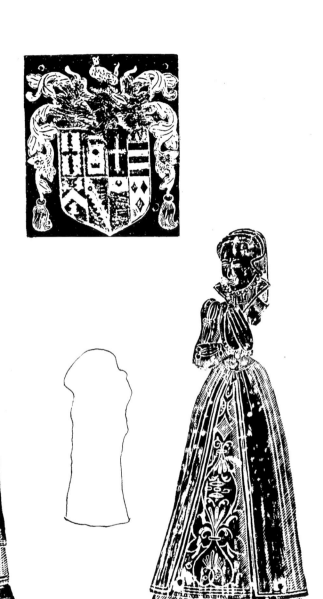

Here vnder this stone lyeth buryed the bodye of Iohn lighe esquier who deceassed the 19. daye of Iannarie anno domini 1575

Froyle I

135

churchyard, maker's name VAUGHAN & BROWN, LONDON, E.C., mur., on marble, N. *IV.* Inscr. James Gillies Benson, D.S.O., D.F.C., 1914-**1987**, mur., on board, Churchyard. *V.* Inscr. Kenneth Dudley Browning, **1994**, on lectern, N. *VI.* Inscr. recording renovation of [south] porch in **1994** by congregation, copper, mur., S.Porch. *VII.* Inscr. with Lat. verse. Raymond Parrott, 1919-**1998**, bronze, mur., on board, Churchyard.

INDENTS & LOST BRASSES. 8. Lost indent, oval-shaped pl., 17th or 18th cent., C. Recorded by Cave (1908) but not found (2006). Pl. 760 x 585 mm.

Ref: *Haines*, II, p.72; *Heseltine, Heraldry*, p.37; *M.B.S. Bulletin*, 23, p.14; *M.B.S. Trans.*, II, p.9, V, pp.301-2; *Mee, Hampshire*, p.169; *M.S.*, p.161, p.753; *Soc. Antiq. MS. 875/6*, pp.50-4; *V.C.H., Hampshire*, II, p.505.

GOODWORTH CLATFORD, St. Peter.

I. Inscr. Major Thomas Arthur Chalk, **1931**, on stall, C. *II.* Inscr. on 3 pls. Gwen Iremonger, **1959**, pos. by husband, Sonny, bronze, on cross, S.C./S.A. *III.* Inscr. recording gift of [south] chapel in **1963** by friends in mem. of Rev. [Robert] Douglas Downes, M.A.(Oxon.), "AFFECTIONATELY KNOWN AND REMEMBERED AS BROTHER DOUGLAS SSF", founder of the Society of St. Francis, Cerne Abbas, Dorset [1930], 1878-1957, bronze, mur., on board, S.C./S.A. *IV.* Inscr. Gladys Olive Brooks, w. and mother, **1973**, copper, on grave marker, Churchyard. *V.* Inscr. Patricia Anne Blake, engr. c.**1980**, on book stand, S.C./S.A. *VI.* Inscr. recording gift of case and book of remembrance in **1982** in mem. of Derek Henry Olden "TO RECORD THE NAMES OF THOSE WHOSE ASHES ARE INTERRED IN THE GARDEN OF REMEMBRANCE", on display case, S.C./S.A. *VII.* Inscr. recording augmentation of bells from 6 to 8 (treble was paid from monies collected in mem. of Ernest Dowling, [bell]ringer and churchwarden; 2nd bell was cast from a bell hung above the guard room at Old Sarum Barracks which came from Taylor [and Sons], of Loughborough in 1924 and given by the R.A.F. Guild of Bellringers to commem. the close connection between par. and R.A.F. Andover) cast in 1986 by the Whitechapel Bell Foundry; hallowed by Rev. Michael [Anthony] Tristram, [M.A., vicar 1985-1992]; installed by Philip Jakeman, of Whitechapel [Bell Foundry] "with the aid of local ringers and supporters"; dedicated in **1986** by Rev. David [Frederick] King, mur., on board, N. *VIII.* Inscr. [Anthony] (Tony) [Hugh] Storer, husband [father and grandfather, 1939-**2003**], and Joan Lake, mother, [pos. by w. and dau., Jane], on bench, Churchyard. *IX.* Inscr. Kenneth Robert Price, 1916-1980, and w. Violet Edith, 1917-**2004**, on grave marker, Churchyard.

INDENTS & LOST BRASSES. 10. Lost indent, ?civilian, kng. and inscr., nearly effaced, N. Recorded by Baigent (c.1850).

Ref: *Brit. Lib. Add. MS. 39966*, f.90.

GOSPORT, (see ALVERSTOKE).

GREYWELL, St. Mary the Virgin.

I. Inscr. recording gift of tablet and 4 oak choir seats by parishioners in mem. of Jethro Grigg, par. clerk for 46 years, ch. servant, **1927**, maker's name F. OSBORNE & CO LTD London, on

Froyle *II*

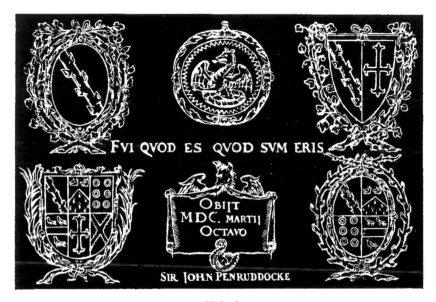

FVI QVOD ES QVOD SVM ERIS

OBIIT
MDC. MARTII
OCTAVO

SIR JOHN PENRUDDOCKE

Hale I

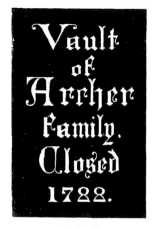

Vault
of
Archer
Family.
Closed
1788.

Hale *II*

choir stall, C. *II*. Inscr. recording gift of [tablet and] 2 altar frontals by par. in mem. of Edwin Poulter, par. clerk 1927-**1968**, on choir stall with no.*I*, C. *III*. Inscr. with verse on oval-shaped pl. Thomas G. Smyth, husband and father, 1915-**1991**, bronze, on gravestone, Churchyard. *IV*. Inscr. William Poulter, son of no.*II*, served ch. for more than 80 years, 1908-**2003**, on choir stall with nos.*I & II*, C.

HALE, St. Mary (new church).

I. Inscr. with 4 shs. and crest. Sir John Penruddocke, **1600**, N. *M.B.S. Trans.*, V, p.304. Inscr. 399 x 594 mm, slab 1850 x 920 mm.

II. Inscr. "Vault of Archer family. Closed **1788**", N.Tr. Inscr. 360 x 229 mm. *III*. Inscr. on celtic cross-shaped pl. encircled with verse on separate circular-shaped pl. Sarah Jane Goff, 1820-1839; Eliza Goff, 1827-**1863**; Caroline Goff, 1821-1842; and Rev. Thomas Goff, 1818-1843, maker's name HART, SON, PEARD & CO. LONDON, mur., on marble, N.Tr. *IV*. Rev. George James Goff, rector 1854-1862, 1826-**1867**, rect. pl., cross and inscr. with verse, maker's name HART, SON, PEARD & CO. LONDON, mur., on marble, C. *V*. Joseph Goff, 1817-**1872**, pos. by widow, rect. pl., inscr. on base of stepped cross and marg. inscr. with verse and 4 evang. symbols on roundels at corners, maker's name HART, SON, PEARD & C⁰, LONDON, mur., on marble, N.Tr. *VI*. Joseph Goff, **1875**, aged 87, and w. Jane, 1874, aged 79, pos. by surviving sons, Robert and Trevor Goff, and by grandson, Joseph Goff, rect. pl., marble inlaid cross in relief, inscr. and marg. inscr. with verse, maker's name HART, SON, PEARD & C⁰ LONDON, mur., on marble, N.Tr. *VII*. Lt.-Col. Trevor Goff, of Everton Grange, Lymington, 4th son of Joseph Goff, 1825-**1888**, pos. by widow, rect. pl., cross and inscr., maker's name HART SON PEARD & C⁰ LONDON, mur., on marble, N.Tr. Rect. pl. 924 x 441 mm. *VIII*. Inscr. recording [north and south chancel] windows pos. by widow in mem. of Lt.-Col. Gerald Lionel Joseph Goff, of Hale Park, J.P. for Hants and Wilts., killed while leading regt. (1st Battn. Argyll and Sutherland Highlanders) at the Battle of Magersfontein, S[outh] Africa, 1855-**1899**, maker's name MAYER & C⁰ LONDON & MUNICH, mur., C. *IX*. Inscr. Lt.-Col. [Gerald Lionel Joseph] Goff, [1st Battn.] Argyll and Sutherland Highlanders, killed at the Battle of Magersfontein, [South Africa], 1855-**1899**, pos. by mother, bronze, on lectern, Crossing. *X*. Inscr. with regt. insignia. Major Cecil Willie Trevor Thomas Goff, D.S.O., East Lancashire Regt., 1860-**1907**, pos. by mother, brothers and sisters, maker's name A & N AUX C.S.L. LONDON, mur., on marble, N.Tr. *XI*. Inscr. Adelaide Henrietta Louisa Hortense Goff, 1833-**1911**, mur., N.Tr. *XII*. Inscr. with regt. insignia in relief. Capt. Betram Lyulph Joseph Goff, Highland Light Infantry, 1857-**1911**, pos. by w., mur., in marble frame, N.Tr. *XIII*. Inscr. Lt.-Col. Ion Malise Goff, King's [(Liverpool)] Regt., [son of Ewen Cameron Goff and w. Ellen Clara (née Constable)], killed in action commanding 2nd Battn. London Irish Rifles at Cassino, [Italy], **1944**, aged 44, [buried at Cassino War Cemetery, Italy], on flowerstand, C. *XIV*. Inscr. Jack Tanner, chorister for 60 years, [**1978**], on choir stall, C. *XV*. Inscr. recording erection of [north transept] doors by friends in mem. of Jack Tanner, served ch. and community for 60 years, **1978**, on door, N.Tr.

Ref: *Gawthorp*, pp.39-40; *Heseltine, Heraldry*, p.37; *M.B.S. Trans.*, V, pp.303-4; *Mee, Hampshire*, p.176; *M.S.*, p.161; *Soc. Antiq. MS. 875/6*, pp.52-3; *V.C.H., Hampshire*, IV, p.578.

Ch. built, 1717.

IN LOVING MEMORY OF LIEUT COL.
TREVOR GOFF, OF EVERTON GRANGE,
LYMINGTON, AND 4TH SON OF
JOSEPH GOFF, ESQ., OF THIS PLACE.
BORN MAR. 25TH 1825. DIED NOV. 17TH 1888.
THIS IS ERECTED BY HIS WIDOW.

Hale *VII*

HAMBLEDON, SS. Peter and Paul.

I. Inscr. Lt. Henry George Hale, R.N., 2nd son of Edward Hale, of Hambledon [House], and w. Caroline, died at sea near Penang, [Malaysia], **1865**, aged 31, maker's name HART & SON, LONDON, mur., C. *II.* Inscr. with verse in raised letters. William Gale Goldsmith, died at Toivoomba, Queensland, [Australia], **1868**, aged 29, pos. by w. Dora, maker's name HART, SON, PEARD & C° LONDON, mur., C. *III.* Inscr. Arthur Higgens, 1848-**1873**, mur., S.C. *IV.* Inscr. [Rev.] Thomas Patteson, vicar for 33 years [1841-**1874**], and w. Rose Sewell, mur., C. *V.* Inscr. recording restoration of ch. in **1876**; [Rev. Dr.] T[homas] White, [M.A., LL.D.], vicar [1874-1897]; J. Gawan and D. Lunn, churchwardens, mur., S.A. *VI.* Inscr. recording dedication of east window by widow, Elizabeth, in mem. of Forrester Wilson, of Whitedale House, **1878**, mur., C. *VII.* Inscr. Ella Mary, w. of Rear-Admiral W.A.J. Heath, C.B., 1837-**1887**, mur., N.C. *VIII.* Inscr. recording dedication [of lectern] by friends and parishioners in mem. of Anne J. Hale, **1888**, maker's name GAWTHORP LONDON, on lectern, N. *IX.* Inscr. [Rev.] Edward Hale, M.A.(Cantab.), eld. son of Edward Hale, of Hambledon [House], and w. Caroline, asst. master at Eton Coll. for 44 years, 1828-**1894**, maker's name GAWTHORP S° LONDON, mur., C. *X.* Inscr. Edward Hale, of Hambledon House, 1870, aged 64, and w. Caroline, **1897**, aged 90, maker's name GAWTHORP S° LONDON, mur., C. *XI.* Inscr. Queen Victoria, 1837-**1901**, mur., N. *XII.* Inscr. with verse. Dora, dau. of W.J.J. Higgens, w. of William Gale Goldsmith, **1909**, aged 70, pos. by relations and friends, mur., C. *XIII.* Inscr. with verse. P[etty] O[fficer] Arthur Edmund Parvin, [R.N., 290747], stoker, [son of William Parvin and w. Catherine, killed] while serving on H.M.S. Bulwark, **1914**, aged 36, pos. by mother and brother, mur., S.A. *XIV.* Inscr. with verse and regt. insignia. 2nd-Lt. Charles Frederic Noel Prince Sealy, 7th [Battn.] Royal Fusiliers, only son of Lt.-Col. C[harles] W[illiam] H[enry] Sealy and [w. Helena Louisa Harris], of Hambledon House, killed in action near Ypres, **1915**, aged 23, maker's name A&N. AUX C.S.L. LONDON, mur., S.C. *XV.* Inscr. in raised letters with enamelled regt. insignia in relief. Major David Grieg Bryce, 76th Punjabis, formerly Lancashire Fusiliers, [son of Archibald Hamilton Bryce and w. Mary, of Edinburgh, husband of Emiline Isabel Bryce, of Fairfield Cottage], died in the Military Hospital, Cawnpore, **1916**, mur., on marble, S.C. *XVI.* Inscr. with verse and enamelled regt. insignia in relief. Capt. John Goldsmith, Royal Marine Light Infantry, eld. son of Edward Goldsmith, [killed] in France, **1917**, aged 34, [buried] at Etaples, maker's name ALLAN G. WYON S° bronze, mur., C. *XVII.* Inscr. recording rehanging of bells in **1918** by subscription and the 5th bell recast in mem. of Patrick Ogilvie, [1826-1906] and [w.] Ellen [Anne, 1827-1913], mur., S.A. *XVIII.* Inscr. John Alexander Wilson, of Westend, 1846-**1922**, mur., S.C. *XIX.* Inscr. Fanny and Rose Agnes Hale, [1926, aged 81], daus. of no.*X*, engr. c.**1930**, mur., below no.*X*, C. *XX.* Inscr. Evelyn Amy Goldsmith, w. of no.*XVI*, **1962**, copper, mur., on brass backing below no.*XVI*, C. *XXI.* Inscr. recording gift of organ case in **1969** in mem. of Emily Leslie Salisbury-Jones, 1874-1966, and dau., Ellaline, 1899-1964, mur., on pillar, N.C./N.A. *XXII.* Inscr. "PART OF A GENEROUS BEQUEST BY RON TURNER FOR THE BELLS AND TOWER **1990**", on Kitchen/Tower. *XXIII.* Inscr. recording gift of seat by widow and dedication in **1997** by [Rev.] Roy [William Henry] Kingston, vicar, in mem. of Admiral Sir Rae McKaig, K.C.B., C.B.E., [of Hill House, 1922-1996], on bench, S.Porch. *XXIV.* Inscr. Gwen Grindler, 1911-**2002**, bronze, on bench, Churchyard.

INDENTS & LOST BRASSES. 25. Indent, upper portion of 2 effs., Churchyard. Dext. eff. 285 remains x c.90 mm remains, sin. eff. 280 remains x c.90 mm remains, slab 760 remains x 750 mm. 26. Indent, priest and inscr., Churchyard. Eff. 780 x c.300 mm, inscr. 105 x 465 mm slab 2060 x 840 mm.

Ref: *Soc. Antiq. MS. 94311.*

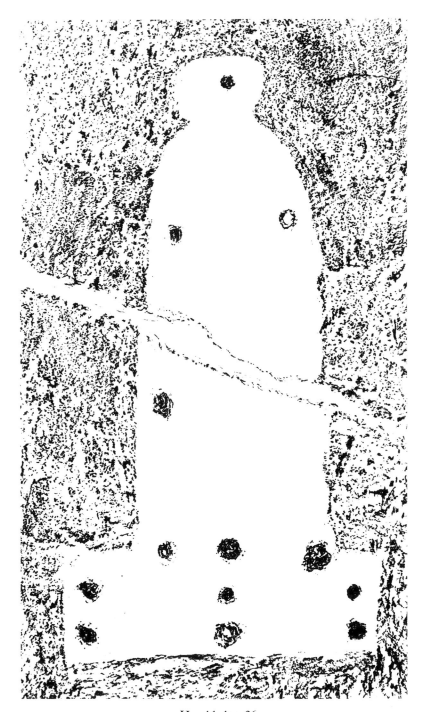

Hambledon 26

HARBRIDGE, All Saints (new church).

I. Inscr. in raised letters recording ch. rebuilt at the sole expense of Welbore Ellis [Herbert, 2nd] Earl of Normanton, of Somerley, [1778-1868], and foundation stone laid in **1838** by Diana, Countess of Normanton, [dau. of George Augustus Herbert, 11th Earl of Pembroke, 1841], bronze, mur., W.Porch/Tower. *II*. Inscr. in raised letters. WELBORE ELLIS, EARL OF NORMANTON BY DEED ENROLLED, DATED THE 29TH OF APRIL **1846** SETTLED £400 3 PER CENT CONSOLS, IN THE NAMES OF HIMSELF, THE LORD BISHOP OF THE DIOCESE AND THE INCUMBENT OF THIS PARISH FOR THE TIME BEING, UPON TRUST, TO APPLY THE DIVIDENDS TO REPAIR FOR EVER THE OUTSIDE AND INSIDE OF THIS CHURCH, THE MONUMENTS AND INSCRIPTIONS THEREON AND THEREIN AND THIS TABLET AND INSCRIPTION THE SURPLUS, IF ANY, TO BE APPLIED TRIENNIALLY TO THE RELIEF OF THE POOR OF THIS PARISH OF HARBRIDGE. THE ACCOUNTS OF THE EXPENDITURE OF THE DIVIDENDS TO BE PRODUCED BY THE INCUMBENT ON THE REASONABLE REQUEST IN WRITING OF ANY PARISHIONER", bronze, mur., W.Porch/Tower. *III*. Inscr. recording engraving and restoration of [south-east nave] window in commem. of "HOLY YEAR" **2000** and in mem. of Tom Sampson, 1922-1999, mur., below window, N.

The inscr. recorded by Cave (1908) as an indent, is a filled-in heating grille aperture.

Ref: *Burke's Peerage and Baronetage*, p.1985, p.2092; *M.B.S. Trans.*, V, p.304; *Soc. Antiq. MS. 875/6*, p.53.

Ch. built, 1838.

HARTLEY MAUDITT, St. Leonard.

I. World War I memorial in raised letters (3 names), maker's name G. MAILE & SON, 367 EUSTON RD LONDON. N.W.1., mur., on board, N. *II*. Inscr. recording presentation [of framed list of rectors 1220-1992 (54 names)] in **1960** by children in mem. of Thomas Shilston Mitchell, O.B.E., 1867-1955, mur., on board below framed list of incumbents, N.

HARTLEY WESPALL, St. Mary the Virgin.

I. Inscr. marg. (mutil.). John [Knottin]gle, esq., **1407**, and son Thomas, C. Marg. inscr. 1904 x 808 x 34 mm, Purbeck slab 2210 x 1070 mm. Style: London B.

II. Inscr. and sh. (3 others lost). John Waspaill, esq., patron of the ch., 1448, and w. Joan, widow of John Pakenham, **1452**, C. Inscr. 120 x 584 mm, upper dext. sh. indent 150 x 120 mm, upper sin. sh. indent 150 x 120 mm, lower dext. sh. indent 150 x 120 mm, lower sin. sh. 155 x 125 mm, Purbeck slab 1515 x 840 mm. Style: London D.

III. Cross, inscr. and marg. inscr. with verse and 4 evang. symbols in quadrilobes at corners. [Rev. Dr.] John Keate, D.D., canon of Windsor, headmaster of Eton Coll. for 24 years [1809-1834], rector for 24 years [1824-1848, 1773-]**1852**, pos. by widow, [Frances, engr. by Messrs. J.G. and L.A.B. Waller], A.T., C. Cross 1120 x 415 mm, inscr. 150 x 535 mm,

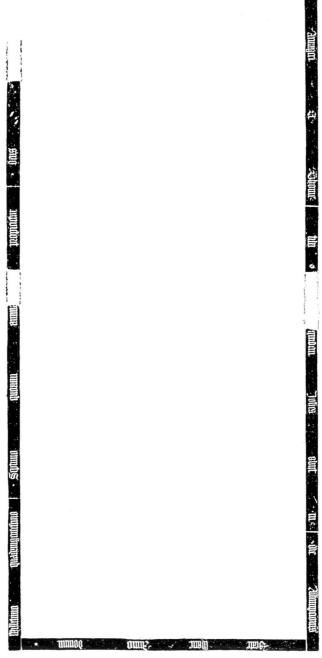

Hartley Wespall I

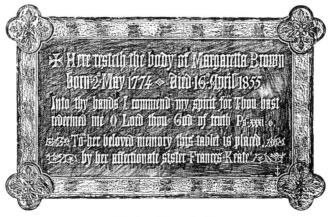

Hartley Wespall II

Hartley Wespall *IV*

Hartley Wespall *III*

145

marg. inscr. 1395 x 705 x 38 mm, upper dext. quadrilobe 133 x 132 mm, upper sin. quadrilobe 135 x 134 mm, lower dext. quadrilobe 134 x 134 mm, lower sin. quadrilobe 134 x 134 mm. See also Eton College Chapel, Bucks. no.*LXXV*. *IV.* Inscr. with verse. Margaretta Brown, 1774-**1855**, pos. by sister, Frances Keate, maker's name WALLER FECIT LONDON (and monogram), mur., on marble, C. Inscr. 455 x 710 mm. *V.* Cross, inscr. and marg. inscr. with verse and quadrilobes at corners. Frances, widow of [Rev. Dr.] John Keate, D.D., **1863**, aged 80, mur., on marble, C. *VI.* Inscr. [Rev.] William Cookesley Thompson, curate, **1866**, and w. Catherine Elizabeth, survived w. by 23 years, maker's name HART, SON, PEARD & Cᵒ LONDON, mur., N. *VII.* Inscr. with verse. Charles Robert Henry Keate, in 1831 entered the civil service of H[onourable] E[ast] I[ndia] C[ompany] S[ervice], died after a short illness at Nagapatam, Madras Pres[iden]cy, [India], 1813-**1835**, and Robert William Keate, M.A.(Oxon.), in 1849 entered the colonial service and held appointments as Lt.-Gov[erno]r and Governor in the West Indies and at Natal, S[outh] Africa, in 1873 appointed Governor-in-Chief of the West Coast Settlements, Africa, died after a few days illness at Cape Coast, 1814-**1873**, pos. by surviving brother and sisters, mur., on marble, N. *VIII.* Inscr. with verse. Mary Steele; also son, Arthur Hudleston Steele, pos. in **1877** by sister, Clara Keate, maker's name HART, SON, PEARD & Cᵒ., LONDON, mur., on marble, N. *IX.* Inscr. with verse, sh. and Chichester diocesan arms. [Rt. Rev.] Richard Durnford, Bishop of Chichester for 25 years [1870-1895], 1802-**1895**, and w. Emma, 4th dau. of Rev. [Dr.] John Keate, D.D., rector, 1812-1884; mar. in the ch. 1840, maker's name BARKENTIN & KRALL LONDON, mur., N. *X.* Inscr. Leslie J. Chamberlain, **1934**, aged 3, bronze, on wooden cross, Churchyard. *XI.* Inscr. recording gift of chair by surviving children in mem. of Richard Durnford, C.B., of Hartley Wespall House, 1843-**1934**, and w. Beatrice Mary, 1857-1927, on chair, C. *XII.* Inscr. recording removal of stone [World War I and II] memorial tablets and font in **1976** from Stratfield Turgis ch., mur., on pillar, N.

Ref: *Haines*, II, p.238; *Heseltine, Heraldry*, p.37; *M.B.S. Trans.*, V, p.305, XV, p.238; *M.S.*, p.161; *Soc. Antiq. MS. 875/6*, p.54; *V.C.H., Hampshire*, IV, p.44.

Ch. essentially, 1868-9.

HAVANT, St. Faith.

I. Thomas Aileward, rector [1397-1413], **1413**, in cope, inscr. with 2 Lat. vv., scroll and 1 sh. (4 others lost); formerly on A.T., N.Tr., mur., N.Tr., now C. *Alcuin Club Colls.*, XXII, p.50; *Builder*, LXV, p.155; *Clinch, Churches*, p.204; *Haines*, p.182 (drg. of orphrey); *M.B.S. Trans.*, II, pt.1, pl.1; *Mee, Hampshire*, p.219 (drg. of eff.); *Suffling*, p.236. Eff. 950 x 273 mm, inscr. 171 x 495 mm, scroll 350 x 208 x 35 mm, sh. 147 x 116 mm, sh. indents 150 x 115 mm, Purbeck slab 2270 x 920 mm. Style: London B.

II. Inscr. Rt. Rev. [Dr.] Michael Solomon Alexander, D.D., 1st anglican Bishop in Jerusalem, father-in-law of Rev. T.G. Halehard, rector, died at Cairo, **1846**, aged 46, mur., C. *III.* Inscr. Jane, widow of Charles Beare Longcroft, 1861, aged 69; also Thomas Craufurd Longcroft, died in London, 1820-1883; w. Katharine, died at Aden, 1854; 1st born son, Hubert, died at Aden, [1853-]1853; only dau., Edith (de St. Croix), died at Tientsin, China, 1884; and yst. son, Harry Longcroft, died at Hove, Brighton, [Sussex], **1884**, mur., W.A. of S.Tr. *IV.* Inscr. on scroll. Okevor Butler Longcroft, 1871, aged 21; Mary Longcroft Longcroft, 1811-1873; Charles John Longcroft, 1815-1877; Franklyn Moody Longcroft, 1848-1880; and Katharina Longcroft, 1845-**1885**, mur., N.Tr. *V.* Inscr. recording erection of [south] window in mem. of

Havant I

Georgiana Frances Pigott, died at Langbrook, **1889**, [aged 74], pos. by brother, Robert Creighton Granville, mur., below window, S.C./S.Tr. *VI.* Inscr. Mary Chignell, **1892**, on window splay, S.A. *VII.* Inscr. on scroll. Charles Needham Longcroft, 1846-**1898**, mur., N.Tr. *VIII.* Inscr. in raised letters with sh. in relief. Capt. Thomas Hodgkinson, R.N., 1882, and w. Jane, **1911**, maker's name GAWTHORP & SONS LONDON, copper, mur., S.Tr. *IX.* Inscr. on scroll. Lt. Thomas Roy Longcroft, [3rd attd.] 2nd [Battn.] Leicestershire Regt., [son of Edward Roy Longcroft and w. Helen Gertrude, killed] at Loos, France, **1915**, [aged 26], mur., N.Tr. *X.* Inscr. with Lat. verse and regt. insignia. Capt. Lawrence Adams Mitchell, M.C., [D Battery, 123rd Brigade], Royal Field Artillery, only child of George A.E. Mitchell and [w.] Elizabeth, of [The Halt], Warblington, killed in action at Briaste, France, **1918**, aged 23, [buried at Belle Vue Cemetery, Briaste], mur., N.Tr. *XI.* Inscr. on scroll. Helen Penelope Longcroft, 1892-1925; Edward Roy Longcroft 1853-1929; and Helen Gertrude Longcroft, 1864-**1951**, mur., N.Tr. *XII.* Inscr. Dorothy Flower, **1959**, copper, mur., on board, S.A. *XIII.* Inscr. recording erection of stations by [Rev. Canon] Philip Howard Duke-Baker, [M.A., hon. canon of Portsmouth Cathedral], rector 1943-**1962**, mur., W.A. of N.Tr. *XIV.* Inscr. Nellie Prudence Paxton, 1892-**1973**, copper, on stall, C. *XV.* Inscr. Alinda May and Hugh Thomas Elliott, 1914-**2000**, mur., S.A.

Ref: *Gent. Mag.*, 1795, I, pp.296-7; *Gent. Mag. Lib. Eng. Topog.*, p.83; *Gittings*, p.28; *Haines*, I, p.77, p.183, II, p.72; *Heseltine, Heraldry*, p.37; *Longcroft, C., A Topographical Account of the Hundred of Bosmere*, 1856, pp.53-4; *M.B.S. Trans.*, I, pt.10, p.10, II, pt.I, pp.63-4, p.337, V, pp.305-6, X, p.10, XV, p.434; *Mee, Hampshire*, p.185; *M.S.*, p.161; *Norris, Memorials*, p.85; *Pevsner, Hampshire*, p.277; *Soc. Antiq. MS. 875/6*, pp.54-5; *V.C.H., Hampshire*, III, p.126.

HAYLING ISLAND, (see HAYLING, NORTH and HAYLING, SOUTH).

HAYLING, NORTH, St. Peter.

I. Inscr. with 4 evang. symbols on roundels at corners recording seating of ch. in **1886** by Mrs. Hardy and family in mem. of Rev. Charles Hardy, B.A., vicar for 46 years [1832-1880], died at Hildenboro, Kent, 1885, aged 81, "THE PARISHIONERS HEREBY EXPRESS THEIR GRATITUDE FOR THE GIFT", mur., on board, N. Inscr. 230-349 x 412-456 mm. *II.* Inscr. with verse recording thank offering of organ light by son, William Leslie [Morrey], ch. organist, and dau., Nora, in mem. of Henry Morrey, of Barlaston, [Staffs.], choirmaster 1903-1918, 1948, and w. Elizabeth, 1953; dedicated in **1961** by Rev. Albert [Charles] Freeman, [M.M., A.K.C.], vicar, on organ, N.A.; from Barlaston, Staffs. *III.* Inscr. recording restoration or organ in **1968** by w., son and dau. in mem. of Ralph Wedgwood, on organ with no.*II*, N.A. *IV.* Inscr. with verse. Krystyna Amblie, dau., 1945-1975, and Simon Amblie, grandson, tragically died, **1988**, aged 18, bronze, on gravestone, Churchyard. *V.* Inscr. recording gift of grille by w. Dorothy E., 1912-**1990**, in mem. of Bernard J. Smith, organist, 1915-1989, on grille, N. *VI.* Inscr. recording presentation [of bench] by Alfreda Reading in mem. of Syd, engr. c.**1990**, on bench, Churchyard. *VII.* Inscr. recording restoration and installation of organ (Father Willis) from Barlaston, Staffs. in 1999 through generosity of parishioners including many descendants of Clement Wedgwood; dedicated in **1999** by archdeacon of Portsmouth at an inaugural concert with Dr. Martin Neary, formerly of Westminster Abbey, on organ with nos.*II & III*, N.A. *VIII.* Inscr. Perry [James] Fox, [son, brother, uncle], 1982-**2000**, pos. by friends, Zowie, Rachael, Hannah, Leah, Lizzie, Craig,

Hayling, North *I*

Hayling, South *IV*

Danny R. Dozer, Mark, Dan W., Ben, Danny E., Steve, Ritchy, Mike, Spud, Gareth, Rob, on bench, Churchyard. *IX.* Inscr. recording planting of tree in mem. of Shreekesh Narsidas (Manny) Laxman, 1948-**2005**, on board, Churchyard.

HAYLING, SOUTH, St. Mary.

I. Inscr. Emma Elizabeth, widow of Capel Hanbury Leigh, of Pontypool, Lord-Lt. of Monmouth, died at South Hayling, **1888**, aged 72, on window splay, S.A. *II.* Inscr. Henry John Trigg, son of Harry Richard Trigg and w. Hannah, formerly of Kingston-on-Thames, [Surrey], died of malarious fever while acting as surveyor to the Colonial Government at Cape Coast Castle, [Ghana], Africa, **1895**, aged 35, on window splay, N.A. *III.* Inscr. Lucy McEuen, 1851-**1897**, maker's name HEATON, BUTLER & BAYNE LONDON, on window splay, N.A. *IV.* Inscr. with verse within border of thistles and 4 evang. symbols at corners. David Painter McEuen, of 24 Pembridge Square, London, and Richmond House, born at Perth Scotland, died at Monte Carlo, 1821-**1911**, maker's name OMAR RAMSDEN ET ALWYN CARR ME FECERUNT, bronze, mur., on board, C. *Weever, J., Memorials and Monuments*, fig.134, p.271. Inscr. 543 x 762 mm. *V.* Inscr. recording dedication of [south-east south aisle] window by friends and parishioners in mem. of D[avid] P[ainter] McEuen, [of 24 Pembridge Square, London, and Richmond House, born at Perth Scotland, died at Monte Carlo, 1821-]**1911**, maker's name HEATON BUTLER & BAYNE, LONDON, on window splay, S.A. *VI.* Inscr. and verse in raised letters with 4 fouled anchors. Sub-Lt. Francis Henry James Startin, R.N.[V.R.], Nelson Battn. R.N. Division, [son of Admiral Sir James Startin, K.C.B., of Wyndlawn], mentioned in despatches for "GALLANT AND DISTINGUISHED SERVICE IN THE FIELD", died of wounds received at Gallipoli, [Turkey], **1915**, aged 23, [buried at Lancashire Landing Cemetery, Turkey], mur., on marble, C. *VII.* Inscr. recording restoration of [south] porch in **1918** by C.H. M[cEuen], E.S. M[cEuen] and E.D. in mem. of David Painter McEuen, of 24 Pembridge Square, London, and Richmond House, [born at Perth Scotland, died at Monte Carlo, 1821-1911], mur., S.Porch. *VIII.* World War I memorial on 2 pls. (78 names), copper, mur., on board, N. *IX.* Inscr. with verse recording dedication of lychgate in **1920** by Rev. H[erbert] G[uildford] Sprigg, M.A., rural dean [of Havant 1917-1922], on lychgate, Churchyard. *X.* Inscr. recording compilation of [board] listing [vicars 1240-1985 (49 names)] to 1889 by E.S. McEuen, churchwarden 1919-**1936**, mur., on list of incumbents board, N.A. *XI.* World War II memorial on 2 pls. (42 names), copper, mur., on board, N. *XII.* Inscr. Roselia Annie Jewry-Harbert, **1961**, aged 95, on prie-dieu, S.A. *XIII.* Inscr. James (Les) Hughes, choirmaster and organist 1958-**1980**, bronze, on organ, Tower. *XIV.* Inscr. in Eng. and Fr. Moss Dollery, 1926-**1985**, on bench, Churchyard. *XV.* Inscr. "THIS HONEYSUCKLE CAME FROM THE RUINED ROYAL ABBEY OF JUMIEGES IN NORMANDY, WHOSE MONKS OWNED SOUTH HAYLING, ORIGINALLY AS A GIFT FROM WILLIAM THE CONQUEROR, AT THE TIME THIS CHURCH WAS BUILT", engr. c.**1985**, on lychgate, Churchyard. *XVI.* Inscr. on round-shaped pl. Hannah Leigh Barnett, **1993**, aged 4 days, on wooden cross, Churchyard. *XVII.* Inscr. with verse on round-shaped pl. Ellen Anne Barnett, sister of no.*XVI*, **1994**, aged 2 hours, on wooden cross with no.*XVI*, Churchyard. *XVIII.* Inscr. with verse. Faith Shirley Lumley-Smith, **1995**, on wooden cross, Churchyard. *XIX.* Inscr. Robert Vine, 1918-**1995**, on chair, Tower. *XX.* Inscr. with verse. on oval-shaped pl. Bridie Anne Michelle Rolfe, 1999-**1999**, on wooden cross, Churchyard.

Ch. essentially, 1869, 1892-3.

Headbourne Worthy I

151

HEADBOURNE WORTHY, St. Swithun.

I. John, son of Simon Kent of Reading, a scholar of Winchester, [died **1434**], in civil dress, inscr. and scroll; formerly N., C., now mur., on marble, C. *Brit. Lib. Add. MS. 39987*, f.27; *Kirby, J.F., Winchester Scholars*, frontis.; *Leach*, opp. p.170; *M.B.S. Trans.*, V, p.307; *Page-Phillips, Children*, fig.16 (eff.); *Slessor, J.H., Headbourne Worthy church*, p.14; *Trivick, Craft*, pl.123, p.63; *Trivick, Picture Book*, pl.154; *V. and A. Mus. List*, pl.54, no.4 (eff.), 2nd edn., pl.60, no.4 (eff.); *Warren*, p.47. Eff. 313 x 95 mm, inscr. 70 x 431 mm, scroll 264 x 142 x 29 mm. Style: London B.

II. Inscr. Capt. Edward Augustus Slessor, Royal Artillery, 1838-**1873**, mur., on marble, N. *III.* Emily Rosetta, w. of Capt. Alfred Matthews, R.N., 1798-**1884**, eff. and inscr., mur., on marble, N. Eff. 423 x 160 mm, inscr. 128 x 409 mm. *IV.* Inscr. on 4 pls. Thomas Courtney and sister, Harriet, **1886**, copper, on screen, N. *V.* Inscr. Frederic George Slessor, M.Inst.C.E., husband of Alice, 1831-**1905**, mur., N. *VI.* Inscr. with ach. [Rev.] John Henry Slessor, [M.A.], eld. son of Major-Gen. John Henry Slessor, of Sidmouth, Devon, fellow of University Coll., Oxford, rector for 44 years [1861-1905], 1821-**1912**, maker's name BARKENTIN & KRALL, LONDON, mur., on marble, N. *VII.* Inscr. on cross-shaped pl. Lt. J[ames] C[harles] M[arjoribanks] Hunt, B Batt[ery], 47th Brigade, R[oyal] F[ield] A[rtillery], son of William Alexander Hunt and w. Isabel Maud, of Headbourne Worthy House], killed in action, **1916**, [aged 21], on wooden cross, Tower. *VIII.* Inscr. in raised letters recording erection of lychgate in **1929** by husband and sons in mem. of Janet Jerome (Nettie Harris), bronze, on lychgate, Churchyard Extension. *IX.* Inscr. Lt.-Col. Herbert Slessor, Royal Marine Artillery, born at Headbourne Worthy Rectory, died at Sidmouth, 1862-1946, and w. Winifred Mary, dau. of William Cotesworth, of Abbotsworthy House, 1872-**1948**, mur., on marble, N. *X.* Inscr. recording gift [of altar rails] in **1966** by Alice Maud Ings, on altar rail, C. *XI.* Inscr. recording substantial improvements and restorations carried out to the ch. 1998-**1999** (including major repairs to the medieval bells) made possible by many benefactors, in particular, Elizabeth (Betty) Balfour, O.B.E., mur., on board, N. *XII.* Inscr. with verse. Edward, Winifred and Pamela Porter and Cyril and Laura Williams, engr. c.**2000**, on bench, Churchyard. *XIII.* Inscr. James Julian Brendan Weeks, 1957-**2004**, on bench, Churchyard Extension.

Ref: *Beaumont*, p.133; *Brit. Lib. Add. MS. 39966*, f.224, *Add. MS. 39987*, f.27; *Duthy*, p.224; *Haines*, I, p.86, II, p.72; *Hampshire N. and Q.*, IV, p.7, p.17; *M.B.S. Trans.*, V, pp.307-8; *Mee, Hampshire*, p.188; *M.S.*, p.161; *Norris, Memorials*, p.90; *Pevsner, Hampshire*, p.286; *Simpson*, p.28; *Soc. Antiq. MS. 875/6*, pp.55-7; *V.C.H., Hampshire*, IV, p.430; *Warren, W.T., Historic Sketches round Winchester*, 1902, pp.47-8.

HEADLEY, All Saints (new church).

I. Civilian and w., c.**1510**; inscr. lost; formerly mur., C., now N. *M.B.S. Trans.*, XV, p.377. Male eff. 375 x 118 mm, female eff. 386 x 138 mm. Style: London G. Rep. by W.G.L. (1994).

II. Inscr. recording erection of reredos in **1882** by widow, Elizabeth, in mem. of John Rouse Phillips, maker's name JONES & WILLIS, mur., on panelling, C. *III.* Inscr. recording gift [of lectern] by 4 sisters; mar. in the ch., 1874, 1874, 1883 and **1886**, on lectern, N. *IV.* Inscr. recording erection of pulpit in **1887** by children in mem. of Elizabeth Phillips, maker's name

In pious memory of Emily Rosetta
wife of Captain Alfred Matthews R.N.
born August 1ˢᵗ 1798. died July 18ᵗʰ 1884.

Headbourne Worthy *III*

Headley I

153

COX & BUCKLEY LONDON, mur., N. *V.* Inscr. Lance-Cpl. Cyril Warrington Rogers, Imperial Light Infantry, yst. son of John Warrington Rogers, Q.C., of Melbourne, Australia, killed at the Battle of Spion Kop, South Africa, **1900**, aged 20, maker's name *JONES & WILLIS*, mur., N. *VI.* Inscr. with Lat. verse. Henry Frederick Baily, M.R.C.S., physician, 1845-**1931**, copper, mur., in wooden frame, N. *VII.* Inscr. recording mosaic (Ecce Homo after Guido Reni) pos. in mem. of Williamina Emma, widow of Admiral Parish, of Beech Hill House, **1932**, copper, mur., below mosaic, N. *VIII.* Inscr. with verse. Charlotte Hannah, w. of Henry Frederick Baily, [M.R.C.S.], 1855-**1938**, mur., on wooden frame with no.*VI*, N. *IX.* Combined World War I (96 names) and II (49 names) memorials on 5 pls., bronze, outside Churchyard. *X.* Inscr. recording gift of font cover by family in mem. of [Rev.] James Spencer Tudor-Jones, [M.A.], rector 1934-**1965**, on font cover, N. *XI.* Inscr. recording [restoration] of organ (new tonal specification and electro-pneumatic action) in **1971** by Wood, Wordsworth & Co., of Leeds with the cost "BORNE FROM THE SALE OF HEATH COTTAGE" given by Mrs. Kay; the pedal flute was given by Mrs. Cooper in mem. of parents, Mr. and Mrs. Wouldham; and the tremulant given by the organist, Lindsay Bleach, F.R.C.O., on organ, C. *XII.* Inscr. recording presentation of [south] porch window in mem. of Major Edward Scott Fiddes, Royal Scots, secretary of the National Playing Fields Association of Scotland 1955-1958, P.C.C. treasurer 1960-1968, **1974**, bronze, mur., S.Porch. *XIII.* Inscr. recording [restoration] of 13th cent. stained glass panel and tablet pos. in **1985** by family "OF A WELL-LOVED PARISHIONER WHO WORSHIPPED IN THIS CHURCH FOR MANY YEARS" 1921-1974, [maker's name Abbey Craftsmen Ltd., of Park Works, Kingsley], bronze; in 2006 loose in C. Inscr. 77 x 127 mm. *XIV.* Inscr. recording renewal of lighting in **1987** through generosity of Mrs. Wendy Simpson, 1919-1983, mur., N. *XV.* Inscr. recording [restoration] of organ in **1997** by Percy Daniel & Co. through legacy of chorister, Nell Goodson, and a grant from the Pilling Trust, on organ with no.*XI*, C.

Ref: *M.B.S. Trans.*, V, p.308, XV, pp.377-8; *Mee, Hampshire*, p.189; *M.S.*, p.161; *Soc. Antiq. MS. 875/6*, p.57.

Ch. built, 1859.

HECKFIELD, St. Michael.

I. John Hall, **1514** (eff. lost), and w. Elizabeth, builders of chantry, inscr.; now mur., N.C. Eff. 490 x 157 mm, inscr. 107 x 644 mm. Style: London G.

II. Inscr., 2 Evang. symbols and rebus. John Creswell, "lorde of this towne at the tyme of the byldyng of thys stepyll & the newe yle & Chapell in this Cherche", **1518**, and w. Isabel; formerly mur., C., now mur., N. Inscr. 86 x 460 mm, dext. evang. symbol 100 x 100 mm, sin. evang. symbol 99 x 99 mm, rebus 103 x 88 mm. Style: London G.

III. Inscr. Thomas Wyfold, gent., **1521**, and ws. Emme and Annes, rel., on step, N.C. Inscr. 102 x 670 mm. Style: London G.

IV. Inscr. Charles Huett, gent., subtreasurer to Queen Elizabeth in Ireland, **1627**, aged 67, mur., vestibule, N.C. Inscr. 119 x 519 mm.

V. Inscr. Charles Huett, gent., son of no.IV, **1652**, aged 53, mur., vestibule, N.C. Inscr. 125 x 434 mm.

Orate pro aiabz Johis hall et Elizabeth conlortis sue quiquidem Johes obyt xxb die mensis Nouembris A dni m b xviij ex cuius sumptibz hec capella construitur quorum aiabus propicietur deus

Heckfield I

Of yo charite pray for the soules of Thomas Gryfold Em & Annes hie wyfes and all hir chyldern the whyche Thomas decelled the xvj day of may the yer of o lord m b xvj on whose soull ihu haue mercy ·

Heckfield III

of Johu Crebbett and Isabell hys wyffe lord of this towne
at the tyme of the byldyng of this chappll & the newe yle of
Chappell in this Cherche whiche John decessyd v day of Ia
..... yn a dm m v rum Du whos sowll yhu have mrcy

Heckfield II

HERE LYETH INTERRED THE BODY OF CHARLES HVETT GENT SVBTRESVRER TO QVEENE ELIZABETH IN IRELAND DECEASED AN° DNI: 1627 ÆTAT SVÆ 67

Heckfield IV

HERE LYETH INTERRED THE BODY OF CHARLES HVETT GENT: SONNE TO THE SAID CHA: HVETT DECEASED AN° DNI: 1652 ÆTAT SVÆ 53

Heckfield V

Heckfield *VI*

VI. Cross, inscr. and marg. inscr. with verse. Lady Frances, [2nd] dau. of [Sir] James [Harris], 1st Earl of Malmesbury, [K.B.], widow of Gen. the Hon. Sir G[albraith] Lowry Cole, G.C.B., [2nd son of 1st Earl of Enniskillen, Governor of Gravesend and Tilbury Fort], 1784-**1847**, pos. by 7 children, [maker's monogram WALLER], mur., on marble, Tower. Cross 720 x 360 mm, inscr. 220 x 550 mm, marg. inscr. 1145 x 720 x 37 mm. *VII.* Inscr. recording dedication of [south-west-centre nave] window by widow, [Jean Mary], in mem. of James Munro Macnabb, [Honourable East India Company Service], **1860**, [aged 71], mur., below window, N. *VIII.* Inscr. with verse. Jane Robina Sneyd, **1878**, mur., Tower. *IX.* Inscr. in raised letters recording dedication of [south-east nave] window in **1884** by children in mem. of Mary Anne Marson, of Highfield Park, mur., below window, N. *X.* Inscr. James Munro Macnabb, H[onourable] E[ast] I[ndia] C[ompany] S[ervice], of Arthurstone, Perthshire, resident at Highfield Park for many years, 1860, aged 71, and w. Jean Mary, dau. of Rev. [Dr.] Donald Campbell, D.D., **1886**, aged 83; also 4th son, John Campbell Erskine, 3rd Bengal Cavalry, killed at Meerut in the [Indian] Mutiny, 1857, aged 19, maker's name GAWTHORP Sᶜ LONDON (and monogram), mur., on marble, N. *XI.* Inscr. recording gift [of lectern] by daus., Emma Laura Shaw Lefevre and Helena St. John Mildmay, in mem. of Rt. Hon. Charles Shaw Lefevre, [1st and last] Viscount Eversley, G.C.B., [Speaker of the House of Commons 1839-1857], 1794-**1888**, on lectern, N. See also Kings Worthy no.*XV*. *XII.* Inscr. recording presentation of lectern in mem. of Rt. Hon. Charles Shaw Lefevre, [1st and last] Viscount Eversley, G.C.B., Speaker of the House of Commons 1839-1857, [1794-]**1888**, mur., N.C. See also Kings Worthy no.*XV*. *XIII.* Inscr. Emma Laura Shaw Lefevre, eld. and last surviving dau. of [Rt. Hon.] Charles [Shaw Lefevre, 1st and last] Viscount Eversley, [G.C.B.], of Heckfield Place, **1899**, aged 78, buried at Kensal Green [Cemetery, Middx.], mur., N.C. *XIV.* Inscr. [Rev.] George James Thomas, M.A., vicar for 29 years [1883-1912], 1840-**1914**, pos. by congregation, mur., below window, C. *XV.* Inscr. Mary Frances Thorne, pos. in **1924** by children, on cross, C. *XVI.* Inscr. in raised letters recording gift of garden of remembrance by husband in mem. of Ethel Rose Stuart-Black, **1960**, bronze, Churchyard.

Ref: *Burke's Peerage and Baronetage*, p.944, p.1736, p.1816; *Haines*, II, p.72; *M.B.S. Trans.*, V, pp.308-10, IX, pp.69-70; *Mee, Hampshire*, p.189; *M.S.*, p.161; *Pevsner, Hampshire*, p.287; *Soc. Antiq. MS. 875/6*, pp.57-9; *V.C.H., Hampshire*, IV, p.49.

HENGISTBURY HEAD, (see BOURNEMOUTH).

HERRIARD, St. Mary.

I. Inscr. recording erection of organ in **1881** by children in mem. of Mary Louisa Ellis Jervoise, on organ, N.A. *II.* Inscr. with 3 shs. "Hugh de Port, 1086; Alexander de Herierd, 1155; Henricus de Herierd, 1167; Germanus de Herierd, 1172; Richard de Herierd, 1187; Sir John de Herierd and son, Richard de Herierd, junior, 1207; sister, Matilda de Herierd and son, Nicholas Sifrewast, 1221; nephew, Fulc de Coudray, 1245; son, Sir Peter de Coudray, 1251; son, Sir Thomas de Coudray and Sir Robert and Lady Agnes Achard (lessees), 1297; son, Sir Thomas de Coudray, 1316; son, Sir Fulc de Coudray, 1349; cousin, Sir Henry de Coudray, 1354; nephew, Edward Coudray, 1365; son, Peter Coudray, 1428; son, Edward Cowdray, c.1460; son, Peter Cowdray, 1464; kinsman, Peter Cowdray, 1483; dau., Elizabeth, 1528 [w.] (1) Richard Poulett, 1532, (2) W[illia]m, 2nd Lord Windsor, 1544, (3) George Puttenham, and son John Poulett, 1561; son,

Sir Richard Paulett, 1580; widow, Lady Anne Poulett, 1614; and dau., Lady Lucy, [w. of] Sir Thomas Jervoise, 1618, lords of the manor, engr. c.**1900**, mur., C. *III.* Inscr. with ach. Sir Thomas Jervoise, Knt., 1587-1654; Thomas Jervoise, 1616-1693; Thomas Jervoise, 1667-1743; Richard Jervoise, 1703-1762; Tristram Huddleston Jervoise, 1736-1794; Rev. George Huddleston Purefoy Jervoise, 1739-1805; George Purefoy Jervoise, 1770-1847; Mary Purefoy Ellis Jervoise, 1776-1849; Francis Jervoise Ellis Jervoise, 1809-1881; and Francis Michael Ellis Jervoise, 1844-1903, [lords of the manor], engr. c.**1900**, mur., C. *IV.* Inscr. [recording gift of altar cross] in **1907** from Violet Lady Beaumont, [O.B.E., only dau. of Frederick Wootton Isaacson, w. of Henry Stapleton, 9th Baron Beaumont, J.P., D.L.], worn, on cross, C. *V.* Inscr. within border of 4 bells and rope. C.T. Burridge, chorister, **1908**, maker's name *J. WIPPELL & C^O L^TD EXETER & LONDON*, mur., N.A. *VI.* Inscr. in raised letters. George Purefoy Valentine Jervoise, [2nd son of Francis Michael Ellis Jervoise, of Herriard Park], district commissioner in the Uganda Protectorate [for 17 years], died at Masindi, [Uganda], **1922**, [aged 42], pos. by friends and fellow officers in Uganda, maker's name A&N C.S.L LONDON, bronze, mur., below window, N. *VII.* Inscr. in raised letters. George Purefoy V[alentine] Jervoise, 2nd son of Francis M[ichael] E[llis] Jervoise, of Herriard Park, district commissioner in the Uganda Protectorate for 17 years, died at Masindi, Uganda, 1922, aged 42, and w. Constance Winifred, **1926**, aged 45; also dau., Anne Penelope, died at Masindi, [Uganda], 1922, aged 5 months, bronze, mur., below no.*VI*, N. *VIII.* Inscr. with verse recording cleaning and restoration of organ and installation of electric blower in **1960** by A.M. J[ervoise] in mem. of husband, Francis Henry Tristram Jervoise, 1872-1959, copper, on organ with no.*I*, N.A. *IX. & X.* Two inscrs. R[ichard] S[omervell] Jervoise, [lord of the manor] 1959-**1961**, [1887-1961], on churchwardens' wands, N. and C. *XI.* Inscr. with sh. Francis Henry Tristram Jervoise, 1872-1959; and Richard Somervell Jervoise, 1887-**1961**, [lords of the manor], mur., C. *XII.* Inscr. Jim Lewis, 1912-1981, and w. Rose, 1911-**1989**, bronze, on bench, Churchyard. *XIII.* Inscr. William (Bill) Hounsell, bellringer, 1912-**1993**, on door, W.Porch/Tower. *XIV.* Inscr. recording restoration of organ in **1993** by family and friends in mem. of Jack Raymond, on organ with nos.*I & VIII*, N.A.

INDENTS & LOST BRASSES. 15. Lost indent, ?4 shs.; in 1908 and 1979 almost completely covered by pew, N.A. Recorded (2 shs.) by Cave (1908) and (2 shs.) by Sadler (1979) but not found (2006). Lower dext. sh. 145 x 120 mm, lower sin. sh. 145 x 120 mm.

Ref: *Burke's Peerage and Baronetage*, p.216; *M.B.S. Trans.*, V, p.310; *Sadler, Dorset and Hampshire,* appx. I, pt.2, p.22; *Soc. Antiq. MS. 875/6*, p.59.

HIGHFIELD, (see PORTSWOOD).

HINTON ADMIRAL, St. Michael and All Angels (new church).

I. Inscr. recording gift of legacy of £1,000, India Annuities, by Mrs. Martha Pyle, of New Sarum, dau. of Joseph Hinxman, of North Hinton; chapel consecrated in **1786**, mur., Vestry. Inscr. 188 x 421 mm. *II.* Inscr. recording payment for organ in **1875** by subscriptions raised by Hon. Mrs. Robinson, on organ, C. *III.* Inscr. Hon. Frederick Noel Somerville, 1867, and Hugh [Somerville], 18th Baron Somerville, [killed while hunting near Withcote Hall, Uppingham, Rutland], 1868, [aged 29], engr. c.**1880**, mur., below window, N. *IV.* Inscr. Rev. Thomas Wyndham, LL.D., 1862; also only son, Thomas [Wyndham], **1881**, mur., below window, N.

V. Inscr. [Fanny], Lady Meyrick, [4th dau. of Christopher Harland, of Ashbourne, Derbys., w. of Sir George Eliott Meyrick Tapps-Gervis-Meyrick, 3rd Bart.], 1892, [pos. in] **1895** [by] Childeroy Compton, on ewer, N. *VI.* Inscr. with verse. Ivor [T.] Davies, ch. worshipper, [husband and father, 1918-]**1987**, bronze, on bench, Churchyard. *VII.* Inscr. Reginald James Weatherhead, 1913-**1992**, on credence table, C.

Ref: *Burke's Peerage and Baronetage*, p.1804; *M.B.S. Trans.*, V, p.310; *Soc. Antiq. MS. 875/6*, p.59.

Ch. built, 1875-83.

HINTON AMPNER, All Saints.

I. Inscr. Katherine, 2nd dau. of Sir Humphrey Drewell of Little Gidding, Hunts., **1599**, aged 9; sh. lost; mur., C. Recorded (sh.) by Pavey (1706). Inscr. 121 x 445 mm.

II. Inscr. Edward, son of John Drewe of St. Decuman's, Devon, **1601**, aged 77; sh. lost; mur., C. Recorded (sh.) by Pavey (1706). Inscr. 118 x 496 mm.

III. Inscr. William, 3rd son of Sir Thomas Stewkeley, 1604-**1606**, mur., C. Inscr. 97-116 x 312 mm.

IV. Inscr. Thomas, eld. son of Sir Hugh Stewkeley, Knt. and Bart., 1635-**1638**; now mur., C. Inscr. 100 x 413 mm.

V. Inscr. and ach. Sir Hugh Stewkeley, Knt. and Bart., **1642**, aged 38 years, 11 months and 20 days, maker's name *Thomas Brome fecit*; now mur., C. *M.B.S. Trans.*, V, p.312 (ach.). Inscr. 648 x 722 mm, ach. 357 x 316 mm.

VI. Inscr. Lady Elizabeth, only child of John Goodwyn of Winchington, Bucks., widow of Sir Thomas Stewkeley, Knt., **1649**, mur., C. Inscr. 244 x 536 mm.

VII. Inscr. with 10 Eng. vv. Elizabeth, 2nd dau. of Sir Hugh Stewkeley, Bart., by Katherine, sole dau. of Sir John Trott of Laverstock, Bart., **1667**, aged 37 weeks, mur., C. Inscr. 305 x 456-463 mm.

VIII. Inscr. Henry Stawell Bilson Legge, Lord Stawell, 1757-**1820**; mar. 1779, Mary, dau. of Asheton, 1st Viscount Curzon, 1760-1804; also son, Henry, 1785-1788, mur., in stone frame, C. *IX.* Inscr. recording erection of [west] window in **1880** by Lavinia A[gnes, w. of Hon. John T.] Dutton, [of Hinton House] in mem. of [Rt. Rev. Dr.] Samuel Wilberforce, D.D., [Bishop of Oxford 1845-1869], Bishop of Winchester [1869-1873, 1805-1873], mur., below window, N. See also Alverstoke no.*VIII*, Alverstoke, or Gosport, Fort Brockhurst no.*XXXIII*, Newport, St. Thomas the Apostle no.*IX*, Petersfield no.*VI*, Ryde, or Swanmore, St. Michael and All Angels no.*III* and Winchester Cathedral no.*X*.

Ref: *Brit. Lib. Add. MS. 39966*, f.298, f.300, *Stowe MS. 845*, ff.39-41; *Heseltine, Heraldry*, p.37; *M.B.S. Trans.*, II, p.62, V, pp.310-4, VIII, p.38; *Mee, Hampshire*, p.193; *M.S.*, pp.161-2; *Norris, Memorials*, p.252; *Soc. Antiq. MS. 875/6*, pp.59-63; *V.C.H., Hampshire*, III, p.322.

ERE LIETH BVRIED KATHERIN DREWELL, SE-
OND DAVGHTER OF SR HVMPHERYE DREWELL
KNIGHT, OF LITELL GIDINGE IN THE COVNTIE OF
NTINGTON, WHO DIED y XXVIIJ OF DECEMB
NNO 1599 BEINGE OF THE AGE OF 9 YERES

Hinton Ampner I

HERE LIETH BVRIED EDWARD DREWE THE SONN
OF JOHN DREWE ESQVIRE LATE OF ST DECVMANS
IN THE COVNTIE OF DEVON, WHO DIED y 29 OF OC:
TOBER, AN 1601. BEINGE OF y AGE OF 77 YERES

Hinton Ampner II

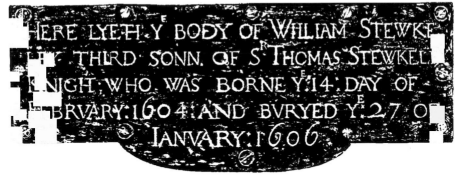

HERE LYETH y BODY OF WILIAM STEWKE
THE THIRD SONN. OF SR THOMAS STEWKELL
KNIGH, WHO WAS BORNE y 14 DAY OF
FEBRVARY 1604 AND BVRYED y 27 O
IANVARY 1606

Hinton Ampner III

HERE LYETH THE BODY OF THOMAS STEWKELEY
EST SONN OF SR HVGH STEWKELEY KNIGHT
BARONETT, WHO WAS BORNE, y 2 DAY OF AVGVST 1635,
BVRYED y FIRST DAY OF APRILL 1638

Hinton Ampner IV

161

M·S·
Hvgonis Stewkeley Militis et Baronetti
Qvod mortale est et corrvptibile,
Hic iacet.
Plvra, viator, si desideres, vicinia
Loqvetvr hospitalitatem, modestiam,
Pietatem, reliqvasq· viri virtvtes
Sic enim ornatvm invenies ædes proximas
Incolvisse. Et hinc lacrymæ. Nam fvisse hvn
Ah, nimis miservm est. At hoc restat vnicvm
Ablatvs in dimidio diervm te valere
Ivbet et vivere, sed memorem læthi.

Vixit ann: xxxviii· men: xi· di· xx·
Devixit xxvii die Sept· 1642

Hinton Ampner V

·Here lyeth the body of the Lady·
Elizabeth Stewkeley widow, of Sir Tho:
mas Stewkeley late of Henton Amner in
the Covnty of Sovthampton Knight ·&
the only child of Iohn Goodwyn of
Winchington in the Covnty of Bvcking
ham·Esqvire· who dyed the ninetenth·
·day of Aprill Anno Dñi Mdcxlviiii·

Hinton Ampner VI

162

Reader within this little Vaule lyes pent
The Ashes of a Female Innocent
Whose early whiter Soule as yet had not
From the defiled World contracted Spott
That day she lived she Dyed yet having spent
Five weeke then to Abrams bosome went
Where now her happy Soule enjoys that Blisse
Which unto little Infants promis'd is
From who this harmlesse was y' should'st know
Looke downe and read th' Inscription here below

HERE LYETH THE BODY OF ELIZABETH STEWKELEY SECOND DAVGHTER OF Sᵣ HVGH STEWKELEY OF THIS PLACE BARRONETT AND DAME KATHERINE HIS WIFE SOLE DAVGHTER OF Sᵣ IOHN TROTT OF LAVERSTOCK IN THIS COVNTY BARRONETT WHO DYED THE 2E DAY OF SEPTEMBER IN THE YEARE OF OVR LORD 1667 BEING OF THE AGE OF 37 WEEKS

Hinton Ampner VII

HABITATION · OF · THINE · HOVSE · AND · THE · PLACE · WHERE · THINE · HONOVR · DWELLETH · LORD · HAVE · LOVED · THE

This Parish Church was rebuilt
to the Honour and Glory of God by
JOHN PEIRSE KENNARD.
in the year of our Lord Mdccclxxii.

This Tablet is placed here by
his children in thankful remembrance
of his deep piety, holy zeal and simple trust
in God's guidance throughout a long life.

PS. XXIV : 8.

Hordle (new church) *IV*

163

HOLDENHURST, St. John the Evangelist (now in Dorset).

I. Henry George Hopkins, of Segrove, Isle of Wight, **1870**, aged 60, mur., below window, C. *II.* Inscr. recording that [west] window was filled with stained glass in **1872** by parishioners in gratitude to Rev. F[rederick] Hopkins, [M.A., curate 1857-1858, vicar 1877-1903], for building the chancel and improving the ch., mur., below window, N. *III.* Inscr. recording erection of lychgate in **1897** by J.E. Cooper Dean in mem. of William Clapcott Dean, of Littledown, and to commem. the 60th year of the reign of Queen Victoria, on lychgate, Churchyard. *IV.* Inscr. recording erection of window on behalf of 5 children, by 2 surviving, in mem. of [parents,] Henry Cecil and [w.] Mary, engr. c.**1900**, mur., below window, N. *V.* Inscr. recording organ subscribed for by friends, parishioners, visitors and a gift from the Carnegie Corporation, of New York, in mem. of Rev. F[rederick] Hopkins, M.A., vicar for over 50 years [curate 1857-1858, vicar 1877-1903]; dedicated in **1913** by Rev. Sydney [Powell] Townend, vicar; [James Edward Harris, 5th] Earl of Malmesbury, [J.P., D.L.], vicar's [church]warden and J.A. Hockey, people's [church]warden, mur., on board, N. *VI.* Inscr. recording installation of electricity in **1955** through generosity of James Ainsworth Hockey, mur., on board, N. *VII.* Inscr. recording restoration of organ in **1958** in mem. of Alice Harding, w. of W.I. Scriven, 1st accompanist to the municipal choir, mur., on organ, N. *VIII.* Inscr. recording presentation [of notice board] in **1995** on baptism of Oliver Meakins, on notice board, N. *IX.* Inscr. Rosemary Deniau, **n.d.**, on bench, Churchyard. *X.* Inscr. Annie Furr and Bill Cherry, **n.d.**, on bench, Churchyard.

Ch. built, 1834 and 1872.

Transferred from Hampshire to Dorset in 1974.

HORDLE, All Saints (old church, now demolished).

INDENTS & LOST BRASSES. 1. Indent, 3 rivets and 2 plugs only, effaced, N.Tr. Non-Purbeck slab 2175 x 950 mm. 2. Lost brass, man in arm., c.1465, N.Tr. Possibly Sir Reginald de Clerke. In private poss. of Gustavus Brander (1781) and presented to Smart Lethieullier. Recorded (lost) by Warner (c.1770). *Bod. Lib. Gough Maps 224*, f.462 (Gough impression); *Brit. Lib. Add. MS. 32478*, f.107 (Craven Ord impression); *Brit. Lib. Maps K. Top. 14*, f.80; *Gough*, II, p.386; *Grose, F., Antiq. of Eng. and Wales*, 1773-87, supplement, I, pl.7, fig.1; *M.B.S. Bulletin*, 103, p.56 (Craven Ord impression); *M.B.S. Trans.*, X, opp. p.484 (Craven Ord impression). Rubbing (by Ord) in British Museum coll. (1781) and impression in Soc. Antiq. coll. (n.d.). Eff. 480 x 175 mm. Style: London D.

Ref: *Bod. Lib. Gough Maps 224*, f.462; *Brit. Lib. Add. MS. 32478*, f.107; *Maps K. Top. 14,* f.80; *Gough*, II, p.386; *Haines*, II, p.76; *Hampshire, Antiquary*, I, p.141; *Hampshire History*, III, p.93; *M.B.S. Bulletin*, 103, p.56; *M.B.S. Trans.*, I, pt.9, p.15, V, pp.314-5, VI, p.386, IX, p.133, p.136, X, p.484, XIV, p.490; *M.S.*, p.170, p.753; *Soc. Antiq. MS. 875/6*, pp.63-4; *Warner*, I, pp.257-8; *Warner, R., Topographical Remarks relating to the south-western parts of Hampshire*, 1793, II, pp.33-4.

Ch. demolished, 1830.

Hordle (old church) 2

HORDLE, All Saints (new church).

I. Inscr. recording gift [of north-east nave window] in **1872** in mem. of [Charles Henry Sydney Raitt, 1855, aged 18, and George Edward Frances Raitt, 1849, aged 8], sons of Charles Robert Raitt and [w.] Anne, [of Downton Lodge], mur., on board below window, N. *II.* Inscr. with verse. Hugh Hamon John Massy, of Hazelhurst, 1867; also children, Dunbar and Narcissa, engr. c.**1875**, mur., on board, N. *III.* Inscr. L.R. and A.W., **1880**, on ewer, Vestry. *IV.* Inscr. with verse and 4 evang. symbols recording rebuilding of ch. in 1872 by John Peirse Kennard, [of Walthamstow, Essex, 1798-1877], pos. by children, engr. c.**1880**, maker's name BARKENTIN & KRALL, LONDON, mur., on board, N. Inscr. 685 x 903 mm. *V.* Inscr. recording presentation of lectern by [children] in mem. of J.A. Russell, of Yeatton [House], **1882**, on lectern, N. *VI.* Inscr. James Tinker, 1906, aged 81, and w. Lucy Elizabeth, **1907**, aged 73, maker's name GAWTHORP, S^C LONDON, mur., on board, N. *VII.* Inscr. William John Crickitt Mello, (w. Susan Charlotte, [1891], and sister, Ellen Mario Mello, [1898], are commem. by ch. windows), died at Folkestone, [Kent], **1909**, aged 75, mur., below window, N. *VIII.* Inscr. Mary Ann Banks, 1832-1900; Ellen Draper, 1835-1896; and Catherine Steel, 1837-**1911**, sisters, maker's name A. R. MOWBRAY & C^O L^TD LONDON & OXFORD, mur., on board, N. *IX.* Inscr. with Lat. verse. Sgt. Archibald Eugene Harris [Logan], Lord Strathcona's Horse, [killed] in the S[outh] Africa[n War], 1863-1900; Capt. Hubert Henderson [Logan], 10th [Battn. (Queen's Own)] Royal West Kent Regt., 1872-**1916**, [buried at Caterpillar Valley Cemetery, Longueval, France]; and Major Lionel Stewart [Logan], Supply and Transport Corps, Indian Army, 1874-1914, [buried at La Gorgue Communal Cemetery, France], sons of Major-Gen. A.G.D. Logan, Indian Army, mur., on board, N. *X.* Inscr. in raised letters. Arthur Wellesley Raitt, son of Charles Robert Raitt and [w.] Anne, of Downton Lodge, 1880, aged 37, and w. Mary, dau. of James Thomson and [w.] Teresa Trapani, of St. Petersburg, [Russia], **1927**, aged 82, copper, mur., on board, N. *XI.* Inscr. John Pemberton Heywood, engr. c.**1930**, mur., C. *XII.* Inscr. [Rev.] Edward Percy Boys-Smith, M.A., vicar 1891-1931, rural dean of Lyndhurst 1927-**1937**, mur., C. *XIII.* Inscr. recording dedication of [electric] light in mem. of Arthur William Price and w. Lilian, served ch. and par. 1931-**1954**, mur., on board with light, N. *XIV.* Inscr. Henry Benjamin Tringham, 1885-**1962**, on processional cross, Vestry. *XV.* Inscr. recording erection of vestry in **1967** with gifts of parishioners and legacy of Arthur George Lunt in mem. of w. Frances Charlotte, 1962, who for 50 years "GAVE HER TIME AND SERVICE TO THE CHURCH AND PEOPLE OF THIS PARISH. HER INTERESTS WERE MANY AND VARIED AND HER LIFE WAS MARKED BY THAT LOVE FOR HUMANITY WHICH WAS BORN OF HER DEEP AND ABIDING CHRISTIAN FAITH", bronze, on cupboard, Narthex. *XVI.* Inscr. Lindsay Anne Whitlock, "a singer in this choir, and a very courageous girl", 1967-**1984**, mur., on board, C. *XVII.* Inscr. Norman Hopkins and [w.] Grace, engr. c.**1990**, on bench, Churchyard. *XVIII.* Inscr. Douglas Howard Jones, 1918-**1999**, bronze, on wooden cross, Churchyard. *XIX.* Inscr. recording opening of "Memorial Hall" in **2005** by Rt. Rev. Michael [Charles] Scott-Joynt, Bishop of Winchester [1995-], mur., on board, Hall Foyer.

Ref: *Burke's Peerage and Baronetage*, p.1469.

Ch. built, 1872.

HURSLEY, All Saints (new church).

I. Inscr. and 10 Lat. vv. John Bowland, park-keeper of Merdon and Winchester for 42 years, **1474**; formerly N., inscr., now on step, C., vv., now mur., Tower. Inscr. 106 x 432 mm, vv. 214 x 320 mm.

Hursley I

Hursley II

II. Inscr. in 6 Eng. vv. Anne Horswell, w. of —— Sternhold, **1559**; formerly mur., C., now mur., Tower. Inscr. 171-194 x 364 mm.

III. Cross with evang. symbols, inscr. and marg. inscr. with roundels at corners. [Rev.] John Keble, vicar 1835-1866, [born at Fairford, Gloucs., died at Bournemouth, 1792-]**1866**, [designed by William Butterfield, engr. by Messrs. J.G. and L.A.B. Waller], C. *Rawdon*, cover (drg.). Cross 1670 x 639 mm, inscr. 119 x 498 mm, marg. inscr. 2040 x 757 x 46 mm, roundels 103 mm dia., slab 2135 x 850 mm. *IV.* Inscr. recording gift of bookcase (which belonged to Rev. John Keble, vicar 1835-1866) to successive vicars by the Misses Young, engr. c.**1900**, copper, on bookcase, N.A. *V.* Inscr. recording rearrangement of choir stalls in **1906** by w. in mem. of Rear-Admiral Francis Durrant, C.M.G., on choir stall, C. *VI.* Inscr. with verse recording presentation [of font] in **1913** by Mr. and Mrs. F.W. Talbot, copper, now mur., on board, N.A.; from Pitt (q.v.). *VII.* Inscr. with verse. Lt. James Shirley Heathcote, [1st Battn.] Coldstream Guards, died of wounds received in the Battle of Loos, [1887-]**1917**, [buried at Kensal Green (All Souls') Cemetery, Middx.], and 2nd-Lt. Martin Arthur Heathcote, M.C., [B Co. 10th Battn.] Royal Fusiliers, killed in action in the Battle of the Somme, [1892-]**1916**, [buried at Heilly Station Cemetery, Mericourt-l'Abbe, France, sons of Arthur Malcolm Heathcote and w. Mary Forbes, 2nd dau. of Rev. James Gavin Young, M.A., vicar 1866-1906], grandsons of Sir W[illiam] Heathcote, 5th Bart., [P.C., 1801-1881], bronze, mur., Tower. *VIII.* World War I memorial in raised letters (6 names), bronze, mur., on board with no.*VI*, N.A.; from Pitt (q.v.). *IX.* Inscr. recording presentation [of lectern] by w. in mem. of Edward Gattey, **1949**, now mur., on board with nos.*VI & VIII*, N.A.; from Pitt (q.v.). *X.* Inscr. recording gift of organ in 1908 by Lady Cooper, C.B.E. and restoration in **1960** by son, Capt. Sir George Cooper, Bart., [J.P., D.L., 1890-1961], bronze, on organ, Organ Chamber. *XI.* Inscr. Phyliss Mary Ashford, 1902-**1977**, on table, Vestry. *XII.* Inscr. recording renovation of bells in **1978** through legacy of Herbert Hunt, mur., N. *XIII.* Inscr. recording renovation of [south aisle] windows in **1978** in mem. of William and Harry Jones, father and son, churchwardens, mur., S.A.

Ref: *Brit. Lib. Add. MS. 39966,* ff.364-6. f.371; *Duthy,* p.339; *Burke's Peerage and Baronetage*, pp.1304-5; *M.B.S. Bulletin*, 52, p.394, p.396; *M.B.S. Trans.*, V, pp.315-6; *M.S.*, p.162; *Pevsner, Hampshire*, p.300; *Rawdon, S.C., All Saints' Church Hursley: a History and Guide*, 1993, pp.24-5, pp.34-6; *Soc. Antiq. MS. 875/6*, pp.64-5; *V.C.H., Hampshire*, III, p.421.

Ch. built, 1846-8.

HURSLEY, or PITT, Good Shepherd (redundant, now a residence).

Inscr. with verse recording presentation [of font] in **1913** by Mr. and Mrs. F.W. Talbot, copper, on font; moved to Hursley (q.v.) (1983). World War I memorial in raised letters (6 names), bronze; moved to Hursley (q.v.) (1983). Inscr. recording presentation [of lectern] by w. in mem. of Edward Gattey, **1949**, on lectern; moved to Hursley (q.v.) (1983).

Ch. built, 1858; closed, 1983.

IBSLEY, St. Martin (new church, redundant, now an Interior and Art Centre).

I. Inscr. Edward Passion, gent., **1599**. Inscr. 114 x 400-407 mm, non-Purbeck slab 1805 x 900 mm.

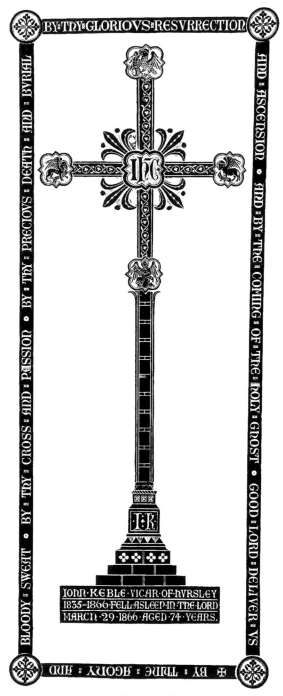

Hursley *III*

INDENTS & LOST BRASSES. 2. Indent, inscr., on same slab as no.*I*. Inscr. 115 x 405 mm.

Ch. built, 1832; closed, 1986; declared redundant, 1991; converted, 1997.

ILFORD, (see BOURNEMOUTH).

ITCHEN ABBAS, St. John the Baptist (new church).

I. Inscr. Rev. Septimus Gillson, M.A., rector for 26 years [1874-1901], **1901**, [aged 60], pos. by friends and parishioners, maker's name *J. WIPPELL & COMP^Y EXETER & LONDON*, mur., S.Tr. *II.* Inscr. with verse. [Capt.] Christopher Byron Simpson, [26th Battn. Royal Fusiliers, son of Byron R Simpson and w. Beatrice], godson, 1893-**1916**, mur., S.Tr. *III.* Inscr. with verse. [Pte.] William Waters Vokes, [200901], 1[st/]4[th Battn.] Hampshire Regt. (Territorials), only son of David Vokes and [w.] Annie, "TAKEN PRISONER APRIL 1916 BY THE TURKS AFTER THE FALL OF KUT AND DIED IN THEIR HANDS AT AFION KARA HISSAR", **1916**, aged 28, [buried at Baghdad (North Gate) War Cemetery, Iraq], maker's name MANNELL & C^O BOURNEMOUTH, mur., N.Tr. *IV.* Inscr. with verse recording dedication of banner ("HUNG AT THE COMMEMORATION OF THE HEROIC DEEDS OF THE FIRST SEVEN DIVISIONS HELD IN LONDON. DEC. 15. **1917**") in mem. of Capt. Noel Spicer Simson, R[oyal] G[arrison] A[rtillery], son of Frederick John Simson and w. Dora, officer] commanding 21st Anti-Aircraft Section, [1915, aged 34, buried at Etaples Military Cemetery, France], and Lt. Kenneth Watson Harvey, R[oyal] F[ield] A[rtillery], 19th H.H.C., 1915, aged 24, buried at Lijssenthoek Military Cemetery, Belgium], "AND THE MEN WHO FELL WITH THEM" during the Battle of Loos, 1915, mur., N. *V.* Inscr. recording recasting of 2 bells in **1949** "THROUGH THE ZEAL AND DEVOTION OF THE YOUTH FELLOWSHIP" in mem. of those [killed in World War II], copper, mur., N. *VI.* Inscr. recording presentation of churchyard extension by Dr. A[rthur] W[alsh] Titherley, [D.Sc., Ph.D., F.I.C.], where the cremated remains of w. Jessie Eleanor were scattered in **1964**, pos. by Charles, Mrs. Gaiger, R. Hall and F.C. Mabey, bronze, on grave marker, Churchyard. *VII.* Inscr. with verse. [Dr.] Arthur Walsh Titherley, D.Sc., Ph.D., F.I.C., engr. c.**1965**, bronze, on grave marker with no.*VI*, Churchyard. *VIII.* Inscr. recording dedication of chair and prayer desk in mem. of Bridget Isaac, **1966**, aged 38, bronze, on prie-dieu, C. *IX.* Inscr. recording restoration of bells in **1990** by gift of Sheila, Lady Douglas-Pennant, [2nd dau. of Stanley Brotherhood, J.P., w. of Admiral the Hon. Sir Cyril Eustace Douglas-Pennant, K.C.B., C.B.E., D.S.O., D.S.C.], of Itchen Lodge, worshipped in the ch. for 21 years, 1988, bronze, mur., N.

INDENTS & LOST BRASSES. 10. Lost brass, eff., inscr. and marg. inscr. William Letham, rector, 1548; with later incised inscr.; C. Recorded (marg. inscr. (mutil.) with eff. and inscr. lost) by Pavey (1703).

Ref: *Brit. Lib. Stowe MS. 845*, f.92; *Burke's Peerage and Baronetage*, p.2096; *M.B.S. Trans.*, V, p.316; *Soc. Antiq. MS. 875/6*, p.65.

Ch. built, 1863, 1867 and 1883.

ITCHEN STOKE, St. Mary
(new church, redundant, now vested in The Churches Conservation Trust).

I. Joan, w. of master John Batmanson, "doctor of Sevell", **1518**, inscr.; formerly on A.T., C., now mur., N. Recorded (in poss. of ?Lord Ashburton) by Haines (1861). Eff. 475 x 155 mm, inscr. 192 x 442 mm. Style: London G.

II. Lady, c.**1525**, kng.; inscr., B.V. Mary and Child, scroll and 2 shs. lost; in 1903 loose in chest at the Vicarage, purchased by Mrs. Rannie, of West Hayes, Winchester, subsequently mounted mur. in chapel of West Hayes School, Winchester, and returned in 1950; formerly on A.T., now mur., N. Recorded (eff. and scroll with inscr., B.V. Mary and Child and 2 shs. lost) by Pavey (1703) and (scroll) by Cave (1903). *Brit. Lib. Add. MS. 39987,* f.48r, f.50r (with scroll); *M.B.S. Trans.,* V, p.318 (with scroll). Illustration (scroll) from rubbing in Soc. Antiq. coll. Rubbing (scroll) in Soc. Antiq. coll. (1903). Eff. 285 x 144 mm, lost scroll 227 x 93 x 28 mm. Style: London F debased.

III. Inscr. on 2 pls. Very Rev. W.D. Conybeare, [Dean of Llandaff, died at Itchen Stoke, 1857], and I.H. Markland, D.C.L., pos. by grandchildren, Crawford, Helen and Charles, engr. **1866**, mur., C. *IV.* Inscr. with verse recording restoration of organ by friends and neighbours in mem. of Mary James, [w. of Edward] Eames, of Stoke Manor, worshipped in the ch. for 15 years, [died at Compton], **1904**, [aged 52], mur., in recess, N. *V.* Inscr. in raised letters. Margaret Susanna Skrine, betrothed 1907, 1883-**1907**, bronze, mur., in marble frame, N. *VI.* World War I memorial (5 names), **1919**, mur., N. *VII.* Inscr. Gunner W[illiam] G[eorge] Jackson, [1693446], 202nd Battery, 127th L.A.A. Regt., R[oyal] A[rtillery], 4th Battn. The Queen's Royal Regt., [son of Ernest Jackson and w. Sarah Ann], **1942**, [aged 30], on vase, N.

INDENTS & LOST BRASSES. 8. Lost brass, four frags. of inscr. (chamfer) bearing the words "one of the kyng's s'jeaunt' at his lawe which lyeth buryed at the whyte ffreers in London on wh"; formerly on A.T., in 1903 loose at Rectory. Recorded (inscr. (chamfer) mutil.) by Pavey (1703) and (inscr. (chamfer) mutil.) by Cave (1903). *M.B.S. Trans.,* V, p.319. Illustration from rubbing in Soc. Antiq. coll. Rubbing in Soc. Antiq. coll. (1903). Inscr. (chamfer) frags. 34 x 335 mm, 34 x 368 mm, 34 x 215 mm and 34 x 311 mm. 9. Lost brass, eff. in swaddling clothes and inscr., Richard Palmer, 1524, aged 8 weeks. Recorded (complete) by Pavey (1703).

Ref: *Brit. Lib. Add. MS. 39966,* f.439, *Add. MS. 39987,* f.48, f.50, *Stowe MS. 845,* ff.109-10; *Duthy,* p.160; *Haines,* II, p.72; *Hants Proc.,* III, p.279; *M.B.S. Bulletin,* 19, p.14; *M.B.S. Trans.,* V, pp.316-9, IX, p.44; *Mee, Hampshire,* p.203; *M.S.,* p.162, p.753; *Pevsner, Hampshire,* p.309; *Soc. Antiq. MS. 875/6,* pp.65-8, *MS. 943/1; V.C.H., Hampshire,* IV, p.194.

Ch. built, 1866; declared redundant, 1973; vested, 1975.

KILMESTON, St. Andrew.

I. Inscr. Rev. Thomas Johnson, M.A., curate for 42 years, 1793-**1867**, pos. by friends and parishioners, mur., on marble, C. *II.* Inscr. with enamelled sh. and crest. Charles Gilbert Heathcote, J.P., of Kilmeston Manor, 3rd son of John Moyer Heathcote, of Conington Castle,

HERE LYETH THE BODY OF EDWARDE
PASSION GENT, WHICH DEPARTED
THIS LIFE THE XIIIJTH DAYE OF APRILL
IN Y^E YERE OF OVR LORD GOD. 1599.

Ibsley *I*

Of yor charite pray for the soule of Johan
Batmanson late the wyffe of walter John
Batmanson docto' of Sebell which Johan
decessed the xvii day of may the yer of ô lord
m̄ b^c xviii on whose soule Jhu have mercy

Itchen Stoke I

172

Itchen Stoke *II*

Itchen Stoke 8

Hunts., barrister-at-law, 1841-**1913**, pos. by children, maker's name CULN GAWTHORP & SONS LONDON, mur., on marble, N. *III.* Inscr. with verse. Lt. John Rory Carden, R.N., Fleet Air Arm, [H.M.S. Audacity, son of Rev. Canon Henry Craven Carden, M.A., rector 1934-1953, and w. Olive], killed in action in the Battle of the Atlantic, **1941**, aged 24, copper, mur., on marble, C. *IV.* Inscr. Margaret Daphne Griffen, [1919-]**2002**, on bench, Churchyard.

KIMPTON, SS. Peter and Paul.

I. Robert Thornburgh, esq., **1522**, in arm., and 2 ws., (1) Alys with 1 son and 1 dau., (2) Anne with 1 son and 6 daus., kng., inscr., sm. cross with the five wounds in top corner and 3 scrolls; 3 shs. lost; mur., A.T., N.Tr. *Brit. Lib. Add. MS. 39987,* f.51r; *M.B.S. Trans.,* V, p.320; *Mee, Hampshire,* p.219 (drg. of effs.). Male eff. 258 x 215 mm, male eff. scroll 172 x 63 x 25 mm, dext. female eff., children and scroll 382 x 223 mm, sin. female eff., children and scroll 343 x 260 mm, inscr. 93 x 662 mm, cross 155 x 110 mm, dext. sh. indent 140 x 115 mm, centre sh. indent 140 x 115 mm, sin. sh. indent 140 x 110 mm, slab 775 x 1240 mm. Style: London F debased.

II. Inscr. Capt. Cecil Dacre More Holbrooke, R[oyal] A[rmy] S[ervice] Corps, son of Rev. Frederick George Holbrooke, M.A., rector [1882-1910], died at Poona, India, **1909**, aged 29, maker's name *JONES & WILLIS LᵀᴰD*, mur., C. *III.* Inscr. Rev. Frederick George Holbrooke, M.A., rector for 29 years [1882-1910], "HE FURNISHED, BEAUTIFIED AND COMPLETELY RESTORED THIS CHURCH AND ERECTED THE ORGAN", **1911**, aged 86, mur., C. *IV* Stepped cross surmounting inscr. with enamelled sh. Charles Foyle Randolph, of Kimpton and Chute, Wilts., eld. son of Rev. Charles Randolph, grandson of George Soley Foyle, 1833-1912, pos. in **1915** by son, Charles Foyle Randolph and w. Edith, maker's name *JONES & WILLIS LᵀᴰD*, mur., C. *V.* World War II memorial in raised letters on 3 pls. (8 names), bronze, mur., on triptych, N.Tr. *VI.* Inscr. in raised letters on 2 pls. recording men of par. who served in World War I (57 names), bronze, mur., on boards, N.Tr. *VII.* Inscr. recording presentation [of chair] by mother as a thank offering for the safe keeping of only son, Humphrey Randolph, during World War I, engr. c.**1920**, on chair, C. *VIII.* Inscr. with verse. Joyce Steele, organist 1947-**1983**, on organ, Gallery/Tower.

INDENTS & LOST BRASSES. 9. Indent, man in arm. and 2 ws., inscr., 4 shs. and inscr. (chamfer), c.1510, on A.T., dexter hf. covered and below no.I., N.Tr. *Sadler, Dorset and Hampshire,* appx. I, pt.2, p.23 (drg.). Male eff. 300 x 50 mm visible, dext. female eff. covered, sin. female eff. 305 x 95 mm, inscr. 90 x 265 mm visible, upper dext. sh. covered, upper sin. sh. 115 x 100 mm, lower dext. sh. covered, lower sin. sh. 115 x 100 mm, inscr. (chamfer) 1360 x 365 x 30 mm, Purbeck coverstone 1400 x 420 mm. Style: London F. 10. Indent, inscr.; in 2005 partly covered by foot pace of altar rails, C. Inscr. 55 x 395 mm, Purbeck slab 1135 visible x 640 mm.

Ref: *Brit. Lib. Add. MS. 39987,* f.51; *Clutterbuck, R.H., Notes on the Parishes of Fyfield, Kimpton, Penton Mewsey, Weyhill and Wherwell, in the County of Hampshire,* 1898, p.64; *Haines,* I, pp.102-3, II, p.72; *M.B.S. Trans.,* V, pp.319-22, VIII, p.375, IX, pp.535-6, X, p.332, XIII, p.335; *Mee, Hampshire,* p.204; *M.S.,* p.162; *Norris, Memorials,* p.205; *Pevsner, Hampshire,* p.310; *Sadler, Dorset and Hampshire,* pt.II, p.19, appx. I, pt.2, pp.23-4, p.41; *Simpson,* p.28; *Soc. Antiq. MS. 875/6,* pp.68-71; *V.C.H., Hampshire,* IV, p.376.

Oft yo'charite pray for the soule of Robert Thornbugh esquier Who body
here restyth and dyed the xu day of may Ju the yere of o' lord god gi b'xxi x
for y' soul of Alys 7 Anne his ladyes 7 all there children olkho' soul thu have mercy

Kimpton I

Kimpton I & 9

175

KINGSCLERE, St. Mary.

I. Cesily Gubard, **1503**, and inscr., very worn; formerly C., S.C., now mur., S.C.; orig. slab in 2005 covered by fitted carpet, S.C. Eff. 377 x 130 mm, inscr. 57 x 295 mm. Style: London F.

II. William Estwood, vicar of Kingsclere, parson of Newnom (Newnham), **1519**, in mass vests. and inscr.; formerly C., S.C., now mur., S.C.; orig. slab in 2005 covered by fitted carpet, S.C. Eff. 440 x 142 mm, inscr. 138 x 494 mm. Style: London G.

III. Inscr. and sh. (mutil.). John Bossewell, gent., "notarye publique", **1580**; another inscr. bearing "Deus in aeternum" lost; formerly N., S.C., now mur., S.C.; orig. slab in 2005 covered by fitted carpet, S.C. Recorded (complete) by Pavey (1704). Illustration from rubbing in Soc. Antiq. coll. Rubbing (inscr. indent) in Soc. Antiq. coll. (1902). Inscr. 113 x 393 mm, inscr. indent 45 x 250 mm, sh. 132 x 113 mm.

IV. Inscr. in 31 Lat. vv. Sir [John] Kingsmill, [died 1558], w. Constance Goring, [died 1581], and children, William, Richard, Roger, Edward, Henry, George and John (twins), Andrew, Thomas, Arthur, Constance, Jane (mar. —— Cooper, gent.), Alice, Anne, Katherine (mar. Richard Trenchard), Margaret, and Mary; sh. lost; engr. c.**1580**; formerly C., rel., S.C., now mur., S.C.; orig. slab in 2005 covered by fitted carpet, S.C. Illustration (sh.) from rubbing in Soc. Antiq. coll. Rubbing (sh.) in Soc. Antiq. coll. (1902). Inscr. 656 x 414 mm, lost sh. 180 x 160 mm.

V. Inscr. Elizabeth, w. of James Hunt of Popham, gent., **1606**; formerly S.C., now mur., S.C.; orig. slab in 2005 covered by fitted carpet, S.C. Inscr. 125 x 440 mm.

VI. Inscr. [Rev.] Richard Nelson Barnes, [M.A.], vicar for 40 years [1849-1889], **1889**, pos. by friends and parishioners, maker's name GAWTHORP. S^c LONDON (and monogram), mur., on marble, S.C. *VII.* Inscr. [Rev.] R[ichard] N[elson] B[arnes, M.A.], vicar 1849-**1889**, [1889], on lectern, N. *VIII.* Inscr. Edward Drake, 1839-1900, engr. **1948**, on chair, Gallery/N. *IX.* Inscr. Charlotte E. Burns, 1844-1922, engr. **1948**, on chair, S.Tr. *X.* Inscr. Eliza Garrett, 1852-1936, engr. **1948**, on chair, Gallery/N. *XI.* Inscr. Philip Sperling, 1911-1940, engr. **1948**, on chair, S.Tr. *XII.* Inscr. Mary E. Ramsey, 1868-1942, engr. **1948**, on chair, S.Tr. *XIII.* Inscr. Walter Chalk, 1881-1943, engr. **1948**, on chair, S.Tr. *XIV.* Inscr. Reginald Parsons, 1878-1945, engr. **1948**, on chair, S.Tr. *XV.* Inscr. George H.T. Seymour, 1881-1946, engr. **1948**, on chair, S.Tr. *XVI.* Inscr. recording presentation [of chair] in **1948** by Kenneth Bartlett, on chair, S.Tr. *XVII.* Inscr. Anita Brown, 1928-**1948**, on chair, S.Tr. *XVIII.* Inscr. Frances Carlyle, 1888-**1948**, on chair, Gallery/N. *XIX.* Inscr. Thomas and Clara Pizzey, engr. **1948**, on chair, S.Tr. *XX.* Inscr. Thomas Knowles Carlyle, 1884-**1964**, on chair with no.*XVIII*, Gallery/N. *XXI.* Inscr. Samuel J. Garrett, 1886-**1966**, on chair with no.*X*, Gallery/N. *XXII.* Inscr. Laura Annie Dudman, 1888-**1967**, on chair, S.Tr. *XXIII.* Inscr. Alfred James Dudman, 1890-**1968**, on chair, S.Tr. *XXIV.* Inscr. Amy E. Parsons, 1884-**1969**, on chair with no.*XIV*, S.Tr. *XXV.* Inscr. recording installation of sound reinforcement system in mem. of Florrie Perkins, "DEARLY LOVED BY THE HOMFRAY FAMILY", 1908-**1973**, mur., S.C. *XXVI.* Inscr. recording that the Kingsclere and District [Branch of the] Royal British Legion [Standard], dedicated in 1948, was laid up in **1976**, mur., on flag-holder, S.Tr. *XXVII.* Inscr. Ernest W. Miller, 1879-1957, and Mary E. Miller, 1881-**1977**, on chair, Gallery/N. *XXVIII.* Inscr. Judith Mary Ridler, 1933-**1979**, on display case, S.Tr. *XXIX.* Inscr. Nell Denness, pos. by family and friends, engr. c.**2000**, on candleholder, N. *XXX.* Inscr. Dorothy Matthew, Rosamond Selsey and Dorothy Aveling, engr. c.**2000**, on votive stand, S.Tr.

Kingsclere I

Of yo charite pray for the soule of S Willm Estwod late vicar of this Churche & plane of Newnom the whiche deceassed y^e xxij day of August the yere of o lord m h^c xix on whose soule ihu have mercy

Kingsclere II

Here lyeth buryed under this stone the bodye
of John Bossewell gentleman and notarye
publique who Deccalied y + day of dereth
in the yeare of our Lorde God A.1580 in hope
of a glorious resurrection to lyfe everlastinge

Kingsclere III

Quem suus est princeps equitis dignabitur honore
longaevillus tibi si longaevalli nomen ad aures
Venerit hic placida compositus pace quiescit
totus et angusto non clauditur ille sepulchro
Fecerat hunc eternum numerosa prole parentem
Re constans Constantia nomine propria coniunx
Quae fuit illustris de sanguine creta Cornish
Crede decem fratres septemque fuisse sorores
Unica quos uno peperit de coniuge coniunx
Primus erat natu Gulielmus in ordine fratrum
Hunc tibi Richardus numerandus et inde Rogerus
Post Adolwardus erat post hunc Henrice husti
Tum Gemini venere Georgius atque Johannes
Ultimus et natu venit qui carmine primus
His minor Andreas et Thomas unior illo
Ultimus Arthurus teris prior nicola coli
Faeminum sexus Constantia maxima natu
Iana secunda fuit generosi sponsa Coperi
Alisiam post hanc illi genuere parentes
Aluisamque suam sequitur soror Anna sororem
Post Katrina nata est qua duxerat olim
Nomine Richardus Trenchardus de nobile natus
Insuper ossa tuos ex ossibus (inclite Thornburgh)
Margarita fuit prognata parentibus illis
Ultima deinde venit numeranda maria sororum
Hic iam quanta potest iniuria temporis esse
Quae tantae sobolis valeat delere parentem
Vivida quin floret virtus non floret caduco
Spiritus est coelis terris sua fama superstes
Si tu Christe tuos vilis sinis esse peremptos
Post cineres salvos serves post funera bonos

Kingsclere IV

HIC IACET CORPVS ELIZABETHÆ HVNT VXOR
IACOBI HVNT DE POPHAM GENEROSI QVÆ FVIT
SEPVLTA DECIMO DIE FEBR. A DNI 1606 CVI FAXIT
DEVS LETIFICAM RESVRRECTIONEM AMEN

Kingsclere V

HERE LYETH REMAINE OF M THOMAS PEARCE DEPOSITED IN THIS PLACE OCTOB THE 5 1674 WHO BY HIS LAST WILL GAVE FOVR HVNDRED POVNDS TO PROVIDE MAIN TENANCE FOR TWO POOR AGED WEAVERS AND FOR THE RELIEF OF TWENTY OTHER POOR WEAVERS OR WEAVERS WIDDOWES HIS DEPARTVRE WAS IN Y 60 YEAR OF HIS AGE GOD AND DID

Kingsclere 36

hic iacet Johes Rolbdou pater magni Johis Rolbdou nup Rectoris Ecclie de kyngesWorthy cuius anime propicietur deus Amen

Kings Worthy I

Orate pro animabz Johis Smythe et Alice uxore eiusdem Qui obiit quinto die mesis Januarij Aº dni millmo ...... lxxxviij Quorum Animabz Propicietur deus Amen

Littleton I

Orate p aia Johannes Smyth quondam firmarius huius Ville, qui obijt viij die mesis Maij Aº dni m̄ qc vº cuius anime ...

Littleton II

181

XXXI. Inscr. recording presentation of processional cross (made of Eng. oak with embedded tesserae from a 6th cent. ch. near Jerusalem by Stan Green) by young musicians of the par. to commem. the Millennium, engr. c.**2000**, on choir stall, C.

INDENTS & LOST BRASSES. 32. Indent, sh.; in 2005 covered by fitted carpet, S.C. Sh. 180 x 155 mm. 33. Lost brass, civilian and 2 ws., inscr. John Woodriffe and ws., Joyce and Agnes, N.Tr. Recorded (partly covered) by Pavey (1704). 34. Lost brass, inscr. Thomas Browne, vicar, 1587. Recorded by Pavey (1704). 35. Lost brass, inscr. James Hunt of Popham, gent., son and heir of Hugh Hunt, 1605, and w. Elizabeth, who had issue John, Richard, Nicholas, Peter and Joan. Recorded by Pavey (1704). 36. Lost brass, inscr. Thomas Pearce, "WHO BY HIS LAST WILL GAVE FOVR HVNDRED POVNDS TO PROVIDE MAINTENANCE FOR TWO POOR AGED WEAVERS AND FOR THE RELIEF OF TWENTY OTHER POOR WEAVERS OR WEAVERS WIDDOWS", 1671, [aged 68]. Illustration from dabbing in Soc. Antiq. coll. Dabbing in Soc. Antiq. coll. Inscr. 245 x 435 mm.

Ref: *Brit. Lib. Add. MS. 39967,* f.118, *Add. MS. 39968,* f.280, *Stowe MS. 845,* f.145, f.147, f.149; *Haines*, II, p.73; *Heseltine, Heraldry*, p.37; *M.B.S. Trans.*, V, pp.322-5; *M.S.,* p.162, p.753; *Pevsner, Hampshire*, p.311; *Sadler, Dorset and Hampshire,* appx. I, pt.2, p.41; *Soc. Antiq. MS. 875/6*, pp.71-4; *V.C.H., Hampshire*, IV, p.264.

Ch. built, 1848-9.

KINGS WORTHY, St. Mary.

I. Inscr. John Rowdoun, father of John Rowdoun, rector, c.**1440**, mur., on stone, C. Inscr. 65 x 549 mm. Style: London B.

II. Inscr. recording gift of [south-east south aisle] window by children in mem. of [Rev.] Henry George Wells, rector [1842-1852, 1805-**1852**], and w. Charlotte, mur., below window, S.A. *III.* Inscr. [Rt. Rev.] T[homas] V[owler] Short, rector 1826-1834, [Bishop of Sodor and Man 1841-1846], Bishop of St. Asaph [1846-1870], and [Rt. Rev.] C[harles] Baring, rector 1834-1842, Bishop of Durham [1861-1879], engr. c.**1860**, on lectern, N. *IV.* Inscr. recording erection of [south-west south aisle] window by brother officers in mem. of Lt. Charles Mosley Turner, 4th Battn. 60th [King's Royal] Rifle [Corps], died at Southampton "From the effects of a Fall From his horse", **1868**, mur., below window, S.A. *V.* Inscr. John Davis Cotesworth, 1889, aged 23, and William Howell Cotesworth, **1890**, aged 29, mur., below window, N. *VI.* Inscr. with verse. Mary Ewer, dau. of Thomas Jacob Turner, widow of Major Henry Otway Mayne, **1906**, aged 75, [buried] in the churchyard, maker's name FRANK SMITH & CO LONDON, mur., on board, S.A. *VII.* Inscr. Albert Vale Barker, chorister, lost with the S.S. Titanic, **1912**, aged 19, mur., N. *VIII.* Inscr. with regt. insignia in relief. Lt. Bryce Stewart, 2nd Battn. Seaforth Highlanders, only child of Col. Bryce Stewart, D.S.O. and w. Georgie, [of Hinton House], killed in action in Mesopotamia, **1916**, aged 22, maker's name A.&N. AUX C.S.L. LONDON, mur., on board, N. *IX.* Inscr. Pte. Frank Mullins, [9336], 2nd Battn. Hampshire Regt., [son of Lloyd Mullins and w. Emily], killed in action in Gallipoli, [Turkey], 1915, [aged 20], pos. by those from the par. who took part "at the Front" in World War I, engr. c.**1920**, mur., on board, N. *X.* Inscr. Lillias Elizabeth Cotesworth, eld. child of William Cotesworth and [w.] Adelaide, of Abbotsworthy House, 1853-**1930**, pos. by relations, maker's name A.&N. C.S.L. LONDON, copper, mur., N. *XI.* Inscr. Charles Mower, bellringer and chorister, **1931**, on notice board,

W.Porch/Tower. *XII.* Inscr. Richard Charles Blake, killed by enemy action, **1942**, aged 34, Churchyard. *XIII.* Inscr. F. Cundell-Blake, 1872-**1961**, Churchyard. *XIV.* Inscr. recording replacement of crystal cross [in mem. of Lt.-Col. Lord Herbert Scott, C.M.G., D.S.O.] stolen in **1982**, on window splay, C. *XV.* Inscr. in raised letters. Lord Eversley, [Rt. Hon. Charles Shaw Lefevre, 1st and last Viscount Eversley, G.C.B., Speaker of the House of Commons 1839-1857, 1794-1888], pos. by E[mma Laura] Shaw Lefevre, engr. c.**1988**, copper, on bench, Churchyard. See also Heckfield nos.*XI & XII. XVI.* Inscr. Horace A. Bulpett, husband, **1992**, bronze, on bench, Churchyard. *XVII.* Inscr. recording that [garden] area was provided by Mrs. Lorna Chorley, J.P. in mem. of husband, Frank Chorley, C.B.E., F.Eng., F.I.E.E., 1926-**1993**, mur., on board, corridor between S.A. and Church Rooms. *XVIII.* Inscr. recording gift of chairs in [south] chapel in mem. of Doris Elsie West, Mothers' Union member, 1900-**1995**, on chair, S.C. *XIX.* Inscr. recording dedication of church rooms in **2000** by Rt. Rev. Michael [Charles] Scott-Joynt, Bishop of Winchester [1995-], mur., on board, S.A.

Ref: *Brit. Lib. Add. MS. 39967*, f.190; *M.B.S. Trans.*, V, p.325; *M.S.*, p.162; *Soc. Antiq. MS. 875/6*, p.74; *V.C.H., Hampshire*, IV, p.432.

Ch. essentially, 1864.

LANGRISH, St. John the Evangelist.

I. Inscr. recording erection of east window by inhabitants in mem. of George Grove Waddington, [1810-]**1870**, buried in family vault at East Meon, mur., on board, C. See also East Meon no.*III. II.* Inscr. recording gift of [nave] window by nephews and nieces in mem. of John Waddington, of Langrish House, [1808-]**1880**, buried in family vault at East Meon, mur., below window, N. See also East Meon no.*III. III.* Inscr. recording erection of [north aisle] window by public subscription in mem. of John Waddington, [of Langrish House, principal ch. benefactor, 1808-**1880**, mur., below window, N.A. See also East Meon no.*III. IV.* Inscr. recording erection of [lych]gate in **1881** in mem. of John Waddington, [of Langrish House, 1808-1880], bronze, on lychgate, Churchyard. See also East Meon no.*III. V.* Inscr. George Lambert, 1911-**1985**, pos. by family and friends, bronze, on bench, Churchyard. *VI.* Inscr. Gwen Keen, sister of no.*V,* 1915-**1997**, bronze, on bench with no.*V,* Churchyard. *VII.* Inscr. "CHRISTS MILLENNIUM **2000**/MR & MRS CHARLES SPINKS CHURCHWARDENS", bronze, on notice board, Churchyard. *VIII.* Inscr. Mary Lambert, [w. of no.*V*], 1910-**2001**, bronze, on bench with nos.*V & VI,* Churchyard.

Ch. built, 1869-70.

LAVERSTOKE, St. Mary the Virgin (new church).

I. Inscr. with ach. and regt. insignia. Capt. Melville Raymond Portal, 2nd Battn. Loyal North Lancashire Regt., eld. son of Melville Portal, [J.P., D.L., High Sheriff 1863] and [w.] Lady Charlotte M[ary Elliott, dau. of 2nd Earl of Minto, G.C.B.], died when employed on special service at Kampala, Uganda, [1856-]**1893**, pos. by brother officers, maker's name HART, SON PEARD & CO LTD, LONDON, bronze, mur., on marble, N.A. *II.* Inscr. in Lat. with ach. recording furnishing of [south] chapel in **1920** by Sir William W[yndham] Portal, [2nd] Bart., [J.P., D.L.,

F.S.A., High Sheriff 1886, 1850-1931], mur., on panelling, S.C. *III.* Inscr. recording gift [of altar cross] in **1970** by Winifred Bull in mem. of husband, Frank [Bull], and son, Desmond [Bull], on cross, S.C. *IV.* Inscr. recording presentation of crucifix ("belonged to Cardinal John Henry Newman, [1801-1890] who, before leaving the Church of England to enter the Roman Catholic Church in 1845, gave it to Melville Portal. Harry Yorke received it as a gift from Melville Portal in 1903 and it was eventually passed on to Kathleen Taylor from whom I inherited it") in **2004** by Mary Taylor Whitten in mem. of mother, Kathleen Yorke Taylor, dau. of [Rev.] Harry Walter Yorke, [M.A.], rector 1903-1920, worshipped in the ch. as a child, 1894-1990; in 2006 loose on board in S.C. Inscr. 135 x 258 mm.

INDENTS & LOST BRASSES. 5. Lost ?brass, angel holding inscr. on scroll. John Portal, [J.P., D.L., 1764-]1848, [engr. by Messrs. J.G. and L.A.B. Waller]. Recorded by Haines (1861).

Ref: *Burke's Peerage and Baronetage*, p.2150; *Haines*, II, p.238.

Ch. built, 1896.

LITTLETON, near WINCHESTER, St. Catherine.

I. Inscr. John Smythe, **1493**, and w. Alice, N. Inscr. 72 x 441 mm, Purbeck slab 1315 x 730 mm. Style: London D.

II. Inscr. John Smyth, "quondam firmarius hujus ville", **1505**; in 1891 in poss. of Dean of Winchester; on same slab as no.I, N. Inscr. 68 x 309 mm. Style: London G.

III. Inscr. with enamelled sh. Rev. Arthur George Garland, M.A.(Cantab.), Lt. 4th Regt. Madras Light Cavalry, rector for 17 years [1871-1888], son of Lewes Peak Garland, of Sandridge, Wilts. and Cadogan Place, Chelsea, grandson of Nathaniel Garland, of Michaelstowe Hall, [Ramsey], Essex, 1822-**1888**, mur., C. *IV.* Inscr. in Lat. [recording gift of reredos in] **1903** by [Rev.] W[alter] N[aish, M.A.], rector [1901-1917], on reredos, C. *V.* Inscr. Kevin Lay, [husband and father, 1963-**1999**], on candleholder, N.

Ref: *M.B.S. Trans.*, II, p.19, p.26, V, p.343; *M.S.*, p.162; *Soc. Antiq. MS. 875/6*, p.75.

Ch. essentially, 1884-5.

LYMINGTON, St. Thomas.

I. Inscr. with ach. Joan, w. of Francis Guidott, gent., **1668**, aged 64; formerly mur., C., now mur., on board, N. *Misc. Gen. et Her.*, N.S. III, p.118. Pl. 266 x 260 mm.

II. Inscr. Tho[ma]s Hunter, gent., **1774**, mur., on board, S.A. *III.* Inscr. Rob[er]t Hamond, **1775**, aged 75, mur., on board, S.A. *IV.* Inscr. recording gift of lectern by daus., Elizabeth Anne Morant, Sibylla Mary Shrubb and Alice Margaret Wykesmith, in mem. of Charles Fluder, M.D., **1860**, and w. Sibylla Jane, 1856, on lectern, N. *V.* Inscr. Robert Rice, of Highfield, died and buried in Brussels, **1865**, aged 59, maker's name H OSBORNE ENGRAVER RYDE I.W., mur., on

Lymington I

Lyndhurst *XIX*

board, S.A. *VI.* Inscr. in Lat. recording gift of [nave] window by w. Emilia in mem. of Richard Blanshard, 1817-**1866**, mur., below window, N. *VII.* Inscr. Chieles Cripps Wilkinson, 1804-**1884**, and w. Caroline, yst. dau. of Sir Louis Versturme, Knt., 1875, aged 71, pos. by nephews and niece, Hutton Versturme, Adolphus Versturme and Alicia North, maker's name GAWTHORP S^C LONDON, mur., on marble, N.A. *VIII.* Inscr. Lt.-Gen. C.D. Creagh-Osborne, C.B., 1823-**1892**, mur., on marble, N.A. *IX.* Inscr. William White, of Up Cerne, Dorset and Fairlie, Isle of Wight, 1865, aged 46, and w. Catherine Mary, **1899**, aged 72, maker's name H. ROSE & SON S^C, SOUTHAMPTON, mur., on marble, N. *X.* Inscr. Martha, widow of Henry Bates Smith, 1859, and daus., Martha Fferis Smith, 1881; Frances Jane Smith, **1900**; Anne Goodenough Smith, 1885; and Lucy Smith, 1891, maker's name GAWTHORP S^C LONDON, mur., N. *XI.* Inscr. Rear-Admiral Hamilton Edward George Earle, **1902**, aged 72, maker's name D. BANKS, mur., on marble, C. *XII.* Inscr. Pte. Arthur W. Kellaway, killed in a railway accident at Barberton, South Africa, while serving as a volunteer during the [South African] War, **1902**, pos. by officers, NCOs and men of A Co. (Lymington) 4th Volunteer Battn. Hampshire Regt., maker's name D. BANKS, mur., on marble, N. *XIII.* Inscr. recording completion of peal of 8 bells (tenor bell dedicated in mem. of Queen Victoria and 2nd new bell presented by Mrs. Haldane), pos. in **1902** to commem. 50 years ministry of Rev. [Canon] B[enjamin] M. Maturin, [M.A., hon. canon of Winchester Cathedral], vicar [1852-1905], rural dean [of Lyndhurst]; William Robinson Hill, M.D. and George Elliott, churchwardens, mur., N. *XIV.* Inscr. William Murdoch, M.A., principal of Solent Collegiate School, 3 times mayor, alderman of the Borough for many years, born at Dufftown, Banfshire, died at Lymington, 1835-**1903**, pos. by old pupils and friends, maker's name D. BANKS, mur., on marble, N.A. *XV.* Inscr. William Alder, died at Lymington, 1899, and Frank Xavier Alder, died at Carnarvon, Australia, **1904**, on cross, C. *XVI.* Inscr. recording renovation and illumination of clock by friends and parishioners in mem. of [Rev. Canon] Benjamin [M.] Maturin, M.A., hon. canon of Winchester [Cathedral], vicar 1852-1905, rural dean [of Lyndhurst], **1905**, aged 89; James Over, mayor; J.P.C. Shrubb and G. Elliott, churchwardens, maker's name D. BANKS. F. HILL PARR ARCHITECT, mur., on marble, C. *XVII.* Inscr. Humphrey Edward Ringler-Thomson, 4th son of John Ringler-Thomson and [w.] Eliza Anne, died at The Brackens, **1907**, [aged 70], maker's name D. BANKS LYMINGTON, mur., N. *XVIII.* Inscr. James Harold Dyer, A.D., only son of James Dyer and [w.] Augusta C., of Westfield, commissioner of Southern Nigeria, served in the Mashonaland Campaign and defence of Mafeking, 1871-**1909**, buried at Afikpo, Southern Nigeria, maker's name D. BANKS, mur., N. *XIX.* Inscr. Laura Marcia, widow of Admiral William Langford Castle, **1911**, aged 85, maker's name H. OSBORNE FECIT RYDE, mur., C. *XX.* Inscr. Martha, widow of Albert Earley, churchwarden 1875-1883, whose [legacy] in 1910 of £1,000 enabled the main roof to be entirely rebuilt in **1911**; J.C.N. King, J.P. and G. Elliott, churchwardens, maker's name D. BANKS, mur., N. *XXI.* Inscr. Harriet Spike and sister, Fanny Haldane, of Holme Mead, by whose benefactions the chapel-of-ease of All Saints and the adjoining hall were built and endowed in 1909 and the stipend of the curate-in-charge provided; in addition the organ was restored and enlarged, an oak pulpit provided, electric light installed, the tower roof restored and other repairs and improvements effected in **1911**, maker's name *J. WIPPELL & C^O L^{TD} EXETER & LONDON*, mur., N. *XXII.* Inscr. 2nd-Lt. Henry Creswell Delamain, [3rd Battn.] Dorset[shire] Regt., 1915, aged 18, [buried in the churchyard], on chair, N. *XXIII.* Inscr. with ach. and regt. insignia. [Capt.] (Brevet-Major) Charles Egerton Hugh Harding, [4th Battn.] Royal Fusiliers, [son of Major Gerald Harding], died in France, 1917, aged 39, buried at Etaples [Military Cemetery], maker's name CULN GAWTHORP & SONS LONDON, mur., N. *XXIV.* Inscr. Sophia Mary Saunders, 1842-**1918**, mur., on marble, N. *XXV.* Inscr. recording appreciation of men and women of par. who served in World War I, mur., on marble, S.A. *XXVI.* Inscr. Edward William Charlton, **1935**, on candleholder, C. *XXVII*. Inscr. Archibald Fryer, verger for over 30 years, 1895-**1986**, on bench, Churchyard. *XXVIII*. Inscr. recording restoration of [chancel] window in **1989** in mem. of Ernest Montague Knight, worshipped in the ch. 1909-1988, 1903-1988, mur., below window, C. *XXIX*. Inscr. recording restoration of [south aisle] window in **1989** in mem. of Edward O'Neil, 1915-1985, mur., on board, S.A. *XXX*. Inscr. Harry Frank Head, 1915-**1990**, mur., C. *XXXI*. Inscr. Brian Cann Donaldson Lane, F.B.H.I., 1932-**1992**, on bench, Churchyard. *XXXII*. Inscr. recording [gift] of tabernacle in mem. of Cicely Eatwell, 1936-**1993**, mur., N.C. *XXXIII*. Inscr. Pauline Joint, 1941-**1997**, on display case, S.A.

INDENTS & LOST BRASSES. 34. Indent, inscr., Churchyard. Inscr. 250 x 315 mm.

Ref: *Heseltine, Heraldry*, p.37; *M.B.S. Trans.*, V, pp.343-4; *M.S.*, p.163; *Soc. Antiq. MS. 875/6*, pp.75-6; *V.C.H., Hampshire*, IV, p.648.

LYNDHURST, St. Michael and All Angels (new church).

I. Inscr. with verse. J[oh]n Coleman, 1729, aged 63, and w. Margaret, **1730**, aged 65, mur., N.A. Inscr. 680 x 579 mm. *II*. Inscr. in Lat. Elizabeth Evelyn, w. of John Pultenay de Northerwood, **1856**, mur., below window, S.Tr. *III*. Inscr. with enamelled ach. and battle honours on scrolls (Egypt, Roleia, Vimiera, Talavera, Busaco, Fuentes D'Onor, Ciudad Rodrico, Badajoz, Salamanca, Vittoria, Chin-Keang-Foo, Shanghai, Woosung, Chapoo, China, Toulouse, Orthes, Nive, Nivelle, Pyrenees) within border of oak leaves and acorns. Lt.-Gen. Sir James Holmes Schordde, K.C.B., Col. 55th Regt. of Foot, A.D.C. to Queen Victoria, died at Elcombe, **1861**, aged 73, buried in the churchyard; bequeathed £100 to the poor, [maker's monogram COX & SON, LONDON], mur., S.Tr. *IV*. Inscr. Admiral Sir Charles Burrard, [2nd] Bart., [son of Gen. Sir Harry Burrard, 1st Bart., 1793-]**1870**, mur., N.Tr. *V*. Inscr. Ensign Herbert Gurney Lushington, 31st Regt., 2nd son of Frederick [Astell] Lushington, and [w.] Margaret [Julia], died at Malta, [1848-]**1871**, mur., S.Tr. *VI*. Inscr. recording completion of organ in **1874** by friends in mem. of Annabella Craufurd, on organ, C. *VII*. Inscr. Lt. Frederick Seton-Karr Lushington, 64th Regt., 3rd son of Frederick [Astell] Lushington, and [w.] Margaret [Julia], died at Glasgow, [1849-]**1874**, mur., S.Tr. *VIII*. Inscr. Ellen Dickson (Dolores), born at Woolwich, died at The Birds Nest, Lyndhurst, 1819-**1878**, mur., N.A. *IX*. Inscr. Richard Bowden Smith, of Vernalls, **1881**, aged 80, maker's name G.T. YOUNG, FECIT. SOUTHAMPTON, mur., N.A. *X*. Inscr. Lawrence H. Cumberbatch, **1885**, aged 58, and w. Harriet, 1877, aged 52, mur., N.Tr. *XI*. Inscr. Louisa, dau. of Sir Henry Lushington, [2nd] Bart., w. of Admiral Sir Charles Burrard, [2nd] Bart., 1801-**1885**, maker's name COX & BUCKLEY LONDON, mur., N.Tr. *XII*. Inscr. recording gift of carved angels in nave by Frederica, [w. of Capt. W.] Norris in mem. of parents, [Admiral] Sir Charles [Burrard, 2nd Bart., 1793-1870], and Lady [Louisa] Burrard, [dau. of Sir Henry Lushington, 2nd Bart., 1801-**1885**], and sisters who worshipped in the ch., mur., N. *XIII*. Inscr. with verse. William Martin Powell, father, engr. c.**1885**, on window splay, S.C. *XIV*. Inscr. with verse. Laura Emmeline, Lady Dickson, [died] at Wilverley Park, **1890**, mur., below window, S.C. *XV*. Inscr. recording erection of cross in **1893** by children in mem. of Frederick Astell Lushington, [J.P., 6th son of Sir Henry Lushington, 2nd Bart., Bengal Civil Service, 1815-1892], and [w.] Margaret Julia, [dau. of James Hay, 15th Earl of Erroll, 1891], mur., N. *XVI*. Inscr. Edward Hammick, par. schoolmaster and organist for 35 years, **1903**, on organ with no.*VI*, C. *XVII*. Inscr. Henry Cumberbatch, **1904**, aged 48, mur., N.Tr. *XVIII*. Inscr. recording gift of altar rails in mem. of Georgina Aide, Charles Burrard, Laura Burrard, Henrietta Lushington,

Clarence Collier, Annabella Craufurd, Anne Frances Cockerell, James Graham Goodenough, Frederick Addington Goodenough, Theresa Harriet Dashwood, William John Papple Dashwood, Edward Pelham Dashwood, Mary Harley Fisher, Jane Fisher, Mary Alexander, Nellie Money, Agnes Georgina Standley, Walter Williams, Harriet Cumberbatch, Arthur Robertson, Louisa Margaret Robertson, Louisa Amelia Emily Robertson, Mary Blanche Robertson, Richard Thomas Pulteney Pulteney, Frances Pulteney Pulteney, John Granville Beaumont Pulteney, Ellen Dickson and Caroline Julia Maskew, maker's name HART, SON, PEARD & C⁰ LONDON, engr. c.**1905**, mur., sedilia, C. *XIX.* Inscr. with enamelled sh., crest, motto and masonic medal with verse on circlet. James Edward Bateman Dashwood, 4th and last surviving son of Vice-Admiral Bateman Dashwood, head of dept. Foreign Office, "FOR THIRTY YEARS A LOYAL SERVANT OF HIS COUNTRY AND QUEEN", 1833-1905, [buried] at Smallvale Cemetery, Bathwick, Bath, [Somerset], pos. in **1906** by dau., maker's name GAWTHORP, S^C. LONDON (and monogram), mur., N.Tr. Inscr. 533 x 533 mm. *XX.* Inscr. Maria Anne, dau. of Col. Saunderson and [w.] Lady Maria, of Northbrook, Bishops Waltham, w. of William George Stevenson, J.P., Scots Guards, of Foxlease Park, **1907**, aged 83; also dau., Marie Louisa, w. of John C. Hibbert, 1906, mur., on marble, S.A. *XXI.* Inscr. William George Stevenson, [J.P.], died at Highfield House, Uxbridge, [Middx.], **1910**, aged 83, mur., S.A. *XXII.* Inscr. Georgina Hutchings, teacher in Lyndhurst Church Schools 1872-**1912**, [pos. by] E. H[utchings] and A.E. H[utchings], copper, on pew, N.A. *XXIII.* Inscr. and cross with verse on separate pl. Beatrice [Harriet, eld. dau. of Frederick Astell] Lushington, [and w. Margaret Julia], **1913**, maker's name HART SON PEARD & C⁰ L^D, mur., S.C. *XXIV.* Inscr. [Rev.] Somerville [Henry] Lushington, [4th son of Frederick Astell Lushington, and w. Margaret Julia, vicar of Thorpe, Surrey 1907-1916, 1856-]**1916**, maker's name HART SON PEARD & C⁰ L^D, mur., S.C. *XXV.* Inscr. with verse and cross on separate pl. Evelyn Cecilia Pulteney (Sister Evangeline), **1917**, maker's name HEATON BUTLER & BAYNE LONDON, copper, mur., S.Tr. *XXVI.* Inscr. with verse and cross on separate pl. Isabella Pulteney, mother, **1920**, maker's name HEATON BUTLER & BAYNE LONDON, copper, mur., S.Tr. *XXVII.* Inscr. [recording gift of pew in] **1925** by M[uriel] P[enelope] C[ooke]-H[urle] in mem. of husband, Col. Edward Forbes Cooke-Hurle, D.S.O., [5th Battn.] Somerset Light Infantry, [1866-1923], on pew, N. *XXVIII.* Inscr. recording gift [of pew] in **1925** by officers of the 5th Battn. Somerset Light Infantry "WHO SERVED UNDER HIM IN THE GREAT WAR" in mem. of Col. E[dward] F[orbes] Cooke-Hurle, D.S.O., [5th Battn. Somerset Light Infantry, 1866-1923], on pew, N. *XXIX.* Inscr. recording gift of 3 pews and cupboards in mem. of Evelyn L. Frere, engr. c.**1925**, copper, on pew, N.Tr. *XXX.* Inscr. recording gift of seat by Mary Jones in mem. of parents, George Jones and [w.] Jane, resident 1864-1908, ch. worshippers, engr. c.**1925**, on pew, N. *XXXI.* Inscr. Richard Congdon Trethewey, sidesman, P.C.C. member, [pos. by] A.S. T[rethewey], engr. c.**1925**, on pew, S.A. *XXXII.* Inscr. Algernon Hay Lushington, eld. son of Frederick [Astell] Lushington, and [w.] Margaret [Julia, 1847-]**1930**, copper, mur., S.Tr. *XXXIII.* Inscr. Harry Ashford, **1932**, and [w.] Eleanor Louisa, [1932], pos. by H.C.A. A[shford], E.L. A[shford], and A.E.N. A[shford], on pew, N.A. *XXXIV.* Inscr. recording seat pos. in mem. of Mabel, w. of Col. Alexander C[aldcleugh] Macleay, C.B., **1933**, on pew, S.A. *XXXV.* Inscr. Thomas Edward Smith, ch. worshipper for 32 years, pos. in **1935** by w. and children, on pew, N. *XXXVI.* Inscr. recording gift of seat by Herbert and Peter Blagrave in mem. of mother, Lady Edward Somerset, 1859-**1939**, on pew, S.A. *XXXVII.* Inscr. Lt. John Howard Shears, R.N., [H.M.S. Formidable], 1941, aged 25, and Capt. Michael William Shears, [138189, 12th Battn.] Hampshire Regt., **1942**, aged 23, [buried at Parkhurst Military Cemetery, Isle of Wight, sons of Albert Ernest Shears and w. Margaret Vaughan], on pew, S.A. *XXXVIII.* Inscr. recording gift [of pew] by parents in mem. of children, Pamela Ayles, 1941, aged 8, and Maurice Ayles, died as a result of an accident, **1948**, [aged 19], on pew, N. *XXXIX.* Inscr. recording gift of chair in mem. of Celine Jones, **1950**, on chair, C. *XL.* Inscr. in raised letters. [Rev.] Frank Robert Cooksley, M.C., M.A., vicar 1928-**1961**, bronze, mur., S.C. *XLI.* Inscr. Wilfrid Percy Hambly, 1887-**1963**, on statue plinth, S.C. *XLII.* Inscr. Vera Cook,

1908-**1975**, on vestment chest, S.Tr. *XLIII*. Inscr. Kathleen Jerrett Dougall, engr. c.**1985**, on chair, S.C. *XLIV*. Inscr. Isaac Ernest Gale, engr. c.**1985**, on chair, S.A. *XLV*. Inscr. Laura Hall, engr. c.**1985**, on chair, S.C. *XLVI*. Inscr. Bill and Harry Harrison, engr. c.**1985**, on bookcase, N.A. *XLVII*. Inscr. Annette Gare and Beatrice Hastings, engr. c.**1985**, on chair, S.C. *XLVIII*. Inscr. Charles Gordon Johnston, engr. c.**1985**, on chair, S.C. *XLIX*. Inscr. Hilda Dilys Lloyd, engr. c.**1985**, on chair, S.C. *L*. Inscr. Alice Mary Long, engr. c.**1985**, on chair, S.C. *LI*. Inscr. William John Lloyd, engr. c.**1985**, on chair, S.C. *LII*. Inscr. Frank Edgar Monckton, engr. c.**1985**, on chair, S.C. *LIII*. Inscr. Wilfred Hugh Payton, engr. c.**1985**, on chair, S.C. *LIV*. Inscr. Edward Victor Vernon, engr. c.**1985**, on chair, S.C. *LV*. Inscr. Charles Young, engr. c.**1985**, on chair, S.C. *LVI*. Inscr. recording dedication of [display] case and book of remembrance ("Records the Names of those whose Ashes are interred in the Garden of Remembrance") in mem. of Frank Cook, 1912-**1989**, on display case, S.A. *LVII*. Inscr. Grahame Nichols, 1914-**1992**, bronze, on bench, Churchyard.

Ref: *Burke's Peerage and Baronetage*, p.1677; *M.B.S. Trans.*, V, p.344; *Soc. Antiq. MS. 875/6*, p.76.

Ch. built, 1858-70.

MAPLEDURWELL, St. Mary.

I. John Canner, in civil dress, and w. Agnes, c.**1525**, with 4 sons and 6 daus., inscr., worn, C. Male eff. 355 x 115 mm, female eff. 336 x 125 mm, inscr. 59 x 500 mm, sons 103-136 x 109 mm, daus. 106-129 x 107 mm, Purbeck slab 1515 x 860 mm. Style: London F debased.

II. Inscr. with verse. Edward Clark, of Hackwood, Bromley, Kent, **1914**, aged 71, [buried] at St. Luke's Cemetery, Bickley, Kent; father, mother and several relatives [buried] in the churchyard, pos. by w. Catherine Alice, maker's name A&N AUX C.S.L LONDON, mur., N. *III*. Inscr. recording gift of altar rails and desk "together with a sum of money for the improvement of the Organ and the upkeep of the Churchyard" in mem. of [Pte.] William [L.] Ackland, [202717, 13th Battn. Gloucestershire Regt., son of Joseph Ackland and w. Fanny, 1918, aged 38, buried at Peronne Communal Cemetery Extension, France]; William Bartlett; [Lance-Sgt.] Alfred Eccott, [5403, 2nd/8th Battn. Royal Warwickshire Regt., son of James Eccott and w. Ada, 1916, aged 20, buried at Merville Communal Cemetery, France]; and [Pte.] Nathaniel [John] Paice, [2554, 1st Battn. Hampshire Regt., son of Charles Paice and w. Ellen, 1918, aged 38, buried at Gonnehem British Cemetery, France], engr. c.**1920**, on desk, N. *IV*. Inscr. [Guardsman] Raymond [Martin] Brown, [2620027, Grenadier Guards, son of Alfred Brown and w. Cassy Adelaide (née Dicker), **1940**, aged 27], on desk with no.*III*, N.

Ref: *Hampshire History*, III, p.285; *M.B.S. Trans.*, V, p.345; *Mee, Hampshire*, p.223; *M.S.*, p.163; *Pevsner, Hampshire*, p.328; *Soc. Antiq. MS. 875/6*, p.77; *V.C.H., Hampshire*, IV, p.152.

MARTIN, All Saints (formerly in Wiltshire).

I. Inscr. with verse. Henry Brouncker, of Boveridge, Dorset, 1841-**1895**, on window splay, N.A. *II*. Inscr. recording erection of reredos in **1896** by widow, [Ellen], and dau., Emily Wylde Browne, in mem. of [Rev.] G.W.B. Daniell, 1st vicar 1854-1870, mur., on board, C. *III*. Inscr. with sh.,

Oſt poure charite pray for the ſoules of Iohn̄ Tanner
& Agnes his wyſe On whois ſoules Ihu haue mercy

Mapledurwell I

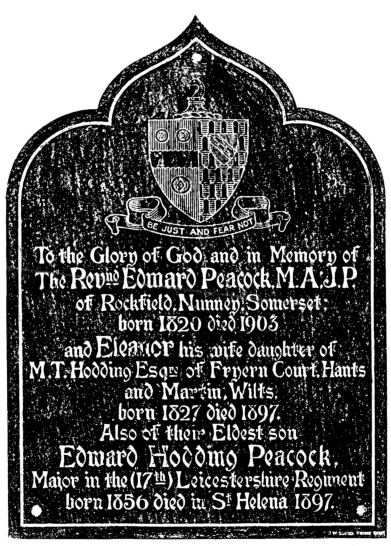

To the Glory of God and in Memory of
The Rev.ⁿᵈ Edward Peacock. M.A. J.P.
of Rockfield, Nunney, Somerset;
born 1820 died 1903
and Eleanor his wife daughter of
M.T. Hodding Esqᵣᵉ of Fryern Court, Hants
and Martin, Wilts.
born 1827 died 1897.
Also of their Eldest son
Edward Hodding Peacock,
Major in the (17ᵗʰ) Leicestershire Regiment
born 1856 died in Sᵗ Helena 1897.

Martin *III*

To our dear Mother Ellen
widow of the Reverend G.W.B. Daniell,
Vicar of this Parish from 1854 to 1870,
Who zealously helped her husband in all his work,
and in the Restoration of this Church.
She fell asleep 16 July 1906. Aged 78 years.

Martin *IV*

191

crest and motto. Rev. Edward Peacock, J.P., M.A., of Rockfield, Nunney, Somerset, 1820-**1903**, and w. Eleanor, dau. of M.T. Hodding, of Fryern Court and Martin, 1827-1897; also eld. son, Major Edward Hodding Peacock, 17th [Battn.] Leicestershire Regt., died in St. Helena, 1856-1897, maker's name J · W · SINGER FROME SOMT, mur., on board, N. Inscr. 471 x 343 mm. *IV.* Inscr. Ellen, widow of Rev. G.W.B. Daniell, [1st] vicar 1854-1870, "Who zealously helped her husband in all his work, and in the Restoration of this Church", **1906**, aged 78, [pos. by children], mur., on board, C. Inscr. 168 x 673 mm. *V.* Inscr. with verse. George Waters, senior, 1901, aged 82, and widow, Harriette, **1907**, aged 81; also 2nd son, George [Waters], 1884, aged 33, maker's name *C. VICUS SC. SARUM*, mur., on marble, N. *VI.* Inscr. recording gift of 2nd bell by dau., Katie Blanche Hibberd, in mem. of Ambrose Blandford and [w.] Blanche, of Tidpit; dedicated in **1934** by archdeacon of Sarum, mur., on board, Tower. *VII.* Inscr. recording gift of treble bell by w. Helena Augusta in mem. of John Read; dedicated in **1934** by archdeacon of Sarum, mur., on board, Tower. *VIII.* Inscr. recording restoration and rehanging of 3 bells (1st hung in 1606, 1657 and 1662) by public subscription and a grant from the White Bequest; rededicated in **1934** by [Ven. Harry William Carpenter, O.B.E., M.A.], archdeacon of Sarum [1914-1936; Rev.] R[ichard] Skilbeck Smith, M.C., M.A., vicar [1932-1945]; G.W. Waters, J.P., vicar's [church]warden and W.M. Lush, people's [church]warden, mur., on board, Tower. *IX.* Inscr. recording restoration of old glass in **1936** with the cost defrayed by Mrs. H.A. Read, on window splay, Baptistry/N.A. *X.* Inscr. in raised letters recording restoration of [grave]stone in **1949** by descendants in mem. of William Lawes, (the Isaac Bawcombe of *Shepherd['s Life: Impressions] of the [South] Wiltshire Downs*, 1910, by W[illiam] H[enry] Hudson), [1800-1886], bronze, on gravestone, Churchyard. *XI.* Inscr. Malcolm Dowson, **1956**, pos. by widow, Joyce, and son, Peter, on altar rail, S.C. *XII.* Inscr. recording presentation of organ blower by widow, Dora, in mem. of Brian Cook, **1959**, on organ blower, Vestry/N.A. *XIII.* Inscr. Rev. E[ric] C[yril] Corke, M.A.(Cantab.), vicar 1946-**1959**, on table, N. *XIV.* Inscr. recording gift of clock in **1966** in mem. of Sir Winston [Leonard Spencer-] Churchill, K.G., [O.M., C.H., T.D., F.R.S., P.C.], "WHOSE INDOMITABLE SPIRIT SO INSPIRED THE PEOPLE OF THESE ISLANDS THAT IN THEIR FINEST HOUR FACED WITH DEFEAT, THEY ACHIEVED FINAL VICTORY", [1874-1965], bronze, mur., on board, south wall outside Tower. *XV.* Inscr. recording gift [of prie-dieu] in **1966** by Sandwith family, on prie-dieu, S.C. *XVI.* Inscr. recording erection of ch. gates in **1978** in mem. of E. Spencer Scott, M.D., of Sweetapples Farm, and [w.] Margaret; in 2006 loose in S.C. Inscr. 127 x 178 mm. *XVII.* Inscr. Tonie Taylor (née Whitehead), w., mother and grandmother, 1917-**1979**; in 2006 loose in S.C. Inscr. 127 x 178 mm. *XVIII.* Inscr. Nell Waters, 1891-**1981**, bronze, on bench, Churchyard. *XIX.* Inscr. recording presentation by Capt. Michael [Hugh] Hutton, [O.B.E., R.N., 1925-2003] and family in mem. of w. [Elizabeth] Ann, "who loved and served this church and village", 1927-**1985**, mur., on board, N. *XX.* Inscr. Ethel Taylor, 1893-**1986**, on pulpit desk, N. *XXI.* Inscr. recording gift of chancel lighting in mem. of Nell Maclean Gouldsbury, 1894-**1989**, mur., on board, C. *XXII.* Inscr. recording renovation of tower clock in mem. of Edmund Horden, son of [Rt. Rev. Hugh Maudsley Hordern, M.A.], Bishop of Lewes [1929-1946], ch. worshipper, 1904-**1992**, mur., on board, Tower. *XXIII.* Inscr. Alan James McGregor, 1920-**1997**, on candleholder, C.

Transferred from Wiltshire to Hampshire in 1895.

MARTYR WORTHY, St. Swithun.

I. Inscr. with verse on lozenge-shaped pl. Edward Bailey, 1802-**1873**, maker's name COX & SONS LONDON, mur., N. Inscr. 712 x 533 mm. *II.* Inscr. Admiral Sir Thomas Pasley, [1st] Bt.,

In loving memory of
Edward Bailey
Born July 15 1802
Died Dec 4 1873.

"I am the Resurrection and the life."

Martyr Worthy *I*

born at Craig, Dumfriesshire, "commanded a division of Lord Howe's Fleet in the Victory over the French Fleet May 29th and June 1st 1794, having his flag in H.M.S. Bellerophon, in which battle he was severely wounded, losing a leg. For his services he was created a Baronet, after holding the Command of Port Admiral at Plymouth 1799-1801, retired to Chilland Cottage, where he died", 1734-1808, buried in the ch., pos. in **1879** by grandson, Admiral Sir Thomas Sabine Pasley, [2nd] Bart., K.C.B., mur., on marble, N. *III.* Inscr. Mary Elizabeth Bailey, w. of no.*I*, 1808-**1892**, mur., below no.*I*, N. *IV.* Inscr. recording erection [of pulpit] by parishioners to commem. the 60th year of the reign of Queen Victoria, **1897**, on pulpit, N. *V.* Inscr. [recording gift of south-east nave window] in **1897** by F. and L.E. Beeston in mem. of 2 infants, mur., below window, N. *VI.* Inscr. recording thank offering [south-west nave window] in **1897** by F. and L.E. Beeston, mur., below window, N. *VII.* Inscr. in Lat. recording dedication [of north-east nave window] in **1897** by Bertha Lampen in mem. of Mary and Florence Field, mur., below window, N. *VIII.* Inscr. recording presentation [of stall] in **1898** by C.J. Cornish-Browne, on stall, C. *IX.* Inscr. M.E. Bishop, headmistress of Chelsea High School, headmistress of Oxford High School, 1st principal of Royal Holloway Coll., and 1st principal of St. Gabriel's Coll., "SHE DIED WORKING", **1913**, pos. by "THREE OXFORD FRIENDS WHO OWE HER MUCH", maker's name A. & N AUX C.S.L LONDON, mur., on board, N. *X.* Inscr. Lt. Owen Nevill Lyte, R[oyal] A[rmy] S[ervice] C[orps], 6th Division Mechanical Transport Co., son of Alfred Owen Lyte and w. Clara], died near Cambrai, **1918**, aged 33, [buried at Premont British Cemetery, France]; 2nd-Lt. John Russell, [D Co. 3rd Battn.] The Buffs [(East Kent Regt.), son of John Russell and w. Catharine, of Parrock Manor, Gravesend, Kent], killed in action at Monchy, 1917, aged 30; and [Pte.] Geoffrey Nevill Hetherington, [81279, B Co.] 15th Battn. Durham Light Infantry, [son of Walter H. Hetherington and w. Margaret], died of wounds at Boulogne, 1918, aged 18, [buried at Boulogne Eastern Cemetery, France], grandsons of Benjamin Nevill, of Chilland, maker's name W^M. MORRIS & C^O L^TD, WESTMINSTER. S.W, mur., on marble, N. *XI.* Inscr. recording gift of organ in **1927** by daus. in mem. of Rev. John [Minet] Freshfield, [M.A., rector of Easton 1899-1919, 1835-1924], and w. [Harriet] Louisa, [1839-**1926**], pos. by parishioners, on board on organ, Organ Chamber. See also Easton no.*VIII.* *XII.* Inscr. recording installation of glass (depicting St. Swithun) [in west window] to commem. 850th anniversary of the ch. and in mem. of Robin Surtees Napier and Charles Antony Wheeler, engr. **1936**, on window splay, N. *XIII.* Inscr. recording renovation [of organ] in **1984** by Keith M. Scudamore, of Bournemouth, on organ with no.*XI*, Organ Chamber.

Ref: *Burke's Peerage and Baronetage*, p.2071.

MEON, EAST, All Saints.

I. Inscr. recording restoration of ch. in **1870**; [Rev.] William Brodic, [M.A.], vicar [1868-1882]; John Christmas and William Ray, churchwardens, maker's name GAWTHORP S^C, LONDON, mur., N.Tr. *II.* Inscr. James Stewart Forbes, 1813-**1871**, mur., S.C. *III.* Inscr. John Horsey Waddington, of Langrish House, 1783-1863, and sons, John [Waddington], 1808-**1880**; George Grove [Waddington], 1810-1870; Thomas Grove [Waddington], 1814-1846; also grandchildren, John Julius, 1835-1847; and Evelyn Charlotte, 1841-1857, children of F[rederick] P[eter] Delme Radcliffe, of Hitchin Priory, buried in [south] chapel vault, mur., S.C. See also Langrish nos.*I, II, III & IV. IV.* Stepped cross surmounting inscr. [Rev.] William Brodic, M.A., rector of New Alresford 1851-1868, vicar 1868-1882, **1882**, aged 61, maker's name GAWTHORP S^C LONDON, mur., N.Tr. *V.* Inscr. recording presentation of pulpit (erected in Holy Trinity, Minories in 1706 and removed when the ch. was dismantled in 1899) in **1906** by Rev. Edward Murray Tomlinson, M.A., vicar of

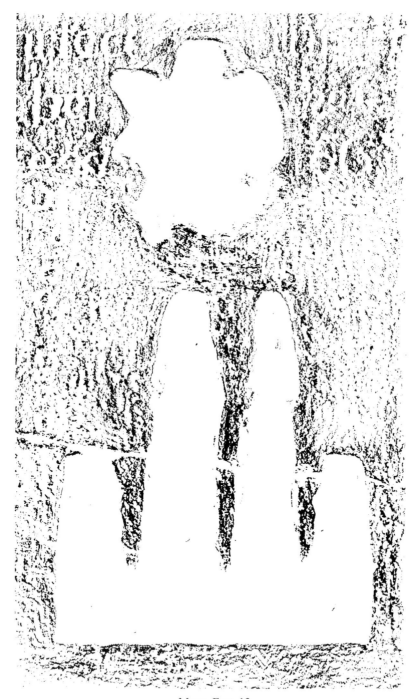

Meon, East 12

Holy Trinity, Minories 1877-1889, vicar 1889-1901, on pulpit, N. *VI.* Inscr. recording [east south chapel] window and reredos were made by Janetta Margaret Errington in mem. of Johanna Agnes[, w. of George] Forbes, 1898, [aged 78], and Ada Mary Hayward, **1909**, S.C. *VII.* Inscr. recording gift of pulpit rail by friends and patients in mem. of Dr. Harold Charles Clifford, churchwarden 1957-1960, 1895-**1960**, on pulpit below no.*V*, N. *VIII.* Inscr. recording presentation [of bench] to Bordean House in mem. of Sheila "WHO LIVED HERE FOR A WHILE", engr. c.**1985**, bronze, on bench, Churchyard. *IX.* Inscr. recording presentation of bell (rung before services at St. Gabriel's ch.) in **1993** by H.M.S. Mercury to "TO MARK THE OCCASION OF ITS CLOSURE AND TO COMMEMORATE THE HAPPY ASSOCIATION SPANNING FIFTY-TWO YEARS", mur., S.Tr. *X.* Inscr. Edward (Ted) Roy Gregory, 1943-**1994**, bronze, on bench, Churchyard. *XI.* Inscr. with verse. Walter Reginal[d] Simpson, [husband and father], 1905-1956, and [w.] Dorcas Hilda (Toni), [mother, grandmother, great-grandmother and great-great-grandmother], 1910-**2004**, on bench, Churchyard.

INDENTS & LOST BRASSES. 12. Indent, civilian and w., inscr., ?2 sons, ?2 daus. and ?Trinity, N.Tr. Male eff. 320 x 80 mm, female eff. 320 x 70 mm, inscr. 105 x 380 mm, sons 125 x 80 mm, daus. 125 x 70 mm, Trinity 245 x 210 mm, slab 1755 x 910 mm, approp. for Ann, w. of Joseph Woodman, 1720, aged 56, and Elizabeth, w. of William Pink, 1729, aged 35. 13. Indent, ?inscr. and scroll, N.Tr. Inscr. 50 remains x c.200 mm, scroll c.235 x c.70 x c.30 mm, slab 710 remains x 450 mm visible.

Ref: *Burke's Peerage and Baronetage*, p.1030; *Mee, Hampshire*, p.144.

MEONSTOKE, St. Andrew.

I. Inscr. on trapezoidal-shaped pl. Edward Plantagenet Hume, R.N., 1848-**1870**, on window splay, C. *II.* Inscr. Thomas, Mary and Catherine Cooper, **1901**, on lectern, N. *III.* Inscr. with verse in raised letters. Mary, w. of Samuel Laing, M.P. for the Orkneys for many years, pos. in **1906** by son-in-law, Charles C[olin] Macrae, of Meonstoke House, on board on window splay, S.C./S.A. *IV.* Inscr. with verse and ach. [2nd-]Lt. Charles Alexander Macrae, Army Service Corps, [killed] on active service in France, **1916**, [buried at St. Riquier British Cemetery, France], and 2nd-Lt. Frank Laing Macrae, 8th [Battn.] Seaforth Highlanders, [killed while] leading his men at the Battle of Loos, 1915, [aged 34], only sons of Charles Colin Macrae and [w.] Cecilia, of Meonstoke House, "BOTH ENLISTED IN THE PUBLIC SCHOOLS BATTALION ON THE OUTBREAK OF THE WAR AND HAVE GIVEN THEIR LIVES FOR THEIR COUNTRY", maker's name G. MAILE & SON, 367, EUSTON R[d] LONDON, mur., on marble, S.C./S.A. *V.* World War I memorial in raised letters (24 names), bronze, on lychgate, Churchyard. *VI.* World War II memorial in raised letters (8 names), bronze, on lychgate with no.*V*, Churchyard. *VII.* Inscr. Alfred James Bignell, [1888-1972], and [w.] Mabel, [1888-**1972**], on altar rail, C.

MEON, WEST, St. John the Evangelist.

I. Inscr. recording ch. foundation stone laid in 1843 by [Rev. Dr.] Henry Vincent Bayley, D.D., rector [1826-1844], 1844, buried in churchyard vault with w.; consecrated in **1846** by [Rt. Rev.] Charles Richard [Sumner], Bishop of Winchester [1827-1869], mur., on marble, C. *II.* Inscr. in Lat. on 2 pls. recording gift of [east] window in mem. of [Rev. Dr.] H[enry] V[incent] Bayley, [D.D.], rector [1826-1844, 1844], engr. c.**1846**, mur., below window, C. *III.* Inscr. recording presentation [of lectern] by parishioners of Clifton Down, St. Peter, to Rev. Alexander Poole, M.A., sacristan and precentor of Bristol Cathedral [1861-1868], "in remembrance of His work among them [as curate] 1862-**1868**", [rector 1891-1899], on lectern, N. *IV.* Inscr. recording presentation of organ in **1877** by Richard Earwaker, of Nottingham; Rev. A[lexander] B[radley] Burton, M.A., rector [1844-1872]; R.J. Challen and Will[ia]m Lewis, churchwardens, on organ, C. *V.* Inscr. recording presentation [of choir stalls] in **1893** by William Benham to commem. 50th anniversary of laying the ch. foundation stone, on choir stall, C. *VI.* Inscr. Rev. William Mussage Kirkwall Bradford, [M.A.], rector for nearly 28 years, [1806-]1872, and w. Mary, [eld. dau. of Rev. Henry Colborne Ridley], **1894**, aged 84, mur., C. *VII.* Inscr. with verse recording erection of [south-east south aisle] window in **1895** by friends in mem. of brothers, John Hicks Arnold, 1892, aged 65, and Matthew Arnold, 1895, aged 67, mur., below window, S.A. *VIII.* Inscr. in Lat. [Rev.] Alexander Poole, M.A., sacristan and precentor [of Bristol Cathedral], rector [1891-1899], and w. Nancy, pos. in **1904** by L[ouisa] E.L. Dutton, on prie-dieu, N. *IX.* Inscr. with verse recording that decoration of the reredos was undertaken through [legacy] of [Rev.] Robert Herbert Fair, [M.A.], rector 1899-**1917**, in mem. of w. Frances Jane; work was extended by family and friends in mem. of stepson, Edmund Nelson Fisher, copper, mur., C. *X.* World War I memorial (30 names), copper, mur., N.A. *XI.* Inscr. recording gift of [north] chapel and altar by friends in mem. of Louisa E.L. Dutton, **1924**, copper, on altar rail, N.C. *XII.* World War II memorial (9 names), maker's name A & N LONDON, copper, mur., N.A. *XIII.* Inscr. with Lat. verse. Major Charles Herbert Fair, D.S.O., 1/19th [Battn.] London Regt. 1914-1918, son of Rev. R[obert] H[erbert] Fair, [M.A., rector 1899-1917], assistant master at Haileybury Coll. for 34 years, chorister for many years, 1885-**1950**, copper, on organ blower, C. *XIV.* Inscr. Joseph Trodd, chorister 1881-**1956**, on choir stall, C. *XV.* Inscr. Thomas Christopher Whitehead, 1st headmaster of Westbury House School 1926-1960, churchwarden 1946-1962, 1889-**1962**, on processional cross, C. *XVI.* Inscr. Jesse Simpson, born at West Meon, died at Port Arthur, Ontario, Canada, 1889-**1966**, bronze, on bench, Churchyard. *XVII.* Inscr. with verse in raised lettters. Charlie Parnell and [w.] Olive, parents and grandparents, engr. c.**2005**, bronze, on bench, Churchyard.

Ref: *Burke's Peerage and Baronetage*, p.337.

Ch. built, 1843-6.

MICHELDEVER, St. Mary the Virgin (new church).

I. Inscr. recording gift of glass in [west] window by William Gale, vicar's churchwarden 1861-**1881**, mur., below window, W.Porch/Tower. *II.* Inscr. recording presentation of lectern by friends and parishioners on re-opening of ch. in **1881** after renovation, mur., N. *III.* Inscr. with verse. Emily Frances Paice, ch. cleaner 1911-**1936**, copper, W.Porch/Tower. *IV.* Inscr. Ernest Witts, 1881-1943, and [w.] Alice, 1879-**1963**, bronze, on wooden cross, Churchyard. *V.* Inscr. Molly Pepper, 1906-**1975**, on stall, N. *VI.* Inscr. F[rances] (Frankie) J[oan] Foot, [1943-**1985**], bronze, on bench, Churchyard. *VII.* Inscr. recording gift of seat by [bell]ringers in mem. of [Walter Henry] (Harry) Symes, [tower] capt., [1907-**1991**], bronze, on bench, Churchyard.

INDENTS & LOST BRASSES. 8. Lost brass, lady, canopy and marg. inscr. Margery de Knyghton, mother of Thomas, 1355, S.A. Recorded (complete) by Pavey (1704).

Ref: *Brit. Lib. Stowe MS. 845*, f.49; *M.B.S. Trans.*, V, p.345; *Soc. Antiq. MS. 875/6*, p.77.

Ch. built, 1880-1.

MICHELMERSH, St. Mary.

I. Inscr. on lozenge-shaped pl. John Wheable, 1728, and w. Alice, 1730; also son, John Wheable, 1720-1827, and w. Phebe, 1756-**1827**, N. Lozenge 539 x 539 mm. *II.* Inscr. recording repair of [south] aisle in **1847** by subscription; [Rev.] John Pierce Maurice, rector [1840-1874]; Henry Symes and John Fay, churchwardens, mur., on pillar, S.A. *III.* Cross in relief with inscr. and verse within border of vine leaves and grapes. [Rev. Canon] Barrington Gore Browne, [M.A.], hon. canon [of Winchester Cathedral], rector 1884-1913, rural dean [of Romsey 1892-1905], 1847-**1914**, [designed by Heywood Sumner, of Fordingbridge], mur., C. *IV.* Inscr. Capt. Stephen H[ugh] Norris, D.S.O. and Bar, D.S.C. and Bar, R.N., [H.M.S. Odyssey, son of Hugh L. Norris and w. Mabel G.], killed on active service at Biograd, Jugo-Slavia, 1903-**1944**, [buried at Belgrade War Cemetery], on lectern, N. *V.* Inscr. Doris Violet Clough, 1897-**1976**, on credence table, C. *VI.* Inscr. Kathleen Marion Sainsbury Hunt, 1902-1991, and William George Hunt, 1905-**1996**, on window splay, C.

INDENTS & LOST BRASSES. 7. Indent, cross with fleur-de-lys terminals between Lombardic letters (I) and (N), inscr., c.1375, curious, C. *Sadler, Dorset and Hampshire*, appx. I, pt.2, p.25 (drg.). Cross 455 x 450 mm, (I) 50 x 25 mm, (N) 50 x 45 mm, inscr. 50 x 315 mm, grey/brown slab 2480 x 985 mm.

Ref: *Earliest English Brasses*, pp.189-90; *M.B.S. Bulletin*, 27, p.15; *M.B.S. Trans.*, V, p.346; *Sadler, Dorset and Hampshire*, appx. I, pt.2, pp.24-5; *Soc. Antiq. MS. 875/6*, p.78.

MILTON, (see PORTSMOUTH).

MONXTON, St. Mary (new church).

I. Alice Swayn, **1599**, aged 98, and son Arthur in civil dress, both kng., inscr. with 4 Eng. vv.; formerly C., N., now mur., N.; orig. slab, N. *M.B.S. Trans.*, V, p.346; *Mee, Hampshire*, p.219 (drg. of effs.). Effs. 282 x 315 mm (1 pl.), inscr. 85 x 555 mm, vv. 87 x 555 mm, non-Purbeck slab 1235 remains x 820 mm. Style: Johnson (script 12).

II. Inscr. Richarda Pore, grand-dau. of Adam Robins, rector, **1606**; formerly C., N., now mur., N.; orig. slab, N. Inscr. 117 x 458 mm, non-Purbeck slab 1740 x 870 mm.

III. World War I memorial (8 names), maker's name J. WIPPELL & Cᴼ Lᵀᴰ, mur., on marble, N. *IV.* World War II memorial (5 names), mur., on marble, N. *V.* Inscr. recording presentation [of notice board] in **1945** by nieces, B. and K. Aldridge, in mem. of Mary Aldridge, ch. worshipper for 90 years, on notice board, Churchyard. *VI & VII.* Two inscrs. Ellen Sabina Hutchens, people's [church]warden 1920-**1946**, [1946, aged 81], on churchwardens' wands, N. *VIII.* Inscr. recording inauguration of endowment fund for ch. maintenance in **1962** through legacy of Mrs. Jessie Brazil, mur., on board, N. *IX.* Inscr. recording presentation of [display] case by Vera Trotter in mem. of husband, Balfour Trotter, **1963**, mur., in display case, N. *X.* Inscr. recording seat pos. in mem. of Benjamin Sydney Whiting, [**1964**], bronze, on bench, Churchyard. *XI.* Inscr. [Louisa] Lily [E.G.] Collacott, [**1965**, aged 87], on flowerstand, C. *XII.* Inscr. with Lat. verse. Norman Potter, "WHO LOVED THIS VILLAGE ALL HIS LIFE", 1920-**1990**, bronze, on bench, Churchyard.

IN
MEMORIAM
JOHN WHEABLE, DIED 1728;
ALICE HIS WIFE, DIED 1730;
JOHN WHEABLE, SON OF THE ABOVE
BORN 1720, DIED 1827;
PHEBE HIS WIFE,
BORN 1756,
DIED 1827.

Michelmersh *I*

Michelmersh 7

Ref: *Brit. Lib. Add. MS. 5836*, f.61; *Haines*, II, p.73; *M.B.S. Trans.*, V, pp.346-7; *Mee, Hampshire*, p.233; *M.S.*, p.163, p.753; *Soc. Antiq. MS. 875/6*, pp.78-9; *V.C.H., Hampshire*, IV, p.380.

Ch. built, 1854.

MOORDOWN, (see BOURNEMOUTH).

MOTTISFONT, St. Andrew.

I. Inscr. and ach. Sir William Sandys, **1628**, C. Inscr. 193 x 427 mm, ach. 184 x 164 mm, black marble slab 2010 x 860 mm.

II. Inscr. in Lat. recording erection of [chancel] window in **1875** by w. Jane in mem. of Rev. [Sir] John Barker Mill, Bart., M.A., 1860, mur., on marble, C. *III.* Inscr. with verse in raised letters within border of oak leaves and acorns. Capt. William Claude Frederick Vaudrey Barker-Mill, Rifle Brigade, killed while leading his men in the Battle of the Somme, **1916**, aged 42, maker's name GAWTHORP & SONS. LONDON, mur., on marble, N. *IV.* Inscr. with verse recording presentation of organ by widow in mem. of Frank Everard Dixon, tenant of Mottisfont Abbey, **1917**, on organ, C. *V.* World War I memorial in raised letters (24 names), maker's name GAWTHORP & SONS. LONDON, mur., on marble, N. *VI.* Inscr. with verse, crest and motto. Arthur Humbert, J.P., of Kimbridge, 1857-**1934**, mur., N. *VII.* Inscr. in raised letters. Richard Meinertzhagen, soldier, traveller, ornithologist and writer, 1878-**1967**, bronze, mur., N. *VIII.* Inscr. recording restoration [of clock mechanism] by P.G.P. Evans, of Romsey, from a gift of E. and K. Buckell, engr. c.**1985**, mur., on board, N. *IX.* Inscr. Christine Olive Shaw, 1894-**1987**, bronze, on bench, Churchyard. *X.* Inscr. with verse on 2 pls. recording that carving was created by Peter Martin from wood removed from the tower due to infestation by wood boring insects during reconstruction in **1990**, on carving, N.

Ref: *Heseltine, Heraldry*, p.37; *M.B.S. Trans.*, V, pp.347-8; *M.S.*, p.163; *Soc. Antiq. MS. 875/6*, pp.79-80; *V.C.H., Hampshire*, IV, p.509.

NATELY SCURES, St. Swithun.

I. Inscr. William Wodall, founder, and Henry Barnes, parson, **1591**, on beam, N. *Brit. Lib. Add. MS. 39968*, f.260v, f.261r. Inscr. 73 x 213 mm.

II. (Formerly M.S.I). Inscr. with 18 Eng. and 2 Lat. vv. John Palmer, **1661**, aged 61, and w. Mary, 1660, aged 50, "TWICE SIXTEEN YEAR WEE LIVD TOGETHER IN SVNSHINE AND IN STORMIE WEATHER IN WEDLOCK BANDS HVSBAND AND WIFE IN IOY LOVE PEACE VOID OF ALL STRIFE AND TEN TIMES CHANGD OVR HABITATION", mur., N. *Brit. Lib. Add. MS. 39968*, f.258r, ff.262v-3r. Inscr. 279 x 381 mm.

III. Inscr. with crest and arms of New Brunswick, Canada. Gen. Thomas Carleton, "Governor of the Province of New Brunswick from its foundation in 1784, until his death in **1817**", pos. by the

Here lyeth buried the body of Alice Swayne Mother unto Arthur Swayne, whose soule ascended into eternall Joye the xth daye of January An° 1599 aged lxxxviij yeres

Christ is to mee as life one earth,
And death to mee is gayne,
Because I trust through him a lone
Salvation to Obtayne

Monxton I

RICHARDA PORE NEPTIS ADAMI ROBINS
RECTORIS HVIVS ECLESIÆ OBIIT XVj MAII
ANN° DOMINI MILL.^{MO} SEXCENT° SEXTO.

Monxton II

MEMORIÆ · SACRVM ·
GVLIELIMVS SANDYS · EQVES AVRATVS EX ·
NOBILI BARONVM DE SANDYS STIRPI
ORIVNDVS, MORIENS RELICTO MAIORVM
MONVMENTO AD VITEM HIC AD FONTEM
IN PROPRIO SVO · DOMINIO SEPELIRI
VOLVIT. OBIJT IN CHRISTO 28 OCTOBRIS
ANNO DNI 1628 ·

Mottisfont I

HERE LIES JOHN PALMER ... AND MARY HIS WIFE
PRISONERS OF HOPE ... TO ETERNALL LIFE
WHO DECEISD
HEE MAY THE ... AGED 6? ... SHEE OCTOBER THE ... AGED
MARY MAKE ROOM ... I WENT BEFORE
TO THEE I COME ... TO OPE DEATHS DORE
AND MY LAST HOME ... I COVLD NOT STAY
THE THE DAY OF DOOM ... BVT NOW GIVE WAY ... BLISSE
THEN SHALL WEE WAKE RISE LIVE FOR ... COME THEN MY DEAR WEEL SLEEP IN
WITH CHRIST A NEVER DVING DAY ... AND IN THE DVST EACH OTHER KISSE
TWICE SIXTEEN YEAR WEE LIVD TOGETHER
IN SVNSHINE AND IN STORMIE WEATHER
IN WEDLOCK BVNDS HVSBAND AND WIFE
IN IOY LOVE PEACE VOID OF ALL STRIFE
AND TEN TIMES CHANGD OVR HABITATION
AND HERE AT LAST WEE FIXD OVR STATION
WHERE AFTER TEN YEARS SPENT WEE HAVE
OBTAIND AT LENGTH A QVIET GRAVE
PALMER ERAM DVM OBITVM MEMO FIT PALMIFER AT NVNC
PALMIFER IN CÆLIS QVI MODO PALMER ERAM
PILGRIMS ON EARTH ARE PILGRIMS SVCH WAS I
MY PILGRIMAGE IS DONE AND HERE I LY

Nately Scures II

202

Nately Scures *I*

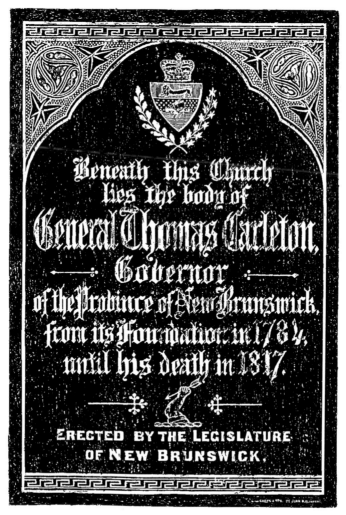

Nately Scures *III*

Legislature of New Brunswick, maker's name R.H. GREEN & SON. ST. JOHN. N.B. CANADA, mur., N. *M.B.S. Bulletin*, 38, p.127 (ach.), p.128 (crest). Inscr. 760 x 510 mm. *IV.* Inscr. with ach. and battle honours on 2 scrolls (Fontenoy 1745, Louisbourg 1758, Quebec 1759, Bellisle 1761, Havannah 1762, Canada 1775). Gen. Sir Guy Carleton, [1st] Baron Dorchester, K.B., Col. 4th Regt. Queen's Own Dragoons, served in the Guards at Fontenoy, Quartermaster-Gen. under Wolfe, "DEFENDED QUEBEC AND SAVED CANADA", created a peer for his services, 1722-1808; mar. Lady Maria, dau. of Thomas, Earl of Effingham, by whom Lt. Guy [Carleton], 3rd Guards, 1773-1793; Thomas [Carleton], 1st R[oya]l Dr[a]g[oon]s, killed at Cateau, [France], 1774-1795; Lt.-Col. Christopher [Carleton], 25th D[ra]g[oon]s, died at Madras, [India], 1775-1806; William [Carleton], 1778-1780; Lancelot [Carleton], 1779-1780; Geo[rge Carleton], wounded at Badajoz, [killed] at Bergen-op-Zoom, [Holland], 1781-1814; Charles [Carleton], R.N., killed on H.M.S. Phoebe, 1786-1799; Capt. Dudley [Carleton], 4th Dragoon [Guards], 1790-1820; [Rev.] Richard [Carleton], rector, 1792-[1869]; Maria, w. of W[illia]m [Orde-Powlett, 2nd] Lord Bolton, [1863]; and Frances, w. of Rev. J. Orde, maker's name BARR, ENGRAVER, LONDON, engr. c.**1860**, mur., N. *V.* Inscr. Lt. Arthur Henry [Carleton], 2nd Baron Dorchester, Royal Horse Guards, 1805-1826, engr. c.**1860**, on window splay, C. *VI.* Inscr. with Lat. verse on cross-shaped pl. encircled. Frances Louisa, dau. of Eusebius Horton, of Catton, w. of Richard Carleton, 1789-**1864**, maker's name BARR, ENGRAVER, LONDON, mur., N. *VII.* Inscr. and cross on separate pl. [Rev. the Hon.] Richard [Carleton], yst. son of Guy [Carleton, 3rd] Baron Dorchester, rector for 50 years, born at London, died at Brighton, [Sussex], 1792-**1869**, mur., below window, C. *VIII.* Inscr. Guy Carleton, 3rd Baron Dorchester, 1811-**1875**, and w. Anne, 1816-1861, on window splay, C. *IX.* Inscr. recording [south-east nave] window pos. by friends in mem. of Capt. Francis Paynton Pigott Carleton, 16th Lancers, of Greywell Hill, **1883**, aged 46, on window splay, N. *X.* Inscr. with verse. Hon. Maria Louisa, dau. of Rev. the Hon. Richard Carleton, sister of [Col.] Dudley [Wilmot Carleton], 4th Baron Dorchester, 1821-**1898**, mur., N. *XI.* Inscr. W.H. Neate, **1905**, on altar, C. *XII.* Inscr. recording recarving of mermaid "BESIDE THE CHURCH DOOR" in **1968** in mem. of Georgina Berry (née Gordon), w. of Walter Black, of Nately Scures House, mother of Alison and Lesley, mur., N.

Ref: *Brit. Lib. Add. MS. 39968*, f.258, ff.260-3; *Burke's Peerage and Baronetage*, p.299; *M.B.S. Bulletin*, 38, pp.127-8; *M.B.S. Trans.*, V, pp.348-9; *Mee, Hampshire*, p.237; *M.S.*, p.163; *Norris, Memorials*, p.255; *Soc. Antiq. MS. 875/6*, pp.80-1; *V.C.H., Hampshire*, IV, p.154.

NETHERTON, St. Michael (old church, now demolished).

INDENTS & LOST BRASSES. 1. Lost brass, ?eff. and inscr.

Ref: *Hampshire, Antiquary*, I, p.41.

Ch. demolished, 1866.

NETLEY ABBEY (now a ruin, maintained by English Heritage).

Man in arm. of the ?Compton family and w. in mantle, c.**1500**, kng., rect. pl. powdered with firebeacons with scrolls, etc.; said to have been formerly in Netley Abbey, discovered in a "poor man's house, where it served as a back to a grate, from which it was obtained for a moderate

Netley Abbey

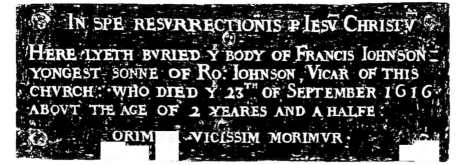

Newton Valence I

gratuity", presented in 1861 by Rev. H. Burnaby Greene, of Longparish, to the Surrey Archaeological Society, Guildford. Recorded ("found in the ruins of Netley Abbey, Hampshire, where it had served for the back of a grate and given to me by Mr Baker jun. bookseller at Southampton") by Gough (1799). *Archaeologia*, XV, opp. p.302; *Bod. Lib. Gough Maps 228*, f.58; *Guillaume*, pl.10; *Surrey Arch. Colls.*, X, opp. p.126. Rect. pl. 498 x 490 mm. Style: London D.

Ref: *Archaeologia*, XV, pp.302-3, XXI, p.550; *Bod. Lib. Gough Maps 228*, f.58; *Guillaume, G., Architectural Views and Details of Netley Abbey*, 1848, p.35; *Hampshire History*, II, pp.373-4; *Kelke, W.H., Notices of Sepulchral Monuments in English Churches*, 1850, p.44; *M.B.S. Trans.*, XIV, p.490; *Surrey Arch. Colls.*, X, pp.126-9.

Abbey established, 1239; dissolved, 1536; ruinous, early 18th cent.

NEWTON VALENCE, St. Mary.

I. Inscr. Francis, yst. son of Ro[bert] Johnson, vicar, **1616**, aged about 2½ years, mur., C. Inscr. 133 x 367 mm.

II. Inscr. with verse. John Hunt, aged 5; Ann Hunt, aged 3; Robert Hewitt, aged 11; Jane Hunt, aged 11; Kitty Kemp, aged 5; Charles Hunt, aged 12; Emily Hunt, aged 1; Isabella Hewitt, aged 9; Henry Hunt, aged 5; and Albert Sawkins, aged 4, all died of diptheria, **1871**, mur., below window, N.C. *III.* Inscr. Algernon T. Lempriere, J.P., M.A., of Pelham, 1835-**1874**, mur., N. *IV.* Inscr. with regt. insignia. Lt. L.C. Maclachlan, Adjutant 1st Battn. King's Royal Rifle [Corps], died at Rawal Pindi, 1868-1895, pos. in **1896** by [brother] officers, mur., on marble, N. *V.* Inscr. recording erection of altar rails in **1899** by children in mem. of [Rev.] Archibald Neil Campbell Maclachlan, M.A.(Oxon.), vicar and patron for 30 years [1860-1890], 1891, maker's name JONES & WILLIS, mur., C. *VI.* Inscr. with verse. Harriet, yst. child of Admiral [George Ouray] Lempriere, of Pelham, **1901**, maker's name JONES & WILLIS, mur., N. *VII.* Inscr. with verse recording gift of altar cross by friends in mem. of Elsie Jean Campbell Maclachlan, 1869-**1903**, maker's name BARKENTIN & KRALL LONDON, mur., in stone frame, N. *VIII.* Inscr. General Thomas Rochfort Snow, Bengal Light Cavalry, served in the Scinde Campaign in 1843-1844 under Sir Charles Napier and was present at the Battles of Meeanee and Hyderabad, the Punjab Campaign and occupation of Lahore 1845, and the Indian Mutiny 1857-1858, 1821-**1904**; also dau., Agnes Gertrude, died at Newton Valence, 1888, aged 23, pos. by w. [Mary Ann Palmer] and children, maker's name H. ROSE & SON, SOUTHAMPTON, mur., C. *IX.* Inscr. Mary Ann Palmer, w. of General Thomas Rochfort Snow for 54 years, 1828-**1905**, pos. by sons and daus., maker's name H. ROSE & SON, SOUTHAMPTON, mur., C. *X.* Inscr. Major-Gen. Cecil Mangles, C.B., 20th Hussars, 1842-**1906**, maker's name *J. WIPPELL & C⁰ Lᵀᴰ EXETER & LONDON*, mur., N. *XI.* Inscr. Ellen, eld. dau. of Admiral George Ouray Lempriere, of Pelham, 1838-**1908**, maker's name A. & N. AUX C.S.L. LONDON, mur., below no.*VI*, N. *XII.* Inscr. with regt. insignia. Major Neil Campbell Maclachlan, 1st Battn. Seaforth Highlanders, died at Nahakki during the Mohmand Expedition on the north-west frontier of India, **1908**, pos. by brother officers, maker's name BARKENTIN & KRALL LONDON, mur., in marble frame, N. *XIII.* Inscr. recording window "DEVISED" by Ulick John Burke and dedication in **1913** by w., mur., below window, N. *XIV.* Inscr. with regt. insignia. Lt.-Col. Henry George Levinge, Norfolk Regt., [eld. son of Henry Corbin Levinge, D.L., killed] in action while commanding 6th Battn. Loyal North Lancashire

Regt. on the heights of Chunuk-Bair in Gallipoli, [Turkey,1864-]**1915**, pos. by w. Maureen [Elizabeth, only dau. of Capt. William Addis Fagan, 12th Lancers], maker's name HERBERT WAUTHIER del F. OSBORNE & CO LTD London, mur., in wooden frame, N. *XV*. Inscr. Lt.-Col. A[lexander] F[raser] C[ampbell] Maclachlan, D.S.O., 60th [King's Royal] Rifle [Corps], killed in action near Fluquières, **1918**, pos. by officers of 13th (S) Battn. Manchester Regt. in gratitude for commanding the battn. 1916-1917, maker's name W^(M.) MORRIS & C^(O.) (WESTMINSTER) L^(TD), mur., N.C. *XVI*. Inscr. Henry Warner, churchwarden for 44 years, 1834-**1921**, and [w.] Robina Selina, 1838-1914, maker's name G. MAILE & SON, LTD 367 EUSTON RD. N.W.1, mur., N.C. *XVII*. Inscr. recording installation of electric light by friends and parishioners and dedication in **1948** by [Rt. Rev. Dr. Mervyn George Haigh, D.D.], Bishop of Winchester [1942-1952], in mem. of [Rev.] Archibald Campbell Maclachlan, [M.A.], vicar 1895-1944, copper, mur., N. *XVIII*. Inscr. recording presentation of organ blower in **1952** by Miss Maclachlan in mem. of brothers, on organ, N.C. *XIX*. Inscr. recording that dorsal curtain behind the altar pos. in mem. of Colin Arthur Jardine, churchwarden and diocesan reader, 1892-**1957**, copper, mur., N. *XX*. Inscr. Lt.-Col. William Henry Middleton, D.S.O., Hampshire Regt., churchwarden for 32 years, 1878-**1967**, mur., N. *XXI*. Inscr. recording restoration of organ in **1985** by w. [Rona Gwenllian (née Harkness)], family and friends in mem. of Rear-Admiral Harry Philip Currey, C.B., O.B.E., 1902-1979, on organ with no.*XVIII*, N.C. *XXII*. Inscr. recording restoration of font in mem. of Gordon Wilson, C.B.E., O.St.J., 1923-**1994**, on font, N.C.

Ref: *Burke's Peerage and Baronetage*, p.1599; *M.B.S. Trans.*, V, p.349; *Mee, Hampshire*, p.242; *M.S.*, p.163; *Soc. Antiq. MS. 875/6*, p.81; *V.C.H., Hampshire*, III, p.29; *Who's Who*, 1967, p.735.

NURSLING, St. Boniface.

I. Inscr. with chronogram, ach., etc. Andrew Mundy, esq., **1632**, aged 61; with incised marg. inscr.; mur., S.C. *M.B.S. Bulletin*, 39, p.137 (ach.); *M.B.S. Trans.*, V, p.350. Inscr. 422 x 422 mm, upper lozenge 267 x 230 mm, lower lozenge 270 x 235 mm, non-Purbeck slab 1755 x 920 mm.

II. Inscr. recording gift [of altar rails] in **1882** by w. and children, Emily, Gilbert, Margaret, Seymour, Wilfred, Osmund, Winifred and Courtenay Hawtrey, as a thank offering for restoration to health in 1878 of [Rev.] H[enry] C[ourtenay] Hawtrey, [M.A., rector 1873-1889], on altar rail, C. *III*. Inscr. on sh.-shaped pl. recording gift [of lectern] by Alicia Boulton in mem. of uncle, Abraham Hodgson Lees, of Upton House, **1883**, aged 74, on lectern, N. *IV*. Inscr. recording gift [of font] by Alicia Boulton in mem. of mother, Emily Lees, of Upton House, **1893**, aged 85, on font plinth, N. *V*. Inscr. recording dedication of [south-east nave] window in **1897** by Emily Barton in mem. of father, [Charles Cutts Barton, 1802-1894], on window splay, N. *VI*. Inscr. Emilia H. Barton, **1900**, copper, on lamp, S.Porch/Tower. *VII*. Inscr. with fouled anchor. Walter Edmund Farmer, R.N., chorister, [drowned] in H.M.S. Cobra in the North Sea, **1901**, aged 18, pos. by friends, maker's name GARRET & HAYSOM, mur., N. *VIII*. Inscr. recording erection of choir stalls by parents and friends, Harold Child and [w.] Isabel, in mem. of Lt. Stephen George Raymond White, Oxfordshire L[igh]t In[fantry] 1899-1901, eld. son of [Rev. George Cecil White, M.A.], rector [1889-1914], died at Umtali, S[outh] A[frica], 1878-**1903**, on stall, C. *IX*. Inscr. with sh. and helm. Col. Fenwick Bulmer de Sales La Terrière, 18th Hussars and Royal Fusiliers, J.P. for Hants and Oxon., yeoman of the guard to Edward VII and George V, h. and representative of family of de Sales, Comtes de Sales de St. Salvy, rescued and restored Grove Place 1895, 1856-**1925**, mur., N. Inscr. 311 x 680 mm. *X.* Inscr. recording gift [churchwardens' wand] by dau., Agnes Worth, in mem. of George Worth, 1830-**1927**, on churchwardens' wand, N. *XI.* Inscr. Margaret Tabitha Collis, **1932**, pos. by M[others'] U[nion] members, on candlesnuffer, C. *XII.* Inscr. Henry Hutton Castle, husband, **1943**, on cross, C. *XIII.* Inscr. recording that ch. heating was provided in **1955** by friends' subscriptions in mem. of Wilfred Varley, [P.C.C.] treasurer, mur., on board, N. *XIV.* Inscr. recording dedication [of processional cross] in **1966** as a thank offering for restoration to health from a serious accident of David Andrews, on processional cross, C. *XV.* Inscr. Henry Thomas Rogers, reader and ch. benefactor, **1985**, [aged 69], mur., on board, N. *XVI.* Inscr. Grace Miriam Warboys, organist for nearly 50 years, **1991**, on choir stall, C.

Ref: *Brit. Lib. Add. MS. 39968,* f.317; *Heseltine, Heraldry*, p.37; *M.B.S. Trans.*, V, p.349, pp.351-2; *M.S.*, p.163; *Soc. Antiq. MS. 875/6*, pp.81-4; *V.C.H., Hampshire*, III, p.439.

OAKLEY, CHURCH, St. Leonard (new church).

I. Robert Warham, in civil dress, and w. Elizabeth (mutil.), both died **1487**, with 4 sons (one a priest in acad., William Warham, Archbishop of Canterbury 1503-1532), inscr.; 2 daus. lost; A.T., S.C./S.A. Recorded (daus. lost) by Pavey (1703). *M.B.S. Trans.*, V, p.277; *Page-Phillips, Children*, fig.21 (sons). Male eff. 457 x 123 mm, female eff. orig. 455 x 170 mm, now 455 x 150 mm, inscr. 70 x 420 mm, sons 114-124 x 91 mm, daus. indent 125 x 55 mm, Purbeck coverstone 1455 x 640 mm. Style: London D.

II. Inscr. recording [south chancel] window pos. in **1869** by [Rev. John Monkhouse, M.A.], rector [1862-1879], in mem. of parents, John Monkhouse and [w.] Margaret, mur., below window, C. *III.* Inscr. recording restoration [of font] in **1869** in mem. of the baptisms of W.W.P., E.J.P., S.J.P., C.M.P., M.A.P., B.P.P. and C.M.P., on font, N. *IV.* Inscr. recording [south south chapel] window pos. by sister, Charlotte Ragwell Purefoy, in mem. of Maude Green Wilkinson, **1869**, mur., below window, old S.C., now Vestry. *V.* Inscr. "In thankful remembrance of blessings received by Mary", **1869**, mur., below window, old S.C., now Vestry. *VI.* Inscr. in Lat. William Warham, born at Malshanger, [Bishop of London 1502-1503], Archbishop of Canterbury [1503-1532], 1450-1532, engr. c.**1870**, mur., below window, S.A. *VII.* Inscr. Elizabeth, widow of John Portal, of Freefolk Priors, **1877**, aged 89, mur., S.C./S.A. *VIII.* Inscr. recording dedication of [north-west north aisle] window by w. and children in mem. of Rev. John Monkhouse, M.A., fellow of Queen's Coll., Oxford, rector for 17 years [1862-1879], **1879**, aged 45, mur., below window, N.A. *IX.* Inscr. recording [north-east north aisle] window pos. by friends and parishioners in mem. of Rev. John Monkhouse, M.A., [fellow of Queen's Coll., Oxford], rector [1862-1879], **1879**, [aged 45], mur., below window, N.A. *X.* Inscr. [Rev. Canon] George Henry Heslop, M.A., fellow of Queen's Coll., Oxford, hon. canon of Carlisle Cathedral, rector, [1822-]**1887**, maker's name FRANK SMITH & Cᵒ LONDON, mur., C. *XI.* Inscr. in Lat. recording gift of [west north aisle window] by children in mem. of [Rev. Canon] George Henry Heslop, M.A., [fellow of Queen's Coll., Oxford], hon. canon of Carlisle Cathedral, rector, 1822-]**1887**, mur., below window, N.A. *XII.* Inscr. with verse. James Gordon Balch, people's churchwarden for 20 years, 1838-**1918**, pos. by friends and parishioners, mur., on pillar, N. *XIII.* Inscr. [Rev.] Francis Glynne Hume, M.A., Queen's Coll., Oxford, rector for 31 years [1887-1918], 1844-**1918**, pos. by friends and parishioners, mur., C. *XIV.* Inscr. [Rev. Canon]

CINERI ○ SACRVM
Selectißimi viri ANDreƐ MVNDy armigeri
hic sepulti
QVI
FIDELITATIS PROTYPVM CHARITATIS SYMBOLVM
PRVDENTIE SPECIMEN PIETATIS EXEMPLVM
PREBENS VIVENDO
ANIMAM COELO, CORPVS SOLO
SVA SVIS LVCTVM OMNIBVS
LIQVIT EXPIRANDO
Tertio die post festum sancti ANDREƐ Apostoli (synonimi)
CRITICE ET QVASI SYMPATHETICE
Anno subscripto cryptico

Vt CererI FVnVs ᴀC pHœnICI CInIs
Vesper ᴀPoLLInI sIC MIHI FInIs
FM nepos patrvo Pientißimo syncero hoc
plorans, plangens parentavit
EƒƐgio

Nursling I

IN REMEMBRANCE OF
COLONEL FENWICK BULMER de SALES La TERRIERE
LATE OF THE 18ᵀᴴ HUSSARS AND ROYAL FUSILIERS.
EXON OF THE KING'S BODY GUARD OF THE YEOMEN OF
THE GUARD TO KING EDWARD VII & KING GEORGE V.
J.P. FOR HANTS & OXON, HEIR TO & REPRESENTATIVE OF THE FAMILY
OF de SALES, COMTES de SALES de Sᵀ SALVY. BORN 1856. DIED 1925.
WHO RESCUED FROM RUIN & RESTORED GROVE PLACE 1895.
"TOUT PASSE"

Nursling IX

209

Orate p aiabz Robecti Washam q obijt pmo die mef Octobris
anno dni cm CCCC lxxxvij et Elizabeth vxor' ei que eciam obijt
eode anno dni xv die Septebris qu aiabus pnciet de' aniē

Oakley, Church I

HERE LYETH THE BODY
OF GYLBARD WYTHER
WHOE DECEASED THE
XXX DAY OF IVNE AN. 1599

Oakley, Church 19

Odiham I

211

George Herbert Jeudwine, M.A., [hon. canon of Winchester Cathedral], rector for 40 years [1919-1960], 1883-**1968**, pos. by friends and parishioners, mur., C. *XV.* Inscr. [Rev.] John Champernowne Litton, rector 1972-**1984**, mur., C. *XVI.* Inscr. Rev. Christopher [Leigh] Atkins, [M.A.], rector 1985-**1996**, on lectern, N.

INDENTS & LOST BRASSES. 17. Lost brass, ?man. in arm. and w., inscr. Nicholas Wareham, 1504, S.C. Recorded (eff. covered) by Pavey (1703). 18. Lost brass, man in arm. of the Wareham family and 2 ws., ?inscr. and 2 shs. Recorded (male eff., female effs. and ?2 shs.) by Pavey (1703). 19. *(Formerly M.S.II)*. Lost brass, inscr. Gylbard Wyther, 1599, N. Recorded (1890) but not found (1930). Illustration from rubbing in Soc. Antiq. coll. Rubbing in Soc. Antiq. coll. (n.d.). Inscr. 92 x 260 mm.

Ref: *Brit. Lib. Stowe MS. 845*, f.103; *Haines*, I, p.172, II, p.73; *M.B.S. Trans.*, V, p.276, p.278; *Mee, Hampshire*, p.251; *M.S.*, p.163; *Norris, Memorials*, p.141; *Pevsner, Hampshire*, p.363; *Soc. Antiq. MS. 875/6*, pp.30-2; *V.C.H., Hampshire*, IV, p.228.

Ch. built, 1869.

ODIHAM, All Saints.

I. Civilian with pouch and dagger and w., c.**1465**; inscr. lost; head renewed in 19th cent.; formerly C., now mur., on slate, N. *M.B.S. Trans.*, V, p.352; *Mee, Hampshire*, p.219 (drg. of effs.). Male eff. 490 x 152 mm, female eff. 450 x 140 mm. Style: London sub B. Rep. by B.S.H.E. (1988).

II. William Goode, vicar of Ponteland, Northumb., rector of Dogmansfield, **1498**, in mass vests., inscr. and 5 Lat. vv. stating he was a native of Leics.; discovered in 1851 under flooring; now mur., on slate, N., vv. now mur., on slate below no.*VII*, N.C. *M.B.S. Trans.*, V, pp.354-5; *Mee, Hampshire*, p.115 (drg. of eff.); *Newcastle Soc. Antiq. Proc.*, 3 S. IX, p.221. Eff. 492 x 174 mm, inscr. 73 x 406 mm, vv. 101 x 295 mm. Style: London G. Rep. by B.S.H.E. (1988).

III. Inscr. (effs., 2 sons, 6 daus., sm. cross and 4 shs. lost); the remains of the brass to John Haydok, esq., **1504**, in arm., and w. Elizabeth; formerly N.A., N.C., now mur., on slate, N.C. Recorded (effs., inscr., sons, cross and 4 shs. with daus. lost) by Pavey (1702). Rubbing (inscr. and 4 shs. with effs., 2 sons, 6 daus. and cross lost) in Soc. Antiq. coll. (1848). Lost male eff. indent 760 x 210 mm, lost female eff. indent 710 x 210 mm, inscr. 80 x 631 mm, lost sons indent c.150 x 75 mm, lost daus. indent 150 x 125 mm, lost cross indent 650 x 295 mm, lost upper dext. sh. 148 x 122 mm, lost upper sin. sh. 143 x 116 mm, lost lower dext. sh. 145 x 107 mm, lost lower sin. sh. 148 x 120 mm. Style: London G. Rep. by B.S.H.E. (1988).

IV. (Formerly M.S.III.A). Lady, c.**1520**, with 9 daus.; inscr. lost; formerly N.C., eff. now mur., on slate with nos.*III* & *V* (daus.), daus. now mur., on slate with nos.*V* (eff.) & *VI.* Eff. 485 x 171 mm, daus. 149-161 x 219 mm. Style: London F. Rep. by B.S.H.E. (1988).

V. (Formerly M.S.III.B). Lady, c.**1520**, with 6 daus.; inscr. lost; formerly N.C., eff. now mur., on slate with nos.*IV* (daus.) & *VI,* daus. now mur., on slate with nos.*III* & *IV* (eff.). Eff. 477 x 165 mm, daus. 135-144 x 192 mm. Style: London F. Rep. by B.S.H.E. (1988).

Hic iacet magist' Willus Goode nup vicarius de ponteland in
northhūbria et 'rector de Dogmalfeld qui obijt xj° die septbris
Anno dūi millmo CCCC°lxxxxvij° cuius aīe ꝓpiciet deus amē

Willūs iacet hic quōdā goode ex patre ortus
Presbiter ꝫ doctor · Artibus Oxonie
Mūē clare emirur quōdā Exeton dom° alma
Hunc gen° ꝫ mores · leᵱctlma terra dat ort°
Pᵱo dui legis hec Carmina funde ᵱces

Odiham II

213

VI. (Formerly M.S.IV). Inscr. Thomas Chapman, **1522**, and w. Agnes, device of a crossbow on inscr.; formerly N.C., now mur., on slate with nos.*IV* (daus.) & *V* (eff.), N.C. Inscr. 84 x 542 mm. Style: London F debased. Rep. by B.S.H.E. (1988).

VII. (Formerly M.S.V). Civilian, c.**1530**; inscr. lost; formerly N., now mur., on slate, N.C. *M.B.S. Trans.*, V, p.357; *Mee, Hampshire*, p.347 (drg.); *Newcastle Soc. Antiq. Proc.*, 3 S. IX, p.221. Eff. 676 x 213 mm. Style: London F debased. Rep. by B.S.H.E. (1988).

VIII. (Formerly M.S.VI). Man in arm., c.**1540**, feet gone; 2 ws., inscr., 6 daus. and 4 shs. lost; 1 son and 5 daus. stolen between 1909 and 1938; palimp., on rev. hand of abbot or bishop on shaft of crosier, c.1320, and pts. of chasuble of abbot or bishop, c.1520; formerly on A.T., N.C., now mur., on slate, N.C.; orig. slab in 2006 almost completely covered by foot pace of altar, N.C. Probably Richard Vass, esq., 1542, and ws. Recorded (male eff., with female effs., inscr., 6 daus. and 4 shs. lost) by Pavey (1702) and (1 son and 5 daus.) by Cave (1908). *M.B.S. Trans.*, V, p.358 (obv. of male eff.); *Palimpsests*, pl.29 (rev.), pl.208 (rev.). Illustration (group of 1 son and 5 daus.) from rubbing in Soc. Antiq. coll. Rubbing (group of 1 son and 5 daus.) in Soc. Antiq. coll. (1865). Male eff. 598 x 248 mm, covered inscr. indent 125 x 860 mm, lost 1 son and 5 daus. 127-144 x 195 mm, upper dext sh. indent 75 visible x 120 mm, upper sin. sh. 75 visible x 120 mm, Purbeck slab 265 visible x 1110 mm. Style: London G (Gyfford). Rep. by B.S.H.E. (1988).

IX. (Formerly M.S.VII). Margaret, 2nd dau. of Thomas Pye, esq., **1636**, aged 6 weeks, in swaddling clothes, inscr. and text with sh.; formerly C., now Vestry/S.C. *M.B.S. Trans.*, V, p.360. Eff. 392 x 126 mm, inscr. 172 x 450 mm, text with sh. 166-173 x 454 mm, black marble slab 1140 x 530 mm visible. Style: London.

X. (Formerly M.S.VIII). Inscr. and ach. Edward Seagar, gent., **1640**; formerly C., now mur., on slate, N.C. Inscr. 131 x 477 mm, ach. 256 x 200 mm. Rep. by B.S.H.E. (1988).

XI. Inscr. with verse, sh. and motto. Rev. William Harriott, M.A., vicar and domestic chaplain to Earl of Beverly, **1847**, aged 57; also children, Emma Louisa, Louisa-Ann and Ellen Anne, died young, mur., on marble, N. *XII.* Inscr. recording 3 east chancel windows filled with glass in **1858** in mem. of Lt.-Col. Charles William Short, [of Bury House], mur., on marble, Vestry/S.C. *XIII.* Inscr. recording presentation [of ewer] in **1893** by par. children, on ewer, Vestry/S.C. *XIV.* Inscr. Clement Pound, husband, **1899**, on prie-dieu, N.C. *XV.* Inscr. recording presentation [of lectern] by widow and children in mem. of Henry Pratt, [church]warden 1894-**1900**, on lectern, S.A. *XVI.* Inscr. George Pound, churchwarden for many years, engr. c.**1900**, on table, N.A. *XVII.* Inscr. with verse in raised letters. Thomas Henry Haddan, B.C.L., M.A., of the Inner Temple and Odiham Close, 1814-1873, and [w.] Caroline Elizabeth, 1829-**1901**, pos. by children, maker's name GAWTHORP, LONDON, bronze, mur., N.A. *XVIII.* Inscr. recording erection of screen in **1912** by son in mem. of Elizabeth, 2nd dau. of William Booth and w. Mary (née Denman), w. of Daniel Pratt, born at East Retford, [Notts.], died at Odiham, 1878, aged 78, on screen, N.C. *XIX.* Inscr. recording gift of chair by nephew, A.B. Pratt, in mem. of David Pratt, benefactor to the chapel, **1913**, on chair, C. *XX.* Inscr. T.T.D., **1913**, on credence table, C. *XXI.* Inscr. with sh., regt. and R.N. insignia within border of oak leaves and acorns. Philip Lutley Sclater, son of William Lutley Sclater, M.A., D.Sc.(Oxon.), of Hoddington, educated at Winchester [Coll.], fellow of Corpus Christi Coll., Oxford, barrister-at-law, fellow of the Royal Society [of London 1861], secretary of the Zoological Society of London for 42 years [1860-1903], "WELL KNOWN THROUGHOUT THE WORLD FOR HIS KNOWLEDGE OF AND

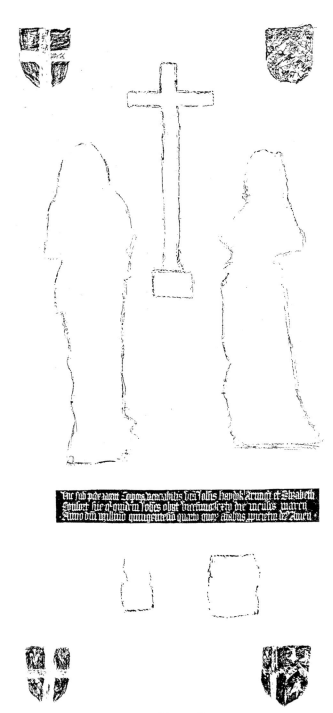

Hic sub pede iacent Corpora venerabilis viri Iohis hanuk Arungi et Elizabeth Consort sue q' quidm Iohes obijt vncesima sexto die ineulus marcij Anno dni mullimo quingenteimo quarto quor' aiabus ppicietur de Amen

Odiham III

215

Odiham *IV*

Odiham *V*

217

Here lieth Thomas Chapman and Agnes his wyffe which Thomas decessid the first day of maye in the yere of oure lord god M⁴cccc xij On whos soules Ihu haue mercy A

Odiham *VI*

Odiham *VII*

218

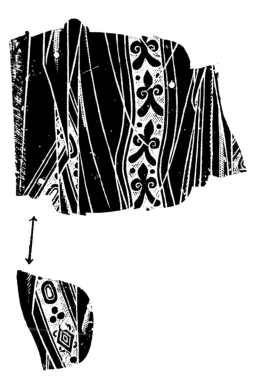

Odiham *VIII* palimpsest reverse

Odiham *VIII*

Suenite ad me et eos non prohibete talium

Luc: cap: XVIII° ver: XVI°

sinite pueruloʒ

et enim regnum dei

Hic iacet sepvlta Margaretta Pye filia secvnda
Thome Pye armiger qve nata decimo septimo die
Novembris Anno Dñi: 1636· novissimṽ reddidit
spiritṽ in manvs redemptoris svi 27° die Decem=
bris seqvent svaviterq in Domino obdormit,
Mors certa, hora incerta,
Da mihi nosse meæ qvæ svnt stata tempora vitæ
Et qvando extremṽ fata fvtvra mihi

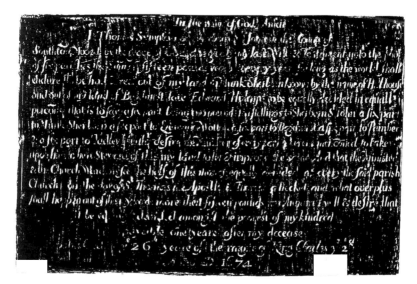

HERE LYETH INTERRED THE BODY OF
EDWARD SEAGAR · GENT WHO DEPARTED
THIS LIFE IN CERTAINE HOPE OF A IOYFVLL
RESVRRECTION Y̆ 11ᵀᴴ OF IVLY A° DÑI 1640·

Odiham *X*

Pamber I

221

WRITINGS ON ZOOLOGICAL SCIENCE", died at Odiham Priory, 1829-1913, buried at Upton Grey; mar. 1862, Jane Anne Eliza, yst. dau. of Sir David Hunter Blair, [3rd] Bart., of Blairquhan, Ayrshire, died at 12 Chester Terrace, London, 1835-**1915**, buried at Upton Grey; also 2nd son, Capt. Bertram Lutley Sclater, Royal Engineers, served in Nyasaland on the staff of Sir Harry Johnston 1891-1892, and in British East Africa 1895-1897 "WHERE HE CONSTRUCTED A ROAD FROM MOMBASA TO VICTORIA NYANZA", born in London, died of fever at Zanzibar, 1866-1897; also 3rd son, Capt. Guy Lutley Sclater, R.N., born at Hoddington, entered the navy in 1882 "SERVED HIS COUNTRY IN MANY PARTS OF THE WORLD AND WAS DISTINGUISHED FOR HIS KNOWLEDGE OF THE APPLICATIONS OF ELECTRICITY IN NAVAL AFFAIRS. ON THE OUTBREAK OF THE GREAT EUROPEAN WAR HE COMMANDED H.M.S. BULWARK AND LOST HIS LIFE WITH ALL HIS SHIP'S COMPANY WHEN THAT VESSEL WAS BLOWN UP IN THE MEDWAY", 1868-1914, buried [in the churchyard], maker's name A & N. AUX C.S.L LONDON, mur., N. *XXII & XXIII.* Two inscrs. recording gift [of candlesticks] in **1918** in mem. of de Courcy Daniell, on candlesticks, Vestry/S.C. *XXIV.* Inscr. with verse. Staff-Capt. John Duke, M.C., 18th Infantry Brigade, master of [Robert May's Grammar] School, 1910-1914, died of wounds in France, **1918**, pos. by friends and old pupils, mur., on board, S.A. *XXV.* Inscr. with verse and regt. insignia. Capt. Geoffrey Harris Gotelee, 7th [Battn.] South Wales Borderers, [son of Arthur Gotelee and w. Esther, of The Old House], killed in action at the Battle of Grand Couronne, Salonika, **1918**, aged 25, mur., on board, N.A. *XXVI.* Inscr. on oval-shaped pl. recording gift [of reredos] by son and dau. in mem. of Thomas Dicker, 1881, and w. Mary Hannah, dau. of Elizabeth Pratt, **1926**, on reredos, N.C. *XXVII.* Inscr. "OUR VERY GALLANT TIM", **1944**, [pos. by] brother officers, NCOs and Guardsmen of 3 Co. 5th B[att]n. Coldstream Guards, on processional cross, Vestry/S.C. *XXVIII.* Inscr. "THIS PLAQUE WAS PLACED HERE WHEN ROBERT MAY'S GRAMMAR SCHOOL (ADJACENT TO THIS CHURCH) WAS CLOSED IN **1951**", mur., on World War I memorial, S.A. *XXIX.* Inscr. Henry James Bransom, bellringer, chorister and churchwarden, 1865-**1956**, and w. Sarah Ann, 1864-1920, on chest of drawers, Vestry/S.C. *XXX.* Inscr. recording erection of screen by parishioners in mem. of Arthur Booth Pratt, ch. servant, churchwarden 1899-1956, 1871-**1956**, bronze, on screen, N. *XXXI.* Inscr. recording installation of refectory in mem. of Barbara Rait Kerr, 1978, engr. **1981**, pos. by family, on kitchenette, N.A. *XXXII.* Inscr. Jim Fleming and [w.] Mabel, engr. c.**1985**, mur., N.C. *XXXIII.* Inscr. recording gift [of screen] in **1995** by church flower arrangers, on screen, S.A. *XXXIV.* Inscr. Neville Lloyd Evans, engr. c.**1995**, on piano, N.A. *XXXV.* Inscr. recording recasting of treble bell and rehanging of bells in **1997** to commem. the coming Millennium; funded by a gift to the Friends of All Saints from the great-niece of Jasper Snowden, [bell]ringer and author, 1844-1885, mur., Tower. *XXXVI.* Inscr. Michael Wentworth, bellringer, "recorded and presented Odiham history" and [w.] Barbara, founded the Odiham Society, [resident] 1975-**1997**, on door, Tower.

INDENTS & LOST BRASSES. 37. Lost indent, inscr.; in 2006 under flooring, N. Recorded by Cave (1908). Inscr. 65 x 460 mm. 38. Lost indent, inscr.; in 2006 under flooring, N. Recorded by Cave (1908). Inscr. 110 x ? mm. 39. Lost ?Indent, effaced; in 2006 under flooring, N. Recorded by Cave (1908).

Nos.*I-VIII & X* were recovered by Rev. Thomas Grey Clarke, vicar, "They were loose for a long time in the old chest, and were collected by me in 1867, and affixed to the wall, as I found that a few archaeological gentlemen had offered our sexton money for them, which he refused".

Ref: *Brit. Lib. Stowe MS. 845*, ff.62-4, *Add. MS. 39964*, f.402, *Add. MS. 39968*, f.353; *Gawthorp*, p.36; *Haines*, I, p.219, II, p.73; *Hampshire, Antiquary*, I, p.6; *Manning*, p.31; *M.B.S.*

Bulletin, 93, p.676; *M.B.S. Trans.*, I, pt.7, p.24, pt.8, p.26, IV, p.121, V, p.353, pp.355-9, p.361-2, IX, p.514, XV, p.181, p.391; *Mee, Hampshire*, p.254; *M.S.*, pp.163-4, p.753; *Norris, Memorials*, p.141, p.247; *Palimpsests*, 102L1-3, p.44, p.xxi; *Pevsner, Hampshire*, p.364; *Simpson*, p.28; *Soc. Antiq. MS. 875/6*, pp.84-94, *MS. 1014/12*; *V.C.H., Hampshire*, IV, pp.96-7.

OVERTON, St. Mary.

I. Inscr. Anthony Budd, churchwarden, **1893**, on lectern, N. *II.* Inscr. recording gift of east window by w. Ellen in mem. of Charles Sprent, **1901**, maker's name HART SON PEARD & Cᵒ Lᴰ LONDON, mur., C. *III.* Inscr. with verse. [Rev. Canon] George Covey Stenning, [M.A., hon. canon of Winchester Cathedral, rector 1896-1910], **1915**, pos. by w., son and dau., maker's name G MAILE & SON. 367, EUSTON Rᴰ *LONDON*, copper, mur., S.A. *IV.* Inscr. Arthur William Strickland, verger 1913-**1919**, mur., on framed picture, N.A. *V.* Inscr. recording gift [of prie-dieu] in **1921** by Mabel Alice Ferguson in mem. of Ellen, [w. of Charles] Sprent, on prie-dieu, C. *VI.* Inscr. with verse. Emily Louisa, w. of [Rev. Canon] George Covey Stenning, [M.A., hon. canon of Winchester Cathedral], rector 1896-1910, **1924**, maker's name G. MAILE & SON Lᵀᴰ 367 EUSTON Rᴰ LONDON, copper, mur., S.A. *VII.* Inscr. Catherine Charlotte Sims-Williams, dau., w. and mother, 1915-**1943**, mur., on board on painting, N.A. *VIII.* Inscr. with verse. Chief Inspector Reginald Stephen Charles Bowles, Hampshire and I[sle] o[f] W[ight] Constabulary, husband and father, **1968**, aged 56, ashes [buried] in the churchyard, bronze, on bench, Churchyard. *IX.* Inscr. recording renovation of organ with tonal improvement in 1978 and installation of bench in **1981**; work carried out by A[nthony] Foster[-]Waite, of Newbury, [Berks.] with the cost met from a gift by Emily Barnett, 1875-1965, on organ, C. *X.* Inscr. recording painting of picture by Miss Edna Hill as a replacement for the orig. stolen in **1981**, mur., on board on painting with no.*VII*, N.A. *XI.* Inscr. on 2 pls. [Sir] Francis Spencer Portal, 5th Bart., [D.L., F.R.S.A., 3rd son of Sir Spencer John Portal, 4th Bart., J.P., High Sheriff 1963], 1903-**1984**, on bookcase, Tower. *XII.* Inscr. recording gift of tapestry altar kneeler by family and friends in mem. of Roy Hudson, churchwarden 1975-1985, 1921-**1985**, on organ with no.*IX*, C. *XIII.* Inscr. Nora Frances Bowles, [w. of no.*VIII*], 1912-**1995**, [pos. by] Angie and Chris, bronze, on bench with no.*VIII*, Churchyard,

Ref: *Burke's Peerage and Baronetage*, p.2149.

OWSLEBURY, St. Andrew.

I. Inscr. with verse and 4 evang. symbols in relief at corners. Rowland Edmond Walter Pery Standish, J.P., D.L., 1893, and w. Caroline Macnamara, **1912**, [both buried] in the churchyard, mur., C. *II.* Inscr. [Rev.] Charles Buston, [M.A.], vicar 1896-1911, **1920**, aged 64, mur., on board below crucifix, N. *III.* Inscr. Sgt. Arthur Sylwood, air gunner, R.A.F., only son of Albert Frederick and [w.] Florence Lush, sidesman for 2 years, killed over Germany, **1942**, aged 22, ?brass, on font cover, Tower. *IV.* Inscr. on 2 pls. recording erection of gates by people of Owslebury and Morestead to commem. the coronation of Queen Elizabeth II in **1953**, bronze, on gates, Churchyard. *V.* Inscr. Mary Shaw, district and city councillor 1972-**1983**, bronze, on gate, outside Churchyard. *VI.* Inscr. recording presentation [of notice board] in **1987** in mem. of Walter [Frederick] Trott, [1962, aged 64], and [w.] Daisy, [1986, aged 86], on notice board, Churchyard.

INDENTS & LOST BRASSES. 7. Lost indent, ?civilian and w., inscr. and sh., C. Recorded by Pavey (1706). 8. Lost indent, ?civilian and w., inscr. and 2 shs., mur., C. Recorded by Pavey (1706).

Ref: *Brit. Lib. Stowe MS. 845*, f.53; *M.B.S. Trans.*, V, p.362; *Soc. Antiq. MS. 875/6*, p.94.

PAMBER, Priory Church of SS. Mary and John the Baptist.

I. Inscr. Benefaction of Thomas Sympson, **1674**, mur., old C., now N. Inscr. 293 x 427 mm.

II. Inscr. in Lat. John Fox, S.T.P., of Queen's Coll., Oxford, **1855**, buried in the churchyard on the south side, bronze, mur., Tower. *III.* Inscr. with verse and ach. Major-Gen. Sir Wyndham Charles Knight, K.C.I.E., C.B., C.S.I., D.S.O., J.P., commanded 4th Bengal Cavalry, son of Capt. William Brodnax Knight, 2nd Dragoon Guards (The Queen's Bays), and w. Louisa Charlotte, 5th son of Edward Knight, of Chawton Park, died at Pamber Place, 1863-**1942**; mar. 1896, Monica Harriet, dau. of Francis Johnston, of Dunsdale Park, Westerham, [Kent], mur., old C., now N. Inscr. 210 x 198 mm. See also Chawton no.*XI.* *IV.* Inscr. Peter Bromhead, benefactor and churchwarden, 1920-**1989**, mur., old C., now N. *V.* Inscr. Roland Edwards, M.B.E., churchwarden, 1907-**1991**, mur., old C., now N.

Ref: *M.B.S. Trans.*, V, pp.362-3; *M.S.*, p.164; *Soc. Antiq. MS. 875/6*, pp.94-5.

PENTON MEWSEY, Holy Trinity.

I. Inscr. with verse. Susan Elizabeth, dau. of [Henry Thynne Lascelles], 4th Earl of Harewood, w. of [Francis] (Frank) [Richard Hugh Seymour] Sutton, J.P., of Penton Lodge, ch. worshipper and par. benefactress "DURING THE 37 YEARS OF HER RESIDENCE IN ITS MIDST", born at Harewood, Yorks., died at Penton Lodge, 1861-**1925**, maker's name *JONES & WILLIS L*^*TD*, mur., on board, N. *II & III.* Two inscrs. John Douglas Rowe, engr. c.**1930**, on churchwardens' wands, N. *IV.* Inscr. Mrs. K. Brace, pos. in **1964** by Penton Sunday School, on vasestand, N. *V & VI.* Two inscrs. Edward Kerswill, churchwarden 1983-**1991**, ?brass, on hymn boards, C.

INDENTS & LOST BRASSES. 7. Lost brass, John Ryche, in civil dress, and inscr., c.1510. *Bod. Lib. MS. Rubbings Phillips/Robinson* 493; *M.B.S. Bulletin*, 32, p.27 (from rubbing in Bod. Lib.). Rubbing (eff.) in Soc. Antiq. coll. (n.d.). Eff. 297 x 95 mm, inscr. 55 x 260 mm. Style: London G.

Ref: *Bod. Lib. MS. Rubbings Phillips/Robinson* 493; *Burke's Peerage and Baronetage*, p.1253; *M.B.S. Bulletin*, 32, pp.26-8.

Ch. essentially, 1888.

PETERSFIELD, St. Peter.

I. Inscr. Anne, dau. of Edmund Goodfellow, esq., w. of Thomas Holt, **1655**; formerly C., now mur., Meeting Room/N.A. Inscr. 230 x 541 mm.

We pray you
remember in the Lord
Major General
Sir Wyndham Charles
Knight
K.C.I.E. C.B. C.S.I. D.S.O. J.P.
Commanded
4th Bengal Cavalry

Son of Captain William Brodnax Knight 2nd
Dragoon Guards (The Queens Bays) and of Louisa
Charlotte his wife, 5-th son of Edward Knight, Esq.
of Chawton Park, Alton. Born 30.11.1863 and died
at Pamber Place on the 10-6-1942. He married in
1896 Monica Harriet, daughter of Francis Johnston
Esq. of Dunsdale Park, Westerham.
Grant him O Lord Eternal Rest and let Light
perpetual shine upon him.

Pamber *III*

Penton Mewsey 7

II. Inscr. Mary, dau. of Richard Love, w. of Thomas Aylwyn, M.D., **1693**, on window splay, Meeting Room/N.A. Inscr. 289 x 410 mm.

III. Inscr. with ach. Thomas Aylwyn, M.D., **1704**; formerly mur., S.A., now on window splay with no.II, Meeting Room/N.A. Pl. 329 x 305 mm. *IV*. Inscr. Mrs. Ann Bott, **1839**, [aged 85], mur., Meeting Room/N.A. Inscr. 155 x 205 mm. *V*. Inscr. with Lat. verse recording [east nave] windows were pos. in mem. of Richard George Pern Minty, **1870**, mur., N. *VI*. Inscr. in Lat. [Rt. Rev. Dr.] Samuel Wilberforce, [D.D.], Bishop of Oxford [1845-1869], Bishop of Winchester [1869]-1873, [1805-1873, pos. in] **1874**, mur., on board, C. See also Alverstoke no.*VIII*, Alverstoke, or Gosport, Fort Brockhurst no.*XXXIII*, Hinton Ampner no.*IX*, Newport, St. Thomas the Apostle no.*IX*, Ryde, or Swanmore, St. Michael and All Angels no.*III* and Winchester Cathedral no.*X*. *VII*. Inscr. recording [east south aisle] window pos. by congregation in mem. of Mary, w. of Rev. John Maunoir Sumner, [M.A.], rector of Buriton-cum-Petersfield, **1875**, mur., on marble below window, S.A. *VIII*. Inscr. recording [south aisle] window pos. by pupils in mem. of Henry John Dayrell Stowe, M.A., of Castle House, **1879**, aged 46, mur., on board below window, S.A. *IX*. Inscr. with Lat. verse in mem. of 2 soldier brothers, eld. and 3rd sons of Capt. and Hon. Mrs. Grenville-Wells, "DIED IN THE SERVICE OF THEIR QUEEN AND COUNTRY IN FOREIGN LANDS", 1884 and **1886**, mur., on board, S.A. *X*. Inscr. recording dedication of [north aisle] window and pulpit by friends and townsmen in mem. of [Dr.] Robert Shackleford Cross, born in the [par.], surgeon for more than 40 years, 1823-**1887**, copper, mur., on board below window, N.A. *XI*. Inscr. recording erection of altar rails in **1891** by Charles S. and Alice Ticehurst in mem. of parents, mur., on board, C. *XII*. Inscr. Thomas Howard, father of Edith E.B. Judge, **1894**, mur., on board, C. *XIII*. Inscr. with Lat. verse. Charlotte Mary, widow of Richard G[eorge] P[ern] Minty, **1899**, aged 79, mur., on board, N.A. *XIV*. Inscr. Capt. Frank Hunnard, D.S.O., Army Service Corps, formerly South Wales Borderers, born in the par., died of enteric fever during the South African [War] at Newcastle, Natal, 1873-**1900**, buried in the cemetery, maker's name GAWTHORP S^c LONDON, mur., on board, N.A. *XV*. Inscr. Lt. John Cecil Hylton Jolliffe, [3rd Battn.] Norfolk Regt., eld. son of Hon. [William] Sydney Hylton Jolliffe, [J.P., D.L.], and [w.] Gertrude [Henrietta], killed in action at Paardeberg, South Africa, [1873-]**1900**, mur., Lady Chapel/Tower. *XVI*. Inscr. with Lat. verse. Thomas Baker, 2nd son of John and Elizabeth Baker, died at Axim, West Africa, **1901**, aged 33, mur., on board, S.A. *XVII*. Inscr. recording dedication of [south aisle] window in mem. of Charlotte Mary Lacell, 1847-**1911**, maker's name HEATON, BUTLER & BAYNE LONDON, copper, mur., on board, S.A. *XVIII*. Inscr. with verse. [Capt. the] Hon. William Sydney Hylton Jolliffe, J.P., D.L., Scots Guards, M.P. for Petersfield 1874-1880, died at The Heath House, [1841-]**1912**, pos. by children and only surviving sister, Hon. [Mary Augusta], Lady Birkbeck, [w. of Sir Edward Birkbeck, 1st and last Bart., K.C.V.O., J.P., D.L., of Horstead Hall, Norf.], maker's name BARKENTIN & KRALL, LONDON, mur., Lady Chapel/Tower. *XIX*. Inscr. with verse and R.N. insignia in relief. Admiral Loftus Francis Jones, R.N., 1836-**1912**, maker's name A & N AUX C.S.L. LONDON, mur., on board, S.A. *XX*. Inscr. Albert Warren Leachman, M.D., 1838-**1914**, on cross, Choir Vestry. *XXI*. Inscr. with verse. Capt. Arthur Henry Wilson, [1st Battn.] East Yorks. Regt., only surviving child of Col. and Mrs. W.H. Wilson, of Broadview, killed in action at Paradis, France, **1914**, aged 39, mur., on board, S.A. *XXII*. Inscr. with H.M.S. Shark insignia in relief. Cmdr. Loftus William Jones, V.C., R.N., H.M.S. Shark, [son of no.*XIX*], "AWARDED THE POSTHUMOUS HONOUR OF THE VICTORIA CROSS "IN RECOGNITION OF HIS MOST CONSPICUOUS BRAVERY AND DEVOTION TO DUTY IN THE COURSE OF THE BATTLE OF JUTLAND"", killed at the Battle of Jutland, [1879-]**1916**, buried at Fiskebackskie, Sweden, maker's name A & N AUX C.S.L. LONDON, mur., on board, S.A. *XXIII*. Inscr. Cmdr. Loftus W[illia]m Jones, V.C., R.N.,

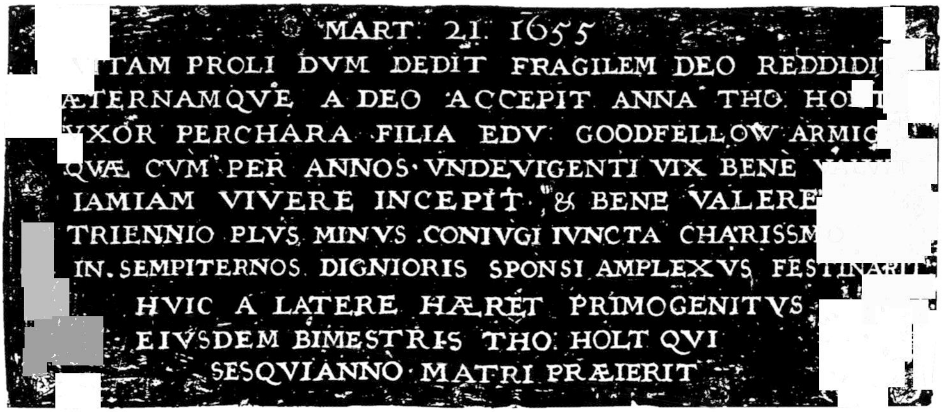

MART: 21. 1655
...TAM PROLI DVM DEDIT FRAGILEM DEO REDDIDI...
...TERNAMQVE A DEO ACCEPIT ANNA THO. HO...
...XOR PERCHARA FILIA EDV: GOODFELLOW ARMI...
QVÆ CVM PER ANNOS· VNDEVIGENTI VIX BENE ...
IAMIAM VIVERE INCEPIT & BENE VALERE...
TRIENNIO PLVS MINVS .CONIVGI IVNCTA CHARISSM...
IN.SEMPITERNOS DIGNIORIS SPONSI AMPLEXVS FESTIN...
HVIC A LATERE HÆRET PRIMOGENITVS
EIVSDEM BIMESTRIS THO. HOLT QVI
SESQVIANNO MATRI PRÆIERIT

Petersfield I

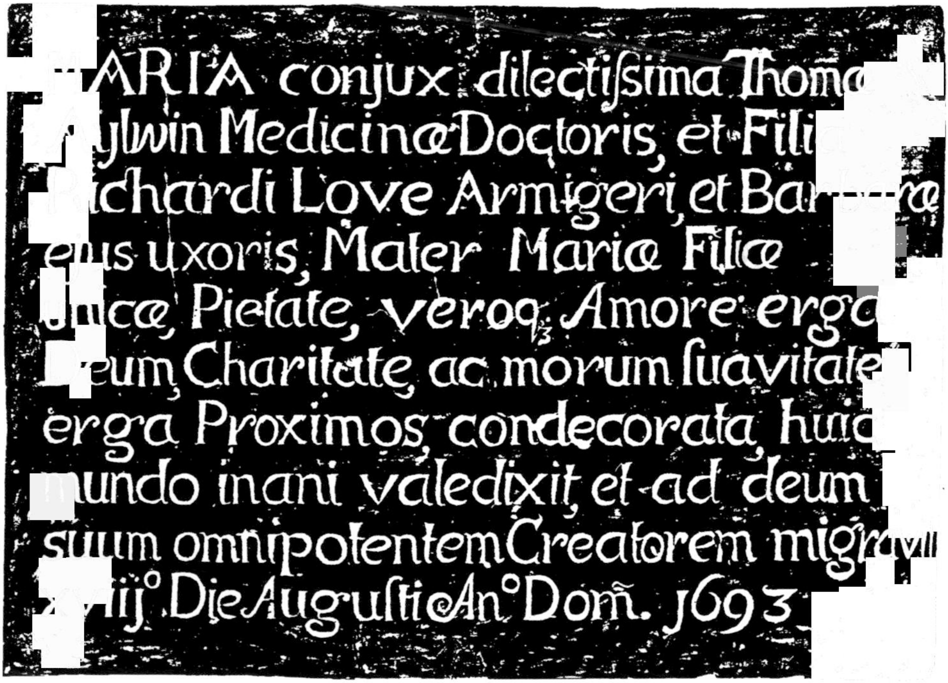

...ARIA conjux dilectissima Thoma...
...ylwin Medicinæ Doctoris, et Fili...
...ichardi Love Armigeri, et Ba----æ
...ens uxoris, Mater Mariæ Filiæ
...nicæ, Pietate, veroq. Amore erga
...eum Charitate, ac morum suavitate
erga Proximos, condecorata, huic
...undo inani valedixit, et ad deum
...suum omnipotentem Creatorem migra...
...ij° Die Augusti An° Dom. 1693

Petersfield II

H.M.S. Shark, [1879-**1916**], bronze, on crucifix, Churchyard. *XXIV*. Inscr. Henry Thomas Keates, **1918**, aged 79, copper, mur., Lady Chapel/Tower. *XXV*. Inscr. Lt.-Col. Gerard Evelyn Leachman, C.I.E., D.S.O., Royal Sussex Regt., political officer, born at Fairley, Petersfield, killed in Mesopotamia, 1880-**1920**, mur., on board, S.A. *XXVI*. Inscr. recording gift and dedication of book of remembrance and [display] case in **1963** in mem. of [Rev.] Francis Jervoise Causton, [M.A.], vicar 1886-1909, and family, bronze, on display case, Lady Chapel/Tower. *XXVII*. Inscr. recording ch. fire in choir vestry at west end of the south aisle (timber roof of the south aisle was destroyed and decorations, furniture and mural tablets severely damaged) in 1962 and restoration carried out by E. Canterbury Ltd., builders, under the direction of Thomas Ford, F.R.I.B.A.; re-hallowed in **1963** by [Rt. Rev. Dr. John Henry Lawrence Phillips, D.D.], Bishop of Portsmouth [1960-1975; Rev. Canon] John Sanderson Long, [M.A.], vicar [1959-1970]; Philip Solesbury, David [S.] Tibbits and Lionel Thompson, churchwardens, bronze, mur., on board, Mezzanine Staircase/S.A. *XXVIII*. Inscr. Marie Louise, [dau. of Rev. Robert Rochfort Forlong, B.A.], w. of Sir Newnham [(Arthur)] Worley, K.B.E., **1966**, bronze, on display case stand, Lady Chapel/Tower. *XXIX*. Inscr. recording gift of clock in mem. of Daisy Ellis, 1885-**1968**, bronze, mur., on board, Clergy Vestry. *XXX*. Inscr. Gordon Jaspar Adlam, 1898-**1969**, on prie-dieu, Lady Chapel/Tower. *XXXI*. Inscr. recording dedication of tablet and electric control of the ch. clock (originally installed in 1856 during the mayoralty of Dr. Robert Shackleford Cross) provided in **1970** by family in mem. of Dr. Robert George Cross, born in the [par.], "PRACTISED MEDICINE HERE FOR NEARLY 40 YEARS", 1863-1932, and w. Margaret Elizabeth, 1861-1926; also eld. dau., Margherita, 1892-1966, mur., on board below window with no.*X*, N.A. *XXXII*. Inscr. recording electric control of the ch. clock (originally installed in 1856 by public subscription during the mayoralty of Dr. Robert Shackleford Cross; Secretaires: Messrs. Duplock and Nichols, churchwardens) in **1970**; design and work of conversion were carried out as a gift by Mr. H.J. Tottle, assistance during the dismantling of the weights and the electric wiring of the clock was given by Walter Butler and the costs paid by the Cross family; the Petersfield Urban District Council were also associated with the project "IN RECOGNITION OF THE VALUE OF THE CHURCH CLOCK TO THE PEOPLE OF PETERSFIELD"; [Rev.] Canon J[ohn] S[anderson] Long, [M.A.], vicar [1959-1970]; D[avid] S. Tibbits and D.C. Francombe, churchwardens, mur., on board, Mezzanine Staircase/S.A. *XXXIII*. Inscr. Hugh Jeffries, 1890-1971, and [w.] Jessie, 1886-**1975**, on bookcase, Meeting Room/N.A. *XXXIV*. Inscr. Sir Lionel Thompson, C.B.E., deputy master of the Royal Mint 1950-1957, churchwarden, [1893-]**1983**, and w. Mary, [dau. of William White, M.D., of Hadfield, Derbys.], 1979, [engr. by Douglas Lincoln], mur., on board, S.A. *XXXV*. Inscr. recording donation [of chair] in **1999** by Caplen family, on chair, N.A. *XXXVI*. Inscr. [recording donation of chair by Miss G. Hancock] in mem. of Richard Hancock, 1902-**1999**, on chair, S.A. *XXXVII*. Inscr. Claude Francis Jackson, 1915-**1999**, and [w.] Stella Howe, 1912-1995, on chair, S.A. *XXXVIII*. Inscr. [recording donation of chair by Miss Gillian Carol Lelliott] in mem. of [mother], Joan Irene Lelliott, 1921-**1999**, on chair, N. *XXXIX*. Inscr. with verse [recording donation of chair] in **1999** by Barry, Yvonne, Nicholas and Victoria Murfitt, on chair, S.A. *XL*. Inscr. recording donation [of chair] in **1999** by [Miss] Sarah [E.] Shadbolt, on chair, N. *XLI*. Inscr. recording donation [of chair] in **2000** by [Miss] Gillian Carol Lelliott, on chair, N. *XLII*. Inscr. William (Bill) Madden, 1906-1993, and [w.] Elizabeth [F.], 1912-**2000**, on chair, N. *XLIII*. Inscr. Anne, w. of Dickie Parsons, 1924-**2000,** on paschal candleholder, N. *XLIV*. Inscr. [recording donation of chair] in **2000** by [Mr. and Mrs. M. Harding] in mem. of Leslie and Mary Pearson, on chair, S.A. *XLV*. Inscr. recording donation [of chair] in **2000** by John and Tricia Witchell, on chair, N. *XLVI*. Inscr. recording donation [of chair] in **2000** by [Mr. T. Austin of the] Lion and Unicorn Players, on chair, N.A. *XLVII*. Inscr. recording "The St. Peter's **2000** Project";

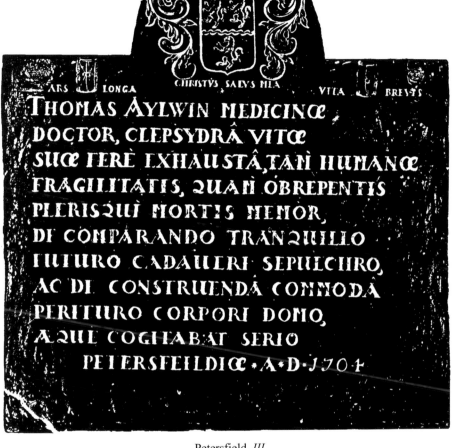

Petersfield *III*

BENEATH THIS SPOT
are Interred the Remains
OF
M.RS ANN BOTE
Who Died 14th April 1839.

Petersfield *IV*

229

major restoration of ch. in 1999 (Portland stone floor laid, west end spaces enclosed with oak and glass screens creating a lady chapel, meeting-room and modern facilities, pews replaced by oak chairs, new lighting installed and heating system refurbished) initiated by [Rev.] Christopher Lowson, [A.K.C.], vicar 1991-1998, and designed by Paul Velluet, R.I.B.A., par. architect; Peter Harrison, R.I.B.A., project architect, F.W. German and Sons, of Alton, main contractor, Tim Wade and Robin Simko, designed and made the chairs; project funded by congregation, local authorities, local businesses, trust funds and individual donors; [Rev. William] Giles Harris-Evans, [A.K.C.], vicar; Gillian Hancock and Simon Mackarness, churchwardens, mur., N.A. *XLVIII.* Inscr. Donald Brooks and June Gander; mar. in the ch. 1949, engr. c.**2000**, on chair, N. *XLIX.* Inscr. Eric [J.] and Edith Carter; mar. in the ch. 1952, engr. c.**2000**, on chair, N. *L.* Inscr. Al and Mary Carder; mar. in the ch. 1954, engr. c.**2000**, on chair, N. *LI.* Inscr. [recording donation of chair by A. (Tony) J. Smee] in mem. of Herbert Thomas Smee, 1890-1957, engr. c.**2000**, on chair, S.A. *LII.* Inscr. [recording donation of chair by Mrs. M. Muir] in mem. of Capt. D.J. Claris, R.N., 1889-1959, engr. c.**2000**, on chair, S.A. *LIII.* Inscr. [recording donation of chair by Mrs. M. Rush] in mem. of Malcolm William Rush, 1914-1970, engr. c.**2000**, on chair, S.A. *LIV.* Inscr. [recording donation of chair by Mr. R.C. Lacey] in mem. of Robert William Lacey, 1913-1971, engr. c.**2000**, on chair, S.A. *LV.* Inscr. [recording donation of chair by Mr. R.H. Parsons] in mem. of Doris Gladys Parsons, 1898-1968, and Sidney Thomas Parsons, 1888-1971, engr. c.**2000**, on chair, N. *LVI.* Inscr. [recording donation of chair by Mr. M. Nation] in mem. of Arthur Nation, 1883-1962, and [w.] Mabel, 1884-1974, engr. c.**2000**, on chair, N.A. *LVII.* Inscr. [recording donation of chair by Mr. D. Francombe] in mem. of Miriam Francombe, 1933-1976, engr. c.**2000**, on chair, S.A. *LVIII.* Inscr. [recording donation of chair by Miss Gillian Carol Lelliott] in mem. of [father], Edward George Lelliott, 1905-1976, engr. c.**2000**, on chair, S.A. *LIX.* Inscr. [recording donation of chair by Mrs. J. Collis] in mem. of Harold Collis, 1915-1977, engr. c.**2000**, on chair, S.A. *LX.* Inscr. [recording donation of chair by Mrs. J.M. Hayne] in mem. of Admiral Sir Charles [(Henry Lawrence)] Woodhouse, K.C.B., 1893-1978, engr. c.**2000**, on chair, N. *LXI.* Inscr. [recording donation of chair by Mrs. M. Gurney] in mem. of mother, Olive Coe, 1885-1979, engr. c.**2000**, on chair, N. *LXII.* Inscr. [recording donation of chair by Mrs. E.M. Viccars] in mem. of Richard T. Viccars, 1919-1979, engr. c.**2000**, on chair, N. *LXIII.* Inscr. [recording donation of chair by Mrs. M. Muir] in mem. of Barbara Sybil Claris, 1898-1981, engr. c.**2000**, on chair, S.A. *LXIV.* Inscr. recording donation [of chair] by Simon and Diana Mackarness in mem. of Peggy Reid, 1914-1982, engr. c.**2000**, on chair, N. *LXV.* Inscr. [recording donation of chair by Mrs. E. White] in mem. of Peter White, 1923-1982, engr. c.**2000**, on chair, N. *LXVI.* Inscr. [recording donation of chair by Mr. H.E. Gorvin] in mem. of Ellen Gorvin, 1936-1985, engr. c.**2000**, on chair, S.A. *LXVII.* Inscr. [recording donation of chair by Mrs. J. Deavin] in mem. of William Edward Rashbrook, 1909-1985, engr. c.**2000**, on chair, N. *LXVIII.* Inscr. [recording donation of chair by Mr. T. Cross] in mem. of Flora Twort, 1893-1985, engr. c.**2000**, on chair, S.A. *LXIX.* Inscr. [recording donation of chair by Mrs. H. Humphreys] in mem. of George Humphreys, 1912-1986, engr. c.**2000**, on chair, N. *LXX.* Inscr. [recording donation of chair by Miss J. Stevens] in mem. of John Kingston Stevens, 1919-1986, engr. c.**2000**, on chair, N. *LXXI.* Inscr. [recording donation of chair by Rev. F.J. Heal] in mem. of Charles Felix Heal, 1907-1987, engr. c.**2000**, on chair, N. *LXXII.* Inscr. [recording donation of chair by Mr. P.E.T. Smith] in mem. of Daphne T. Coxon, 1923-1988, engr. c.**2000**, on chair, N. *LXXIII.* Inscr. [recording donation of chair by Mrs. Susan Fisher] in mem. of Wilfred O. Fisher, 1904-1988, engr. c.**2000**, on chair, N. *LXXIV & LXXV.* Two inscrs. [recording donation of chairs by Mr. M. Brown] in mem. of Maggie Gladwell, 1915-1988, engr. c.**2000**, on chairs, N. and S.A. *LXXVI.* Inscr. [recording donation of chair by Mr. R.C. Lacey] in mem. of Jessie Emily Lacey, 1913-1988, engr. c.**2000**, on chair, N.A. *LXXVII.* Inscr. recording gift [of chair] by family in mem. of Elizabeth Mathias (née Mackarness), 1952-1988, engr. c.**2000**, on chair, S.A. *LXXVIII.* Inscr. [recording donation of chair by Mrs. B. Toogood] in mem. of Sidney Alfred Toogood, O.B.E., 1912-1989, engr. c.**2000**, on chair, S.A. *LXXIX.* Inscr. [recording donation of chair by Ms Jo Gooderham] in mem. of Rosemary Twiddy, 1940-1989, engr. c.**2000**, on chair, S.A. *LXXX.* Inscr. [recording donation of chair by Mrs. B. Rolfe] in mem. of Nancy Davies, 1914-1990, engr. c.**2000**, on chair, N. *LXXXI.* Inscr. recording donation [of chair] by family in mem. of Frederick Roy Maitland, 1920-1990, engr. c.**2000**, on chair, N. *LXXXII.* Inscr. [recording donation of chair by Mr. B.J. Hargreaves] in mem. of Sam Hargreaves, 1909-1991, engr. c.**2000**, on chair, N. *LXXXIII.* Inscr. [recording donation of chair by Mrs. A. Hutchings] in mem. of Cmdr. Kenneth Wedgwood Spooner, R.N., 1917-1991, engr. c.**2000**, on chair, N. *LXXXIV.* Inscr. [recording donation of chair by Mrs. O. Gooch] in mem. of Leslie Gooch, 1921-1992, engr. c.**2000**, on chair, N. *LXXXV.* Inscr. [recording donation of chair by Mrs. Lillie Jessie Pyle] in mem. of Victor Charles Pyle, 1919-1992, engr. c.**2000**, on chair, N. *LXXXVI.* Inscr. [recording donation of chair by Mrs. M. Ray] in mem. of Alan John Ray, 1924-1992, engr. c.**2000**, on chair, S.A. *LXXXVII.* Inscr. [recording donation of chair by Mr. M. Thomas] in mem. of Stan Thomas, 1915-1991, and [w.] Chris, 1917-1992, engr. c.**2000**, on chair, S.A. *LXXXVIII.* Inscr. [recording donation of chair by Mrs. Rene Thomson] in mem. of Harold Thomson, 1918-1992, engr. c.**2000**, on chair, N.A. *LXXXIX.* Inscr. [recording donation of chair by Capt. B.H. Kent] in mem. of Leslie Kent, 1890-1980, and [w.] Margaret, 1901-1993, engr. c.**2000**, on chair, N. *XC.* Inscr. [recording donation of chair by Mrs. E.M. Kilvert] in mem. of [Rev.] Canon Robert [Wynne] Kilvert, [M.A.], priest in the Portsmouth Diocese for 54 years, 1913-1993, engr. c.**2000**, on chair, S.A. *XCI.* Inscr. [recording donation of chair by Mrs. J. Milner-Smith] in mem. of Barry Milner-Smith, 1947-1993, engr. c.**2000**, on chair, S.A. *XCII.* Inscr. [recording donation of chair by Miss J. Tully] in mem. of John Benjamin Tully, 1898-1993, engr. c.**2000**, on chair, N. *XCIII.* Inscr. [recording donation of chair by Mr. T. Bensted] in mem. of James Bensted, 1911-1994, and [w.] Gwenyth, 1908-1993, engr. c.**2000**, on chair, N. *XCIV.* Inscr. [recording donation of chair by Mr. N. Lyster-Binns] in mem. of Elaine Binns (née Coltman), 1905-1994, engr. c.**2000**, on chair, S.A. *XCV.* Inscr. [recording donation of chair by Mrs. J.M. Hayne] in mem. of Barbara [Margaret] Woodhouse, [dau. of Dr. H.M.] Brownfield, [w. of no.*LX*], 1904-1994, engr. c.**2000**, on chair, N. *XCVI.* Inscr. [recording donation of chair by Mr. J. Deavin] in mem. of Bernard Deavin, 1910-1995, and Millicent Deavin, 1907-1992, engr. c.**2000**, on chair, N. *XCVII.* Inscr. [recording donation of chair by Miss G. Hancock] in mem. of Winifred Hancock, 1907-1995, engr. c.**2000**, on chair, S.A. *XCVIII.* Inscr. [recording donation of chair by Mrs. D.I. Ford] in mem. of Ernestine R. Willis, 1908-1995, engr. c.**2000**, on chair, N. *XCIX.* Inscr. [recording donation of chair by Mrs. J.E. Atkinson] in mem. of Thomas Edward Barnes, 1914-1983, and w. Elsie, 1919-1996, engr. c.**2000**, on chair, N.A. *C.* Inscr. [recording donation of chair by Rev. Canon Ronald Harry Granger, M.A., hon. canon of Portsmouth Cathedral, vicar 1970-1990] in mem. of June Mary Granger, 1929-1996, engr. c.**2000**, on chair, S.A. *CI.* Inscr. [recording donation of chair by Mr. and Mrs. P. Young] in mem. of Ursula Home, 1906-1996, engr. c.**2000**, on chair, S.A. *CII.* Inscr. [recording donation of chair by Mrs. E.M. Astill] in mem. of Charles Rogers, 1910-1996, engr. c.**2000**, on chair, N.A. *CIII.* Inscr. Stuart Edwin Day, 1908-1985, and [w.] Norah Farmer, 1900-1997; mar. in the ch. 1937, engr. c.**2000**, on lectern, N. *CIV.* Inscr. Roger Goodchild, 1934-1992, and [w.] Joanne Louisa, 1970-1997, engr. c.**2000**, on chair, N. *CV.* Inscr. [recording donation of chair by Mr. J.H. Lunt] in mem. of Marjorie Lunt, 1912-1997, engr. c.**2000**, on chair, N.A. *CVI.* Inscr. [recording donation of chair by Mr. and Mrs. Penny] in mem. of Michael Penny, 1980-1997, engr. c.**2000**, on chair, S.A. *CVII.* Inscr. [recording donation of chair by Mr. J.A. Perris] in mem. of Brenda Perris, 1921-1997, engr. c.**2000**, on chair, N. *CVIII.* Inscr.

[recording donation of chair by Mrs. A.R. Scholfield] in mem. of Charles Perry, 1908-1986, and [w.] Amy, 1911-1997, engr. c.**2000**, on chair, S.A. *CIX.* Inscr. [recording donation of chair by Mrs. D.I. Ford] in mem. of R.W. Gaspard Willis, 1905-1997, engr. c.**2000**, on chair, S.A. *CX.* Inscr. [recording donation of chair by Mr. N. Morris] in mem. of Sybil Ballance, 1909-1998, engr. c.**2000**, on chair, N. *CXI.* Inscr. [recording donation of chair by Mr. K.J. Brisley] in mem. of Hilda Brisley, 1907-1998, engr. c.**2000**, on chair, N. *CXII.* Inscr. [recording donation of chair by Mrs. S. Marriner] in mem. of June Rosemary Collins, 1940-1998, engr. c.**2000**, on chair, N. *CXIII.* Inscr. [recording donation of chair by Mr. and Mrs. P. Smith] in mem. of Irene Elford, 1908-1998, engr. c.**2000**, on chair, S.A. *CXIV.* Inscr. [recording donation of chair by Miss A. Clarke] in mem. of Marguerite J (Peggy) Foord, 1998, engr. c.**2000**, on chair, S.A. *CXV.* Inscr. [recording donation of chair by Mrs. M.J. Poore] in mem. of Mary Poore, 1934-1998, engr. c.**2000**, on chair, N. *CXVI.* Inscr. [recording donation of chair by Mrs. S. Lowson] in mem. of Reggie Rowell, 1922-1998, engr. c.**2000**, on chair, S.A. *CXVII.* Inscr. [recording donation of chair by Miss J. Stevens] in mem. of Hilary Margaret Stevens, 1919-1998, engr. c.**2000**, on chair, S.A. *CXVIII.* Inscr. [recording donation of chair by Michael Suthers] in mem. of Di Suthers, 1902-1998, engr. c.**2000**, on chair, N. *CXIX.* Inscr. [recording donation of chair by Mrs. N.M. Scott] in mem. of Joan Frances Wise, 1908-**1998**, on chair, N. *CXX.* Inscr. with verse [recording dedication of chair by Mr. M.J. Wise] in mem. of Joan Frances Wise, 1908-1998, engr. c.**2000**, on chair, N. *CXXI.* Inscr. recording donation [of chair] by Richard [L.] and Roma Bennetts, engr. c.**2000**, on chair, S.A. *CXXII.* Inscr. recording donation [of chair] by dau., [Miss] Dorothy [W. Benson], in mem. of parents, George Benson and [w.] Grace, engr. c.**2000**, on chair, S.A. *CXXIII.* Inscr. with Lat. verse recording donation [of chair] by [Dr.] Colin [M.] Bisset and [w.] Joan, engr. c.**2000**, on chair, N. *CXXIV.* Inscr. [recording dedication of chair by Mr. D. Parsons] in mem. of Mary Le Blancq, engr. c.**2000**, on chair, S.A. *CXXV.* Inscr. recording donation [of chair] by Elizabeth Blenkinsop, engr. c.**2000**, on chair, N. *CXXVI.* Inscr. [recording donation of chair by Mrs.] Barbara Toogood in mem. of parents, Joe Borzone and [w.] Grace, engr. c.**2000**, on chair, S.A. *CXXVII.* Inscr. recording donation [of chair] by Leslie and Margaret Bowden, engr. c.**2000**, on chair, S.A. *CXXVIII.* Inscr. recording donation [of chair] by Ken and Elsa Bulmer, engr. c.**2000**, on chair, N. *CXXIX.* Inscr. recording donation [of chair] by Dorothy Burges, engr. c.**2000**, on chair, N. *CXXX.* Inscr. recording donation [of chair] by Leslie Burges, engr. c.**2000**, on chair, N.A. *CXXXI.* Inscr. recording donation [of chair] by [Mrs.] Daisy Cattermole, engr. c.**2000**, on chair, N. *CXXXII.* Inscr. Clancy and Sarah L. Cave, engr. c.**2000**, on chair, S.A. *CXXXIII.* Inscr. [recording donation of chair by Mrs. J. Easlick] in mem. of Kate Cole and "Others unnamed who have given long service to St Peter's", engr. c.**2000**, on chair, N. *CXXXIV.* Inscr. Geoff and Jean Coombs, engr. c.**2000**, on chair, N. *CXXXV.* Inscr. recording donation [of chair] by [Rev. John] Allan Crace, [D.S.C.], engr. c.**2000**, on chair, S.A. *CXXXVI.* Inscr. recording donation [of chair] by [Mrs.] Rosemary Crace, engr. c.**2000**, on chair, S.A. *CXXXVII.* Inscr. [recording donation of chair by Miss E. Bowen] in mem. of Dorothy Crossley, engr. c.**2000**, on chair, N.A. *CXXXVIII.* Inscr. recording donation [of chair] by Mark and Rosemary Dancer, engr. c.**2000**, on chair, S.A. *CXXXIX.* Inscr. recording donation [of chair] by Philip and Jane Daubeney, engr. c.**2000**, on chair, N. *CXL.* Inscr. [recording donation of chair by Mrs. M. Ellis] in mem. of Stephen and Edith Daughtry, engr. c.**2000**, on chair, S.A. *CXLI.* Inscr. "In Gratitude for the privilege of serving God in St Peter's", John and Joyce Deavin, engr. c.**2000**, on chair, N.A. *CXLII.* Inscr. recording gift [of chair] by [Mrs.] Lee Edmunds in gratitude for grandchildren, engr. c.**2000**, on chair, N. *CXLIII.* Inscr. recording donation [of chair] by David and Jillie Francombe, engr. c.**2000**, on chair, N.A. *CXLIV.* Inscr. Bernard and Alma Gatrill, engr. c.**2000**, on chair, S.A. *CXLV.* Inscr. recording donation [of chair] by Chief Inspector John Gibson, retd., and family, engr. c.**2000**, on chair, N.A. *CXLVI* Inscr.

recording donation [of chair] by Bill and Pearl Gosney, engr. c.**2000**, on chair, N.A. *CXLVII.* Inscr. [recording donation of chair by Miss S.F. Goulder] in mem. of 3 generations of Goulder family who have worshipped in the ch., engr. c.**2000**, on chair, N.A. *CXLVIII.* Inscr. recording donation [of chair] by Mark and Derrie Greef in mem. of Jack and Eva Greef, engr. c.**2000**, on chair, S.A. *CXLIX.* Inscr. recording donation [of chair] by Mark and Derrie Greef, engr. c.**2000**, on chair, S.A. *CL.* Inscr. recording donation [of chair] by Dennis and Pat Green in golden wedding year, engr. c.**2000**, on chair, S.A. *CLI.* Inscr. recording donation [of chair] by Philip and Denise Griffiths, engr. c.**2000**, on chair, N. *CLII.* Inscr. recording donation [of chair] by [Capt.] John [P.] and [Mrs.] Jane Gunning, engr. c.**2000**, on chair, N. *CLIII.* Inscr. recording gift [of chair] by Ron and Hanna Hallett, engr. c.**2000**, on chair, N. *CLIV.* Inscr. recording donation [of chair] by Keith and Violet Hawthorne, engr. c.**2000**, on chair, S.A. *CLV.* Inscr. recording donation [of chair] by [Rear-Admiral A.] Paul and [Mrs. E.] (Rue) Hoddinott, engr. c.**2000**, on chair, S.A. *CLVI.* Inscr. recording donation [of chair] by benefactor, [Rear-Admiral A. Paul and Mrs. E. (Rue) Hoddinott], engr. c.**2000**, on chair, N. *CLVII.* Inscr. recording donation [of chair] by [William H.] (Bill) and Margery Howes, engr. c.**2000**, on chair, N. *CLVIII.* Inscr. recording donation [of chair] by Chris and Deanna Jacobs, engr. c.**2000**, on chair, N. *CLIX.* Inscr. [recording donation of chair by Mrs. J. Watts] in mem. of Pat Kille, engr. c.**2000**, on chair, N. *CLX.* Inscr. [recording donation of chair by P.C.C.] in mem. of Pat Kille, benefactor, engr. c.**2000**, on chair, N.A. *CLXI.* Inscr. recording donation [of chair] by Mark and Derrie [Greef] in mem. of Leslie and Derrie Lambert, engr. c.**2000**, on chair, N.A. *CLXII.* Inscr. [recording donation of chair by Miss M. Lamport] in mem. of Patrick John Lamport, engr. c.**2000**, on chair, S.A. *CLXIII.* Inscr. [recording donation of chair by Mr. and Mrs. T.J. Shepherd] in mem. of Ethel Lewis, engr. c.**2000**, on chair, N. *CLXIV.* Inscr. [recording donation of chair by Mrs. S. Lowson] in mem. of auntie Trudy and uncle Dick, engr. c.**2000**, on chair, S.A. *CLXV.* Inscr. recording donation [of chair] by [Mrs.] Felicity Mackilligin, engr. c.**2000**, on chair, N. *CLXVI.* Inscr. [recording donation of chair by Dr. G. Mani] in mem. of George D. Mani, grandfather of B.E. Sunil, engr. c.**2000**, on chair, N. *CLXVII.* Inscr. recording donation [of chair] by Elaine and Brian Marshall, engr. c.**2000**, on chair, N. *CLXVIII.* Inscr. [recording donation of chair by Mrs. J. Martin] in mem. of John and Christopher Martin, engr. c.**2000**, on chair, S.A. *CLXIX.* Inscr. recording gift [of chair] by Michael Mates, [M.P.] and [w.] Christine, engr. c.**2000**, on chair, S.A. *CLXX.* Inscr. recording dedication [of chair] by dau., [Mrs.] Joan [Campbell in mem.] of Mr. and Mrs. William Norton, engr. c.**2000**, on chair, S.A. *CLXXI.* Inscr. recording donation [of chair] by Oakley family, engr. c.**2000**, on chair, N. *CLXXII.* Inscr. recording donation [of chair] by [Rev.] Juliet Grace in mem. of parents, Charles Old and [w.] Olive, engr. c.**2000**, on chair, S.A. *CLXXIII.* Inscr. recording donation [of chair] by Frederick Payne in mem. of [w.] Olive, engr. c.**2000**, on chair, N. *CLXXIV.* Inscr. recording donation [of chair] by Stanley and Freda Pettitt, engr. c.**2000**, on chair, S.A. *CLXXV.* Inscr. recording donation [of chair] by Steve [W.] Pibworth, of The Petersfield Forge, engr. c.**2000**, on chair, S.A. *CLXXVI.* Inscr. recording donation [of chair] by George and Shirley Pickup, engr. c.**2000**, on chair, S.A. *CLXXVII.* Inscr. recording donation [of chair] by [Miss] Molly Rimington, engr. c.**2000**, on chair, S.A. *CLXXVIII.* Inscr. recording donation [of chair] by [Mrs.] June Carlyle-Scott, engr. c.**2000**, on chair, N.A. *CLXXIX.* Inscr. [recording donation of chair by Mrs. June Carlyle-Scott] in mem. of John and Pansy Scott, engr. c.**2000**, on chair, S.A. *CLXXX.* Inscr. [recording donation of chair by Mrs. S.J. Newman] in mem. of parents, Joseph Shepherd and [w.] Winifred, engr. c.**2000**, on chair, N. *CLXXXI.* Inscr. [recording donation of chair by A. (Tony) J. Smee] in mem. of Edith Smee, engr. c.**2000**, on chair, S.A. *CLXXXII.* Inscr. recording donation [of chair] by Tony and Dorothy Smee, engr. c.**2000**, on chair, N. *CLXXXIII.* Inscr. recording donation [of chair] by [Mrs.] Janet Stapleton in mem. of Harry [Stapleton], engr.

c.**2000**, on chair, N.A. *CLXXXIV.* Inscr. recording donation [of chair] by John [T.] Starbuck, in mem. of parents, Sydney Starbuck and [w.] Gladys, engr. c.**2000**, on chair, S.A. *CLXXXV.* Inscr. recording donation [of chair] by Desmond [H.] and Jeanne Taylor, engr. c.**2000**, on chair, S.A. *CLXXXVI.* Inscr. recording donation [of chair] by [Mrs.] Rene Thomson, engr. c.**2000**, on chair, N. *CLXXXVII.* Inscr. [recording donation of chair by Mrs. M. Vincent] in mem. of Percy and Beryl Vincent, engr. c.**2000**, on chair, N.A. *CLXXXVIII.* Inscr. recording donation [of chair] by the makers, Tim Wade, of Wales, and Robert Imko, of Slovakia, engr. c.**2000**, on chair, S.A. *CLXXXIX.* Inscr. with Fr. verse [recording donation of chair by Lady C.M. Vincent] in mem. of Rev. Edward Gibson Walton, engr. c.**2000**, on chair, N.A. *CXC.* Inscr. [recording donation of chair by Mrs. M. Somerset-Ward] in mem. of Adrian Somerset-Ward, engr. c.**2000**, on chair, N. *CXCI.* Inscr. recording donation [of chair] by Brenda Tierney in loving memory of parents, Kenneth Wittey and [w.] Margaret, engr. c.**2000**, on chair, S.A. *CXCII.* Inscr. [recording donation of chair by Mr. K.J. Woodman] in mem. of Leonard Woodman, husband of Brenda, [father] of Kenneth and Margaret, engr. c.**2000**, on chair, N. *CXCIII.* Inscr. recording donation [of chair] by [Mr. P. Elborough of] Channel Safety Systems Ltd., engr. c.**2000**, on chair, N.A. *CXCIV.* Inscr. recording donation [of chair] by [Mr. Bill Gosney of] Littlejohn Bathrooms Ltd., engr. c.**2000**, on chair, N. *CXCV.* Inscr. recording gift [of chair] by Mothers' Union members, engr. c.**2000**, on chair, S.A. *CXCVI.* Inscr. [recording donation of chair by Mrs. C. Coffin] in mem. of son, Simon Charles Clarke, 1960-**2001**, on chair, N. *CXCVII.* Inscr. [recording donation of chair by Rev. F.J. Heal] in mem. of John Nicholas Heal, 1936-**2001**, on chair, S.A. *CXCVIII.* Inscr. [recording donation of chair by Mr. D.F. Hiscock] in mem. of Arthur Hiscock, 1978, and [w.] Doris, **2001**, on chair, S.A. *CXCIX.* Inscr. [recording donation of chair by Mrs. G.E. Denten] in mem. of Archie Kelsey, 1901-1975, and [w.] Freda, 1903-**2001**, on chair, N. *CC.* Inscr. Leslie Nation, 1915-**2001**, and [w.] May, 1922-1986, on chair, N.A. *CCI.* Inscr. [recording donation of chair by Miss C. Tully] in mem. of Jenny Tully, [lay] reader 1944-**2001**, on chair, S.A. *CCII.* Inscr. [recording donation of chair by Mrs. B.M. Cutting] in mem. of Jacqueline Cole, 1948-**2002**, on chair, N. *CCIII.* Inscr. recording donation [of chair] by [William] (Bill) [A.] Grace in **2002** in mem. of parents, on chair, N. *CCIV.* Inscr. [recording donation of chair by Mrs. M. Sharples] in **2002** in mem. of parents, Walter Long and [w.] Margaret, on chair, S.A. *CCV.* Inscr. [recording donation of chair by Rev. F.J. Heal] in mem. of Gertrude Marion Heal, 1905-**2003**, on chair, N. *CCVI.* Inscr. Gwen Holland, 1919-**2003**, on chair, S.A. *CCVII.* Inscr. [recording donation of chair by Mr. A.J. Smee] in mem. of Dorothy Smee, 1926-**2003**, on chair, N.A. *CCVIII.* Inscr. [recording donation of chair by Mrs. A. Wright] in mem. of Gwen Armstead, 1901-**2004**, on chair, N. *CCIX.* Inscr. Susie Fisher, [w. of no.*LXXIII*], 1912-**2004**, on chair, S.A. *CCX.* Inscr. Donald Frederick Hiscock, 1934-**2004**, and w. Charlotte Louise, 1963-1966, on chair, N. *CCXI.* Inscr. Lily Jessie Pyle, [w. of no.*LXXXV*], 1916-**2004**, on chair with no.*LXXXV*, N. *CCXII.* Inscr. [recording donation of chair by Mrs. K. Banting] in mem. of Ted Banting, 1923-**2005**, on chair, N. *CCXIII.* Inscr. Marion Joyce Scott, 1917-2005, and Richard David Scott, 1942-**2006**, on chair, N.

Ref: *Brit. Lib. Add. MS. 14296*, f.61; *Burke's Peerage and Baronetage*, p.1404; *Heseltine, Heraldry*, p.37; *M.B.S. Bulletin*, 38, p.134, 39, p.144; *M.B.S. Trans.*, V, pp.363-4; *M.S.*, p.164; *Soc. Antiq. MS. 875/6*, pp.95-6; *V.C.H., Hampshire*, III, p.119; *Who's Who*, 1967, p.3033, p.3356.

PITT, (see HURSLEY).

POKESDOWN, (see BOURNEMOUTH).

PORTCHESTER, St. Mary.

I. Inscr. Emily Monk, **1889**, on lectern, N.Tr. *II.* Inscr. recording restoration and re-opening of ch. in **1889**; [Rev.] A[lexander] Arthur Headley, vicar [1884-1889]; W.E. Baker and W.R. Allcot, churchwardens, mur., N. *III.* Inscr. in raised letters recording erection of west window by children in mem. of William Stares, **1907**, bronze, mur., vestibule, N. *IV.* Inscr. recording east window pos. in mem. of 2nd-Lt. John Sturgess Eldred, [2nd Battn.] Leinster Regt. [attd. 2nd Battn. Royal Irish Rifles], yst. son of Fleet-Paym[a]st[e]r [Capt.] E.H. Eldred, [C.B.E.], R.N., great-grandson of Lt. W. Sturgess, R.N., died at Boulogne of wounds received in action at Ypres, 1914, aged 20, [buried at Boulogne Eastern Cemetery, France], mur., C. *V.* World War I memorial on 3 pls. (33 names), maker's name FOSTER, SOUTHSEA, mur., in wooden frame, N. *VI.* Inscr. Mary Elizabeth, dau. of Rear-Admiral John Ingles, w. of Vice-Admiral Cunningham Robert de Clare Foot, born and died at Dinan, [France], 1869-**1926**, "COMMITTED TO THE DEEP OFF THE NEEDLES", maker's name CULN GAWTHORP, & SONS L[TD] LONDON, copper, mur., N. *VII.* Inscr. recording renovation and restoration of lychgate (built to commem. diamond jubilee of Queen Victoria, 1897) by people of Portchester to commem. silver jubilee of George V, **1935**, bronze, on lychgate, Churchyard. *VIII.* Inscr. recording tablet and desk pos. in **1935** by friends and scholars in mem. of Richard Bennetts, schoolmaster for over 40 years, [church]warden and choirmaster for many years, on prie-dieu, Crossing. *IX.* Inscr. William Arthur Humber, 1863-**1938**, on altar, C. *X.* Inscr. recording dedication of furnishings by dau. in mem. of Sister Joanna Stevens, **1966**, aged 74, on shelf, N. *XI.* Inscr. recording repair and restoration of lychgate in **1993** by voluntary subscription and dedication in mem. of "ALL THOSE WHO HAVE LOVED PORTCHESTER, THE CASTLE AND ST MARY'S CHURCH", bronze, on lychgate with no.*VII*, Churchyard. *XII.* Inscr. Stan Jackman, 1915-1990, and [w.] Hazel, 1918-**1996**, on lectern, N. *XIII.* Inscr. Tim Collins, partner, 1965-1998, and dog, Mutley, 1991-**1998**, bronze, on bench, Churchyard. *XIV.* Inscr. with verse. Douglas Porter, 1913-**2004**, and [w.] Edna, 1913-2003, on bench, Churchyard.

PORTSEA, St. Mary.

I. Inscr. Cmdr. William Ponsonby Johnson, R.N., 2nd son of William Ponsonby Johnson and [w.] Mary, of Walton House, Cumberland, **1864**, aged 46, buried in Portsea Cemetery "WHERE ALSO LIE HIS WIFE AND CHILD", mur., N.A. *II.* Inscr. with verse. Capt. Basil Hall, R.N., 1788-1844, [buried in the churchyard]; also son, Capt. Basil Sidmouth De Ros Hall, R.N., died at Mayence, Germany, 1833-**1871**, mur., S.A. *III.* Inscr. on maltese cross-shaped pl. in mem. of Gunner Cain Mahony, R.N.; Stoker Evans Trevethan; Shipwright Will[ia]m Finnigan; E.R. Artificer James C. Hutchings; Caulker Will[ia]m Spencer; Ord[inar]y-Seaman Fred[eric]k Williams; Bandmaster Luigi Gonzaga; E.R. Artificer Will[ia]m H. Towner; Stoker Lucius Steed; and Gun[ne]r Will[ia]m C. Soder, R[oyal] M[arine] Art[iller]y, of H.M.S. Dreadnought, Mediterranean Station, 1884-**1887**, pos. by shipmates, mur., S.A. *IV.* Inscr. George Pele, **1889**, on lectern, N. *V.* Inscr. with verse on maltese cross-shaped pl. in mem. of Lt. James Erskine; W[illia]m Aug[ustine] Harvey, secretary; Thomas Stubbs, smith; Ch[ief-]Yeo[man] Edw[ar]d Cotter, sig[na]ls; G[unner] Benj[amin] McAnnally, M[arine] A[rtillery]; G[unne]rs-Mate W[illia]m Matthews; G[unner] Joseph Younger, M[arine] A[rtillery]; A[ble-]S[eaman] David Buchanan;

A[ble-]S[eaman] Alfred Shilvock; A[ble-]S[eaman] Henry Wardley; A[ble-]S[eaman] George Jordan; George Wilkie, dom[estic]; and G[unner] Fred G Kelsall, M[arine] A[rtillery], died during the commission of H.M.S. Boadicea, Flag Ship, East Indies, 1888-**1891**, mur., S.A. *VI.* Inscr. Ass[istan]t-Engineer Frank Waterfield; Bandsman Alexander Cunningham; Leading Stoker William Little; Ord[inar]y-Seaman Edward Woodley; William H. Pond, domestic; A[ble-]S[eaman] James Isaac; Stoker Joshua J. Tregaskis; Stoker Henry Warr; Stoker James Aishfield; Gunner George Hicks, R[oyal] M[arine] A[rtillery]; A[ble-]S[eaman] John Gould; Ord[inar]y-Seaman Charles Bowers; Leading-Seaman Charles Fossey; and Francis P. Tempany, domestic, died during the 1st commission of H.M.S. Trafalgar, Mediterranean [Station], 1890-**1893**, pos. by officers and men, maker's name COX & BUCKLEY LONDON, mur., N.A. *VII.* Inscr. with ach. and R.N. insignia on quadrilobe-shaped pl. in mem. of Staff-Surgeon J.A. Collot, 1894, aged 44 years; Stoker J. Norton, 1893, aged 23; Ord[inary-Seaman] C. Morrison, 1895, aged 18; B.I.C. R. Nichols, 1893, aged 17; Pte. G. Paddon, R[oyal] M[arines], 1895, aged 20; Pte. H. Yeates, R[oyal] M[arines], 1893, aged 29; A[ble-]S[eaman] Ernest L. Bell, 1895, aged 27; A[ble-]S[eaman] Sam[ue]l Woolley, 1894, aged 25; Ord[inary-Seaman] Step[he]n J. Smith, 1895, aged 19; Gunner J. Whyte, R[oyal] M[arine] A[rtillery], 1895, aged 37; and Ord[inary-Seaman] George Carter, 1895, aged 19, at Malta; Gunner H. Hobson, R[oyal] M[arine] A[rtillery], 1895, aged 25; and Ord[inary-Seaman] G.W. Godfrey, 1895, aged 19, at Boudroum, [Turkey]; and Painter J.H. Trueman, 1896, aged 31, at Salonica, [Greece], died during 2nd commission of H.M.S. Collingwood, Mediterranean Station, 1893-**1896**, pos. by officers and ship's company, mur., S.C. *VIII.* Inscr. Major Richard Dyneley Jennings-Bramly, 1st Battn. Gordon Highlanders, [killed] at Dargai, India, **1897**, on prie-dieu, N.A. *IX.* Inscr. with verse. William Linington, **1901**, aged 76, ch. worshipper for many years, maker's name FOSTER, MARMION ROAD, SOUTHSEA, mur., S.C. *X.* Inscr. recording dedication of organ screen in 1901 by friends and relations of "MEN WHO SERVED THEIR COUNTRY" in the [South African] War 1899-**1902** in mem. of Sir Walter Bartelot, [1st] Bart., [C.B.]; Frederick Nance Aylen; and [Major] Alfred William Jennings-Bramly, [19th Hussars, killed in action at Lake Banagar, South Africa, 1901], on organ, N.A. *XI.* Inscr. with enamelled insignia in relief and battle honours (Mons, Marne, Aisne, Ypres) in mem. of 1st British Expeditionary Force of **1914**, "OLD CONTEMTIBLES", pos. by Portsmouth and District Branch of the Old Contemptibles Association "WHO WORSHIPPED IN THIS CHURCH", bronze, mur., on board, S.C. *XII.* Inscr. with regt. insignia. Sgt. William Goodwillie, [12562], 1st [Battn.] Dorset[shire] Regt., killed in action "IN A GALLANT ATTEMPT TO SAVE TWO OF HIS OFFICERS" near Thiepval, France, **1916**, [buried at Miraumont Communal Cemetery, France], mur., S.A. *XIII.* Inscr. Leonard K.H. Hackman, L.R.C.P., M.R.C.S., vicar's [church]warden for 6 years, **1917**, aged 59, mur., N.A. *XIV.* Inscr. recording gift of candlesticks and picture in **1919** by Emily Louisa Wright, mur., on board on pillar, C. *XV.* Inscr. with verse. Fanny Dommett, **1928**, mur., on board, Narthax. *XVI.* Inscr. with verse. "IN PROUD AND ENDURING MEMORY OF OUR FALLEN COMRADES AT DUNKIRK WHOSE SACRIFICE ENABLED US TO COMPLETE THE TASK THEY HAD SO NOBLY BEGUN", pos. by Portsmouth Branch of the Dunkirk Veterans' Association, 1939-**1940**, bronze, mur., on board, S.A. *XVII.* Inscr. John Read, "WHO HELPED TO BEAUTIFY THIS MISSION CHURCH", 1879-1930, and w. Lilian Elizabeth, 1879-**1955**, mur., on board, Narthax. *XVIII.* Inscr. on sh.-shaped pl. recording gift of raised pew-tops in **1970** in mem. of Charles Richard Kennett, chorister for over 20 years, on choir stall, C. *XIX.* Inscr. Canon Walter John Smith, M.A., vicar 1944-1961, "MINISTERED TO REBUILD THE LIFE OF THIS PARISH AFTER THE SECOND WORLD WAR", 1898-**1973**, and w. Olive Margaret, mur., S.A. *XX.* Inscr. Mantell Thomas Lofthouse, 1906-1973, and w. Barbara Mary, 1905-**1975**, mur., on board, S.C. *XXI.* Inscr. P[etty-]O[fficer] K.I. McCallum, A.E., killed on H.M.S. Glamorgan in the Falklands War, **1982**, aged 27, copper, on grave marker, Churchyard. *XXII.* Inscr. Mary Blackmore and Catharine Jane Blackmore, ch. benefactors, engr. c.**1985**, mur., on board, N. *XXIII.* Inscr. Frederick Benjamin Coley, B.Mus., F.R.C.O., F.L.C.M. (Hon.), choirmaster and organist for 44 years, 1906-**1994**, mur., on board, S.C. *XXIV.* Inscr. Bill Ward, 1924-**1997**, on grave marker, Churchyard.

Ref: *M.B.S. Bulletin*, 51, p.371.

Ch. built, 1887-9.

PORTSMOUTH, Cathedral Church of St. John the Evangelist (R.C.).

I. Inscr. on 2 pls. recording consecration of cathedral in **1887** by [Rt. Rev.] John [Vertue], 1st Bishop of Portsmouth [1882-1900, 1826-1900]; Henry [Fitzalan-Howard], 15th Duke of Norfolk, [K.G.], The Empress Eugenie, [John Patrick Crichton-Stuart, K.T., 3rd] Marquis of Bute, Lord Edmund Talbot, Lord and Lady Arundell of Wardour, Lady Gray, Canon Horan, G.M. Arnold, Canon Ballard, F. Stapleton-Bretherton, Baron Boeslager, Harriet Barton, Lady Bulkeley, V. Ballard, Rt. Rev. Provost Cahill, L.T. and L. Cave, M. Cody, Rev. W.B. Drewe, J. Denny, M. Dunn, Rev. B. Doran, J. Driscoll, Sir John Stanley Errington, G.B. Eyston, R.E. Froude, J. Gainsford, M. Oughton-Giles, G. Gould, J.S. Hansom, J. Hayes, J.J. Kavanagh, M. Digby-Lloyd, J.G. Leeming, Canon Mount, Monsignor McCarthy, M. MacGregor, Rev. F. O'Hare, T.F. O'Reilly, Rev. E. Reardon, M. Reiner, Rev. W. Stone, Countess Tasker, C.E. and A. Vertue, E.G. Ward, C.A. Webber, A. Winthrop, C. West, J. Weld and T. Wickham, benefactors, mur., in stone frame, N. *II.* Inscr. with verse, enamelled sh., motto and 2 enamelled medals within border of oak leaves and acorns with 2 enamelled shs. and 2 monogram shs. at corners. Engineer-Lt. Francis James Charlton, R.N., son of Edward Charlton, M.D., D.C.L., and w. Margaret, born at Hexham, [Northumb.], died as a result of an accident at Portsmouth, 1874-**1908**, pos. by brother officers, maker's name John Hardman & C[o.] Birm[m.], mur., W.Porch. *III.* Rt. Rev. John Baptist Cahill, 2nd Bishop of Portsmouth [1900-1910, 1841-]**1910**, in pontifical vests. with mitre, recumbent on mattress, canopy with 2 shs. in side shafts, inscr. with Lat. verse recording donation of Stations of the Cross, maker's name HARDMAN B'HAM, mur., on marble, N.A. *IV.* Inscr. Bugler Edward Alexander Harding, [RMA/15303], Royal Marine Artillery, H.M.S. Colossus, 4th Battle Sqdn., Grand Fleet, **1918**, aged 15, pos. by shipmates, maker's name T. PRATT & SONS, LONDON, mur., on board, W.Porch. *V.* Inscr. with verse recording foundation of a "Mass to be said in perpetuity on November 11th each year" by the Portsmouth Branch of the Catholic Womens League in mem. of those [killed] in World War I, maker's name S.H. VINCENT MIDDLE ST. SOUTHSEA, mur., on board, W.Porch.

Ref: *M.B.S. Bulletin*, 51, p.371.

Ch. built, 1882.

PORTSMOUTH, Cathedral Church of St. Thomas of Canterbury.

I. Inscr. recording presentation of window by dau., Emily, in mem. of parents, Benjamin Richards, 1848, and [w.] Ann, **1866**, on Organ Gallery/C. *II.* Inscr. recording repair and regilding [of Golden Barque weathervane] in **1873** by E. Gray, of Broad Street;

[Rev.] E[dward] P[ierce] Grant, [M.A.], vicar [1868-1899]; W.D. King and W.H. Saunders, churchwardens, bronze, on weathervane, N.Tr. *III*. Inscr. Robertson Fernie, **1885**, mur., below window, old C., now Chapel of St. Thomas. *IV*. Inscr. Susan, dau. of Cmdr. H. Craddock, R.N., w. of Capt. F.W. Paull, R.N., 1819-**1885**; also children, Susan Mary Hoare, [buried] at West Brompton Cemetery, and Louis Philippe Paull, [buried] in the churchyard, on Organ Gallery/C. *V*. Inscr. recording erection of [north-centre] window in **1886** by friends in mem. of George Rahe, architect, mur., below window, old C., now Chapel of St. Thomas. *VI*. Inscr. Assistant-Paymaster Richard Read, H.M.S. Alecto, died off Elmina, west coast of Africa, **1887**, aged 37, pos. by "mess mates", on Organ Gallery/C. *VII*. Inscr. Howard Ware (Jack) Rogers, only child of Capt. George Burridge Rogers, 48th (Northamptonshire) Regt., and [w.] Maud, **1887**, aged 11, maker's name FRANK SMITH & Cᴼ LONDON, W.C., mur., on marble, old C., now Chapel of St. Thomas. *VIII*. Inscr. Mary Palmer, [killed] in a fire at Hill's, High Street, **1888**, pos. by naval officers, mur., on marble, Inner N.A. of C. *IX*. Inscr. 2nd-Lt. Edward Macrae Ross, 2nd Battn. Seaforth Highlanders Ross-shire Buffs (The Duke of Albany's), 3rd son of Horatio S.I. Ross, grandson of Horatio Ross, of Rossie, Forfarshire, died at Ferozepore, India, **1893**, aged 22, pos. by brothers officers, maker's name BARKENTIN & KRALL, LONDON, mur., on marble, old C., now Chapel of St. Thomas. *X*. Inscr. Selina Jane, w. of Rev. T[homas] D[uodecimus] Platt, [B.A.], vicar [of Portsea, Holy Trinity 1854-1902], **1896**, maker's name HART SON PEARD & Cᴼ Lᴰ LONDON, on Organ Gallery/C. *XI*. Inscr. recording presentation [of frag. of ensign flown by H.M.S. Victory at the Battle of Trafalgar] in mem. of Frederick Thomas Durell Durell, 1814-**1897**, mur., on frame of oak from H.M.S. Victory, Navy Aisle/Outer S.A. of C. *XII*. Inscr. [Rev.] Thomas Duodecimus Platt, B.A., son of Hon. Sir Thomas Joshua Platt, one of the Barons of H.M. Court of Exchequer, vicar of Portsea, Holy Trinity, for 48 years [1854-1902], **1902**, maker's name HART SON PEARD & Cᴼ Lᴰ LONDON, on Organ Gallery/C. *XIII*. Inscr. recording presentation [of lectern] in **1903** by Edward VII, on lectern, old N., now C. *XIV*. Inscr. recording gift of railing in **1904** by W[illiam] H[enry] and L. Barrell in mem. of Henry Lewis Barrell, 1891-1897, Martha Lewis, 1817-1891, and Harry Lewis, 1819-1901, mur., on panelling, old N.Tr., now Lady Chapel. *XV*. Inscr. Capt. William Payne, J.P., Volunteer [Battn.] Hampshire [Regt.], eld. son of Capt. Thomas Payne, of Dolgelly, Borough treasurer for 25 years, **1904**, aged 79, pos. by yst. brother, Edward Payne, Borough resident for 50 years, copper, mur., in marble frame, old C., now Chapel of St. Thomas. *XVI*. Inscr. recording dedication of [centre north aisle of choir] window in **1904** by officers and men of 3rd (D.C.O.) Volunteer Battn. Hampshire Regt. in mem. of Pte. Charles French, Pte. Guy Ford, Pte. Charles Hodgkins, Pte. William E. Jackson, Lance-Cpl. William Moody and Pte. Ernest R. Wrighton, mur., in stone frame, Outer N.A. of C. *XVII*. Inscr. recording gift of oak (from which the poor box and post of the mayor's desk in the mayor's pew are made once formed pt. of the battleship, H.M.S. Tremendous (built at Woolwich in 1784, fought under Admiral Lord Howe in 1794, cut-down to a 50 gun frigate and re-named the Grampus in 1845, paid off 4 years later, converted into a powder bulk and broken up in 1897) and the cost of making the ceiling panels of the pulpit sounding board including the gilded stars (of timber from H.M.S. Tremendous, Queen Charlotte, Actaeon and Chesapeake and the central rose from H.M.S. Victory) by congregation at the ch. restoration in **1904**, mur., on pillar, old S.A., Inner S.A. of C. *XVIII*. Inscr. recording dedication of [centre south aisle of choir] window in **1905** by Portsmouth Grammar School boys in mem. of Old Portemuthians: Capt. R.H.E.G. Holt, R[oyal] A[rmy] M[edical] C[orps]; Lt. H.N. Field, 1st Battn. Devon[shire] Regt.; R.W. Pearson, Rifle Brigade; H.A.F. Watson, 1st Battn. Royal Dublin Fusiliers; Cpl. P. Hetherington, Thorneycrofts Mounted Infantry; Pte. F.N. Aylen, City Imperial Volunteers; C.A.H. Baddeley, Imperial Light Infantry; G. Ford, 3rd (D.C.O.) Volunteer Battn. Hampshire Regt.; and Trooper P.D.O. Salkeld, Cape Police, mur., in stone frame, Navy Aisle/Outer S.A. of C. *XIX*. Inscr.

Thomas King, J.P., mayor of the Borough 1894-1895, alderman 1895-[1907], ch. worshipper for many years, **1907**, aged 66, on Organ Gallery/C. *XX*. Inscr. with Lat. verse and enamelled ach. in relief. George Long, son of Walter Long, of Preshaw House, 1823-**1909**, mur., on marble, old C., now Chapel of St. Thomas. *XXI*. Inscr. with regt. insignia. "ROLL OF PAST & PRESENT OFFICERS (of 8th Battn. Hampshire Regt. who served in South Africa 1900-1902) WHO SUBSCRIBED TO THE FUND FOR DEFRAYING THE COST OF THE COLOURS also of THE COLOUR PARTY & DETACHMENT WHO RECEIVED THEM" in **1909** from [Edward VII] at Windsor Castle, on box, Outer N.A. of C. *XXII*. Inscr. recording repair [of Golden Barque weathervane] in **1912** by G. Russell, coppersmith, and regilding by E.T. Foster, decorator, under the supervision of Harold Wyllie; [Rev.] R[obert] S[umner] Medlicott, [M.A.], vicar [1903-1915]; Alfred Bishop and Charles T. Wood, churchwardens, bronze, on weathervane with no.*II*, N.Tr. *XXIII*. Inscr. with enamelled sh. William Henry Saunders, F.S.A., archaeologist, "A RELIABLE AND PAINSTAKING HISTORIAN OF HIS NATIVE TOWN. CLOSELY IDENTIFIED WITH THIS CHURCH FOR OVER 60 YEARS", born and died at Portsmouth, 1832-**1913**, pos. by townsmen, mur., on marble, old C., now Chapel of St. Thomas. *XXIV*. Inscr. with verse. Engineer-Lt. F[rank] N[orman] Bennett and w. Ada May (née Bevis), [killed] in the H.M.S. Natal disaster at Invergordon, **1915**, mur., on marble, old S.Tr., now Chapel of Healing and Reconciliation. *XXV*. Inscr. with verse. Lt.-Col. Charles Ford, V.D., solicitor, "BY HIS WILL A BENEFACTOR TO THE PORTSMOUTH EYE & EAR HOSPITAL AND OTHER CHARITIES", [1845-]**1918**, "HIS ASHES REPOSE BEHIND THIS TABLET", pos. by brothers and sister, copper, mur., on marble, old S.Tr., now Chapel of Healing and Reconciliation. *XXVI*. World War I memorial (7 names); pos. by staff and employees of Portsmouth Corporation Electricity Supply, mur., on board, Organ Gallery/C. *XXVII*. Inscr. Margery Sylvia Pink, dau., **1919**, aged 23, [pos. by] J.E. P[ink] and J.F. P[ink], on Organ Gallery/C. *XXVIII*. Inscr. William Henry Barrell, secretary of Phoenix Mark Lodge 2 for 15 years, 1858-**1922**, pos. by brethren, on Organ Gallery/C. *XXIX*. Inscr. recording that Lady Chapel windows commem. James Gieve, J.P., 1888, and w. Emma, 1919; also dau., Emma Elizabeth (Bessie), 1919, and eld. son, John William Gieve, J.P., **1923**, mur., on panelling, old N.Tr., now Lady Chapel. *XXX*. Inscr. on oval-shaped pl. Col. Frank Stubington, V.D., J.P., D.L., Hampshire Regt., **1923**, aged 69, on stall, Inner S.A. of C. *XXXI*. Inscr. Jeanie Norris, **1927**, copper, on processional cross, old S.Tr., now Inner S.A. of C. *XXXII*. Inscr. Phyllis Andrews and Alice Bray, pos. by sister, Dapnne Hill, engr. c.**1930**, on lectern, C. *XXXIII*. Inscr. Dr. and Mrs. James Green and family, engr. c.**1930**, on settle, Navy Aisle/Outer S.A. of C. *XXXIV*. Inscr. recording presentation of churchwardens' wands by family in mem. of Paymaster Rear-Admiral George Grant, [church]warden 1920-**1941**, lay canon [of Portsmouth Cathedral], on choir stall, old S.A., now Inner S.A. of C. *XXXV*. Inscr. recording gift of arches in mem. of 155 officers and men of H.M.S. Isis [killed] in action off the coast of Normandy during combined operations for the liberation of Europe, **1944**, bronze, mur., on triptych, Navy Aisle/Outer S.A. of C. *XXXVI*. World War II memorial (27 names); members of Portsmouth Corporation Electricity Supply, copper, mur., Organ Gallery/C. *XXXVII*. Inscr. recording restoration of Golden Barque weathervane (erected in 1710 and made of oak and copper from H.M.S. Victory) in **1958**; Vice-Admiral J[ocelyn] S[tuart] C[ambridge] Salter, C.B., D.S.O. and Bar, O.B.E., [admiral-]superintendent [H.M. Dockyard Portsmouth 1954-1957]; S.H. Watson, M.I.N.A., manager, Construction Dept.; "executed" and presented by J. Evans & Son (Portsmouth) Ltd., plinth constructed and presented by A.E. Hadley Ltd.; Very Rev. E[ric] N[oel] Porter Goff, M.A., provost, copper, on plinth, N.Tr. *XXXVIII*. Inscr. "THIS SHIP, FOR MANY YEARS A WEATHER-VANE ON THE TOWER OF THIS CHURCH AND A GUIDE TO MARINERS ENTERING PORTSMOUTH HARBOUR IN FORMER TIMES, WAS BLOWN DOWN IN THE GALES OF DECEMBER 1954, WAS RESTORED IN 1958 BY MEMBERS OF THE CATHEDRAL BUSINESS MENS COMMITTEE

AND NOW RESTS HERE AS A REMINDER OF PAST GLORIES AND A CHALLENGE TO US TO MAINTAIN AND CARE FOR THIS ANCIENT BUILDING, STILL INCOMPLETE, WHICH AS THE CATHEDRAL OF THE DIOCESE OF PORTSMOUTH SEEK TO SERVE THE PEOPLE OF THESE DAYS", engr. **1958**, bronze, on plinth with no.*XXXVII*, N.Tr. *XXXIX*. Inscr. recording construction of plinth for Golden Barque [weathervane] with nos.*XXXVIII & XXXIX* forged from the orig. keel bolts from H.M.S. Victory, engr. **1958**, copper, on plinth with nos.*XXXVII & XXXVIII*, N.Tr. *XL*. Inscr. Evette, goddau., **1976**, aged 15, [pos. by] Paul and Pamela Gawthorpe, bronze, on book stand, old N.Tr., now Lady Chapel. *XLI*. Inscr. in raised letters with Piscataqua Pioneers insignia in relief. Capt. John Mason, R.N., treasurer of the Army, capt. of Southsea Castle, Governor of the colony of Newfoundland, patentee and founder of New Hampshire, America, vice-admiral of New England, 1586-1635, buried at Westminster Abbey, [pos. by] Piscataqua Pioneers, 1623-**1977**, bronze, old C., now Chapel of St. Thomas. See also Portsmouth, Royal Garrison Church no.*LXXXI*. *XLII*. Inscr. recording erection of statue of St. John the Baptist (by David Wynne, orig. in the ch. of St. John the Baptist, Rudmore) in **1983** in mem. of Anthony Marchbank Carrick, scholar of Winchester Coll., scholar elect of King's Coll., Camb. 1932-1949, and as a permanent reminder of the work of Winchester Coll., bronze, on board statue plinth, old, S.A., now Inner S.A. of C. *XLIII*. Inscr. Mrs. Edna Irene Ayres, Wren, 1903-**1984**, bronze, on bench, Churchyard. *XLIV*. Inscr. with enamelled sh. in relief recording gift of [south-east chapel] window by D-Day and Normandy Fellowship [in mem. of Admiral Sir Bertram Home Ramsay, K.C.B., K.B.E., M.V.O., son of Brig.-Gen. William Alexander Ramsay, allied naval C.-in-C., commanded seaborne forces at Dunkirk 1940 and Normandy 1944, killed in action, 1945, aged 61, buried at St. Germain-en-Laye New Communal Cemetery, France; also those under his command killed during these operations]; unveiled in **1984** by Queen Elizabeth the Queen Mother and dedicated by [Rt. Rev. and Rt. Hon. Robert Alexander Kennedy Runcie], Archbishop of Canterbury [1980-1991], copper, mur., on panelling, old S.Tr., now Chapel of Healing and Reconciliation. *XLV*. Inscr. Jack and Eileen Blair, [pos. by] R. B[lair], engr. c.**1985**, bronze, on bench, Churchyard. *XLVI*. Inscr. Patricia Hodgson, engr. c.**1985**, bronze, on bench, Churchyard. *XLVII, XLVIII, XLIX & L*. Four inscrs. Henry C. Lockyer, engr. c.**1985**, bronze, on benches, Churchyard. *LI*. Inscr. Ken Makins, engr. c.**1985**, bronze, on bench, Churchyard. *LII*. Inscr. Rodney Watson Gieve, 1901-**1989**, reunited with father, James Watson Gieve, J.P., 1927, and other family members, mur., on panelling, old N.Tr., now Lady Chapel. *LIII*. Inscr. with verse and enamelled H.M.S. Fiji insignia in relief in mem. of 233 men "WHO GAVE THEIR LIVES WHEN H.M.S. FIJI WAS LOST AFTER HEAVY AIR ATTACK DURING THE BATTLE FOR CRETE 34° 35 N 23° 12E", 1941, engr. c.**1991**, mur., on panelling, Navy Aisle/Outer S.A. of C. *LIV*. Inscr. with enamelled H.M.S. Cossack insignia in relief in mem. of Capt. E[dward] L[yon] Berthon, [D.S.O. and Bar, D.S.C., R.N., son of Claude T Berthon and w. Annie, 1941, aged 47], and 158 officers and ratings of the ship's company who died as a result of enemy action, 1941, pos. in **1994** by survivors and members of the H.M.S. Cossack Association, mur., on panelling, Navy Aisle/Outer S.A. of C. *LV*. Inscr. with verse and enamelled Fleet Air Arm insignia in relief in mem. of "Aircrew members of The British Pacific and East Indies Fleets operating from H.M. Aircraft Carriers who lost their lives during air attacks on enemy held territory or were captured and subsequently executed. Remembering also comrades in arms of allied services including the United States Army Twentieth Air Force who lost their lives in similar circumstances in South East Asia and the Pacific in 1942-45", engr. **1995**, mur., on panelling, Navy Aisle/Outer S.A. of C.

INDENTS & LOST BRASSES. 56. Lost brass, inscr. Henry, son of Joseph and Jean Cook, 1696; also father, Joseph Cook, 1705, aged 47, [signed by Ridge, schoolmaster, Portsmouth], Churchyard. Recorded by Pavey (c.1716).

Ref: *Brit. Lib. Add. MS. 14296*, f.37; *M.B.S. Bulletin*, 23, p.12, p.14; *M.B.S. Trans.*, V, pp.364-5; *Soc. Antiq. MS. 875/6*, pp.96-7.

PORTSMOUTH, Royal Garrison Church (maintained by English Heritage).

I. Inscr. Admiral Sir Thomas Foley, G.C.B., Rear-Admiral of England, "ONE OF NELSON'S PALADINS", led the British line in command of [H.M.S.] Goliath (74 guns) at the Battle of the Nile [1798] and was Nelson's flag capt. at the Battle of Copenhagen [1801], died C.-in-C. Portsmouth, **1833**; mar. Lucy, dau. of James FitzGerald, 1st Duke of Leinster, buried in the ch., pos. by John Beresford Herbert, mur., C. Inscr. Capt. William Simpson, R.N., [buried] in the ch., 1790-**1838**, mur., N.; moved to Alverstoke, or Gosport, Fort Brockhurst (q.v.). *II.* Inscr. recording that colours of 7th (Royal Fusiliers) [Regt. of Foot] were [laid up] in **1849** by Lt.-Gen. Lord Frederick FitzClarence, G.C.H., Lt.-Governor of Portsmouth [1847-1851], who commanded the regt. 1825-1832, [1799-1854], mur., C. See also Alverstoke, or Gosport, Fort Brockhurst no.*XI*. *III.* Inscr. recording gift of 2 standards in mem. of Lt. Henry Tryon, 1st Battn. Rifle Brigade, [killed] in the Crimea "WHILE IN COMMAND OF THE GALLANT AND SUCCESSFUL ATTACK AGAINST THE RUSSIAN RIFLE PITS", **1854**, pos. by mother, mur., C. *IV.* Inscr. Major Heneage Wynne, 86th Light Infantry, [killed] at the Battle of Inkerman, **1854**; in 2006 loose in C. *V.* Inscr. in mem. of officers and men of the Black Sea Fleet [killed] 1854-]**1855**; in 2006 loose in C. Inscr. recording erection of pulpit by shipmates stationed in the Baltic, Cape of Good Hope and East Indies in mem. of seamen and marines of H.M.S. Penelope killed at Bomarsund [in the Baltic Sea] or "DIED IN THE SERVICE OF THEIR COUNTRY", **1858**, mur., N.; moved to Alverstoke, or Gosport, Fort Brockhurst (q.v.). *VI.* Inscr. 11 Officers and 361 NCOs and men of the 67th (South Hampshire) Regt. who died on service in India, China and the Cape 1858-**1865**, on window splay, C. Inscr. recording gift of [west nave] window by widow, Maria Wilhemia, in mem. of Gen. Sir Charles Menzies, K.C.B., K.H., knt. of Charles III [of Spain], Col. of Royal Marine Artillery, A.D.C. to Queen [Victoria, 1783-]**1866**, mur., below window, N.; moved to Alverstoke, or Gosport, Fort Brockhurst (q.v.). Inscr. recording erection of [west] window in mem. of Lt.-Col. H.J.P. Booth; Capt. G.R. Mure; Capt. R.F.T. Hamilton; Capt. F. Utterton; Capt. A.R. Close; Lt. F.G.E. Glove; Ensign G.I. Langland; Sgt.-Major J. Vance; Sgt. M. Clifford; Cpl. J. Wheeler; Bugler J. Blackwall; Pte. J. Audley; Pte. G. Bradbrook; Pte. S. Bolton; Pte. P. Fitzgerald; Pte. H. Goff; Pte. J. Holbrook; Pte. J. Holohan; Pte. S. Hornsby; Pte. R. Johnson; Pte. I. Lane; Pte. T. Madden; Pte.J. Maher; Pte. J. Mcguire; Pte. R. Phelan; Pte. F. Pratt; Pte. G. Robbins; Pte. F. Trann; Pte. W.H. Varlow; and Pte. H. Wilkinson, of the 43rd Monmouthshire Light Infantry killed in action or died of wounds during the New Zealand War 1863-**1866**, mur., below window, N.; moved to Alverstoke, or Gosport, Fort Brockhurst (q.v.). *VII.* Inscr. with verse recording dedication of [east nave] window in mem. of 2nd-Capt. Morgan Crofton Molesworth, Royal Engineers, "HE LABOURED FOR THE RESTORATION OF THIS CHURCH", **1867**, aged 30; formerly mur., below window, N.; in 2006 loose in C. *VIII.* Inscr. Eliza Angelina, w. of Col. George H. Willis, C.B., Quartermaster-Gen. Southern District, **1867**, on window splay, C. *IX.* Inscr. recording gift of [south-west chancel] window by relations and friends in mem. of Lt.-Gen. the Hon. Henry Edward Butler, [2nd son of Henry Thomas Butler, 2nd Earl of Carrick], served in Egypt and the Peninsular War, died in Paris, [1780-]1856; also sons, Capt. Henry Thomas [Butler], 55th Regt. [of Foot, killed] at [the Battle of] Inkerman, [1823-]1854; Capt. Charles George [Butler], 86th Regt. [of Foot], died of fever at Bombay, [India], 1854, aged 31, [Rev.] Pierce [Butler], rector of Ulcombe, Kent, chaplain to H.M. Forces in the Crimea [1854-1855, 1826-]**1868**; and Capt. James Armar [Butler], Ceylon Rifle Regt., died of wounds received at the defence of Silistria [in the Turkish War], [1827-]1854, on window splay, C. *X*. Inscr. recording gift of [south-centre chancel] window by [brother] officers in mem. of Col. Colin Frederick Campbell, Major 46th (South Devon) Regt. [of Foot], died at Simla, **1868**, aged 44, on window splay, C. *XI*. Inscr. recording gift of [south-east chancel] window by [brother] officers in mem. of Col. Arthur George Vesey, Col. commanding 46th (South Devon) Regt. [of Foot], died on return to England at Suez, **1868**, aged 49, on window splay, C. Inscr. recording gift of [south nave] window by [brother] officers, NCO's and [men] in mem. of comrades of 46th (South Devon) Regt. [of Foot, killed] in the Crimea, Corfu and the 3 presidencies of Bengal, Madras and Bombay 1854-**1868**, mur., below window, N.; moved to Alverstoke, or Gosport, Fort Brockhurst (q.v.). Inscr. recording gift of [west nave] window by friends in mem. Major-Gen. Sir John William Gordon, K.C.B., Royal Engineers, **1870**, aged 55, mur., below window, N.; moved to Alverstoke, or Gosport, Fort Brockhurst (q.v.). Inscr. recording dedication of [north] nave window by widow, [Catherine, only dau. Capt. John Street, Royal Artillery] in mem. of Col. Edwin Wodehouse, C.B., [Royal Artillery], A.D.C. to Queen [Victoria], eld. son of Vice-Admiral the Hon. Philip Wodehouse, died at Portsmouth, [1817-]**1870**, mur., below window, N.; moved to Alverstoke, or Gosport, Fort Brockhurst (q.v.). Inscr. Town-Major Henry White, 74th (Highlanders) [Regt. of Foot], "AFTER MUCH ACTIVE SERVICE IN THE WARS OF HOLLAND AND THE PENINSULA WHERE HE WAS FOUR TIMES SEVERELY WOUNDED. HE WAS 25 YEARS TOWN MAJOR OF THIS GARRISON", 1849, aged 69, and w. Jean, died at Durham, **1870**, aged 90, pos. by son, Lt.-Col. George Francis White, 31st Regt. [of Foot], mur., N.; moved to Alverstoke, or Gosport, Fort Brockhurst (q.v.). *XII*. Inscr. recording erection of reredos in mem. of Col. and Brig.-Gen. Sir William West Turner, K.C.S.I., C.B., Royal Fusiliers and 97th Regt. [of Foot], "A DISTINGUISHED SOLDIER WHOSE MILITARY TALENTS WERE CONSPICUOUSLY BROUGHT TO NOTICE DURING THE WAR IN THE CRIMEA AND IN CHINA AND IN THE INDIAN MUTINY OF 1857-58 MERITED THE SPECIAL APPROBATION OF HIS SOVEREIGN", died after 30 years service at Naples, [Italy], **1871**, aged 48, mur., C. *XIII*. Inscr. Alfwine, Bishop of Winchester 1032-1047, pos. by [Rt. Rev. Dr.] Samuel [Wilberforce, D.D., Bishop of Oxford 1845-1869], Bishop of Winchester [1869-1873, 1805-1873], engr. **1872**, on choir stall, C. *XIV*. Inscr. Vice-Admiral Horatio, Viscount Nelson, K.B., killed at [the Battle of] Trafalgar, [1758-]1805, pos. by Capt. H.R.H. the Duke of Edinburgh, K.G., engr. **1872**, on choir stall, C. *XV*. Inscr. Gen. Sir John Moore, K.C.B., killed at [the Battle of] Corunna, [1761-]1809, pos. by Lt.-Gen. [George Frederick Upton, 3rd] Viscount Templetown, K.C.B., engr. **1872**, on choir stall, C. *XVI*. Inscr. Gen. Sir Alexander Dickson, G.C.B., Royal Artillery, [1777-]1840, pos. by officers of 12th Brigade, R[oyal] A[rtillery], engr. **1872**, on choir stall, C. *XVII*. Inscr. Gen. [Rowland Hill, 1st] Viscount Hill, G.C.B., [2nd son of Sir John Hill, 3rd Bart.], C.-in-C. 1828-1842, [1772-]1842, pos. by nephew, Viscount Hill, engr. **1872**, on choir stall, C. *XVIII*. Inscr. Gen. Sir John McDonald, G.C.B., Col. of 42nd (Royal Highland) Regt., 1776-1850, pos. by Lt.-Gen. the Hon. Sir James Yorke Scarlett, G.C.B., engr. **1872**, on choir stall, C. *XIX*. Inscr. Lt.-Gen. [the Hon.] Sir Hercules [Robert] Pakenham, K.C.B., [3rd son of Edward Michael Pakenham, 2nd Baron Longford], Lt.-Governor of Portsmouth for 8 years, [1781-]1850, pos. by dau. Elizabeth [Catherine, w. of Thomas] Thistlethwayte, engr. **1872**, on choir stall, C. See also Southwick no.*VI*. *XX*. Inscr. Field-Marshal Arthur [Wellesley, 1st] Duke of Wellington, K.G., G.C.B., G.C.H., [P.C., F.R.S., 1769-]1852, pos. by Field-Marshal H.R.H. the Duke of Cambridge, K.G., engr. **1872**, on choir stall, C. *XXI*. Inscr. Lt.-Gen. Sir Charles James Napier, G.C.B., [1782-]1853, pos. by widow, [Frances, dau. of William Philips, and widow of Richard Alcock], and nephew, Major-Gen. W.C.E. Napier, engr. **1872**, on choir stall, C. *XXII*. Inscr. Capt. Henry Thomas Butler, 55th Regt. [of Foot]. killed at [the Battle of] Inkerman, [1823-]1854, pos. by [brother] officers, engr. **1872**, on choir stall, C. See also no.*IX*. *XXIII*. Inscr. Capt. James Armar

Butler, Ceylon Rifle Regt., died of wounds received at the defence of Silistria [in the Turkish War, 1827-]1854, pos. by brother, engr. **1872**, on choir stall, C. See also no.*IX*. *XXIV*. Inscr. Col. George Carpenter, C.B., 41st (Welsh) Regt. of Foot, "FELL AT THE HEAD OF HIS REGT" at the Battle of Inkerman, 1854, pos. by son, George [Carpenter], engr. **1872**, on choir stall, C. *XXV*. Inscr. Lt.-Gen. the Hon. Sir George Cathcart, K.C.B., [3rd son of William Schaw Cathcart, 1st Earl Cathcart], killed at [the Battle of] Inkerman, [1794-]1854, pos. by [Alan Frederick Cathcart, 3rd] Earl Cathcart, [D.L.], engr. **1872**, on choir stall, C. *XXVI*. Inscr. Major-Gen. Henry William Adams, C.B., died of wounds received at the Battle of Inkerman at Scutari, 1855, aged 49, pos. by officers of 49th Regt. [of Foot], engr. **1872**, on choir stall, C. *XXVII*. Inscr. Lt.-Gen. Sir George Charles D'Aguilar, K.C.B., Col. of 23rd Royal Welsh Fusiliers, [1784-]1855, engr. **1872**, on choir stall, C. *XXVIII*. Inscr. Col. Thomas Graham Egerton, C.B., [killed] while commanding the 77th Regt. "AT THE CAPTURE OF THE RUSSIAN RIFLE PITS", 1855, aged 42, pos. by [brother] officers, engr. **1872**, on choir stall, C. *XXIX*. Inscr. Lt.-Gen. Sir George [Thomas] Napier, K.C.B., [brother of no.*XXI*, 1784-]1855, pos. by children, engr. **1872**, on choir stall, C. *XXX*. Inscr. Capt. Sir Robert Newman, [2nd] Bart., [eld. son of Sir Robert William Newman, 1st Bart.], Grenadier Guards, killed at the Battle of Inkerman, 1855, aged 32, pos. by [brother], Sir Lyndston Newman, [3rd] Bart., [J.P., D.L.], engr. **1872**, on choir stall, C. See also Mamhead, Devon no.*III*. *XXXI*. Inscr. Field-Marshal [Fitzroy James Henry Somerset, 1st Baron] Raglan, G.C.B., [P.C., yst. son of 5th Duke of Beaufort], died at [the Siege of] Sevastopol, [1788-]1855, engr. **1872**, on choir stall, C. *XXXII*. Inscr. Major.-Gen. Thomas Fox Strangeways, [grandson of Stephen Fox Strangeways, 1st Earl of Ilchester], killed at the Battle of Inkerman, [1790-]1855, pos. by friends, engr. **1872**, on choir stall, C. See also Melbury Sampford, Dorset no.*VI*. *XXXIII*. Inscr. in mem. of 12 chaplains [killed] during the Crimean War [1854-1856], pos. by Army Chaplains', engr. **1872**, on choir stall, C. See also Alverstoke, or Gosport, Fort Brockhurst no.*XX*. *XXXIV*. Inscr. in mem. of 51 officers of Army Medical Dept. [killed] during the Crimean War [1854-1856], pos. by Army Medical Dept., engr. **1872**, on choir stall, C. *XXXV*. Inscr. in mem. of Etonians [killed] during the Crimean War [1854-1856], pos. by Etonians, engr. **1872**, on choir stall, C. *XXXVI*. Inscr. in mem. of Harrovians [killed] during the Crimean War [1854-1856], pos. by Harrovians, engr. **1872**, on choir stall, C. *XXXVII*. Inscr. in mem. of officers of 49th (Hertfordshire) Regt. [killed] during the Crimean War [1854-1856], pos. by [brother] officers, engr. **1872**, on choir stall, C. *XXXVIII*. Inscr. Lt.-Gen. Sir Henry William Barnard, K.C.B., "DIED IN COMMAND OF THE FORCE BEFORE DELHI" [in the Indian Mutiny, 1798-]1857, pos. by Col. W.A. Moore Barnard, engr. **1872**, on choir stall, C. *XXXIX*. Inscr. Sir James McGrigor, [1st] Bart., K.C.B., M.D., Director-Gen. Army Medical Dept., [1771-]1858, aged 87, pos. by [brother] officers, engr. **1872**, on choir stall, C. *XL*. Inscr. in mem. of Rugbeians [killed] during the Crimean War [1854-1856] and Indian Mutiny [1857-1858], pos. by Rugbeians, engr. **1872**, on choir stall, C. *XLI*. Inscr. in mem. of officers, NCOs and [men] of 8th (King's) Regt. killed or died of disease during the Indian Mutiny [1857-1858], engr. **1872**, on pew, C. *XLII*. Inscr. Gen. Sir William F[rancis] P[atrick] Napier, K.C.B., [brother of nos.*XXII* & *XXX*, 1785-]1860, pos. by 4 daus., engr. **1872**, on choir stall, C. *XLIII*. Inscr. Lt.-Gen. Sir James Outram, G.C.B., [K.S.I., 1803-]1863, pos. by friends, engr. **1872**, on choir stall, C. *XLIV*. Inscr. Gen. the Rt. Hon. Sir George Brown, G.C.B., K.H., [1790-]1865, pos. by Col. G[eorge] H. Willis, C.B., Quartermaster-Gen. Southern District, engr. **1872**, on choir stall, C. *XLV*. Inscr. Gen. Sir Harry D. Jones, G.C.B., [Royal] Engineers], 1866, aged 75, pos. by friends, engr. **1872**, on choir stall, C. *XLVI*. Inscr. Rev. Pierce Butler, [rector of Ulcombe, Kent], chaplain [to H.M. Forces] in the Crimea, [1854-1855, 1826-]1868, pos. by widow, engr. **1872**, on choir stall, C. See also no.*IX*. *XLVII*. Inscr. Major-Gen. Frank Adams, C.B., 1869, aged 60, pos. by officers of 28th Regt., engr. **1872**, on choir stall, C. *XLVIII*. Inscr. Admiral Sir Henry Ducie Chads, G.C.B., 1788-1869, pos.

by sons and daus., engr. **1872**, on choir stall, C. See also Portsmouth, or Southsea, St. Jude no.*XII*. *XLIX*. Inscr. Capt. Arthur Wellesley Cassan, 65th Regt., Military Knight of Windsor, died at Portsmouth, 1870, aged 75, pos. by widow, Grace, engr. **1872**, on choir stall, C. *L*. Inscr. Major-Gen. Sir J. William Gordon, K.C.B., Royal Engineers, 1870, aged 56, pos. by Lt.-Gen. Lord William Paulet, G.C.B., [4th son of Charles Ingoldsby Paulet, 13th Marquess of Winchester], engr. **1872**, on choir stall, C. *LI*. Inscr. Capt. Christopher Hore Hatchell, 43rd L[igh]t Infantry, drowned in Cork Harbour, 1870, aged 33, pos. by [brother] officers, engr. **1872**, on choir stall, C. *LII*. Inscr. Col. John Hinde King, C.B., [Col.] commanding 2nd Battn. Grenadier Guards, 1870, aged 44, pos. by brothers and sisters, engr. **1872**, on choir stall, C. *LIII*. Inscr. Col. Edwin Wodehouse. C.B., Royal Artillery, A.D.C. to Queen [Victoria], died at Portsmouth, 1870, aged 53, pos. by widow and children, engr. **1872**, on choir stall, C. *LIV*. Inscr. Field-Marshal Sir Alexander Woodford, G.C.B., G.C.M.G., 1870, aged 88, pos. by dau., [Susan Upton], Viscountess Templetown and [husband, Gen. George Frederick Upton, 3rd] Viscount Templetown, K.C.B., engr. **1872**, on choir stall, C. *LV*. Inscr. [Lt.-]Gen. the Hon. Sir James Yorke Scarlett, G.C.B., [2nd son of Sir James Scarlett, Knt., 1st Baron Abinger, Lt.-Governor of Portsmouth 1857-1860, 1799-]1871, pos. by widow, Lady Scarlett, [Charlotte Anne, 2nd dau. and coh. of John Hargreaves], engr. **1872**, on choir stall, C. *LVI*. Inscr. recording erection of stalls in **1872** in mem. of "THE OFFICERS WHOSE NAMES ARE INSCRIBED ON THEM", on stall, C. Inscr. on 2 pls. recording erection of [north nave] window in **1872** by [brother] officers in mem. of officers (18 names), 250 NCO's and [men] of 82nd Regt. Prince of Wales Volunteers killed in action or died since the regt. embarked for the Crimea in 1855, mur., below window, N.; moved to Alverstoke, or Gosport, Fort Brockhurst (q.v.). Inscr. recording erection of [north nave] window in **1872** by [brother] officers in mem. of Col. R.J. Straton, C.B.; Major H.A. Macdonald; [Major] R.H. Willington; [Major] W.N.M. Orpen; Capt. W. Gair; [Capt.] H.S. Weighall; Lt.-Adjutant G. Cook; Lt. A.T. Butts; [Lt.] A. Bishop; Ensign A.L. Heming; [Ensign] C.J. Arnold; [Ensign] F.P. Ferguson; [Ensign] H.N. Moore; and 515 NCO's and [men] of 77th (East Middlesex) Regt. [of Foot, killed] 1856-1872, mur., below window, N.; moved to Alverstoke, or Gosport, Fort Brockhurst (q.v.). *LVII*. Inscr. Capt. Sir Henry Martin Blackwood, [2nd] Bart., died while in command of H.M.S. Vengeance, at [Portsmouth, 1801-]1851, and w. Harriet Louisa, [yst. dau. of John Matthew Bulkeley], **1873**, [both buried] in Haslar Cemetery, pos. by surviving children, on stall, C. Inscr. recording dedication of [south nave] window in **1873** by widow, Augusta, [dau. of George Boyle, 4th Earl of Glasgow, G.C.H., F.R.S.], in mem. of Lt.-Gen. Lord Frederick FitzClarence, G.C.H., A.D.C. to William IV and Queen Victoria, son of William IV, entered the Coldstream Guards 1814, Lt.-Col. 1824, commanded the 11th Regt. of Infantry and 7th (Royal Fusiliers) Regt. of Foot, Lt.-Governor of Portsmouth 1847-1851, Col. 36th Regt., C.-in-C. of H.M. Forces and Honourable East India Companies Army in Bombay 1852, died at Poorundhur, India, 1799-1854, mur., below window, N.; moved to Alverstoke, or Gosport, Fort Brockhurst (q.v.). Inscr. Capt. D[aniel] G[reen] Clery, [1869]; Capt. E[dward] M[ontagu] Kemp; Lt. and Adjutant H[enry] A[rthur] G[rey] Todd; Surgeon J. B[enjamin] Lane; and Sub-Lt. G.A. Monroe, 1st Battn. 4th (King's Own Royal) Regt. [of Foot], pos. in **1874** by brother officers; moved to Alverstoke, or Gosport, Fort Brockhurst (q.v.). Inscr. in mem. of officers, NCOs and men killed or died of disease during the Ashanti Expedition, [West Africa], 1873-**1874**, pos. by Rt. Hon. Gathorne-Hardy, M.P., on pew, N.; moved to Alverstoke, or Gosport, Fort Brockhurst (q.v.). Inscr. Major Thomas Oldfield, Royal Marines, killed at the defence of Acre, [Syria], 1799, aged 43, engr. c.**1875**, mur., below window, N.; moved to Alverstoke, or Gosport, Fort Brockhurst (q.v.). *LVIII*. Inscr. recording presentation of chalice, flagon and 2 patens in mem. of Rt. Hon. William Cornwallis, G.C.B., yst. brother of Charles Cornwallis, [1st] Marquess Cornwallis, Governor-Gen. of India 1770, [1738-1805], Admiral of the White, Commander of the Channel Fleet 1805, Vice-Admiral of England, died at Newlands, [1744-]1819, pos. by god-dau., Theresa Cornwallis West, engr. c.**1875**, mur., C. Inscr. with verse. F.M.F.M., 1831 and M.F.F.M., 1835, engr. c.**1875**, on pew, N.; moved to Alverstoke, or Gosport, Fort Brockhurst (q.v.). Inscr. Gen. Lord [Robert] Edward H[enry] Somerset, G.C.B., [3rd] son of Henry [Somerset], 5th Duke of Beaufort, [K.G., D.C.L.], knt. of the Tower and Sword of the Order of Maria Theresa and St. Vladimir of Russia, 1776-1842; pos. by [only] son, Major-Gen. E[dward] A[rthur] Somerset, C.B., and [grand-]dau., engr. c.**1875**, on pew, N.; moved to Alverstoke, or Gosport, Fort Brockhurst (q.v.). Inscr. Capt. the Hon. [Granville] Charles Cornwallis Eliot, 1st Battn. Coldstream Guards, killed while Acting-Adjutant at the Battle of Inkerman, [1828-]1854; pos. by father, [Edward Granville Cornwallis Eliot, 3rd] Earl of St. Germans, G.C.B., [P.C., LL.D.], engr. c.**1875**, on pew, N.; moved to Alverstoke, or Gosport, Fort Brockhurst (q.v.). Inscr. Lt.-Col. F.J. Elliot, [killed] while commanding the 79th Cameron Highlanders at Varana, 1854, pos. by M.E., engr. c.**1875**, on pew, N.; moved to Alverstoke, or Gosport, Fort Brockhurst (q.v.). Inscr. Major-Gen. Bucknell Escourt, Adjutant-Gen., died "FROM ILLNESS BROUGHT ON BY OVER EXERTION" before [the Siege of] Sevastopol, [1802-]1855, pos. by widow, [Caroline Carew], engr. c.**1875**, on pew, N.; moved to Alverstoke, or Gosport, Fort Brockhurst (q.v.). Inscr. in mem. of 12 chaplains [killed] during the Crimean War [1854-1856], pos. by Chaplain's Dept., engr. c.**1875**, mur., below window, N.; moved to Alverstoke, or Gosport, Fort Brockhurst (q.v.). Inscr. in mem. of officers, NCOs and [men] of Coldstream Guards killed or died of disease during the Crimean War [1854-1856], pos. by regt., engr. c.**1875**, on pew, N.; moved to Alverstoke, or Gosport, Fort Brockhurst (q.v.). Inscr. in mem. of 8 officers, 7 NCOs and 233 [men] of 34th (Cumberland) Regt. [of Foot] killed or died of disease during the Crimean War [1854-1856], pos. by regt., engr. c.**1875**, on pew, N.; moved to Alverstoke, or Gosport, Fort Brockhurst (q.v.). Inscr. in mem. of officers, NCOs and [men] of 95th (Derbyshire) Regt. [of Foot] killed or died of disease during the Crimean War [1854-1856], pos. by regt., engr. c.**1875**, on pew, N.; moved to Alverstoke, or Gosport, Fort Brockhurst (q.v.). Inscr. in mem. of officers, NCOs and [men] of 68th (Durham Light Infantry) [Regt. of Foot] killed or died of disease during the Crimean War [1854-1856], pos. by regt., engr. c.**1875**, on pew, N.; moved to Alverstoke, or Gosport, Fort Brockhurst (q.v.). Inscr. in mem. of officers, NCOs and [men] of 77th (East Middlesex) Regt. [of Foot] killed or died of disease during the Crimean War [1854-1856], pos. by regt., engr. c.**1875**, on pew, N.; moved to Alverstoke, or Gosport, Fort Brockhurst (q.v.). Inscr. in mem. of officers, NCOs and [men] of 9th (East Norfolk) Regt. [of Foot] killed or died of disease during the Crimean War [1854-1856], pos. by regt., engr. c.**1875**, on pew, N.; moved to Alverstoke, or Gosport, Fort Brockhurst (q.v.). Inscr. in mem. of officers, NCOs and [men] of Grenadier Guards killed or died of disease during the Crimean War [1854-1856], pos. by regt., engr. c.**1875**, on pew, N.; moved to Alverstoke, or Gosport, Fort Brockhurst (q.v.). Inscr. in mem. of officers, NCOs and [men] of 47th (Lancashire) Regt. [of Foot] killed or died of disease during the Crimean War [1854-1856], pos. by regt., engr. c.**1875**, on pew, N.; moved to Alverstoke, or Gosport, Fort Brockhurst (q.v.). Inscr. in mem. of officers, NCOs and [men] of Royal Engineers killed or died of disease during the Crimean War [1854-1856], pos. by regt., engr. c.**1875**, on pew, N.; moved to Alverstoke, or Gosport, Fort Brockhurst (q.v.). Inscr. in mem. of officers, NCOs and [men] of Scots Fusilier Guards killed or died of disease during the Crimean War [1854-1856], pos. by regt., engr. c.**1875**, on pew, N.; moved to Alverstoke, or Gosport, Fort Brockhurst (q.v.). Inscr. in mem. of Rugbeians killed or died of disease during the Indian Mutiny [1857-1858], pos. by Rugby [school]masters, engr. c.**1875**, on pew, N.; moved to Alverstoke, or Gosport, Fort Brockhurst (q.v.). Inscr. in mem. of officers, NCOs and [men] of 64th (2nd Staffordshire) Regt. [of Foot] killed or died of disease during the Indian Mutiny [1857-1858], pos. by regt., engr. c.**1875**, on pew, N.; moved to Alverstoke, or Gosport, Fort Brockhurst (q.v.). Inscr. [Rt. Rev. Dr.] Samuel Wilberforce, D.D., [Bishop of Oxford 1845-1869], Bishop of Winchester [1869-1873, 1805-1873], engr. c.**1875**, on pew, N.; moved to Alverstoke, or Gosport, Fort Brockhurst (q.v.). Inscr. Lt. Charles Rufus Robson, R.N., only son of Rev. J. Stuart Robson, only brother of Ensign William James Stuart Robson, 17th Regt., engr. c.**1875**, mur., below window, N.; moved to Alverstoke, or Gosport, Fort Brockhurst (q.v.). Inscr. recording dedication of nave gas standards in mem. of Major-Gen. Charles Richard Sackville-West, 6th Earl De La Warr, K.C.B., Viscount Cantelupe and Baron West, 2nd son of George John [Sackville-West], 5th Earl De La Warr, [officer] of the Legion of Honour, received the Crimea medal and 4 clasps, [knt. of the] Medjidie (3rd class), Sardinian and Turkish medals; entered the army in 1833 as ensign in the 43rd (Light Infantry) [Regt. of Foot] and in 1864 became Major-Gen., A.D.C. to Sir Hugh Gough in the Sikh War 1845, fought at Moodkee, Ferozshah and Sobraon (wounded) and received [Crimea] medal and 3 clasps and C.B., present at the Battles of Alma [1854], Balaclava [1854] and Inkerman [1854] and "SHARED IN THE ATTACKS" of the Redan [at the Siege of Sevastopol 1855], commanded a brigade in the expedition against Kinburn [1855], 1815-1873, pos. in **1876** by kinswomen by mar., Theresa Cornwallis West, mur., N.; moved to Alverstoke, or Gosport, Fort Brockhurst (q.v.). *LIX.* Inscr. recording presentation [of missal stand] in **1877** by Gen. Sir [Charles] Hastings Doyle, K.C.M.G., Commander Southern District, Lt.-Governor of Portsmouth; Col. North, M.P.; and Perry Doyle, C.B., in mem. of father, Lt.-Gen. Sir Charles William Doyle, G.C.B., C.B., [1770-1842], on missal stand, C. *LX.* Inscr. recording dedication of altar vases in mem. of Elizabeth Mary, w. of Rev. C.A. Assheton Craven, M.A., principal chaplain to garrison forces, died at Southsea, **1880**, mur., C. Inscr. Major Charles Covey, 68th (Durham Light Infantry) [Regt. of Foot], died at Mejah, near Allahabad, India, **1881**, mur., N.; moved to Alverstoke, or Gosport, Fort Brockhurst (q.v.). Inscr. Capt. Henry Humphries, commanded mounted infantry, Sgt.-Major 2nd Battn. Royal Inniskillen Fusiliers (108th Regt. [of Foot)] for 10 years, promoted to Lt. 2nd Battn. Welsh Regt. (69th [(South Lincolnshire Regt. of Foot)] 1881, "PROCEEDING TO EGYPT IN 1882 HE WAS APPOINTED PROVOST MARSHAL AND AFTERWARDS TO THE MOUNTED INFANTRY, WHICH CORPS HE COMMANDED WITH GREAT DISTINCTION IN THE CAMPAIGN IN THE SUDAN IN 1884", died at Cairo, Egypt, **1884**, aged 35, pos. by brother officers of Military Police and Mounted Infantry Corps, mur., below window, N.; moved to Alverstoke, or Gosport, Fort Brockhurst (q.v.). Inscr. Major James Anderson Morice, Royal Marines, [killed] in the 1st Battle of El Teb, **1884**, pos. by brother officers and friends, mur., below window, N.; moved to Alverstoke, or Gosport, Fort Brockhurst (q.v.). Inscr. with verse. Admiral Robert FitzGerald Gambier, R.N., of Anglesey Terrace, chairman of the Sailors Home at Portsea for many years, 1803-**1885**, mur., N.; moved to Alverstoke, or Gosport, Fort Brockhurst (q.v.). *LXI.* Inscr. Anna [Rodney], 1882, and Rebecca Rodney, [**1885**] on choir stall, C. Inscr. with regt. insignia and colours. Pte. J. Wakefield, Pte. T. Kay, Pte. W. Gatley, Pte. H. Spiers and Pte, T. Wilks "LOST THEIR LIVES THROUGH INJURIES RECEIVED AT AN EXPLOSION OF GAS" at Cambridge Barracks, **1887**, pos. by NCOs and [men] of 2nd Battn. Worcestershire Regt., mur., N.; moved to Alverstoke, or Gosport, Fort Brockhurst (q.v.). *LXII.* Inscr. recording dedication of altar rails in **1889** by Gen. Sir George Willis, K.C.B., [1822-1900], on step, C. *LXIII.* Inscr. Ven. H.P. Wright, senior chaplain to H.M. Forces [1st Class], archdeacon [of Columbia 1861-1865, Royal Garrison Church 1866-1876 and Vancouver Island 1877-1880], chaplain to H.R.H. the Duke of Cambridge, K.G., 1814-**1892**, pos. by [2nd] w. Marian L., on choir stall, C. *LXIV.* Inscr. Gen. the Hon. Sir Leycester Smyth, C.B., K.C.M.G., Governor of Gibralter [1890-1891], Lt.-Governor of Portsmouth, 1829-1891, pos. in **1893** by Lt.-Gen. H.R.H. the Duke of Connaught and Strathearn, K.G., K.C.B., Lt.-Gov. of Portsmouth, on choir stall, C. Inscr. Constance Adelaide Newton, pos. by M. St. Quintin, engr. c.**1900**, on pew, N.; moved to

Alverstoke, or Gosport, Fort Brockhurst (q.v.). Inscr. Richard William Ford, clerk of the peace, [1822-]1900, and [w.] Emma, [1832-]1892, pos. in **1902** by [son], Archibald [Ford, 1846-1930], mur., N.; moved to Alverstoke, or Gosport, Fort Brockhurst (q.v.). *LXV.* Inscr. [recording lectern] pos. in **1902** by congregation and garrison in mem. of Queen Victoria, [1819-1901], on lectern, C. Inscr. recording gift of bench by children and sister in mem. of Helen Wolseley Cox, president of Guild of St. Helena, 1840-**1905**, on pew, N.; moved to Alverstoke, or Gosport, Fort Brockhurst (q.v.). Inscr. Rev. Joseph Barnaby Charles Murphy, M.A., chaplain to [H.M.] Forces [at Aldershot 1887-1890, Portsmouth 1890-1895 and Colchester 1899-1903], pos. in **1908** by friends, mur., N.; moved to Alverstoke, or Gosport, Fort Brockhurst (q.v.). Inscr. recording restoration of chapel in **1908** by friends in mem. of [Rev.] Joseph Barnaby Charles Murphy, M.A., chaplain to [H.M.] Forces [at Aldershot 1887-1890, Portsmouth 1890-1895 and Colchester 1899-1903], mur., N.; moved to Alverstoke, or Gosport, Fort Brockhurst (q.v.). Inscr. William and Ellen French, **1909**, on pew, N.; moved to Alverstoke, or Gosport, Fort Brockhurst (q.v.). Inscr. Capt. Henry Hann, **1909**, pos. by dau., Bertha Morley, mur., N.; moved to Alverstoke, or Gosport, Fort Brockhurst (q.v.). Inscr. George Long, 1823-**1909**, pos. by dau. Jane Long, on pew, N.; moved to Alverstoke, or Gosport, Fort Brockhurst (q.v.). Inscr. "A THANKOFFERING FOR THE DAILY EUCHARIST LENT", **1910**, on pew, N.; moved to Alverstoke, or Gosport, Fort Brockhurst (q.v.). Inscr. Lysander Maybury, M.D., **1911**, on pew, N.; moved to Alverstoke, or Gosport, Fort Brockhurst (q.v.). Inscr. pos. by sisters of Guild of St. Helena, **1911**, on pew, N.; moved to Alverstoke, or Gosport, Fort Brockhurst (q.v.). Inscr. "A THANKOFFERING FOR THE DAILY EUCHARIST LENT", **1911**, on pew, N.; moved to Alverstoke, or Gosport, Fort Brockhurst (q.v.). Inscr. Josephine Price Heap, only dau. of William Price, M.D., of Cincinatti, Ohio, [America]; also eld. grandson, Lt. R[obert] C[unynghame] Slade-Baker, M.C., 1st Battn. Royal Berkshire Regt., [son of Brig.-Gen. Arthur Slade-Baker and w. Caroline Fisher], **1917**, [aged 21, buried at Beuvry Communal Cemetery extension, France], mur., N.; moved to Alverstoke, or Gosport, Fort Brockhurst (q.v.). Inscr. Jessie P.A.L., w. of Col. W.F. Graham, R[oyal] A[rtillery], **1918**, aged 58, pos. by husband and daus., Ethel D. Sargeaunt and Dorothy Harrison-Baker, mur., N.; moved to Alverstoke, or Gosport, Fort Brockhurst (q.v.). Inscr. Lt.-Col. and Battn.-Col. F[rederick] J[ohn] Evelegh, Oxfordshire Light Infantry and Royal Garrison Regt.; also [sons], Major C.N. Evelegh, Duke of Cornwall's Light Infantry; Lt.-Col. E[dmund] G[eorge] Evelegh, Royal Marine Light Infantry and Nelson Battn. R.N. Division, [1915, buried at Skew Bridge Cemetery, Turkey]; and Capt. R[osslyn] C[urzon] Evelegh, [2nd Battn.] Oxford and Bucks. Light Infantry, [1914, aged 29, buried in Soupir Churchyard, France], [pos. in] **1921**, mur., N.; moved to Alverstoke, or Gosport, Fort Brockhurst (q.v.). Inscr. Rose Mills, lifelong ch.worshipper, **1922**, on pew, N.; moved to Alverstoke, or Gosport, Fort Brockhurst (q.v.). Inscr. E[dith] M. C[larkson, 1922], pos. in **1924**, on pew, N.; moved to Alverstoke, or Gosport, Fort Brockhurst (q.v.). Inscr. Edith [M.] Clarkson, 1922, pos. in **1924** by family, on pew, N.; moved to Alverstoke, or Gosport, Fort Brockhurst (q.v.). *LXVI.* Inscr. Laura Emily Dominic, 1824, and Mira Elizabeth Rodwell, **1924**, pos. by members of Guild of St. Helena, on choir stall, C. *LXVII.* Inscr. Maurice Percy Berkeley Portman, R.N., **1928**, on hymn board, C. *LXVIII.* Inscr. recording presentation [of processional cross] by sisters of Guild of St. Helena and the widow of a naval officer in mem. of Helen Nicholson, engr. **1929**, on processional cross, C. *LXIX.* Inscr. recording gifts of donors augmented in **1929** by subscriptions from the congregation [for no.*LXVIII*], on pew, N. *LXX.* Inscr. recording that colours of 67th South Hampshire Regt. (presented in 1846 at Cork) were damaged in the blitz, **1941**, mur., on board, C. *LXXI.* Inscr. with verse. Lt. Ian Granville Sharp, Royal Marines, eld. son of [Major] Douglas [Charles Granville] Sharp, of Southsea, and [w.] Katherine [Utten Mary], died on active service in Ceylon, **1943**, aged 23, [buried in Kandy War Cemetery, Sri Lanka], mur., C. *LXXII.* Inscr. Edward Chevers, 1798, and w. Elizabeth, 1787, [grandparents]; also mother, Ann, w. of Forbes MacBean Chevers, 1825, pos. by Surgeon-Major Norman Chevers, M.D., Bengal Army; erected in **1948** by surviving children of Norman Chevers and w. Emily to replace orig. destroyed by enemy action, mur., on board, C. *LXXIII.* Inscr. recording donation of Portsmouth and District 8th Army O[ld] C[omrades] A[ssociation] book of remembrance by life Vice-President F.A.J. Grant and donation of display case by Vice-President Bill North, engr. c.**1955**, on display case, C. *LXXIV.* Inscr. recording reconstruction of pews (damaged in 1941 through enemy action) in **1957** by 71 Water Transport Co. Workshops, R[oyal] E[lectrical and] M[echancial] E[ngineers, on pew, C. *LXXV.* Inscr. with verse. Capt. Ernest Henry Coulter, Royal Hampshire Regt., 1879-**1959**, mur., on board, C. *LXXVI.* Inscr. with verse. Major Douglas Charles Granville Sharp, Royal Field Artillery, husband of Katherine [Utten Mary], father of Ian, Ann, Douglas and Peter, churchwarden for 21 years, **1960**, aged 64, mur., C. *LXXVII.* Inscr. with regt. insignia recording that standard of Portsmouth and District No.1 Branch Royal Army Service Corps Association was laid up in 1963; dedicated to founder member W[arrant] O[fficer Class] 1 (R.S.M.) James Davies, R[oyal] A[rmy] S[ervice] C[orps] in mem. of members who served in the garrison and worshipped in the ch. 1886-**1965**, mur., on board, C. *LXXVIII & LXXIX.* Two inscrs. recording dedication of replacement [south-west and south-centre chancel] window (destroyed in 1941 [through enemy action]) in **1967** by Ven. J[ohn] R[oss] Youens, O.B.E., M.C., Chaplain-Gen. [1966-1974, hon. chaplain to Queen Elizabeth II 1969-1985], mur., below nos.*IX & X*, C. *LXXX.* Inscr. recording dedication of replacement [south-east chancel] window (destroyed in 1941 [through enemy action]) in **1970** by Ven. J[ohn] R[oss] Youens, C.B., O.B.E., M.C., Chaplain-Gen. [1966-1974, hon. chaplain to Queen Elizabeth II 1969-1985], mur., below no.*XI*, C. *LXXXI.* Inscr. in raised letters with Piscataqua Pioneers insignia in relief. Capt. John Mason, R.N., treasurer of the Army, capt. of Southsea Castle, Governor of Newfoundland, patentee and founder of New Hampshire, America, Vice-Admiral of New England, 1586-1635, buried at Westminster Abbey, pos. by John Scribner Jenness, Charles Levy Woodbury, Charles Wesley Tuttle, Alexander Hamilton Ladd, Charles Henry Bell, Eliza Appleton Haven and Charlotte Maria Haven, of New Hampshire, [America], engr. **1977**, mur., C. See also Portsmouth, Cathedral Church of St. Thomas of Canterbury no.*XLI. LXXXII.* Inscr. Rev. Fred Mason, padre to [Portsmouth and District] 8th Army Old Comrades Association, **1982**, aged 86, mur., C. *LXXXIII.* Inscr. with verse and insignia recording installation of [north-west chancel] window by Portsmouth and District 8th Army Old Comrades Association in mem. of comrades who died while supporting sea and air forces in Egypt, Alamein, Tunisia, Sicily and Italy 1941-1945; dedicated in **1984** by Rev. George Hughes, padre, and unveiled by Field-Marshal Lord Carver, G.C.B., C.B.E., D.S.O., M.C., mur., below no.*VI*, C. *LXXXIV.* Inscr. Robert John Claridge, 1928-**1986**, and [w.] Shirley Ann (née Doble), 1932-1985; mar. in the ch. 1953, [buried in the churchyard], on choir stall, C. *LXXXV.* Inscr. with Lat. verse recording installation of [south-west chancel] window to "all Gunners past & present" by Portsmouth [Branch of the] Royal Artillery Association; dedicated by Major the Rev. C[hristopher] J[ames] S[ambrooke] Burne, D.S.O. and unveiling of plaque in **1987** by Major-Gen. B. Davis, C.B., C.B.E., on window splay with no.*VIII*, C. *LXXXVI.* Inscr. with verse. Albert Ernest Watts, verger for many years, 1894-**1988**, mur., C. *LXXXVII.* Inscr. Leslie James Carter, 5th Battn. Hampshire Regt and 8th Army, 1917-**1990**, on choir stall, C. *LXXXVIII.* Inscr. Major E.W. (Nick) Cornick, R[oyal] A[rmy] S[ervice] C[orps]/R[oyal] E[lectrical and] M[echancial] E[ngineers, 8th Army, husband, father and grandfather, 1915-**1993**, on choir stall, C.

Ref: *Burke's Peerage and Baronetage*, p.16, p.211-2, p.271, pp.488-9, p.499, p.755, p.1104, p.1337, p.1408, p.1492, p.1702, p.1963, p.2054, p.2203, p.2351, p.2622.

Ch. bombed, 1941.

PORTSMOUTH, or MILTON, St. James.

I. Inscr. on oval-shaped pl. Alfred Godley Crewe, surgeon in the Bengal Army, India, born at Breadsall, Derbys., died at Milton, aged 63, pos. by w. and dau., engr. c.**1900**, mur., on marble, S.A. *II.* Inscr. in raised letters. Bonner Harris Mumby, M.D., D.Ph., V.D., 1856-**1914**, bronze, mur., S.A. *III.* Inscr. in raised letters. Ethel Frances Wollaston, 1858-**1934**, bronze, mur., N.A. *IV.* Inscr. in raised letters. Ellen Marianne Mumby, [w. of no.*II*], 1856-**1953**, bronze, with no.*II*, S.A.

Ch. built, 1841; demolished and rebuilt, 1913.

PORTSMOUTH, or SOUTHSEA, St. Jude.

I. Inscr. Robert Shean, [1858], and Harriett Vallancer, [**1858**], husband and sister, pos. by Elizabeth Shean, mur., below window, Choir Vestry. *II.* Inscr. recording tablet and window pos. by widow in mem. of Thomas Ellis Owen, J.P., founder of ch., [1805-]**1862**; also [widow], mur., below window, old S.A., now South Room. *III.* Inscr. Catherine Owen, [widow of no.*II*], **1865**, mur., below no.*II*, old S.A., now South Room. *IV.* Verse on base of stepped cross and marg. inscr. with 4 evang. symbols on roundels at corners. [Rev.] Thomas Richard Brownrigg, M.A., 1st incumbent, **1869**, aged 47, pos. by congregation, mur., on board, C. *V.* Inscr. with verse. Rev. James, M. Fitz-Maurice, M.A., of Hawarden, Flintshire, 1800-1853, and w. Mary, died at Southsea, 1800-**1869**, pos. by children, maker's name HART, SON, PEARD & C⁰, LONDON, mur., on stone, old N.A., now North Room. *VI.* Inscr. Lydia, w. of Jeremiah Owen, brother of [Thomas Ellis Owen, J.P.], founder of ch., **1873**, aged 66, mur., on marble, Choir Vestry. *VII.* Inscr. with verse recording erection of pulpit, clergy stall and lectern by congregation in mem. of Emmeline, w. of Rev. [Canon] J[oseph] S[ewell] Blake, M.A., [hon. canon of Winchester Cathedral, 2nd] vicar [1869-1909], **1876**, on pulpit, N. *VIII.* Inscr. Lt. John Warrington Leckie, 2nd Battn. Worcestershire (late 36th) Regt., son of Lt.-Col. John Davies Leckie, Bombay Army, died at Teddington, [Middx.], **1886**, aged 24, pos. by brother officers, maker's name COX & BUCKLEY LONDON, mur., on board, Choir Vestry. *IX.* Inscr. Major John Le Cocq Robilliard, Royal Marine Artillery, of H.M.S. Nelson, "DROWNED · BY · THE · CAPSIZING OF · A · BOAT · IN · JERVIS · BAY", New South Wales, [Australia], **1887**, aged 39, pos. by officers of H.M.S. Nelson, mur., on marble, N. *X.* Inscr. with crest and motto. Matilda, w. of A. Slocock, **1888**, maker's name JONES & WILLIS, mur., old S.A., now South Room. *XI.* Robert Crosse, 1879, aged 91; also dau., Frances Henrietta Willis, died at Southsea, **1889**, rect. pl., canopy, inscr. with Lat. verse, sh., crest and motto, mur., on board, N. *XII.* Inscr. Caroline Frances, dau. of Admiral Sir Henry [Ducie] Chads, G.C.B., 1823-**1905**, maker's name JONES & WILLIS, mur., on board, Choir Vestry. See also Portsmouth, Royal Garrison Church no.*XLVIII*. *XIII.* Inscr. with verse. Elizabeth Cottam, **1922**, ch. worshipper for many years, mur., on marble, N. *XIV.* Inscr. with verse in raised letters. Capt. Edward Madden, R.N., died while in command of H.M.S. Hector off Netley, 1876; also widow, Catherine, died at 2 St. Helens Parade, **1922**, bronze, mur., N. *XV.* Inscr. recording dedication of chapel in mem. of [Rt. Rev. Dr.] E[rnest] G[raham] Ingham, [M.A., Hon.D.D.], Bishop [of Sierra Leone 1883-1897], vicar 1912-**1926**, mur., on board, N. *XVI.* Inscr. with verse. Charles William Bevis, J.P., F.R.I.B.A., husband of Florence, churchwarden 1915-1925, **1927**, bronze, mur., N. *XVII.* Inscr. Arderne Hulley, of One House, Rainow, Cheshire and Natal, [South Africa], 1836-**1927**; also 2nd son, Lt. A.H.B. Hulley, Royal Field Artillery, died in Netley Hospital, 1918, [buried in Netley Military Cemetery], mur., N.

XVIII. Inscr. Edward George Woolhouse, 1925, and w. Emma Elizabeth, **1936**, of Eversley, Southsea, worshipped in the ch. for 50 years, pos. by sons and daus., mur., N. *XIX.* Inscr. Brig.-Gen. Sir Robert [Augustus William] Colleton, [9th and last] Bart., C.B., [1854-]**1938**, and w. Edith, [3rd dau. of Thomas Robert Abraham], 1936, mur., on marble, N.

Ch. built, 1851.

PORTSMOUTH, or SOUTHSEA, St. Simon.

I. Inscr. recording erection of [south chancel] window by tutors and school-fellows of Eastman's Royal Naval Academy in mem. of Nennbery Bright Smith, 2nd son of Rev. G.A. Bright Smith, drowned at Shanklin, 1856-**1872**, mur., on board, C. *II.* Inscr. with verse recording presentation of pulpit by family in mem. of Emma Sarah Lush, w. and mother, **1885**, on pulpit, N. *III.* Inscr. recording communion rails pos. by widow in mem. of Commissary-Gen. Robert Clement Major, **1895**, mur., on board, C. *IV.* Inscr. Sarah Richards, **1895**, pos. by sister, Emily Richards, on lectern, N. *V.* Inscr. recording tablet pos. in **1902** "OVER THE PULPIT AND ELECTRIC LIGHT INSTALLED" in mem. of Rev. Frederick Baldey, 1st vicar [1868-1901, 1901, aged 73], maker's name E A FOSTER ENGRAVER, mur., on board, N. *VI.* Inscr. Jacob Parkins, chorister for 36 years, **1916**, aged 66, pos. by choir, maker's name FOSTER, SOUTHSEA, mur., on board, C. *VII.* Inscr. [Rev.] Nathaniel Vickers, M.A., vicar 1905-1919, bronze, mur., C. *VIII.* World War I memorial on 3 pls. (146 names), **1919**, mur., in wooden frame, N.A. *IX.* Inscr. with verse. Godfrey Charles Brian Parish, F.R.G.S., colonial secretary of the Gambia, died of yellow fever, **1934**, aged 37, [buried] at Bathurst, Gambia, mur., C. *X.* Inscr. Edward James Smee, churchwarden for many years, 1879-**1963**, on chair, C. *XI.* World War II memorial, engr. c.**1990**, mur., on board below no.*VIII*, N.A. *XII.* Inscr. with verse. Lt.-Cmdr. the Rev. Peter [Anthony] Lewis, [hon. curate], 1925-**1998**, mur., on board, old N., now Meeting Room.

Ch. built, 1864-6.

PORTSWOOD, (see SOUTHAMPTON).

PRIVETT, Holy Trinity (redundant, now vested in The Churches Conservation Trust).

I. Inscr. recording building of ch. 1876-1878 and consecration in **1878** by [Rt. Rev. Dr.] Edward Harold [Browne, M.A., D.D.], Bishop [of Winchester 1873-1891], maker's name HART, SON, PEARD & CO. LONDON, mur., in recess, C. *II.* Inscr. [Rev.] Edward Pedder, M.A. of Brasenose Coll., Oxford, hon. canon of Manchester Cathedral, vicar for 18 years, **1881**, on lectern, N. *III.* Inscr. with verse in raised letters with ach. in relief. William Nicholson, of Basing Park, "THIS CHURCH WHICH HE BUILT AND WHEREIN HE WORSHIPPED IS THE LASTING MEMORIAL", 1824-**1909**, bronze, mur., N.A. *IV.* Inscr. with verse in raised letters. Eliza Hansford, 1835-**1911**, maker's name OMAR RAMSDEN ET ALWYN CARR ME FECERUNT, bronze, mur., N.A. *V.* Inscr. [Pte.] Harry Foyle, [41285, 1st Battn. Duke of Cornwall's Light Infantry, son of Harry Foyle and w. Edith], chorister, died in France, **1918**, [aged 19], bronze, on hymn board, N.

Ch. declared redundant, 1975; vested, 1980.

QUARLEY, St. Michael.

I. Inscr. "IN · REMEMBRANCE · OF · HAPPY · WORK · AND · WORSHIP · AT · S^T · ELIZABETH'S · KENSINGTON · T · J · E · **1896**", on ewer, C. *II*. Inscr. Edith Alexandrina, dau. of Rev. J[ohn] G[eorge] H[enry] Hill, [M.A.], brother of [the Royal Hospital of] St. Katharine, rector [1873-1899], widow of A.P. Wilson, 1858-**1949**, mur., N. *III*. Inscr. recording donation [of bench] in **2000** in mem. of Willie James Futcher, [1898-1972], and [w.] Emma Charlotte, [1908-2000], on bench, Churchyard. *IV*. Inscr. Harry Davis, 1892-1980, and [w.] Elsie, 1893-1983; also Bob Hodges, 1910-1996, and [w.] Ann, 1914-**2000**, on bench, Churchyard.

RINGWOOD, SS. Peter and Paul (new church).

I. John Prophete, prebendary of Lincoln, Dean of Hereford and York, **1416**, in cope with SS. Michael, John the Baptist, Peter, Paul, —— Winifred, Katherine, Barbara, Margaret, on orphreys, single canopy (much mutil.); marg. inscr. and 6 shs. lost; formerly C., now A.T., S.A. *Beaumont*, p.91 (eff.); *Bod. Lib. Gough Maps 223*, f.48; *Gent. Mag.*, 1807, II, p.1001; *Gent. Mag. Lib. Eng. Topog.*, fig.3, p.98; *Hants Proc.*, VII, opp. p.76 (eff.); *M.B.S. Portfolio*, I, pt.5, pl.2; *Portfolio Book*, pl.123. Eff. orig. 1683 x 505 mm, now 1642 x 505 mm, canopy orig. 2025 x 690 mm, now 350 x 595 mm, sh. indents 160 x 135 mm, marg. inscr. indent 2085 x 1135 x 30 mm, Purbeck slab 2100 remains x 1200 mm remains. Style: London A. Rep. by W.G.L. (2006).

II. Inscr. Thomas Dyer, surgeon, **1853**, aged 60, on window splay, C. *III*. Inscr. with enamelled sh. recording erection of [east] window by widow, Lady Caroline Morant, and sons, John, Hay and William, in mem. of John Morant, of Brokenhurst, lord of the manor of Ringwood and Brokenhurst [Park], 1787-**1857**, on window splay, C. *IV*. Inscr. recording erection of east window by w. Lady Caroline Morant, and sons, John, Hay and William, in mem. of John Morant, of Brokenhurst, lord of the manor of Ringwood and Brokenhurst Park, [1787-]**1857**, maker's name COX & BUCKLEY · LONDON, on step, C. *V & VI*. Two inscrs. recording erection of [north-east and south-east chancel] windows by friends and parishioners in mem. of Rev. Charles Henry Maturin, M.A., vicar and rector of Harbridge for 16 years [1845-1862], **1862**, aged 62, on window splays, C. *VII*. Inscr. recording erection of tablet and 2 chancel windows by friends and parishioners in mem. of Rev. Charles Henry Maturin, M.A., vicar and rector of Harbridge for 16 years [1845-1862], **1862**, [aged 62], mur., on marble, S.A. *VIII*. Inscr. in Lat. Ann Mary, eld. dau. of Henry Tremenheere Johns and [w.] Anne Eliza, w. of Herbert Lucas, 1847-**1868**, on window splay, C. *IX & X*. Two inscrs. on scroll-shaped pl. [Rev.] Richard Holmes Tuck, M.A., vicar [1862-1868], **1868**, on window splays, C. *XI*. Inscr. in Lat. recording [chancel] window pos. by husband in mem. of Anne Eliza, w. of Henry Tremenheere Johns, 1824-**1870**, on window splay, C. *XII*. Inscr. recording [erection] of [south] chancel window by public subscription in mem. of Stephen Street, churchwarden for 33 years, **1877**, aged 76, on window splay, C. *XIII*. Inscr. Harcourt Sumner Campbell, died at Fort St. George, Madras, [India], 1872, aged 6, and Gordon Harry, died at Wimborne, [Dorset], **1878**, aged 10, sons of Lt.-Col. Thomas Dyer, Madras Staff Corps, and w. Ellen, on window splay, C. *XIV*. Inscr. recording presentation of reredos by friends and parishioners in mem. of [Rev. Canon] George Williams, B.D., senior fellow of King's Coll., Camb., hon. canon of Winchester Cathedral, author of *The Holy City*, vicar of Ringwood and Harbridge for 9 years, "HE · WILL · LONG · BE · REMEMBERED · FOR · HIS · EMINENT · PERSONAL · HOLINESS, · HIS · DEEP · THEOLOGICAL · LEARNING, · HIS · STRENUOUS · EFFORTS · TO · PROMOTE · THE · RE-UNION · OF · CHRISTENDOM · AND · HIS · TENDER · LOVE ·

FOR · THE · SOULS · COMMITTED · TO · HIS · CHARGE", born at Eton, died at Harbridge, 1814-**1878**, mur., on marble, N. *XV*. Inscr. Elizabeth, w. of John Clark Holliday, organist for 18 years, **1881**, aged 44, on window splay, C. *XVI*. Inscr. [Col.] Thomas Dyer, Deputy-Adjutant General Madras Army, [1831-]**1882**, on window splay, C. *XVII*. Inscr. recording chancel window pos. by brother officers and friends in Madas in mem. "OF · THE · COMPANION · WHOSE · DEATH · FROM · AN · ACCIDENT · THEY · DEEPLY · DEPLORE", Col. Thomas Dyer, Deputy-Adjutant General Madras Army, born at Ringwood, died at Madras, [India], 1831-**1882**, mur., on marble, N. *XVIII*. Inscr. recording erection of [north chancel] window by friends in mem. of Samuel Sumner Dyer, M.D., "THE BELOVED PHYSICIAN", **1885**, on window splay, C. *XIX*. Inscr. with verse. Samuel Sumner Dyer, M.D., churchwarden for 14½ years, [**1885**], pos. by friends; "TO FURTHER PERPETUATE HIS MEMORY A SUM OF MONEY WAS SUBSCRIBED TO FORM A FUND IN THE HANDS OF TRUSTEES: FOR THE ASSISTANCE AND MAINTENANCE OF PERSONS IN THE PARISHES OF RINGWOOD UNION: REQUIRING THE BENEFIT OF HOSPITALS AFFORDING TREATMENT IN SPECIAL CASES", mur., on marble, S.C./S.Tr. *XX*. Inscr. recording erection of font by parishioners and dedication in **1885** in mem. of [Rev.] William Frederick Witts, M.A., fellow of King's Coll., Camb., vicar for 6 years [1878-1884], on font plinth, N. *XXI*. Inscr. Mary Jane Gosse, dau. of William Hamper, F.S.A. and w. Jane, 1878; also yst. dau., Lydia Anna Dawson, **1889**, on window splay, C. *XXII & XXIII*. Two inscrs. in Lat. recording [choir stalls] pos. by W.D.B. and [w.] K.E.B. in mem. of parents, S.R., 1885; C.A.R., 1895; W.P.B., 1900; and E.B., **1901**, on choir stalls, C. *XXIV*. Inscr. recording restoration [of font] in **1903** in mem. of Ellen Mary, widow [of Rev. William Frederick Witts, M.A.], on font plinth with no.*XX*, N. *XXV*. Inscr. [Cpl.] Robert [Gundry] Hodges, [202876, 2nd/4th Battn. Hampshire Regt., son of George Hodges and w. Eliza, of Ash, Somerset], par. worker for 16 years, husband and father, killed in France, **1918**, aged 38, pos. by w., Ellen Lyne, mur., S.C./S.Tr. *XXVI*. Inscr. recording presentation of altar in **1927** by daus. in mem. of Charles Farnell Brown and w. Alice, on altar, N. *XXVII*. Inscr. Ellen, widow of Col. Thomas Dyer, died at Hayling Island, **1933**, [aged 91], on window splay with no.*XVI*, C. *XVIII*. Inscr. recording presentation [of churchwardens' wand] in **1945** by Frank [Wyatt] Pilbrow [and w. Mabel Agnes] in mem. of only dau., Nancy, 1933, aged 4, on churchwardens' wand, N. *XXIX*. Inscr. recording presentation [of churchwardens' wand] in **1945** by Frank [Wyatt] Pilbrow [and w. Mabel Agnes] in mem. of eld. son, [Aircraftsmen 2nd Class] Keith Wyatt [Pilbrow, 1896653], R.A.F.[V.R., killed] on active service, 1944, aged 18, [buried in Ringwood Cemetery], on churchwardens' wand, N. *XXX*. Inscr. Margaret Edith Green, infant Sunday school superintendent 1933-**1948**, on cross, N. *XXXI*. Inscr. recording presentation [of prie-dieu] by family and friends in mem. of G. Norman Meachen, M.D.,(Lond.), organist 1941-1955, **1955**, on prie-dieu, S.C. *XXXII*. Inscr. recording presentation [of prie-dieu] by family in mem. of Eleanor Broomfield, 1879-**1964**, on bench front, S.C./S.Tr. *XXXIII*. Inscr. Frank Wyatt Pilbrow, clerk to Ringwood and Fordingbridge R.D.C., 1896-**1965**, on churchwardens' wand, N. *XXXIV*. Inscr. Florence Emily Green, 1884-**1971**, on cupboard, S.C. *XXXV*. Inscr. Henry Albert King, 1902-**1974**, on cabinet, N.Tr. *XXXVI*. Inscr. (Reggie) Heath, "A FRIEND OF RINGWOOD GUIDING", **1982**, on flowertrough, N. *XXXVII*. Inscr. Margaret Heath, M.B.E., district commissioner and president of Girl Guides, **1984**, on flowertrough, N. *XXXVIII*. Inscr. Marjorie Isabella King (née Coates), w. of no.*XXXV*, 1907-**1990**, on cabinet with no.*XXXV*, N.Tr. *XXXIX*. Inscr. recording dedication [of organ] in **1990** by Rev. John R[ichard] Turpin, M.A., vicar [1985-], on organ console, Crossing. *XL*. Inscr. recording gift of organ by w. and dau. in mem. of Pat Cross, accountant, ch. friend, engr. c.**1990**, on organ console with no.*XXXIX*, Crossing. *XLI*. Inscr. recording donation [of bench] in **1991** by Geoffrey Osborne Building Ltd., bronze, on bench, Churchyard. *XLII*. Inscr. recording gift of porch by Miss Olive Bursey, 1908-**1993**, in mem. of [parents], Walter Bursey, par. clerk

Ringwood I

and verger, 1877-1951, and [w.] Louisa, 1881-1967; also sister, Lilian, 1905-1988, mur., vestibule, S.A. *XLIII.* Inscr. with verse recording gift of [display] case in mem. of Jean Sharp, 1925-**1993**, on display case, N. *XLIV.* Inscr. Jean Sharp, 1925-**1993**, on bench, Churchyard. *XLV.* Inscr. recording donation of seat [in **1995**] by Normandy Veterans' Association to commem. 50 years "SINCE THE CESSATION OF HOSTILITIES IN EUROPE AND THE FAR EAST BETWEEN 1939 AND 1945", on bench, Churchyard. *XLVI.* Inscr. recording gift of books of remembrance in mem. of George Walter Carpenter, 1906-**1996**, on display case with no.*XLIII*, N. *XLVII.* Inscr. Rene Melton, **1998**, on bench, Churchyard. *XLVIII.* Inscr. Ada, w. and mother, 1924-**1999**, bronze, on bench, Churchyard.

INDENTS & LOST BRASSES. 49. Lost brass, civilian and w., kng., inscr. and 3 shs. Richard Line, founder of the Free School, mur., A.T., S.Tr. *Gent. Mag.*, II, p.1001.

Ref: *Antiquary*, XXI, p.193; *Beaumont*, p.90; *Bod. Lib. Gough Maps 223*, f.48; *Gent. Mag.*, 1807, II, p.1001; *Gent. Mag. Lib. Eng. Topog.*, p.98; *Gittings*, p.28; *Gough*, II, pt.2, p.49; *Haines*, II, p.73; *Hampshire History*, III, p.141; *Hampshire N. and Q.*, IV, pp.75-6; *Hants Proc.*, VII, pp.75-7; *M.B.S. Bulletin*, 65, p.96, 86, p.528, 93, p.676; *M.B.S. Trans.*, V, p.367, IX, p.116, X, p.10, XIII, p.211; *Mee, Hampshire*, p.288; *M.S.*, p.164; *Norris, Memorials*, p.62, p.66, p.85; *Simpson*, p.28; *Soc. Antiq. MS. 875/6*, pp.98-9, *MS. 1014/12*; *V.C.H., Hampshire*, IV, p.612.

Ch. built, 1853-5.

ROCKBOURNE, St. Andrew.

I. Inscr. P.J.C. R[adcliffe], 1891-**1893**, on lectern, N. *II.* Inscr. A.D.C., **1894**, mur., below window, Choir Vestry. *III.* Inscr. in raised letters on cross-shaped pl. Theresa Jane Furse, 4th dau. of Rev. William Johnson Yonge, [M.A., rector 1824-1875], 1833-**1900**, bronze, Churchyard. *IV.* Inscr. recording presentation of tower clock face by Marjorie Hawkins in mem. of husband, Lt.-Col. Brian Hawkins, O.B.E., Royal Berkshire Regt., churchwarden 1956[-1960], **1960**, bronze, mur., S.A. *V.* Inscr. with verse recording gift of choir and vestment furnishings in mem. of Jessie Milroy Martin, 1903-**1965**; in 2006 loose in Choir Vestry. Inscr. 51 x 114 mm. *VI.* Inscr. Minnie Barnett Parker, 1898-**1969**, on credence table, C. *VII.* Inscr. Sir William Radcliffe van Straubenzee, M.B.E., [great-great-grandson of no.*III*], "*A Faithful Servant of Church and State*", 1924-**1999**, on display case, N.

INDENTS & LOST BRASSES. 8. Lost indent, 4 frags. with civilian and w., inscr. and 4 shs., c.1500; formerly on A.T., now N.C. Recorded by Cave (1908) but not found (2006). Effs. c.530 mm, inscr. ? x 495 mm, shs. 125 x 100 mm, slab 1830-2135 x 950 mm.

Ref: *M.B.S. Trans.*, V, p.368; *Soc. Antiq. MS. 875/6*, pp.100-1.

ROMSEY, Abbey Church of SS. Mary and Ethelflaeda.

I. Inscr. John Hayward. "SOMTIME MAYOR OF THIS TOWNE", **1619**, aged 58, mur., C. Inscr. 244 x 418 mm.

Ringwood I *after Gent. Mag.*

Ringwood 49 *after Gent. Mag.*

HERE LYETH Ẏ BODY OF IOHN HAYWARD · SOMTIME MAYOR OF THIS TOWNE: WHO TRVSTED IN CHRIST IESVS FOR Ẏ REDEMTION OF HIS SOVLE: HEE DIED Ẏ 13ᵀᴴ OF NOVEMBER · 1619 · ÆTATIS SVÆ · 58 ·

Romsey, Abbey I

II. Inscr. with verse recording dedication of [south aisle] window in mem. of Caroline Maria, yst. dau. of Hon. and Rev. [Canon] Gerard T[homas] Noel, [M.A.], vicar [1841-1849], engr. c.**1845**, mur., S.A. of N. *III*. Inscr. with verse. Charlotte Christiana, 3rd dau. of Hon. and Rev. [Canon] Gerard Thomas Noel, M.A., [vicar 1841-1849; mar. 1832], Rev. James Drummond Money, rector of Sternfield, Suff., by whom 11 children, [died] at Romsey, **1848**, mur., Chapel of St. Anne/S.A. of C. *IV*. Inscr. William Footner, **1851**, aged 88, and w. Charlotte, **1844**, aged 79; also dau., Elizabeth, **1807**, aged 9, [buried] in vault [beneath south aisle], mur., in stone frame, S.A. of N. *V*. Inscr. with verse recording that [south] "CHAPEL WAS FITTED UP FOR DIVINE SERVICE" in **1855** by Susan, widow [and 2nd w.] of Hon. and Rev. [Canon] Gerard T[homas] Noel, M.A., vicar [1841-1849; Rev.] C[harles] Avery Moore, vicar [1855-1860]; W[illia]m Jenvy and J. Perry, churchwardens, mur., Chapel of St. Anne/S.A. of C. *VI*. Inscr. with verse. Charlotte Sophia, dau. of Sir Lucius O'Brien, Bart., 1st w. of Hon. and Rev. Gerard T[homas] Noel, M.A., by whom 3 sons, who died in infancy, and 6 daus., **1838**, [buried] (1) in Winchester Cathedral, (2) with husband in the south [aisle], pos. by surviving daus., engr. c.**1855**, mur., in stone frame, N.A. of N. *VII*. Inscr. with verse. Hon. and Rev. [Canon] Gerard T[homas] Noel, M.A., vicar for 10 years [1841-1849, hon.] canon of Winchester Cathedral, 2nd son of Sir Gerard [Noel] Noel, [2nd] Bart., and [1st] w. [Diana], Baroness Barham, [only child of Sir Charles Middleton, 1st Bart., 1st Baron Barham], 1782-1851, buried in the south [aisle], pos. by widow, [2nd w.] Susan, [dau. of Sir John Kennaway, Bart.], engr. c.**1855**, mur., in stone frame, S.A. of N. *VIII*. Inscr. on quadrilobe-shaped pl. Job Fifield, of Standbridge, **1840**, aged 73, and w. Mary, **1839**, aged 64; also son, Job Fifield, [junior], **1858**, aged 51, maker's name GAWTHORP S^c LONDON, mur., on board, Chapel of St. Ethelflaeda/Retrochoir. *IX*. Inscr. Robert George Linzee, of Jermyns, **1889**, aged 69, pos. in **1891** by widow and family, maker's name FRANK HIGHMAN, SALISBURY, on pulpit plinth, N. *X*. Inscr. [Dr.] M. Foster, D.D., **1896**, on frontal chest, N.Tr. *XI*. Inscr. on scroll-shaped pl. recording gift towards organ restoration in mem. of Joseph Ellershaw and Fanny Pepper, engr. c.**1900,** on organ, Chapel of St. Lawrence/N.A. of C. *XII*. Inscr. with verse. Engineer-Officer Arthur Ward, "who died in the brave fulfilment of his duty in the foundering of" S.S Titanic, **1912**, pos. by friends and townsmen, mur., on board, N.A. of N. *XIII*. Inscr. with verse in raised letters with sh. and regt. insignia in relief. 2nd-Lt. Charles Townsend Cobbold, 27th Battery, [32nd Brigade], R[oyal] F[ield] A[rtillery], yst. son of A[ugustus] Hills Cobbold and only son of [w.] Ellen, of Brownhill House, Nursling, [killed] in action near Les Boufs, France, **1916**, aged 23, copper, mur., on board, Chapel of St. Mary/Retrochoir. *XIV*. Inscr. with verse. Joseph (Joe) Hassall, 2nd son of Joseph Hassall and w. Mary Wall, born at Klerksdorp, S[outh] Africa, died at La Paz, Bolivia, South America, 1903-**1929**, on chest, Chapel of St. Lawrence/N.A. of C. *XV*. Inscr. recording gift of cupboard by daus., Eva and Ada Drew, in mem. of Frank Frederick Drew, churchwarden, **1932**, on cupboard, N.A. *XVI*. Inscr. recording thank offering in **1935** by S.E.P.W. and J.M.W., on B.V. Mary and Child, C. *XVII*. Inscr. recording gift of notice board by w. and family in mem. of [Pte.] Clifford Stanley Upson, [14353069, 2nd Battn. Dorsetshire Regt.], killed in action in Burma, **1944**, [aged 31, buried at Kohima War Cemetery, India], on notice board, S.A. of N. *XVIII*. Inscr. W.R. Chandler, 1883-**1954**, on pulpit plinth, N. *XIX*. Inscr. Ernest Hall and [w.] Lilian, engr. c.**1955**, on bench front, N.Tr. *XX*. Inscr. in raised letters [recording presentation of] flag of the Supreme Allied Commander of South-East Asia flown in Singapore in 1945 by Admiral the Lord Louis Mountbatten, [G.C.V.O., C.B., D.S.O.], later Admiral of the Fleet [1st] Earl Mountbatten of Burma, [1900-1979], engr. c.**1970**, mur., on Board, N. *XXI*. Inscr. in raised letters [recording presentation of] flag of the Viceroy of India flown in Delhi in 1947 by His Excellency Rear-Admiral the Viscount Mountbatten of Burma, [K.G., G.C.S.I., G.C.I.E., G.C.V.O., K.C.B., D.S.O., P.C.], later Admiral of the Fleet [1st] Earl Mountbatten of Burma,

[1900-1979], engr. c.**1970**, mur., on Board, N. *XXII.* Inscr. Nicholas [Timothy Charles] Knatchbull, [4th son of Sir John Ulick Knatchbull, 16th Bart., 7th Baron Brabourne, 1964-1979], and Doreen [Geraldine Browne, C.I., D.St.J.], Lady Brabourne, [3rd dau. of George Ulick Browne, 6th Marquess of Sligo, F.S.A., F.Z.S., F.R.G.S., w. of Sir Michael Herbert Rudolf Knatchbull, 15th Bart., 5th Baron Brabourne, G.C.S.I., G.C.I.E., M.C., J.P., 1979], aged 83, died with Lord Mountbatten, [Admiral of the Fleet Louis Francis Albert Victor Nicholas Mountbatten, 1st Earl Mountbatten of Burma, K.G., G.C.B., O.M., G.C.S.I., G.C.I.E., G.C.V.O., D.S.O., P.C., 1900-]**1979**, on family pew, C. *XXIII.* Inscr. recording gift [of prie-dieu] by Dorothy A. Clapp in mem. of [Rev.] Walter Edward Morris, engr. c.**1980**, on prie-dieu, Chapel of St. Anne/S.A. of C. *XXIV.* Inscr. Capt. Cecil Edward (Hatch) Hatchley, master mariner, 1902-**1982**, on offertory box/table, S.A. of N. *XXV.* Inscr. George Edward Goulding, chorister and deputy-organist, 1902-**1983**, copper, Chapel of St. Lawrence/N.A. of C. *XVI.* Inscr. Douglas Athersuch and [w.] Nellie, engr. c.**1985**, on chair, Chapel of St. Anne/S.A. of C. *XXVII.* Inscr. Doris Chandler, engr. c.**1985**, on chair, Chapel of St. Annc/S.A. of C. *XXVIII.* Inscr. Gladys Hilda Dark, engr. c.**1985**, on chair, Chapel of St. Anne/S.A. of C. *XXIX.* Inscr. Mr. and Mrs. H. Darke, engr. c.**1985**, on chair, Chapel of St. Anne/S.A. of C. *XXX.* Inscr. Margery Deare, engr. c.**1985**, on chair, Chapel of St. Anne/S.A. of C. *XXXI.* Inscr. Clayton Drew, engr. c.**1985**, on chair, Chapel of St. Anne/S.A. of C. *XXXII.* Inscr. Dorothy Gay, engr. c.**1985**, on chair, Chapel of St. Anne/S.A. of C. *XXXIII.* Inscr. E. Gay, engr. c.**1985**, on chair, Chapel of St. Anne/S.A. of C. *XXXIV.* Inscr. Frank Edward Gay, engr. c.**1985**, on chair, Chapel of St. Anne/S.A. of C. *XXXV.* Inscr. G. Gay, engr. c.**1985**, on chair, Chapel of St. Anne/S.A. of C. *XXXVI.* Inscr. Walter Lionel Gay, engr. c.**1985**, on chair, Chapel of St. Anne/S.A. of C. *XXXVII.* Inscr. W.R. Gilks, engr. c.**1985**, on chair, Chapel of St. Anne/S.A. of C. *XXXVIII.* Inscr. R. Gunner, engr. c.**1985**, on chair, Chapel of St. Anne/S.A. of C. *XXXIX.* Inscr. Alice C. Hayward, engr. c.**1985**, on chair, Chapel of St. Anne/S.A. of C. *XL.* Inscr. M.H.W. Hayward, engr. c.**1985**, on chair, Chapel of St. Anne/S.A. of C. *XLI.* Inscr. W.E. and E.M. Herbert, engr. c.**1985**, on chair, Chapel of St. Anne/S.A. of C. *XLII.* Inscr. F.R. Iliff, engr. c.**1985**, on chair, Chapel of St. Anne/S.A. of C. *XLIII.* Inscr. A.H. and M.M. Johnston, engr. c.**1985**, on chair, Chapel of St. Anne/S.A. of C. *XLIV.* Inscr. L.L. Kelsey, engr. c.**1985**, on chair, Chapel of St. Anne/S.A. of C. *XLV.* Inscr. W. Lehmann, engr. c.**1985**, on chair, Chapel of St. Anne/S.A. of C. *XLVI.* Inscr. H.G. Mackrell, engr. c.**1985**, on chair, Chapel of St. Anne/S.A. of C. *XLVII.* Inscr. E.C. Osborne, engr. c.**1985**, on chair, Chapel of St. Anne/S.A. of C. *XLVIII.* Inscr. Bill Radclyffe, engr. c.**1985**, on chair, Chapel of St. Anne/S.A. of C. *XLIX.* Inscr. R.A. Radclyffe, engr. c.**1985**, on chair, Chapel of St. Anne/S.A. of C. *L.* Inscr. E. Sales, engr. c.**1985**, on chair, Chapel of St. Anne/S.A. of C. *LI & LII.* Two inscrs. Merle Sauage, engr. c.**1985**, on chairs, Chapel of St. Anne/S.A. of C. *LIII.* Inscr. A.C. Taylor, engr. c.**1985**, on chair, Chapel of St. Anne/S.A. of C. *LIV.* Inscr. M.A. Upson, engr. c.**1985**, on chair, Chapel of St. Anne/S.A. of C. *LV.* Inscr. W. Upson, engr. c.**1985**, on chair, Chapel of St. Anne/S.A. of C. *LVI.* Inscr. Bernard Wiggins, engr. c.**1985**, on chair, Chapel of St. Anne/S.A. of C. *LVII.* Inscr. recording gift of cross and candlesticks by w. in mem. of Gerald Cairncross, server, 1928-**1986**, mur., on board, Chapel of St. Ethelflaeda/Retrochoir.

INDENTS & LOST BRASSES. 58. Indent, ?nun or lady, inscr., 15th cent., nearly effaced, N.A. of N./N. *Sadler, Dorset and Hampshire*, pt.II, p.21 (drg.). Eff. 470 x c.250 mm, inscr. 75 x 620 mm, Purbeck slab 1140 remains x 1020 mm. 59. Indent, abbess, in mantle with crosier, inscr. (chamfer) and 4 roundels, c.1510, A.T., Chapel of St. Mary/Retrochoir; 4 shs. (3 shs. a modern restoration), mur., in stone panels of A.T., lost. Possibly Joyce Rowse, abbess 1502-1515. *Sadler, Dorset and Hampshire,* appx. I, pt.2, p.29 (drg.). Eff. 870 x 295 mm, inscr. (chamfer) 2075 x 895 x 35 mm, roundels 115 mm dia., Purbeck coverstone 2105 x 920 mm;

Romsey, Abbey 59

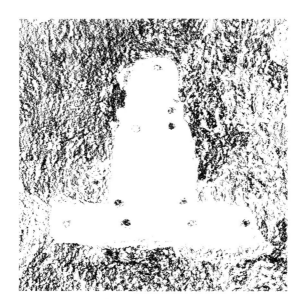

Romsey, Abbey 58

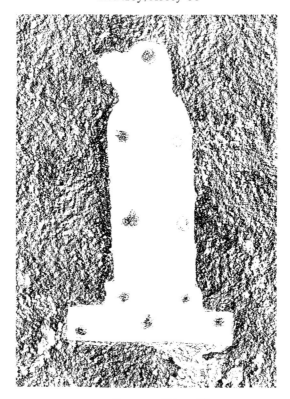

Romsey, Abbey 60

north panel: sh. mur. indent 170 x 140 mm; west panel: dext. sh. mur. 168 x 141 mm, centre sh. mur. 168 x 138 mm, sin. sh. mur. 168 x 139 mm. Style: London G. 60. Indent, abbess, in mantle with crosier, inscr., c.1520, N.A. of N. Possibly Anne Westbrook, abbess 1515-1523. *Sadler, Dorset and Hampshire*, pt.II, p.20 (drg.). Eff. 660 x 230 mm, inscr. 75 x 400 mm, Purbeck slab 2170 x 1075 mm. Style: London ?F. 61. Indent, inscr., N.Tr. Inscr. 80 x 500 mm, Purbeck slab 340-470 remains x 850-860 mm remains. 62. Indent, inscr., Chapel of St. Lawrence/N.A. of C. Inscr. 65 x 340 mm, Purbeck slab 2005 x 695 mm visible.

Ref: *Burke's Peerage and Baronetage*, p.333, pp.1062-3, p.2467; *M.B.S. Trans.*, V, pp.368-9; *M.S.*, p.164; *Sadler, Dorset and Hampshire*, pt.II, pp.20-1, p.38, appx. I, pt.2, p.28.

ROWNER, St. Mary the Virgin.

I. Inscr. with verse. Sarah, w. of William Poore, of Brockhurst, **1769**, aged 65; formerly mur., N., now mur., S.A. Inscr. 458 x 358 mm. *II*. Inscr. with fig. of time, setting sun, cherub and cherub's heads in relief. John Castleman, of Bridgmerry, friend, husband and father, **1778**, aged 62, mur., in marble frame, S.A. Inscr. 506 x 307 mm. *III*. Inscr. Katie, w. of Col. R[owland] H[ill] Martin, [C.B., C.M.G., C.I.E.], 21st Hussars, of Fleetlands, died at Secunderabad, India, **1895**, mur., below window, S.A. *IV*. Inscr. with verse recording erection of lychgate by friends and parishioners in mem. of [Rev.] Edward Shapland Prideaux-Brune, M.A., [2nd son of Charles Prideaux-Brune and w. Ellen], rector 1884-1919, [born at Padstow, Cornwall, 1853-**1928**], copper, on lychgate, Churchyard. *V*. Inscr. recording presentation [of piano] by sisters, Margaret and Mabel, in mem. of Lt.-Col. Hugh Worthington, R.M.A., engr. c.**1930**, bronze, on piano, N. *VI*. Inscr. [Rev.] Francis Neville Davis, [M.A., F.S.A., F.R.Hist.S., rector 1919-1937, editor of the *Proceedings of the Hampshire Field Club* 1928-1938], **1954**, bronze, mur., S.A. *VII*. Inscr. Sophie Westrope Barker, grandmother, 1888-**1972**, on votive stand, N. *VIII*. Inscr. recording dedication of garden in **1977** to commem. silver jubilee of Queen Elizabeth II, bronze, on bench, Garden. *IX*. Inscr. A[dah] L[ouisa] A[nne] P[rideaux]-B[rune, 1947], pos. in **1977** by [husband, Sir] H[umphrey] I[ngelram] P[rideaux]-B[rune, K.B.E., C.M.G., 1886-1979], bronze, on bench, Churchyard. *X*. Inscr. H[ugh] T[reverbyn] P[rideaux]-B[rune], pos. in **1977** by [brother, Sir] H[umphrey] I[ngelram] P[rideaux]-B[rune, K.B.E., C.M.G., 1886-1979], bronze, on bench, Garden. *XI*. Inscr. Jack Brindley, 1900-**1983**, and [w.] Louise, 1901-1981, on display case, S.A. *XII*. Inscr. Edward William Gascoigne, 1930-**1993**, on grave marker, Churchyard. *XIII*. Inscr. with verse. Marcus [John] Juniper, [son, brother and] friend, [1982-**1997**], pos. by Year 11 Bridgemary Community School, bronze, on bench, Churchyard. *XIV*. Inscr. Eileen McFarlane, mother, 1941-**1997**, on bench, Churchyard. *XV*. Inscr. recording dedication [of bench] by John's boys in mem. of uncle, Philip Hurdle, 1920-**1999**, on bench, Churchyard. *XVI*. Inscr. recording restoration of lychgate in **1999** by donations from Rowner Masonic Lodge and Provincial Grand Lodge of Hampshire and Isle of Wight, copper, on lychgate with no.*IV*, Churchyard. *XVII*. Inscr. on oval-shaped pl. recording gift [of chair] in mem. of Roy V. Thompson, 1942-**2000**, on chair, N. *XVIII*. Inscr. with verse. Frank Kellett, 1914-2004, and [w.] Marjorie, 1915-**2004**, on wooden cross, Churchyard. *XIX*. Inscr. Joy A.M. Thompson, [w. of no.*XVII*], 1941-**2004**, on chair, N. *XX*. Inscr. Thomas Parsonage, 1934-**2005**, on wooden cross, Churchyard.

Ref: *M.B.S. Trans.*, V, p.369; *Soc. Antiq. MS. 875/6*, p.101; *Who's Who*, 1967, p.2475.

Ch. originally nave and chancel with north aisle and north chapel; ch. restored in 1874 with north aisle widened to become a new nave, the old nave a south aisle and the old chancel an organ

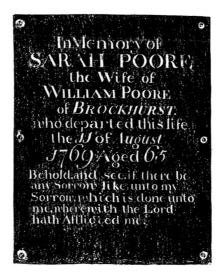

In Memory of
SARAH POORE
the Wife of
WILLIAM POORE
of *BROCKHURST*
who departed this life
the *11* of *August*
1769 Aged *65*

Behold and see if there be
any Sorrow like unto my
Sorrow which is done unto
me wherewith the Lord
hath Afflicted me.

Rowner *I*

In Memory of
M. John Castleman
of *BRIDGMERRY*
who Died Feb. 11. 1778
AGED 62
A loving Friend, a tender
Husband & a kind Father.

Rowner *II*

chamber (restored in 1950 as a south chapel); in 1965 a new extension was added to the west of the old ch. to create a nave with the old nave becoming an extended chancel; ch. destroyed by fire, 1990; rebuilt, 1992.

SHERBORNE, MONK, All Saints.

I. Inscr. with sh. (mutil.). William Dobson, rector, **1653**, mur., on board, N. Inscr. 321 x 466 mm.

II. Inscr. Benefaction of Thomas Sympson, **1674**, mur., on board, N. Inscr. 305 x 436 mm.

III. Inscr. Lt.-Col. Bickerstaff, J.P. for Lancashire, 6th D[ragoon] G[uar]ds Carabineers, served in the Indian Mutiny [1857-1858], 1823-**1894**, maker's name HART · SON · PEARD · & · Cᵒ Lᴰ · LONDON, mur., on board, N. *IV.* Inscr. with verse. Blanche, w. of Major-Gen. Lukin, Royal Artillery, died at The Priory, **1908**, maker's name CULN GAWTHORP Sᶜ LONDON, mur., on board, N. *V.* Inscr. Lt.-Col. Lionel Trevor Goff, Royal Artillery, died at Queen's House, **1953**, aged 76, mur., on board, N. *VI.* Inscr. recording presentation [of chair] by friends of Mrs. Mary Bishop in recognition of 55 years service to the ch. 1926-**1981,** bronze, on chair, C. *VII.* Inscr. Charles [William] Pritchard, par. council chairman, churchwarden and treasurer, [1938-1993, pos. in] **1995**, bronze, on bench, Churchyard.

INDENTS & LOST BRASSES. 8. Indent, civilian and inscr., c.1520, nearly effaced, N.Porch. Eff. c.375 x c.115 mm, inscr. 75 x 385 mm, Purbeck slab 1435 x 650 mm.

Ref: *Heseltine, Heraldry*, p.37; *M.B.S. Trans.*, V, pp.370-1; *Mee, Hampshire*, p.233; *M.S.*, p.164; *Sadler, Dorset and Hampshire,* appx. I, pt.2, p.26; *Soc. Antiq. MS. 875/6*, pp.102-3; *V.C.H., Hampshire*, IV, p.234.

SHERBORNE ST. JOHN, St. Andrew.

I. Raulin Brocas, in civil dress, and his sister Margaret, c.**1385**, hf. eff. with Fr. inscr., mur., in recess, N.C. *Burrows*, opp. p.129; *Cameron*, I; *Haines*, p.134 (drg.); *M.B.S. Trans.*, VI, p.2, XVII, p.226; *Mee, Hampshire*, p.219 (drg. of male eff.); *Norris, Craft*, fig.168 (photo.); *Page-Phillips, Children*, fig.1 (effs.). Male eff. 174 x 149 mm, female eff. 172 x 139 mm, inscr. 75 x 427 mm, Purbeck slab 430 visible x 300 mm visible. Style: London C.

II. Bernard Brocas, esq., **1488**, in arm. with tabard, kng. to a cross now lost, below is a skeleton in shroud (mutil.), inscr., ach., 2 shs. (1 mutil.) and marg. inscr. in 8 Lat. vv. (mutil.); formerly N., now N.C. Recorded (marg. inscr. more complete) by Burrows (1886). *Burrows*, opp. p.164; *Cameron*, II; *Death in Towns*, pl.13.8, p.205; *M.B.S. Trans.*, VI, p.3; *Norris, Craft*, fig.240 (photo.). Male eff. 510 x 282 mm, shroud 141 x 610 mm, inscr. 44 x 507 mm, cross indent c.365 x c.200 mm, ach. 357 x 210 mm, upper dext. sh. 134 x 110 mm, upper sin. sh. 135 x 110 mm, marg. inscr. 1864 x 642 x 33 mm, Purbeck slab 2130 x 1200 mm. Style: London F.

III. John Brocas, esq., son and h. of William Brocas, esq., **1492**, in arm., and 2 ws., (1) Anne, dau. of Edward Longford, esq., with 2 sons and 3 daus., (2) Anne, dau. of John Rogers, esq., with 5 sons and 1 dau.; inscr. and ?4 shs. lost; N.C. Recorded (2 shs.) by George (1686) and (pt. of

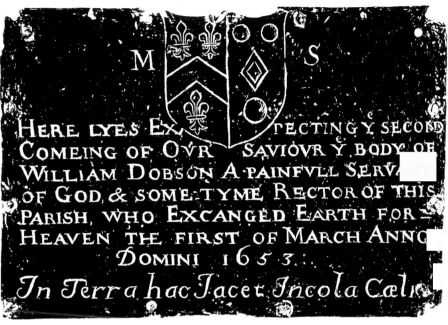

HERE LYES EX...PECTING Y SECOND
COMEING OF OVR SAVIOVR Y BODY OF
WILLIAM DOBSON A PAINFVLL SERVANT
OF GOD, & SOME-TYME RECTOR OF THIS
PARISH, WHO EXCANGED EARTH FOR
HEAVEN THE FIRST OF MARCH ANNO
DOMINI 1653.
In Terra hac Iacet Incola Cæli

Sherborne, Monk I

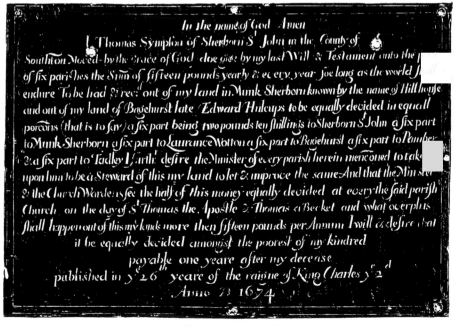

In the name of God Amen
I Thomas Symplon of Sherborn S.t John in the County of
Southton Moved by the Grace of God doe give by my last Will & Testament unto the
of six parishes the Sum of fifteen pounds yearly & every year soe long as the world shall
endure To be had & rec.t out of my land in Munk Sherborn known by the name of Hillhouse
and out of my land of Baghurst late Edward Hulcups to be equally decided in equall
porcons (that is to say) a six part being two pounds ten shillings to Sherborn S.t John a six part
to Munk Sherborn a six part to Laurance Wotton a six part to Baghurst a six part to Pamber
& a six part to Tadley Earth desire the Minister of every parish herein mencoṇed to take
upon him to be a Steward of this my land to let & improve the same And that the Minister
& the Church Wardens see the half of this money equally decided at every the said parish
Church on the day of S.t Thomas the Apostle & Thomas a Becket and what overplus
shall happen out of this my lands more then fifteen pounds per Annum I will & desire that
it be equally decided amongst the poorest of my kindred
payable one yeare after my decease
published in y.e 26.th yeare of the raigne of King Charles y.e 2.d
Anno D 1674

Sherborne, Monk II

Raulin broras ⁊ margarete la four gisount ici
Dru pour la grace d'lour almes eyt mci ame

Sherborne St. John I

Orate p ana Johis Brocas Arnng'i quodm filij et herebis Wilti Brocas Armigi
qui quom Uilms derelict london xxvj die Apuilis Anno Regni Rege Rici teren pmo
Et sepult' eir in eccha hofpitalis Sci Barthi in Smythfeld in Capella bte Marie
Et jdicti Johes obiit Sed die mapi A' dm mj° CCCC° lxxxxij A' Regni
Regis Henrici vij Septimo · Quorum Animabus Propicietur de' Amen

Sherborne St. John IV

264

Sherborne St. John II

265

Sherborne St. John III

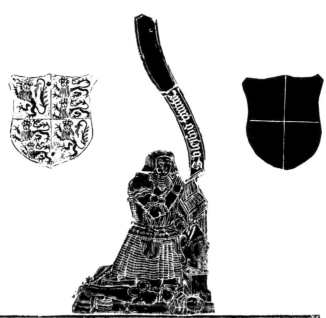

Sherborne St. John V

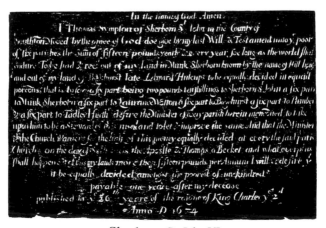

Sherborne St. John VI

inscr.) by Burrows (1886). *Burrows*, opp. p.168; *Cameron*, III. Male eff. 522 x 185 mm, dext. female eff. 466 x 166 mm, sin. female eff. 481 x 125 mm, inscr. indent c.70 x c.590 mm, dext. children 165-172 x 210 mm, sin. children 175-178 x 148 mm, sh. indents effaced, Purbeck slab 1555 x 810 mm. Style: London D.

IV. John Brocas, esq. (son and h. of William Brocas, esq., who died in London in 1483, and was buried in the church of the hospital of St. Bartholomew, Smithfield, in the chapel of the B.V.M.), **1492**, in arm., kng., inscr., Trinity and 3 shs. (2 mutil. and another lost); 1 sh. stolen between 1992 and 2006; N.C. Recorded (complete) by Cave (1908), by Stuchfield (1978) and by Lack (1992). *Burrows*, opp. p.167; *Cameron*, IV; *M.B.S. Trans.*, VI, p.5. Eff. 310 x 234 mm, inscr. 120 x 536 mm, Trinity 162 x 98 mm, upper dext sh. 121 x 103 mm, upper sin. sh. 125 x 104 mm, lower dext. sh. indent 125 x 105 mm, lower sin. sh. 123 x 106 mm, Purbeck slab 480 remains x 815 mm remains. Style: London D. Rep. by H.K.C. (1973).

V. William Brocas, of Beaurepair, "buryed in this chapell", died 1506, in arm., kng.; he left 2 daus. and cohs., Anne, mar. and died s.p., and Edith, mar. to Rauff Pexsall, esq. (who pos.), by whom she had 2 sons, John (dec.), and Richard "yet living, sole heir to the said Edith", inscr., scroll and 2 shs., engr. c.**1535**; upper pt. of scroll and sin. sh. renewed; mur., in recess, N.C. Recorded (scroll complete and 1 sh. lost) by George (1686). *Burrows*, opp. p.172; *Cameron*, V; *Haines*, p.235 (drg. of shoulder piece). Eff. 230 x 193 mm, inscr. 175 x 450 mm, scroll 134 remains x 62 x 25 mm, renewed upper pt. of scroll 116 x 50 x 26 mm, dext. sh. 130 x 123 mm, renewed sin. sh. 134 x 115 mm, Purbeck slab 625 visible x 500 mm visible. Style: London G (Gyfford, script 1).

VI. Inscr. Benefaction of Thomas Sympson, **1674**, mur., in wooden frame, N. Inscr. 280 x 410 mm.

VII. Inscr. recording erection of [south-east nave] window by widow, Martha, in mem. of William Lyde Wiggett Chute, of The Vyne, **1879**, aged 79, mur., in stone frame below window, N. *VIII.* Inscr. in Lat. recording gift [of altar cross] in **1910** by H.M. S-B, on cross, N.A. *IX.* Inscr. Gertrude Carmela Bromhead, **1947**, pos. by Daphne, John and Peter, on prie-dieu, C. *X & XI.* Two inscrs. A.G.W., **1954**, on churchwardens wands, N. *XII.* Inscr. Victor Merryweather, chorister for 74 years, **1982**, on choir stall, C.

INDENTS & LOST BRASSES. 13. Indent, rivets only, effaced, Tower. Non-Purbeck slab 1820 x 795 mm.

Ref: *Burrows, M., Family of Brocas of Beaurepaire*, 1886; *Cameron, H.K., Brasses to the family of de Brocas in the church of Sherborne St John*, 1974; *Gawthorp*, p.95; *Haines*, I, p.56, p.93, p.139, p.164, p.166, p.169, p.213, p.235, II, p.73; *Hants Proc.*, VIII, p.187; *Heseltine, Heraldry*, p.37; *M.B.S. Bulletin*, 6, p.5, 62, p.45, 93, p.676; *M.B.S. Trans.*, II, p.86, III, p.117, VI, pp.1-8, VII, p.241, IX, p.357, X, p.332, XIII, p.221, XV, p.426, XVII, p.224, p.249; *Mee, Hampshire*, p.309; *M.S.*, p.164; *Norris, Memorials*, p.64, p.137, p.139, p.149, p.158, p.207; *Pevsner, Hampshire*, p.501; *Sadler, Dorset and Hampshire*, appx. I, pt.2, p.30; *Soc. Antiq. MS. 875/6*, pp.106-13, *MS. 1014/12*; *Squibb*, pp.228-9; *V.C.H., Hampshire*, IV, p.169.

SHERFIELD–ON–LODDON, St. Leonard.

I. Inscr. and ach. Edmund, 2nd son of Sir Edmund Molyneux, K.B., justice of the common bench, "QVI PER DECENNIVM FVIT A SECRETIS PRÆNOBILI VIRO HENRICO SIDNEIO HIBERNIÆ

PRÆFECTO SVMMO : ET WALLIÆ PRÆSIDI", born 1532, died [**1589**], date not filled in, "CVIVS ANIMÆ PROPICIETVR DEVS", mur., on marble, N. Inscr. 206 x 542 mm, ach. 316 x 275 mm, Petworth slab 620 x 620 mm.

II. Mary, elder dau. and coh. of Stephen Hadnoll, esq., w. of Francis Palmes "OF, FRANCIS, ON CORBET, Yᴱ HEIR", died in childbed, **1595**, aged 33, with 11 children, Guy, Margaret, Thomas Ellen, William, Ann (dec., buried at Ashwell, Rutland), Brian, Andrew, Stephen, Jane and Mary, all kng., rect. pl. with inscr. and 3 shs., mur., N. *M.B.S. Trans.*, VI, p.10. Rect. pl. 555 x 508 mm. Style: Johnson. See also Otley, Yorks. no.I.

III. Stephen Hadnall, esq., born in Salop, one of the privy chamber to Queen Mary, died at Launcelevye in 1590, in civil dress, kng.; mar. Margaret, dau. of Thomas Atkins, esq., had 2 daus. and cohs., Mary, mar. to Sir Frances Palmes, and Anne, mar. to Sir Hampden Poulett; his widow mar. Sir Richard Lewkenor, chief justice of Chester, and pos. in **1600**, inscr. and ach., mur., in Petworth marble frame, C. *M.B.S. Trans.*, VI, p.12. Eff. 350 x 199 mm, inscr. 255 x 521 mm, ach. 204 x 173 mm, Petworth frame 980 x 745 mm. Style: Johnson.

IV. Inscr. F.G. B[arker], 1866, and V.A. B[arker], **1867**, on font plinth, N. *V.* Inscr. recording presentation of organ in **1869** by George William Barker, of Stanlake Park, Berks., "AS A DYING TOKEN OF THE INTEREST HE FELT IN THE CHURCH AND PARISH" of which his brother, [Rev.] Alfred Gresley Barker, [M.A.], was rector [1863-1875], on organ, Organ Chamber. *VI.* Inscr. F.M. B[arker], 1873, and E.M.L. B[arker], **1878**, on font plinth with no.*IV*, N. *VII.* Inscr. A[rthur] P[rescott] B[arker], churchwarden 1936-1960, 1882-1973], 1883, and [Rev. Canon] J[ohn] B[ramston] B[arker], M.A., hon. canon of Winchester Cathedral, rector 1913-1925, 1969, aged 86], **1883**, on font plinth with nos.*IV & VI*, N. *VIII.* Inscr. L.A. B[arker], **1883**, maker's name COX & BUCKLEY LONDON, on font plinth with nos.*IV, VI & VII*, N. *IX.* Inscr. with verse. John Bramston Stane, of Buckfield, 1803-**1888**, pos. by sister, Maria Elizabeth Beckford, mur., Choir Vestry. *X.* [Rev.] William Pulleine Lysaght, [M.A.], rector 1875-**1890**, pos. by friends, rect. pl., canopy, cross, inscr. with verse in raised letters, Alpha-Omega symbols in roundels and separate inscr. in raised letters, C. Rect. pl. 910 x 610 mm, inscr. 78 x 615 mm. *XI.* Inscr. Leonard Arthur, born and baptised **1895**, on ewer, N. *XII.* Inscr. recording that pulpit was "ENRICHED" in **1897** in mem. of Fanny Tucker, 1840-1894, maker's name JONES & WILLIS, on pulpit, N. *XIII.* Inscr. with Lat. verse and R.F.C. insignia. Major Leonard Arthur Tilney, M.C., Officer of the Order of the Crown and Croix de Guerre, Belgium, Lt. [40th Sqdn.] Royal Horse Guards, Sqdn.-Cmdr. Royal Flying Corps, [son of Col. R.H. Tilney, D.S.O. and w. Daisy F.M.], killed in aerial action over enemy lines, **1918**, aged 22½, buried [at Cabaret-Rouge British Cemetery, Souchez], near Dourges, [France], grave 1314, on choir stall, C. *XIV.* Inscr. J.B. B[arker], **1921**, on cross, C. *XV.* Inscr. with verse. Agnes Barker, **1923**, pos. by family "TO MARK THE SPOT WHERE SHE WORSHIPPED FOR MANY YEARS", maker's name CULN J. WIPPELL & Cᵒ Lᵀᴰ, mur., N. *XVI.* Inscr. recording installation of electric belfry lighting by Sherfield-on-Loddon Branch of the [Royal] British Legion in mem. of Jim Ilsley, "WHO MET HIS DEATH ON HIS WAY TO RING FOR THE EVENING SERVICE", **1933**, [aged 50], mur., S.Porch/Tower. *XVII.* Inscr. commem. 850th anniversary [of the ch.] in **1967**; [Rev.] J[ohn] C[ripps] Brashaw, M.A., B.Sc., rector [1943-1970]; P.C.E. Sims and A.A. Bucknall, churchwardens, on sanctuary lamp, C. *XVIII.* Inscr. Herbert Humphreys Mundy, headmaster of Sherfield School 1927-1955, lay reader 1927-**1970**, on bookcase, N. *XIX.* Inscr. recording reordering of the sanctuary and dedication in **1982** by w. and children in mem. of Stanley Ivor George Tosswill, naval architect, churchwarden, 1925-1980, mur., on board, C. *XX.* Inscr. recording restoration of organ in **1989**

HIC IACET EDMVNDVS MOLYNEVX SECVNDVS FILIVS
EDMVNDI MOLYNEVX MILITIS BALNEI, FACTVS IN
CORONATIONE REGIS EDWARDI SEXTI: VNVS IVSTI
CIARIORV COMMVNIS BANCI: QVI PER DECENNIVM FVIT
A SECRETIS PRÆNOBILI VIRO HENRICO SIDNEIO
HIBERNIÆ PRÆFECTO SVMMO: ET WALLIÆ PRÆSIDI:
OBIIT DIE MENSIS ANNO DOMINI ET
NATVS ERAT ANNO DOMINI 1532: DIE 23 MENSIS
DECEMBRIS: CVIVS ANIMÆ PROPICIETVR DEVS:

Sherfield-on-Loddon I

NOT WSTANDING THROVGH
BEARINGE OF CHILDREN
SHE SHALBE SAVED,
&c. I. TINO. 2. CA.

MARY E. THELDER, COHEIRE, OF, STEPHEN, HADNOLL, ESQVIER
WAS, MARIED, TO, FRANCIS, PALMES, OF, FRANCIS, ON, CORBET, Y, HEIR
HE, BEGATT, ON, HER GVY, MARGARETT. THOMAS, AND ELLEN
WILLM, AN, BRIAN, ANDREW, STEPHEN, IANE, & MARY. IVST. A LEVE
AN, DIED, ATT, ASHWELL, IN, RVTLAND, & THEIR, BVRIED, LIETH
THE, REST, LIVE, BVT, MARY, ON, MARY, IN, CHIELDBED, DEPTETH
SHEE, DIED, THE, XXI, OF, MARCHE 1595
AND, IN, THE, XXXIII, YEARE, OF, HER, AGE
E. REGINÆ, 37

Sherfield-on-Loddon II

HERE LYETH THE BODY OF STEPHEN HADNALL ESQ BORNE
IN SHROPSHIRE WHO WAS OF THE PRIVIE CHAMBER TO THE
LATE QVEENE MARYE. HEE MARIED MARGARETT ATKINS
DAVGHTER OF THOMAS ATKINS ESQVIRE AND BY HER
HAD ISSVE TWO DAYGHTERS HIS HEIRES. VIZ MARY HIS
ELDEST DAVGHTER MARIED TO FRAVNCIS PALMES
KNIGHT ANNE HIS YOVNGER DAVGHTER MARIED TO HAMP
DEN POVLETT KNIGHT. AND DIED AT LAVNCELEVYE
THE FIRST DAY OF APRILL A° DÑI 1590. 32 ELIZ: RÑE
IN REMEMBRANCE WHEROF THIS MONVMENT IS SET
VP AT THE CHARGES OF MARGARET HIS SAID WIEFE
NOW WIFE TO Sᵗ RICHARD LEWKENOR KNIGHT CHIEFE
IVSTICE OF CHESTER A° DÑI 1600.

Sherfield-on-Loddon III

by J.W. Walker & Sons for Michael Abrams, organist, and family, in mem. of Ivy Lawrence, 1974, Marjorie Abrams, 1986, and Reg Lawrence, 1987, on organ with no.*V*, Organ Chamber. *XXI.* Inscr. James P. Daly, 1925-**1990**, bronze, on wooden cross, Churchyard. *XXII.* Inscr. Tom Doggart, 1915-**1992**, bronze, on wooden cross, Churchyard. *XXIII.* Inscr. Mary Jean Schmieder, 1927-**1996**, on wooden cross, Churchyard. *XXIV.* Inscr. Robert Charles Hewett, [father and grandfather], 1925-**1998**, bronze, on wooden cross, Churchyard. *XXV.* Inscr. recording installation of sound system and dedication in **1999** in mem. of George Willson, ch. member, 1926-1997, on sound system case, N. *XXVI.* Inscr. David (Dave) George Armstrong, son, brother and uncle, 1959-**2000**, bronze, on wooden cross, Churchyard.

Ref: *Brasses as Art and History*, p.56; *Heseltine, Heraldry*, pp.37-8; *M.B.S. Trans.*, VI, pp.9-13, IX, p.38; *Mee, Hampshire*, p.310; *M.S.*, p.165; *Soc. Antiq. MS. 875/6*, pp.114-7; *V.C.H., Hampshire*, IV, p.107.

Ch. essentially, 1866 and 1872.

SILCHESTER, St. Mary the Virgin.

I. Cross and inscr. Percy Barnard Cooper, Duke of Cambridge's Own Imperial Yeomanry, killed in action at Vlakfontein, South Africa, **1901**, aged 22, pos. by "FRIENDS AND COLLEAGUES WITH WHOM HE WAS ASSOCIATED IN READING, AS A MARK OF RESPECT AND HIGH APPRECIATION OF HIS GALLANTRY", maker's name *C. LOVEGROVE. READING*, mur., N. *II.* Inscr. recording that bench-ends were designed and carved by dau. and son-in-law, Ellen and Henry Sealy, in mem. of Mary, widow of Henry Newnham Davis, **1909**, maker's name *J. WIPPELL & C⁰ Lᵀᴰ EXETER & LONDON*, on pew, N. *III.* Inscr. recording presentation [of lectern] in **1927** by Mothers' Union members, on lectern, N. *IV.* Inscr. recording presentation [of prie-dieu] in **1927** by Mothers' Union members, on prie-dieu, N. *V.* Inscr. with verse. Eleanor, dau. of John Ramsden Armitage, J.P., w. of [Dr.] John Robertson, D.D., 1861-**1930**, copper, mur., N. *VI.* Inscr. Cicely Joan, w. of Thomas Hartley, 1889-**1965**, bronze, on bench, Churchyard. *VII & VIII.* Two inscrs. Henry Mahaffey, 1930-**1984**, on bookcases, N. *IX.* Inscr. recording presentation [of bench] in **1987** by Stephen [William Turner Gray] Goddard, [1908-1991], and [w.] Sybil [Winifred, 1914-1988], in mem. of Goddard family "WHO LOVED THIS CHURCH THROUGH MANY GENERATIONS", bronze, on bench, Churchyard. *X.* Inscr. Michael Gibson Crabtree, resident 1976-1990, 1941-**1992**, bronze, on bench, Churchyard. *XI.* Inscr. in raised letters. Arthur John Lovegrove, husband and father, 1972, engr. c.**2000**, bronze, on bench, Churchyard.

SOBERTON, SS. Peter and Paul.

I. Inscr. with ach. (coffin pl.). Elizabeth, [only dau. of Rev. Edward Turnour, of Stapleford Tawney, Essex], widow of [Sir] Thomas Lewis, **1754**, aged 82, mur., on board, S.Tr. Pl. 381 x 278 mm. *II.* Inscr. in Lat. Caroline Palmer, 1826-**1860**, mur., S.A. *III.* Inscr. recording restoration and re-opening of ch. in **1881** at a cost of "about" £1,800 mainly contributed by the public, mur., N.A. *IV.* Inscr. with enamelled ach. in relief. Charles Richard Pink, F.R.I.B.A., president of the Architectural Association 1885-1886, born in the par., died at Hyde, near Winchester, 1853-**1889**, pos. in the ch. "RESTORED UNDER HIS DIRECTION" by friends in the Architectural Association, London, mur., S.A. *V.* Inscr. with regt. insignia. Capt.

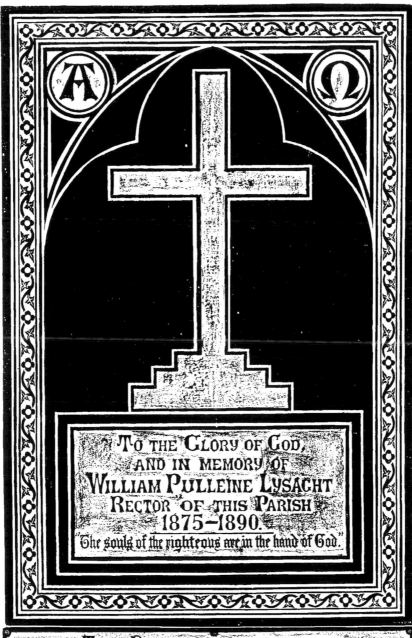

Sherfield-on-Loddon X

273

George Wheeler Morley, Royal Inniskilling Fusiliers, son of Lt.-Col. G.L. Morley, took part in the Tirah Campaign, Indian Frontier 1897-1898, the Natal Campaign 1899-1900, present at the Battles of Spion Kop, Vaal Krantz and Railway Hill, died at Mooi River Hospital, **1900**, [aged 27], maker's name A. & N. AUX C.S.L. LONDON, mur., C. *VI.* Inscr. Maria Dorothea, w. of Capt. John King, 59th Regt., **1901**, aged 81, mur., S.Tr. *VII.* Inscr. Frank Goodison, **1910**, on cross, C. *VIII.* Cross surmounting inscr. Mary Sophia Morley, par. worker for 35 years, **1913**, maker's name A. & N. AUX C.S.L. LONDON, mur., below no.*V*, C. *IX.* Inscr. within border of laurel leaves. Cpl. William Hugh Twynam, [16391], 7th Battn. Canadian [Infantry (British Columbia] Regt.), killed in action in France, 1915, [aged 33]; Staff-Sgt. John Twynam, [131, 1st] South African Mounted Rifles, killed by lightening at Windhoek while on duty, 1914, [buried at Barnea Siding Burial Ground, Bethlehem, South Africa]; Lt. Hugh Twynam, R.N.R., drowned in [H.M.] Submarine [E.36], **1917**, [aged 29]; Lt. Godfrey Twynam, 11th Battn. Border Regt., killed in action in France, 1916, [buried at Waggon Road Cemetery, Beaumont-Hamel]; Capt. Geoffrey Matthew George Culley, 11th Battn. [(Queen's Own)] Royal West Kent Regt., [son of Matthew T. Culley and w. Eleanor, of Coupland Castle, Northumberland], husband of Elizabeth Frances, [of Corscombe, Dorset], killed in action in France, 1916, [aged 33, buried at Bulls Road Cemetery, Flers]; sons and son-in-law of John Twynam and [w.] Mary [Rachel], of Soberton House, mur., on board, N. *X.* Inscr. recording erection of screen in **1938** by Soberton Towers School as a thank offering "FOR THE SPIRITUAL GUIDANCE GIVEN TO THE BOYS" by Rev. J[ohn] Godefroy, [M.A., vicar, 1920-1947], on screen, N. *XI.* Inscr. Brenda Ponton, 1920-**1992**, on missal stand, C. *XII.* Inscr. Brenda Ponton, 1920-**1992**, ?brass, on paschal candleholder, S.A. *XIII.* Inscr. Alfred [Hezekiah Bower, 1914-1997] and Jack Bower, [husband, father and grandfather, 1918-**1997**], bronze, on bench, Churchyard.

INDENTS & LOST BRASSES. 14. Indent, lady, kng., inscr., ?religious device and scroll, nearly effaced, cross in niche on dext. side, mur., A.T., S.Tr.; 3 shs., mur., in stone panels of A.T. Eff. c.340 x c.170 mm, inscr. 85 x c.405 mm, device effaced, scroll c.170 x c.215 x c.25 mm, cross 310 x 205 mm, dext. sh. 150 x 125 mm, centre sh. 150 x 125 mm, sin. sh. 145 x 120 mm, slab 765 x 1380 mm.

Ref: *Heseltine, Heraldry*, p.37; *M.B.S. Trans.*, VI, pp.13-4; *Soc. Antiq. MS. 875/6*, pp.117-8.

SOMBORNE, KING'S, SS. Peter and Paul.

I. Two civilians, c.**1385**; inscr. lost; rel., C. *Brit. Lib. Add. MS. 39987,* ff.16-7r; *Gent. Mag.*, 1858, ii, p.559 (dext. eff.); *Haines*, p.164 (drg. of dext. eff.); *Hewitt, Armour*, II, p.254 (dext. eff.); *Macklin, Br. of Eng.*, p.59; *M.B.S. Portfolio*, I, pt.6, pl.1; *Mee, Hampshire*, p.347 (drg. of dext. eff.); *Portfolio Book*, pl.57. Dext. eff. 736 x 205 mm, sin. eff. 726 x 198 mm, Purbeck slab 2710 x 1015 mm. Style: London B. Rep. by B.S.H.E. (1978).

II. Inscr. recording erection of pulpit by James Reeves in mem. of [w.] Sophia Sarah, **1882**, on pulpit, N. *III.* Inscr. with verse. Colour-Sgt. George Weston, Mounted Infantry, 2nd Battn. Hampshire Regt., died of wounds at Charles Town, South Africa, **1902**, maker's name *JONES & WILLIS*, mur., on board, C. *IV.* World War I memorial (21 names), **1919**, maker's name A & N C.S.L., bronze, mur., in stone frame, C. *V.* Inscr. recording addition of treble bell by public subscription in **1927**, mur., on board, Baptistry/N. *VI.* Inscr. recording illumination of tower clock by par. to commem. silver jubilee of George V, **1935**, mur., on board, Baptistry/N.

Somborne, King's I

VII. Inscr. Montague William [Edwards], 1854-1936, and Reginald Henry [Edwards, 1854-]**1945**, twin sons of Thomas Edwards and [w.] Sarah, of Compton Manor, on credence table, C. *VIII.* Inscr. recording restoration of organ in **1952** in mem. of Lt.-Col. Godfrey Christopher Firbank, M.C., Coldstream Guards, of Furze Down, died at Hoplands, 1947, "*HIS ASHES ARE SCATTERED ON THE ESTATE HE OWNED AND LOVED*", on organ, S.A. *IX.* Inscr. recording repair of organ in **1980** in mem. of Mollie Wells, 1912-1979, on organ with no.*VIII*, S.A. *X.* Inscr. Arthur Cummings, 1900-**1986**, on bench, Churchyard. *XI.* Inscr. Mary Jeffries, 1905-**1996**, on grave marker, Churchyard. *XII.* Inscr. Alfred John Richardson, 1926-**1996**, on grave marker, Churchyard. *XIII.* Inscr. recording restoration of east window (south panel) in **2000** by churchwardens and ws. to commem. [silver] wedding anniversaries; Andrew Johnson and [w.] Kathy and Derek Buckles and [w.] Jayne, mur., on board, C.

Ref: *Brit. Lib. Add. MS. 39987*, ff.16-7; *E. & S.*, p.29; *Haines*, I, pp.163-4, II, p.74; *M.B.S. Bulletin*, **93**, p.676; *M.B.S. Trans.*, VI, pp.14-5, VII, p.238, p.241, XVI, p.207; *Mee, Hampshire*, p.205; *M.S.*, p.165; *Norris, Memorials*, p.58; *Pevsner, Hampshire*, p.312; *Simpson*, p.28; *Soc. Antiq. MS. 875/6*, pp.118-9, *MS. 1014/12*; *V.C.H., Hampshire*, IV, p.479.

SOMBORNE, LITTLE, All Saints
(redundant, now vested in The Churches Conservation Trust).

INDENTS & LOST BRASSES. 1. Indent, inscr. Inscr. 60 x 410 mm, Purbeck slab 1650 x 650 mm.

Ch. declared redundant, 1974; vested, 1975.

SOUTHAMPTON, God's House or Hospital Chapel of St. Julian.

I. Priest, c.**1500**, in cope; head and inscr. lost; formerly loose on board in C., mur., on a board, N., now C. Eff. 842 remains x 309 mm, inscr. indent 165 x 400 mm, Purbeck slab 1930 x 885 mm. Style: London G.

II. Inscr. recording presentation [of chair] in **1887** by Mr. and Mrs. J.H. de Carteret, on chair, C.

Ref: *Haines*, II, p.74; *Hampton,* p.73; *M.B.S. Trans.*, VI, p.15; *M.S.*, p.165; *Soc. Antiq. MS. 875/6*, p.119.

SOUTHAMPTON, Holy Rood (redundant, now a ruin and Merchant Navy Memorial).

I. Inscr. recording restoration of "Quarter Jacks" and replacement of bells in **1897** by Sir Frederick Perkins, [Knt., J.P., D.L.], M.P. for Southampton [1874-1880], 5 times Chief Magistrate, in mem. of father, Richard Hopkins Perkins, resident in the par., ch. worshipper for more than 50 years; [Rev.] L[ancelot] White Atkins, [B.A.], vicar [1895-1900]; William W. Paul and David H. Corke, churchwardens, mur., on marble, Tower. *II.* Inscr. recording removal from orig. site in St. John's churchyard in **1958** of family tomb of Richard Taunton, mcht.-adventurer, benefactor, twice mayor, founder of Taunton's School [1760], 1684-1752, mur., south wall

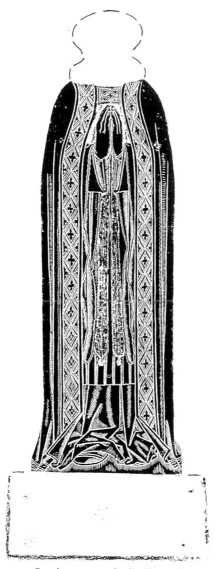

Southampton, God's House I

HERE LYETH THE BODYE OF AVERIN WALLOP THE WIFE OF
WILLM WALLOP ESQ. WHOSE BODYE HERE LYETH SHE LYVED
IN THE FEARE OF GOD A RELIGIOVS & VERTVOVS GENTLEWOMAN
AND SHE DYED IN THE TRVE FAITH OF IESVS CHRIST. THVRS
DAYE TH IX OF APRILL IN THE YEARE OF OVR LORD 1601
AND IN THE XLIII YEARE OF THE QVEENE ELIZABETH

Southampton, Holy Rood 4

outside, C. *III*. Inscr. "THE WATCH ASHORE HAS DEDICATED THIS CORNER GARDEN TO THE EVERLASTING MEMORY OF RELATIVES & FRIENDS WHO LOST THEIR LIVES AT SEA", engr. c.**1960**, bronze, mur., S.A.

INDENTS & LOST BRASSES. 4. *(Formerly M.S.I)*. Lost brass, inscr. Averin, w. of William Wallop, esq., 1601; purchased in 1926 by Rt. Rev. St. John Basil Wynne Wilson, Bishop of Bath and Wells 1921-1937, "for half-a-crown at a sale of antique furniture" of the late Dr. Fitzjames Molony, at Porlock, Somerset, subsequently identified by J. Challenor Smith, F.S.A. in 1927 and returned in 1928; mur., on stone, C. Illustration from rubbing in Soc. Antiq. coll. Rubbing in Soc. Antiq. coll. (n.d.). Inscr. 154 x 622 mm. Rep. by W.E.G. (c.1928).

Ref: *M.B.S. Trans.*, VII, p.41, p.247, p.297; *M.S.,* p.753; *Squibb*, p.216.

Ch. bombed, 1940.

SOUTHAMPTON, or PORTSWOOD, Christ Church.

I. Verse on base of stepped cross with evang. symbols and marg. inscr. with roundels at corners. Joshua Arthur Brandon, architect of the ch., [1822-]**1847**, pos. by friends, [maker's monogram WALLER], N.A. Cross 1910 x 756 mm, vv. 116 x 500 mm, marg. inscr. 2205 x 985 x 45 mm, roundels 135 mm dia., slab 2370 x 1160 mm. *II.* Inscr. with verse recording [south] window pos. [in **1848**] by [Rev.] T[homas] MacCalmont in mem. of 2 sisters, Elizabeth Anne MacCalmont, 1821-1840, and Margaret Jane MacCalmont, 1817-1848, [buried] at South Stoneham, mur., below window, S.C./Tower. *III.* Col. Eyre John Crabbe, commanded 74th (Highlanders) [Regt. of Foot] and served regt. for 39 years, Knt. of Hanoverian Guelphic Order, J.P. for Hants and Borough of Southampton, **1859**, aged 68 years, [buried] in the churchyard, rect. pl. crucifixion under single canopy, bust, inscr., verse, 3 enamelled shs. (1 with Hanoverian order suspended), 2 medals and battle honours (Toulouse, Orthes, Nive, Nivelle, Salamanca, Badajoz, Ciuad Rodrigo, Busaco), mur., on pillar, N. Rect pl. 1405 x 682 mm. *IV.* Harriet Louisa, [1st] w. of Col. Eyre John Crabbe, K.H., [J.P.], "Activated by her sincere piety and love to God she mainly assisted by large donations to the building and completing of this Church · Unobtrusive in her numerous charities to the poor kind and affectionate in all the relations of life, she died lamented as she lived beloved and respected", 1848, aged 60, lady on bracket, 4 enamelled shs. and marg. inscr. with roundels at corners, [maker's monogram WALLER], engr. **1878**, C. Eff. 1319 x 511 mm, bracket 306 x 566 mm, shs. 161 x 131 mm, marg. inscr. 1875 x 837 x 39 mm, roundels 98 mm dia., slab 1975 x 930 mm. *V.* Inscr. William Berrett, of Lea Hurst, Portswood Road, **1891**; bequeathed £500 to the churchwardens for the benefit of the poor, maker's name H. ROSE & SON. SOUTHAMPTON, mur., N.A. *VI.* Inscr. with verse in raised letters. Rev. [Preb.] Frederic Edward Wigram, [M.A.], prebendary of St. Paul's Cathedral [1881-1895], hon. secretary of the Church Missionary Society 1881-1895, [vicar] 1864-1880 "DURING WHICH TIME THE PRESENT CHANCEL WAS BUILT AND THE CHURCH ENLARGED", [died] at Hampstead, **1897**, [aged 62], maker's name HART, SON, PEARD & C⁰, LTD., LONDON, mur., N. *VII.* Inscr. with verse. Lt. Thomas Peere William Nesham, [38th Battery], Royal Field Artillery, only son of [Rear-]Admiral Nesham and w. Constance, "killed while Gallantly Serving his guns at Tweebosch", 1880-**1902**, on lectern, N.A. *VIII.* Inscr. with verse and 2 shs. Morris Miles, **1908**, [maker's name GARRET & HAYSOM *SOUTHAMPTON*], mur., on marble, S.C./Tower. *IX.* Inscr. Emily Georgina, widow of Rev. Thomas McCalmont, 1826-**1912**, pos. by children, maker's name

Southampton, or Portswood *I*

279

Southampton, or Portswood *III*

Southampton, or Portswood *IV*

H. ROSE & Co. SOUTHAMPTON, mur., on marble, N.A. *X.* Inscr. with regt. insignia. Lt. Guy Fitzgerald Wharton, 2nd Battn. Durham Light Infantry [attd. 1st Battn. King's Own Yorkshire Light Infantry, son of John Henry Turner Wharton and w. Edith], died of wounds at the 2nd Battle of Ypres, **1915**, aged 20, [buried at Brandhoek Military Cemetery, Belgium], mur., N. *XI.* Inscr. in Lat. recording gift [of altar cross] (made by W.G.H.) by H. and E.B. in **1918**; [Rev. Canon] R[obert] A[ndrew] M[itchell, M.A., hon. canon of Winchester Cathedral], vicar [1903-1920], on cross, C. *XII.* Inscr. with verse in raised letters and R.A.F. insignia in relief. Flight-Lt. Owen Cecil Chave, [82955, pilot, 15th Sqdn.], R.A.F.V.R., Bomber Command, [son of Sir Benjamin Chave, K.B.E.], killed in action, **1943**, aged 29, [buried at Heverlee War Cemetery, Belgium], mur., S.A. *XIII.* Inscr. Wilfrid Guy Kimber, **1946**, aged 46, bronze, mur., on board, W.Porch. *XIV.* Inscr. recording presentation [of credence table] in **1957** to Highfield Infant Sunday School in mem. of Joan Rowe (née Barnard), on credence table, N.A. *XV.* Inscr. with Knt. bachelor insignia on 2 pls. recording dedication of [west] porch in mem. of Sir Sidney Guy Kimber, Knt., hon. freeman of the Borough and mayor 1918-1920, [1873-]1949, and w. Helen Sarah, **1958**, bronze, mur., on board, W.Porch. *XVI.* Inscr. Florence Nellie Sheppard, 1892-**1964**, on umbrella stand, W.Porch. *XVII.* Inscr. Doris Brandon, 1900-**1975**, bronze, on bench, Churchyard. *XVIII.* Inscr. Herbert Collins, architect and "Worker for Peace", **1975**, on stall, N. *XIX.* Inscr. Capt. O.W. (Peter) Salisbury, engr. c.**1980**, on lectern, N.

Ref: *M.B.S. Bulletin*, 93, p.676; *Pevsner, Hampshire*, p.572; *Reader, E., Highfield Church, Southampton 1847-1994*, p.21, p.37, p.42; *Soc. Antiq. MS. 1014/12*.

Ch. built, 1846-7, 1855, 1878, 1915 and 1955.

SOUTHBOURNE, (see BOURNEMOUTH).

SOUTHSEA, (see PORTSMOUTH).

SOUTHWICK, St. James.

I. John White, esq., "fyrst Owner of yᵉ Priory & Manor of Suthwike aft[er] yᵉ Surrender & deptyng of yᵉ Chanons from yᵉ same", died 1567 (date added), in arm., and 1st w. Katherine, only dau. of William Pound of Drayton, esq., by Mary, dau. and coh. of Thomas Haynes of the Isle of Wight, esq., died **1548**, with 5 sons and 4 daus.; appropriated effs. of c.1520, 1 son (lost), 2 daus., 5 shs. and inscr. (chamfer) added in 1548 and palimp., on rev 2 shs., 1504, pt. of civilian, c.1500, pt. of 15th cent. inscr., pt. of shroud, c.1500, and frags. of 2 15th cent. effs.; A.T., N.C./C.; 8 shs. (6 lost; 1 sh. (sin. sh. of south panel) stolen between 1964 and 1969), mur., in stone panels of A.T. *Brit. Lib. Add. MS. 14296*, f.14 (drg. of 2 shs.); *Hants Proc.*, III, opp. p.85; *M.B.S. Trans.*, XV, p.170 (daus.), p.175 (details of inscr. (chamfer)), p.276, p.278 (photo. of tomb); *Palimpsests*, pl.49 (approp. effs., children with slab and rev. of sh.), pls.193-4 (rev.). Male eff. 485 x 167 mm, female eff. 482 x 163 mm, sons orig. 167-175 x 164 mm, now 165-175 x 200 mm, daus. 162-166 x 190 mm, dext. sh. 184 x 156 mm, sin. sh. 190 x 161 mm, inscr. (chamfer) orig. 2060 x 925 x 47 mm, now 2025 x 925 x 47 mm, Purbeck coverstone 2125 x 885 mm; north panel: dext. sh. mur. indent 185 x 155 mm, centre sh. mur. indent 185 x 155 mm, sin. sh. mur. indent 185 x 155 mm; south panel: dext. sh. mur. 186 x 157 mm, centre sh. mur. 190 x

167 mm, sin. sh. mur. indent 185 x 155 mm; east panel: sh. mur. indent 185 x 155 mm; west panel: sh. mur. indent 185 x 155 mm. Style: London F (appropriated effs.) and G (Fermer, script 6). Rep. by B.S.H.E. (1983 and 1985).

II. Inscr. (mutil.) (eff. and 2 shs. lost). Anne, dau. of Lewes Wyngfeld, esq., widow of Anthony Pound of Drayton, esq., 2nd w. of John White, esq., [1557]; palimp., on rev. section (broken in 2 along lower section of baselard) from below belt of civilian showing belt and baselard, c.1405; now mur., in marble frame, N.C./N.A.; facsimile of palimp., mur., on board, N.C./N.A.; orig. slab, mur., N.A. Recorded (inscr. complete with eff. and 2 shs. lost) by Pavey (1702). *Palimpsests*, pl.194 (rev.). Illustration (complete) from rubbing in Soc. Antiq. coll. Rubbing (complete) in Soc. Antiq. coll. (n.d.). Eff. 300 x 190 mm, inscr. orig. 150 x 525 mm, now 130 x 525 mm, dext. sh. c.230 x c.205 mm, sin. sh. c.230 x c.205 mm, Purbeck slab 1360 x 785 mm. Style: London G (script 6, obv.), London A (rev.). Rep. by B.S.H.E. (1983).

III. & IV. Two inscrs. "ECCLESIÆ DE SOUTHWICK IN COM: SOUTHTON RICARDUS . NORTON . PATRONUS D : D : D", engr. **early 17th cent.**, on candlesticks, C.

V. Inscr. with verse. Jeffery Darnley, son of Lt.-Col. Alex[ande]r [Borthwick] and Mrs. [Katherine] Borthwick, [dau. of Thomas Thistlethwayte and w. Elizabeth Catherine], died at Southwick, 1881-**1884**, maker's name *J. WIPPELL & C[O] L[TD] EXETER & LONDON*, mur., on board, N.C./N.A. *VI.* Inscr. with enamelled sh. and crest. Thomas Thistlethwayte, 1809-**1900**, and w. Elizabeth Catherine, dau. of Lt.-Gen. the Hon. Sir Hercules [Robert] Pakenham, K.C.B., 1823-1885, maker's name T. PRATT & SONS, LONDON, mur., on marble, C. See also Portsmouth, Royal Garrison Church no.*XIX.* *VII.* Inscr. "TO THE GLORY OF GOD ALL SAINTS MISSION G. & H.W. **1900**" on missal stand, Vestry. *VIII.* Inscr. with ach. on separate pl. Alexander Edward Thistlethwayte, eld. son of Thomas Thistlethwayte [and w. Elizabeth Catherine], 1854-**1915**, mur., on marble, C. *IX.* World War I memorial (14 names), mur., on marble, N.A. *X.* Capt. Arthur Henry Thistlethwayte, Grenadier Guards, 1857-1924; also brother, Robert Richard [Thistlethwayte], 1863-**1934**, [sons of no.*VI*], rect. pl., triple canopy, inscr. and ach. in semi-relief, mur., on stone, C. *XI.* World War II memorial (2 names), mur., on marble below no.*IX*, N.A. *XII.* Inscr. with verse. Lt. David Mudford, R.N., fighter pilot, [killed], **1950**, aged 23, copper, mur., on board, N.A. *XIII.* Inscr. Rear-Admiral Frederic Arthur Buckley, C.B., "HE LIVED FOR HIS COUNTRY HIS SERVICE AND HIS FRIENDS", 1952, pos. in **1953** by Southwick Ex-Services Men's Club, mur., on marble, N.A. *XIV.* Inscr. with Lat. verse and R.A.F. insignia. Flying-Officer Stanley Evelyn Crook, fighter pilot, 92nd Sqdn., R.A.F., [killed] over Middlesbrough Bay, **1958**, aged 22, mur., on board, N.A. *XV.* Inscr. Eva, w. of Rear-Admiral F[rederic] A[rthur] Buckley, [C.B.], born at Odense, Denmark, "HER GAY, COURAGEOUS, LOVING SPIRIT ENRICHED THE LIFE OF THIS VILLAGE FROM 1914 TO 1962", mother, 1890-**1962**, mur., on marble, N.A. *XVI.* Inscr. Arthur Sandilands Borthwick, [son of no.*V*], 1879-1968, and w. Vera [Janet, dau. of William Bethel-Hervey], 1886-**1977**, mur., on marble, C.

Ref: *Brasses as Art and History*, p.133; *Brit. Lib. Add. MS. 14296*, ff.14-5, *Add. MS. 39970*, f.58r, *Stowe MS. 845*, ff.124-5; *Burke's Peerage and Baronetage*, p.1648; *Haines*, II, p.74; *Hants Proc.*, III, pp.79-87, XXIV, p.75; *Heseltine, Heraldry*, p.38; *Manning*, p.31; *M.B.S. Bulletin*, 21, p.6, 93, p.676; *M.B.S. Trans.*, VI, pp.15-8, XIII, pp.453-4, XV, p.143, p.147, p.151, p.153, p.168, pp.170-3, p.177, p.275, pp.277-81, p.392, XVI, p.256; *Mee, Hampshire*, p.338; *M.S.*, p.165; *Palimpsests*, 139L1-21, p.49, p.xiii, p.xv, L448-1, p.xiii, p.xv; *Pevsner, Hampshire*, p.605; *Simpson*, p.28; *Soc. Antiq. MS. 875/6*, pp.119-22, *MS. 1014/12*; *V.C.H., Hampshire*, III, p.165.

Southwick I

Southwick I palimpsest reverse

Southwick II obverse and palimpsest reverse

285

SPARSHOLT, St. Stephen.

I. Rev. Edward Stewart, vicar 1842-1875, 1808-**1875**, rect. pl., canopy, cross, inscr., verse, sh. and crest, maker's name HART, SON, PEARD & CO. LONDON, mur., on marble, C. *II.* Inscr. on 2 pls. James Pern Fitt, of Westley, **1878**, aged 68, on pulpit, N. *III.* Inscr. David Cecil Bostock, 1909-**1926**, on font plinth, S.A. *IV.* Inscr. Eleanor Lewington, [engr. **1948**], on candleholder, C. *V.* Inscr. John Lewington, [engr. **1948**], on candleholder, C. *VI.* Inscr. recording renovation of organ and installation of 2 stops by family, friends and parishioners in mem. of Louisa Dyson Cobb, organist 1917-1968, [1896-**1969**], on organ, N.A. *VII.* Inscr. Alice Thackeray May, headmistress of Sparsholt Church of England School 1929-1963, P.C.C. secretary 1929-1969, 1896-**1969**, on prie-dieu, N. *VIII.* Inscr. recording refurbishment of gates in **2005** in mem. of Vera [May] Edwards, [2004, aged 81], on gate, Churchyard.

SPRINGBOURNE, (see BOURNEMOUTH).

STEVENTON, St. Nicholas.

I. Inscr. with verse recording [east] window pos. in **1883** in mem. of Rev. John James Digweed, M.A. of Pembroke Coll., Oxford, maker's name MAYER & CO 149, NEW BOND ST., on reredos, C. *II.* Inscr. Jane Austen, [ch.] worshipper, 1775-1817, pos. in **1936** by great-grandniece, Emma Austen-Leigh, maker's name F. OSBORNE & CO LTD · LONDON W.C.1., copper, mur., N. See also Winchester Cathedral no.*VI. III.* Inscr. recording presentation by friends in mem. of Evelyn Audrey Tatlow, **1971**, aged 48; in 2005 loose in Vestry/N. *IV.* Inscr. recording presentation [of bookcase] by w. and friends in mem. of Albert Titheridge, churchwarden and ch. worker, [**1972**], on bookcase, Vestry/N. *V.* Inscr. Dorothy Annie Grey, ch. worshipper for 34 years, 1907-**1981**, mur., N. *VI.* Inscr. [Rev.] Geoffrey R[aymond] Turner, rector 1976-**1992**, on bench, Churchyard. *VII.* Inscr. recording refurbishment of 2 medieval bells and a 3rd bell (dated 1670) in **1995** with donations from American and Canadian members of the Jane Austen Society of North America and gratitude of P.C.C. and Friends of St. Nicholas Church, Steventon, mur., on board, Tower.

STOKE CHARITY, St. Michael.

I. Thomas Wayte, esq., **1482**, in arm., inscr., fig. of Our Lord in Pity, scroll and 1 sh. (3 others lost), A.T., N. *Brit. Lib. Add. MS. 39987,* f.183r (drg. before restoration by Baigent), *Add. MS. 39987,* f.34; *Hants Proc.,* III, opp. p.1; *Mann,* pl.8 (eff.); *M.B.S. Trans.,* VI, p.19, XI, p.96 (Our Lord), XIII, p.334 (Our Lord); *Norris, Memorials,* fig.239. Eff. 672 x 209 mm, inscr. 60 x 398 mm, Our Lord 274 x 275 mm, scroll 263 x 51 mm, upper sin. sh. 119 x 95 mm, Purbeck slab 1495 x 700 mm. Style: London F. Rep. by W.G.L. (1995).

II. Thomas Hampton, esq., **1483**, in arm., and w. Isabel (upper hf. lost), with 2 sons and 6 daus., inscr., Trinity, 2 scrolls and 4 shs., A.T. C. *Brit. Lib. Add. MS. 39970,* f.177r (drg. of tomb by Baigent), *Add. MS. 39987,* ff.35v-6r; *Hampton,* pl.5a, between pp.160-1 (upper pt. of male eff.); *Hants Proc.,* III, opp. p.4; *M.B.S. Trans.,* VI, p.21; *Page-Phillips, Children,* fig.19 (children). Male eff. 816 x 226 mm, male eff. scroll 303 x 83 mm, female eff. orig. 825 x 257 mm, now 451 x 257 mm, female eff. scroll 307 x 59 mm, inscr. 83 x 629 mm, children 189 x 319 mm,

Stoke Charity I

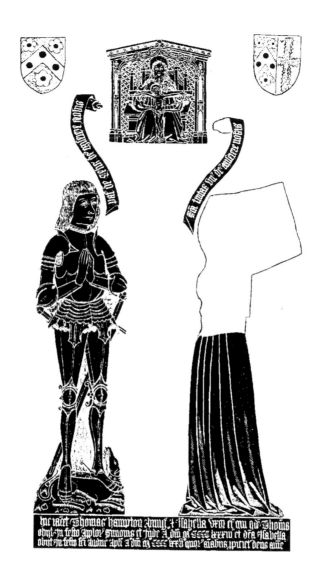

Stoke Charity II

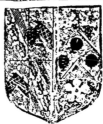

f your charite I desire you to praye for the Soule of Richard Waller Squyer
whos bodye here lyeth in Sauthern a clere is r towre of this Towne ⁊ also right
here leyd vnder this stone: being born: the xviii The vii of September yᵉ yere of
Incarnacion of oͬ lorde. M CCCC lii: God bryng his soule to his saluaciō amē

Stoke Charity III

Worldly Ioy lande me her
us perkhū squyer continue my tȳe
se be my helpe mayde modyr and wyfe
in thy bondes I leue my lyfe

Dn̄... peri aluī ⁊ Ioha...
que Iohanna ob...rt x⁰ die July Anni
CCCC° xxxī° ...

Stoke Charity III palimpsest reverse

289

Trinity 257 x 258 mm, upper dext. sh. 144 x 115 mm, upper sin. sh. 145 x 115 mm, lower dext. sh. 140 x 120 mm, lower sin. sh. 144 x 117 mm, Purbeck slab 1950 x 940 mm. Style: London F. Rep. by W.G.L. (1995).

III. Inscr. (mutil.) and 2 shs. Richard Waller, esq., "late lorde of this towne", **1552**, "god bring his soule to his salvacion"; palimp., on rev. 2 inscrs., c.1490 and 1532, and pts. of 2 ladies, c.1500 (one links with Somerton, Oxon. no.VII); N.C. *M.B.S. Trans.*, IX, p.333 (obv.), p.334 (rev.), XVI, p.172 (obv.); *Page-Phillips, 16th Cent. Workshop*, p.2 (rev.); *Palimpsests*, pl.64 (rev.). Inscr. orig. 95 x 703 mm, now 95 x 670 mm, dext. sh. 163 x 142 mm, sin. sh. 169 x 143 mm, Purbeck slab 1980 x 900 mm. Style: London G (Fermer, script 6). Rep. by R.H.P. (1955) and W.G.L. (1995).

IV. Inscr. recording restoration of east window in **1907** by widow in mem. of [Rev.] Charles Balston, [M.A., B.D.], fellow of Christ Church Coll., Oxford., rector for 38 years 1846-1884, mur., C. *V.* Inscr. recording restoration of [north-chapel] window in **1917**, on window splay, N.C. *VI.* Inscr. recording restoration of Hampton Chapel in **1946** in mem. of William Austin and Penelope Elizabeth Horn, of Old Stoke, mur., N.C. *VII.* Inscr. recording conservation of tomb in **1993** by sister, Hon. Angela [Mildred] Baring, in mem. of Alexander St. Francis Vincent [Baring], 6th Baron Ashburton, K.G., K.C.V.O., 1898-1991, mur., above A.T., N.

Ref: *Brit. Lib. Add. MS. 39970*, f.177, f.183, f.186, *Add. MS. 39987*, ff.34-6; *Burke's Peerage and Baronetage*, p.116; *Gittings*, p.63; *Haines*, II, p.74; *Hampton*, pp.73-4; *Hants Proc.*, III, pp.1-26; *Heseltine, Heraldry*, p.38; *Lloyd, C.B., Short History of Stoke Charity*, [1927], pp.6-7, p.16; *M.B.S. Trans.*, VI, p.18, p.20, pp.22-4, IX, pp.331-2, XI, pp.96-7, XIII, p.331, XV, p.144, pp.147-8, p.172, pp.508-9, XVI, p.171, pp.173-4, p.243; *Mee, Hampshire*, p.349; *M.S.*, p.165; *Norris, Memorials*, p.139, p.148, p.202, p.205; *Palimpsests*, 163L1-7, p.53; *Pevsner, Hampshire*, p.613; *Soc. Antiq. MS. 875/6*, pp.122-7; *V.C.H., Hampshire*, III, pp.450-1.

STRATFIELD SAYE, St. Mary the Virgin (new church).

I. Inscr. with 8 Lat. vv. George Dabrigecort, esq., lord of the manor, **1558**; the vv. composed by his son Thomas who pos.; mur., on board, C. Inscrs. 310 x 399 mm and 32 x 224 mm. Style: London G (script 9).

II. Inscr. with Lat. vv., etc. Eustace Dabrigecort, **1594**; formerly mur., C., now mur., on board, N. Inscr. 509 x 387 mm. Style: Johnson.

III. Inscr. with verse. Cpl. George Miles, 2nd Battn. Royal West Kent Regt., [killed] at the Battle of Abou Klea, **1885**, aged 21, maker's name COX & BUCKLEY LONDON, mur., N. *IV.* Inscr. in raised letters on anvil-shaped pl. recording erection [of lychgate] by husband in mem. of Anna Ansell, **1896**, bronze, on lychgate, Churchyard. *V.* Inscr. with verse within border of thistles. Rev. Horace George Monro, M.A., rector 1878-1903, 1831-1920, and w. Margaret Isabella, dau. of Rev. A.H. Duthie, 1832-**1920**, maker's name A. & N. C.S.L. LONDON, mur., C. *VI.* Inscr. Catherine [Pakenham, 3rd dau. of 2nd Baron Longford], w. of 1st Duke of Wellington, 1772-1831; Arthur [Wellesley, eld.] son of Lord Charles Wellesley, 1845-1846; [Major-Gen.] Lord Charles Wellesley, [2nd son of 1st Duke of Wellington], 1808-1858; [Lt.-Gen.] Arthur Richard [Wellesley], 2nd Duke of Wellington, [K.G.], 1807-1884; [Augusta] Sophia [Anne, only

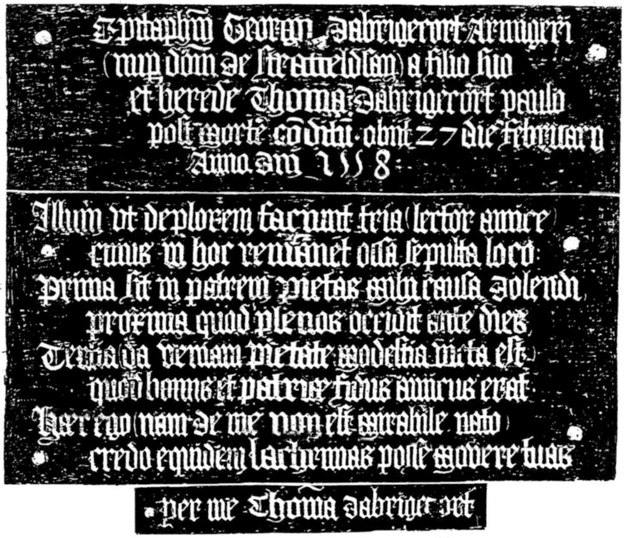

Stratfield Saye I

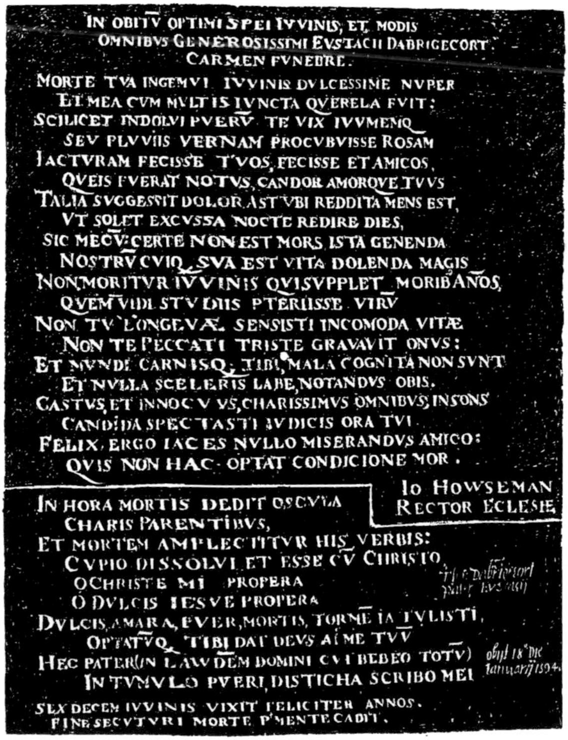

Stratfield Saye II

child of Rt. Hon. Henry Manvers Pierrepont, 3rd son of 1st Earl Manvers], Lady Charles Wellesley, 1819-1893; [Lt.-Col.] Henry [Wellesley], 3rd Duke of Wellington, [D.L.], 1846-1900; [Lady] Elizabeth [Hay, dau. of 8th Marquess of Tweeddale], widow of 2nd Duke of Wellington, 1820-1904; ashes of Kathleen [Emily Bulkeley, dau. of Capt. Robert Williams], w. of 4th Duke of Wellington, 1848-1927; Arthur Charles [Wellesley], 4th Duke of Wellington, [K.G., G.C.V.O., D.L.], 1849-1934; Arthur Charles [Wellesley], 5th Duke of Wellington, [J.P.], 1876-1941; [Hon. Lilian] Maud, [Glen Coats, yst. dau. of 1st Baron Glentanar], widow of 5th Duke of Wellington, 1885-**1946**, buried in vault beneath north transept, mur., N.Tr. *VII*. Inscr. with regt. insignia recording sqdn. standard of Royal Horse Guards (The Blues) (presented to the regt. in 1927 by George V on Horse Guards Parade after "being carried in the service of Sovereign and Country for 26 years") pos. in **1953** by Lt.-Col. The Marquess Douro, M.V.O., M.C., commanding officer; Field Marshal [Arthur Wellesley, 1st] Duke of Wellington, K.G., [G.C.B., G.C.H., P.C., F.R.S., 1769-1852], Col. of The Blues, mur., N.Tr.

INDENTS & LOST BRASSES. 8. Indent, ?man in arm., inscr., ach. and 1 sh., nearly effaced, W.Porch. Eff. c.680 x c.230 mm, inscr. c.150 x c.600 mm, ach. c.150 x c.140 mm, sh. c.140 x c.120 mm, non-Purbeck slab 1955 x 890 mm. 9. Indent, ?man in arm. and w., inscr., 2 groups of children, inscr., device, scroll and 2 shs., c.1470, nearly effaced, W.Porch. Male eff. c.640 x c.240 mm, female eff. c.630 x c.240 mm, inscr. c.110 x c.650 mm, sons c.310 x c.260 mm, daus. c.310 x c.280 mm, children inscr. c.60 x c.900 mm, device and scroll effaced, shs. c.165 x c.135 mm, Purbeck slab 2330 x 1050 mm remains. 10. Indent, civilian and w., ?holding an inscr. between them, 2 inscrs., 1 dau., device, scroll and sh., c.1490, W.Porch. *Sadler, Dorset and Hampshire*, pt.II, p.23 (drg.). Male and female effs. with rect. pl. 615 x 710 mm, inscrs. 115 x 560 mm and 30 x 510 mm, dau. 170 x 170 mm, device 150 x 70 mm, scroll 275 x 110 x 30 mm, sh. 140 x 110 mm, non-Purbeck slab 2010 x 1090 mm. 11. Indent, ?eff. and inscr., effaced, W.Porch. Slab 1880 x 915 mm. 12. Indent, inscr. and ?oval-shaped pl., N. Inscr. 130 x 650 mm, pl. effaced, Purbeck slab 1650 x 770 mm. 13. Lost brass, inscr. and sh. Nicholas Darbridgecourt, 1400, w. Mary, S.C. Recorded by Ashmole (c.1660). 14. Lost brass, inscr. Thomas Darbridgecourt, 1466, and w. Alice, S.C. Recorded by Ashmole (c.1660). 15. Lost brass, inscr. Thomas Darbridgecourt, 1485, S.C. Possibly no.10. Recorded by Ashmole (c.1660).

Ref: *Bod. Lib. MS. Ashmole 1107*, p.311; *Burke's Peerage and Baronetage*, p.1110, p.1649, p.2690, p.2784-6; *Haines*, II, p.76; *M.B.S. Trans.*, VI, pp.24-6; *M.S.*, p.166; *Sadler, Dorset and Hampshire*, pt.II, pp.22-5; *Soc. Antiq. MS. 875/6*, pp.127-9.

Ch. built, 1754-8.

STROUDEN PARK, (see BOURNEMOUTH).

SUTTON, BISHOP'S, St. Nicholas.

I. Man in arm. and w. (effs. mutil.), c.**1520**; inscr. lost; formerly C., mur., C., rel., C.; orig. slab, C. Possibly Lewis Wingfield and w., 1504. Recorded (inscr. lost) by Duthy (1839). *Brit. Lib. Add. MS. 39987*, f.43r. Male eff. 698 x 182 mm remains, female eff. 642 remains x 174 mm, inscr. indent effaced, Purbeck slab 1750 remains x 920 mm. Style: London F.

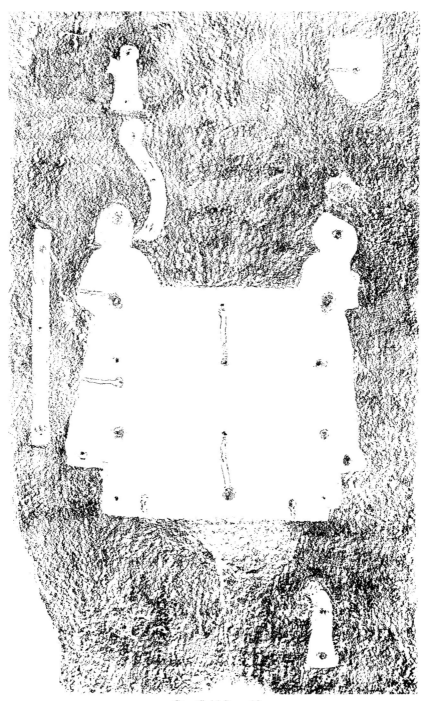

Stratfield Saye 10

II. World War I memorial (14 names), **1919**, mur., C. *III.* Inscr. recording gift [of organ] in **1929** by sister, [Jane] Augusta Lasham, [1941, aged 86], in mem. of Henry James Lasham, on organ, N. *IV.* Inscr. recording gift [of font cover] in **1940** by Mothers' Union members, copper, on font cover, N. *V.* World War II memorial (4 names), maker's name F. OSBORNE & CO LTD London W.C.1., mur., C. *VI.* Inscr. with verse. Pte. Anthony John Sheppard, Gloucestershire Regt., killed in action in Korea, **1951**, maker's name F. OSBORNE & CO LTD London W.C.1., mur., C. *VII.* Inscr. Robert Steele, 1893-**1969**, and [w.] Norah Esme, 1891-1967, bronze, on lectern, N. *VIII.* Inscr. recording repair to the tower in **1983** through generosity of family in mem. of Theophila Mary Gardner, 1902-1982, bronze, mur., on pillar, N. *IX.* Inscr. John Charles Twelftree, 1935-**1990**, bronze, on bench, Churchyard.

INDENTS & LOST BRASSES. 10. Indent, inscr. and sh., C. Inscr. 95 x 420 mm, sh. 150 x 125 mm, Unio Purbeck slab 2130 x 835 mm.

Ref: *Brit. Lib. Add. MS. 39987*, f.43; *Duthy*, p.119; *Haines*, II, p.74; *Hampshire, Antiquary*, I, p.71; *M.B.S. Bulletin*, 23, p.14; *M.B.S. Trans.*, I, pt.7, p.28, V, pp.259-60; *Mee, Hampshire*, p.61; *M.S.*, p.166; *Pevsner, Hampshire*, p.103; *Sadler, Dorset and Hampshire,* appx. I, pt.2, p.41 (drg.); *Soc. Antiq. MS. 875/6*, pp.13-4; *V.C.H., Hampshire*, III, p.44.

TADLEY, St. Peter.

I. Inscr. Benefaction of Thomas Sympson, **1674**, mur., in wooden frame, N. Inscr. 289 x 416 mm.

II. Inscr. Lt. Donald Perceval Lynden-Bell, 1st [Battn.] Royal Irish Fusiliers, [son of Col. Charles Perceval Lynden-Bell, J.P., of Fairlawn House, killed while] leading his men in attack at the 2nd Battle of Ypres, **1915**, aged 19, [buried at New Irish Farm Cemetery, Ieper, West Vlaanderen, Belgium], maker's name *JONES & WILLIS L^{TD}*, on board on window splay, N. *III.* Inscr. Capt. T[homas] E[dward] Painton Jones, [1st/6th Battn. London Regt. (City of London Rifles), killed] in France, **1916**, pos. by widow, mur., N. *IV.* Inscr. recording insertion of chancel panelling in mem. of 2nd-Lt. John Bertram Greenup, [5th Battn. attd. 1st Battn.] Rifle Brigade, [son of Rev. Dr. Albert William Greenup, M.A., Litt.D., of The Rectory, Great Oakley, Essex], scholar of Wadham Coll., Oxford, [killed] in action near Poelcappelle, **1917**, aged 19, mur., on board, C. *V.* Inscr. Ellen Amelia Stacey, 1853-**1941**, on missal stand, C. *VI.* Combined World War I (30 names) and II (4 names) memorials, mur., on board, N. *VII.* Inscr. Lily Emily Gray, **1954**, on processional cross, C. *VIII.* Inscr. Lionel Grant Courtney Clack, organist and verger, 1913-**1967**, mur., on board, C. *IX.* Inscr. A.W. Liversidge, 1922; H.B. Howard, 1948; J.J. Morland, 1954; C.H. Nicholson, 1963; D. McMillan, 1979; T.D.J. Curry, 1981; and V.J. Latson, **1995**, [churchwardens], on churchwardens' wand, N. *X.* Inscr. W. Kernutt, 1925-1935; F.E. Hussey, 1936; S.G. Wilmot, 1950; C.R. Andrews, 1955; W.L. Singleton, 1964; M.L. Fussell, 1970; T.D.J. Curry, 1973; A.T. Ellis, 1977; Mrs. P. Brown, 1988; C.A. Hunt, 1996; A.K. Jones, 1999; and M.B.C. Ridley, **2000**, [churchwardens], on churchwardens' wand, N.

Ref: *M.B.S. Trans.*, V, p.363, VI, pp.26-7; *Mee, Hampshire*, p.355; *M.S.*, p.166; *Soc. Antiq. MS. 875/6*, pp.129-30; *V.C.H., Hampshire*, IV, p.220.

Sutton, Bishop's I

In the name of God Amen
I, Thomas Symskin of Sherborn St John in the County of
Southton Moved by the grace of God doe give by my last Will & Testament unto the poor
of six parishes the Sum of fifteen pounds yearly & every year soe long as the world shall
endure To be had & rec out of my land in Monk Sherborn known by the name of Hill house
and out of my land of Peakhurst late Edward Thilcups to be equally divided in equall
porcons (that is to say a six part being two pounds ten shillings to Sherborn St John a six part
to Monk Sherborn a six part to Lawrence Wotton a six part to Baghurst a six part to Pamber
& a six part to Tadley I smth desire the Minister of every parish herein menconed to take
upon him to be a Steward of this my land to let & improve the same And that the Minister
& the Church Wardens see the half of this money equally decided at every the said parish
Church on the day of St Thomas the Apostle & Thomas a Becket and what overplus
shall happen out of this my lands more then fifteen pounds per Annum I will & desire
it be equally decided amongst the poorest of my kindred
payable one yeare after my decease
published in ye 26th yeare of the raigne of King Charles ye 2d
Anno D 1674

Tadley I

295

THROOP, (see BOURNEMOUTH).

THRUXTON, SS. Peter and Paul.

I. Sir John Lysle, Lord of Wodynton in the Isle of Wight, husband of Lady Elizabeth Lysle, died 1407, engr. c.**1425**, in arm., triple canopy, 4 shs. and marg. inscr., C. *Ashdown, Armour*, p.202 (eff.); *Bod. Lib. Gough Maps 223*, f.23, *227*, ff.49-52; *Boutell, Series* (3 pls.); *Brit. Lib. Add. MS. 39987*, ff.22-3r; *Franklyn*, p.33, 2nd edn., p.36; *Gittings*, fig.27, p.34; *Gough*, II, pl.7, p.23; *Hants Proc.*, VI, p.116; *Hewitt, Armour*, III, p.384 (eff.); *Macklin, Br. of Eng.*, p.151; *M.B.S. Portfolio*, II, pl.8; *Mee, Hampshire*, p.347 (drg. of eff.); *Portfolio Book*, pl.149. Male eff. 1512 x 462 mm, canopy 2349 x 847 mm, upper dext. sh. 148 x 122 mm, upper sin. sh. 150 x 132 mm (lead), lower dext. sh. 148 x 122 mm, lower sin. sh. 149 x 121 mm, marg. inscr. 2580 x 1086 x 40 mm, Purbeck slab 2740 x 1310 mm. Style: London D. Rep. (1963) and by W.G.L. (1997).

II. Inscr. Rev. Donald Christopher Baynes, B.C.L., 3rd son of Sir Christopher Baynes, Bart., of Harefield Place, Middx., [curate 1847-1864], died at Winchester, **1884**, aged 76, buried in the churchyard, pos. by relatives in England and Italy, mur., N.A. *III.* Inscr. with verse and cross on separate pl. Harry Noyes, of Thruxton Manor, 1844, [aged 65], and [w.] Catherine, 1850, [aged 70]; also [children], Henry Crine [Noyes], 1873, and w. Sarah Haighton, 1893; Samuel Frederick [Noyes], 1890, and w. Charlotte, 1886; Catherine Eliz[a]b[e]th, 1852; Sarah, w. of G.A.F. Wilks, 1879; Mary, w. of J.S. Ayerst, 1889; and Anna, **1906**, mur., in stone frame, N. *IV.* Inscr. with regt. insignia. Major Donald Baker, Indian Army, **1907**, [aged 42], pos. by brother officers of 102nd King Edward's Own Grenadiers, maker's name GAWTHORP Sᶜ LONDON, mur., on marble, C. *V.* Inscr. with verse and regt. insignia. Major Roger Dyke Baker, East Lancashire Regt., Brigade-Major 38th Infantry Brigade 13th Division, yst. son of Rev. Henry De Foe Baker, [B.A.], rector [1896-1898, served at] Waziristan 1901, Somaliland (medals with clasps) 1904, Dardanelles 1915, and Gallipoli (mentioned in despatches), "THOUGH WOUNDED AT DAWN, HE LED HIS MEN ALL DAY, UNTIL AT NIGHT HE FELL MORTALLY WOUNDED", **1915**, aged 36, buried at [East Mudros Military Cemetery], Lemnos, [Greece], maker's name CULN. GAWTHORP & SONS · LONDON, mur., on marble, N. *VI.* Inscr. Edwin Nixon, chorister for 45 years including organist for 21 years, churchwarden for 9 years, and school headmaster for 35 years, **1929**, aged 75, on choir stall, C. *VII.* Inscr. recording gates in mem. of Thomas Charles Wise, **1963**, bronze, on board on gate post, Churchyard. *VIII.* Inscr. recording donation of gates in mem. of Clive John Brookes, 1965-**1984**, mur., on board, S.Porch. *IX.* Inscr. George (Jack) Forest, [1904-**1984**], on tree post, Churchyard. *X.* Inscr. David Hugh Matyear, 1934-**2003**, on bench, Churchyard.

INDENTS & LOST BRASSES. 11. Indent, inscr. (chamfer). _____ de Lisle, and w., c.1520, A.T., C.; 4 shs., mur., in stone panels of A.T. Inscr. (chamfer) 1765 x 600 x 45 mm, Purbeck coverstone 1805 x 640 mm, shs. mur. 155 x 125 mm.

Ref: *Bod. Lib. Gough Maps 223*, f.23, *227*, ff.49-52; *Brit. Lib. Add. MS. 39987*, ff.22-3; *Gittings*, p.54; *Gough*, II, pt.2, p.23; *Haines*, I, p.189, II, p.74; *Hampshire History*, III, p.156; *Hants Proc.*, VII, pp.75-6; *Heseltine, Heraldry*, p.38; *M.B.S. Trans.*, VI, pp.27-8, X, p.111, XIV, p.490, XV, p.242, p.244, XVI, p.192; *Mee, Hampshire*, p.356; *M.S.*, p.166; *Norris, Memorials*, p.76; *Pevsner, Hampshire*, p.620; *Simpson*, p.28; *Soc. Antiq. MS. 875/6*, pp.130-1; *V.C.H., Hampshire*, IV, p.390.

Thruxton I

297

TICHBORNE, St. Andrew.

I. Inscr. (2 shs. lost). Anne, dau. of Robert Whyte of Suthwerborne, w. of Nicholas, son of John Tycheborne, **1519**, N.A. Recorded (complete) by Pavey (1702). Illustration (complete) from rubbing in Soc. Antiq. coll. Rubbing (complete) in Soc. Antiq. coll. (1853). Inscr. 194 x 522 mm, dext. sh. indent 145 x 120 mm remains, sin. sh. indent 140 x 125 mm, freestone slab 1395 remains x 620 mm remains. Style: London G.

II. Inscr. George Marx, 1835, aged 58, and w. Selina, 1826, aged 29; also children, George, 1820, aged 6 months; James Digges Chambers, 1824, aged 1; Selina Catherine Rush, 1825, aged 6 months; and Emma Anne, **1844**, aged 21, maker's name MORING LONDON, mur., N. *III.* Inscr. on 2 pls., cross and inscr. (chamfer). Sir Edward Doughty, Bart., 3rd son of Sir Henry Tichborne, 7th Bart.; in 1826 assumed the surname of Doughty on succeeding to the estates of Elizabeth, [only dau. and h. of Henry] Doughty, of Snarford Hall, Lincs.; mar. 1827, Mary Katharine, 5th dau. of James Everard, 9th Baron Arundell of Wardour, born at Irnham Hall, Lincs., died at Tichborne Park, 1795-**1872**; by whom [son], Henry, [1829-1835] and [dau.], Katharine [Mary Elizabeth, w. of Sir Joseph Percival Pickford Radcliffe, 3rd Bart., 1906]; in 1845 succeeded eld. brother, Sir Henry Tichborne as 9th Bart., 1732-1853, pos. by widow, A.T., N.A.; 3 shs., mur. in stone panels of A.T. *IV.* Inscr. Anna Maria Selina, dau. of Wadham Locke, M.P., of Rowdeford, Wilts., w. of Francis [J.P.] Marx, of Arle-Bury, born at Rowde, died at Arle[-]Bury, 1807-**1875**, mur., N. *V.* Inscr. Francis J.P. Marx, J.P., of Arle-Bury, son of George Marx, 1816-**1876**, mur., on marble, N. *VI.* Inscr. Henrietta, dau. of George Marx, w. of Oliver Calley Codrington, of Deane House, Kilmeston, **1882**, aged 64, mur., N. *VII.* Inscr. Capt., George Francis Marx, J.P., 68th Durham Light Infantry, of Arle[-]Bury, son of Francis and Selina Marx, 1849-**1883**, mur., N. *VIII.* Inscr. recording presentation [of bench] by parishioners in mem. of [Rev.] Arthur Percy Skene, [B.A.], rector 1943-**1966**, bronze, on bench, Churchyard. *IX.* Inscr. [recording presentation of] copy painting by Corregio (1514-1523) in mem. of Sir Anthony [Joseph Henry Doughty] Doughty Tichborne, 14th Bart., [1914-]**1968**, and w. Antonia, [twin dau. of Sir Harold Snagge, K.B.E.], 1966, mur., on board suspended from painting, N. *X.* Inscr. recording presentation in **1971** by William George [Henry] May, of Tichborne Park, on retirement as churchwarden and treasurer after 40 years, [1889-1979], copper, on pew, N. *XI.* Inscr. Lionel Ottley, churchwarden for 13 years, 1924-**1996**, mur., Baptistry/S.A.

INDENTS & LOST BRASSES. 12. Indent, inscr., N.A. Inscr. 90 x 425 mm, Purbeck slab 2330 x 905 mm remains.

Ref: *Brit. Lib. Stowe MS. 845*, f.118; *Gent. Mag.*, 1810, I, pp.305-6; *Gent. Mag. Lib. Eng. Topog.*, p.111; *Heseltine, Heraldry*, p.38; *M.B.S. Trans.*, VI, pp.28-9; *M.S.*, p.166; *Sadler, Dorset and Hampshire*, appx. I, pt.2, p.41; *Soc. Antiq. MS. 875/6*, pp.131-3; *V.C.H., Hampshire*, III, p.338; *Who's Who*, 1967, p.3052.

TISTED, EAST, St. James.

I. Inscr. with 6 Lat. vv. Richard Burdon, pastor for 27 years, **1615**, aged 58, mur., Tower. Inscr. 225 x 554 mm.

II. Inscr. with chronogram. Thomas Emes, born at Bugden [Buckden], Hunts., pastor for 24 years, **1663**, mur., Tower. Inscr. 187 x 248 mm.

Ihū haue mcy of the sowle of Anne Bycheborne oon of
the doughters of Robt Whyte of Suthwerborne elsewher
late the wyfe of Richas Tycheborne of Tycheborne sōne
of John Tycheborne brother & heire of Wullm ye eldeſt sone
of the seid Johā Whyche Anne deyed this worlde the
xxiiij day of ffebruary the yere of ō lord god iō bᶜⁱᵛ

Tichborne I

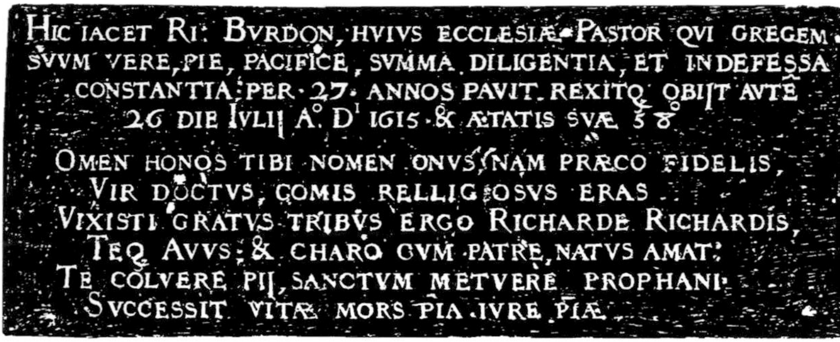

HIC IACET RI: BVRDON, HVIUS ECCLESIÆ PASTOR QVI GREGEM
SVVM VERE, PIE, PACIFICE, SVMMA DILIGENTIA, ET INDEFESSA
CONSTANTIA PER 27 ANNOS PAVIT, REXITQ OBIJT AVTĒ
26 DIE IVLIJ Aº Dⁱ 1615 & ÆTATIS SVÆ 58
OMEN HONOS TIBI NOMEN ONVS, NAM PRÆCO FIDELIS,
VIR DOCTVS, COMIS RELLIGIOSVS ERAS
VIXISTI GRATVS TRIBVS ERGO RICHARDE RICHARDIS,
TEQ AVVS: & CHARO CVM PATRE, NATVS AMAT:
TE COLVERE PIJ, SANCTVM METVERE PROPHANI
SVCCESSIT VITÆ MORS PIA IVRE PIÆ
Tisted, East I

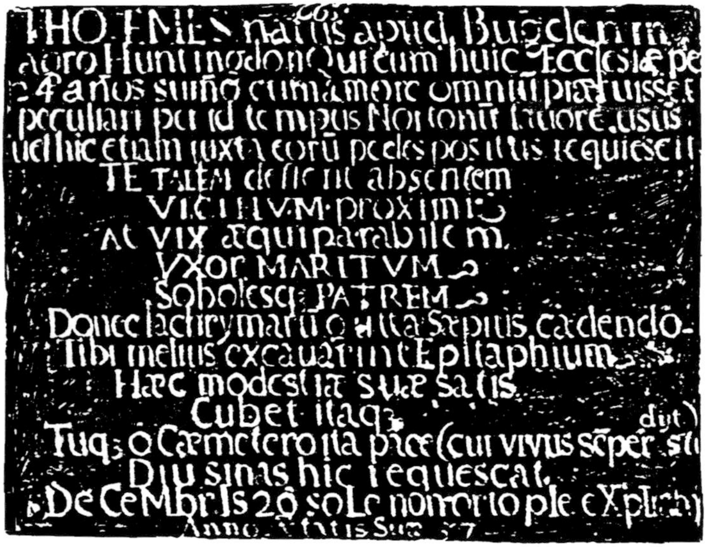

THO. EMES natus apud Bugden in
agro Huntingdon Qui cum huic Ecclesiæ pe
24 años sum̄o cum amore omnium præfuisset
peculiari per id tempus Nortonii favore usus
vel hic etiam juxta eorū pedes positus requiescit
TE TALEM deflent absentem
VICINUM proximi
At vix æquiparabilem.
UXOR MARITUM
Sobolesq PATREM
Donec lachrymarum gutta sæpius cadendo
Tibi melius excavarint Epitaphium
Hæc modestia suæ satis.
Cubet itaq
Tuq; o Cæmeterio ita pace (cui vivus sēper studuit)
Diu sinas hic requiescat.
Decembris 20
Anno ætatis Suæ 57
Tisted, East II

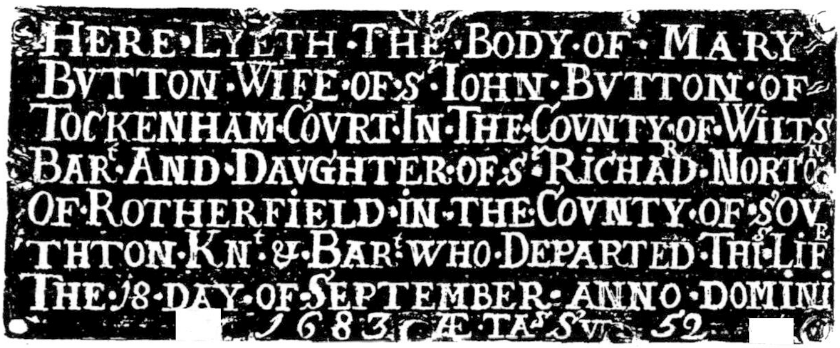

HERE·LYETH·THE·BODY·OF·MARY
BVTTON·WIFE·OF·Sᴿ·IOHN·BVTTON·OF
TOCKENHAM·COVRT·IN·THE·COVNTY·OF·WILTS
BARᵀ·AND·DAVGHTER·OF·Sᴿ·RICHARD·NORTON
OF·ROTHERFIELD·IN·THE·COVNTY·OF·SOVTHTON·KNᵀ·&·BARᵀ·WHO·DEPARTED·THIS·LIFE
THE·18·DAY·OF·SEPTEMBER·ANNO·DOMINI
1683·ÆTAᵀˢ·SVÆ·52
Tisted, East III

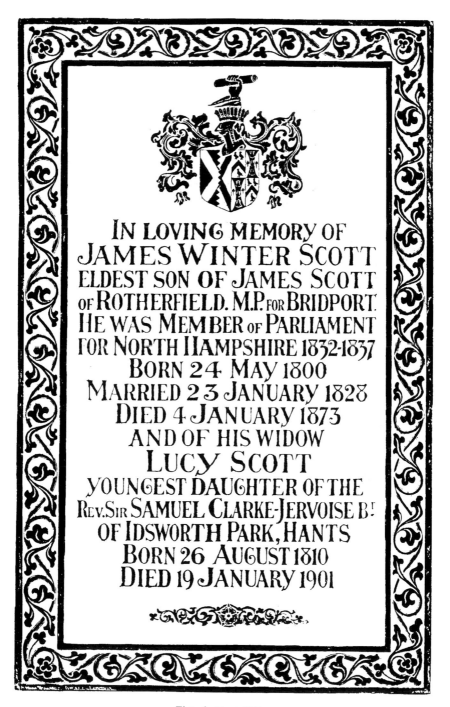

IN LOVING MEMORY OF
JAMES WINTER SCOTT
ELDEST SON OF JAMES SCOTT
OF ROTHERFIELD. M.P. FOR BRIDPORT.
HE WAS MEMBER OF PARLIAMENT
FOR NORTH HAMPSHIRE 1832-1837
BORN 24 MAY 1800
MARRIED 23 JANUARY 1828
DIED 4 JANUARY 1873
AND OF HIS WIDOW
LUCY SCOTT
YOUNGEST DAUGHTER OF THE
REV. SIR SAMUEL CLARKE-JERVOISE BT
OF IDSWORTH PARK, HANTS
BORN 26 AUGUST 1810
DIED 19 JANUARY 1901

Tisted, East *VII*

III. Inscr. **Mary**, dau. of Sir Richard Norton of Rotherfield, Knt. and Bart., w. of Sir John Button, of Tockenham Court, Wilts., Bart., **1683**, aged 52, N. Inscr. 144 x 356 mm, Petworth marble slab 1870 x 890 mm.

IV. Inscr. with ach. Walter Jervoise Scott, [J.P.], 2nd son of James Winter Scott, of Rotherfield Park, [barrister-at-law of the Inner Temple], died at the Valley of Lagoons, Queensland, Australia, 1835-**1890**, mur., C. *V.* Inscr. with ach. George Arthur Jervoise Scott, [J.P., D.L.], of Rotherfield Park, eld. son of James Winter Scott and w. Lucy Clarke Jervoise, [barrister-at-law of the Inner Temple], died at sea near Aden, 1833-**1895**, mur., N. *VI.* Inscr. with verse in raised letters and ach. in relief. Capt. Richard William Spicer, 16th Lancers, 1828-1892; also son, Lt. Arthur Reginald William Spicer, 3rd Battn. King's Royal Rifle Corps, fought at the Battle of Spion Kop and throughout the Natal Campaign 1899-1900, died at Elandsfontein, **1901**, aged 22, maker's name BARKENTIN & KRALL · LONDON, mur., N. *VII.* Inscr. in raised letters with ach. in relief. James Winter Scott, [J.P., D.L.], eld. son of James Scott, of Rotherfield, M.P. for Bridport, M.P. for North Hampshire 1832-1837, [High Sheriff 1864], mar. 1828, 1800-1873; also widow, Lucy, yst. dau. of Rev. Sir Samuel Clarke Jervoise, [1st] Bart., of Idsworth Park, 1810-**1901**, maker's name BARKENTIN & KRALL · LONDON, mur., N. Inscr. 465 x 285 mm. *VIII.* World War I memorial (3 names), **1919**, maker's name CULN GAWTHORP & SONS LONDON, mur., S.A. *IX.* Inscr. John George Adnams, clerk and sexton for 22 years, **1936**, maker's name OSBORNE & CO LTD London, mur., Tower. *X.* Inscr. Mary Angela, dau. of Major-Gen. Lord Charles Wellesley, of Conholt Park, grand-dau. of Arthur [Wellesley], 1st Duke of Wellington, w. [of George Arthur Jervoise Scott], 1850-**1936**, mur., below no.*V*, N. *XI.* World War II memorial (5 names), **1945**, bronze, mur., S.A. *XII.* Inscr. recording festal frontal and kneelers for the altar commem. Florence Dennis, "DEVOTED AND BELOVED TEACHER OF EAST TISTED'S CHILDREN FOR 25 YEARS", 1908-**1997**, mur., C.

Ref: *Burke's Peerage and Baronetage*, p.2390, p.2786; *M.B.S. Bulletin*, 39, p.149; *M.B.S. Trans.*, VI, pp.29-30; *M.S.*, p.166; *V.C.H., Hampshire*, III, p.34.

Ch. essentially, 1846.

TITCHFIELD, St. Peter.

I. Inscr. with sh. and crest recording erection of [west south aisle] window in **1870** by daus., Emily Hornby and Louisa Hornby, in mem. of John Hornby, of The Hook, 1832, aged 67, and w. Jane, 1846, aged 73, buried in the chancel, on window splay, S.A. *II.* Emily, dau. of John Hornby and [w.] Jane, of The Hook, born at The Hook, died at Belmore, Cowes, **1876**, aged 68, rect. pl., canopy, inscr., verse, enamelled lozenge and 4 evang. symbols in quadrilobes at corners, mur., S.A. *III.* Inscr. with sh., 3 crests and motto. Capt. William O'Bryen Hoare, R.N., 2nd son of Sir Joseph Wallis Hoare, [3rd] Bart., and Lady Harriet [O'Bryen], born at Youghal, co. Cork, Ireland, died at Worthing, Sussex, [1807-]**1886**, pos. by [dau.], Mary L[ouisa] Hoare, mur., S.A. *IV.* [Rev.] Francis John Cosser, [son of Rev. Walter M. Cosser, M.A., vicar 1852-1887, and w. Sophia A.L.], **1889**, aged 36, rect. pl., inscr. on base of stepped cross and marg. inscr. with verse and roundels at corners, maker's name T. PRATT & SONS, TAVISTOCK Sᵀ LONDON, mur., on marble, S.A. *V.* Inscr. Charlotte, dau. of Capt. James Bradshaw, R.N., M.P., widow of William Hornby, of The Hook, **1890**, aged 67, maker's name GAFFIN. REGENT Sᵀ· LONDON, mur., S.A. *VI.* Inscr. Alice Gilberta, w. of Rev. Reginald A[rthur] R[ichard] White, M.A., [F.R.G.S.,

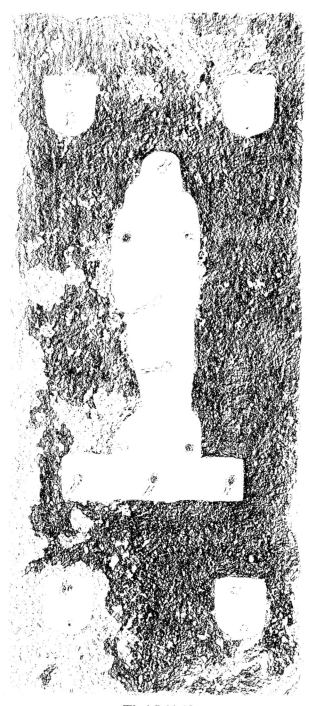

Titchfield 18

F.Z.S.], vicar [1887-1907], **1896**, on lectern, N.C./N.A. See also West Cowes, St. Faith no.*I.* *VII.* Inscr. with verse. Mary Louisa Hoare, [dau. of no.*III*], **1907**, [pos. by sister] E[lizabeth] C[lotilde] H[oare], maker's name CATON. 64 DUKE S^T LONDON. W, mur., S.A. *VIII.* Inscr. with verse. Elizabeth Clotilde Hoare, [dau. of no.*III*], **1910**, maker's name CATON. 491 OXFORD. S^T. W, mur., S.A. *IX.* Inscr. with verse in mem. of mother, brothers and sisters, engr. c.**1920**, on screen, C. *X.* Inscr. in raised letters with regt. insignia in relief. Major-Gen. Sir Harington Owen Parr, K.C.B., C.M.G., commandant 7th D.C.O. Rajputts 1915-1919, died near Thorncombe, Dorset, 1867-**1928**, pos. by commandant, British officers, Indian officers, NCOs and men of regt. in which he served from 1891-1919, bronze, mur., N.A. *XI.* Inscr. L.M.H. and A.L.H., 1909-**1934**, on flowerstand, C. *XII.* Inscr. Frederick Charles Love, chorister for 52 years, tower capt., churchwarden, "FRIEND TO FOUR VICARS OF TITCHFIELD", 1884-**1964**, and w. Bessie, bronze, on choir stall, C. *XIII.* Inscr. Capt. A.E. Johnston, C.B.E., R.N., churchwarden for 30 years 1935[-**1965**], "In whose name the vestry once on this site was dedicated", mur., Mezzanine Staircase/S.A. *XIV.* Inscr. Celia M. Hales, 1929-**1985**, on bookcase, N. *XV.* Inscr. [Rev. Thomas] (Tom) [Warwick Winstanley] Pemberton, [M.A.], vicar 1973-**1990**, "BY WHOSE INSPIRATION THESE CHAPTER ROOMS WERE BUILT", mur., on board, Mezzanine Staircase/S.A. *XVI & XVII.* Two inscrs. Roma Haslam, **1998**, on chairs, N.

INDENTS & LOST BRASSES. 18. Indent, man in arm., inscr. and 4 shs., c.1520, S.C. *Sadler, Dorset and Hampshire*, pt.II, p.26 (drg.). Eff. 925 x 250 mm, inscr. 120 x 535 mm, upper dext. sh. 165 x 150 mm, upper sin. sh. 170 x 150 mm, lower dext. sh. 170 x 145 mm, lower sin. sh. 165 x 150 mm, Unio Purbeck slab 2090 x 910 mm. Style: London G.

Ref: *Burke's Peerage and Baronetage*, p.1346; *Norris, Memorials*, p.224; *Sadler, Dorset and Hampshire*, pt.II, p.26.

TYTHERLEY, WEST, St. Peter (new church)

I. Anne, dau. and coh. of Thomas Hampton, gent., w. of Mawrice Whitehede, esq., **1480**, inscr., N. *M.B.S. Trans.*, VI, p.31; *Mee, Hampshire*, p.115 (drg. of eff.). Eff. 578 x 202 mm, inscr. 79 x 435 mm. Style: London F.

II. Inscr. Robert, son and h. of John Whytehede, esq., c.**1490**, N. Inscr. 58 x 183 mm. Style: London D.

III. Inscr. with sh. Sir Henry Whithed, Knt., and w. Dame Anne, dau. of James Weston of Lichfield, Staffs., esq., **1629**, N. Inscr. 343 x 178-494 mm.

IV. Inscr. with sh. Lucy, dau. of Rob[er]t Love of St. Needes (St. Neots), Hunts., gent., 2nd w. of Richa[r]d Whithed of Tuderly, esq., **1652**, N. Inscr. 127 x 262 mm.

V. Inscr. Christian, 5th dau. of Richard Whithed of Tuderly, esq., w. of William Thomas of Gray's Inn, esq., died in childbed, **1655**, and infant son Richard, N. Inscr. 223 x 474 mm.

VI. Inscr. recording presentation [of organ] in **1834** by Hon. B[artholomew] Bouverie, [3rd son of William Bouverie, 1st Earl of Radnor, 1753-1835], on organ, N. *VII.* Inscr. recording erection of chancel and window in mem. of Thomas Baring, M.P., of Norman Court, [2nd son of

Tytherley, West I

Tytherley, West II

305

Sir Thomas Baring, 2nd Bart.], 1799-**1873**, on step, C. *VIII.* Cross and inscr. with verse on 4 pls. Elizabeth Baring, 1826-**1897**, pos. by 4 children, mur., on marble, C. *IX.* Inscr. Mary Faithfull Cotesworth, 1896-**1903**, on cross, C. *X.* Inscr. recording gift [of lectern] in **1906** by Francis Baring, of Norman Court, in mem. of mother, on lectern, N. *XI.* Inscr. with verse and enamelled regt. insignia. Sapper William Alfred Bristow, [143269, 72nd Field Co.] R[oyal] E[ngineers], son [of William Bristow and w. Emma] and brother, chorister and confirmed in the ch., **1918**, aged 29, buried at Baghdad [(North Gate) War Cemetery, Iraq], maker's name *F. HIGHMAN & SON, L^{TD} SALISBURY*, mur., on marble, C. *XII.* Inscr. recording gift of altar with riddel posts, dorsal and ornaments by Baring family; consecrated and dedicated in **1927** by [Rt. Rev. Frank Theodore Woods], Bishop of Winchester [1923-1932], copper, mur., C. *XIII.* Inscr. Geoffrey Beale, 1902-**1981**, and grandson, Philip Low, 1956-1977, buried in France, bronze, on sundial, Churchyard. *XIV.* Inscr. Sidney John Jacobs, churchwarden, **1985**, on hymn board, N. *XV.* Inscr. Rev. Henry G[eorge] Kelsey, M.A., 1900-**1985**, pos. by family, mur., on board, N. *XVI.* Inscr. Joan Beale, w. of no.*XIII*, 1905-**1996**, bronze, on sundial with no.*XIII*, Churchyard. *XVII.* Inscr. Denys Morley Green, churchwarden for 40 years, 1919-**1998**, on gate, Churchyard.

Ref: *Burke's Peerage and Baronetage*, p.1994, p.2200; *Heseltine, Heraldry*, p.38; *M.B.S. Trans.*, VI, pp.30-2; *Mee, Hampshire*, p.379; *M.S.*, p.166; *Norris, Memorials*, p.144; *Pevsner, Hampshire*, p.648; *Soc. Antiq. MS. 875/6*, pp.133-5; *V.C.H., Hampshire*, IV, p.523.

Ch. built, 1833.

WALLOP, FARLEIGH, St. Andrew (new church).

I. Inscr. Dame Elizabeth, dau. and sole h. of Robert Corbett of Morton Corbett, esq., by Anne, dau. of John, Lord St. John of Bletsoe, w. of Sir Henry Wallop of Farley Wallop, **1624**, left 1 son and 5 daus. then living, much corroded; in 1863 loose in the Wallop vault; now mur., S.Tr. Inscr. 218 x 481 mm.

II. Inscr. on heart-shaped pl. (?coffin pl.). Sir Henry Wallop, Knt., **1642**, aged 73, mur., S.Tr. Inscr. 190 x 175 mm.

III. Inscr. in raised letters recording installation of electrical heating and lighting in **1949** in mem. of Kate Yolland, w. of Richard Wallis Cory, J.P., of Langdon Court, Devon; grandmother of Bridget [Cory, C.St.J.], Countess of Portsmouth, [only dau. of Capt. Patrick Bermingham Croban, R.N., of Owlpen Old Manor, Uley, Gloucs., 2nd w. of Gerard Vernon Wallop, 9th Earl of Portsmouth, 1911-1979], bronze, mur., S.Tr. *IV.* Inscr. recording gift [of stool] by family in mem. of Ellen Annie Burgess, ch. caretaker 1931-**1967**, [w. and mother, 1967, aged 66], on stool, Vestry/N.Tr. *V.* Inscr. recording donation [of churchyard gate] in **1995** by family in mem. of [Robert Dunkley] (Bob) Fordham, [husband, father and grandfather, 1929-1994], on gate, Churchyard.

INDENTS & LOST BRASSES. 6. Indent, man in arm. of the Wallop family and w., inscr., Trinity, 2 scrolls and 4 shs., c.1520; in 2006 partly covered by panelling, A.T., C. *Sadler, Dorset and Hampshire*, pt.2, p.17 (drg.). Male eff. 705 x 185 mm visible, male eff. scroll 290 x 90 x 25 mm, female eff. 685 x 220 mm, female eff. scroll 290 x 115 x 25 mm, inscr. 55 x 525 mm visible, Trinity 170 x 105 mm, upper dext. sh. 120 visible x 35 mm visible, upper sin. sh. 135 x

HEERE LIE THE BODIES OF S[R] HENRY
WHITHED K[T] AND DAME ANNE HIS
WIFE THE DAVGHTER OF IAMES WESTON
OF LICHFIELD IN THE COVNTY OF
STAFFORD ESQ. 1629

Tytherley, West III

HEARE LIETH THE BODY OF LVCY THE SECOND
WIFE OF RICHAD WHITHED OF TVDERLY IN THE
COVNTY OF SOVTH[N] ESQ THE DAVGHTER OF
ROBT DOVE OF S[T] NEEDES IN THE COVNTY OF
HVNTINGTON GENT WHO DYED THE ZI DAY
OF SEPTEMBER 1652

Tytherley, West IV

HERE LYE THE BODIES OF CHRISTIAN Y[E] FIFTH
DAVGHTER OF RICHARD WHITHED OF TVDERLY ESQ
AND WIFE OF WILLIAM THOMAS OF GRAYS INN ESQ
AND OF RICHARD THE ONELY LIVEING OFFSPRING
BETWIXT THEM SHE DYED IN CHILDBED ON SVNDAY
THE 3[D] OF FEB[RY] ANNO DN: 1655 LEAVEING THIS
ISSVE TO SVRVIVE VNTILL THE 16TH DAY OF MAY
FOLLOWING WHEN IT AGAINE FROM MEE
RETVRNED TO HIS MOTHER

Tytherley, West V

Wallop, Farleigh I

ANNE DODINGTON WIDDOWE WIFE
OF IOHN DODINGTON OF BREAMOR
IN THIS COVNTY OF SOVTHTON ESQ
ELDEST DAVGHTER OF S^T HENRY
WALLOP KNIGHT & DAME ELIZABETH
HIS WIFE DAVGHTER & HEIRE OF
ROBERT CORBETT OF MORETON
CORBETT IN Y^E COVNTY OF SALOP ESQ
WHO RESIGNED HER SOVLE INTO
THE HANDS OF HER REDEEMER IESVS
CHRIST THE XXVIII DAY OF DE-
CEMBER IN THE YFARE OF OVR
LORD GOD 1656

Wallop, Farleigh 9

Wallop, Farleigh 6

110 mm, lower dext. sh. 95 visible x 100 mm visible, lower sin. sh. 140 x 110 mm, Purbeck coverstone 1715 x 570-620 mm visible. Style: London F. 7. Indent, lady, inscr. and 2 shs., c.1530, N. and C. *Sadler, Dorset and Hampshire*, appx. I, pt.2, p.20 (drg.). Eff. 445 x 130 mm, inscr. 135 x 225 mm visible, upper dext. sh. 130 x 100 mm, upper sin. sh. 130 x 105 mm, Purbeck slab 1335 remains x 465 mm remains and 665 remains x 300 mm remains. Style: London F. 8. Indent, ?marg. inscr., 18 rivets, 20 plugs and 5 plug holes only, effaced, at entrance to S.Porch, Churchyard. Purbeck slab 1285 remains x 485 mm remains. 9. *(Formerly M.S.II)*. Lost brass, inscr. Anne, widow, eld. dau. of Sir Henry Wallop, Knt. and w. Dame Elizabeth, dau. and h. of Robert Corbett of Moreton Corbett, Salop, w. of John Dodington of Breamor, 1656; in 1863 loose in the Wallop vault. Illustration from rubbing in Soc. Antiq. coll. Rubbing in Soc. Antiq. coll. (n.d.). Inscr. 218 x 270 mm.

Ref: *Burke's Peerage and Baronetage*, p.2162; *Haines*, II, p.74; *M.B.S. Bulletin*, 5, p.13; *M.B.S. Trans.*, VI, p.33; *Mee, Hampshire*, p.162; *M.S.*, p.166; *Sadler, Dorset and Hampshire*, pt.2, p.16, appx. I, pt.2, pp.19-21, p.41; *Soc. Antiq. MS. 875/6*, p.136; *V.C.H., Hampshire*, III, p.365.

Ch. built, c.1750, essentially 1871-2.

WALLOP, NETHER, St. Andrew.

I. Dame Mary Gore, prioress [of Amesbury], **1436**, in kirtle, veil head-dress, barbe and mantle, inscr. and scroll (both mutil.); sh. lost; N. *Bertram, Brasses*, fig.49, p.97; *Brit. Lib. Add. MS. 39987*, f.28r; *M.B.S. Trans.*, VI, p.34; *Mee, Hampshire*, p.115 (drg. of eff.); *Specimens of Lettering*, no.165 (lettering). Eff. 724 x 234 mm, inscr. 88 x 390 mm, scroll orig. 102 x 192 x 23 mm, now 80 x 184 x 23 mm, sh. indent 160 x 140 mm, Purbeck slab 2645 x 1070 mm. Style: London D.

II. Inscr. recording gift [of font cover] in **1882** by ws. and daus. of parishioners in mem. of Fanny Adeline, w. of Rev. Edm[un]d Lacon, [M.A.], vicar [1875-1919], on font cover, N. *III & IV*. Two inscrs. Marian, widow of Rev. Walter Blunt, **1886**, on candelabrum, C. *V*. Inscr. recording ch. clock pos. in **1887** by parishioners to commem. [golden jubilee of] Queen Victoria, maker's name FRANK SMITH & C⁰ LONDON, mur., on panelling, Tower. *VI*. Inscr. Walter Morrison Pothecary, 1892, aged 51, and w. Georgina, **1907**, aged 71; also only son, Frederick William [Pothecary], died at sea, 1890, aged 27, mur., N.A. *VII*. Inscr. in raised letters recording gift of [east north aisle] window in **1909** by Philip Shuttleworth Darnell and w. Julia Elinor, on window splay, N.A. *VIII*. World War I memorial (18 names), pos. by parishioners, maker's name *F. HIGHMAN & SON, L^{TD} SALISBURY*, mur., on board, N.A. *IX*. Inscr. Frank Pothecary, of Fifehead Manor, 1922, and w. Alice, **1928**, copper, mur., N.A. *X*. Inscr. E. Sherwood, engr. c.**1950**, on churchwardens' wand, N. *XI*. Inscr. M. Sherwood, engr. c.**1950**, on churchwardens' wand, N. *XII*. Inscr. recording restoration and conversion of ch. clock to automatic winding in **1977** by parishioners to commem. silver jubilee of Queen Elizabeth II, mur., on panelling, Tower. *XIII*. Inscr. Mrs. R., 1897-**1979**, bronze, on bench, Churchyard. *XIV*. Inscr. Ruth Osmond, 1906-**1985**, on stool, N.A. *XV & XVI*. Two inscrs. Olive Mona Hughesdon, 1914-1980, engr. c.**1985**, on pews, N.A. *XVII*. Inscr. Tony Gallop, 1935-1982, engr. c.**1985**, on credence table, N.A. *XVIII*. Inscr. recording gift [of table] by B.H. Becker, engr. c.**1985**, on table, N.A. *XIX*. Inscr. recording gift [of pew] by Betty Combes, engr. c.**1985**, on pew, N.A. *XX*. Inscr. recording gift [of stool] by Rose Kermode, engr. c.**1985**, on stool, N.A. *XXI*. Inscr. in mem. of Lynwood family, engr. c.**1985**, on pew, N.A. *XXII*. Inscr. recording donation [of pew] by Hugh and Stuart Fraser Richards, engr. c.**1985**, on pew, N.A.

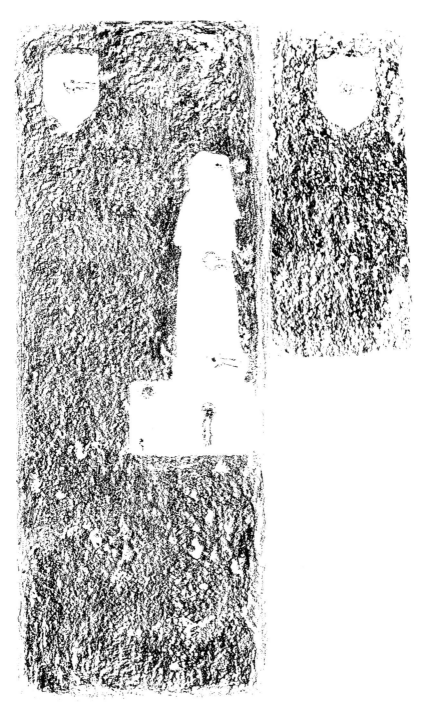

Wallop, Farleigh 7

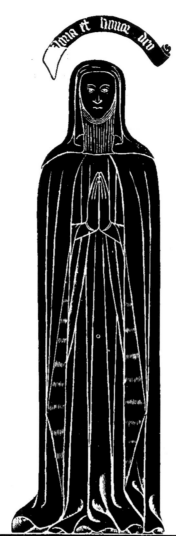

Wallop, Nether I

312

Wallop, Nether 27

XXIII. Inscr. recording presentation [of pew] by Linda Sherwood in mem. of parents, engr. c.**1985**, on pew, N.A. *XXIV.* Inscr. Nancy Helen Turner, engr. c.**1985**, on pew, N.A. *XXV.* Inscr. [recording gift of pew] from Simon White and family, engr. c.**1985**, on pew, N.A. *XXVI.* Inscr. recording restoration and reglazing of east window in **1997** in mem. of [Major] Bertram William Jepson Turner, M.C., C[roix] de G[uerre], D.L., of Garlogs, 1919-1995, mur., on board, C.

INDENTS & LOST BRASSES. 27. Indent, abbot or bishop, single canopy and super-canopy, inscr. and 2 shs., c.1400, N.A. *Sadler, Dorset and Hampshire*, pt.II, p.18 (drg.), appx. I, pt.2, p.27 (drg.). Eff. 1765 x 470 mm, canopy 2640 x 930 mm, canopy inc. super-canopy 2710 x 1035 mm, inscr. 100 x 1055 mm, dext. sh. 150 x 120 mm, sin. sh. 150 x 120 mm, Purbeck slab 2965 x 1310 mm remains. Style: London A.

Ref: *Brit. Lib. Add. MS. 39987,* f.28; *Gawthorp*, p.92; *Gittings*, p.30; *Haines*, I, p.87, II, p.74; *Manning*, p.31; *M.B.S. Trans.*, VI, p.33, p.35; *Mee, Hampshire*, p.238; *Moody*, p.198; *M.S.*, pp.166-7; *Norris, Memorials*, p.88; *Pevsner, Hampshire*, p.344; *Sadler, Dorset and Hampshire*, pt.II, pp.18-9, appx. I, pt.2, p.26; *Simpson*, p.28; *Soc. Antiq. MS. 875/6*, pp.136-8; *V.C.H., Hampshire*, IV, p.529.

WALTHAM, NORTH, St. Michael (new church).

I. Inscr. **William Pink**, M.A., fellow of Magdalen Coll., Oxford, 1628, aged 27, and brother John, **1629**, aged 23, mur., in wooden frame, C. Inscr. 437 x 482 mm.

II. Inscr. recording erection of [east] window in mem. of Rev. William Fraser, chaplain to H[onourable] E[ast] I[ndia] C[ompany] S[ervice], rector, 1842, aged 53, and 1st w. Margaret, 1826, buried at Bhauryulpore; also children, Isabella May, 1839, aged 14, and Roderick, 1841, aged 18; also widow, Mary, **1865**, aged 67, buried in the churchyard, mur., below window, C. *III.* Inscr. recording [south-east chancel] window and western windows pos. in **1868** by friends and parishioners in mem. of Rev. Henry Carey, M.A., rector 1863-1867 "during which time he effected the rebuilding of this Church", 1867, aged 59, on window splay, C. *IV.* Inscr. with verse. [Rev. Canon] William Lewery Blackley, [M.A., F.S.S.], hon. canon of Winchester Cathedral, curate-in-charge of Frensham 1855-1867, rector 1867-1883, vicar of King's Somborne 1883-1889, vicar of Westminster, St. James the Less 1889-[1902], 1902, aged 71, pos. in **1904** by widow, maker's name H. ROSE & SON. SOUTHAMPTON, mur., on board, N. *V.* Inscr. Rolfe Evans, 1962-**1995**, on table, N. *VI.* Inscr. Richard Neil Jebbitt, husband and [father] to Jayne, Holly and Matthew, [1960-**2001**], on bench, Churchyard.

Ref: *M.B.S. Trans.*, VI, pp.35-6; *M.S.*, p.167; *Soc. Antiq. MS. 875/6*, pp.138-9; *V.C.H., Hampshire*, IV, p.222.

Ch. built, 1865-6.

WARBLINGTON, St. Thomas à Becket.

I. Inscr. with verse recording chancel windows filled with glass in **1859** by Rev. W[illia]m Norris, M.A., rector [1827-1878], in mem. of w. Emily, dau. of Charles Short, of Woodlands,

¶ M S

...uc appulêre duo fratres ex
...nestâ et antiquâ familiâ Pinkoru...
...undi Quorũ natu maior Gulielm...
...ium Magifter Theologus Soci...
...ll: Mag: Oxon: & Philofophiæ
...ector Scientiarum Linguarum
...itiâ et infigni pietate claruit
...iit An° Dn'. 1628 Decemb 24
Ætatis fuæ 27 Iunior autē eo...
...annes iuvenis modeftus ac
...robus Obijt An° D' 1629 Marti...
Ætatis fuæ vicefimo tertio
T M

Waltham, North I

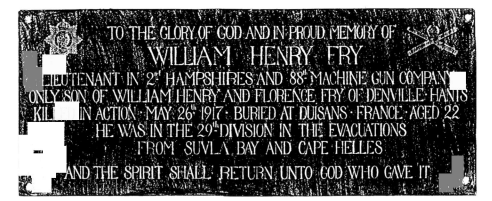

TO THE GLORY OF GOD AND IN PROUD MEMORY OF
WILLIAM HENRY FRY
LIEUTENANT IN 2ᵈ HAMPSHIRES AND 88ᵗ MACHINE GUN COMPANY
ONLY SON OF WILLIAM HENRY AND FLORENCE FRY OF DENVILLE HANTS
KILLED IN ACTION MAY 26ᵗʰ 1917 BURIED AT DUISANS FRANCE AGED 22
HE WAS IN THE 29ᵗʰ DIVISION IN THE EVACUATIONS
FROM SUVLA BAY AND CAPE HELLES
AND THE SPIRIT SHALL RETURN UNTO GOD WHO GAVE IT

Warblington *VIII*

1859, aged 66; also son, William Thomas, "LOST IN THE AUSTRALASIAN SEAS", "HE EMBARKED ON BOARD THE WYVERN, WHICH SAILED FROM NELSON, IN NEW ZEALAND, FOR SYDNEY, NEW SOUTH WALES, ON THE 1ST OF JULY 1856, AND WAS NEVER HEARD OF MORE", 1856, aged 26, mur., C. *II.* Inscr. recording [east south chapel] window filled with glass in mem. of Capt. William Butler Fellowes, 3rd Madras Cavalry, of Adbury House, 2nd son of Sir James Fellowes, M.D., F.R.S., joined regt. in 1841 and served for more than 20 years, "HE WAS ON FIELD SERVICE IN THE SOUTHERN MAHRATTA COUNTRY FROM NOVEMBER 1844 TO JUNE 1845, AND WAS ENGAGED WITH THE REBELS IN THE RAM GHAUT ON THE 1ST 4TH 18TH AND 29TH OF JANUARY 1845", husband and father, **1872**, aged 50, mur., below window, S.C. *III.* Inscr. recording [east north chapel] window filled with glass in mem. of Anne Norris, dau. of Rev. William Norris, [M.A.], rector 1789-1827, **1872**, [aged 81], mur., below window, N.C. *IV.* Inscr. John Russell Reeves, 1879-**1886**, [buried] in family vault at St. Mary's, Wimbledon, copper, mur., below window, N.A. *V.* Inscr. Rev. William Norris, [M.A.], curate for 9 years [1818-1827] and rector for 51 years [1827-1878], born and died at The Rectory "LIVED THERE NEARLY 98 YEARS", 1795-**1893**, mur., below window, S.A. *VI.* Inscr. [Rev.] Paulus Æmilius Singer, [M.A.], **1901**, aged 69, on window splay, C. *VII.* Inscr. with verse. Capt. Eric Perry Coventry Black, R.N., H.M.S. Natal, and w. Violet, "WHO DIED WITH HIM", **1915**, maker's name A&N. C.S.L. LONDON, mur., N. *VIII.* Inscr. with verse and 2 regt insignia. Lt. William Henry Fry, 2nd [Battn.] Hampshire [Regt. attd.] 88th Co. Machine Gun Co., only son of William Henry Fry and [w.] Florence [Ann], of Denville, "HE WAS IN THE 29th DIVISION IN THE EVACUATIONS FROM SUVLA BAY AND CAPE HELLES", killed in action, **1917**, aged 22, buried at Duisans [British Cemetery, Etrun], France, mur., on marble, N.A. Inscr. 265 x 654 mm. *IX.* Inscr. 2nd-Lt. Victor Thomas James Rainey, 2nd Battn. Devon[shire] Regt., son of William Rainey and [w.] Harriet M[atilda], killed in action at Ypres, **1917**, aged 19, [buried at Lancashire Cottage Cemetery, Belgium], mur., S.A. *X.* Inscr. in raised letters with regt. insignia in relief. Lt. John William Ronald Campbell, M.C., 3rd [Battn.] Worcestershire Regt., 2nd son of Gen. Sir William Campbell, K.C.B., R.M.A., and [w.] Frances Maria, great-grandson of Rev. William Norris, [M.A.], rector 1827-1878, killed in France, **1918**, [aged 24], maker's name CULN GAWTHORP & SONS · LONDON, mur., C. *XI.* Inscr. with Lat. verse and regt. insignia in relief. Capt. Gilbert Hume Norris, [13th Battn.] King's Royal Rifle Corps, son of Rev. William Burrell Norris, [M.A., curate 1875-1878, and] rector [1878-1928], and w. Constance, died of wounds received in action in France, **1918**, aged 31, [buried at Lijssenthoek Military Cemetery, Belgium], maker's name CULN GAWTHORP & SONS LONDON, mur., in wooden frame, C. *XII.* Inscr. with verse, 2 regt. insignia in relief and 2 enamelled medal ribbons. Capt. George Gordon Paine, M.C., 2nd Battn. attd. 6th [Battn.] Royal Berkshire Regt., killed in action at Aveluy Wood, France, **1918**, aged 24, [buried at Varennes Military Cemetery, France]; also Pte. James Horace Paine, [760380], 1st Battn. [London Regt.] (Artists' Rifles), killed in action near Cambrai, 1917, aged 19, [sons of George Cuthbert Paine and w. Agnes May], mur., on board, C. *XIII.* Inscr. recording erection of reredos in **1919** by rector and parishioners as [World War I] memorial (30 names), mur., on board, C. *XIV.* Inscr. Beatrice L. Beauchamp, president of Warblington C[hurch] W[orkers] G[uild] 1937-**1947**, on pulpit, N. *XV.* Inscr. Christopher and Millicent Wilkins, engr. c.**1950**, on cupboard, Vestry. *XVI.* Inscr. recording that lighting was provided in **1951** in mem. of Henry Curwen Biscoe-Smith, 1934, aged 67, and w. Louisa Margaret, 1938, aged 68, bronze, mur., N. *XVII.* Inscr. Nora Tinson Wale, **1963**, on candlestick, Vestry. *XVIII.* Inscr. recording presentation [of processional cross] by Miss J. Edith Dunning in mem. of John Dunning, [w.] Helena and family, engr. c.**1980**, on processional cross, Vestry. *XIX.* Inscr. recording dedication of [south-centre west] window in mem. of George Halsted, 1884-1957, and [w.] Nellie, 1887-1973; also daus., Helen Webber, 1916-**1982**, and Heather Lofts, 1923-1965,

Warblington 24

[buried] in Warblington Cemetery; also sons, Henry Norman [Halsted], 1913-1942, and Tony [Halsted], 1915-1918, on door below window, C. *XX.* Inscr. recording restoration of organ in **2000** with funds donated by Miss Joan Hawes, on organ, N. *XXI.* Inscr. recording restoration of [nave] windows and installation of loop system the gift in **2000** of the Guild of Friends of Warblington Church to commem. 70th anniversary, on organ with no.*XX*, N. *XXII.* Inscr. Mr. and Mrs. R. Swadling, engr. c.**2000**, on organ seat, N. *XXIII.* Inscr. recording refurbishment of baptistry in **2005** by the Guild of Friends of Warblington Church to commem. 75th anniversary, on cupboard, Baptistry/N.A.

INDENTS & LOST BRASSES. 24. Indent, civilian and w., inscr., 2 shs. and 2 roundels, c.1535, nearly effaced, C. *Sadler, Dorset and Hampshire*, pt.II, p.27 (drg.). Male eff. c.470 x 165 mm, female eff. c.465 x 185 mm, inscr. 255 x 520 mm, dext. sh. 155 x 145 mm, sin. sh. 160 x 140 mm, dext. roundel 105 mm dia., sin. roundel 105 mm dia., Purbeck slab 2725 x 1010 mm, approp. for Frances, dau. of Richard ?Cotton and w. Elizabeth, 1637, aged 12. Style: London.

The monument to a priest, in gown, kng., inscr., scroll and sh. Raffe Smalpage, chaplain to Earl of Southampton, Lord Chancellor, parson, 1558, recorded by Pevsner (1967) as a brass, is an incised slab.

Ref: *Gent. Mag.*, 1795, II, pp.638-40; *Gent. Mag. Lib. Eng. Topog.*, p.115; *Haines*, II, p.76; *Heseltine*, *Heraldry*, p.38; *M.B.S. Trans.*, VI, p.36, X, pp.97-101, XI, pp.113-4; *Mee, Hampshire*, p.371; *Pevsner, Hampshire*, p.641; *Sadler, Dorset and Hampshire*, pt.II, p.27; *Soc. Antiq. MS. 875/6*, p.139; *V.C.H., Hampshire*, III, p.139.

WARNBOROUGH, SOUTH, St. Andrew.

I. Robert Whyte, esq., lord of the manor, son of John Whyte, esq., 1512, in arm. of the period c.1480, kng., with a large hand pointing to a scroll, inscr., engr. c.**1490**; Trinity and 4 shs. lost; mur., A.T., C. Recorded (2 shs.) by Pavey (1706). *Brasses as Art and History*, fig.99, p.130; *Brit. Lib. Add. MS. 39971,* f.230 (drg. by Baigent), *Harl. MS. 4944,* ff.62-4; *Clinch, Costume*, p.210 (eff.); *Lewis*, fig.61A, p.85; *M.B.S. Portfolio*, III, pl.3; *Mee, Hampshire*, p.115 (drg. of eff.); *Portfolio Book*, pl.283. Male eff. 465 x 369 mm, inscr. 115 x 464 mm, Trinity indent 220 x 125 mm, hand 126 x 99 mm, scroll 255 x 120 x 31 mm, upper dext. sh. indent 125 x 105 mm, upper sin. sh. indent 125 x 105 mm, lower dext. sh. indent 130 x 110 mm, lower sin. sh. indent 130 x 110 mm, Purbeck slab 865 x 700 mm, Purbeck coverstone 2290 x 1040 mm. Style: London D.

II. Inscr. recording grant of £25.00 in **1869** by The Incorporated Church Building Society "TOWARDS RESEATING AND RESTORING THIS CHURCH, BY WHICH ADDITIONAL ACCOMMODATION HAS BEEN OBTAINED FOR 46 PERSONS, THE ENTIRE AREA WILL ACCOMMODATE 205, AT THE LEAST. THE SITTINGS ARE ALL FREE AND SUBJECT TO ALLOTMENT BY THE CHURCHWARDENS, SUITABLE PROVISION BEING MADE FOR THE POORER INHABITANTS"; [Rev. Dr.] Cha[rle]s Montague Style, [M.A., D.D.], rector [1866-1917]; T.H. Wayne and H. Bennett, churchwardens, mur., S.C./S.A. *III.* Inscr. Thomas Moore Wayne and w. Frances, 1868-**1870**, on window splay, C. *IV.* Inscr. with verse recording erection [of west window] by friends in mem. of George Doubleday, **1890**, on window splay, Vestry/N. *V.* Inscr. Thomas Harrison Harrison Wayne, lord of the manor, and w. Emma Tucker; also dau.,

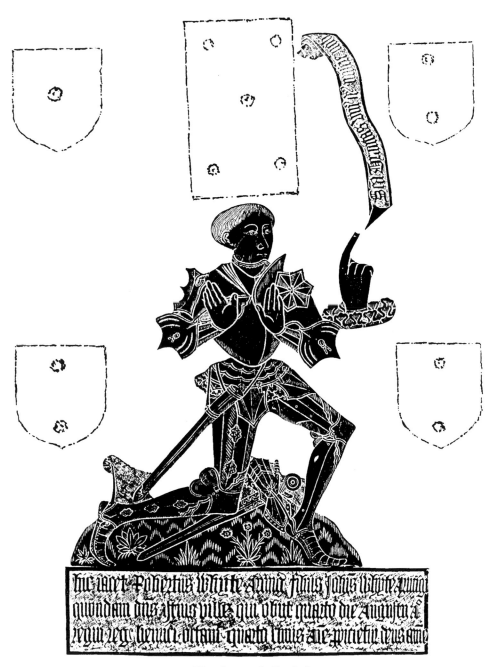

Warnborough, South I

Irene Effield Harrison, buried at Cromhall, Gloucs., and grandson, John Wayne Bakewell, [pos. in] **1937** [by] M.B., mur., on board, C. *VI.* Inscr. recording erection [of pulpit desk] by friends in mem. of [Rev.] Henry Douglas Oldfield, M.C., rector 1935-**1950**, on pulpit desk, N. *VII.* Inscr. recording erection [of screen] by family in mem. of Annie Mary Janaway, of Ford Farm, **1953**, bronze, on screen, N. *VIII.* Inscr. Jack Carter, 1901-**1959**, bronze, on wooden cross, Churchyard. *IX.* Inscr. recording that [south] porch was enclosed in **1960**, the gift of surviving children, Ewan, Lancelyn and Donald, in mem. of Theodora Gawne, churchwarden for many years, 1942, on door, S.Porch. *X.* Inscr. Gilbert Dicker, 1911-**1977**, pos. by friends, mur., on board, S.C./S.A. *XI.* Inscr. recording erection of chandeliers by friends in mem. of Ewan Gawne, 1889-**1978**, mur., on board, C. *XII.* Inscr. George H. Janaway, of Ford Farm, 1881-1966, and dau., Dorothy Darnell, 1918-**1978**, bronze, on screen, N. *XIII.* Inscr. with verse recording donation of [north-east nave] window by widow and stepmother, Freida Olive, in mem. of Leonard Ewart Jones, **1982**, aged 90, and "HIS TOTALLY BLIND SON", Alwyn [Jones], 1980, aged 58, mur., N. *XIV.* Inscr. with verse. Evelyn Louie Knight, 1910-**1991**, bronze, on bench, Churchyard. *XV.* Inscr. recording restoration of ch. clock (1825) in **1994** by apprentices and Serco staff at Princes Marina Coll., Aborfield, [Berks.], mur., on chiming apparatus case, Vestry/N. *XVI.* Inscr. with verse. Alec William Forbes, [1920-**1995**], bronze, on bench, Churchyard Extension. *XVII.* Inscr. Alice and Albert Taylor, engr. c.**1995**, on wooden cross, Churchyard. *XVIII.* Inscr. with verse. Arthur Henry Knight, 1905-**1997**, bronze, on bench with no.*XIV*, Churchyard.

INDENTS & LOST BRASSES. 19. Lost ?brass, lady in heraldic mantle, kng., inscr. and sh. Elizabeth, dau. of Sir Thomas White, Knt., w. of Lord Chidioke Paulett, who had issue William, Elizabeth, Katherine, Susan, 1560, mur., C. Recorded by Pavey (1706). *Brit. Lib. Add. MS. 39971*, f.230r (drg. by Baigent). 20. Lost brass, eff., inscr. and ?4 shs. [Sir] Thomas [?White, Knt., 1570]. Recorded (sh., White imp. a cross between 6 martlets, with eff., inscr. and ?3 shs. lost) by Pavey (1706). *Brit. Lib. Add. MS. 39971*, f.230 (drg. by Baigent). 21. Lost brass, inscr. Richard White, esq., lord of the manor, 15__, and w. Ellen, 1597. *Brit. Lib. Add. MS. 39971*, f.242 (drg. by Baigent).

Ref: *Brasses as Art and History*, p.128; *Brit. Lib. Add. MS. 39971*, ff.230-1, f.242, *Harl. MS. 4944*, ff.62-4; *Stowe MS. 845*, f.42, f.44; *Haines*, II, p.74; *Heseltine, Heraldry*, p.38; *Lewis*, pp.84-5; *M.B.S. Trans.*, VI, pp.36-8, IX, pp.426-7, X, pp.11-2; *Mee, Hampshire*, p.337; *M.S.*, p.167; *Norris, Memorials*, pp.137-8; *Pevsner, Hampshire*, p.603; *Soc. Antiq. MS. 875/6*, pp.139-41.

WARNFORD, Our Lady.

I. Inscr. in raised letters. Betty Freda Clarke, worshipped in the ch. for 54 years, 1912-**1993**, bronze, on grave marker, Churchyard. *II.* Inscr. Ron Clarke, husband of no.*I*, worshipped in the ch. for 62 years, 1913-**2001**, bronze, on grave marker, Churchyard.

WEEKE, or WYKE, St. Matthew.

I. Figure of St. Christopher and inscr. to William Complyn, **1498** (date added), and w. Annes, "Also this be ye dedis yᵗ ye said Willm hath down to this Church of Wike yᵗ is to say frest dedycacion of yᵉ Church xlˢ & to make nawe bellis to yᵉ sam Church xᶠ also gave to yᵉ halloyeng

Here lyeth Willm̄ Complyn
& Annes his wife ye whiche
Willm̄ dwellid ye xxi day of
Maij ye yere of oure lord
M.ccccc.xxx vii And Also this be
ze redis yt ze said Willm̄ hath
do[v]en to this Church of Wike
yt is to lay here dedicacion
of ye Church &c & to make
newe bellis to ye sam Church
&c allso gave to ye hallowing
of ye grettest bell iij li viii d
& for ye testimonyall of the
dedicacion of ye sam Church
iiijs viij d on whos soules
Ihū have mercy Amen

Weeke I

of ye grettest bell vi^s. viii·d & for ye testimonyall of the dedicacion of ye sam Church vi^s. viii·d", mur., N. *Arch. Jour.*, III, p.84, and *Winchester vol.*, 1845; *Baigent, F.J., Hist. of Wyke Church*, 1865, frontis.; *Beaumont*, p.159; *Bertram, Brasses*, fig.85(c), p.135 (saint); *Bouquet, Church Brasses*, fig.60, p.105 (saint); *Boutell, Br. and Slabs*, p.140 (saint); *Brit. Lib. Add. MS. 39987*, f.42r; *Calendar of the Anglican Church*, 1851, p.203 (saint); *Haines*, I, p.105 (drg. of saint); *Hants Proc.*, VII, p.78; *Moody*, p.85; *Oxford Man.*, p.48 (saint); *Trivick, Craft*, pl.180, p.70 (saint); *Trivick, Picture Book*, pl.99 (saint); *V. and A. Mus. List*, pl.56, no.5 (saint), 2nd edn., pl.62, no.5 (saint). Fig. 218 x 110 mm, inscr. 307 x 186-192 mm, Purbeck slab 560 x 345 mm. Style: London F.

II. Inscr. [Pte.] Thomas Harold Drake, [125, East African Mounted Rifles], killed in action at Longido, E[ast] Africa, **1914**, aged 30, [buried at Dar Es Salaam War Cemetery, Tanzania], on altar rail, C. *III.* Inscr. Capt. Charles William Pleydell-Bouverie, R.N., [1850-]**1921**, [pos. by w.] I[sabella] J[ane] P[leydell]-B[ouverie], on prie-dieu, N. *IV.* Inscr. [Chaplain 2nd Class] Ralph Henry Whitrow, T.D., C.F., [40452, Royal Army Chaplains' Dept., son of Benjamin Whitrow and w. Mary], rector 1937-1944, killed on active service, **1944**, [aged 47, buried at Winchester (West Hill) Old Cemetery], on choir stall, C. *V.* Inscr. recording gift of plain glass in [south chancel] windows in **1957** in mem. of Percy John and Helen Heather, mur., C.

INDENTS & LOST BRASSES. 6. Indent, ?rose, nearly effaced, N. Rose 95 mm dia., Purbeck slab 685 remains x 485 mm remains.

Ref: *Brit. Lib. Add. MS. 39987*, f.42; *Burke's Peerage and Baronetage*, p.2200; *Haines*, I, p.106, II, p.74; *Hampshire N. and Q.*, IV, pp.23-4; *Hants Proc.*, VII, pp.77-79; *Manning*, p.31; *M.B.S. Bulletin*, 68, p.159; *M.B.S. Trans.*, VI, p.39, XV, p.432; *Mee, Hampshire*, p.375; *M.S.*, p.167; *Norris, Memorials*, p.205; *Pevsner, Hampshire*, p.693; *Sadler, Dorset and Hampshire,* appx. I, pt.2, p.30; *Simpson*, p.29; *Soc. Antiq. MS. 875/6*, pp.142-4; *V.C.H., Hampshire*, III, p.452.

WELLOW, EAST, St. Margaret of Antioch.

I. Inscr. with verse. William Empson, yst. son of Rev. W[illiam] H[enry] Empson, M.A., vicar [1844-1883], 1853-**1870**, maker's name GAWTHORP S^C LONDON, mur., on marble, S.A. *II.* Inscr. (chamfer). [Rev.] William Henry Empson, [M.A.], vicar 1844-1883, **1883**, and Emily Frances Empson, 1857; also yst. son, William Empson, 1853-1870, Churchyard. *III.* Cross and inscr. with verse. [Rev.] William Henry Empson, [M.A.], vicar 1844-1883, **1883**, maker's name GAWTHORP S^C LONDON, mur., on marble, S.A. *IV.* Inscr. recording erection of font by only surviving son in mem. of [Rev.] William Henry Empson, M.A., vicar for 39 years [1844-1883, 1883], engr. c.**1885**, on font, N. *V.* Inscr. with verse recording gift of lectern in **1898** by Etheldred Elizabeth Fisher, on lectern, N. *VI.* Inscr. Charles William Empson, J.P., M.A., eld. son of Rev. W[illiam] H[enry] Empson, [M.A.], vicar [1844-1883], **1919**, aged 70, and w. Katharine Leslie (née Gillies), 1918, aged 55, mur., on marble, S.A. *VII.* Inscr. recording presentation of organ in **1927** by [Mr.] and Mrs. J.J. Crosfield, on organ, N. *VIII.* Inscr. recording installation of electric organ blower by husband and children in mem. of Violet Cornelia Makin, died at Eastlands, West Wellow, **1952**, copper, on organ with no.*VII*, N. *IX.* Inscr. Jessie Pilbrow, of Woodington House, **1975**, ashes scattered in the churchyard, bronze, on bench, Churchyard. *X.* Inscr. in raised letters. Clara Whiting, 1896-**1979**, bronze, on grave marker, Churchyard. *XI.* Inscr. Mrs. Joyce Wilkins, organist for 25 years, **1981**, on organ with nos.*VII* & *VIII*, N. *XII.* Inscr. Wellow and District Branch of the Royal British Legion, orig. standard 1932-**1982**, on beam below standard, N. *XIII.* Inscr. recording demolition of orig. war memorial plinth (erected in 1920) by traffic accident and resiting in **1984**, bronze, on plinth, outside Churchyard. *XIV.* Inscr. James (Jimmy) Roy Stokes, 1962-**1988**, pos. by friends "AT POINTERS", on bench, outside Churchyard. *XV.* Inscr. Cathy Lane, pos. by friends "IN THE MIDLAND", engr. c.**1990**, on bench, Churchyard Extension. *XVI.* Inscr. [Frederick James] (Jim) Daniels, [husband and father], 1932-**1993**, [pos. by] w. Ann, and son, Raymond, bronze, on bench, Churchyard Extension. *XVII.* Inscr. Margaret Parkinson, S.R.N., S.C.M., 1906-**1993**, on pew, S.A. *XVIII.* Inscr. John Lee, 1949-**2002**, pos. by w. and children, on bench, Churchyard Extension.

WESTBOURNE, (see BOURNEMOUTH).

WHITCHURCH, All Hallows.

I. Richard Brooke, 1593, in civil dress, and w. Elizabeth [Twyne], 1599, mar. 41 years, with 3 sons, Richard, Thomas, Robert, and 3 daus., Elizabeth, Barbara, Dorothy, inscr. in 20 Eng. vv. and 3 shs.; Robert their yst. son, citizen of London, mcht.-adventurer and goldsmith pos. in **1603**; now mur., S.A. *Bouquet, Church Brasses,* fig.37, p.71 (head of female eff.); *M.B.S. Portfolio,* IV, pl.5; *Mee, Hampshire,* p.347 (drg. of effs. and children); *Portfolio Book,* pl.392. Male eff. 728 x 272 mm, female eff. 686 x 274 mm, inscr. 480 x 657 mm, sons 205 x 277 mm, daus. 172 x 265-274 mm, dext. sh. 162 x 138 mm, sin. sh. 162 x 138 mm, centre sh. 139 x 116 mm. Style: Johnson (script 12).

II. Inscr. recording gift [of lectern] in **1885** by Charles Edney, of The Manor, on lectern, N. *III.* Inscr. recording erection of [south-east south aisle] window by w., family and brother, Ven. Archdeacon Dudley, of Christchurch, New Zealand, in mem. of [Rev.] William Mason Dudley, M.A., vicar for 44 years [1842-1886], chaplain to Union for 30 years [1846-1876], rector of Laverstoke for 24 years [1846-1870], 1803-**1886**, on window splay, S.A. *IV.* Inscr. with verse. Emma, w. of George Edney, of The Manor, **1886**, aged 47, mur., below window, S.A. *V.* S[outh] African War memorial (7 names), 1900-1902, pos. in **1902** by inhabitants of Whitchurch and neighbouring district, maker's name H · OSBORNE · DES[r] · ENGr · RYDE I · W, mur., on board, N.A. *VI.* Inscr. with crest and motto. Tobias Rustat Hemsted, 1880, aged 69, and w. Mary Ann, 1882, aged 68; also son, Henry Hemsted, 1916, aged 79, w. Ellen, **1921**, aged 80, and Ellen Mary Hilhouse Hemsted, 1917, aged 51, mur., N. *VII.* Inscr. recording donation [of display case] by Whitchurch Branch of the Royal British Legion in mem. of Mrs. F. Dance, engr. c.**1930**, on display case, S.A. *VIII.* Inscr. recording erection of organ in **1935** by parishioners and C.C.D. in mem. of M.E.C.D., 1930, bronze, on organ, C. *IX.* Inscr. recording restoration of picture in **1939** by T[om] A[ugustine] Edney Hayter, mur., on picture frame, N.A. *X.* Inscr. Charles Nichols, **1944**, on table, N.C. *XI.* Inscr. Tom Augustine Edney-Hayter, J.P., **1945**, aged 91, and w. Emma Harriet, eld. dau. of George Edney, of The Manor, 1944, aged 85, mur., on board below no.*IX*, N.A. *XII.* Inscr. Jennifer Anne Sossick (née Kail), 1936-**1973**, on grave marker, Churchyard. *XIII.* Inscr. Jack Kelland, 1909-**1976**, bronze, on bench, Churchyard. *XIV.* Inscr. recording presentation [of display case] to Whitchurch Branch of the Royal British Legion by Reg Smith in mem. of father, engr. c.**1985**, on display case, Baptistry/S.A. *XV.* Inscr. Elsie Dorothea Baynham, M.B.E., 1896-**1988**, mur., on board, C.

Ref: *Brit. Lib. Stowe MS. 845*, f.81; *Haines*, II, p.74; *Hampshire N. and Q.*, II, p.42; *Heseltine, Heraldry*, p.38; *M.B.S. Trans.*, VI, pp.40-1; *Mee, Hampshire*, p.381; *M.S.*, p.167; *V.C.H., Hampshire*, IV, p.303.

WICKHAM, St. Nicholas.

I. Inscr. with 2 angels holding crown within border of oak leaves and acorns with roundels at corners. Rear-Admiral Sir Francis Aug[ustu]s Collier, C.B., K.G.H., died while in command at Hong Kong, 1849, aged 63, and 1st w. Eliza, dau. of Thomas Osborne, of the Island of Antigua, died at Versailles, [France], 1828; also [children], Ellen, w. of Major F. English, 35th Regt., died at Moulmeim, [Burma], **1856**, and Georgina and Francis, died young, [maker's monogram GAWTHORP], mur., on stone, N.Tr. *II.* Inscr. recording re-opening of ch. in **1862** after restoration and addition of tower, mur., on board, W.Porch/Tower. *III.* Inscr. Col. Hardress Saunderson, Gren[adier] Guards, son of Col. Saunderson, of Castle Saunderson, Ireland, **1865**, and w. Lady Maria, dau. of John, last Earl of Carhampton, 1861, pos. by children, mur., on board, N. *IV.* Inscr. with verse. Katherine, dau. of Thomas Thistlethwayte, of Southwick Park, widow of Rear-Admiral Sir Francis Augustus Collier, C.B., K.G.H., **1894**, aged 85; also sons, Francis Guitton, 1836-1843; Gulston Gordon, 1837-1837; and Lt. Alexander Thistlethwayte Collier, R.N., 1839-1861, mur., on board, N.Tr. *V.* Inscr. Capt. Herbert Parker, South Wales Borderers, killed in action at Suntai, W[est] Africa, **1899**, [aged 26], mur., on board, N. *VI.* Inscr. with Lat. verse, sh. and regt. insignia. Major John Trefusis [Carpenter-Garnier, 1st Battn.] Scots Guards, eld. son of John Carpenter-Garnier and [w.] Mary, of Rookesbury Park, mortally wounded at the Battle of the Aisne, France, 1874-**1914**, [buried in the churchyard at Vendresse, France], mur., on board, N. *VII.* Inscr. with crest. Capt. Dick Macdonald Porteous, D.S.O., 1st [Battn.] Argyll and Sutherland Highlanders, only son of Lt.-Col. and Mrs. J.J. Porteous, nephew of Lt.-Col. and Mrs. H.R. Farquhar, of Park Place, killed in action near Ypres, **1915**, [aged 31], maker's name A&N. AUX. C.S.L. LONDON, mur., N.Tr. *VIII.* Inscr. [Lt.-]Col. Charles Edward Radclyffe, D.S.O., Rifle Brigade and [11th Battn.] Essex Regt., only son of Charles Edward Radclyffe and [w.] Constance Albuera, killed at Hulluch, France, **1915**, aged 50, maker's name A&N. AUX. C.S.L. LONDON, mur., on board, N. *IX.* Inscr. recording gift of shrine by widow, [Theresa Caroline], in mem. of Lt.-Col. Charles Edward Radclyffe, D.S.O., [Rifle Brigade and] 11th Battn. [Essex Regt.], killed while commanding the Essex Regt. at [the Battle of] Loos, **1915**, [aged 50], mur., on triptych, N. *X.* Inscr. with verse, crest, regt. insignia in relief and battle honours (South Africa 1900-1902, Gallipoli 1915). Fanny, dau. of J. Wayte, widow of G. Woodroffe-Hicks, **1917**; also Lt. Surtees Sheffield, [13th Battn. attd.] 2nd [Battn.] Hampshire Regt., [killed] at Achi-Baba, [Turkey], 1915, mur., N.Tr. *XI.* Inscr. Frederick A. Hawker, 1893, aged 42; also eld. son, Arthur F.B. Hawker, 1886, aged 10; yst. son Lt. C.W. Seymour Hawker, [13th Battn.] Hampshire Regt., "DIED OF ILLNESS CONTRACTED DURING THE WAR", 1918, aged 29, [buried at Vevey (St. Martin's) Cemetery, Switzerland]; and yst. dau., Irene Laura Maud Hawker, **1919**, mur., N.Tr. *XII.* Inscr. William Wheatley, churchwarden and sidesman for 42 years, **1938**, aged 73, pos. by grandchildren, mur., on board, N. *XIII.* Inscr. recording restoration of pews by Charles Edward Mott-Radclyffe, M.P., in mem. of mother, Theresa Caroline, [only dau. of John Stanley Mott, J.P., of Barningham Hall, Norf.], widow of Lt.-Col. Charles Edward Radclyffe, D.S.O., Rifle Brigade, of Little Park, 1868-**1941**, on pew, N. *XIV.* Inscr. with Lat. verse. Lt. John Prideaux Carpenter-Garnier, [240641, 2nd Battn.] Scots Guards, son of George Carpenter-Garnier and [w.] Cheston [Isolda], killed in action near Salerno, Italy, 1921-**1943**, [buried at Salerno War Cemetery, Italy], copper, mur., on board with no.*VI*, N. *XV.* Inscr. recording gift

Pietatis opus

This graue' old greise' hath swallowed up with wide and open' mouth,
the' bodie' of good Richard Brooke, of whitchurch, hampton south,
And Elzabeth his wedded wife, twise twentie yeares and one,
Sweete Ihus hath their soules in heaven, & ground fleh skin and bone,
In Ianuarie'(worne' with age') deir sixterith died her,
From Christ full fiftene' hundred yeares, and more' by ninetie' three',
But death hir tooke of life' in May, deir twentith did vntwine',
From Christ full fifteene' hundred yeares, and more' by xvii time'
They left behinde' them well to liue', and growne' to good degree',
First, Richard, Thomas, Robert Brooke, the' yongest of the' three',
Elzabeth, and Barbara, then Dorathee' the' last,
All six the' knot of Nature's loue', and kindnes keeping fast.
This 'Toome' stone' with the' Plate' thereon, thus grauen takes a large'
Did Robert Brooke, the' yongst sonne' make of his proper charge,
A Citzen of london state', by faithfull service free',
Of Marchant greate' adventurers, a brother (borne' is her.
And of the' Indian Companie' (come' gaine' or losse') a lim,
And of the' Goldsmithe' liverie, All these' God giues to him:
This Monument of memorie' in loue' performed her,
December thirtie' one' from Christ sixterne' hundred and three':

Anno Domini 1603, laus Deo,

Whitchurch I

325

[of lectern] by son and dau. in mem. of Logan Sutherland Stansfield, 1859-1936, and w. Mary, 1869-**1946**, on lectern, N. *XVI.* Inscr. in raised letters. Sqdn.-Leader Walter Riley Adkins, R.A.F., **1956**, aged 60, bronze, on gravestone, Churchyard. *XVII.* Inscr. R.G.G. Warwick, father, **1956**, [pos. by] Brian, Richard and David, bronze, on altar, S.C. *XVIII.* Inscr. Edward Morris Lea, 1925-**1973**, on door, N.Tr. *XIX.* Inscr. recording gift of bookcase by children, Mary, Brian, Richard and David, in mem. of Dorothy Alice Warwick, **1979**; in 2006 loose in bookcase, S.C. *XX.* Inscr. Rev. J[ohn] G. Rashleigh, [B.A.], rector for 56 years [1805-1861], 1782-1868, engr. c.**1990**, copper, on bench, Churchyard. *XXI.* Inscr. Rev. R[ichard] Parker, [M.A.], rector 1863-1892, engr. c.**1990**, copper, on bench, Churchyard. *XXII.* Inscr. [Sir] Charles Edward Mott-Radclyffe, [Knt., M.P.], of Barningham Hall, Norf., [only] son of [Lt.-Col.] Charles Edward Radclyffe, [D.S.O.] and [w.] Theresa Caroline, 1911-**1992**, mur., on board, N. *XXIII.* Inscr. Jean Hill, "FOR HER SUPPORT & DEVOTION TO St. NICHOLAS CHURCH AND THE VILLAGE OF WICKHAM", engr. c.**1995**, bronze, on bench, Churchyard. *XXIV.* Inscr. Derek Harry West, husband, father and grandfather, 1929-**1996**, bronze, on grave marker, Churchyard. *XXV.* Inscr. Elizabeth Wilson (Tiney), [w., mother, grandmother and great-grandmother, **2003**, aged 74], on bench, Churchyard. *XXVI.* Inscr. Mario Avonda, 1914-1986, and Giuseppe Avonda, 1947-1984, engr. **2004**, on chair, S.C. *XXVII.* Inscr. Eileen Carpenter-Garnier, 1916-1987, engr. **2004**, on chair, S.C. *XXVIII.* Inscr. H.C. (Bert) Palmer, 1896-1990, engr. **2004**, on chair, S.C. *XXIX.* Inscr. Archer Hirst, 1905-1992, and [w.] Pixie, 1907-1988, engr. **2004**, on chair, S.C. *XXX.* Inscr. Harold F. Kendrick, 1920-1992, engr. **2004**, on chair, S.C. *XXXI.* Inscr. Michael Arcedeckne-Butler, 1933-1993, engr. **2004**, on chair, S.C. *XXXII.* Inscr. George Carpenter-Garnier, 1911-1993, engr. **2004**, on chair, S.C. *XXXIII.* Inscr. Kenneth C. Simmons, 1921-1993, engr. **2004**, on chair, S.C. *XXXIV.* Inscr. Hamish Thoms, 1902-1989, and [w.] Vera, 1911-1993, engr. **2004**, on chair with no.*XXIX*, S.C. *XXXV.* Inscr. E.R. (Duggie) Cadogan, 1909-1997, engr. **2004**, on chair, S.C. *XXXVI.* Inscr. Geoffrey Ian Randell, 1976-1998, engr. **2004**, on chair, S.C. *XXXVII.* Inscr. Edna Dawson, 1914-2000, engr. **2004**, on chair, S.C. *XXXVIII.* Inscr. Mick Johnston, 1934-2000, engr. **2004**, on chair, S.C. *XXXIX.* Inscr. Vera Turner, 1910-2000, engr. **2004**, on chair, S.C. *XL.* Inscr. Grace Barfoot (née Beckett), 1910-2001, engr. **2004**, on chair, S.C. *XLI.* Inscr. Edmund David Bellis, 1942-2001, engr. **2004**, on chair, S.C. *XLII.* Inscr. Eric F. Case, 1913-2001, engr. **2004**, on chair, S.C. *XLIII.* Inscr. Ellen Childs, 1917-2001, engr. **2004**, on chair, S.C. *XLIV.* Inscr. Rosalind Holladay, 1947-2001, engr. **2004**, on chair, S.C. *XLV.* Inscr. Group-Capt. Andrew K. Hunter, 1916-2001, engr. **2004**, on chair, S.C. *XLVI.* Inscr. Peter John Alexander (Alex), 1940-2002, engr. **2004**, on chair, S.C. *XLVII.* Inscr. Edna Doris Baird, 1915-2003, engr. **2004**, on chair, S.C. *XLVIII.* Inscr. Edith Ward, 1903-2003, engr. **2004**, on chair, S.C. *XLIX.* Inscr. Reg Amey, 1917-**2004**, and [w.] Thelma, 1921-2000, on bench, Churchyard. *L.* Inscr. recording donation [of chair] in **2004** by John Leach and [w.] Jean, on chair, S.C. *LI.* Inscr. Moya Pratt, "LOLLIPOP LADY", 1934-**2004**, on chair, S.C. *LII.* Inscr. Joan Helen Sharp, 1926-**2004**, on chair, S.C. *LIII.* Inscr. with verse on 2 pls. Eric Charles Walder, husband and father, 1927-**2004**, on wooden cross, Churchyard.

INDENTS & LOST BRASSES. 54. Lost indents, 10 gravestones "on which have been arms, pourtraitures and inscriptions on brass plates which are all gone", "As you enter ye Church under your feet lie several stones which had been inlaid with brass after ye old manner, one with a cross", N. Recorded by Pavey (1705).

Ref: *Brit. Lib. Add. MS. 14296*, f.16, *Stowe MS. 845*, f.131; *M.B.S. Trans.*, VI, pp.41-2; *Soc. Antiq. MS. 875/6*, pp.144-5; *Who's Who*, 1967, p.2186.

WIDLEY, St. Mary Magdalene (old church, now demolished).

INDENTS & LOST BRASSES. 1. ?Indent, sh.; with incised marg. inscr.; Dorothy, eld. dau. of Sir William Forth, of Buttley Abbey, Suff., Knt., w. of Nicholas Southcote, 1643, N. Sh. 375 x 305 mm, non-Purbeck slab 1875 x 940 mm.

Ref: *M.B.S. Trans.*, VI, p.42; *Soc. Antiq. MS. 875/6*, p.145.

Ch. rebuilt, 1849; demolished, 1953.

WINCHESTER, Cathedral Church of Holy Trinity, SS. Peter, Paul and Swithun.

I. Frag. of marg. inscr. in Lombardics, "OCTAVA DIE MENSIS . . . M . . . S", **late 13th cent.**, partly under Wykeham Chantry/N. Frags. 515 x 50 mm visible, 270 x 25 mm remains and 470 x 30 mm remains, Purbeck slab 3195 x 1090 mm.

II. Inscr. (chamfer). William Edington, [Bishop of Winchester 1346-1366], **1366**, A.T., Edington Chantry/N. Inscr. (chamfer) 1880 x 670 x 35 mm.

III. Inscr. (chamfer). William Wykeham, [Bishop of Winchester 1366-1404], **1404**, A.T., Wykeham Chantry/N. Inscr. (chamfer) 1962 x 750 x 52 mm.

IV. (Formerly M.S.II). Inscr. Richard Boles, killed at Alton, 1641; "*Ricardus Boles Wiltoniensis in Art : Mag : Composuit Posuitque Dolens. An. : Dm : 1689*", mur., on pillar, N. Inscr. 333 x 237 mm. See Alton no.*XIII.*

V. Inscr. with ach. "*THOMAS CHEYNEY, S.T.P. HUJUSCE ECCLESIÆ DECANUS DONO DEDIT A.D. 1756*", on chandelier, S.Tr. *VI.* Inscr. with verse. Jane Austen, novelist, "known to many by her writings, endeared to her family by the varied charms of her Character, and ennobled by Christian Faith and Piety", born at Steventon, 1775-1817, buried in the cathedral, pos. in **1872** by [nephew], Rev. J[ames] E[dward] Austen[-Leigh, M.A., from proceeds of biographical *Memoir* of 1870, designed by Thomas Henry Wyatt], mur., in stone frame, N.A. of N. Collected Reports of the Jane Austen Society 1949-1965, 1967, p.215; *Greenwood, D., Who's Buried where in England?*, 2nd edn., 1991, p.203 (photo.); *Wheeler, M., Jane Austen and Winchester Cathedral*, 2003, p.5. See also Steventon no.*II.* *VII.* Inscr. [Rev. Canon] Benjamin Prowting Clement, M.A., son of Capt. Benjamin Clement, R.N., and w. Ann Mary, minor canon [of Winchester Cathedral] for 34 years, **1873**, aged 60, maker's name SEARGENT WINTON, mur., in stone frame, N.A. of N. *VIII.* Inscr. with verse and enamelled sh. Harriet, Countess of Guilford, only dau. of Lt.-Gen. Sir Henry Warde, G.C.B., of Dean House, 1804-**1874**; mar. (1) 1826, Francis, 6th Earl of Guilford, eld. son of [Rt. Rev.] Brownlow North, Bishop of Winchester [1781-1820, 1861]; by whom 5 sons and 2 daus., (2) 1863, John Lettsom Elliot, of Pimlico, Middx., commoner of Winchester Coll., mur., in stone frame, N.A. of N. *IX.* Inscr. in raised letters with regt. insignia in relief. Col. Peter Burton Roe, 4th Battn. 60th [King's] Royal Rifle Corps, Adjutant-Gen. Madras 1869-1872, 1821-**1875**, pos. by brother and sister, Robert and Kate Roe, maker's name *Gaffin, Regent St London*, mur., in stone frame, S.A. of N. *X.* Inscr. with separate enamelled sh. recording erection of screen (northern portion) in **1875** by private contributions in mem. of [Rt. Rev. Dr.] Samuel Wilberforce, D.D., [Bishop of Oxford 1845-1869], Bishop [of Winchester] 1869-1873,

[1805-1873], on screen, C. See also Alverstoke no.*VIII*, Alverstoke, or Gosport, Fort Brockhurst no.*XXXIII*, Hinton Ampner no.*IX*, Newport, St. Thomas the Apostle no.*IX*, Petersfield no.*VI* and Ryde, or Swanmore, St. Michael and All Angels no.*III*. *XI*. Inscr. with separate enamelled sh. recording erection of screen (southern portion) in **1875** by private contributions in mem. of [Very Rev.] Thomas Garnier, D.C.L., Dean [of Winchester] 1840-1872, on screen, C. See also Bishopstoke no.*II*. *XII*. Inscr. with enamelled ach. and regt. insignia. Capt. the Hon. Edward Courtenay Vaughan, 4th Battn. Rifle Brigade, 3rd son of [Ernest Augustus Vaughan], 4th Earl of Lisburne, died at Umballa, India, [1841-]**1876**, pos. by friends in regt., mur., in stone frame, N.A. of N. *XIII*. Inscr. enamelled ach. and regt. insignia. Capt. Cornelius Davenport Broadbent, 4th Battn. Rifle Brigade, son of Rev. C[ornelius] F. Broadbent, died at Umballa, India, **1877**, aged 40, pos. by friends in regt., mur., in stone frame, N.A. of N. *XIV*. Inscr. Lt.-Col. Charles Williamson, 60th [King's] Royal Rifle [Corps, 3rd son of Sir Hedworth Williamson, 7th Bart.], died at Whitburn, Co. Durham, 1833-**1877**, on lectern plinth, N. *XV*. Inscr. with regt. insignia. Major Francis FitzPatrick, died "AFTER A SERVICE OF OVER 40 YEARS IN THE 2ND BATTALION 60TH RIFLES FOR 25 OF WHICH HE WAS ITS PAYMASTER AND WAS WITH IT DURING THE KAFFIR MUTINY AND THE CHINA WAR 1860", 1822-1879, pos. in **1880** by "FRIENDS WHO SERVED WITH HIM", maker's name HART SON PEARD & Cᵒ LONDON, mur., in stone frame, S.A. of N. *XVI*. Inscr. with regt. insignia. in mem. of officers, NCOs and men of 4th Battn. Rifle Brigade "WHO : DIED : ON : THE : CAMPAIGN : IN : AFGHANISTAN : AND : ON : THE : RETVRN : MARCH : TO INDIA : BETWEEN : 20 : NOVᴿ : 1878 : AND : 13 : JVLY : 1879" (85 names), pos. in **1880** by comrades, mur., in stone frame, N.A. of N. *XVII*. Inscr. with verse, badge, regt. insignia and Alpha-Omega symbols. Capt. Edward Hugh Crofton, Rifle Brigade, yst. son of Col. Hugh Denis Crofton, grandson of Sir Morgan G[eorge] Crofton, [3rd] Bart., of Mohill, Co. Leitrim, [Ireland], 1854-**1882**, maker's name HART SON PEARD & Cᵒ Lᴰ, mur., in stone frame, N.A. of N. *XVIII*. Inscr. with verse. [Rev. Canon] Edward Joseph Rose, [M.A.], rector of Weybridge, [Surrey], hon. canon [of Winchester Cathedral], rural dean, **1882**, maker's name HART SON PEARD & Cᵒ LONDON, mur., in stone frame, N.A. of N. *XIX*. Inscr. with regt. insignia within border of oak leaves and acorns recording erection of [south aisle of nave] window in mem. of officers, NCOs and [men] of 60th King's Royal Rifle Corps "WHO LOST THEIR LIVES IN THE SERVICE OF THEIR COUNTRY DURING THE AFGHAN, ZULU, TRANSVAAL AND EGYPTIAN CAMPAIGNS"; 2nd Battn. – Afghan Campaign: killed (4 names), died of disease (58 names) – Transvaal Campaign 1880-1881: died of disease (5 names) – Sudan 1884: killed (1 name); 3rd Battn. – Zulu Campaign 1879: killed (1 name), died of wounds (2 names), died of disease (50 names) – Transvaal Campaign 1880-1881: killed (60 names), died of wounds (7 names), drowned (1 name) – Egyptian Campaign **1882**: killed (4 names), died of wounds (5 names): Staff – Capt. Edward Walter Home Crofton, A.D.C., died of cholera, Afghan Campaign, mur., below window, S.A. of N. *XX*. Inscr. with regt. insignia. Major Mordaunt Charles Boyle, King's Royal Rifle Corps, died while Brigade-Major in Nile Expeditionary Force at Kurot on the Nile, **1885**, [aged 34], pos. by brother Riflemen, mur., in stone frame, S.A. of N. *XXI*. Cross and incised inscr. [Very Rev.] John Bramston, [M.A., B.D.], vicar of Great Baddow, [Essex], 1831-1840, vicar of Witham, [Essex], 1840-1872, [hon. canon of Rochester Cathedral 1863-1872], Dean [of Winchester] 1872-1883, 1802-**1889**, C. *XXII*. Inscr. with regt. insignia. Major Robert Henley, King's Royal Rifle Corps, died at Ovington, **1889**, aged 37, pos. by brother officers, mur., in stone frame, S.A. of N. *XXIII*. Inscr. with verse and regt. insignia. Lt.-Col. Arthur James Nixon, commanding 3rd Battn. Rifle Brigade, served with regt. through the Crimean War [1854-1856] and Indian Mutiny [1857-1858], died at Aldershot, 1875, aged 46; also 2nd son, Lt. Edward Stopford Nixon, 1st Battn. Rifle Brigade, died of cholera at Bareilly, India, **1889**, aged 26, mur., in stone frame, N.A. of N. *XXIV*. Inscr. with regt. insignia. Lt.-Col. Robert Cradock Davies,

Winchester, Cathedral I

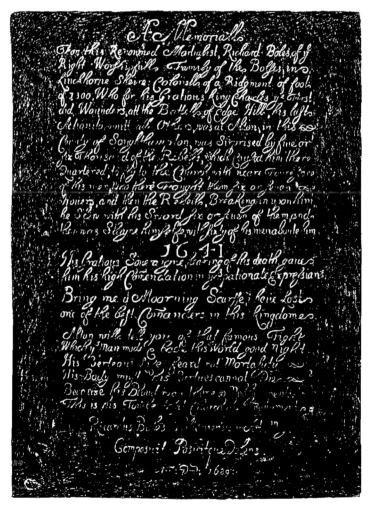

Winchester, Cathedral *IV*

Major King's Royal Rifle Corps, died at Shawford, **1890**, aged 45, pos. by brother officers, mur., in stone frame, S.A. of N. *XXV.* Inscr. with verse. Emily Winifreda Nixon, widow of no.*XXIII*, died at Winchester, **1891**, aged 55, mur., below no.*XXIII*, N.A. of N. *XXVI.* Inscr. with regt. insignia. Major Humphrey David Parry Okeden, King's Royal Rifle [Corps], **1894**, aged 44, pos. by brother officers, mur., in stone frame, S.A. of N. *XXVII.* Inscr. with enamelled ach. and 3 regt. insignia in relief. Capt. Frederick Eyre Lawrence, Rifle Brigade, son of General Sir Arthur [Johnstone] Lawrence, K.C.B., Col.-Commandant 2nd Battn. Rifle Brigade, killed while on special service at Mboyani, East Africa, **1895**, aged 33, maker's name HART, SON, PEARD & C[O], LTD, LONDON, mur., in stone frame, N.A. of N. *XXVIII.* Inscr. with verse in raised letters with regt. insignia and V.C. medal in relief. Lt. Frederick Hugh Sherston Roberts, V.C., King's Royal Rifle [Corps], only surviving son of Field-Marshal [The Rt. Hon. Sir Frederick Roberts] Lord Roberts, [Baron Roberts, V.C., K.G., K.P., G.C.B., G.C.S.I., G.C.I.E.], and w. Nora, "Who · fell · mortally · wounded · in · an · attempt · to save · the British · guns · at · the · battle · of · Colenso on · the · 15ᵗʰ December · **1899** · and · who · died two · days · afterwards Aged · 27 · years · and · 11 · months", bronze, mur., S.A. of C. *XXIX.* Inscr. with regt. insignia. Lt.-Col. Robert George Buchanan Riddell, commanding 3rd Battn. King's Royal Rifle [Corps], "FELL IN ACTION AT THE HEAD OF HIS BATTALION ON THE HEIGHTS OF SPION KOP. NATAL", **1900**, aged 45, pos. by w., mur., in stone frame, S.A. of N. *XXX.* Inscr. with regt. insignia. Major-Gen. Hugh Parker Montgomery, of Tyrella, Co. Down, Ireland, Lt.-Col. commanding 2nd Battn. 60th [King's] Royal Rifle [Corps], served regt. for 29 years, died at Winchester, **1901**, aged 72, pos. by brother officers, mur., in stone frame, S.A. of N. *XXXI.* Gen. William Charles Forrest, C.B., Col. 11th (P[rince] A[lbert's] O[wn]) Hussars and 4th/7th Dragoon Guards, served in the Crimean [War] 1854-1855, mentioned in despatches, Brevet Lt.-Col., 1819-**1902**, eff. of army officer on horseback in relief, inscr. with verse in raised letters, ach. and battle honours (Balaclava, Sevastopol, Inkerman and Tcherrade), bronze, mur., in stone frame, S.A. of N. *XXXII.* Inscr. with regt. insignia. Col. Montagu Charles Brudenell Forestier Forestier-Walker, Lt.- Col. commanding 1st Battn. King's Royal Rifle [Corps], accidentally killed while Ass[istan]t-Adj[utan]t-Gen. of Army of Occupation at Helouan, Egypt, **1902**, pos. by brother, mur., in stone frame, S.A. of N. *XXXIII.* Cross and inscr. with verse in raised letters. [Very Rev.] William Richard Wood Stephens, [M.A., B.D., F.S.A.], Dean [of Winchester] 1895-1902, **1902**, aged 63, C. *XXXIV.* Inscr. Col. Montagu Hall, commanded 101st Royal Bengal Fusiliers and 1st Royal Munster Fusiliers, fought under the colours in many actions in Burmah and India, "SERVED WITH HAVELOCK'S FORCE, TOOK PART IN THE RELIEF DEFENCE AND CAPTURE OF LUCKNOW, AND LED A STORMING PARTY ON THE HIRN KHANNAH 1857-1858", died at Ryde, I[sle of] W[ight], **1904**, aged 72, mur., N.A. of N. *XXXV.* Inscr. with verse. [Rev.] Canon Edward Huntingford, D.C.L., hon. canon [of Winchester] Cathedral, headmaster of Eagle House School, Hammersmith 1848-1860, Wimbledon 1860-1874, 1820-**1905**, pos. by pupils and assistant masters, mur., in marble frame, S.A. of C. *XXXVI.* Inscr. with verse. Elizabeth, w. of [Rt. Rev. Dr.] Edward Harold Browne, [M.A., D.D.], Bishop of Winchester [1873-1890], 1819-**1906**, maker's name BARKENTIN & KRALL, LONDON, S.A. of N. *XXXVII.* Inscr. with verse in raised letters with separate regt. insignia in relief. Capt. Arthur George Nixon, Rifle Brigade, eld. son of Col. Arthur James Nixon, Rifle Brigade, died at Tiverton, [Devon], 1857-**1906**, pos. by w. and children, mur., in marble frame, N.A. of N. *XXXVIII.* Inscr. with verse and regt. insignia. Capt. Robert Francis Dalrymple, King's Royal Rifle Corps, died at Eliri, Soudan, **1908**, aged 29, maker's name CULN GAWTHORP, S[C] LONDON, mur., S.A. of N. *XXXIX.* Inscr. with regt. insignia. Major Charles L.E. Robertson Eustace, D.S.O., King's Royal Rifle [Corps], died at Cairo, Egypt, **1908**, pos. by brother officers, maker's name CULN GAWTHORP, LONDON, mur., S.A. of N. *XL.* Inscr. with enamelled regt. insignia. Lt.-Col. Sir Frederick Brydges Major Henniker, [5th] Bart., commanded 2nd Battn.

60th [King's Royal] Rifle [Corps], died at sea, [1862-]**1908**, mur., S.A. of N. *XLI.* Inscr. with regt. insignia. Major William Greer Turle, King's Royal Rifle [Corps], "desperately wounded and gazetted as killed at the siege of Delhi 1857", **1909**, mur., S.A. of N. *XLII.* Inscr. in raised letters with regt. insignia in relief. Lt. Colin Douglas Eyre, King's Royal Rifle Corps, 1880-**1910**, mur., S.A. of N. *XLIII.* Inscr. with regt. insignia. Col. Henry Peter King-Salter, Rifle Brigade, died while in command of 2nd Battn. at Calcutta, [India], 1861-**1910**, pos. by brother officers, maker's name HART SON PEARD & Cᵒ Lᴰ LONDON, mur., on marble, N.A. of N. *XLIV.* Inscr. with sh. recording dedication of 4 chapel windows in **1910** by [Rev. Canon] Arthur Sutton Valpy, [M.A., F.S.A., hon.] canon [of Winchester Cathedral], to commem. 15th anniversary of installation, mur., on board, Epiphany Chapel/W.A. of N.Tr. *XLV.* Inscr. Col. Llewellyn Wavell, Bengal Staff Corps, 3rd son of Major-Gen. Wavell, K.F., K.C.S., F.R.S., attd. 1st European Bengal Fusiliers and served with regt. throughout the Indian Mutiny 1857, fought in the China War 1860 and Afghan War 1870, born at Somborne Park, died at Farnborough, 1839-**1910**, [pos. by w.], maker's name A&N AUX C.S.L LONDON, mur., N.A. of N. *XLVI.* Inscr. in raised letters with regt. insignia in relief. Major William Barnett, King's Royal Rifle Corps, died at Winchester, 1868-**1912**, pos. by brother officers, mur., S.A. of N. *XLVII.* Inscr. in raised letters. Capt. Montagu A[lfred] Nixon, 5th Battn. Rifle Brigade, yst. son of nos.*XXIII & XXV*, 1866-**1917**, [buried at Winchester (West Hill) Old Cemetery], mur., on marble below no.*XXXVII*, N.A. of N. *XLVIII.* Inscr. with regt. insignia in mem. of officers of the 1st European Bengal Fusiliers (now 1st Battn. The Royal Munster Fusiliers) who served under the colours 1845-**1921** (35 names), maker's name A & N. AUX. C.S.L. LONDON, mur., in stone frame, N.A. of N. *XLIX.* Inscr. recording that altar and ornaments pos. in **1924** by friends in mem. of John Ronald Moreton Macdonald, of Largie, and Henry Wynyard Kaye, of Magdalene Coll., Oxford, Waynflete Chantry/Retrochoir. *L.* Inscr. [Rt. Rev.] Frank Theodore Woods, Bishop of Winchester 1924-**1932**, "carried this staff which records the names of parishioners to which he walked and commemorates his pastoral care and wide social concern", mur., below staff, N.Tr. *LI.* Inscr. recording gift [of music stand] by "an old chorister" in mem. of Dr. William Prendergast, [**1933**], on music stand, C. *LII.* Inscr. recording gift [of altar cross] by w., son and dau. in mem. of Guy Townsend Rose, 1889-**1954**, on cross, N. *LIII.* Inscr. Jane, 1884, and Mary, 1939, daus. of Charles Mayo, F.R.C.S., lifelong friends of Cathedral; also Anne, w. of James Mayo, B.D., LL.D., **1960**, and son, Major Robert Hobart Mayo, O.B.E., F.R.Ae.S., R[oyal] F[lying] C[orps], inventor of Mayo Composite Aircraft, [1891-]1957, mur., N.A. of N. *LIV.* Inscr. recording renewal of quire lighting in **1977** made possible by a grant from the Friends of [Winchester] Cathedral, bronze, on choirs stall, C. *LV.* Inscr. in raised letters. William Walker, [M.V.O.], diver, ". . . who saved the Cathedral with his own hands . . . 1906-1911", 1869-1918, engr. **2001**, bronze, on statue plinth, Retrochoir.

INDENTS & LOST BRASSES. 56. Indent, ?2 effs. under sm. double canopy supported on a bracket with long shaft rising from base, marg. inscr. and 2 quatrefoils, c.1420, nearly effaced, N. Effs. c.600 mm x ? mm, canopy effaced, bracket effaced, marg. inscr. 3020 x 1120 x 30 mm, Purbeck slab 3190 x 1290 mm. 57. Indent, ?priest, hf. eff. with head on cushion, and inscr., early 15th cent., nearly effaced, N. Eff. c.600 x 335 mm, inscr. 65 x 620 mm, Unio Purbeck slab 2310 x 1025 mm. 58. Indent, inscr. (chamfer). Cardinal Henry Beaufort, 1447, A.T., Beaufort Chantry/Retrochoir; 14 shs. (restoration possibly after the Civil War), mur., in stone panels of A.T. Recorded (1 fillet inscribed "Tribularer, si nescirem misericordias tuas") by Milner (1801). Inscr. (chamfer) upper 2840 x 1030 x 55 mm, lower 2940 x 1135 x 50 mm. 59. Indent, civilian and inscr., nearly effaced, c.1450, N.A. of N. *Sadler, Dorset and Hampshire*, pt.II, p.29 (drg.). Eff. c.480 x c.135 mm, inscr. c.100 x c.510 mm, Purbeck slab 2395 x 1070 mm. 60. Indent, monk and inscr., mid 15th cent., nearly effaced, N. *Sadler, Dorset and Hampshire*, pt.II, p.28 (drg.). Eff. 515 x 130 mm, inscr. 90 x 345 mm, Purbeck slab 2110 x 820 mm. 61. Indent, priest, hf. eff. in mass vests., and inscr., mid-late 15th cent., nearly effaced, S.Tr. Eff. c.230 mm, inscr. 100 x 540 mm, Purbeck slab 3410 x 1440 mm. 62. Indent, priest, hf. eff. in mass vests., and inscr., mid-late 15th cent., N.A. of N. *Sadler, Dorset and Hampshire*, pt.II, p.30 (drg.). Eff. 365 x 180 mm remains, inscr. 75 x 275 mm remains, slab 1605 x 545 mm remains, approp. for Joan H____, 17th cent. 63. Indent, priest in acad. and inscr., c.1480, N.A. of N. *Sadler, Dorset and Hampshire*, pt.II, p.31 (drg.). Eff. 485 x 145 mm, inscr. 90 x 420 mm, Purbeck slab 1780 x 660 mm. 64. Indent, prior in pontifical vests. with mitre and crosier, triple canopy with super-canopy, Trinity, 4 shs. and marg. inscr. with 4 evang. symbols in quadrilobes at corners, c.1490, S.A. of C. Probably Thomas Hunton, prior 1470-98. *M.B.S. Portfolio*, IV, pl.18, *M.B.S. Trans.*, VIII, opp. p.207 (photo.); *Portfolio Book*, pl.253; *Sadler, Dorset and Hampshire*, pt.II, p.35 (drg.). Eff. 1780 x 520 mm, canopy 3085 x 900 mm, shs. 120 x 110 mm, marg. inscr. 3120 x 1130 x 40 mm, upper dext. quadrilobe 150 x 150 mm, upper sin. quadrilobe 150 x 150 mm, lower dext. quadrilobe 150 x 150 mm, lower sin. quadrilobe 150 x 150 mm, Purbeck slab 3310 x 1270 mm. 65. Indent, inscr. and 4 shs., 15th cent., S.A. of N. Inscr. c.130 x c.650 mm, shs. 165 x 135 mm, Purbeck slab 2755 x 1195 mm. 66. Indent, bishop in pontifical vests. with mitre and crosier, triple canopy with super-canopy with SS. in shafts, inscr., 4 gartered shs. and inscr. (chamfer). Thomas Langton, Bishop of Winchester [1493-1501], 1501, A.T., Langton Chantry/Retrochoir; 8 shs., mur., in stone panels of A.T. *Bod. Lib. Gough Maps 226*, f.144; *Bracken, Noble Order of the Garter*, fig.64, p.71 (drg.); *Sadler, Dorset and Hampshire*, pt.II, p.33 (drg.). Eff. 1020 x 282 mm, canopy 2100 x 810 mm, inscr. 265 x 560 mm, gartered shs. 185 x 150 mm, inscr. (chamfer) 2250 x 950 x 45 mm, shs. mur. 135 x 115 mm, Purbeck slab 2340 x 1025 mm. 67. Indent, prior in pontifical vests. with mitre and crosier, canopy with super-canopy and 2 shs. in shafts, inscr., 1 sh. and marg. inscr. with 4 evang. symbols in quadrilobes at corners, c.1520, nearly effaced, Retrochoir. Possibly Robert Westgate, prior 1450-1470, or Thomas Silkstead, prior 1498-1524. Eff. 1970 x c.510 mm, canopy 3350 x 1200 mm, sh. 110 x 90 mm, marg. inscr. 3350 x 1370 x 50 mm, upper dext. quadrilobe 140 x 140 mm, upper sin. quadrilobe 140 x 140 mm, lower dext. quadrilobe 140 x 140 mm, lower sin. quadrilobe 140 x 140 mm, Purbeck slab 3740 x 1520 mm. 68. Indent, eff. in pontifical vests. with mitre and crosier, canopy and marg. inscr., c.1520, rivets and plugs only, nearly effaced, S.Tr. Possibly Robert Westgate, prior 1450-1470, or Thomas Silkstead, prior 1498-1524. Purbeck slab 3330 x 1300 mm. 69. Indent, priest in acad. and inscr., late 15th or early 16th cent., nearly effaced, S.A. of Retrochoir. Eff. 1050 mm, inscr. 105 x 780 mm, Purbeck slab 2360 x 1050 mm. 70. Indent, cross and inscr., nearly effaced, early 16th cent., S.A. of N. Cross c.750 x c.50 mm, inscr. c.70 x c.370 mm, Purbeck slab 2140 x 880 mm. 71. Indent, cross and inscr., nearly effaced, early 16th cent., S.A. of N. Cross c.450 x ? mm, inscr. c.100 x c.350 mm, Purbeck slab 2165 x 890 mm. 72. Indent, priest in cope and inscr., mid 16th cent., nearly effaced, S.A. of N. Possibly William Kingsmell, last prior, 1st Dean, 1548. Eff. c.950 mm, inscr. 85 x 510 mm, Unio Purbeck slab 2005 x 715 mm. 73. Indent, inscr., N.A. of N. Inscr. 80 x 490 mm, Purbeck slab 1460 x 690 mm. 74. Indent, inscr., S.Tr. Inscr. c.85 x 275 mm, Purbeck slab 1715 x 570 mm. Recorded by Bertram (1979) and by Rogers (2003) but not found (2007). 75. Indent, ?inscr., 1 rivet and 6 plugs only, effaced, N.A. of N. Inscr. c.250 x c.500 mm, Unio Purbeck slab 1190 remains x 1110 mm remains. 76. Indent, inscr., 7 plugs only, effaced, S.A. of N. Inscr. c.100 x c.400 mm, Purbeck slab 1920 x 905 mm remains. 77. Indent, inscr., 4 plugs only, effaced, S.A. of N. Inscr. c.90 x c.540 mm, Purbeck slab 3100 x 1050 mm remains. 78. Indent, inscr.; partly filled with cement; N. Inscr. 110 x 815 mm, Unio Purbeck slab 2145 x 900 mm. 79. Indent, inscr., N. Inscr. 55 x 425 mm, Purbeck slab 2150 x 875 mm. 80. Indent, inscr., N. Inscr. 85 x 580 mm,

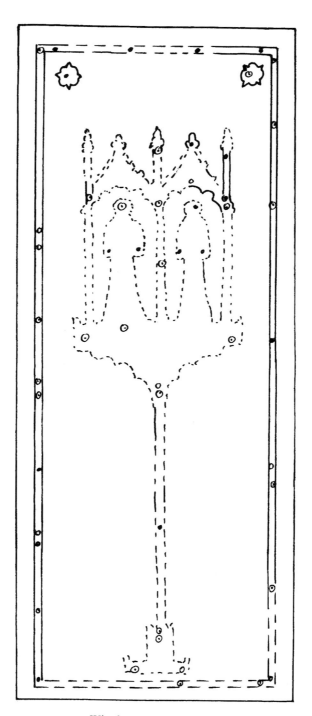

Winchester, Cathedral 56

Winchester, Cathedral 64

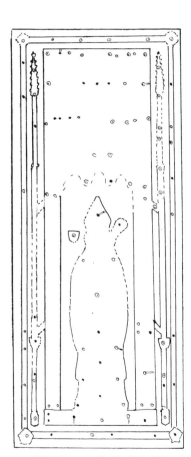

Winchester, Cathedral 67

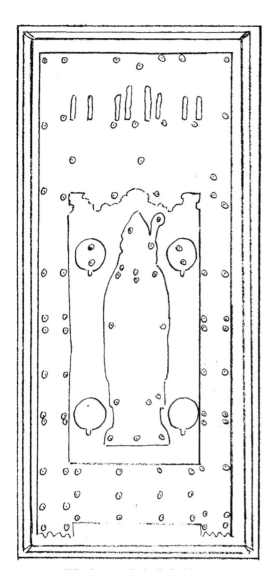

Winchester, Cathedral 66

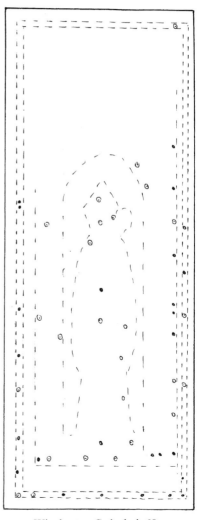

Winchester, Cathedral 68

335

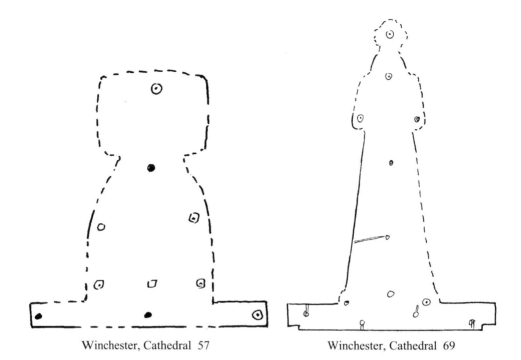

Winchester, Cathedral 57

Winchester, Cathedral 69

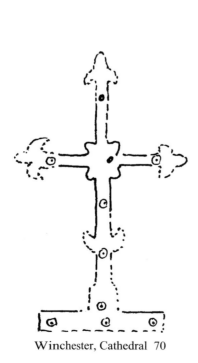

Winchester, Cathedral 70

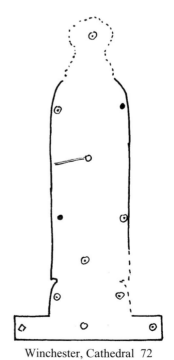

Winchester, Cathedral 72

336

Purbeck slab 2480 x 1090 mm. 81. Indent, inscr., 1 plug only, effaced, S.Tr. Inscr. c.60 x c.380 mm, Purbeck slab 1200 remains x 870 mm remains. 82. Indent, 1 plug only, S.Tr. Purbeck slab 1110 remains x 460 mm remains. 83. Lost brass, inscr. (chamfer). Thomas Cooper, [Bishop of Lincoln 1571-1594, Bishop of Winchester 1584-1594], 1594, S.A. of C. Recorded by Henry, Earl of Clarendon (1715), by Warner (1795) and (lost) by Woodward, Willis and Lockhart (1858). 84. Lost indent, ?civilian and inscr. Recorded by George (1686). 85. Lost indent, canopy and marg. inscr., ?16th cent., 1 rivet only, effaced, S.Tr. Recorded by Cave (1911) and by Bertram (1979) but not found by Bertram (2003). Purbeck slab 170 remained x 190 mm remained.

Ref: *Bod. Lib. Gough Maps 226*, f.144; *Bracken, Noble Order of the Garter*, p.71; *Brayley, E., and Britton, J., The Beauties of England and Wales*, VI, 1805, p.59, pp.60-1; *Burke's Peerage and Baronetage*, p.693, p.1189, p.1312, p.1627, p.2835; *Busby, Companion Guide*, p.39; *Clarendon, Earl of, and Gale, S., The History and Antiquities of the Cathedral Church of Winchester*, 1715, pp.74-5, p.86, p.30; *Earliest English Brasses*, p.190; *Hampshire History*, I, p.67, pp.72-3, p.75, p.78; *Hampshire N. and Q.*, III, p.11; *Hampton*, pp.76-7; *M.B.S. Bulletin*, 27, p.15; *M.B.S. Trans.*, II, p.237, V, p.253, VI, pp.121-4, pp.326-7, IX, p.366, XVIII, p.207, XIV, p.490; *Milner, History*, II, p.27, p.29, pp.31-2; *Milner, Survey*, II, pp.27-30, p.60, pp.66-70, pp.78-9, p.127; *M.S.*, p.167; *Norris, Memorials*, p.84, p.94, p.254, p.261; *Sadler, Dorset and Hampshire*, pt.II, pp.28-38, appx. I, pt.2, pp.30-2, p.42; *Selwyn and Blount, Winchester Cathedral: Its Monuments and Memorials*, 1919, p.11, pp.186-7, p.299; *Soc. Antiq. MS. 875/6*, pp.146-9; *Squibb*, p.208; *Warner*, I, pp.258-9; *Warton*, I, p.59, p71; *Winchester, Description*, p.105.

WINCHESTER, College Chapel and Cloisters.

I. (Formerly M.S.III). Inscr. William Clyff, first chaplain "istius capelle" [in the cloisters, now the north library], **1433**; formerly mur., W.Cloister, now mur., Chantry Chapel. *Lithograph by F.J. Baigent.* Inscr. 85 x 391 mm. Style: London D.

II. (Formerly M.S.XXXIV). Frag. of scroll "cognoscere sortem", c.**1450**; in 2007 loose in Bursary. Possibly belonging to no.*XLIX*. Scroll 68 x 200 remains x 40 mm. Style: Norwich 1.

III. (Formerly M.S.VI). Inscr. William Ball, fellow, **1472**, mur., W.Cloister. Inscr. 71 x 307 mm. Style: London D.

IV. (Formerly M.S.VII). Edward Tacham, fellow, **1473**, hf. eff. in cope, inscr., mur., W.Cloister. *Alcuin Club Colls.*, XXII, p.61; *Brit. Lib. Add. MS. 39987,* f.38r, f.60r (eff. only); *M.B.S. Trans.*, VI, p.132. Eff. 319 x 247 mm, inscr. 87 x 422 mm. Style: London sub B.

V. (Formerly M.S.VIII). John Taknell, fellow, **1494**, ¾ eff. in mass vests., inscr.; formerly E.Cloister, now mur., W.Cloister. *Brit. Lib. Add. MS. 39987,* f.38r, f.60r (eff. only); *M.B.S. Trans.*, VI, p.133. Eff. 298 x 144 mm, inscr. 79 x 377-384 mm. Style: London D.

VI. (Formerly M.S.X). Inscr. John Fylde, **1507**; formerly S.Cloister, now mur., W.Cloister. Inscr. 101 x 417 mm. Style: London G.

VII. (Formerly M.S.XII). Inscr. John Curteys, fellow, **1509**; formerly S.Cloister, now mur., W.Cloister. Inscr. 107 x 521 mm. Style: London G.

Orate p aïa dñi Will Chiff pñm Capellaïu
uiti Capelle qui obijt xxiiij die meñ marcij
A dñi mj CCCC xxxvij Cuj aïe ppiciet dé ame

Winchester, College *I*

Winchester, College *II*

Orate pro T I Dri Will'mu Yall quod anc
loc? iu collegio qui obijt vij die maij anno
dñi millo CCCC Lf Ef? cui aïe ppiciet dé anï

Winchester, College *III*

Orate p aïa Johïs Kylde qui obijt xxiij die
meñs ffebruary anno dñi qñtimo CCCC
septimo cui aïe ppicietur deus amen

Winchester, College *VI*

hic iacet dñs Joynes Twteys quodam socius huius
collegij qui obijt penultima die meñs Jannary A dñ
qñ qñngentesimo nono cuius aïe ppicietur deus amen

Winchester, College *VII*

338

Winchester, College *IV*

Winchester, College *V*

VIII. (Formerly M.S.XIII). John Gylbert, fellow, **1514**, ¾ eff. in mass vests., inscr.; formerly E.Cloister, now mur., E.Cloister. *Alcuin Club Colls.*, XXII, p.42; *Brit. Lib. Add. MS. 39987,* f.45r; *M.B.S. Trans.*, VI, p.134. Eff. 400 x 170 mm, inscr. 118 x 421 mm. Style: London G.

IX. (Formerly M.S.XIV). John Erewaker, fellow, **1514**, ¾ eff. in mass vests., inscr.; formerly E.Cloister, now mur., E.Cloister. *Brit. Lib. Add. MS. 39987,* f.45r; *M.B.S. Trans.*, VI, p.135. Eff. 407 x 167 mm, inscr. 119 x 459 mm. Style: London G.

X. (Formerly M.S.XV). Inscr. Richard Skynner, fellow, **1514**; formerly E.Cloister, now mur., E.Cloister. Inscr. 116 x 460 mm. Style: London G.

XI. (Formerly M.S.XVI). Inscr. John Hopkyns, conduct, **1514**; formerly S.Cloister, now mur., S.Cloister. Inscr. 118 x 454 mm. Style: London G.

XII. (Formerly M.S.XIX). Inscr. John Dere, M.A., fellow, **1527**; formerly E.Cloister, now mur., E.Cloister. Inscr. 77 x 347 mm. Style: London G.

XIII. Inscr. John Webb, fellow, **1532**, mur., organ gallery, C. Inscr. 52 x 425 mm. Style: London G.

XIV. (Formerly M.S.XX). John White, warden, died 1560, in rich cope, inscr. in 20 Eng. vv. and marg. inscr., facsimile engr. 1882; formerly Ante-chapel, now, C. A portion of the original eff., engr. c.**1548**, is palimp., on rev. a portion of the eff. of a widow, c.1420; in 2007 in reversible frame in fellows library safe. John White was afterwards Bishop of Lincoln 1554-1556, translated to Winchester in 1556, deprived in 1559, and buried in the cathedral. Recorded (partly covered and marg. inscr. lost) by Haines (1861). *Alcuin Club Colls.*, XXII, p.59 (obv. and rev. of eff.); *Brit. Lib. Add. MS. 39987,* f.55r (eff. and pt. of inscr.); *Hants Proc.*, III, opp. p.80 (obv. and rev. of eff.); *Leach*, opp. p.288 (eff. and vv.); *M.B.S. Trans.*, VI, p.131 (obv. and rev. of eff.); *Palimpsests*, pl.51 (rev.). Illustration (eff. more complete and pt. of lost inscr.) from rubbing in Soc. Antiq. coll. Rubbing (eff. more complete and pt. of lost inscr.) in Soc. Antiq. coll. (n.d.). Eff. 785 remains x 333 mm remains, eff. (facsimile) 1326 x 362 mm, inscr. (facsimile) 268 x 728 mm, shs. (facsimile) 153 x 117 mm, marg. inscr. (facsimile) 2174 x 892 x 40 mm. Style: London G (Gyfford) (obv.), London ?D (rev.).

XV. (Formerly M.S.XXI). Inscr. with 6 Lat. vv. John Dolber, M.A., fellow, **1560**, mur., in stone frame, W.Cloister. Inscr. 260 x 505 mm. Style: London G (script 6).

XVI. (Formerly M.S.XXIII). Inscr. with 4 Lat. vv. John Clerke, priest, fellow, **1571**, mur., in stone frame, N.Cloister. Inscr. 128 x 410 mm. Style: London G (script 10).

XVII. (Formerly M.S.XXIV). Inscr. John Scotte, priest, fellow, **1575**, mur., in stone frame, N.Cloister. *Baigent, F.J., Hist. of Wyke Ch.*, 1865, p.36. Inscr. 99 x 400 mm. Style: London G (script 10).

XVIII. (Formerly M.S.XXV). Inscr. with 4 Lat. vv. George Flower, M.A., **1578**, mur., in stone frame, N.Cloister. Inscr. 128 x 420 mm. Style: London G (script 10).

XIX. (Formerly M.S.XXVI). Inscr. Philip Dereux, priest, **1578**, mur., in stone frame, N.Cloister. Inscr. 90 x 410 mm. Style: London G (script 10).

Winchester, College *VIII*

Winchester, College *IX*

Winchester, College *X*

Winchester, College *XI*

Winchester, College *XII*

Winchester, College *XIII*

Winchester, College *XV*

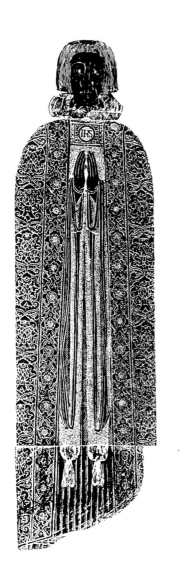

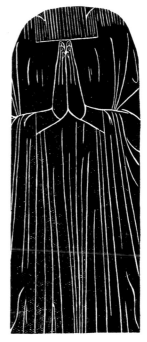

Winchester, College *XIV*
palimpsest reverse

Winchester, College *XIV*

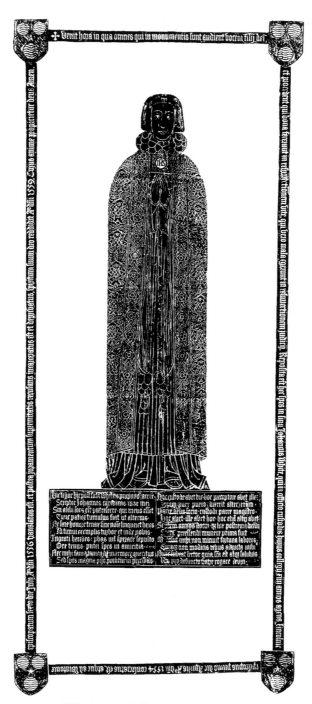

Winchester, College *XIV* (facsimile)

344

Epita. Jo. Clerke

Vilanus Joannes iacet hoc sub marmore Clerkus
... fuit hic quondam presbiter et socius
In terra roleos solitus bullare liquores
In celo vivus nunc quoq gaudet aquis
Obiit x die mensis Junii 1571.

Winchester, College *XVI*

positum ob memoriā Jo: Scotte plūmeri nuper
socij istius Collegij cui? corpus prope hoc monu=
mentū lapide sub marmoreo humatum conditur
Obiit vij die mēsis Dece: A° dm. 1575

Winchester, College *XVII*

Epita: Georgij Flower in artibus magistri
Georgius hoc floris sub marmore dormit
Floruerat, sed flos ille reduces erat.
septem socius vix hic transegerat annos.
Mors pede qui pulsat floris ut hic abeat
Obijt 15 die Novembris A°.1578.

Winchester, College *XVIII*

A fronte huius monumenti humi est corpus Philippi
Derette presbiteri nuper istius Collegij Capellani .2
coductorij huri iciū in Collegio gruin in pauperes heri
benefici atq pū : Obiit 14 die mēsis Februarij A°.1578.

Winchester, College *XIX*

XX. (Formerly M.S.XXVII). Inscr. with 4 Eng. vv. Edmund Hodson, clerk, fellow, **1580**, mur., in stone frame, W.Cloister. Inscr. 125 x 332 mm. Style: London G (script 10).

XXI. (Formerly M.S.XXVIII). Inscr. with 4 Lat. vv. Thomas Larke, fellow, **1582**, mur., in stone frame, E.Cloister. Inscr. 128 x 440 mm. Style: London (script 12).

XXII. (Formerly M.S.XXIX). Inscr. with 6 Lat. vv. Thomas Jones, B.C.L., fellow, **1585**, mur., in stone frame, W.Cloister. Inscr. 212 x 424 mm. Style: London (script 12).

XXIII. (Formerly M.S.XXX). Inscr. with 4 Lat. vv. Thomas Davison, fellow, **1586**, mur., in stone frame, **W.**Cloister. *Baigent, F.J., Hist. of Wyke Ch.*, 1865, p.36. Inscr. 118 x 368 mm. Style: London (script 12).

XXIV. (Formerly M.S.XXXI). Inscr. with 4 Lat. vv. Robert Watton, fellow, **1596**, mur., in stone frame, E.Cloister. Inscr. 150 x 488 mm. Style: Johnson.

XXV. (Formerly M.S.XXXII). Inscr. with 6 Lat. vv. Thomas Geffres, S.T.B., fellow, **1605**, mur., in stone frame, W.Cloister. Inscr. 220 x 508 mm. Style: Johnson.

XXVI. (Formerly M.S.XXII). Inscr. with 6 Lat. vv. William Adkins, M.A., fellow, 1561, engr. c.**1605**, mur., in stone frame, W.Cloister. Inscr. 205 x 552 mm. Style: Johnson.

XXVII. (Formerly M.S.XXXIII). Inscr. and sh. John Harris, D.D., warden, **1658**, aged 70; formerly Ante-chapel, now mur., on stone, N.Cloister. Inscr. 412 x 745 mm, sh. 345 x 314 mm.

XXVIII. Inscr. Frances Elizabeth, dau. of John Lucius Dampier and w. Margaret Sarah, 1833-**1839**, bronze, mur., on buttress outside Chantry Chapel. *XXIX.* Inscr. George William Chard, Mus.Doc., coll. and cathedral organist for 47 years, 1849, aged 84, and w. Amelia, **1850**, [aged 84, both buried] at the base of the buttress, pos. by dau., Amelia Poore, bronze, mur., on buttress outside N.Cloister. *XXX.* Inscr. Benjamin Long, Mus.Bac., organist, **1850**, aged 48, [buried] at the base of the buttress, bronze, mur., on buttress outside N.Cloister. *XXXI.* Cross and inscr. in Lat. Arthur Moberly, 2nd son of [Rt. Rev. George Moberly,] headmaster [1835-1866, Bishop of Salisbury 1869-1885], scholar [1851-1858, 1840-]**1858**, mur., on marble, E.Cloister. *XXXII.* Cross and inscr. in Lat. George Prothero Roch, commoner [1856-1858], **1858**, aged 14, pos. by 4 fellow pupils, mur., S.Cloister. *XXXIII.* Cross with Lat. verse and inscr. in Lat. [Rev.] William Henry Gunner, M.A., rector of Winchester, St. Swithun [1852-1859], assistant master for 23 years [1836-1859], chaplain for 20 years [1839-1859, 1812-]**1859**, mur., on marble, E.Cloister. *XXXIV.* Cross and inscr. in Lat. Sydney Law Malet, scholar [1857-1860, 1843-]**1860**, pos. by fellow pupils, maker's name *C H OSBORNE. S^c WINTON*, mur., on marble, S.Cloister. *XXXV.* Inscr. in Lat. G[eorge] T[addy] Daniel, [son of James Daniel, of Ramsgate, Kent], commoner [1858-1861, **1861**], pos. by P.C., C.E.M., W.A.J., W.P.T., J.H.W. and P.C.H., mur., on marble, S.Cloister. *XXXVI.* Inscr. in Lat. Francis George Eyre, of New Coll., Oxford, scholar [1853-1859, 1840-]**1861**, pos. by 3 Wykehamists, mur., on marble, S.Cloister. *XXXVII.* Cross and inscr. in Lat. James Leatham Birley, [son of Thomas Hornby Birley], commoner [1861-1866], died at Oxford, [1847-]**1866**, pos. by fellow pupils, mur., on marble, E.Cloister. *XXXVIII.* Inscr. in Lat. recording restoration of east wall of chapel in **1866** by William Erle, scholar [1804], chief justice of the common pleas, [1794-1880], on reredos, C. *XXXIX.* Inscr. on base of stepped cross, inscr., marg. inscr. with verse and 4 evang. symbols on roundels at corners. Robert Marriott, of Christ Church, Oxford, commoner [1861-1865, 1846-]**1868**, maker's name HART & SON, LONDON, mur., on marble,

Edmunde Hodson Clerke and fellow [of]
this College, died the vij of August. 15 8[.]

Who so thou art, with lovinge harte
Stonde, reade, and thinck on me:
for as I was so nowe thou arte
and as I am so shalte thou be

Winchester, College *XX*

Epitaphium Magistri Thomæ Larke
nuper socij istius Collegij Obr: 16 May. [....]

Qui precor hoc tumulo, dicor prænomine Thomæ
Cognomen ferit dulcis Alauda mihi.
Bis septem menses, ter septem præsbyter annos
hic colui, cuius nunc fervor ore, Deum.

Winchester, College *XXI*

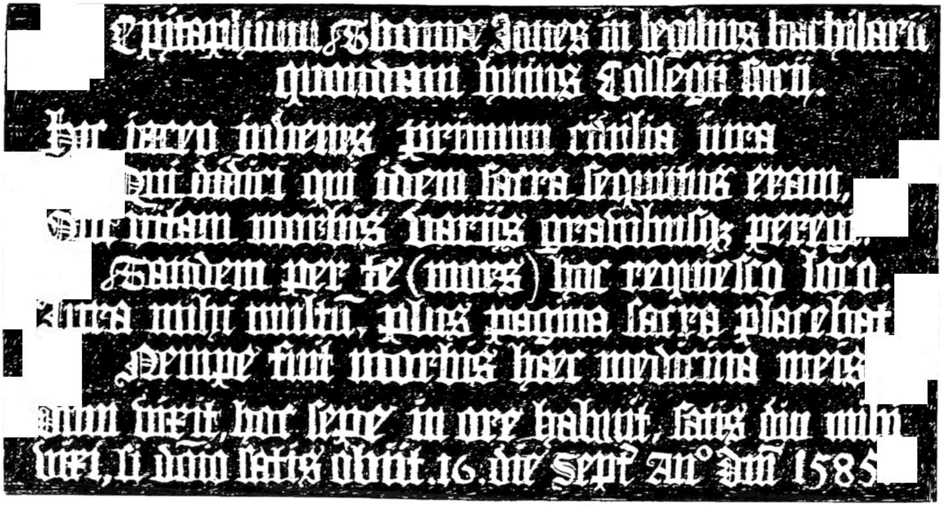

Epitaphium Thomæ Jones in legibus bachilarij
quondam huius Collegij socij.

Hic iaceo inheus primum civilia iura
qui didici qui idem sacra secuutus eram,
Dum vitam morbis varijs gravibuszs pergi.
Tandem per te (mors) hoc requiesco loco.
Iura mihi multu, plus pagina sacra placebat
Nempe fuit morbis hæc medicina meis.
Dum vixit, hoc sepe in ore habuit, satis diu mihi
vixi, si diu satis obijt. 16. die Sept Añ° Dñi 1585.

Winchester, College *XXII*

347

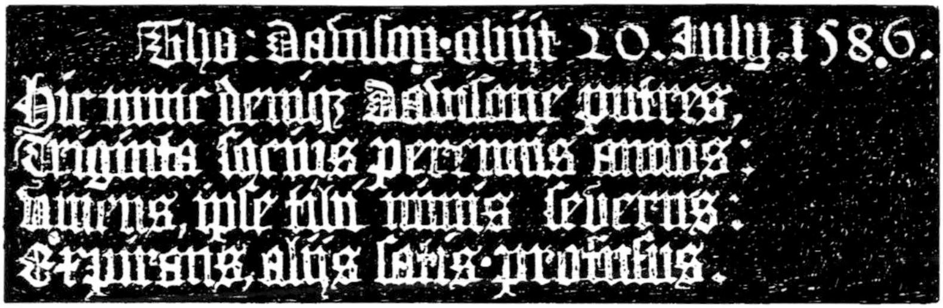

Tho: Dawlton obijt 20. July 1586.
Hic nunc demu Dawltone putres,
Triginta socius per omnes annos:
Vivens, ipse tibi nimis severus:
Expirans, alijs satis profusus.

Winchester, College *XXIII*

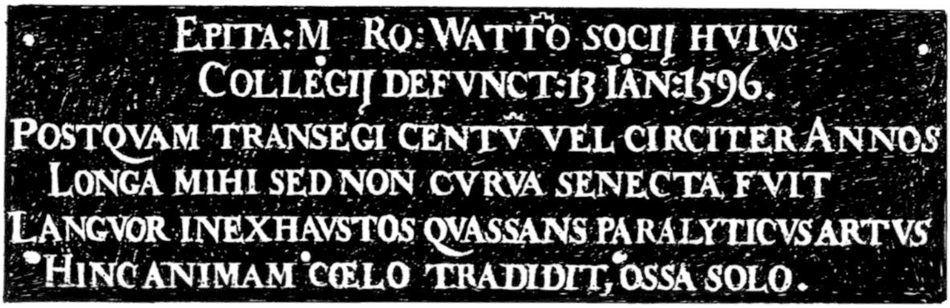

EPITA:M Ro: WATTO SOCIJ HVIVS
COLLEGIJ DEFVNCT:13 IAN:1596.
POSTQVAM TRANSEGI CENTV VEL CIRCITER ANNOS
LONGA MIHI SED NON CVRVA SENECTA FVIT
LANGVOR INEXHAVSTOS QVASSANS PARALYTICVS ARTVS
HINC ANIMAM CŒLO TRADIDIT, OSSA SOLO.

Winchester, College *XXIV*

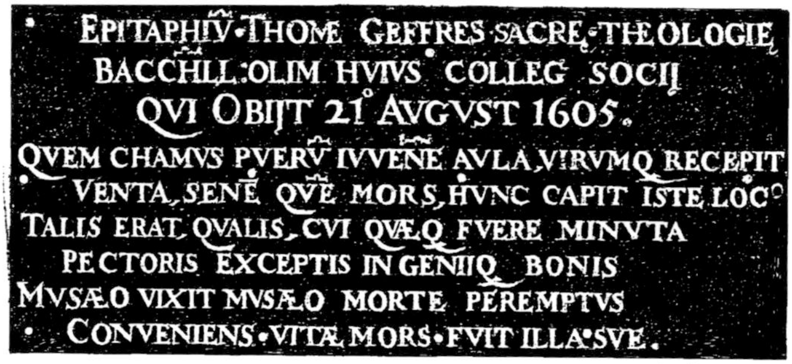

EPITAPHIV THOMÆ GEFFRES SACRÆ THEOLOGIÆ
BACCHLL:OLIM HVIVS COLLEG SOCIJ
QVI OBIJT 21° AVGVST 1605.
QVEM CHAMVS PVERV IVVENÊ AVLA VIRVMQ RECEPIT
VENTA SENÊ QVÊ MORS HVNC CAPIT ISTE LOC°
TALIS ERAT QVALIS, CVI QVÆQ FVERE MINVTA
PECTORIS EXCEPTIS INGENIIQ BONIS
MVSÆO VIXIT MVSÆO MORTE PEREMPTVS
CONVENIENS VITÆ MORS FVIT ILLA SVE.

Winchester, College *XXV*

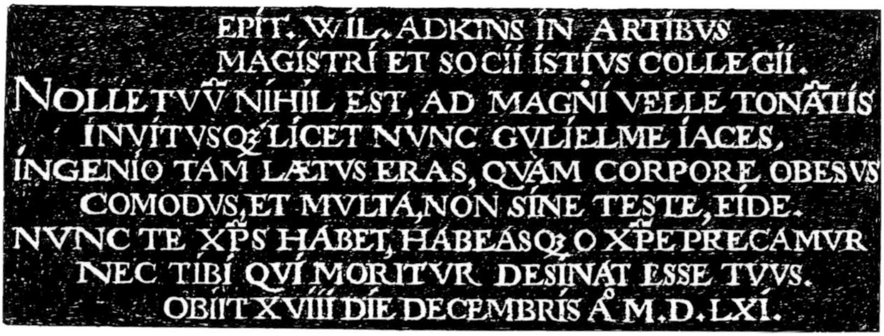

EPIT. WIL. ADKINS IN ARTIBVS
MAGISTRI ET SOCII ISTIVS COLLEGII.
NOLLE TVV NIHIL EST, AD MAGNI VELLE TONATIS
INVITVSQ LICET NVNC GVLIELME IACES,
INGENIO TAM LÆTVS ERAS, QVAM CORPORE OBESVS
COMODVS, ET MVLTA, NON SINE TESTE, EIDE.
NVNC TE XPS HABET, HABEASQ O XPE PRECAMVR
NEC TIBI QVI MORITVR DESINAT ESSE TVVS.
OBIIT XVIII DIE DECEMBRIS A M.D.LXI.

Winchester, College *XXVI*

348

Winchester, College *XXVII*

Winchester, College *XLIV*

S.Cloister. Cross 598 x 362 mm, inscr. 103 x 340 mm, marg. inscr. 791 x 447 x 28 mm, roundels 180 mm dia. *XL.* Cross and inscr. in Lat. Selwyn William Moberly, yst. son of [Rt. Rev. George Moberly,] headmaster [1835-1866], Bishop of Salisbury [1869-1885], commoner [1864-1871, brother of no.*XXXI,* 1854-]**1871**, pos. by fellow pupils, mur., on marble, E.Cloister. *XLI.* Inscr. in Lat. Rev. Charles Henry Ridding, [B.C.L., scholar 1836-1844], 2nd master, [fellow, 1825-]**1871**, mur., in stone frame, N.Cloister. *XLII.* Inscr. [Rt. Rev.] Edward Ash Were, S.T.P., [chaplain 1877-1880, suffragan] Bishop [of Derby 1880-1909, suffragan Bishop of Stafford 1909-1915, 1846-1915], **1874**, mur., Chantry Chapel. *XLIII.* Cross and inscr. in Lat. with Lat. verse. Clement Empson, [commoner 1874-1876], 1860-**1876**, mur., on marble, S.Cloister. *XLIV.* Martin White Benson, eld. son of [Rt. Rev.] Edward White [Benson], Bishop of Truro [1877-1882, Archbishop of Canterbury 1882-1896], scholar [1874-1878] and prefect, **1878**, aged 17 years, 5 months and 21 days, ¾ eff. in school uniform, inscr. in Lat. with Lat. verse and Chi Rho monogram and scroll. Eff. 295 x 234 mm, inscr. 189 x 482 mm, scroll 35 x 231 x 30 mm, mur., in stone frame, E.Cloister. *XLV.* Inscr. Edward Hatton Montagu Bowles, only son of Major Edward Bowles, 60th [King's Royal] Rifle [Corps, commoner] 1875-1881, exhibitioner 1876 and prefect 1879, died suddenly at Mürren, Switzerland, **1881**, mur., S.Cloister. *XLVI. (Formerly M.S.I).* John Morys, first warden, 1413, in almuce, inscr., facsimile engr. **1882**; formerly Ante-chapel, now, C. Recorded (inscr. lost) by Haines (1861). *Bardfield, S., Thatcham, Berks., and its Manors,* I, p.350; *Brit. Lib. Add. MS. 39987,* f.2v; *Leach,* opp. p.132 (eff.). Illustration (lost eff.) from rubbing in Soc. Antiq. coll. Rubbing (lost eff.) in Soc. Antiq. coll. (n.d.). Lost eff. 957 x 265 mm, eff. (facsimile) 956 x 270 mm, inscr. (facsimile) 153 x 550 mm. Style: London B. *XLVII. (Formerly M.S.II).* John Wyllyngale, fellow, 1432, hf. eff. in cope, inscr., facsimile engr. **1882**; formerly Ante-chapel, now, C. Illustration from rubbing in Soc. Antiq. coll. Rubbing (lost eff. (mutil.) and lost inscr.) in Soc. Antiq. coll. (n.d.). Lost eff. orig. 485 x 253 mm, 357 x 253 mm remained, eff. (facsimile) 385 x 261 mm, lost inscr. 92 x 508 mm, inscr. (facsimile) 95 x 508 mm. Style: London E. *XLVIII. (Formerly M.S.IV).* Nicholas North, fellow, 1445, hf. eff. in cope, inscr., facsimile engr. **1882**; formerly Ante-chapel, now, C. *Brit. Lib. Add. MS. 39987,* f.6v, ff.29-32; *Litho. by E. Baigent.* Illustration (lost brass complete) from rubbing in Soc. Antiq. coll. Rubbing (lost brass complete) in Soc. Antiq. coll. (n.d.). Lost eff. 412 x 283 mm, eff. (facsimile) 413 x 286 mm, lost inscr. 85 x 448 mm, inscr. (facsimile) 90 x 450 mm. Style: London D. *XLIX (Formerly M.S.V).* Robert Thurberne, warden, 1450, in cope, inscr. and scroll, facsimile engr. **1882**; now, C. Recorded (inscr. lost) by Haines (1861). *Brit. Lib. Add. MS. 39987,* f.4v; *Haines,* I, p.76 (drg. of upper hf. of eff.); *Trivick, Craft,* pl.76 (upper hf. of eff.). Illustration (lost eff. (mutil.) with scroll indent) from rubbing in Soc. Antiq. coll. Rubbing (lost eff. with scroll indent) in Soc. Antiq. coll. (n.d.). Lost eff. 1200 remained x 345 mm, eff. (facsimile) 1204 x 364 mm, inscr. (facsimile) 134 x 762 mm, scroll indent c.345 x c.380 x c.35 mm, scroll (facsimile) 375 x 396 x 39 mm. Style: Norwich 1. *L. (Formerly M.S.IX).* John Bedell, mayor of the city [in 1496], formerly scholar of the coll., 1498, in civil dress, inscr., facsimile engr. **1882**; formerly Ante-chapel, now, C. *Brit. Lib. Add. MS. 39987,* f.8v, ff.39-40r; *Leach,* opp. p.173; *Lithograph by F.J. Baigent.* Illustration (lost brass) from rubbing in Soc. Antiq. coll. Rubbing (lost eff. with inscr. (mutil.)) in Soc. Antiq. coll. (n.d.). Lost eff. 568 x 205 mm, eff. (facsimile) 571 x 195 mm, lost inscr. 65 x 327 mm remained, inscr. (facsimile) 69 x 439 mm. Style: London D. *LI. (Formerly M.S.XI).* Thomas Lyrypyn, priest, fellow, 1509, ¾ eff. in mass vests., inscr. and scroll, facsimile engr. **1882**; now, C. *Brit. Lib. Add MS. 18478,* f.45v (Suckling drg.), *Add. MS. 39987,* f.6v; *M.B.S. Trans.,* VI, p.127. Illustration (lost brass with scroll indent) from rubbing in Soc. Antiq. coll. Rubbing (lost brass with scroll indent) in Soc. Antiq. coll. (n.d.). Lost eff. 298 x 154 mm, eff. (facsimile) 301 x 165 mm, lost inscr. 79 x 373 mm, inscr. (facsimile) 82 x 376 mm, scroll indent c.300 x 90 x 30 mm, (facsimile) scroll 298 x 104 x 30 mm. Style: London F variant. *LII. (Formerly M.S.XVII).* Inscr. (eff. lost). William Ernle,

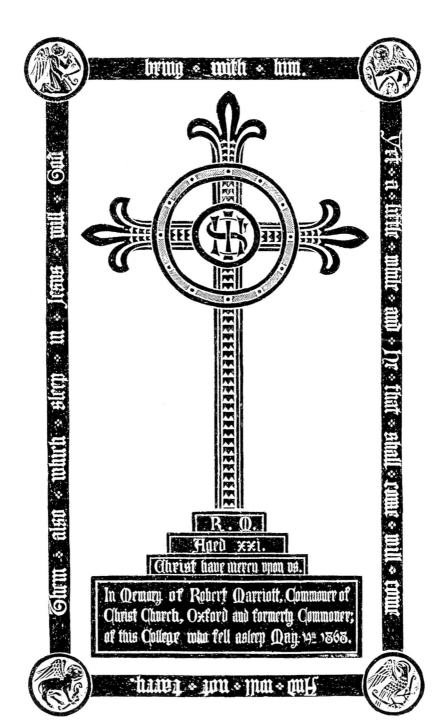

bring · with · him.

Yet a little while and He that shall come will come

And will not tarry.

Them · also · which · sleep · in · Jesus · will · God

R. M.

Aged XXI.

Christ have mercy vpon vs.

In Memory of Robert Marriott, Commoner of Christ Church, Oxford and formerly Commoner; of this College who fell asleep May 14th 1868.

Winchester, College *XXXIX*

Winchester, College *XLVI* (lost)

hic iacet magisst Iohes Morys primus Custos huius Collegii qui obijt die undecim egilia virginum Anno dni M°. CCCC°. XIIJ°. et Anno regni Regis Henrici quinti primo. littera dnicali A. Cui aie propicietur deus Amen

Winchester, College *XLVI* (facsimile)

352

Winchester, College *XLVII* (lost)

Winchester, College *XLVII* (facsimile)

353

Winchester, College *XLVIII* (lost)

Winchester, College *XLVIII* (facsimile)

354

Winchester, College *XLIX* (lost)

Winchester, College *XLIX* (facsimile)

Winchester, College *L* (lost)

Winchester, College *L* (facsimile)

Winchester, College *LII* (lost)

Winchester, College *LII* (facsimile)

356

Winchester, College *LI* (lost)

Winchester, College *LI* (facsimile)

357

"in decretis bacallarius", fellow of New Coll., Oxford, chaplain to the Bishop of Winchester, 1521, facsimile engr. **1882**; formerly Ante-chapel, now, C. Recorded (eff. lost) by Haines (1861). Illustration (lost inscr.) from rubbing in Soc. Antiq. coll. Rubbing (lost inscr.) in Soc. Antiq. coll. (n.d.). Lost inscr. 120 x 502 mm, (facsimile) inscr. 123 x 504 mm. Style: London G. *LIII. (Formerly M.S.XVIII)*. John Barratte, B.A., fellow, 1524, in acad., kng., inscr., facsimile engr. **1882**; formerly Ante-chapel, now, C. *Brit. Lib. Add. MS. 39987*, f.52r; *M.B.S. Trans.*, VI, p.128. Illustration (lost brass) from rubbing in Soc. Antiq. coll. Rubbing (lost brass) in Soc. Antiq. coll. (n.d.). Lost eff. 375 x 140 mm, (facsimile) eff. 374 x 139 mm, lost inscr. 66 x 545 mm, (facsimile) inscr. 69 x 546 mm. Style: London F debased. *LIV*. Inscr. with verse. Lt. Rawdon Hardy, Royal Fusiliers, commoner [1873-1876], died of fever at Bellary, Madras, [India, 1858-]**1882**, pos. by "OLD SCHOOL FRIENDS", maker's name T. PRATT & SONS ENGRAVERS, TAVISTOCK S[T] LONDON, mur., on marble, S.Cloister. *LV*. Inscr. in raised letters. [Rev.] Robert Charles Lenny Tomlinson, B.A., son of Cmdr. R[obert] C[osby] Tomlinson, R.N., scholar [1871-1876], "HIS EARNEST WORK AS A PARISH PRIEST WAS SUDDENLY CUT SHORT BY A FATAL CARRIAGE ACCIDENT", [died at Weston-super-Mare, Somerset, 1857-]**1883**, bronze, mur., on marble, S.Cloister. *LVI*. Inscr. in Lat. Francis Ward Montagu, scholar [1877-1882], died [of typhoid at Poona], India, [1864-]**1885**, pos. by friends, mur., on stone, S.Cloister. *LVII*. Inscr. in Lat. Arthur Rhodes Cobb, [commoner 1877-1883, died of typhoid, 1864-1886], and Henry Francis Eckersley, [13th Regt. Somerset Light Infantry, commoner 1877-1883], "who once shared a room", [killed leading an attack at Mingyan, Burma, 1863-]**1886**, pos. by fellow pupils, mur., in stone frame, W.Cloister. *LVIII*. Inscr. in Lat. Ernest Charles Read, of New Coll., Oxford, scholar [1873-1880, assistant master 1884-1885, master at] Marlborough [School 1885-1886], died at Honiton, [Devon, 1861-]**1886**, mur., in stone frame, W.Cloister. *LIX*. Inscr. in Lat. [Lt.] Eustace Hervey Stockdale, [68th] (Durham Light Infantry) [Regt. of Foot], commoner [1877-1884], died of [typhoid] fever [at Allahabad], India, [1864-]**1886**, mur., in stone frame, W.Cloister. *LX*. Inscr. in Lat. Herbert Ross Webbe, of New Coll., Oxford, commoner [1869-1875, 1856-]**1886**, pos. by relatives and friends, mur., in stone frame, W.Cloister. *LXI*. Inscr. with battle honours (Balaklava, Alma, Inkerman, Sevastopol, Lucknow). Gen. William Lygon Pakenham, 4th Earl of Longford, G.C.B., Col. Northumberland Fusiliers, commoner 1831-1836, 1819-**1887**, "THUS ENDING A LIFE SPENT IN THE SERVICE OF HIS COUNTRY AND FOR THE BENEFIT OF HIS FELLOW MEN", maker's name GAWTHORP S[C]. LONDON, mur., on stone, N.Cloister. *LXII*. Inscr. in Lat. Gerald Frederick Hornby, commoner [1876-1881, 1862-]**1890**, pos. by comrades, maker's name *HART SON PEARD & C[O] LONDON*, mur., on stone, W.Cloister. *LXIII*. Inscr. with verse. Philip Bonham-Carter, 8th son of Henry Bonham-Carter and [w.] Sibella, commoner in the house of Rev. J[ohn] T[rant] Bramston, [M.A., assistant master 1868-1908, chaplain 1877-1913], 1888-[1891], **1891**, [aged 16], mur., on marble, W.Cloister. *LXIV*. Inscr. Frank St. Clair Grimwood, of Merton Coll., Oxford, I[ndian] C[ivil] S[ervice], 2nd son of Jeffery Grimwood Grimwood, commoner [1867-1874], deputy commissioner of Assam, [India], "BRITISH RESIDENT AT MANIPUR. WHERE HE WAS TREACHEROUSLY MURDERED", **1891**, aged 37, mur., on marble, S.Cloister. *LXV*. Inscr. with verse and Christ The Good Shepherd. Archibald Edward Vernon-Harcourt, yst. son of Leveson Francis Vernon-Harcourt and [w.] Alice, [commoner 1889-1891], of Culver's Close, died at Winchester, [1875-]**1891**, mur., in stone frame, W.Cloister. Inscr. 235 x 796 mm. *LXVI*. Inscr. in Lat. with Lat. verse. [2nd-Lt.] Francis Ainger Burnett, 1st Battn. (Shropshire Light Infantry) [53rd Regt. of Foot], commoner [1880-1885], drowned [in S.S. Bokhara en-route from Shanghai to Hong Kong, 1868-]**1892**, mur., on marble, W.Cloister. *LXVII*. Inscr. 2nd-Lt. W[illia]m Alexander Lindsay, 31st [Battn.] East Surrey Regt., only son of W[illia]m Lindsay, (commoner 1858-1865), commoner 1887-1891, died at Agra, [India], **1894**, aged 20, mur., on marble, W.Cloister. *LXVIII*. Inscr. with verse. [Rev.] George Pascal Keble Houssemayne Du Boulay, M.A., "a faithful Soldier and Missionary of CHRIST

Orate p eis dm Johis Barrett i artib baccallrary quond locrij hui colleg q obijt xiij die may a sj b xxiij on me pat te

Winchester, College *LIII* (lost)

Orate p eis dm Johis Barrett i artib baccallrary quond locrij hui colleg q obijt xiij die may a sj b xxiij on me pat te

Winchester, College *LIII* (facsimile)

baptized and trained for HIS service within these walls", died at Umba, east coast of Central Africa, 1866-**1895**, mur., in marble frame, W.Cloister. *LXIX.* Inscr. in Lat. William Hill Corrie, scholar for 9 years [1848-1857], died as a result of a railway crash at St. Neots station, [Hunts., 1839-]**1895**, maker's name *J. WIPPELL & COMP*ᵞ *EXETER & LONDON*, mur., on marble, W.Cloister. *LXX.* Inscr. Henry Harold Godwin, commoner [1893-1895, 1879-]**1895**, pos. by fellow pupils, mur., in stone frame, W.Cloister. *LXXI.* Inscr. with verse. Oswald George Arthur, Bengal Civil Service, [commoner 1882-1888], exhibitioner 1883-1886, scholar of Christ Church [Coll.], Oxford 1888, acting deputy commissioner of Jubbulpore, [India], died of cholera "while engaged on Famine Relief Work", [1869-]**1896**, mur., on marble, W.Cloister. *LXXII.* Inscr. Gen. Sir W[illiam] Pollexfen Radcliffe, K.C.B., [3rd son of Rev. Walter Radcliffe], Col.-Commandant 20th Regt., commoner 1837-1841, **1897**, aged 74, mur., on marble, N.Cloister. *LXXIII.* Inscr. in Lat. Arlingham Jacob Toye, assistant master for 30 years [1869-1899, 1842-] **1899**, pos. by friends and [pupils], mur., in stone frame, W.Cloister. *LXXIV.* Inscr. in Lat. Percy Robert Turner Toynbee, scholar 1865-1870, [1851-]**1899**, pos. by friends, bronze, mur., on marble, W.Cloister. *LXXV.* Inscr. in Lat. with Lat. verse. Leonard Tabor Fisher, commoner [1894-1900, 1881-]**1900**, pos. by pupils, mur., in stone frame, W.Cloister. *LXXVI.* Inscr. in Lat. [Rev.] Charles Halford Hawkins, assistant master for 39 years [1861-1900], chaplain for 7 years [1863-1900], 1838-**1900**, pos. by friends and pupils, mur., in stone frame, W.Cloister. *LXXVII.* Inscr. in Lat. with Lat. verse. Ronald Laurence Fyffe, son of Charles Alan Fyffe, M.A., commoner [1900-1901, 1887-]**1901**, maker's name BARKENTIN & KRALL, LONDON, mur., in stone frame, W.Cloister. *LXXVIII.* Inscr. in mem. of 3 commoners. [Rev.] James Edward Austen Leigh, M.A., of Exeter Coll., Oxford, [commoner 1814-1816], vicar of Bray, Berks., 1798-1874; Cholmeley Austen Leigh, M.A., fellow of Trinity Coll., Oxford, scholar [1842-1847], 1829-1899; and Charles Raymond Austen Leigh, B.A., of Trinity Coll., Oxford, [commoner 1888-1892], 1874-**1901**, grandfather, father and son, maker's name HART · SON · PEARD · & · Cᴼ · Lᴰ · LONDON, mur., in marble frame, W.Cloister. *LXXIX.* Inscr. in raised letters with regt. insignia in relief. Lt. Lionel Wilfred de Sausmarez, 60th [King's Royal] Rifle [Corps], commoner 1888-1892, served with regt. during the [South African] War 1899-1900 and took part in the defence of Ladysmith, "AS A SPECIAL SERVICE OFFICER HE COMMANDED A COMPANY IN THE EXPEDITION AGAINST THE "MAD MULLER" IN SOMALILAND", died at Burao of wounds accidentally received, **1901**, aged 26, bronze, mur., in marble frame, W.Cloister. *LXXX.* Inscr. with verse. Arthur Edward Turner, R[oyal] E[ngineers], eld. son of Edward John Turner [assistant master 1869-1909] and [w.] Celia, [commoner 1885-1888], died at Simla, [India], **1901**, aged 29, maker's name *J. WIPPELL & COMP*ᵞ*., EXETER & LONDON*, mur., in stone frame, W.Cloister. *LXXXI.* Inscr. with verse. Robert Dolling, school missioner in St. Agatha's, Landport, [Portsmouth] 1885-1895, [1851-**1902**], pos. by Wykehamists, mur., in stone frame, E.Cloister. *LXXXII.* Inscr. Edward Chernocke Downes, 2nd son of Lt.-Col. Charles Villiers Downes, of Aspley Guise House, Beds., commoner 1900[-1902, 1886-]**1902**, mur., in stone frame, N.Cloister. *LXXXIII.* Inscr. in Lat. Lionel [Pigot] Johnson, of New Coll., Oxford, scholar [1880-1886], died in London, 1867-**1902**, mur., in stone frame, E.Cloister. *LXXXIV.* Inscr. in Lat. Clifford Wyndham Holgate, M.A., commoner [1872-1877], chancellor of the Diocese of Salisbury, 1859-**1903**, mur., in stone frame, E.Cloister. *LXXXV.* Inscr. in Lat. Robert Ker Parr, B.A., scholar [1887-1893], assistant master for 4 years [1900-1904], **1904**, aged 30, pos. by headmaster, [Herbert Murray Burge], mur., in stone frame, W.Cloister. *LXXXVI.* Inscr. in Lat. [Rev.] George Richardson, M.A., of St. John's Coll., Camb., assistant master [1867-1873], 2nd master for 16 years [1873-1899], **1904**, aged 65, maker's name BARKENTIN & KRALL. LONDON, mur., in stone frame, W.Cloister. *LXXXVII.* [Rt. Rev.] George Ridding, S.T.P., [son of no.*XLI*, scholar, 2nd master 1863-1867, headmaster 1867-1884], Bishop of Southwell [1884-1904, fellow 1895-1904], **1904**, aged 77, eff., inscr. in Lat. and sh. with mitre, maker's name BARKENTIN & KRALL, LONDON, C. *Meara*,

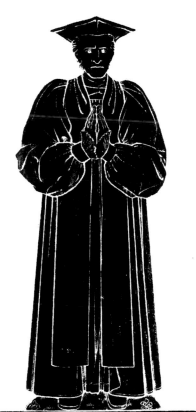

S·M·GEORGII·RIDDING·S·T·P·EPISCOPI
PRIMI·SOVTHWELLENSIS·QVI·HVJVSCE
COLLEGII·INTRA·MVROS·NATVS·FVIT·SCHO
LARIS·HOSTIARIVS·INFORMATOR·SOCIVS·
OBDORMIVIT·IN·CHRISTO·DIE·XXX°·MENS·
SEXTILIS·HCMIV·AETATIS·SVAE·LXXVII°

Winchester, College *LXXXVII*

Victorian Brasses, pl.65, p.120. Eff. 975 x 371 mm, inscr. 191 x 531 mm, sh. 443 x 419 mm. *LXXXVIII.* Inscr. with verse in raised letters and regt. insignia in relief. Lt. Sutton Aylmer Davies, 2nd **Battn**. East Lancashire Regt., scholar [1888-1894], drowned at Poona, [India], 1875-**1905**, bronze, mur., on marble, S.Cloister. *LXXXIX.* Inscr. [Rev.] Edmund William Sergeant, [M.A.], assistant master 1865-1882, 1835-**1905**, maker's name *JONES & WILLIS. L*ᵀᴰ, mur., in stone frame, W.Cloister. *XC.* Inscr. in Lat. with Lat. verse. John A[lexander] T[rant] Bramston, commoner [1892-1899], **1906**, aged 26, pos. by father, [Rev. John Trant Bramston, M.A., scholar 1856-1861, assistant master 1868-1908, chaplain 1877-1913], mother and sister, maker's name BARKENTIN & KRALL, LONDON, mur., in stone frame, W.Cloister. *XCI.* Inscr. in Lat. Edward Hastings Buckland, B.A., assistant master for 17 years [1888-1906, 1864-]**1906**, maker's name BARKENTIN & KRALL. LONDON, pos. by 2 friends, mur., in stone frame, W.Cloister. *XCII.* Inscr. in Lat. with Lat. verse. Kenneth John Freeman, scholar [1895-1901], assistant master [1905-1906], **1906**, aged 25, pos. by friends, mur., in stone frame, W.Cloister. *XCIII.* Inscr. in Lat. with Lat. verse. John Hamilton Mitchell, commoner [1902-1908, 1889-]**1907**, mur., in stone frame, E.Cloister. *XCIV.* John Hanbury Rowe, [son of Rev. T.B. Rowe], scholar [1903-1907, died at Bournemouth, 1890-]**1907**, rect. pl. bust of boy in semi-relief, inscr. in Lat. with Lat. verse on scroll in raised letters, Alpha-Omega symbols and Chi Rho monogram in relief, bronze, mur., in marble frame, E.Cloister. *XCV.* Inscr. in Lat. with Lat. verse. Arthur Sergius Bigg-Wither, [son of Rev. Fitzhugh Bigg-Wither], commoner [1902-1907], **1907**, aged 18, mur., in stone frame, N.Cloister. *XCVI.* Inscr. in Lat. with Lat. verse. G[eorge] Malcolm McConnel, commoner [1906-1908, 1893-]**1908**, mur., in stone frame, N.Cloister. *XCVII.* Inscr. in Lat. Francis Hornby Birley, [J.P., son of Thomas Hornby Birley, commoner 1863-1868], brother of no.*XXXVII*, husband and father, [1850-]**1910**, pos. by sons, mur., in stone frame, E.Cloister. *XCVIII.* Inscr. in Lat. Thomas Frederick Kirby, M.A., bursar for 33 years [1877-1910, 1836-]**1910**, pos. by warden and fellows, mur., in stone frame, N.Cloister. *XCIX.* Inscr. in Lat. Edmund Henry Girdlestone, son [of Rev. Henry Girdlestone, rector of Landford], scholar "of Founder's Kin" [1840-1842, 1827-]1842, pos. in **1912**, pos. by brothers, mur., in stone frame, E.Cloister. *C.* Inscr. in Lat. Frederick Morshead, scholar [1848-1853], assistant master for 37 years [1868-1905], alderman for 27 years, twice mayor [1873 and 1876], **1914**, aged 78, mur., in stone frame, W.Cloister. *CI.* Inscr. with verse on scroll and sh. George Donath Lascelles Harcourt, only son of George Harcourt and [w.] Mary, [commoner 1913-1915], died at Winchester, [1899-]**1915**, mur., in stone frame, N.Cloister. *CII.* Inscr. [Dr.] Edwin Freshfield, LL.D., [F.S.A., son of James William Freshfield, of Reigate, Surrey, commoner, fellow 1888-1895, solicitor to the Bank of England, 1832-**1918**], mur., Chantry Chapel. Inscr. 88 x 386 mm. *CIII.* Inscr. Joseph Heap, of Liverpool, [commoner 1919-1923], "came to Culver's Close Sept. 1919 died on his summer holiday", 1905-**1923**, mur., in stone frame, N.Cloister. *CIV.* Inscr. [Rev.] Arthur George Bather, [M.A., assistant master 1894-1928], chaplain for 24 years [1902-1928, 1868-]**1928**, mur., Chantry Chapel. *CV.* Inscr. with verse. John William George Mills, commoner for 1 year [1936-1937], 1923-**1937**, mur., in stone frame, N.Cloister. *CVI.* Inscr. Field-Marshal Archibald Percival [Wavell], Earl Wavell, P.C., G.C.B., G.C.S.I., G.C.I.E., C.M.G., M.C., Viscount Wavell of Cyrenaica and of Winchester, Viscount Keren of Eritrea and of Winchester, scholar [1896-1900], Col. Black Watch, Viceroy and Governor-Gen. of India, Constable of H.M. Tower of London, soldier, statesman, poet, 1883-1950, buried in the cloister; also only son, Major Archibald John Arthur [Wavell], 2nd Earl Wavell, M.C., Black Watch, commoner [1929-1934], "BURIED IN KENYA WHERE HE DIED IN BATTLE", 1916-**1953**, mur., in stone frame, N.Cloister. *CVII.* Inscr. in Lat. Ruthven O[liphant] Hall, scholar [1931-1936], bursar [1961-1982], 1917-**1983**, on music stand, C. *CVIII.* Inscr. recording gift of organ in **2005** by pupil [Graham Starforth Hill, scholar 1940-1945,] in mem. of Sydney Watson, [assistant] master of music 1938-1945, [1903-1991], on organ, Chantry Chapel.

In loving memory of ARCHIBALD EDWARD VERNON-HARCOURT, of Culver's Close, Winchester College, younger son of Leveson Francis and Alice Vernon-Harcourt, who died at Winchester, 13th April, 1791 aged 15 years. "Thanks be to God which giveth us the Victory through Our Lord Jesus Christ."

Winchester, College *LXV*

In Thy kingdom remember LORD Thy servant Edwin Freshfield Doctor of Laws formerly a fellow of this College

Winchester, College *CII*

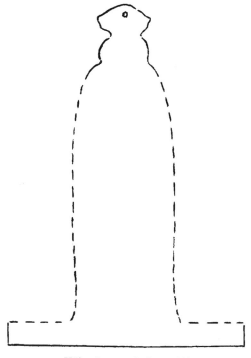

Winchester, College 111

INDENTS & LOST BRASSES. 109. Indent, priest, hf. eff. in mass vests. and inscr., c.1450, N.Cloister. *Sadler, Southern England,* appx. I, p.18 (drg.). Eff. 350 x 200 mm, inscr. 75 x 395 mm, Purbeck slab 1650 x 700 mm. 110. Indent, priest, hf. eff. in mass vests. and inscr., c.1450, N.Cloister. *Sadler, Southern England,* appx. I, p.19 (drg.). Eff. 335 x 200 mm, inscr. 95 x 430 mm, Purbeck slab 1525 x 670 mm. 111. Indent, priest in cope and almuce, inscr., c.1460, W.Cloister. *Sadler, Dorset and Hampshire,* appx. I, pt.2, p.39 (drg.). Eff. 855 x c.210 mm, inscr. 65 x 635 mm, Purbeck slab 2600 x 1050 mm. 112. Indent, ?eff. and inscr., 8 plug holes only, effaced, E.Cloister. Eff. c.315 x ? mm, inscr. c.125 x 495 mm, Purbeck slab 1980 x 785 mm. 113. Indent, ?priest, hf. eff. and inscr., 2 plugs and 1 plug hole only, effaced, N.Cloister. Eff. 270 x ? mm, inscr. c.95 x c.330 mm, Purbeck slab 805 remains x 545 mm. 114. Indent, eff. and inscr., 6 rivets only, effaced, W.Cloister. Eff. c.310 x c.90 mm, inscr. c.60 x c.400 mm, Purbeck slab 1590 x 650 mm. 115. Indent, priest, hf. eff. and inscr., nearly effaced, W.Cloister. Eff. c.340 x c.190 mm, inscr. c.85 x c.330 mm, Purbeck slab 1585 x 645 mm. 116. Indent, inscr., E.Cloister. Inscr. 75 x 345 mm, Purbeck slab 1870 x 780 mm. 117. Indent, inscr., E.Cloister. Inscr. 100 x 285 mm, Purbeck slab 1565 x 670 mm. 118. Indent, inscr., 1 plug and 2 plug holes only, effaced, N.Cloister. Inscr. c.80 x c.310 mm, Purbeck slab 1620 x 750 mm. 119. Indent, inscr., W.Cloister. Inscr. 65 x 340 mm, Purbeck slab 1720 x 760 mm. 120. Indent, inscr., nearly effaced, W.Cloister. Inscr. c.85 x c.485 mm, Purbeck slab 1550 x 735 mm. 121. Lost brass, inscr. Henry Kesewyk, 1409, Ante-chapel. Recorded by Wood (c.1690) and by Warton (1773). 122. Lost brass, inscr. William Laus, fellow, 1417, W.Cloister. Recorded by Wood (c.1690), by Warton (1773) and by Milner (1801). 123. Lost brass, inscr. John Cleir, fellow, 1421, Ante-chapel. Recorded by Wood (c.1690) and by Warton (1773). 124. Lost brass, inscr. William Walynford, fellow, 1439, Ante-chapel. Recorded (lost) by Wood (c.1690) and by Warton (1773). 125. Lost brass, inscr. John Bowke, 3rd warden of New Coll., Oxford, 1442. Recorded (lost) by Wood (c.1690) and by Warton (1773). 126. Lost brass, inscr. John Frances, fellow, 1445, Ante-chapel. Recorded by Wood (c.1690) and by Warton (1773). 127. Lost brass, inscr. Richard Boweman, fellow, 1464, E.Cloister. Recorded by Wood (c.1690). 128. Lost brass, inscr. William Nyghtyngale, fellow, 1467. Recorded by Wood (c.1690) and by Warton (1773). 129. Lost brass, inscr. John Beckynton, fellow, 1473, Ante-chapel. Recorded by Wood (c.1690) and by Warton (1773). 130. Lost brass, inscr. Richard Dene, M.A., 13th headmaster, 1494, W.Cloister. Recorded by Wood (c.1690) and by Warton (1773). 131. Lost brass, eff, inscr. and scroll. John Wyght, fellow, 1494, Ante-chapel. Recorded by Wood (c.1690). 132. Lost brass, Joan Bedell, w. of no.*L*, 1497, Ante-Chapel. Recorded by Wood (c.1690) and by Warton (1773). 133. Lost brass, marg. inscr. with evang. symbols at corners. Michael [Cleve, warden 1489-1501], Ante-chapel. Recorded by Wood (c.1690) and by Warton (1773). 134. Lost brass, inscr. Thomas Ashburne, fellow, 1516, Ante-chapel. Recorded by Wood (c.1690) and by Warton (1773). 135. Lost brass, inscr. Richard Cole, conductor, 1519, S.Cloister. Recorded by Wood (c.1690) and by Warton (1773). 136. Lost brass, inscr. Maurice Morrys, clerk, 1523, S.Cloister. Recorded by Wood (c.1690) and by Warton (1773). 137. Lost brass, inscr. Thomas Ryve, fellow, 1524, W.Cloister. Recorded by Wood (c.1690) and by Warton (1773). 138. Lost brass, inscr. Thomas Beche, B.C.L., fellow, 1531, W.Cloister. Recorded by Wood (c.1690) and by Warton (1773). 139. Lost brass, inscr. in 6 Lat. vv. Thomas Basset, fellow and vice-warden, 1555, pos. by C. Johnson, mur., Ante-chapel and Cloister. Recorded by Wood (c.1690) and by Warton (1773). 140. Lost brass, inscr. in 8 Lat. vv. John Leffe, D.C.L., 1557, aged 66, Ante-chapel and Cloister. Recorded by Wood (c.1690) and by Warton (1773). Illustration from rubbing in Soc. Antiq. coll. Rubbing in Soc. Antiq. coll. (n.d.). Inscr. 324 x 386 mm. 141. Lost brass, inscr. in 4 Lat. vv.

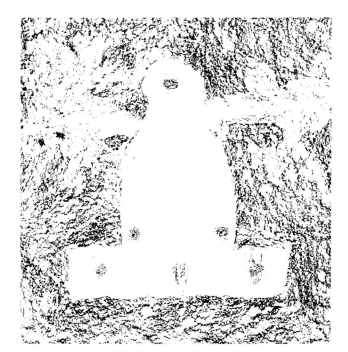

Winchester, College 109

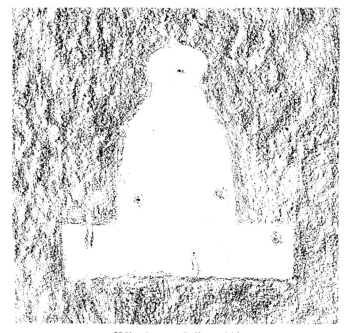

Winchester, College 110

Thomas Vole, fellow, 1558, Ante-chapel. Recorded (lost) by Wood (c.1690) and by Warton (1773). 142. Lost brass, inscr. in 10 Lat. vv. Thomas Stempe, LL.D., 11th warden 1581. Recorded (lost) by Wood (c.1690) and by Warton (1773). 143. Lost brass, inscr. in 6 Lat. vv. John Boles, M.A., fellow, 1610, mur., W.Cloister. Recorded by Wood (c.1690). 144. Lost brass, inscr. in 4 Lat. vv. Thomas Emes, chaplain for 33 years, 1629, mur., W.Cloister. Recorded by Wood (c.1690) and by Warton (1773). 145. Lost brass. inscr. with 4 Lat. vv. and ach. Nicholas Love, S.T.D., warden for 17 years, pos. by B.M., engr. c.1630, Ante-chapel. Recorded by Wood (c.1690) and by Warton (1773). 146. Lost brass, inscr. William Turner, clerk, 1644, mur., E.Cloister. Recorded by Wood (c.1690). 147. Lost brass, inscr. John Gray, 16__, N.Cloister. Recorded by Wood (c.1690). 148. Lost brass, inscr. Edward _____, W.Cloister. Recorded (inscr. mutil.) by Wood (c.1690) and by Warton (1773). 149. Lost brass, ?priest, ?warden, inscr., and scroll, Ante-Chapel. Recorded (eff. and scroll with inscr. lost) by Wood (c.1690) and (scroll with eff. and inscr. lost) by Warton (1773).

In 1681 the brasses were removed to the ante-chapel when the floor of the chapel was repaved with black and white marble. Nine original brasses (listed by Mill Stephenson as nos.I, II, IV, V, IX, XI, XVII, XVIII & XX) mysteriously disappeared during the restoration of the chapel in 1875 having again being taken up and reputedly placed in safe-keeping. Facsimiles (nos.*XIV, XLVI, XLVII, XLVIII, XLIX, L, LI, LII & LIII*) were engraved in 1882 at the cost of Dr. Edwin Freshfield, LL.D., F.S.A., solicitor to the Bank of England.

Ref: *Beaumont*, p.141; *Bod. Lib. MS. Wood D.4*, ff.34-49; *Brit. Lib. Add MS. 18478*, f.41, *Add. MS. 39987*, ff.2-9, ff.29-32, ff.38-40, f.45, f.52, f.55, f.60; *Burke's Peerage and Baronetage*, p.1649; *Haines*, I, pp.75-6, p.79, p.81, p.85, p.95, p.183, II, pp.74-5; *Hampshire, Antiquary*, I, p.71; *Hampshire History*, I, pp.186-91; *Hants Proc.*, III, pp.79-87, X, pp.279-80; *Heseltine, Heraldry*, p.38; *Leach*, p.494; *Manning*, p.31; *M.B.S. Bulletin*, 28, p.6, 68, p.159; *M.B.S. Trans.*, I, pt.10, p.10, II, p.237, IV, pp.121-2, p.333, V, p.244, VI, pp.124-42, p.214, VIII, p.355; *Milner, History*, II, pp.120-1, p.123; *Milner, Survey*, II, p.96, pp.159-60, pp.162-3; *M.S.*, pp.167-9, p.753; *Norris, Memorials*, pp.85-6, p.168, p.182, p.264, p.282, p.284; *Palimpsests*, 140L1, p.49; *Pevsner, Hampshire*, p.701; *Sadler, Dorset and Hampshire*, appx. I, intro., xvii, pt.2, pp.38-42; *Sadler, Southern England*, appx. I, pp.17-9; *Simpson*, pp.28-9; *Soc. Antiq. Lond. Proc.*, 2 S. IX, p.18; *Soc. Antiq. MS. 875/6*, pp.149-66; *V.C.H., Hampshire*, V, p.16; *Warton*, I, pp.101-2, p.104, p.109, pp.111-3, pp.116-7, pp.119-20, p.127, p.131, pp.133-41, pp.154-5, p.157, pp.195-8, p.203; *Winchester, Description*, pp.29-36, pp.38-40, pp.46-52, pp.54-8.

WINCHESTER, Hampshire County Museum Service.

I. Six sons and 4 daus. in shrouds, from brass to Philip Astley, esq., **1467**, and 4 ws., Lettis, Margaret, Elizabeth, Alice, at Standon, Herts.; purchased in 1912 by Herbert Druitt for £5 from the Old Curiosity Shop, 45 High Street, Poole, Dorset and bequeathed in 1934 on death to the Red House Museum, Christchurch. Accession no. HMCMS:CRH1979.44/1-2. *Bertram, Rare Brass Rubbings*, fig.10 (children). Sons 133-135 x 129 mm, daus. 127-129 x 100 mm. *II.* Inscr. Winifred, w. (1) of John Beconshaw, by whom John and Amy, (2) of Richard Ailif, **1570**, from Ewhurst (q.v.); deposited in 1982 by Lt.-Col. Richard Mayfield of Ewhurst House. Accession no. HMCMS/DA:1982.98. *M.B.S. Bulletin*, 33, p.42. Inscr. 120 x 320 mm. Style: London.

Ref: *M.B.S. Bulletin*, 33, pp.42-3; *M.S.*, pp.582-3.

Winchester, College 140

Winchester, Hampshire County Museum Service *1*

WINCHESTER, Magdalen Hospital.

Frag. of inscr. ". . . ag . . ./. . .ue . . .", c.**1425-50**; discovered in 2001 during a *Time Team* excavation; deposited with Winchester, Museums Service (q.v.).

INDENTS & LOST BRASSES. 1. Lost brass, inscr. John Ebden, D.D., prebendary of Winchester Cathedral, master, "gave £200 to augment the income of the Master and Poor of this foundation", 1614, aged 98, mur., C. Recorded by Warton (1773).

Ref: *Warton*, I, p.210.

WINCHESTER, Museums Service.

I. Frag. of inscr. ". . . ag . . ./. . .ue . . .", c.**1425-50**; discovered in 2001 during a *Time Team* excavation at Magdalen Hospital (q.v.). Accession no. AY30. Frag. of inscr. 62 x 32 mm. Style: London ?B.

II. (Formerly M.S.I). Trinity, c.**1500**; purchased in 1922 for £3 together with no.*III* and said to have come from Farringdon (q.v.). Accession no. WINCM:LH443.2. *M.B.S. Trans.*, X, p.91. Trinity 157 x 101 mm. Style: London.

III. (Formerly M.S.II). Two sons, c.**1515**; purchased in 1922 for £3 together with no.*II* and said to have come from Farringdon (q.v.) are from brass to man in arm. and 2 ws., c.1515, at Blewbury, Berks. (q.v.). Accession no. WINCM:LH443.1. *Berks.*, p.17. Sons 153 x 75 mm. Style: London F variant.

Ref: *Berks.*, p.16; *M.B.S. Bulletin*, 68, p.159; *M.B.S. Trans.*, X, p.90; *M.S.*, p.828.

WINCHESTER, St. Bartholomew Hyde.

I. Inscr. in 4 Lat. vv. Edmund Poore, **1599**; formerly mur., C., now mur., on board, N. Inscr. 130 x 551 mm. Style: Johnson.

II. Inscr. recording [north] aisle built in **1859** by William Barrow Simonds, of Abbotts Barton, [1820-1912], in mem. of parents, [William Simonds, 1858, aged 71, and w. Helen, 1846, aged 48], mur., on board, N.C. *III.* Inscr. recording chancel rebuilt in **1859** by Rev. William Williams, M.A., vicar [1833-1869], Walter Davies Williams, M.D., Rev. T.P. Wright and w. Eliza Phillippa in mem. of parents, William Williams and w. Martha, mur., on board, C. *IV.* Inscr. "AN ANCIENT STOUP OF THE CHURCH OF HYDE ABBEY ACCIDENTALLY FOUND ON NOVEMBER 12TH **1879**, AND PLACED HERE BY THE VICAR AND CHURCHWARDENS", mur., S.Porch. *V.* Cross surmounting inscr. Lt.-Gen. Francis Carey, 26th Cameronians, died at Gatehouse, N[ew] B[runswick, Canada], 1887, aged 68; also sons, Lt. Francis Peter [Carey], died on board H.M.S. Indus, **1889**, aged 39, and Reginald William Cyril [Carey], died at Torquay, [Devon], 1889, aged 21, mur., on marble, N.A. *VI.* Cross in relief and inscr. on scroll-shaped pls. [Rev.] George James Athill, M.A., vicar 1895-**1897**, pos. by widow and children, C. *VII.* Inscr. Thomas Charles Langdon, F.R.C.S., 1905, and w. Mary Ann, **1913**, on statue plinth, N. *VIII & IX.* Two inscrs.

Winchester, Hampshire County Museum Service *II*

Winchester, Museums Service *I*

Winchester, Museums Service *II*

Winchester, Museums Service *III*

369

Fred Holway, server, **1918**, worn, on candleholders, C. *X.* World War I memorial (75 names), copper, mur., in wooden frame, N. *XI.* Inscr. recording renovation and rededication of organ in **1939 in** mem. of Hubert Miller Carey and sister, Caroline, son and dau. of no.*V*, on organ, C. *XII.* Inscr. [Rev.] William Riddell Parr, M.A., vicar 1934-**1941**, bronze, on choir stall, C. *XIII.* Inscr. May E. Hill, **1958**, bronze, on choir stall, C. *XIV.* Inscr. Miss Elsie Gates, 1906-**1975**, on aumbry, N.C. *XV.* Inscr. L.K. Fearon, engr. c.**1980**, on credence table, C. *XVI.* Inscr. recording planting of [Oriental Hawthorn] (Crataegus Laciniata) in **1985** in mem. of June Woods (née Higgs), 1933-1982, bronze, on tree post, Churchyard. *XVII.* Inscr. recording planting of [Oriental Hawthorn] (Crataegus Laciniata) in **1990** in mem. of Florence Marion Higgs, 1907-1989, bronze, on tree post, Churchyard. *XVIII.* Inscr. Jean Mary Moss, **1993**, on display case, N.A. *XIX.* Inscr. Rosemary Tayler, 1928-**1994**, on book stand, N.C. *XX.* Inscr. Kathleen Grace (Tass) Mills, engr. c.**1995**, bronze, on bench, Churchyard. *XXI.* Inscr. Alan Michael House, 1923-**1998**, on choir stall, C. *XXII.* Inscr. Dorothy May Bryan, 1914-**1999**, on choir stall with no.*XIII*, C. *XXIII.* Inscr. Brenda Lowe, 1928-**2003**, on choir stall with nos.*XIII & XXII*, C.

INDENTS & LOST BRASSES. 24. Indent, ?man in arm., hf. eff., inscr. and sh., c.1450; formerly C., N., now Tower. Eff. 400 mm, inscr. 250 x 380 mm, sh. 145 x 120 mm. 25. Lost brass, inscr. Isabella, mother of Edward Hocley, M.A., vicar, 1483. Recorded by Warton (1773).

Ref: *Hampshire History*, I, p.173; *M.B.S. Trans.*, VI, p.143; *M.S.*, p.169, p.753; *Soc. Antiq. MS. 875/6*, p.167; *V.C.H., Hampshire*, V, p.70; *Warton*, I, p.203.

WINCHESTER, St. Cross.

I. John de Campeden, warden of the hospital, [canon of Southwell, **1382**], in cope (mutil.), with inscr., shs. of the Passion and Trinity and marg. inscr. with text from Job XIX, 25-27 and evang. symbols in quadrilobes at corners; formerly N., rel., C. *Alcuin Club Colls.*, XXII, p.47 (eff.); *Bardfield, S., Thatcham, Berks., and its Manors*, I, p.348; *Bertram, Brasses*, fig.82(b), p.130 (detail); *Bouquet, Church Brasses*, fig.25, p.67; *Boutell, Series*; *Brit. Lib. Add. MS. 39987,* ff.25-6r; *Carter, J., Specimens of Anc. Sculpture and Painting*, II, p.46; *Gittings*, fig.18, p.26 (eff. and inscr.); *Leach*, p.78; *M.B.S. Portfolio*, IV, pl.7; *M.B.S. Trans.*, XIII, p.336 (sh. of the Passion); *Mee, Hampshire*, p.347 (drg. of eff.); *Portfolio Book*, pl.60. Eff. 1809 x 554 mm, inscr. 65 x 494 mm, dext. sh. 168 x 128 mm, sin. sh. 166 x 120 mm, marg. inscr. 2338 x 869 x 37 mm, upper dext. quadrilobe 102 x 102 mm, upper sin. quadrilobe 102 x 102 mm, lower dext. quadrilobe 101 x 102 mm, lower sin. quadrilobe 102 x 101 mm, Purbeck slab 2375 x 1000 mm. Style: London B. Rep. by H.F.O.E. (1956).

II. Inscr. in 8 Eng. vv. John Newles, a brother of the hospital, esquire and servant for 30 yeares to Cardinal Beaufort, **1452**, N. Inscr. 246 x 470 mm, Purbeck slab 2145 x 925 mm. Style: London D.

III. Inscr. William Saundres, chaplain, **1464**, S.Tr. Inscr. 73 x 360 mm, Purbeck slab 1550 x c.660 mm. Style: London D.

IV. Richard Harward, "decretorum doctoris", warden, **1493**, in cap and almuce; inscr. restored by 1905; formerly N., rel., C. Recorded (inscr. mutil. and in Porter's Lodge) by Warton (1773) and (inscr. lost) by Haines (1861). *Alcuin Club Colls.*, XXII, p.67; *Beaumont*, p.88; *Brit. Lib.*

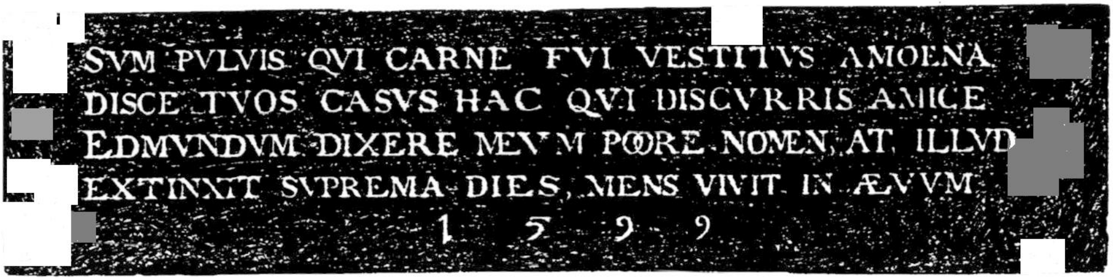

SVM PVLVIS QVI CARNE FVI VESTITVS AMOENA
DISCE TVOS CASVS HAC QVI DISCVRRIS AMICE
EDMVNDVM DIXERE MEVM PŒRE NOMEN AT ILLVD
EXTINXIT SVPREMA DIES MENS VIVIT IN ÆVVM
1 5 9 9

Winchester, St. Bartholowew Hyde I

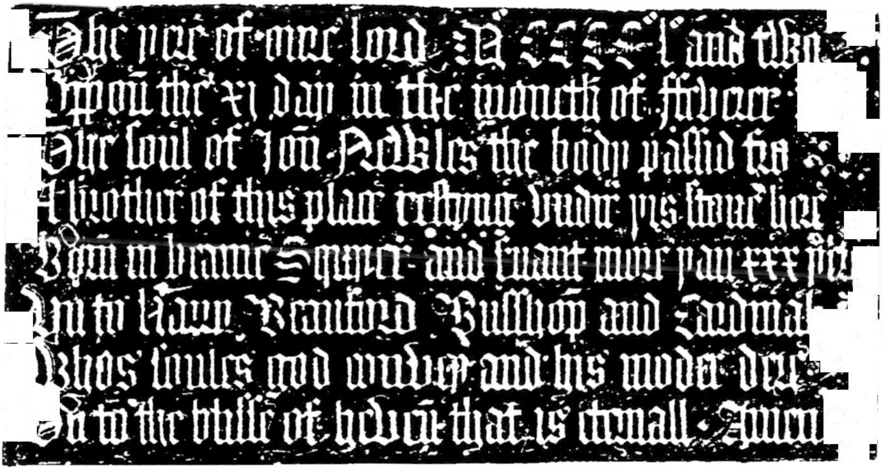

Winchester, St. Cross II

Winchester, St. Cross III

Winchester, St. Cross V

371

Winchester, St. Cross I

372

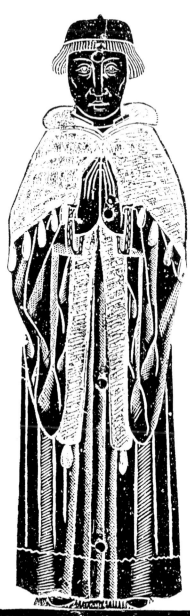

Orate p ãia Wñi Ricardi Halward decretorum doctoris ac
nuper huius hospitalis magistri qui obiit   die Aprilis A·
dñi M᷑·CCCC·nonogesimo tertio Cui᷑ ãie ppicietur dens

Winchester, St. Cross IV

Add. MS. 39987, f.37; *Gawthorp*, pl.22, opp. p.65; *M.B.S. Trans.*, VI, p.146; *Mee, Hampshire*, p.219 (drg. of eff.); *Page-Phillips' Macklin*, p.55 (drg. of eff.). Eff. 656 x 196 mm, inscr. 89 x 392 mm, Purbeck slab 1065 x 565 mm. Style: London G.

V. Inscr. John, son of John and Agatha Wayte, **1502**; formerly S.C., now N. Inscr. 89 x 452 mm, Purbeck slab 2220 x 1020 mm. Style: London G.

VI. Thomas Lawne, rector of Mottisfont, **1518**, in mass vests., inscr.; formerly Tower, now rel., C. *Brit. Lib. Add. MS. 39987*, ff.46r-7r; *M.B.S. Trans.*, VI, p.148. Eff. 965 x 304 mm, inscr. 130 x 550 mm, Purbeck slab 1400 x 660 mm. Style: London F variant.

VII. Inscr. (mutil.). Elizabeth Wroughton, "Gentlewoman", **1551**; palimp., on rev. 2 lines of drapery; on same slab as no.26, C. *M.B.S. Trans.*, XVI, p.66 (obv.), p.67 (with no.26); *Palimpsests*, pl.57 (rev.). Inscr. 89 x 424 mm. Illustration (complete) from rubbing in Soc. Antiq. coll. Rubbing (complete) in Camb. coll. (1847) and (complete) in Soc. Antiq. coll. (n.d.). Inscr. 89 x 424 mm. Style: London G (Fermer, script 6). Rep. (1967) and by B.S.H.E. (1996).

VIII. Inscr. Alexander Ewart, a brother of the hospital, **1569**, S.Tr. Inscr. 194 x 427 mm, Purbeck slab c.1780 x 730 mm.

IX. Inscr. "LOVE NEVER FAILETH JANUARY 24TH **1900**", on cross, C. *X.* Inscr. in raised letters recording rebuilding and enlargement of organ in **1907** by husband, [Rev. the Hon. Alan Brodrick, M.A.], master [1901-1909], in mem. of [w.] Emily Hester, [dau. of Philip Melvill, 1906], maker's name HART · SON · PEARD · & Cᴼ · LD. · LONDON, on organ, S.Tr. *XI.* Inscr. in raised letters recording tower clock pos. in **1907** by 4 children in mem. of Emily Hester, [dau. of Philip Melvill, w. of Rev. the Hon. Alan] Brodrick, [1906], maker's name HART · SON · PEARD · & Cᴼ · LD. · LONDON, mur., on pillar, Crossing. *XII.* Inscr. in raised letters recording east window and chapel fittings pos. by friends and parishioners of St. Faith in **1907** in mem. of Emily Hester, [dau. of Philip Melvill], w. of [Rev. the Hon. Alan] Brodrick, [M.A.], master [1901-1909], 1906, maker's name HART · SON · PEARD · & Cᴼ · LD · LONDON, mur., S.C. of C. *XIII.* Inscr. in raised letters recording erection of [west north transept] window in **1908** by William Barrow Simonds in mem. of 6 family members [buried] in the transept, bronze, mur., below window, N.Tr. *XIV.* Inscr. with verse in raised letters recording gift of [east north chapel] window in mem. of [Rev. the Hon.] Alan Brodrick, [M.A., 4th son of Rev. William John Brodrick, 7th Viscount Midleton], master 1901-**1909**, [1840-1909, pos. by] A.G.B.R., bronze, mur., N.C. of C. *XV.* Inscr. Caroline Merriott, **1913**, on ewer, Vestry. *XVI.* Inscr. with verse in raised letters with regt. insignia in relief. Lt. Charles George Edric Clowes, [1st Battn. attd. 3rd Battn.] King's Royal Rifle [Corps, son of Major Charles Edward Clowes], born in the par., baptised in the ch., [killed] in action near Ypres, 1892-**1915**, [buried at] Bailleul [Communal] Cemetery, [France], bronze, mur., in stone frame, S.A. *XVII.* Inscr. with verse on scroll-shaped pl. Capt. Jervoise Purefoy Causton, [1st Battn.] Hampshire Regiment, son of [Francis Jervoise Causton, M.A.], master [1909-1928, and w. Laura Georgina], killed in action at Bethune, France, **1918**, [aged 24, buried at Gonnehem British Cemetery, France], on reredos, N.C. of C. *XVIII.* Inscr. recording restoration of north choir chapel "in remembrance of those Parishioners of Sᵗ Faith who fell gallantly in defence of their King and Country in the Great War of 1914-1918"; dedicated in **1918** by [Rt. Rev. Edward Stuart Talbot,] Bishop of Winchester [1911-1923], mur., in stone frame, N.C. of C. *XIX.* World War I memorial in raised letters on 2 pls. (20 names), bronze, mur., in stone frame, N.C. of C. *XX.* Inscr. Charles Henry Gamblin, organist for many years,

Winchester, St. Cross VI

375

1834-**1921**, pos. by Winchester Choral Society members and friends, on organ with no.*X*, S.Tr. *XXI*. Inscr. George John Douglas Walters, **1963**, aged 64, bronze, on display case, N.C. of C. *XXII*. Inscr. Jules Alexander Cornelius William West, **1965**, on table, Vestry. *XXIII*. Inscr. Brig. Alexander Buchanan Dick, T.D., M.B., R[oyal] A[rmy] M[edical] C[orps], 1915-**1976**, pos. by w. and family, on chair, Vestry. *XXIV*. Inscr. Harold Kay, senior Beaufort brother, 1913-**2005**, on votive stand, S.C. of C.

INDENTS & LOST BRASSES. 25. Indent, priest in mass vests. and inscr. John Prews, rector of Mechelmarsh, 1418, S.Tr. Recorded (complete) by Schnebbelie (1788) and (complete) by Gough (c.1790). *Bod. Lib. Gough Maps 223*, f.50 (drg.); *M.B.S. Trans.*, XIV, p.481 (Schnebbelie drg.); *Sadler, Dorset and Hampshire*, appx. I, pt.2, p.37 (drg.). Illustration (headless eff.) from rubbing in Soc. Antiq. coll. Rubbing (headless eff.) in Soc. Antiq. coll. (n.d.). Eff. 365 x 115 mm, inscr. 110 x 500 mm, Purbeck slab c.2540 x 1035 mm. Style: London B. 26. Indent, priest, hf. eff. in almuce with master's staff and inscr., c.1440, C. Possibly John Forest, master 1426-1444. *M.B.S. Trans.*, XVI, p.67 (with no.VII); *Sadler, Dorset and Hampshire*, appx. I, pt.2, p.33 (drg.). Eff. 260 x 170 mm, inscr. 85 x 420 mm, Purbeck slab 1685 x 735 mm. Style: London D. 27. Indent, priest in acad., c.1470, S.Tr. *Sadler, Dorset and Hampshire*, appx. I, pt.2, p.36 (drg.). Eff. 565 remains x 110 mm remains, Purbeck slab 705 remains x 420 mm remains. 28. Indent, priest and civilian, inscr., c.1500, C. *Sadler, Dorset and Hampshire*, appx. I, pt.2, p.35 (drg.). Male eff. 270 x 100 mm, female eff. 260 x 100 mm, inscr. 215 x 435 mm, Purbeck slab 1700 x 805 mm. 29. Indent, ?priest in mass vests. and inscr., nearly effaced, N.Tr. Eff. c.300 x c.80 mm, inscr. 70 x 270 mm, Purbeck slab 1545 x 710 mm. 30. Indent, inscr., S.C. of C. Inscr. 60 x 370 mm, Purbeck slab 1410 x 765 mm. 31. Indent, ?inscr., 3 rivets only, effaced, N.Tr. Purbeck slab 1570 x c.600 mm. 32. Lost brass, marg. inscr. in ?Lombardics. Peter de St. Marie, master 1289-96. Recorded by Carter (1787). 33. Lost ?brass, John Berton, vicar of St. John's, N. Recorded by Warton (1773). 34. Lost, ?brass, John Turke, a brother of the hospital. Recorded by Warton (1773).

Ref: *Beaumont*, p.87, p.89; *Bod. Lib. Gough Maps 223*, f.50; *Brit. Lib. Add. MS. 39987*, ff.25-6, f.37, ff.46-7; *Burke's Peerage and Baronetage*, p.1810; *Carter, J., Specimens of the Ancient Sculpture and Wallpainting*, 1787, II, p.46; *Duthy*, p.288; *Earliest English Brasses*, p.190; *Gawthorp*, p.76, p.87; *Gittings*, p.28; *Gough*, II, pt.2, p.354; *Haines*, I, p.57, p.79, p.102, p.144, II, p.75; *Hampshire History*, I, pp.227-8; *Hampshire N. and Q.*, II, pp.75-6; *Manning*, p.31; *M.B.S. Trans.*, I, pt.9, pp.8-10, pt.10, p.7, II, p.237, III, p.15, VI, pp.143-5, p.147, p.149, IX, p.116, p.529, X, p.10, p.37, XI, p.317, XIII, p.211, p.335, XIV, p.481, p.490, XV, p.144, p.147, p.449, XVI, pp.66-8, p.136; *Mee, Hampshire*, p.413; *Milner, Survey*, II, p.189; *M.S.*, p.169; *Norris, Memorials*, p.62, pp.70-1, p.146, p.169; *Palimpsests*, 154L2, p.51; *Pevsner, Hampshire*, p.711; *Sadler, Dorset and Hampshire*, appx. I, pt.2, pp.33-7, p.42; *Sadler, Southern England*, appx. I, p.17; *Simpson*, p.28; *Soc. Antiq. MS. 875/6*, pp.167-73; *V.C.H., Hampshire*, V, p.65; *Warton*, I, pp.232-6; *Winchester, Description*, pp.19-21.

WINCHESTER, St. John the Baptist.

I. Inscr. "JACOBI MINGAY ARMIGERI DOMINI REGI E CONSILTARIIS *ANNO DOMINI* **1791** EX DONO", on chandelier, N. *II*. Inscr. with verse. Francis Alleyne Menzies, of New Coll., Oxford, 1856-**1879**, pos. by friends at Oxford "IN APPRECIATION OF HIS LIFE OF PURITY AND IN RECOGNITION OF HIS MANY CHRISTIAN VIRTUES", maker's name COX & SONS, LONDON, mur.,

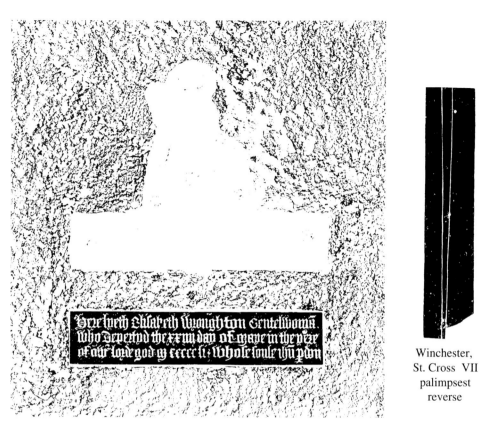

Here lyeth Elisabeth Wrioughton Gentelwoman. Who Departyd the xxviij day of maye in the yere of our lorde god m ccccc li; Whose soule jhu pdon

Winchester, St. Cross VII & 26

Winchester,
St. Cross VII
palimpsest
reverse

Under this stone resteth Alexander, Swaet: late brother of this place, who departed: this transitorie lyfe to Almighttie god the :xvij: daye of Julij: M : D : LXix : Beati mortui qui in domino moriuntur

Winchester, St. Cross VIII

377

Winchester, St. Cross 25

hu iacc Johes pzeles quondm Rectoz Ecctie de
mechelmerssh qui obiit xiii die menß Aprilis Anno
dm sp' AAAA° xvii cuius aie pinietur deus Ame,

Winchester, St. Cross 25 *after Schnebbelie*

378

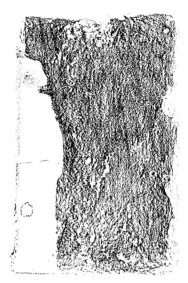

Winchester, St. Cross 27

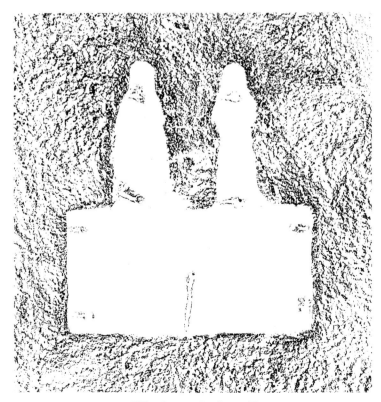

Winchester, St. Cross 28

N.A. *III*. Inscr. recording erection of modern glass in [east south chapel] window, 2 [south south chapel] windows, rood fig. on screen and gates below by bequest of [Rev.] Malise Cunninghame Graham, curate, [1860-**1885**], mur., S.C. *IV*. Inscr. Rev. William Menzies, M.A., of Queen's Coll., Camb., rector [of Winnal] for nearly 34 years [1853-1886], chaplain of the Royal Hants County Hospital for many years [1855-1870], **1886**, aged 81, pos. by parishioners, widow, son and surviving brother, [maker's name COX & SONS, LONDON], mur., N.A. *V*. Inscr. Anne Elizabeth Cunninghame Graham Bontine, born on board H.M.S. Barham, off La Guaira, [Venezuela], 1828-**1925**, mur., C. *VI*. Inscr. recording restoration of pulpit in **1925** by son, R.B. Cunninghame Graham, in mem. of Anne Elizabeth Cunninghame Graham Bontine, [1828-1925], pos. by parishioners "MINDFUL OF MANY BENEFITS RECEIVED FROM THIS FAMILY", bronze, on pulpit step, N. *VII*. Inscr. Eleanor Louisa Steel, **1951**, bronze, on table, S.A. *VIII*. Inscr. recording presentation of display case in **1975** by Jno Steel & Son Ltd., [funeral directors], in display case, S.C. *IX*. Inscr. recording donation of new [north aisle] doorway by w. Brigid in mem. of Mel Crofton, 1931-**2003**, on door, N.A. *X*. Inscr. recording gift of piano by Crofton family who worshipped in the ch. 1972-**2005**, on piano, S.A.

INDENTS & LOST BRASSES. 11. Indent, inscr. with ?scroll issuing, nearly effaced, N. Inscr. c.60 x 490 mm, ?scroll 400 x 100 x 45 mm, slab 1450 visible x 1050 mm. 12. Indent, inscr. (chamfer), A.T., N.C. Inscr. (chamfer) 1940 x 765 x 35 mm, coverstone 1970 x 815 mm

Ref: *M.B.S. Trans.*, VI, p.149; *Sadler, Dorset and Hampshire,* appx. I, pt.2, p.41; *Soc. Antiq. MS. 875/6*, p.173.

WINCHESTER, St. Lawrence-in-the-Square.

I. Inscr. Thomas Lloyd, parishioner and churchwarden "FOR SOME YEARS", **1892**, aged 61, pos. by friends and parishioners, mur., on marble. *II*. Inscr. recording presentation [of bench] by friends and parishioners to Rev. H[enry] M[anning] Richards, M.A., on resignation as rector 1871-**1894**, on bench. *III*. Inscr. Harry White Phillips, churchwarden for 36 years, **1926**, aged 82, pos. by friends and parishioners, mur., on marble. *IV*. Inscr. [Most Rev. and Rt. Hon. Frederick] Donald Coggan, [1st Baron Coggan of Canterbury and Sissinghurst, P.C., M.A., D.D.], Archbishop of Canterbury 1974-1980, 1909-**2000**, on bench, W.Porch/Tower.

WINCHESTER, St. Maurice (now demolished).

(Formerly M.S.I). Jane, Anne, Anne and John, children of John Bond, "born and died within three years", **1612**, 4 infants in swaddling clothes on a tomb, inscr. with 8 Lat. vv.; their father pos.; mur., N.A.; moved to Winchester, St. Swithun-upon-Kingsgate (q.v.) (1959). *M.B.S. Trans.*, VI, p.150.

(Formerly M.S.II). Inscr. with 8 Eng. vv. Fridiswide, w. (1) of Charles Newboulte, "TWICE MAIOR OF THIS CITIE", (2) of George Johnson, "MINISTER OF GODS' WORDE, AND ONE OF THE MASTERS OF THE COLLEDG", **1626**, very lightly engr., mur., N.A.; moved to Winchester, St. Swithun-upon-Kingsgate (q.v.) (1959).

INDENTS & LOST BRASSES. 1. Lost brass, Alicia, w. of John Pescod of Littleton, gent., 1624, by whom, Henry, Andrew, Elizabeth. Recorded by Warton (1773). 2. Lost brass, inscr.

Jane, w. of Thomas Entwesle of Oxford, gent., 1647, aged 61, pos. by husband. Recorded by Warton (1773). 3. Lost brass, inscr. William Craddocke, gent., twice mayor, 1684, aged 61, mur., on pillar. Recorded by Warton (1773).

Ref: *Busby, Companion Guide*, p.120; *Gawthorp*, p.36; *Hampshire History*, I, p.160; *M.B.S. Trans.*, VI, pp.149-51, XI, p.45; *M.S.*, pp.169-70, p.753; *Norris, Memorials*, p.232; *Soc. Antiq. MS. 875/6*, pp.173-5; *V.C.H., Hampshire*, IV, p.73; *Warton*, I, pp.195-8.

Ch. essentially, 1842; demolished (except tower), 1957.

WINCHESTER, St. Swithun-upon-Kingsgate.

I. (Formerly WINCHESTER, St. Maurice M.S.I). Jane, Anne, Anne and John, children of John Bond, "born and died within three years", **1612**, 4 infants in swaddling clothes on a tomb, inscr. with 8 Lat. vv.; their father pos.; mur., on marble; from Winchester, St. Maurice (q.v.). Children 113 x 119 mm, inscr. 308 x 463 mm.

II. (Formerly WINCHESTER, St. Maurice M.S.II). Inscr. with 8 Eng. vv. Fridiswide, w. (1) of Charles Newboulte, "TWICE MAIOR OF THIS CITIE", (2) of George Johnson, "MINISTER OF GODS' WORDE, AND ONE OF THE MASTERS OF THE COLLEDG", **1626**, very lightly engr., mur., in stone frame; from Winchester, St. Maurice (q.v.). Inscr. 327 x 248 mm.

III. Cross with Lat. inscr. and Eng. verse on circlet. John Payne, 1812, aged 32, and w. Eliza, **1862**, aged 82, on marble on window splay. *IV.* Inscr. Frances Helena, w. of [Rev.] John Henry Hodgson, M.A., rector 1885-1895, died at Alpes Maritimes, Nice, France, 1906, aged 40, and Florence Louise, w. of [Rev.] Francis Thomas Mudge, M.A., rector 1895-1905, died at Williamsport, Pennsylavania, **1907**, aged 47, maker's name CULN GAWTHORP S^c LONDON, on window splay.

Ref: *M.B.S. Trans.*, XI, p.45.

WINCHFIELD, St. Mary.

I. Inscr. and 2 shs. (another lost). Elizabeth, dau. of Anthony Niccolls of Paddington, esq., w. (1) of Laurence Rudyerd of Winchfield, esq., (2) of Richard Tilney of Rotherwick, esq., by whom she had 3 sons and 3 daus., **1652**, aged 68; in 2006 partly covered by pews, N.A. Illustration (upper sin. sh.) from rubbing in Soc. Antiq. coll. Rubbing (upper sin. sh.) in Soc. Antiq. coll. (1849). Inscr. 310 x 384 mm visible, upper dext. sh. indent c.170 x c.165 mm, upper sin. sh. covered, lower sh. 223 x 196 mm, Purbeck slab 1780 x 680 mm visible.

II. Inscr. and 3 shs. Frances, dau. of Sir Francis Gamull of Chester, Knt. and Bart., of Chester, by Christian, dau. of Sir Richard Grosvenor of Eaton, Cheshire, Knt. and Bart., w. of Benjamin Rudyerd, esq., **1652**, aged 27, had 6 children whereof now are living 2 sons and 1 dau.; formerly C., now N.A. Inscr. 279 x 509-520 mm, upper dext. sh. 200 x 167 mm, upper sin. sh. 198 x 170 mm, lower sh. 208 x 186 mm, black marble slab 1840 x 915 mm.

M S

IN PRÆ-IMMATVRAM MORTEM IIII INFANTVLORṼ, INTRA
TRES ANNOS ET NATORVM, ET HEV RVRSVS
DENATORVM: EPITAPHIVM.

QVATTVOR INFANTES VRNÀ CONDVNTVR IN ISTA,
EXTINCTVS VITÆ ET LIMINE QVISQ SVÆ.
Iana DIES BIS-QVINQVE VIDENS, MACRO-BIA DICI,
PRÆ RELIQVIS POTERAT TEMPORA SI NVMERES.
Anna DIES QVATVOR TANTVM TRES Anna SECVNDA
VIXIT Ioannes VAGIIT, ET MORITVR.
NEMPE IGITVR POSSENT QVAM VERE DICERE, Vt Hora.
Vita FVGAX ORITVR, DEMORITVRQ CITO
Ioh. Bond PATER, M. P. Aº Dᴺᴵ CIƆIƆCXII.

Winchester, St. Swithun-upon-Kingsgate *I*

Winchester, St. Swithun-upon-Kingsgate *II*

382

HERE LIETH Y BODY OF ELIZAB: TI
DAVGHTER OF ANTHONY NICCOLL
PADDINGTON ESQ, WIDDOW OF RIC
TILNEY OF ROTHERWEK ESQ, WHO MAR
HER WHEN SHE WAS Y WIDDOW OE LA
RVDYERD OF WINCHEEILD ESQ, BY
SHE HAD ISSVE 3 SONNES 3 DAVGE
AGED 68 SHE DEPARTED THIS LIF
THE 17 OF IANVARY
1652

COVERED

Winchfield I

HERE LIETH THE BODY OF FRANCES RVDYERD
WIFE TO BENIAMIN RVDYERD OF WINCHFEILD &c
THE DAVGHTER OF S.R FRANCIS GAMVIL KN.T &
BARONET OF CHESTER AND CHRISTIAN HIS WIFE
WHO WAS Y.E DAVGH.RT OF S.R RICHARD GROSVENOVR
KN.T &. BARONET OF ETON IN Y.E COVNTY OF CHESTER
AGED 27. AND HAD ISSVE 6 CHILDREN WHEREOF
NOW ARE LIVING 2 SONNES AND ONE DAVGHTER
THE OTHER 3 ARE DEAD BEFORE THEIR MOTHER
SHE DEPARTED THIS LIFE Y.E 16 OF AVG.st 1652.

Winchfield II

HERE LIES Ỹ BODY OF FRANCES RVDGERD
DAVGHTER TO BENIAMIN RVDGERD ESQ:
AND FRANCES HIS WIFE SHE DEPARTED
THIS LIFE ON THE 24ᵗʰ OF DECEMBER
1659 IN THE 9ᵗʰ YEARE OF HER AGE
EPITAPH
Here lies a iewell of unvalewed price
Her Father wore her at his heart
Transplanted to the eternall Colonies
Where better set she shines her part

Winchfield III

III. Sh. and lozenge; inscr. lost; for Frances, dau. of Benjamin and Frances Rudyerd, **1659**, aged 9; in 2006 almost completely covered by pews, N.C. Illustration (inscr.) from rubbing in Soc. Antiq. coll. Rubbing (inscr.) in Soc. Antiq. coll. (1849). Lost inscr. 237 x 352 mm, sh. 161 visible x 38 mm visible, lozenge 201 visible x 85 mm visible, black marble slab 1370 x 715 mm.

IV. Inscr. [Rev.] Charles Frederic Seymour, [M.A.], rector for 41 years [1849-1890], ch. restorer 1850-1851, 1818-**1897**, mur., C. *V.* Inscr. with Lat. verse. Capt. G[erald] H[ugh] Fitzgerald, 4th Dragoon Guards [(Royal Irish), eld. son of Lord Maurice Fitzgerald and w. Lady Adelaide Jane Frances Forbes, of Johnstown Castle, co. Wexford, Ireland], killed in action, [1886-]**1914**, [buried at Bourg-et-Comin Communal Cemetery, France], mur., on pillar, N.C. *VI.* Inscr. with verse. Lt.-Cmdr. H. John C. Abercrombie, R.N., only son of Sir John and Lady Abercrombie, died suddenly on board H.M.S. Devonshire, 1916-**1952**, copper, on ewer, N. *VII.* Inscr. Joan Margaret, w. of Peter Adams, mother of George, Davan and Linda, 1917-**1953**, copper, mur., on pillar, N. *VIII.* Inscr. with verse. Sir Kinahan Cornwallis, G.C.M.G., C.B.E., D.S.O., [administrator and diplomat], 1883-**1959**, mur., on board, N. *IX.* Inscr. recording donation [of painting of ch.] by daus., Edna and Christine, in mem. of Molly Blay, **1996**, mur., on board with framed painting, N.A. *X.* Inscr. with verse. [Rev.] Kenneth Sutton Bradley, [A.L.C.D.], rector of Winchfield and Dogmersfield 1953-1972, 1908-**1998**, mur., on board, N. *XI.* Inscr. John and Hilary McGinty, engr. c.**2000**, bronze, on bench, Churchyard.

INDENTS & LOST BRASSES. 12. Indent, ?eff. and inscr., 1 rivet, 1 plug and 1 plug hole only, effaced, at entrance to S.Porch, Churchyard. Purbeck slab 1015 remains x 630 mm remains.

Ref: *Brit. Lib. Add. MS. 39972,* f.140; *Burke's Peerage and Baronetage*, p.1582; *Hampshire, Antiquary*, I, p.5; *Heseltine, Heraldry*, p.38; *M.B.S. Trans.*, VI, pp.151-3; *M.S.*, p.170, p.753; *Sadler, Dorset and Hampshire,* appx. I, pt.2, p.40; *Soc. Antiq. MS. 875/6*, pp.175-7; *V.C.H., Hampshire*, IV, p.112.

WINSLADE, St. Mary (new church, redundant, now a residence).

I. Inscr. Elizabeth, w. of Henry Pinck of Kempshot, **1625**, aged 80, C. Inscr. 174 x 408 mm, slab 1520 x 620 mm.

INDENTS & LOST BRASSES. 2. Lost brass, civilian; with incised inscr.; Henry Pincke, of Kempshot, 1611. Recorded by Pavey (1702). 3. Lost brass, inscr. Henry Pincke, of Kempshot, gent., 1672, [aged 64]. Recorded by Pavey (1702).

The monument to William, eld. son of William Pincke, citizen and druggist of London, 1679-91, recorded by Pavey (1702) as a brass, is a ledger.

Ref: *Brit. Lib. Stowe MS. 845*, f.101; *M.B.S. Trans.*, VI, pp.154-5; *M.S.*, p.170; *Soc. Antiq. MS. 875/6*, pp.177-8.

Ch. built, 1816; declared redundant, 1978, converted, 1983.

WINTON, (see BOURNEMOUTH).

HEERE LYETH BVRYED THE BODY OF
ELIZABETH PINCK WIFE OF HENRY
PINCK OF KEMPSHOT WHO DECESED
THE 24TH DAYE OF APRILL AT THE AGE
OF LXXX YEARES AN DOM 1625

Winslade I

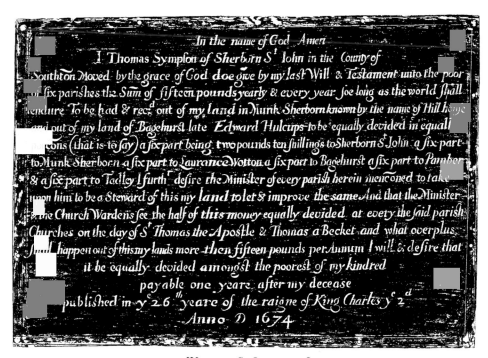

In the name of God Ameri
I Thomas Symplon of Sherborn St John in the County of
Southton Moved by the grace of God doe give by my last Will & Testament unto the poor
of fix parishes the Sum of fifteen pounds yearly & every year foe long as the world shall
endure To be had & recd out of my land in Munk Sherborn known by the name of Hill house
and out of my land of Bagehurst late Edward Hulcups to be equally devided in equall
portions (that is to fay) a fix part being two pounds ten shillings to Sherborn St John a fix part
to Munk Sherborn a fix part to Laurance Wotton a fix part to Bagehurst a fix part to Pamber
& a fix part to Tadley I furth defire the Minister of every parish herein menconed to take
upon him to be a Steward of this my land to let & improve the same And that the Minister
& the Church Wardens fee the half of this money equally devided at every the faid parish
Churches on the day of St Thomas the Apostle & Thomas a Becket and what overplus
shall happen out of this my lands more then fifteen pounds per Annum I will & defire that
it be equally devided amongst the poorest of my kindred
payable one yeare after my decease
published in ye 26th yeare of the raigne of King Charles ye 2d
Anno D 1674

Wootton St. Lawrence I

387

WONSTON, Holy Trinity.

I. Inscr. recording dedication of north and south chancel windows in **1884** by friends and parishioners in mem. of Rev. Lewis Welsh Owen, M.A., hon. canon of Winchester Cathedral, rector for 14 years [1870-1884, 1884, aged 70], mur., C. *II.* Inscr. recording dedication of altar in mem. of [Rev.] Charles Pierrepont Hutchinson, [M.A.], rector 1888-**1898**, [1898, aged 66], maker's name CULN GAWTHORP, LONDON, mur., C. *III.* Inscr. in Lat. recording gift [of lectern] in **1909** by H. S[mith] and C.W. S[mith] in mem. of parents, Lancelot Smith and William Harrison and [w.] Elizabeth, on lectern, N. *IV.* Inscr. recording presentation [of prie-dieu] "towards the Restoration" in **1909** by M. Carta Sturge, on prie-dieu, N. *V.* Inscr. recording restoration of [north and south chancel] windows (destroyed by fire in 1908) in **1909** by family of no.*I* and by friends and parishioners, maker's name CULN GAWTHORP, LONDON, mur., below no.*I*, C. *VI.* Inscr. Emma Johnson, **1938**, aged 92, bronze, on wooden cross, Churchyard. *VII.* Inscr. in raised letters recording installation of amplifier system by Esmée Blackadder in mem. of husband, Roy Blackadder, **1971**, mur., N. *VIII.* Inscr. Alice [Muriel, w. of Ernest] Spillane, [**1972**, aged 60, pos. by husband], bronze, on bench, Churchyard. *IX.* Inscr. in raised letters commem. repair and rehanging of peal of bells in **1981** by Whitechapel Bell Foundry and "73rd year in which Mr Richard Smith, Captain of the Tower, has rung in this church", mur., N. *X.* Inscr. in raised letters. Rev. V[ictor] W[illiam] Norriss, [B.A.], rector 1971-**1986**, on altar rail, C. *XI.* Inscr. in raised letters. John Edwin Bone, 1911-**1989**, sidesman, reader and friend, on bookcase, N. *XII.* Inscr. [Louis] (Bob) [Shafe, husband, father and grandfather, 1922-1994], and Tony Shafe, [son, husband and father, 1951-]**1994**, pos. by family, on bench, Churchyard. *XIII.* Inscr. Tommy Green, 1938-**2000**, on wooden cross, Churchyard.

Ch. damaged by fire, 1908; restored 1909.

WOODCOTT, St. James.

I. Inscr. Emma Mary Corbett, 1974-**1974**, mur., on wallsafe.

Ch. built, 1853.

WOODMANCOTE, St. James.

I. Inscr. Charles Holdaway, **1896**, [aged 70], and [w.] Anne, [1906, aged 88], on pulpit desk, N. *II.* Inscr. [recording lectern made from] "WINCHESTER CATHEDRAL OAK FELLED 1086" in **1897** in mem. of Charles Holdaway, [1896, aged 70], and [w.] Anne, [1906, aged 88], on lectern, N. *III.* Inscr. recording restoration of ch. to commem. diamond jubilee of Queen Victoria, **1897**; [Rev.] G.N. Godwin, B.D., vicar; W[illiam] T[homas] Holdaway and G.H. King, churchwardens, mur., N. *IV.* Inscr. [Rev.] Stephen Bonnett, vicar for 16 years, engr. c.**1910**, on cross, C. *V.* Inscr. Everil E.M. Bonnett, **1950**, on hymn board, N. *VI & VII.* Two inscrs. Judy Tower, 1924-**1988**, on churchwardens' wands, N. *VIII.* Inscr. recording restoration of [south-east nave] window in **1995** in mem. of Bertie Tower, [1922-1991], and [w.] Judy, [1924-1988], parishioners 1978-1991, on window splay, N. *IX.* Inscr. recording restoration of [south-west nave] window in **1995** in mem. of Georgina M[abel] R[uth] Welling, [1944-1994], parishioner 1977-1994, on window splay, N. *X.* Inscr. Nancy McTaggart, "SHE LOVED THIS CHURCH", 1931-**1999**; in 2007 loose on bookcase in N.

Ch. built, 1855.

WOOTTON ST. LAWRENCE, St. Lawrence.

I. Inscr. Benefaction of Thomas Sympson, **1674**, mur., in wooden fame, N. Inscr. 309 x 434 mm.

II. Inscr. on 5 pls. Rev. Lovelace Bigg-Wither, J.P., M.A., of Manydown [Park] and Tangier [Park], born at Wymering, died at Brighton, [Sussex], 1805-**1874**, [maker's name FORSYTH SC BAKER Sᵀ LONDON], mur., on marble, N.A. *III.* Inscr. Arthur Fitz-Walter Bigg-Wither, 2nd son of Lovelace Bigg-Wither, died at Southsea, 1887, aged 52, and dau., Eva Mary Orde, w. of H. Teviot Kerr, died in India, **1895**, maker's name GAWTHORP, Sᶜ LONDON (and monogram), mur., on marble, N.A. *IV.* Inscr. Thomas Plantagenet Bigg-Wither, C.E., F.R.G.S., 10th son of Lovelace Bigg-Wither, died on voyage home from India, 1890, aged 44; also Lancelot Frith Bigg-Wither, 6th son of Lovelace Bigg-Wither, died at Gopalpore, India, **1898**, aged 58, maker's name GAWTHORP, Sᶜ LONDON, mur., on marble, N.A. *V.* Inscr. Melita Maria, 2nd w. of Arthur Fitz-Walter Bigg-Wither, **1901**, aged 68, pos. by son, maker's name GAWTHORP Sᶜ LONDON, mur., on marble, N.A. *VI.* Inscr. Emma Jemima, widow [of Rev. Lovelace Bigg-Wither, J.P., M.A.], died at Brighton, [Sussex], **1901**, aged 91, maker's name GAWTHORP, Sᶜ LONDON, mur., on marble below no.*II*, N.A. *VII.* Inscr. Jessy Maria, w. of [Rev.] C[harles] S[legg] Ward, M.A., vicar [1876-1908], 1889; also sons, Oswald [Ward], 1876; Cyril [Ward], 1892; and Denis [Ward], **1903**, mur., N.A. *VIII.* Inscr. [Sir] Edward Bates, 1st Bart., [J.P., D.L.], of Manydown Park, [1816-]1896, and [2nd] w. Ellen, [dau. of Thomas Thompson, of Hessle, Yorks.], **1905**, aged 83; also 4th [and yst.] son, Wilfred Imrie Bates, 1886, aged 29, copper, mur., C. *IX.* Inscr. Major Edward J. Bigg-Wither, Capt 28th Regt., 4th son of Lovelace Bigg-Wither, 1837-**1909**, maker's name GAWTHORP & SONS LONDON, mur., on marble, N.A. *X.* Inscr. [Rev.] Charles Slegg Ward, [M.A.], vicar 1876-1908, 1840-**1913**, mur., below no.*VII*, N.A. *XI.* Inscr. Col. Archibald Cuthbert Bigg-Wither, F.R.A.S., Bengal Infantry and P.W.D. India, 9th son of Lovelace Bigg-Wither, born at Tangier Park, died at Peel, I[sle] o[f] M[an], 1844-**1913**, maker's name CULN GAWTHORP & SONS, LONDON, copper, mur., N.A. *XII.* Inscr. Norah Ellen, eld. dau. of Sydney E[ggers] Bates, [J.P., M.A., 3rd son of no.*VIII*], of Manydown [Park], and w. Elizabeth Jessie, [3rd dau. of Col. George Grenville Malet], 1881-**1922**, mur., C. *XIII.* Inscr. [Rev.] Reginald Fitzhugh Bigg[-]Wither, [M.A.], 7th son of Lovelace Bigg[-]Wither, rector of Worting 1879-1898, rector of Wonston 1898-1911, 1842-**1929**, maker's name CULN GAWTHORP & SONS, Lᵀᴰ LONDON, copper, mur., on marble, N.A. *XIV.* Inscr. with verse recording dedication of children's corner in mem. of [Aircraftsman 2nd Class Edgar] Donald Balaam, [1423820], R.A.F.[V.R, son of Edgar Henry Balaam and w. Blanche], killed on active service, **1942**, [aged 20], on table, N.A. *XV.* Inscr. Edward John Kent, 1911-**1984**, pos. by family, bronze, on bench, Churchyard.

INDENTS & LOST BRASSES. 16. Indent, cross, inscr. and 4 scrolls, c.1400, curious, C. Cross 410 x 410 mm, inscr. 40 x 210 mm, upper dext. scroll 55 x 80 x 30 mm, upper sin. scroll 60 x 85 x 30 mm, lower dext. scroll 50 x 85 x 25 mm, lower sin. scroll 55 x 85 x 30 mm, Purbeck slab 1670 x 635 mm.

Ref: *Burke's Peerage and Baronetage*, p.196; *M.B.S. Trans.*, VI, pp.154-5; *M.S.*, p.170; *Soc. Antiq. MS. 875/6*, pp.178-9; *V.C.H., Hampshire*, IV, p.242.

Ch. built, 1864.

WORLDHAM, EAST, St. Mary the Virgin.

I. Inscr. recording restoration of [west] window in **1865** by surviving children in mem. of William Cooper, of The Grove, Kentish Town, and w. Mary, eld. dau. of John Eggar of the Manor House; also son, James Cooper and "the three who in one year were removed from their Home on Earth", mur., N. See also Bentley no.*V.* *II.* Inscr. recording gift of organ by parents and relations in mem. of Mabel Alice Palmer, **1902**, mur., on board, N. *III.* Inscr. with verse recording gift of frontal in **1903** by Florrie, Edward and Maggie in mem. of mother, S.B., 1901; in 2006 loose in N. *IV.* Inscr. Phyliss Trigwell, 1905-1963, and William Trigwell, churchwarden 1958-1967, 1888-**1975**, mur., C. *V.* Inscr. recording presentation of bell to Mrs. A.L. Thomas on retirement as headteacher of East Worldham Church of England School, 1954-**1979**, on display stand, C. *VI.* Inscr. recording replacement of organ (casson positive) commem. no.*II*, "IN CONTINUAL USE", 1903-**1991**, mur., on board with no.*II*, N.

WORLDHAM, WEST, St. Nicholas.

I. Inscr. in Lat. recording restoration of font in **1889** by Winchester Coll., on font plinth, N. *II.* Inscr. William Brock, O.B.E., churchwarden 1896-1956, 1870-**1962**, on cupboard, N. *III.* Inscr. William George Brock, churchwarden 1956-**1982**, [1905-1982], pos. by W.W. and H.M., benefice churchwardens, on cross, C.

WYKE, (see WEEKE).

WYMERING, SS. Peter and Paul.

I. Inscr. Benjamin Caesar, choirmaster, **1881**, on choir stall, C. *II.* Inscr. [recording gift of north-west north aisle window by] Emma [Low, w. of Richard William] Ford, [1823-]**1892**, in mem. of mother, on window splay, N.A. See also Alverstoke, or Gosport, Fort Brockhurst no.*XLII.* *III.* Inscr. Arthur William Cockburn Astley, aged 4 years and 4 months, [1867], engr. **1895**, mur., below window, S.A. *IV.* Inscr. with verse. William Edmonds, godfather of Lucy Rendle Edmonds, baptised **1897**, on ewer, S.A. *V.* Stepped cross surmounting inscr. with verse. Ernest, son of J. and R. Scullard, died at the Cameroons, West Coast of Africa, **1897**, [aged 27], mur., N.A. *VI.* Inscr. with Lat. verse, ach., 16 shs. and 4 medals. Arthur Collett Nightingale, yst. son of Capt. Geoffrey Nightingale, Grenadier Guards, and w. Mary, [only dau. of Thomas] Knowlys, [grandson of Sir Edward Nightingale, 10th Bart.], J.P. for Stirling, joined 93rd (Sutherland Highlanders) Regt. [of Foot] 1854, Col. commanding [2nd Battn.] (Princess Louise's) Argyll and Sutherland Highlanders, commanded 91st regimental district 1888-1893, died at Snowdown House, Stirling, 1837-**1899**, mur., N. *VII.* Inscr. with Lat. verse, lozenge, sh. and 2 crests. Dame Virginie-Marie, dau. of Don Pedro Garcia (descended from the Counts of Castille), [2nd w. of Peter] Hesketh-Fleetwood, [1st] Bart., M.P., of Rossall Hall, Lancs., founder of Fleetwood, [Lancs.], died at Wymering Manor, **1900**, aged 87, mur., S.C./S.A. *VIII.* Inscr. with Lat. verse. Richard William Ford, of Wymering Manor, licensed reader in the par. for many years, died at The Chestnuts, Porchester, [1822-]**1900**, mur., N.A. See also Alverstoke, or Gosport, Fort Brockhurst no.*XLII.* *IX.* Inscr. with verse. Richard William Ford, [of Wymering Manor, 1822-**1900**], and w. Emma [Low, 1823-1892], pos. by son, Douglas Morey Ford, [1851-1916],

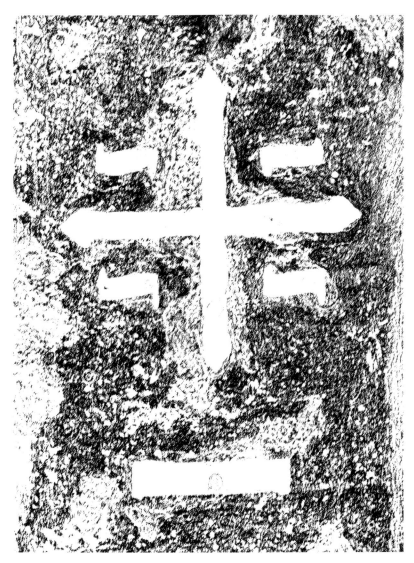

Wootton St. Lawrence 16

Orate p nia Johe Veans Johis Hellblot ⁊
Et siue Robm Bingele an̄ aie p̄nor dz

Yateley I

mur., N.A. See also Alverstoke, or Gosport, Fort Brockhurst no.*XLII*. *X*. Inscr. William Tennant, killed near Johannesburg, [South Africa], **1900**, copper, mur., on sundial, south wall outside S.Porch. *XI*. Inscr. Katherine, w. of [Lt.-Col. Charles Shea] Hunt, pos. by grandchildren, engr. c.**1900**, on window splay, S.C./S.A. *XII*. Inscr. Thomas Brown Baker, 1827-**1901**, 1st lay reader in the par., and w. Anne Martell, 1826-1884, on lectern, N. *XIII*. Inscr. with Lat. verse. Arthur William Martin, 2nd son of William Billett Martin, of Paul's Grove, and w. Lucy, ch. worshipper, [died] at Johannesburg, [South Africa], **1903**, maker's name OSBORNE · FECIT · RYDE, mur., S.A. *XIV*. Inscr. with Lat. verse and sh. [Rev.] Russell Day, [M.A.], fellow of King's Coll., Camb., assistant-master of Eton Coll. [1851-1874], vicar of Lytchett Minster, Dorset [1874-1881], rector of Horstead, Norf. for 24 years [1881-1904], worshipped and ministered in the ch., **1904**, [aged 76], on wooden frame, S.A. *XV*. Inscr. with Lat. verse within border of oak leaves and acorns. Henry Edward Chalmers Martin, died at Greenfields, Bakersfield, California, 1894, aged 25, and Doveton Arthur William Martin, M.R.C.S., L.R.C.P., dis[tric]t-surgeon of N[orth] Rhodesia, died at Salisbury, S[outh] Rhodesia, **1904**, aged 36, only sons of Henry Arthur Martin, M.D., and w. Eleanor Blanche, resided in Cosham and worshipped in the ch., maker's name OSBORNE · FECIT · RYDE · I · W, mur., N.A. *XVI*. Inscr. with verse. John Stares, **1905**, chorister for 25 years, copper, mur., Organ Chamber. *XVII*. Stepped cross surmounting inscr. with verse. George Peel, of Great Farm, **1907**, pos. by widow, Mary, mur., S.C./S.A. *XVIII*. Inscr. with verse. Charles V. Clarke, lost with the [S.S.] Titanic, **1912**, aged 29, [pos. by widow], maker's name GARRET & HAYSOM. SOUTHAMPTON, mur., N.A. *XIX*. Inscr. Charles Tennant, brother of no.*X*, **1912**, copper, mur., below no.*X*, south wall outside S.Porch. *XX*. Inscr. recording gift of [font] cover by family in mem. of Archibald Henry Ford, A.M.I.C.E., [1846-**1930**], and only son, Major Charles Cobbett Ford, R[oyal] A[rtillery], R.O., on font cover, S.A. *XXI*. Inscr. recording reordering of chancel in **1987** in mem. of Norman Whyte, organist for over 50 years, 1979, and Norah Luke, treasurer for over 30 years, 1986, mur., on board, Organ Chamber.

INDENTS & LOST BRASSES. 22. Lost brass, inscr. William Waite, 1448, S.A. Recorded by Pavey (1705). 23. Lost brass, ?civilian, inscr. and sh. Recorded (sh. with eff. and inscr. lost) by Pavey (1705).

Ref: *Brit. Lib. Stowe MS. 845*, f.136; *Burke's Peerage and Baronetage*, pp.1969-70; *Heseltine, Heraldry*, p.38; *M.B.S. Trans.*, VI, p.42; *Soc. Antiq. MS. 875/6*, p.145.

YATELEY, St. Peter.

I. Inscr. Joan, dau. of Robert Dyngele, w. of John Hewlot, c.**1450**; formerly C., now mur., on board, Tower. Inscr. 70 x 360 mm. Style: London D. Rep. by W.G.L. (1982).

II. William Lawerd, **1517**, in civil dress, and w. Agnes, with 9 sons and 1 dau., inscr.; male eff. stolen c.1979; formerly N., now Tower. *Brit. Lib. Add. MS. 39987*, f.56r. Illustration (male eff.) from rubbing in Soc. Antiq. coll. Rubbing (male eff.) in Soc. Antiq. coll. (n.d.). Lost male eff. 468 x 126 mm, female eff. 470 x 150 mm, inscr. 160 x 520 mm, children 150 x 265 mm, Purbeck slab c.1635 x 650 mm. Style: London F variant. Rep. by W.G.L. (1982).

III. William Rygg, **1532**, in civil dress, and w. Tomysyn, with 4 sons and 7 daus., inscr.; formerly S.A., now Tower. *Brit. Lib. Add. MS. 39987*, f.54r. Male eff. 475 x 165 mm, female eff. 475 x 150 mm, inscr. 90 x 450 mm, sons 115 x 95 mm, daus. 115 x 160 mm, Purbeck slab 1710 x 635 mm. Style: London G (script 4). Rep. by W.G.L. (1982).

pray for the soules of wilham lalberd & Agnes
his wyf the whiche wilham decessed the xbij day
of August the yere of our lord god m⁵ lt xbij
on whose soules Jhu haue mercy Amen

Yateley II

IV. Elizabeth, dau. of Robert Morflett, esq., **1578** (lower hf. of eff. lost); by her 1st husband Edward Ormsby she had 4 sons and __daus., by her 2nd Andrew Smith she had 3 sons and 3 daus.; inscr., 2 scrolls (1 mutil.) and 1 sh. (another lost); palimp., on rev. pt. of civilian, c.1500, and worn Flemish border, 14th/15th cent.; formerly C., now Tower; facsimile of palimp. sh., mur., on board, Tower. *Brit. Lib. Add. MS. 39987,* f.57r; *Palimpsests,* pl.185 (rev.), pl.191 (rev.), pl.224 (rev.). Illustration (dext. sh.) from rubbing in Soc. Antiq. coll. Rubbing (dext. sh.) in Soc. Antiq. coll. (n.d.). Female eff. orig. 458 x 180 mm, now 185 x 140 mm, inscr. 80 x 455 mm, dext. sh. indent 145 x 120 mm, dext. scroll orig. 65 x 200 x 44 mm, now 65 x 170 x 44 mm, sin. sh. 150 x 125 mm, sin. scroll 65 x 205 x 44 mm, Purbeck slab 1465 x 600 mm. Style: London G (script 10). Rep. by W.G.L. (1982).

V. Civilian, c.**1590**, (mutil.); inscr. lost; formerly N., now Tower. *Brit. Lib. Add. MS. 39987,* f.47r, f.58r. Eff. 475 x 180 mm, inscr. indent 125 x 435 mm, black marble slab 1215 x 600 mm. Style: Johnson. Rep. by W.G.L. (1982).

VI. Inscr. Georgina, w. of William Stevens, of Hilfield, **1863**, aged 43, on board on window splay, old C., now Chapel. *VII.* Inscr. William Stevens, of Hilfield, **1871**, aged 74, on board on window splay, old C., now Chapel. *VIII.* Inscr. James Wapshare, of Lyburn, father of no.*VI,* **1874**, aged 90, on board on window splay, old C., now Chapel. *IX.* Inscr. (mutil.) and sh. recording gift of screen in **1886** by John Gilliam Stilwell, of Townfield and Bregsells, Surrey, J.P. for Middx. and Westminster, [1886, aged 92], in mem. of son, John Pakenham Stilwell, [J.P.], of Hilfield, [1832-1921], and grandson, [Lt.-Col. Geoffr]ey Holt Stilwell, [V.D., T.D., M.A., 1865-1927], copper, mur., old Churchwardens' Vestry, now Retrochoir. *X.* Inscr. and ach. John Gilliam Stilwell, 1886, aged 92, and widow Ellen Mary, dau. of John Tingcombe, of Hartley, Devon, 1804-**1887**, maker's name effaced, copper, mur., old Churchwardens' Vestry, now Retrochoir. Inscr. 183 x 183 mm, ach. 184 x 184 mm. *XI.* Inscr. Capt. Henry Browne Mason, R.N., engr. c.**1890**, on window splay, old C., now Chapel. *XII.* Inscr. Lt. Edmund Ward Thompson, Prince of Wales' Own Grenadiers, Bombay Staff Corps, and w. Lilian Clara; mar. in the ch. 1892; lost in S.S. Roumania off the coast of Portugal on passage out to India, **1892**, rect. pl., inscr. with verse on base of stepped cross, maker's name JONES & WILLIS, mur., on board, Church. Inscr, 661 x 432 mm. *XIII.* Inscr. recording that colours of King's Own were [laid up] in mem. of Capt. George Mason, lived at the Manor House for many years, engr. c.**1900**, maker's name *JONES & WILLIS LTD*, mur., old C., now Chapel. *XIV.* Inscr. John Pakenham Stilwell, J.P., of Hilfield, churchwarden, president of the Diocesan Guild of Bellringers, 1832-**1921**, and w. Georgina Elizabeth, 1842-1916, on organ, old N., now Church. *XV.* Inscr. on sh-shaped pl. recording presentation of King's Colours (carried in action at the Battle of Egmont-op-Zee, the Siege of Copenhagen, the Peninsular War, the War with the United States of America and the Battle of Waterloo which were presented in 1799 by Prince of Wales to 4th (King's Own) Regt. of Foot) by Emily Mary, dau. of Capt. George Mason, of the Manor House, who served regt. from 1825-1838; restored to the regt. in **1927** by vicar and churchwardens where "IT NOW HANGS IN THE MEMORIAL CHAPEL OF THE REGIMENT AT LANCASTER", mur., old C., now Chapel. Inscr. 305 x 309 mm. *XVI.* Inscr. Lt.-Col. Geoffrey Holt Stilwell, V.D., T.D., M.A., 4th Battn. Hampshire Regt., lay reader, churchwarden, 1865-**1927**, maker's name A&N. C.S.L. LONDON, copper, mur., on board, old C., now Chapel. *XVII.* Inscr. M.A. S[mith], **1930**, copper, on grave marker, Churchyard. *XVIII.* Inscr. on scroll and verse on sh. suspended from sword. Edith Margaret, w. of Col. W.H. Gribbon, C.M.G., C.B.E., King's Own Royal Regt., died at Little Halt, **1934**, bronze, on gravestone, Churchyard. *XIX.* Inscr. S. Smith, **1938**, copper, on grave marker with no.*XVII,* Churchyard. *XX.* Inscr. Lt.-Col. William Byron Stilwell,

Pray for the Soules of Wullm Wgr and Gonwfa hys wyf the whiche Wullm decessed the XXIX day of Augst y yer of o lord m v°XXXy On whose soules Ihu hvue mcy

Yateley III

Yateley IV

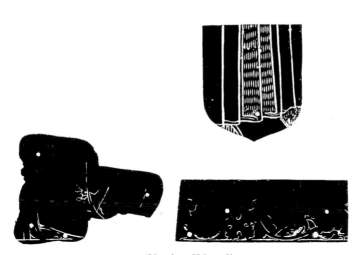

Yateley IV palimpsest reverse

Yateley V

IN LOVING MEMORY OF ELLEN
MARY, WIDOW OF JOHN GILLIAM
STILWELL, ESQ. AND DAUGHTER
OF JOHN TINGCOMBE OF HARTLEY,
IN THE COUNTY OF DEVON,
GENTLEMAN. SHE WAS BORN 2ND
OCTOBER, 1804, AND ENTERED
INTO REST 14TH JULY, 1887.
SHE SURVIVED HER HUSBAND
FOURTEEN MONTHS, HE HAVING
DIED 30TH MAY, 1886, AGED
92 YEARS.

Yateley *X*

Yateley *XII*

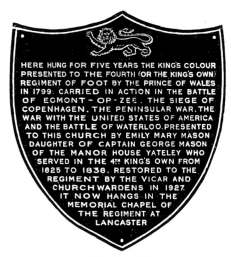

HERE HUNG FOR FIVE YEARS THE KING'S COLOUR
PRESENTED TO THE FOURTH (OR THE KING'S OWN)
REGIMENT OF FOOT BY THE PRINCE OF WALES
IN 1799: CARRIED IN ACTION IN THE BATTLE
OF ECMONT - OP - ZEE, THE SIEGE OF
COPENHAGEN, THE PENINSULAR WAR, THE
WAR WITH THE UNITED STATES OF AMERICA
AND THE BATTLE OF WATERLOO. PRESENTED
TO THIS CHURCH BY EMILY MARY MASON
DAUGHTER OF CAPTAIN GEORGE MASON
OF THE MANOR HOUSE YATELEY WHO
SERVED IN THE 4TH KING'S OWN FROM
1825 TO 1838. RESTORED TO THE
REGIMENT BY THE VICAR AND
CHURCH WARDENS IN 1927.
IT NOW HANGS IN THE
MEMORIAL CHAPEL OF
THE REGIMENT AT
LANCASTER

Yateley *XV*

D.S.O., 1st/4th Battn. Hampshire Regt. (T.A.), 1880-1959, and w. Blanche (née Lipscomb), 1884-**1964**, on organ with no.*XV*, old N., now Church. *XXI.* Inscr. recording gift [of processional cross] in **1981** in mem. of Philip Bradford, A.R.I.B.A., 1917-1973, on processional cross, old C., now Chapel. *XXII.* Inscr. with verse. Ida Elizabeth Fullbrook, 1908-**1982**, bronze, on grave marker, Churchyard. *XXIII.* Inscr. John Grant Stilwell, soldier, churchwarden, organist and benefactor, 1895-**1982**, copper, mur., old C., now Chapel. *XXIV.* Inscr. in raised letters. Lt.-Col. Eric Carmichael Brown, 1885-**1983**, and Col. Vincent Christopher Brown, O.B.E., D.S.C., [Royal Marines attd. H.Q. 3rd Division], 1893-1940, [buried at Dunkirk Town Cemetery, France, sons of Col. Francis David Millett Brown, V.C., I.S.C., and w. Jessie Doris (née Child)], bronze, on lychgate, Churchyard. *XXV.* Inscr. recording presentation [of bench] in **1987** by Guy Fullbrook, bronze, on bench, Churchyard. *XXVI.* Inscr. with verse. Leslie Alfred Tilston Fullbrook, 1909-**1995**, bronze, on grave marker, Churchyard. *XXVII.* Inscr. recording planting of [mountain ash] (Sorbus Aucuparia) in celebration for the [baptism] in **1999** of Joshua Paul Benjamin Rason, on tree post, Churchyard. *XXVIII.* Inscr. Beattie Divall, 1915-**2000**, on bench, Churchyard. *XXIX.* Inscr. Shirley Ann George, "SONGSTRESS", 1947-**2000**, on music stand, old Churchwardens' Vestry, now Retrochoir. *XXX.* Inscr. recording planting of [mountain ash] (Sorbus Aucuparia) in celebration for the [baptism] in **2002** of Timothy Stuart Barnabas Rason, on tree post, Churchyard.

INDENTS & LOST BRASSES. 31. Lost brass, ?civilian and inscr. Richard Gale, 1513, N. Recorded by Warner (1795).   32. Lost brass, civilian and inscr. Probably no.V. Recorded (inscr. lost) by Warner (1795).

Ref: *Brit. Lib. Add. MS. 39987*, f.47, f.54, ff.56-8; *Gent. Mag.*, 1794, II, pp.984-6; *Gent. Mag. Lib. Eng. Topog.*, pp.151-2; *Haines*, II, pp.75-6; *Heseltine, Heraldry*, p.38; *M.B.S. Trans.*, VI, pp.155-7, XIII, pp.442-4; *Mee, Hampshire*, p.419; *M.S.*, p.170; *Palimpsests*, L426, p.vi, L426-2/4, p.xi, L426-2/4, p.xxxviii; *Pevsner, Hampshire*, p.727; *Soc. Antiq. MS. 875/6*, pp.179-81; *V.C.H., Hampshire*, IV, p.25; *Warner*, I, p.315, p.317.

Ch. destroyed by fire, 1979; rebuilt, 1980-1.

The following churches have been searched but no brasses have been found:

Eldon, Upper (St. Mary, redundant, now vested in The Churches Conservation Trust); Bournemouth, or Moordown (Church of the Holy Epiphany); and Bournemouth, or Queen's Park, (St. Barnabas).

The following churches have not been searched:

Ampfield (St. Mary); Appleshaw (St. Peter); Ashmansworth (St. James); Beaulieu (Blessed Virgin and Holy Child); Beauworth (St. James); Bentworth (St. Mary); Bishops Waltham (St. Peter); Bisterne (St. Paul); Blackmoor (St. Matthew); Blendworth (Holy Trinity); Boarhunt (St. Nicholas); Boldre (St. John the Baptist); Bossington (St. James); Botley (All Saints); Bradley (All Saints); Braishfield (All Saints); Bramshaw (St. Peter); Bransgrove (St. Mary); Brockenhurst (St. Peter); Broughton (St. Peter); Bullington (St. Michael and All Angels); Catherington (All Saints); Cheriton (St. Michael and All Angels); Chilcomb (St. Andrew); Chilworth (St. Denys); Clanford (St. James); Clatford, Upper (All Saints); Cliddesden (St. Leonard); Compton (All Saints); Crux Easton (St. Michael and All Angels); Dean, East (St. Winifred); Dibden (All Saints); Durley (Holy Cross); Ecchinswell (St. Lawrence); Ellisfield (St. Martin); Empshott (Holy Rood); Exbury (St. Katherine); Farnborough (St. Peter); Fawley (All Saints); Froxfield (St. Peter-on-the-Green); Fyfield (St. Nicholas); Grateley (St. Leonard); Greatham (St. John the Baptist); Hartley Witney (St. John the Evangelist); Hartley Witney (St. Mary, redundant, now vested in The Churches Conservation Trust); Hawkley (SS. Peter and Paul); Highclere (St. Michael and All Angels); Holybourne (Holy Rood); Houghton (All Saints); Hound (St. Mary the Virgin); Hurstbourne Priors (St. Andrew); Hurstbourne Tarrant (St. Peter); Idsworth (St. Hubert); Kingsley (All Saints); Knights Enham (St. Michael and All Angels); Lasham (St. Mary); Leckford (St. Nicholas); Linkenholt (St. Peter); Liss (St. Mary); Litchfield (St. James the Less); Lockerley (St. John the Evangelist); Longparish (St. Nicholas); Longstock (St. Mary); Long Sutton (All Saints); Mattingley (dedication unknown); Medstead (St. Andrew); Milford-on-Sea (All Saints); Minstead (All Saints); Morestead (dedication unknown); Newnham (St. Nicholas); Newtown (SS. Mary the Virgin and John the Baptist); Northington (St. John the Evangelist); Otterbourne (St. Matthew); Ovington (St. Peter); Plaitford (St. Peter); Ropley (St. Peter); Rotherwick (dedication unknown); St. Mary Bourne (St. Peter); Selborne (St. Mary); Shalden (SS. Peter and Paul); Sherfield English (St. Leonard); Shipton Bellinger (St. Peter); Sopley (St. Michael and All Angels); Southampton (St. Mary); Southampton (St. Michael); Steep (All Saints); Stockbridge (St. Peter); Stoneham, North (St. Nicholas); Stoneham, South (St. Mary); Stratton, East (All Saints); Sydmonton (St. Mary); Tangley (St. Thomas of Canterbury); Tidworth, South (St. Mary); Timsbury (St. Andrew); Tisted, West (St. Mary Magdalen); Tufton (St. Mary); Tunworth (All Saints); Twyford (St. Mary); Tytherley, East (St. Peter); Up Nately (St. Stephen); Upton Grey (St. Mary); Vernham Dean (St. Mary the Virgin); Wallop, Over (St. Peter); Weston Patrick (St. Lawrence); Weyhill (St. Michael and All Angels); Wherwell (St. Peter and Holy Cross); Wield (St. James); Winnall (St. Martin); Woodhay, East (St. Martin); Wolverton (St. Katherine); and Worting (St. Thomas of Canterbury).

CHRONOLOGICAL LIST OF FIGURE BRASSES WITH STYLES OF ENGRAVING

[1381]	London B	Crondall I
[1382]	London B	Winchester, St. Cross I
c.1385	London C	Sherborne St. John I
c.1385	London B	Somborne, King's I
1413	London B	Havant I
1413	London B	Winchester, College *XLVI*
1416	London A	Ringwood I
1418	London B	Winchester, St. Cross 25
c.1425	London D	Thruxton I
c.1430	London D	Bramshott I
1432	London E	Winchester, College *XLVII*
1434	London B	Headbourne Worthy I
1436	London D	Wallop, Nether I
1445	London D	Winchester, College *XLVIII*
1450	Norwich 1	Winchester, College *XLIX*
1452	London D	Bramley I
c.1465	London D	Hordle (old church) 2
c.1465	London sub B	Odiham I
1467	London	Winchester, Hampshire County Museum Service *I*
1473	London sub B	Winchester, College *IV*
1480	London F	Tytherley, West I
1482	London F	Stoke Charity I
1483	London F	Stoke Charity II
1487	London D	Oakley, Church I
1488	London F	Sherborne St. John II
c.1490	London F	Candover, Brown I
c.1490	London D	Warnborough, South I
1492	London D	Sherborne St. John III
1492	London D	Sherborne St. John IV
1493	London G	Winchester, St. Cross IV
1494	London D	Winchester, College *V*
1498	London G	Odiham II
1498	London F	Weeke I
1498	London D	Winchester, College *L*
c.1500	London D	Netley Abbey
c.1500	London G	Southampton, God's House I
1503	London F	Kingsclere I
1509	London F variant	Winchester, College *LI*
c.1510	London F	Alton I
c.1510	London ?F	Alton II
c.1510	London G	Headley I
c.1510	London G	Penton Mewsey 7
1514	London G	Heckfield I
1514	London G	Winchester, College *VIII*
1514	London G	Winchester, College *IX*
c.1515	London F variant	Winchester, Museums Service *III*
1517	London F variant	Yateley II
1518	London G	Itchen Stoke I
1518	London F variant	Winchester, St. Cross VI
1519	London G	Kingsclere II
c.1520	London F debased	Bramley II
c.1520	London G	Candover, Brown 6
c.1520	London F	Odiham *IV*
c.1520	London F	Odiham *V*
c.1520	London F	Sutton, Bishop's I
1522	London F debased	Kimpton I
1524	London F debased	Winchester, College *LIII*
c.1525	London F debased	Itchen Stoke *II*
c.1525	London F debased	Mapledurwell I
1529	London G	Bramley III
c.1530	London F debased	Odiham *VII*
1532	London G	Yateley III
c.1535	London G	Sherborne St. John V
c.1540	London G	Odiham *VIII*
1548	London F and G	Southwick I
c.1548	London G	Winchester, College *XIV*
1563	London G	Crondall II
1568	London G	Fordingbridge I
1575	London G	Froyle I
1578	London G	Yateley IV
c.1580	Johnson	Dummer III
1590	Johnson	Dogmersfield I
c.1590	Johnson	Yateley V
1595	Johnson	Sherfield-on-Loddon II
1599	Johnson	Monxton I
1600	Johnson	Sherfield-on-Loddon III
1603	Johnson	Whitchurch I
1605	Johnson	Dean, Prior's I
1606	Johnson	Basingstoke II
1607	Johnson	Candover, Preston I
1621	Johnson	Basingstoke III
1636	London	Odiham *IX*
1641	Francis Grigs	Crondall III

411

417

424

427

431

Isle of Wight

ARRETON, St. George.

I. Harry Hawles, "long tyme steward of the yle of Wyght", c.**1430**, in arm., head lost, inscr. in 4 Eng. vv.; sh. lost; S.C. Recorded (complete) by Tomkins (1796), (complete) by Brettell from Tomkins (1840) and (head lost) by Holloway (1848). *Brit. Lib. Add. MS. 39987*, f.24r; *Holloway*, p.152 (headless); *Staines*, p.2 (headless); *Stone*, I, pl.5. Eff. 770 x 216 mm, now 665 x 216 mm, inscr. 125 x 353 mm, sh. indent 150 x 125 mm, Purbeck slab 2050 x 880 mm. Style: London B.

II. Inscr. William Colnett of Comblie, gent., **1594**, aged 69, mur., in stone frame, north wall outside C. Inscr. 155 x 420 mm.

III. Inscr. in 24 Eng. vv. William Serle, **1595**, aged 59, mur., in Petworth marble frame, S.A. Inscr. 570 x 433 mm, Petworth frame 840 x 600 mm.

IV. Inscr. George Serle, c.**1600**, mur., S.A. Inscr. 185 x 504 mm.

V. Inscr. Capt. Henry Geary, son of Cmdr. Thomas Geary, R.N., of Newport, killed in action at [the Battle of] Rolica, [Portugal], 1773-1808, and w. Frances, dau. of Benjamin Joliffe, M.D., of Broadfields, died at East Sheen, [Surrey], 1783-**1862**; also children, Capt. Henry Geary, R[oyal] A[rtillery], died at sea, 1802-1844; Frances, w. of Rev. James Joliffe, of Padmore, died at Stoke Charity, 1804-1836; Frederick Augustus Geary, of Inland Revenue Office, died at Putney, [Surrey], 1805-1854; and Mary Geary, died at Camberwell, [Surrey], 1808-1830, mur., on marble, C. *VI.* Inscr. Frederick Roache, **1882**, aged 81, mur., S.A. *VII.* Inscr. Elizabeth Roache, widow of William Foquett, yst. sister of no.*VI*, **1888**, mur., S.A. *VIII.* Inscr. recording erection of organ in **1888** in mem. of Elizabeth Wallbridge, buried in the churchyard, and Lt. John Phelips, R.N., brother of the vicar, died at sea during the ch. restoration in 1885, maker's name JONES & WILLIS, on organ, S.A. *IX.* Inscr. on oval-shaped pl. within border of musical instruments. Annie Whale, organist for 28 years, 1884-**1912**, pos. by friends, maker's name H. OSBORNE ENG^R RYDE, mur., S.A. *X.* Inscr. with verse in raised letters and regt. insignia. Capt. Charles Seymour Pittis, M.C., 8th Battn. Hampshire Regt. (Isle of Wight Rifles), eld. son of Seymour Pittis, of Hale, and w. Kate, killed in action near Gaza, **1917**, aged 21, [buried at Gaza War Cemetery, Israel], maker's name CULN GAWTHORP & SONS LONDON, bronze, mur., on marble, N. *XI.* Inscr. George Eric Pittis, of Hale, **1925**, aged 21, on table, S.A. *XII.* Inscr. recording installation of electric lighting by parishioners to commem. the coronation of Queen Elizabeth II in **1953**, mur., on board on pillar, C. *XIII.* Inscr. Lt.-Gen. Sir Henry Le G. Geary, K.C.B., Col.-Commandant R[oyal] A[rtillery], 1837-1918; also sons, Lt. Henry G.F. Geary, R.A., 1870-1897, and Lt.-Col. John A. Geary, R.A., D.S.O., 1877-**1967**, mur., on marble, C. *XIV.* Inscr. recording that the Burma Star memorial window, standard and roll of honour relate to past history and the involvement of Isle of Wight branch of the Burma Star Association, 1952-**1999**, on display case, S.A. *XV.* Inscr. recording chair was made from an old bell frame in **2001** by Paul Wise, chair maker and bellringer, mur., on board, N.

INDENTS & LOST BRASSES. 16. Indent, civilian and w., inscr. and 2 shs., c.1500, S.C. *Sadler, Dorset and Hampshire,* appx. I, p.44 (drg.). Male eff. 405 x 105 mm, female eff. 405 x 105 mm, inscr. 75 x 585 mm, shs. 140 x 125 mm, Unio Purbeck slab 1745 x 730 mm. Style: London G. 17. Indent, sh., S.A. Sh. 165 x 130 mm, slab 1340 x 375 mm remains. 18. Lost brass, ?civilian and w., inscr. and shs. _____Voryes, nearly effaced, on A.T., S.C. Possibly no.16. Recorded (lost) by Oglander.

here is v̇ buried vnder this graue ⁊ ⁊
harry hawbles his soule god saue ⁊ ⁊
longe tyme stewçard of the yle of wyght ⁊ ⁊
haue mçy on hym god ful of myght ⁊ ⁊

Arreton I

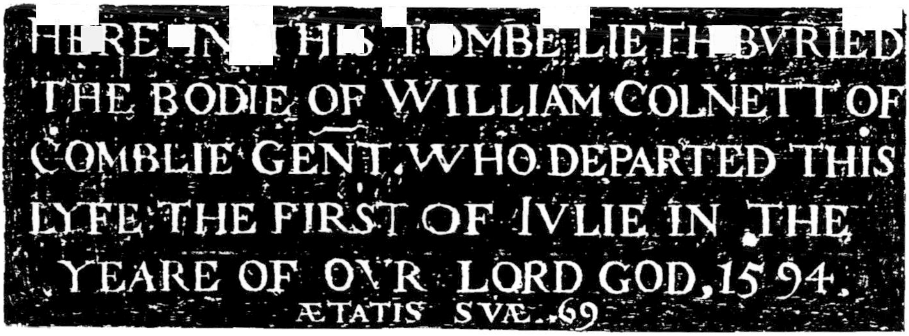

HERE IN THIS TOMBE LIETH BVRIED
THE BODIE OF WILLIAM COLNETT OF
COMBLIE GENT. WHO DEPARTED THIS
LYFE THE FIRST OF IVLIE IN THE
YEARE OF OVR LORD GOD, 15 94.
ÆTATIS SVÆ 69

Arreton II

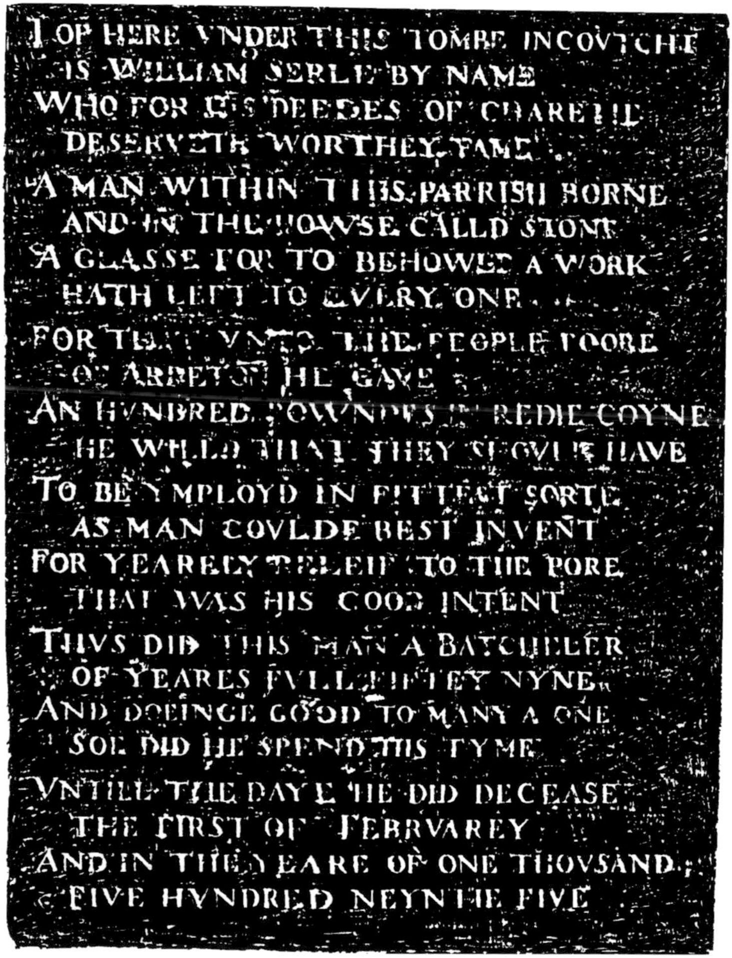

LO HERE VNDER THIS TOMBE INCOVTCHE
IS WILLIAM SERLE BY NAME
WHO FOR HIS DEEDES OF CHARETIE
DESERVETH WORTHEY FAME
A MAN WITHIN THIS PARRISH BORNE
AND IN THE HOWSE CALLD STONE
A GLASSE FOR TO BEHOWLD A WORK
HATH LEFT TO EVERY ONE
FOR THAT VNTO THE PEOPLE POORE
OF ARRETON HE GAVE
AN HVNDRED POWNDES IN REDIE COYNE
HE WILLD THAT THEY SHOVLD HAVE
TO BE YMPLOYD IN FITTEST SORTE
AS MAN COVLDE BEST INVENT
FOR YEARELY RELEIF TO THE PORE
THAT WAS HIS GOOD INTENT
THVS DID THIS MAN A BATCHELER
OF YEARES FVLL FIFTEY NYNE
AND DOEINGE GOOD TO MANY A ONE
SO DID HE SPEND THIS TYME
VNTILE THE DAYE HE DID DECEASE
THE FIRST OF FEBRVAREY
AND IN THE YEARE OF ONE THOVSAND
FIVE HVNDRED NEYNTIE FIVE

Arreton III

437

Ref: *Arch. Jour.*, II, p.83; *B.A.A. Jour.*, I, p.54; *Brettell*, 2nd edn., p.146; *Brit. Lib. Add. MS. 39959*, f.469, *Add. MS. 39987*, f.24; *Haines*, II, p.76; *Holloway, H.R., Walks round Ryde*, 1848, pp.152-3, p.155; *Jeans*, p.35; *Long*, pp.192-6; *Manning*, p.31; *M.B.S. Trans.*, II, pp.2-3, p.6, VIII, p.208; *Mee, Hampshire*, p.425; *M.S.*, p.171; *Pevsner, Hampshire*, p.731; *Sadler, Dorset and Hampshire*, appx. I, pt.2, p.44, p.52; *Simpson*, p.28; *Staines*, p.1; *Stone*, I, p.7; *Tomkins*, II, p.132; *V.C.H., Hampshire*, V, p.149.

ARRETON, or HAVENSTREET, St. Peter.

I. Lt. Charles Kent, R.N., of H.M.S. Dauntless, only brother of Rev. Frederic Kent, incumbent of the district, died of yellow fever at Barbadoes, "with fourteen brother officers, victims of the same deadly pestilence", **1852**, aged 28, [buried] at St. Matthew's Church, [Barbadoes], pos. by "one left to mourn the untimely loss of a most noble heart", rect. pl., ship in full sail within a quatrefoil and inscr., [engr. by John Hardman & C⁰· Birmᵐ·], mur., on marble, C. *II.* Inscr. recording gift of altar in **1900** by dau., Eleanor Maud, in mem. of Emma Barry, 1899, on altar, C. *III.* World War I memorial in raised letters (20 names), copper, mur., in wooden frame, N.

Ref: *Haines*, II, p.238 (under Ryde).

Ch. built, 1852.

BARTON, (see NEWPORT).

BEMBRIDGE, Holy Trinity.

I. Inscr. with verse. Charlotte Elizabeth, w. of John Le Mesurier, **1853**, mur., N. *II.* Inscr. Robert Watson, coastguard, **1883**, maker's name HART SON PEARD & C⁰ LONDON, mur., S.A. *III.* Inscr. in Lat. Claud Davenport Thomas, **1891**, aged 16, mur., N. *IV.* Inscr. recording gift of sacrarium pavement in **1893** by grandmother in mem. of Claud Davenport Thomas, 1891, aged 16, mur., C. *V.* Inscr. recording gift of altar steps in **1893** by widow, Madame Poclet, and son, Rev. Edward Howard Francis, M.A., vicar [1891-1906], in mem. of Dayrell Joseph Thackwell Francis, M.D., F.R.C.P.L., 1887, mur., C. *VI.* Inscr. recording [gift of] altar rails in **1893** in mem. of Rev. Canon [John] Le Mesurier, [M.A.], vicar [1851-1891], mur., C. *VII.* Inscr. recording gift of [south aisle] window by dau., Louisa, in mem. of Jeremiah Dennett, engr. c.**1895**, mur., S.A. *VIII.* Inscr. recording gift of [south aisle] window by sister, Louisa, in mem. of John William Dennett, engr. c.**1895**, mur., S.A. *IX.* Inscr. Walter Varnham, 1881, and w. Louisa Emily, **1909**, maker's name HAMNER & CO LTD LONDON, mur., N. *X.* Inscr. Annie Louisa, w. of Joseph Basil Dennison, **1912**, maker's name H. OSBORNE ENGᴿ RYDE, mur., S.A. *XI.* Inscr. with regt. insignia in relief. Capt. Archibald Campbell Dennison, 2nd Battn. Royal Highlanders Blackwatch, killed at the Battle of Loos, **1915**, mur., in wooden frame, S.A. *XII.* World War I memorial, on screen, N. *XIII.* Inscr. Molière Tabuteau, churchwarden 1907-1916, and w. Elizabeth Harriet; also children, Ethel, Claude, Kathleen, Helen, Reginald, Winifred, Madeline, Renée and Rupert, **1964**, mur., S.A.

Ch. built, 1845-6.

THE REWARDE OF SINNE IS DEATH, EVERLAS-
TINGE LIFE IS THE GIFTE OF GOD THROVGH OV^R
LORD AND SAVIOVR IESVS CHRISTE, WHEREFOR
ALL YE THAT LOVE THE LORD, DOE THIS, HATE
ALL THINGS THAT ARE EVELL, FOR HE DOTHE
KEPE THE SOVLES OF HIS FROM SVCHE AS
WOVLDE THEM SPILL. GEORGE SERLE

Arreton IV

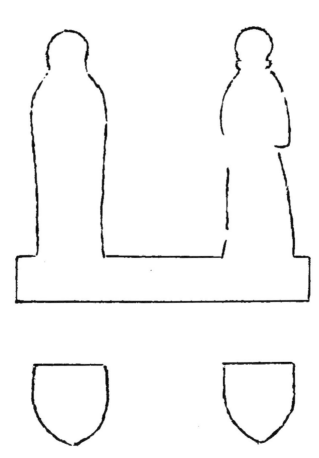

Arreton 16

BINSTEAD, Holy Cross.

I. Inscr. Thomas Yarel, **1844**, N. *II.* Inscr. [Rev.] William Dickonson, rector, 1794, aged 73, and w. Jane, 1807, aged 90; also Ann White, 1783, aged 69, engr. c.**1850**, mur., C. *III.* Inscr. William Banning, of Liverpool, died at Ryde, **1857**, aged 72, [buried] in the new [churchyard], mur., in stone frame, N. *IV.* Inscr. Major Alleyne Cox Yarel, 1st Battn. 47th North Lancashire Regt., died at Camp Ziarat, Beluchistan, [Pakistan], 1846-**1886**, maker's name FRANK SMITH & C^{O.} 13, SOUTHAMPTON S^{T.} STRAND LONDON, mur., on marble, N.A. *V.* Inscr. John N[icholas] Hathway, **1902**, on lectern, N. *VI.* Inscr. John Nicholas Hathway, [church]warden for many years, [**1902**], on font cover, N.A. *VII.* World War I memorial (29 names), maker's name H. OSBORNE RYDE, mur., C. *VIII.* Inscr. recording dedication of panelling in **1932** by [Rt. Rev. Dr. Ernest] Neville [Lovett, D.D.], 1st Bishop of Portsmouth [1927-1936], on screen, N. *IX.* Inscr. recording gift of sanctuary lamp in **1941** by parishioners in mem. of [Rev.] Cecil Sumner Stooks, [M.A.], rector 1927-1939; in 2005 loose on board in C. *X.* Inscr. recording gift of [north aisle] window in **1988** by [children] in mem. of John Henry Venus, [w.] Phillis and family, on window splay, N.A.

BONCHURCH, St. Boniface (old church).

I. Inscr. recording gift of prayer desk in **1933** by 2 daus. in mem. of Jonathan George Jolliffe, on prie-dieu, C. *II.* Inscr. recording installation of electricity in **1980** in mem. of George and Russell Mursell, mur., on board, N.

BONCHURCH, St. Boniface (new church).

I. Inscr. in Lat. recording [chancel] window pos. by [Rev.] Ranulph Henry Feilden and [w.] Phoebe Sara in mem. of Ranulph William [Feilden], **1858**; Frances Caroline [Feilden], 1858; and Elizabeth Helen [Feilden], 1840, mur., below window, C. *II.* Inscr. Edith Swinburne, 1840-**1863**, mur., below window, S.Tr. *III.* Inscr. in Lat. recording [north transept] window pos. by dau., Phoebe Sara Feilden, in mem. of Sir Robert Arbuthnot, Knt., 1853, and w., 1822; also only son, George Arbuthnot, **1865**, mur., below window, N.Tr. *IV.* Inscr. in Lat. recording [chancel] window pos. by widow, Phoebe Sara Feilden, in mem. of Rev. Ranulph Henry Feilden, **1870**, mur., below window, C. *V.* Inscr. in Lat. recording [chancel] window pos. by William Feilden, gent., and dau., Phoebe Sara Feilden, in mem. of daus., Cecilia, 1846, and Maria Anna, **1873**, mur., below window, C. *VI.* Inscr. recording donation in **1873** of £50 by Hampshire Diocesan Church Association and accepted by the building committee towards the erection of the south transept on condition that "ALL SITTINGS SHOULD BE UNAPPROPRIATED AND FREE FOR THE POOR OF THE PARISH"; [Rev.] H[enry] J[ohn] Maddock, M.A., rector [1869-1895]; H. Rhoades and D. Day, churchwardens, mur., S.Tr. *VII.* Inscr. in Lat. recording erection of [nave] window by brother and sisters in mem. of Edward Arthur Feilden, 1836-1874; also George Robert Fielden, 1843-**1874**, mur., below window, N. *VIII.* Inscr. in Lat. recording that [nave] window was filled with stained glass by family in mem. of William Sewell, S.T.P., fellow of Exeter Coll., Oxford, **1874**, aged 70, mur., N. *IX.* Inscr. in Lat. recording [west nave] window pos. in **1874** by uncle in gratitude for a young man's recovery from serious illness, mur., below window, N. *X.* Inscr. in Lat. recording [nave] window pos. by son and dau. in mem. of mother, Phoebe Sara Feilden, 1804-**1876**, mur., below window, N. *XI.* Inscr. Admiral Charles Henry Swinburne, 1797-**1877**, mur., below window, S.Tr. *XII.* Cross with enamelled nativity scene under triple canopy with angel holding inscribed scroll under single canopy at base surmounting inscr. with verse. Susan Harriet Feilden, 1826-**1887**, mur., N. *XIII.* Cross on 2 steps and inscr. E. Constance Maude, 1854-**1889**, maker's name HART SON PEARD & Cᴼ LONDON, mur., N. *XIV.* Cross on 3 steps with angel holding inscribed scroll under single canopy with flying buttresses at base surmounting inscr. [Rev.] Ludovic Charles André Mouton, rector, **1895**, aged 49, mur., C. *XV.* Inscr. Major William Morrison Bell, died at The Lilies, **1900**, aged 65, pos. by nieces and nephews, maker's name A & N AUX C.S.L. LONDON, mur., N. *XVI.* Inscr. Harry Fenn Rowlands, B.A.(Oxon.), missionary C[hurch] M[issionary] S[ociety], died in the earthquake at Kangra, Punjab, India, **1905**, aged 35, maker's name A & N AUX C.S.L. LONDON, mur., N. *XVII.* Cross surmounting inscr. recording gift of stall in **1911** by friends and pupils in mem. of Elizabeth [M.] Sewell, worshipped in the ch. for over 50 years, on stall, N. *XVIII.* Inscr. recording gift of service books in **1911** in mem. of Ellen M. Sewell, Elizabeth M. Sewell and Emma F. Sewell, mur., N.Tr. *XIX.* Inscr. Clara Constance Porter, 2nd dau. [of Stephen Canning Day and w. Edith Maude], **1912**, aged 39, Churchyard. *XX.* Inscr. with regt. insignia. Lt.-Col. Edmund Emerson Bousfield, 123rd Outram Rifles attd. 1st Battn. [King George's Own] Gurkha Rifles [(The Malaun Regt.), son of Edmund Collingwood Bousfield and w. Louisa], killed in action in France, **1915**, aged 45, [buried] at St. Vaast [Post Military Cemetery], Richebourg[-L'Avoue], maker's name AKED CLEGG ENGRAVER WAKEFIELD, mur., on board, N. *XXI.* Inscr. Edward James, 2nd son of Stephen Canning Day and w. Edith Maude, **1916**, aged 8, with no.*XIX*, Churchyard. *XXII.* Inscr. Kate Florence Riddick, eld. dau. [of Stephen Canning Day and w. Edith Maude], **1925**, aged 53, with nos.*XIX & XXI*, Churchyard. *XXIII.* Inscr. recording presentation [of prie-dieu] by daus., Maria and Joan, in mem. of Ida Cholmondeley, engr. c.**1930**, on prie-dieu, N. *XXIV.* Inscr. Daniel Day, **1933**, aged 86, with nos.*XIX, XXI & XXII*, Churchyard. *XXV.* Inscr. in raised letters. Pamela, eld. dau. of George Dudley and [w.] Ruth, w. of Robert Dalton, died at Corning, N[ew] Y[ork], U.S.A., **1934**, aged 32, bronze, mur., on board, N. *XXVI.* Inscr. Clara Georgina, w. of Daniel Day, **1936**, aged 89, with nos.*XIX, XXI, XXII & XXIV*, Churchyard. *XXVII.* Inscr. recording gift of reredos and sanctuary panelling in **1937** by w. in mem. of Charles Harvey Combe, mur., on panelling, C. *XXVIII.* Inscr. recording gift of altar rail [in **1937**] by sister, Dorothy, in mem. of Charles Harvey Combe, mur., on panelling, C. *XXIX.* Inscr. [Rev.] William Forster Haire, chaplain to R.A.N.R. and Missions to Seamen, "THE GREATER PART OF HIS MINISTRY WAS DEVOTED TO THE WELFARE OF SEAFARING MEN IN AUSTRALIAN PORTS AND AT ANTWERP", rector 1931-**1938**, on organ, C. *XXX.* Inscr. Alice Ann Venables, **1938**, pos. by sister, E. Maud Venables, on choir stall, C. *XXXI.* Inscr. Daniel Day, 2nd son [of Stephen Canning Day and w. Edith Maude], **1938**, aged 63, with nos.*XIX, XXI, XXII, XXIV & XXVI*, Churchyard. *XXXII.* Inscr. recording restoration of organ in mem. of Mary Liddelow, chorister for many years; also brother, Flying Officer John Coulthard, [133021, 29th Sqdn., R.A.F.V.R., son of Tom Peacock Coulthard and w. Priscilla Annie May, of Coulsdon, Surrey, 1940, aged 19], missing in action, **1943**, on organ, C. *XXXIII.* Inscr. recording presentation [of processional cross] by w. in mem. of Sir John Martin-Harvey, [**1944**, aged 80, buried at East Sheen, Surrey], on processional cross, C. *XXXIV.* Inscr. Stephen Canning Day, eld. son [of Stephen Canning Day and w. Edith Maude], **1945**, aged 76, with nos.*XIX, XXI, XXII, XXIV, XXVI & XXXI*, Churchyard. *XXXV.* Inscr. Edith Maude, w. of Stephen Canning Day, **1955**, aged 77, with nos.*XIX, XXI, XXII, XXIV, XXVI, XXXI & XXXIV*, Churchyard. *XXXVI.* Inscr. Hephzibah Brackley, [grandmother], 1882-**1965**, Churchyard. *XXXVII.* Inscr. Betty, w. of Daniel Day, **1966**, aged 89, with nos.*XIX, XXI, XXII, XXIV, XXVI, XXXI, XXXIV & XXXV*, Churchyard. *XXXVIII.* Inscr. [Rev.] Adolphus Eric Lockley, rector 1960-1967, **1967**, mur., N. *XXXIX.* Inscr. J.E., 1923-**1973**, on bench, Churchyard. *XL.* Inscr. Daniel Day, son of Daniel Day and no.*XXXVII*, **1974**, aged 60, with nos.*XIX, XXI, XXII, XXIV, XXVI, XXXI, XXXIV & XXXV*, Churchyard. *XLI.* Inscr.

Gwladys M. Williams, L.R.A.M., organist 1921-**1978**, on organ, C. *XLII.* Inscr. recording gift of piano by friends and pupils in mem. of Gwladys M. Williams, L.R.A.M., organist 1921-**1978**, on piano, N.Tr. *XLIII.* Inscr. Arthur Winston Lewis, 1908-**1983**, on chair, C. *XLIV.* Inscr. recording restoration of St. Boniface [nave] window in **1988** in mem. of Frederick Perriman and [w.] Ethel Agnes, 1939-1957, mur., on board, N. *XLV.* Inscr. Stephen Canning, eld. son of Stephen Canning Day and no.*XXXV*, **1992**, aged 86, with nos.*XIX, XXI, XXII, XXIV, XXVI, XXXI, XXXIV, XXXV, XXXVII & XL*, Churchyard. *XLVI.* Inscr. Eleanor Mary, w. of Daniel Day, **1993**, aged 82, with nos.*XIX, XXI, XXII, XXIV, XXVI, XXXI, XXXIV, XXXV, XXXVII, XL & XLV*, Churchyard. *XLVII.* Inscr. Edith Muriel, eld. dau. of Stephen Canning Day and no.*XXXV*, **1994**, aged 88, with nos.*XIX, XXI, XXII, XXIV, XXVI, XXXI, XXXIV, XXXV, XXXVII, XL, XLV & XLVI*, Churchyard. *XLVIII.* Inscr. recording restoration of St. Luke [nave] window in **1994** in mem. of Leslie John Russell, churchwarden 1966-1994, mur., on board, N. *XLIX.* Inscr. Helen Maria, yst. dau. of Stephen Canning Day and no.*XXXV*, **2001**, aged 85, with nos.*XIX, XXI, XXII, XXIV, XXVI, XXXI, XXXIV, XXXV, XXXVII, XL, XLV, XLVI & XLVII*, Churchyard.

Ch. built, 1847-8.

BRADING, St. Mary the Virgin.

I. Inscr. George Oglander, esq., 1567, and w. Alice Hamond, engr. c.**1630**, mur., A.T., S.C. Inscr. 157 x 436 mm.

II. Inscr. Sir William Oglander, Knt., 1608, and w. Ann Dillington, engr. c.**1630**, mur., on stone panel of A.T., S.C. Inscr. 153 x 430 mm.

III. Inscr. George Oglander, esq., eld. son of Sir John Oglander, Knt., died at "Cawne", Normandy, **1632**, aged 23, mur., S.C. Inscr. 66 x 124 mm.

IV. Inscr. Sir John Oglander, Knt., deputy lieutenant of the Island, **1655**, aged 70, and w. Frances, yst. dau. of Sir George Moore of Loseley, 1644, aged 52, mur., on stone panel of A.T., S.C. Inscr. 126 x 644 mm.

V. Inscr. Rev. T. Waterworth, B.D., vicar, **1790**, aged 70, C. *Brit. Lib. Add. MS. 39962,* f.226r. *VI.* Inscr. Elizabeth, widow of Rev. T. Waterworth, **1814**, aged 77, C. *VII.* Inscr. recording presentation [of lectern] in **1875** by John [Rogerson], 10th Lord Rollo, [J.P., D.L., 1835-1916]; Rev. John Glover, M.A., vicar [1862-1884], on lectern, N. *VIII.* Inscr. with sh. recording [west south aisle] window pos. by friends and parishioners in mem. of Rev. John Glover, M.A. of Trinity Coll., Camb., vicar for 21 years [1862-1884], **1884**, aged 61, maker's name H. OSBORNE ENGR RYDE, mur., on board below window, S.A. *IX.* Inscr. on circular-shaped pl. Kathleen Lucy, dau. of C[harles] Meeves, [M.R.C.S.] and [w.] C[lara] M[aria], w. of H. Milner White, LL.D., **1890**, aged 33, maker's name BENHAM & FROUD LD, LONDON, mur., S.A. *X.* Cross on 4 steps and inscr. Clara Maria, w. of Charles Meeves, M.R.C.S., of Sandown, for 49 years, 1820-**1895**, mur., S.A. *XI.* Inscr. on circular-shaped pl. Isabel Clara, dau. of C[harles] Meeves, [M.R.C.S.] and [w.] C[lara] M[aria], widow of Sydney Hownam-Meek, C.E., LL.D., **1898**, aged 44, maker's name BENHAM & FROUD LD, LONDON, mur., S.A. *XII.* Inscr. Rev. Legh Richmond, M.A. of Trinity Coll., Camb., rector of Turvey, Beds., chaplain to H.R.H. the Duke of Kent, curate-in-charge of Brading and Yaverland 1797-1805, author of *The Annals of the Poor,*

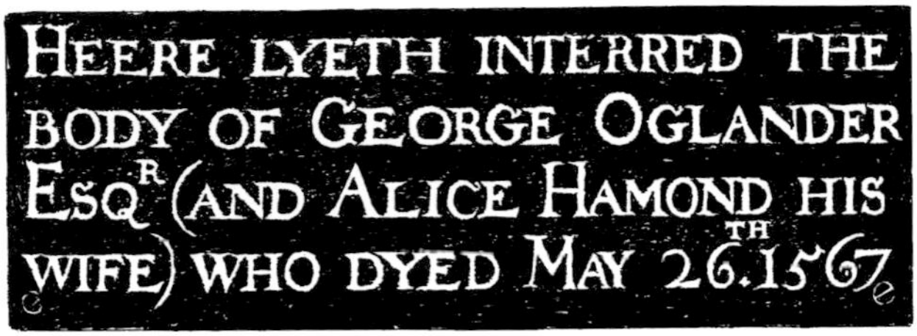

HEERE LYETH INTERRED THE
BODY OF GEORGE OGLANDER
ESQ^R (AND ALICE HAMOND HIS
WIFE) WHO DYED MAY 26.15'67

Brading I

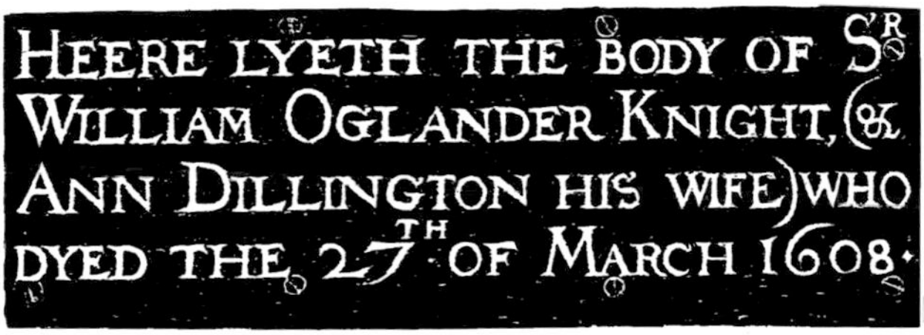

HEERE LYETH THE BODY OF S^R
WILLIAM OGLANDER KNIGHT, (&
ANN DILLINGTON HIS WIFE)WHO
DYED THE 27TH OF MARCH 1608·

Brading II

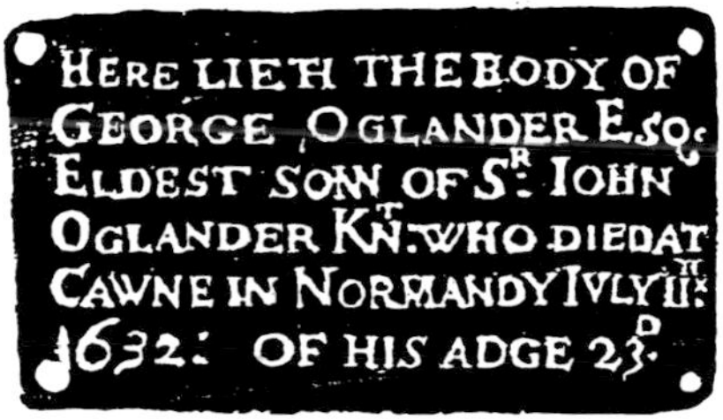

HERE LIETH THE BODY OF
GEORGE OGLANDER ESQ.
ELDEST SONN OF S^R IOHN
OGLANDER KN^T. WHO DIED AT
CAWNE IN NORMANDY IVLY II:
1632: OF HIS ADGE 23^D.

Brading III

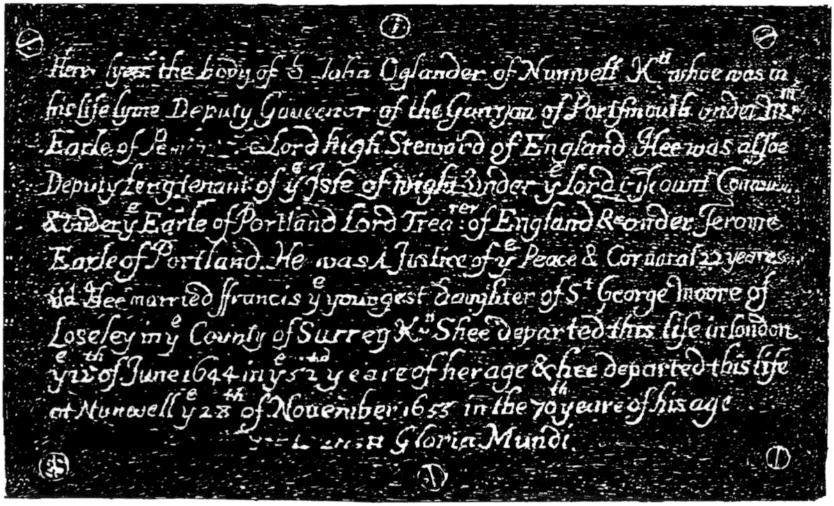

Here lyeth the body of Sr Iohn Oglander of Nunwell K^tt whoe was in
his life tyme Deputy Gouernor of the Garyson of Portsmouth under the
Earle of Pe...... Lord high Steward of England Hee was alsoe
Deputy Lentenant of ye Isle of Wight under ye Lord Viscount Conway
& under ye Earle of Portland Lord Trea^rer of England & under Ierome
Earle of Portland. He was A Iustice of ye Peace & Coronal 22 yeares.
old Hee married ffrancis ye youngest daughter of St George Moore of
Loseley in ye County of Surrey K^t. Shee departed this life in London
ye 12 of Iune 1644 in ye 52 yeare of her age & hee departed this life
at Nunwell ye 28 of Nouember 1655 in the 70 yeare of his age
...... Gloria Mundi.

Brading IV

443

[1772-1827], pos. in **1898** with the consent of Rev. E[dgar] Sumners, [M.A.], B.D., vicar [1884-1906] and rural dean [of East Wight 1893-1906], and descendants of the 2nd, 3rd and 4th generations, maker's name J.W. SINGER & SONS FROME & LONDON, mur., on marble, S.A. *XIII.* Inscr. Charles Meeves, M.R.C.S., of Sandown, **1905**, aged 87, maker's name A & N AUX C.S.L. LONDON, mur., S.A. *XIV.* Inscr. William Henry Gordon, 3rd son of John Grimes Harvey and [w.] Frances, died of fever at sea 17° 40' N. 40° 40' W., **1906**, aged 21, maker's name GAWTHORP Sᶜ LONDON, mur., N.A. *XV.* Inscr. Malcolm Edward Harvey, drowned off Cape Horn, **1908**, aged 20, mur., N.A. *XVI.* Inscr. recording presentation [of reredos] in **1909** by husband, [John Rogerson, 10th Lord Rollo, J.P., D.L.], in mem. of Agnes Bruce, Lady Rollo, [eld. dau. of Lt.-Col. Robert Knox Trotter, of Ballindean, Perthshire, 1906], mur., C. *XVII.* Inscr. Ralph Squibb, verger for 30 years, **1978**, on door, N. *XVIII.* Inscr. Peter Wetherick, 1914-**1980**, on bench, Churchyard. *XIX.* Inscr. Elsie, w. of Ralph Squibb, **1986**, on door with no.*XVII*, N.

Ref: *Brasses as Art and History*, p.70; *Brit. Lib. Add. MS. 39962,* f.226; *Burke's Peerage and Baronetage*, p.2286; *Jeans*, p.7; *Long*, p.xxvii, p.167; *M.B.S. Trans.*, II, p.3; *M.S.*, p.171; *Stone*, I, pp.15-6; *V.C.H., Hampshire*, V, p.168.

BRADING, or LAKE, Good Shepherd.

I. Inscr. recording erection of organ in **1901** in mem. of "HAPPY DAYS PASSED IN LAKE", on organ, C. *II.* Inscr. [Sgt.] F[rederick] E[rnest] Booker, [3/4967, 2nd Battn. Hampshire Regt., 1915, aged 35]; G.A. King; and [Rifleman] R[aymond] Trinder, [1952, 1st/8th Battn. Hampshire Regt., 1915], choristers killed in World War I, maker's name *JONES & WILLIS Lᵀᴰ*, mur., on board, N.C. *III.* Inscr. Henry Charles Fanner, organist 1906-**1919**, on organ with no.*I*, C. *IV.* Inscr. Rev. W[illiam] T[ownsend] Storrs, B.D., [M.R.C.S.], vicar for 29 years [1881-1910], "THROUGH WHOSE ZEAL THIS CHURCH WAS ERECTED", maker's name A. L. MOORE & SON, LONDON. W.C., engr. c.**1920**, mur., S.A. *V.* Inscr. with verse recording dedication of [south aisle] window in mem. of ch. worshippers killed in World War I, maker's name *JONES & WILLIS Lᵀᴰ*, engr. 1922, mur., on board, S.A. *VI.* Inscr. recording dedication of [north chapel] in mem. of Janet Mitchell Richardson, "TO HER VISION, FAITH AND CHARITY WAS LARGELY DUE THE BIRTH OF THE PARISH OF LAKE 4 NOVEMBER 1930", **1931**, mur., N.C. *VII.* Inscr. Bertram William Baker, organist 1919-**1933**, on organ with nos.*I & III*, C. *VIII.* Inscr. William Barnes, **1949**, and [w.] Alice, 1947, pos. by family, mur., N.A. *IX.* Inscr. Ellen Porter, benefactress, **1951**, mur., S.A. *X.* Inscr. Alan Lionel Marshall, organist 1933-**1953**, on organ with nos.*I, III & VII*, C. *XI.* Inscr. Charles Finch, churchwarden 1956-**1963**, mur., N.A. *XII.* Inscr. John Henry Lacey, engr. c.**1970**, mur., N.A. *XIII.* Inscr. Muriel Deborah Outram, L.R.A.M., A.R.C.M., engr. c.**1975**, on organ with nos.*I, III, VII & X*, C.

Ch. built, 1892.

BRADING, or SANDOWN, Christ Church.

I. Inscr. with sh. recording dedication of [north aisle] window by friends to Rev. William Thomas, rector of Llangibby, preacher for 16 years, founder of the ch. in 1845 and minister, [vicar 1856-**1862**], maker's name GAWTHORP Sᶜ LONDON, mur., N.A. *II.* Inscr. Elizabeth Bell, w. of [Rev.] William M[olland] Lee, [M.A.], vicar [1862-1873], rector of Yaverland [1869-1873], **1873**, aged 70, mur., S.A. *III.* Inscr. recording enlargement of ch. in **1874**;

[Rev.] Gilbert S[parshott] Karney, M.A., vicar [1871-1881]; G.C. Bailie and James Dove, churchwardens, mur., S.C. *IV.* Inscr. recording erection of organ in **1875**; [Rev.] Gilbert S[parshott] Karney, M.A., vicar [1871-1881]; W.A. Davidson, M.D. and James Dove, churchwardens, on organ, N.A. *V.* Inscr. Jessie, dau. of Major-Gen. Sir John M. Caskill, K.C.B., widow of Col. Hugh Mitchell, Madras Native Infantry, died at The Bays, **1887**, aged 72, maker's name HART SON PEARD & Cº LONDON, mur., S.A. *VI.* Inscr. Maurice Robert Fitzgerald Collis, 1889-**1890**, mur., N.A. *VII.* Inscr. E.E.B., engr. c.**1900**, on lectern, N. *VIII.* Inscr. W.A.G., M.J.G., J.A.G., T.M.G., E.G., S.G., E.G., engr. c.**1900**, mur., N.A. *IX.* Inscr. James Ranson Baass, M.Inst.C.E., superintending engineer Uganda Railway, died at Fort Tiernan, **1902**, aged 41, buried at Nairobi, British East Africa, mur., on marble, S.A. *X.* Inscr. within border of oak leaves and acorns. William Garland, churchwarden for 35 years, Sunday school superintendent for many years, **1911**, aged 72, pos. by widow and friends, maker's name H. OSBORNE FECIT RYDE, mur., on board, N.A. *XI.* Inscr. Frederick Armstrong Boucher, of Blundellsands, Lancs., yst. son of John Bishop Boucher, of Shrewsbury, [Salop], husband of Lilian Boucher, died at Shanghai, [China], **1914**, aged 44, mur., S.A. *XII.* Inscr. with verse and regt. insignia in relief. Lt.-Col. Hugh Edward Richard Boxer, D.S.O., [1st Battn.] Lincolnshire Regt., yst. son of Lt. Edward [W.F.] Boxer, R.N., [killed] at Hooge, near Ypres, **1915**, aged 44, [pos. by w.], maker's name CULN GAWTHORP & SONS LONDON, bronze, mur., on marble, S.A. *XIII.* Inscr. Mary, dau. of Lt.-Col. Henry Grove, 23rd Light Dragoons, w. of Major J.F. Wyley, 22nd Regt., died at Broadstone, Dorset, **1915**, pos. by brother, maker's name J. WIPPELL & Cº LTD, mur., N.A. *XIV.* Inscr. Henry Martin Barker, M.D., churchwarden for many years, **1917**, pos. by congregation, friends and patients, maker's name A. L. MOORE & SON, LONDON. W.C., mur., S.A. *XV.* Inscr. Cpl. Walter Henry Mumby, [DM2/207454, 895th] M.T. [Co.], A[rmy] S[ervice] C[orps], 2nd son of John Washington Mumby, of Riverhead, Sevenoaks, [Kent], drowned by torpedoing of the transport "Arcadian" in the East Mediterranean, **1917**, mur., on board, N.A. *XVI.* World War I memorial in raised letters (27 names); "IMPROVEMENTS TO THE ORGAN AND THE INSTALLATION OF AN ELECTRIC BLOWER FORM A FURTHER PORTION OF THE WAR MEMORIAL", **1919**, maker's name H. OSBORNE FECIT RYDE, in wooden frame on organ, N.A. *XVII.* Inscr. Robert William Collis, L.R.C.P., churchwarden for several years, **1920**, pos. by congregation, friends and patients, maker's name A. L. MOORE & SON, LONDON. W.C., mur., N.A. *XVIII.* Inscr. Arthur Caseford, "WHO MADE THE SUPREME SACRIFICE", **1940**, on altar, S.C. *XIX.* Inscr. recording dedication of [south] chapel in **1948** to commem. the ch. centenary, mur., S.C. *XX.* Inscr. [Rev.] Arthur Osmond Neve, vicar 1954-**1965**, copper, mur., on board, S.A. *XXI.* Inscr. Clara Edith Mathias, M.D., benefactor, **1978**, on pew, N. *XXII.* Inscr. Arthur Henry Jenkins, chorister and verger, 1913-**1983**, on choir stall, C. *XXIII.* Inscr. recording seat of Arthur Henry Jenkins, ch. servant for 50 years, [1913-**1983**], on pew, N. *XXIV & XXV.* Two inscrs. James Stanley Piles, churchwarden emeritus, 1909-**1986**, on prie-dieus, C.

Ch. built, 1845, 1861 and 1874.

BRADING, or SANDOWN, St. John the Evangelist.

I. Inscr. recording gift [of lectern] in **1881** by George Paulson and Elizabeth Wragge, on lectern, N. *II.* Inscr. recording erection of [south aisle] window by friends in mem. of Lance-Cpl. Ashley William Arnell, 1st Volunteer Co. Hampshire Regt., died of enteric fever contracted during the Transvaal War, **1901**, aged 21, mur., below window, S.A. *III.* Inscr. recording ch. re-decoration and reheating; also oak work placed around the chancel, 6 stained glass windows in the east, 1 in the north and a new pulpit 1907-**1912**; [Rev.] John Agg Large, M.A., vicar [1906-1917]; A. Douglas and T.E. Porter, churchwardens, maker's name ROSE & CO. SOUTHAMPTON, mur., on board, N. *IV.* Inscr. Lance-Cpl. A[rthur] G[ordon] C[layton] Cumming, [201135], 2nd/4th Battn. Hampshire Regt., [son of William Hugh Cumming and w. Augusta Mary, **1916**, aged 28], on prie-dieu, C. *V.* Inscr. recording presentation [of south porch doors] by w. in mem. of Herbert George Bull, lifelong chorister, **1963**, mur., S.Porch. *VI.* Inscr. Arthur J. Dixon, **1965**, mur., S.C. *VII.* Inscr. Lily Allen, pos. by Sandown Afternoon Townswomen's Guild, engr. c.**1965**, mur., S.C. *VIII.* Inscr. recording dedication of altar (designed and constructed by John B.R. Rowe from reclaimed orig. ch. furniture) in **2002** by Rt. Rev. Dr. Kenneth [William] Stevenson, Bishop of Portsmouth [1995-], on altar, N.

Ch. built, 1880-1.

BRADING, or SANDOWN, St. Patrick (R.C.).

I. Inscr. [Rev.] John Flynn, priest for 34 years [1909-1943], erected the ch. [1929], **1943**, mur., N.C. *II.* Inscr. [Rev.] Andrew Speakman, priest 1964-1997, **1998**, mur., N.C.

Ch. built, 1929.

BRIGHSTONE, St. Mary the Virgin.

I. Inscr. James Blair Preston, **1858**, mur., S.A. *II.* Inscr. on lozenge-shaped pl. Rev. E. McAll, M.A., restored the ch., **1866**, maker's name BRANNON NEWPORT, mur., on pillar, C. *III.* Inscr. in Lat. George Francis Preston, **1869**, mur., C. *IV.* Inscr. on trapezoidal-shaped pl. Robert H. Inglis Synnot, **1872**, mur., C. *V.* Inscr. Mary Marian Harriet Aylward, **1917**, mur., S.A. *VI.* Inscr. Peter Heylyn Heygate, R.A.F., **1936**, mur., S.A. *VII.* Inscr. [Rev.] Arthur William Harvey Grindon, M.A., Mus.Bac., rector 1934-**1945**, mur., S.C. *VIII.* Inscr. [Rev.] Ralph Headley Charlton, rector 1946-**1972**, and w. Barbara, mur., S.C. *IX.* Inscr. Ann Ellen Attrill, **1980**, mur., S.C.

The monument to Thomas and Francis Wavell, father and son, 1718, recorded by Lewis (1892) as a brass, is in slate.

Ref: *M.B.S. Trans.*, II, p.3.

BROOK, St. Mary the Virgin.

I. Inscr. [Rev.] Collingwood Forster Fenwick, rector 1833-**1856**, mur., C. *II.* Inscr. with sh. [Rev.] Thomas Bowreman, rector for 35 years, last male descendant, 1844, and w. Elizabeth, 1850; also 3rd dau., Jane, 1810, aged 3, and eld dau., Mary Stoddard, w. of Thomas John Blackford, **1864**, mur., N. *III.* Inscr. Mary Elizabeth Frances Browne, **1865**, aged 18 months, mur., N.A. *IV.* Inscr. [Rev.] John Pellew Gaze, M.A., priest for 37 years, [rector 1859-1891], **1891**, maker's name GAWTHORP Sᶜ LONDON, mur., C. *V.* Inscr. William Amelius Aubrey de Vere, 10th Duke of St. Albans, P.C., [1840-]**1898**, maker's name GAWTHORP Sᶜ LONDON, mur., C. *VI.* Inscr. [Rev.] Robert Leslie Morris, M.A., rector 1892-**1909**, mur., C. *VII.* Inscr. recording installation of electric light by brother, [Sir] Hugh [Michael Sealy, 3rd Bart., 1st] Lord Sherwood, in mem. of Sqdn.-Leader Nigel [Richard William] Sealy, [son of Sir Charles Hilton Sealy, 2nd Bart., J.P., D.L., and w. Hilda Lucy, killed on active service, 1902-1943], engr. c.**1950**, mur., N. *VIII*. Inscr. Margaret Stone, organist for 50 years, engr. c.**1975**, on organ, C.

Ref: *Burke's Peerage and Baronetage*, p.2338, p.2431.

Ch. built, 1864.

CALBOURNE, All Saints.

I. Man in arm., c.**1380**; canopy and inscr. lost; once on A.T., slab and tomb destroyed, rel., mur., S.A. Recorded (eff. with canopy) by Tomkins (1796) and (eff. with canopy) by Baigent from Tomkins (1840). *Brettell*, 1st edn., p.201, 2nd edn., between pp.54-5 (after Tomkins); *Brit. Lib. Add. MS. 39987*, f.20r (eff. only), *Add. MS. 39993*, f.L (with pt. of canopy); *M.B.S. Bulletin*, 74, p.285 (from Tomkins); *Staines*, p.7; *Stone*, II, pl.71; *Tomkins*, II, p.55 (with pt. of canopy). Illustration (eff. more complete and canopy) from rubbing in Soc. Antiq. coll. Rubbing (eff. more complete and canopy) in Soc. Antiq. coll. Eff. 1210 x 330 mm, lost canopy 1615 x 455 mm. Style: London B.

II. Inscr. and sh. Arthur Price, rector for 22 years, **1638**, aged 59; his w. Jane pos.; mur., C. *Staines*, p.7. Inscrs. 162 x 470 mm and 48 x 380 mm, sh. 215 x 155 mm.

III. Inscr. Daniel Evance, rector, born in London in 1613, died at Calbourne, **1652**, rect. pl. with figs. of Time and Death, anagram and 8 Eng. vv.; "HANNA HS MOVRNFVL RELICT" pos.; mur., C. *Stone*, II, pl.70. Rect. pl. 350 x 303 mm. Style: London.

IV. Inscr. "Elizabeth, his wife", **1764**, aged 64, copper, mur., C. *V*. Inscr. John Newen, 1760, and w. Charity, 1762; also grandson, John Barlow, surgeon, 1778; dau., Elizabeth Newen, 1783; and son, James Newen, **1800**, maker's name Jas. Wood fecit, on tomb, Churchyard. *VI*. Inscr. with figs. of Time and Death. John Bull, 1792, aged 77, and w. Elizabeth, **1814**, aged 89, maker's name Jas. Wood sculpt., on tomb, Churchyard. *VII*. Inscr. Richard Barlow, grandson of no.*V*, son of Richard and Mary Barlow, 1818, and sister, Mary, **1822**, on tomb with no.*V*, Churchyard. *VIII*. Inscr. Arthur Price, [rector for 22 years], 1638, [aged 59], engr. c.**1845**, C. *IX*. Inscr. Richard Dove, [rector], 1650, engr. c.**1845**, C. *X*. Inscr. Nevill Heath, [rector], 1685, engr. c.**1845**, C. *XI*. Inscr. Thomas Terrell, [rector], 1739, engr. c.**1845**, C. *XII*. Inscr. John Fisher, [rector], 1787, engr. c.**1845**, C. *XIII*. Inscr. Rev. John Vicars, M.A., rector 1877-1912, **1916**, mur., C. *XIV*. Inscr. [Ven.] Lewen Greenwood Tugwell, LL.D., rector 1912-1928, archdeacon 1922-1928, **1937**, maker's name MAILE LTD. ENGRAVERS. 367, EUSTON Rᴰ LONDON, mur., C.

Nos. *VIII-XII* mark the sites of stone slabs which were covered/lost during the restoration of the ch. completed in 1842.

Ref: *Brettell*, 2nd edn., p.149; *Brit. Lib. Add. MS. 39963*, ff.70-2, *Add. MS. 39987*, f.20, *Add. MS. 39993*, f.L; *Haines*, II, p.76; *Heseltine, Heraldry*, p.37; *Long*, p.56; *Manning*, p.31; *M.B.S. Bulletin*, 40, p.166, 48, p.311, 74, p.285; *M.B.S. Trans.*, I, pt.10, p.26, II, pp.3-4, X. p.241; *Mee, Hampshire*, p.440; *M.S.*, p.171; *Norris, Memorials*, p.252, *Pevsner, Hampshire*, p.736; *Simpson*, p.28; *Staines*, pp.3-4; *Stone*, II, p.12; *Tomkins*, II, p.55; *V.C.H., Hampshire*, V, p.221.

Calbourne I

Abijt non Obijt ⦿Præijt non Perijt⦿

HERE LYETH BVRYED THE BODY OF M.ᴿ ARTHVR
PRICE WHO WAS RECTOR OF THIS PARISH 22
YEARES AND DIED THE 26ᵀᴴ OF OCTOBER 1638
BEING AGED 59 YEARES
FOR WHOSE PIOVS MEMORIE IANE HIS DEARE
WIFE CAVSED THIS MEMORIALL

Calbourne II

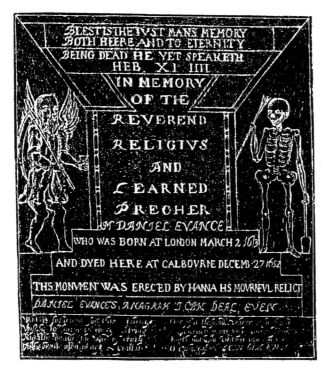

Calbourne III

449

CARISBROOKE, Castle.

I. Inscr. with initials "Q. Eliz", **1598**, above gate.

II. Inscr. Hon. Manners Powlett Orde-Powlett, died an infant, and Hon. Charles Powlett Orde-Powlett, **1806**, aged 13, sons of [Thomas Orde-Powlett, 1st] Lord Bolton, Governor of Isle of Wight [1791-1807], Chapel of St. Nicholas/C. See also Basing no.*III. III.* [Lady] Adela Charlotte Cochrane, [3rd dau. of John Edward Cornwallis Rous, 2nd Earl of Stradbroke, w. of Lt. Thomas Belhaven Cochrane, M.V.O., R.N., Deputy-Governor of Isle of Wight 1899-1910], 1862-**1911**, pos. by brothers and sisters, rect. pl., angel, hf. eff., holding chalice under canopy, inscr. and marg. inscr. with verse and 4 evang. symbols in quadrilobes at corners, Chapel of St. Nicholas/N. Rect. pl. 1015 x 610 mm. *IV.* Inscr. recording presentation of 3 centre lights of east window by friends in mem. of Lady Adela [Charlotte] Cochrane, [1862-**1911**], maker's name F. OSBORNE & CO LTD, on reredos, Chapel of St. Nicholas/C. *V.* Inscr. recording erection of altar painting by [mother], Beatrice, [H.R.H.] Princess Henry of Battenburg in mem. of Lt. [H.R.H. Prince] Maurice [of Battenburg, K.C.V.O., son of H.R.H. Prince Henry of Battenburg, K.G., P.C.], 1st Battn. King's Royal Rifles, killed near Ypres, [1891-]**1914**, on reredos, Chapel of St. Nicholas/C. *VI.* Inscr. recording gift of 2 outer panels of east window in mem. of [Rt. Rev. Dr.] James Macarthur, D.D., Bishop of Bombay 1898-1903, Bishop of Southampton 1903-1921, archdeacon of Isle of Wight, 1906[-1922, 1848-]**1922**, maker's name CULN J. WIPPELL & CO LTD, on reredos, Chapel of St. Nicholas/C.

Ch. rebuilt, 1738; demolished, 1856; rebuilt 1904.

Ref: *Bod. Lib. MS. Gough Misc. Antiq. 15*, f.123; *Burke's Peerage and Baronetage*, p.2546; *M.B.S. Trans.*, II, pp.4-5.

CARISBROOKE, St. Mary.

I. Sh. (4 others lost) for William Keeling, [1578-**1620**], N. Sh. 280 x 250 mm, sh. indents 170 x 145 mm, Purbeck slab 2480 x 1090 mm.

II. Inscr. Margaret, w. of Robert Reeves, **1640**, on tomb, Churchyard. Inscr. 144 x 540 mm.

III. Inscr. Robert Clarke, **1771**, aged 79, and w. Lydia, 1766, aged 65, on tomb, Churchyard. *IV.* Inscr. William Clarke, **1801**, aged 66, and w. Hannah, 1795, aged 56, on tomb, Churchyard. *V.* Inscr. Hannah Mortimer, **1824**, on tomb, Churchyard. *VI.* Inscr. Robert Clarke, **1825**, aged 61, on tomb, Churchyard. *VII.* Inscr. Richard Clarke, 1817, aged 81, and w. Lydia, **1828**, aged 90, on tomb, Churchyard. *VIII.* Inscr. Rev. Edward Dickinson Scott, M.A., of Queen's Coll., Oxford, vicar with the chapels of Newport and Northwood, **1857**, aged 58, Churchyard. *IX.* Inscr. John Mortimer, husband of no.*V*, **1858**, on tomb with no.*V*, Churchyard. *X.* Inscr. with enamelled sh. Col. Sir Faithful Fortescue, Knt., son of John Fortescue, of Buckland Filleigh, Devon and [w.] Susannah, dau. of Sir John Chichester, of Raleigh, "HE WAS A DISTINGUISHED ROYALIST OFFICER AND FOUGHT IN SEVERAL BATTLES OF THE GREAT CIVIL WAR. AT THE RESTORATION HE BECAME A GENTLEMAN OF THE PRIVY CHAMBER TO KING CHARLES THE SECOND. HAVING LEFT LONDON TO AVOID THE CONTAGION OF THE PLAGUE HE RETIRED SOON AFTERWARDS BEING THEN OF A GREAT AGE", died at Bowcombe, 1666, pos. in **1866** by eld.

Carisbrooke, Castle *III*

Carisbrooke, St. Mary *I*

male representative, Thomas Fortescue, Lord Clermont, [1815-1887], maker's name HART & SON, LONDON, mur., on marble, N. See also Buckland Filleigh, Devon no.*V. XI*. Inscr. with verse. Col. William Sadler, 4th King's Own Regt., 1863, and w. Constantia Emma, **1874**, mur., S.A. *XII*. Inscr. recording lectern and table pos. by parishioners and relations in mem. of [Rev.] Edmund Bouchier James, M.A., vicar for 34 years [1858-1892], **1892**, mur., N. *XIII*. Inscr. Capt. Hugh McIntosh, 16th Light Dragoons and 101st [Regt. of] Foot, 1832, and w. Elizabeth, 1858; also grandson, Gen. Sir Henry [Dermot] Daly, G.C.B., [C.I.E.], **1895**, and w. Susan, 1874, maker's name A. & N. AUX C.S.L. LONDON, mur., N. *XIV*. Inscr. with verse and regt. insignia. Lt.-Col. Henry Alan Vallings, 29th Punjabis, [son of Henry Vallings and w. Marie, husband of] Gertrude, [killed] in action at Mbuyuni, East Africa, **1915**, aged 49, [buried at Taveta Military Cemetery, Kenya]; also son, Alan Frederick Dudley, died at Dalhousie, India, 1904, aged 7 months, mur., on marble, N. *XV*. Inscr. Harris Nicolas Pinnock, 1846-**1922**, and w. Augusta Isabel, 1847-1919, pos. by children, maker's name Sidney Hunt del, F. Osborne & Co., L^{D.}, London, mur., S.A.

INDENTS & LOST BRASSES. 16. Indent, inscr., on tomb with no.*II*, Churchyard. Inscr. 330 x 190 mm. 17. Indent, 2 inscrs., on tomb, Churchyard. Inscrs. 115 x 250 mm. 18. Lost ?indents, "several old stones robbed of their effigies and inscriptions". Recorded by Suckling (1832).

Ref: *Brit. Lib. Add MS. 18478*, f.41; *Hampshire History*, III, p.55; *Heseltine, Heraldry*, p.37; *M.B.S. Trans.*, II, pp.4-5; *M.S.*, p.171; *Soc. Antiq. MS. 943/1*; *Staines*, pp.4-5.

CHALE, St. Andrew.

I. Inscr. recording dedication of 5 windows and 2 bells in **1898** by George Arnold Hearn, of U.S.A., to commem. ancestors, mur., S.C. *II*. Inscr. Grace Arnold Hearn Wheeler, **1899**, on organ, S.C. *III*. Inscr. Joseph Graves, B.A., M.B., medical officer of health, Isle of Wight Rural District, **1907**, maker's name H. OSBORNE RYDE, mur., S.A. *IV*. Inscr. Hilda Somerville, **1908**, Churchyard. *V*. Inscr. Major Harold Frederick Harrison Strugnell, R[oyal] M[arines] L[ight] I[nfantry], **1919**, mur., S.A. *VI*. Inscr. Gladys Elizabeth Mary Way, **1919**, mur., S.C. *VII*. Inscr. Gladys Elizabeth Mary Way, **1919**, Churchyard. *VIII*. Inscr. [Rt. Rev. Dr.] Gerard Trower, [M.A., Hon. D.D.], Bishop of Likoma and N[orth-]W[est] Australia [1902-1927], rector [1927-1928, 1860-]**1928**, mur., C. *IX*. Inscr. Doris Eleanor Joye Hawthorn, **1929**, mur., S.A. *X*. Inscr. [Rev.] Charles William Heald, [M.A.], rector for 41 years [1885-1926], **1930**, mur., C. *XI*. Inscr. Henry Way, 1936, and w. Christina Isabella, **1955**, Churchyard.

COWES, EAST, St. James.

I. Inscr. recording gift of font by mother, A.P. P[owys] in mem. of Philip Barrington Lybbe Powys, **1868**, aged 20, on font, N. *II*. Inscr. John Prendergast Vereker, 3rd Viscount Gort of Limerick, Baron Kiltarton [of Gort], representative peer for Ireland, Col. of Limerick Artillery Militia, M.P. for Limerick, died at East Cowes Castle, [1790-]1865; also 1st w. Maria, eld. dau. of Standish O'Grady, 1st Viscount Guillamore, died at Dublin, 1854; also 5 children, Charles, died at Rockbarton, Limerick, [1817-]1819; Capt. Richard Vereker, 60th King's Royal Rifles, died at Rangoon, Burma, [1829-]1865; Capt. Adolphus Edward Vereker, 20th Regt. [of Foot], died at Yokohama, Japan, [1833-]1864; Maria Corinna, w. of Lt.-Col.

452

Christian Montieth Hamilton, 92nd Gordon Highlanders, died at Hafton House, Argyll, 1856; and Julia Georgina, died at London, [1856]; also 2nd w. Elizabeth Mary, only dau. and h. of John Jones, solicitor of Westminster, widow of George Tudor, M.P. for Barnstaple, built the chancel, died at East Cowes Castle, **1880**, maker's name MATTHEWS & SONS, 135 OXFORD ST, LONDON W, mur., Vestry. *III.* Inscr. Octavia, yst. dau. of George Shedden, of Spring Hill, 1817-**1900**, on lectern, N. *IV.* Inscr. John Fox, Sunday school teacher for over 60 years, sidesman for 21 years, **1911**, aged 79, pos. by subscription, mur., S.A. *V.* Inscr. Henry William Glasspell, chorister for 17 years, **1911**, aged 33, mur., C. *VI.* Inscr. Richard Lihou Robertson, vicar's [church]warden for 37 years, **1926**, aged 82, on font cover, N. *VII.* Inscr. on lozenge-shaped pl. James Sholto Cameron Douglas, D.M.(Oxon.), 1879-**1931**, on altar, S.C./S.A. *VIII.* Inscr. recording dedication of children's corner in **1931** by Rt. Rev. [Dr.] Ernest Neville Lovett, D.D., Bishop of Portsmouth [1927-1937]; panelling made by A. Hounsell and J. Jackman, sidesmen; wood given by H.W. Brading in mem. of mother, Lydia Brading, 1930; Rev. [Dr.] R[eginald] S[tewart] Moxon, [M.A.], D.D., vicar [1929-1937]; Rev. P[hilip] H[oward] Duke Baker, B.A., [curate 1929-1934]; J. Taylor and H.W. Brading, churchwardens, mur., on panelling, S.C./S.A. *IX.* Inscr. recording erection of screen by husband, Col. Starling Meux Benson, [J.P., 17th Lancers], in mem. of Eleanor, Viscountess Gort, [dau. and coh. of Robert Smith Surtees, of Hamsterley Hall, Rowlands Gill, Newcastle-upon-Tyne, w. of John Gage Prendergast, 5th Viscount Gort, J.P.], of East Cowes Castle, **1933**, on screen, N. *X.* Inscr. Thomas William Smith, chorister for 66 years, **1938**, aged 73, mur., C. *XI.* Inscr. H. (Harry) W. Brading, eld. son of W[illia]m H. Brading, 1866-**1955**, on chair, N.A. *XII.* Inscr. Archer Coles Brading, son of W[illia]m H. Brading, 1881-**1957**, on chair, N.A. *XIII.* Inscr. Ronald Jackman, organist 1897-1950, 1961, and w. Patience, **1961**, on choir stall, C. *XIV.* Inscr. Annie Lampard, **1964**, on lectern, N. *XV.* Inscr. Uffa Fox, C.B.E., R.D.I., naval architect, "WORLD FAMOUS AS THE DESIGNER, BUILDER AND HELMSMAN OF SMALL BOATS WHOSE PERFORMANCES WERE ASTOUNDING TO ALL. THE AIRBORNE LIFEBOAT OF WORLD WAR II WAS HIS MOST SATISFYING ACHIEVEMENT AS MANY LIVES WERE SAVED", 1898-**1972**, mur., S.A. *XVI.* Inscr. recording presentation [of bench] by [father], Patricia and Hilda in mem. of Ivy May Jane Moorby, **1973**, on bench, Churchyard. *XVII.* Inscr. in raised letters. Charles Reader, **1989**, aged 86, on bench, Churchyard. *XVIII.* Inscr. in raised letters. Grace Reader, **1991**, aged 86, on bench with no.*XVII*, Churchyard.

Ref: *Burke's Peerage and Baronetage*, pp.1135-7; *Who's Who,* 1967, p.1075.

Ch. built, 1831-3 and rebuilt 1868.

COWES, WEST, Holy Trinity.

I. Inscr. Sarah, w. of Rev. [Maximilian] Geneste, **1856**, mur., C. *II.* Inscr. Rev. Maximilian Geneste, incumbent for 23 years, **1860**, mur., C. *III.* Inscr. recording restoration of ch. by husband and children in mem. of Julia Maw, **1879**, mur., C. *IV.* Inscr. Midshipman Algernon Charles Willes Watson, R.N., died on board H.M.S. Bellerophon, **1887**, aged 17½, buried at Charlottetown P[rince] E[dward] Island, [Canada], maker's name THOMAS PRATT & SONS ENGRAVERS, mur., on marble, N. *V.* Inscr. Philip Percival, Royal Horse Guards, **1897**, pos. by friends and members of the Royal Yacht Squadron, mur., on marble, N. *VI.* Cross surmounting inscr. Lt.-Col. George Charles Keppel Johnstone, Grenadier Guards, **1912**, pos. by widow and children, mur., on marble, N. *VII.* Inscr. Henry Haren Wheeler, sidesman and churchwarden for 46 years, **1927**, pos. by friends, mur., N. *VIII.* Inscr. recording rebuilding of organ in **1987** in mem. of Sir [John William)] Max Aitken, [2nd] Bt., D.S.O., D.F.C., [eld. son of William Maxwell, 1st Baron Beaverbrook, P.C.], Royal Yacht Squadron member, 1910-1985, on organ, N.

Ref: *Burke's Peerage and Baronetage*, p.222.

Ch. built, 1832 and 1862.

COWES, WEST, St. Faith.

I. Inscr. recording presentation of organ in **1909** by Rev. Reginald A[rthur] R[ichard] White, M.A., [F.R.G.S., F.Z.S.], and [w. Alice Gilberta], on organ, C. See also Titchfield no.*VI.*

Ch. built, 1909.

COWES, WEST, St. Mary the Virgin.

I. Inscr. James Moore, **1839**, aged 74, and [w.] Elizabeth, 1820, aged 59, mur., S.A. *II.* Inscr. recording west nave window pos. by Mary, widow of Rev. W.H. Parker, M.A., and Harriet, widow of Sir Charles Fellows, in mem. of parents John Eames, **1851**, and [w.] Harriet, 1836; also brother, Robert W[illia]m Eames, 1848, and [grandparents], James Davis, 1786, and [w.] Mary, 1822, all buried in nave vault, N. See also Newport, or Barton no.*II.* *III.* Inscr. Helen, w. of Pascall Atkin, **1853**, aged 35, mur., S.A. *IV.* Inscr. Elizabeth, w. of Admiral [Edward] Ratsen, **1860**, mur., N.A. *V.* Inscr. Pascall Ratsen Atkin, **1862**, aged 20, mur., S.A. *VI.* Inscr. Elizabeth, w. of James Moore, **1865**, aged 55, mur., S.A. *VII.* Inscr. Admiral Edward Ratsen, **1867**, mur., N.A. *VIII.* Inscr. Guybon Henry Damant, M.A., Bengal Civil Service, deputy-commissioner and political officer of the Naga Hills Assam, killed by the Nagas while in the discharge of his duty at Khonoma, **1879**, mur., N.A. *IX.* Inscr. recording gift [of lectern] by 8 children in mem. of [Rev.] John Breeks Atkinson, M.A., incumbent for 47 years, **1880**, aged 82, and w. Jane Isabella, 1855, aged 49, on lectern, N. *X.* Inscr. Emily Octavia, yst. dau. of Henry Baynes Ward, **1883**, mur., Tower. *XI.* Inscr. Harriet, last surviving dau. of George Ward, widow of Capt. J.L. Beckford, R.N., **1886**, mur., Tower. *XII.* Inscr. Atweek Penton, churchwarden for 14 years, **1886**, pos. by congregation, maker's name COX & BUCKLEY LONDON, mur., N. *XIII.* Inscr. James Duff Ward, Bengal Civil Service, grandson of George Ward, **1891**, mur., Tower. *XIV.* Inscr. Henrietta Mary, sister of James Duff Ward, **1897**, maker's name OSBORNE ENG^R RYDE, mur., Tower. *XV.* Inscr. Charity Florence, sister of James Duff Ward, **1900**, maker's name OSBORNE ENG^R RYDE, mur., Tower. *XVI.* Inscr. [Dr.] Thomas Arnold, D.D., headmaster of Rugby School 1828-1842, born at West Cowes, privately baptised 1795, 1795-1842, maker's name H. OSBORNE ENG^R RYDE, engr. c.**1900**, mur., S.A. *XVII.* Inscr. Henry James Damant, resident for 55 years, **1901**, aged 83, maker's name A & N AUX C.S.L. LONDON, mur., N.A. *XVIII.* Inscr. in raised letters. Sub-Lt. Victor William Cooke, R.N.R., 2nd and last surviving son of John William Cooke and [w.] Hildegard Eugenia, accidentally killed at sea, **1903**, aged 18, copper, mur., N.A. *XIX.* Inscr. in raised letters. John Parsons Rubie, churchwarden 1877-1890, **1905**, mur., N.A. *XX.* Inscr. Elizabeth Johnson, w. of Henry James Damant, **1906**, aged 83, maker's name A & N AUX C.S.L. LONDON, mur., N.A. *XXI.* Inscr. Henry Edward Civil, superintendent of Cross Street Sunday School, **1912**, pos. by teachers and scholars, maker's name W. BALLARD COWES, mur., S.A.

XXII. Inscr. recording dedication of panelling in **1913** in mem. of Robert Taylor, organist, and William Robert Rowe, chorister, on organ, C. *XXIII.* Inscr. recording erection of mosaic in **1916** by parishioners in mem. of [Rev.] Andrew Hamilton McElwee, [M.A., B.C.L., curate 1901-1902 and] vicar 1902-1915, mur., N. *XXIV.* Inscr. with regt. insignia. Capt. Donald White Ratsey, [D Co.] 8th Battn. Hampshire Regt. (Isle of Wight Rifles), killed at Suvla Bay, 1915, [aged 31]; Capt. Clayton Ratsey, [C Co.] 8th Battn. Hampshire Regt. (Isle of Wight Rifles), killed at Suvla Bay, 1915, [aged 29]; and Lt. Stephen Gilbert Ratsey, [8th Battn.] Hampshire Regt. (Isle of Wight Rifles), killed in the 1st Battle of Gaza, **1917**, [aged 24, buried in the Gaza War Cemetery]; sons of Thomas White Ratsey and [w.] Lucy Margaret, maker's name H. OSBORNE ENGR RYDE, mur., on marble, N.A. *XXV.* Inscr. Henry Charles Mogridge, **1918**, aged 79, mur., N.A. *XXVI.* Inscr. with regt. insignia. [Pte.] Arthur Frederick Richardson, [57521], 10th Battn. Worcestershire Regt., died of wounds while a prisoner of war [at Bruillet, France], **1918**, aged 19, [buried at Marfaux British Cemetery, France]; also Thomas Edward Richardson, chief engineer S.S. Sangara, died at Kotonou, West Africa, 1913, aged 32, [sons of Thomas Richardson and w. Sarah], maker's name H. OSBORNE FECIT RYDE, mur., on board, N.A. *XXVII.* Inscr. Rev. A[rthur] S[elwyn] Harrison, M.A., vicar 1920-**1924**, pos. by parishioners, maker's name W. BALLARD ENGR COWES, mur., C. *XXVIII.* Inscr. recording gift of electric blowing instrument by sons and dau. in mem. of W.E. Moon, organist 1872-**1924**, on organ, C. *XXIX.* Inscr. recording eff. carved in olive wood and cross made from part of orig. oak beam from Winchester Cathedral in mem. of T.H. Clark, engr. c.**1930**, mur., S.A. *XXX.* Inscr. Reginald William Wyatt, lost at Eddystone Lighthouse, 1940, and Ronald James Wyatt, lost off Farne Islands, **1940**, maker's name F. OSBORNE & CO LTD LONDON W.C.1., mur., N.A. *XXXI.* Inscr. John William Bromley, organist for 60 years, organist at the ch. 1944-**1969**, on organ, C.

Ref: *V.C.H., Hampshire*, V, p.271.

Ch. built, 1867.

COWES, WEST, St. Thomas of Canterbury (R.C.).

I. Inscr. Valentine Eglé Exshaw, **1888**, maker's name John Hardman & Co. Birmm., mur., N.

Ch. built, 1796.

FRESHWATER, All Saints.

I. Man in arm., of the Compton family, c.**1365**, with sh. on jupon, scroll in Fr. from hands; canopy and inscr. lost; formerly mur., on board, Vestry, now rel., mur., N.A. *Bouquet, Church Brasses*, fig.20, p.52; *M.B.S. Portfolio*, III, pl.27; *Portfolio Book*, pl.48; *Staines*, p.9; *Stone*, II, pl.83. Eff. 870 x 195 mm, slab 1105 x 255 mm. Style: London A.

II. Inscr. Josias Rogers Woodford, **1811**, on tomb, Churchyard. *III.* Inscr. Benefaction of Joseph Squire, by will dated **1846** left £100 to the rector to use for the poor of the par. annually, mur., on marble, N. *IV.* Inscr. recording erection of pulpit in mem. of Col. the Hon. F[rancis] Grosvenor-Hood, [grandson, of Henry, 2nd Viscount Hood], commanded the Grenadier Guards at Alma, [killed] in the trenches at Sebastopol, [1809-]**1854**, on pulpit, N. *V.* Inscr. Philip Stanhope Worsley, M.A.,

Freshwater, All Saints I

456

Freshwater, All Saints 21

Freshwater, All Saints 22

1866, maker's name BENHAM & FROUD, LONDON, mur., on stone, C. *VI.* Inscr. Capt. William Pearson Crozier, R.N., **1868**, mur., C. *VII.* Inscr. Col. Rawson John Crozier, B.N.I., **1871**, mur., C. *VIII.* Inscr. recording erection of east window by widow, Caroline, in mem. of [husband], William George Shedden, 1872; also parents, Admiral of the Fleet Sir Gordon Eden Hamond, [2nd Bart.], G.C.B., [1779-]1862, and w. Elizabeth, [dau. of John Kimber, of Fowey, Cornwall], 1872; also brothers, Vice-Admiral Sir Andrew Snape Hamond-Graeme, [3rd Bart., 1811-]**1874**, and Cmdr. Gordon Eden William Hamond, R.N., [1814-]1847, C. *IX.* Inscr. Frances Margaret Crozier, **1876**, mur., C. *X.* Inscr. recording erection [of chancel] window by w. Sarah in mem. of Samuel Burkett, contractor, restored the ch., **1882**, mur., C. *XI.* Inscr. Julia, w. of Admiral Richard Crozier, **1883**, mur., on marble, C. *XII.* Inscr. Pearson Frank Crozier, died at sea, **1892**, mur., C. *XIII.* Inscr. recording dedication of 6 bells (5 given by Hon. Mrs. Grosvenor and Mrs. Martin, Lord Tennyson, Col. Crozier, Mr. and Mrs. Healey, Mr. and Mrs. Morrian and Mrs. Tankard) in **1895**; [Rev.] Joseph Merriman, [M.A.], D.D., rector [1891-1905]; Alfred Hollis, M.D. and Jonathan Gilbert, churchwardens, mur., N. *XIV.* Inscr. recording insertion of stained glass in **1902** by Francis W. Pixley and Emmeline Watson Munro in mem. of parents, Thomas Pixley, 1891, and w. Caroline, 1891, mur., N.A. *XV.* Inscr. Margaret Elizabeth Worsley, **1905**, maker's name BENHAM & FROUD, LONDON, mur., on marble, N.A. *XVI.* Inscr. Emily Ursula Ann Clogstoun, died at Ajinere, **1907**, mur., on marble, C. *XVII.* Inscr. in raised letters. Richard Bowland Cross, **1911**, mur., N. *XVIII.* Inscr. in raised letters. Alfred Hollis, M.D., churchwarden for 25 years, **1915**, mur., C. *XIX.* Inscr. in raised letters. Major Thomas Ffoster Chamberlain, R[oyal] A[rtillery], churchwarden, **1918**, mur., N. *XX.* Inscr. William J. Young, chorister, **1949**, on choir stall, C.

INDENTS & LOST BRASSES. 21. Indent, man in arm. and w., double canopy, inscr., 2 scrolls and 2 shs., c.1385; formerly Churchyard, now mur., S.C. Possibly Roger de Affeton. Recorded (lost) by Tomkins (1796). *Sadler, Dorset and Hampshire,* appx. I, p.45 (drg.); *Stone,* II, pl.83. Male eff. 940 x 250 mm, female eff. 900 x 250 mm, canopy 1700 x 810 mm, inscr. 115 x 910 mm, scrolls 30 x 100 mm, dext. sh. 150 x 105 mm, sin. sh. 150 x 105 mm, slab 2335 x 1100 mm. Style: London A. 22. Indent, lady, scroll from hands, single canopy, marg. inscr., c.1390; formerly Churchyard, now mur., S.C. *Sadler, Dorset and Hampshire,* appx. I, p.47 (drg.). Eff. c.1100 x c.280 mm, canopy c.1700 x c.390 mm, marg. inscr. c.1700 x c.390 x 30 mm, slab 2010 x 785 mm. Style: London A.

Ref: *Brit. Lib. Add MS. 39965,* f.470; *Burke's Peerage and Baronetage,* p.1145, p.1366; *Haines,* II, p.76; *Heseltine, Heraldry,* p.37; *History of the Isle of Wight,* 1781, p.268; *Jeans,* p.56; *M.B.S. Trans.,* I, pt.10, p.26, II, pp.5-6; *Mee, Hampshire,* p.455; *M.S.,* p.171, p.755; *Norris, Memorials,* p.54, *Pevsner, Hampshire,* p.744; *Sadler, Dorset and Hampshire,* appx. I, pt.2, pp.45-7; *Staines,* p.5; *Stone,* II, pp.32-3; *Tomkins,* II, p.67; *V.C.H., Hampshire,* V, p.245; *Worsley,* p.268.

FRESHWATER, St. Agnes.

I. Inscr. Rt. Hon. Sir Alfred Comyns Lyall, K.C.B., G.C.I.E., [1835-]**1911**, maker's name *J. WIPPELL & C⁰ L^{TD} EXETER & LONDON,* mur., N. *II.* Inscr. Eleanor, dau. of Sir Henry Taylor, widow of Rev. C[harles] S[eymour] Towle, **1911**, maker's name *J. WIPPELL & C⁰ L^{TD} EXETER & LONDON,* mur., N. *III.* Inscr. in raised letters. Susan, widow of Lewis Ffytche, **1913**, aged 88, mur., N. *IV.* Inscr. [Cpl.] Francis Bygott, [15/74], 15th [Battn.] West Yorkshire Regt. [(Prince of Wales's Own), eld. son of James Bygott and w. Mary], killed in action in France,

1916, aged 21, [buried at Auchonvillers Military Cemetery], mur., N. *V.* Inscr. Hon. Arthur Ralph Douglas Elliot, 2nd son of [William Hugh Elliot], 3rd Earl of Minto, [K.T., D.L., barrister-at-law, M.P. for Roxburghshire 1880-1892, and for Durham 1898-1906, editor of the *Edinburgh Review* 1895-1912, 1846-]**1923**, maker's name *Singers Frome*, mur., N. *VI.* Inscr. Marjorie Lovis Tennyson, dau. of Stephen [Louis] Simeon, grand-dau. of Sir John Simeon, [3rd] Bart., M.P. [for Isle of Wight], w. of William [Edward Frank] Macmillan, god-dau. of Alfred, [1st] Lord Tennyson, **1934**, mur., N. *VII.* Inscr. recording gift of seats in choir and other seats in the ch. by dau. and grandchildren in mem. of Kathleen Millicent Fryer, 1898-**1968**, mur., C.

Ref: *Burke's Peerage and Baronetage*, p.1836, p.2448.

Ch. built, 1908.

FRESHWATER, or TOTLAND, Christ Church.

I. Inscr. recording gift [of lectern] in **1875** by Capt. W. Wood, R[oyal] A[rtillery], on lectern, N. *II.* Inscr. Catherine Elizabeth, widow of Rev. George May, vicar of Lyddington, Wilts., 1873; also dau., Anne Elizabeth Catherine, **1877**, pos. by dau.-in-law and sister-in-law, Anna Maria May, mur., N. *III.* Inscr. "THE WOOD OF THIS LYCHGATE WAS TAKEN FROM THE TIMBERS OF H.M.S. THUNDERER 74 GUNS WHICH FOUGHT ON THE LEE LINE AT TRAFALGAR", engr. c.**1900**, bronze, in wooden frame on lychgate, Churchyard. *IV.* Inscr. Frederic Wildman Burnett, **1904**, on lychgate, Churchyard. *V.* Inscr. Samuel John Thacker, A.R.I.B.A., died in London, **1905**, aged 73, [buried] at Rottingdean, [Sussex], mur., N. *VI.* Inscr. George Pickering, 1877, aged 89, and w. Lydia Frances, **1906**, aged 74, pos. by family, maker's name GAWTHORP Sᶜ LONDON, mur., N. *VII.* Inscr. in raised letters recording installation of electric lighting in **1937** by w. in mem. of James Ernest Neecham, C.B.E., mur., C. *VIII.* Inscr. Edith M.V. Osborne, organist 1911-**1947**, on organ, C. *IX.* Inscr. Rev. F[rederick] G[eorge] Ralph, [A.L.C.D.], vicar 1960-**1974**, on door, S.Porch. *X.* Inscr. recording presentation of bell by family in mem. of Henry J. Rouse, Mara L. Rouse and Emid L. Rouse, engr. c.**1975**, mur., C. *XI.* Inscr. recording gift of doors by Waring family in mem. of parents, [William S.O. Waring and w. Ada Blanche], brother, [Major] Sam[uel Carden Ondeslowe] Waring, M.C. and Bar, [71096, 2nd Battn. King's Own Royal Regt. (Lancaster), 1941, aged 25], and nanny, Annie Stephens, engr. c.**1975**, on door, N. *XII.* Inscr. Guy Chandos Harcourt, O.B.E., 1903-**1976**, on prie-dieu, C.

Ch. built, 1875, 1888, 1905 and 1910.

FRESHWATER, or TOTLAND, St. Saviour (R.C.).

I. Inscr. with regt. insignia. Lt. Charles John Wingfield Pakenham, 2nd Battn. Hampshire Regt., [son of Major Charles Pakenham, of Headon Hall, Alum Bay], killed in action at the Dardanelles, **1915**, aged 23, mur., S.A. *II.* Inscr. with regt. insignia. Sgt. William Edmund White, [4/10151], 10th Battn. Durham Light Infantry, [son of William White and w. Mary], killed in action in France, **1916**, aged 38, mur., N.

Ch. built, 1923.

GATCOMBE, St. Olave.

I. Inscr. Katherine, dau. of Richard Ouiat, w. of Capt. Thomas Urry, **1644**, N. Inscr. 167 x 465 mm, slab 1845 x 815 mm.

II. Inscr. and sh. Jane, w. of Tho[mas] Urry, gent., **1650**, aged 82, N. Inscr. 282 x 563 mm, sh. 208 x 186 mm, slab 2030 x 920 mm.

III. Inscr. with ach. Penelope, w. of Thomas Urry, **1665**, [aged 20], worn, N. Inscr. 224 x 314 mm, slab 1890 x 945 mm.

IV. Inscr. recording renovation of organ in **1951** in mem. of Lt.-Col. Sir [(Claud)] Vere [Cavendish] Hobart, [2nd] Bart., D.S.O., O.B.E., J.P., D.L., [only son of Sir Robert Henry Hobart, 1st Bart., K.C.V.O., C.B.], worshipped in the ch. [for more than 25 years, 1870-]1947, on organ, C. *V.* Inscr. recording gift of lamp bracket in mem. of [Rev.] Thomas Cyril Lister Farrah, rector 1954-**1957**, mur., C. *VI.* Inscr. recording dedication of audio system in mem. of [Rev.] James Evans, rector 1965-**1973**, mur., C. *VII.* Inscr. [recording gift of bench] by A. and F. Taylor and F. and A. Burt in mem. of Chorley, Helen and George Burt, engr. c.**1975**, on bench, Churchyard. *VIII.* Inscr. Cicily Mary Oldham, engr. c.**1975**, on bench, Churchyard. *IX.* Inscr. Richard Henry Upton and [w.] Alice Maud Ann, engr. c.**1975**, on bench, Churchyard. *X.* Inscr. Arthur John William and [w.] Ada, engr. c.**1975**, on bench, Churchyard. *XI.* Inscr. Dorothy Brown, organist for more than 50 years, 1904-**2000**, on organ, C.

INDENTS & LOST BRASSES. 12. Indent, inscr. and 2 shs.; in 2005 partly covered by choir stalls, C. Inscr. 120 x 525 mm, shs. 150 x 125 mm, slab 915 visible x 1080 mm.

Ref: *Burke's Peerage and Baronetage*, p.1349; *Hampshire History*, III, pp.57-8; *Sadler, Dorset and Hampshire*, appx. I, pt.2, p.52.

GODSHILL, All Saints.

I. Inscr. Richard Legge, eld. son of Thomas Legge of Stenburie, **1641**, aged 33, on tomb, Churchyard. Inscr. 167 x 442 mm.

II. Inscr. Rebecca, dau. of Thomas Hardley and [w.] Rebekah, **1823**, aged 22, on tomb, Churchyard. *III.* Inscr. Rebekah Hardley, **1834**, on tomb, Churchyard. *IV.* Inscr. Thomas Hardley, **1842**, on tomb with no.*III*, Churchyard. *V.* Inscr. recording erection of [north aisle] window by friends and parishioners in mem. of [Rev.] Thomas Ratcliffe, M.A., curate for 14 years [1853-1867] and vicar for 25 years [1867-1892], **1892**, mur., N.A. *VI.* Inscr. recording dedication of [chancel] window by surviving children, Wentworth H. Ratcliffe, Hilda F.R. Ratcliffe and Mildred E. Ratcliffe, in mem. of Frances S. Ratcliffe, **1931**, mur., C.

INDENTS & LOST BRASSES. 7. Indent, civilian, inscr. and 2 shs., c.1500, nearly effaced, N.A. *Sadler, Dorset and Hampshire,* appx. I, p.50 (drg.). Eff. c.525 x 165 mm, inscr. 85 x 400 mm, shs. 130 x 100 mm, slab 2030 x 850 mm. 8. Indent, ?lady, 4 shs. and marg. inscr., nearly effaced, N.A. *Sadler, Dorset and Hampshire,* appx. I, p.48 (drg.). Eff. 760 x 330 mm, shs. 145 x 125 mm, marg. inscr. 1700 x 760 x 30 mm, Purbeck slab 1740 visible x 1060 mm.

HERE LYETH THE BODIE OF KATHE
RINE VRRY WIFE OF CAPTAINE THO
MAS VRRY, DAVGHTER OF RICHARD
OVIAT. SHEE DECEASED THE 8TH OF
MARCH ANNO DNI. 1644

Gatcombe *I*

HERE LYETH INTERRED THE
BODY OF IANE VRRY THE WIFE
OF THO. VRRY GENT. WHO. DE-
PARTED THIS LIFE. Y 8TH OF IVLY
1650 AGED 82 YEARES

Gatcombe *II*

HEARE LYETH INTERRED THE BODY OF PENELOPE VRRY Y WIFE OF THOMAS
VRRY WHO DEPARTED THIS LIFE. Y EIGHTH DAY OF
MAY 1665 IN Y 21 YEARE OF HER AGE

Gatcombe *III*

461

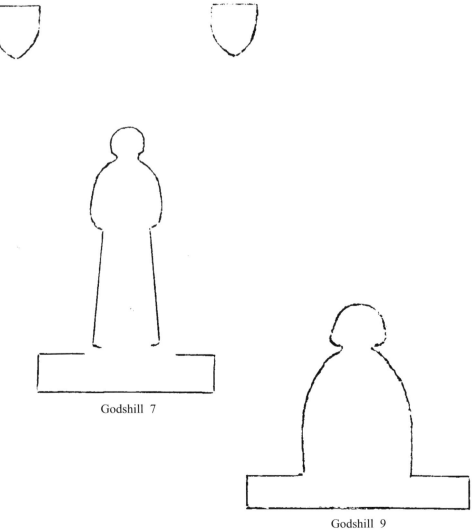

HERE SLEEPETH Y BODY OF RICHARD
LEGGE Y ELDEST SONNE OF THOMAS
LEGGE OF STENBVRIE WHO CHEARETVLLY
GAVE HIS SOVLE TO CHRIST HIS SAVIOVR
Y 15TH OF DECEMBER AO DNI 1641 AGED
33 YEARES

Godshill 1

Godshill 7

Godshill 9

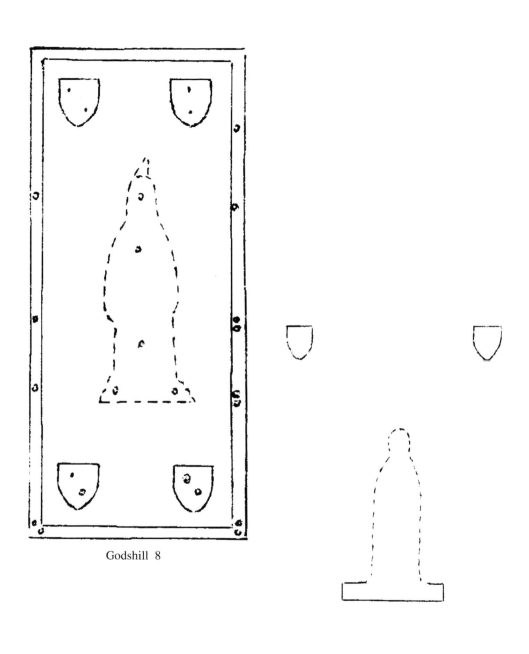

Godshill 8

Godshill 10

9. Indent, priest, hf. eff. and inscr., c.1500, S.Tr. *Sadler, Dorset and Hampshire,* appx. I, p.49 (drg.). Eff. c.305 x 195 mm, inscr. 65 x 455 mm, slab 1490 x 620 mm. 10. Indent, ?priest, inscr. and 4 shs., nearly effaced, S.Tr. *Sadler, Dorset and Hampshire,* appx. I, p.51 (drg.). Eff. c.650 x 225 mm, inscr. 75 x 455 mm, shs. 160 x 125 mm, slab 2130 x 915 mm. 11. Indent, inscr., S.Tr. Inscr. 60 x 450 mm, slab 1825 x 820 mm. 12. Lost brass, inscr. and sh. Anne, dau. of Sir John Leigh, widow of Sir James Worsley, 1557, N.A. Possibly no.7. Recorded (lost) by Oglander. 13. Lost brass, ?civilian and w., inscr. _____ Fry, N.C. Recorded (effs. loose in "ye stores" with inscr. lost) by Oglander. 14. Lost brass, prior and inscr., S.Tr. Recorded by Oglander. 15. Lost indents, "several brasses have been stripped off from the old monuments, which are said to have belonged to the families of Aula, Heyno and Fry". Recorded by Worsley (1781), by Tomkins (1796) and by Oglander.

Ref: *Brit. Lib. Add MS. 39966,* f.56; *Long,* pp.184-5; *M.B.S. Trans.,* II, p.6; *M.S.,* p.171; *Sadler, Dorset and Hampshire,* appx. I, pt.2, pp.48-52; *Soc. Antiq. MS. 943/1; Staines,* p.5; *Tomkins,* II, p.131; *Worsley,* p.213.

GURNARD, (see NORTHWOOD).

HAVENSTREET, (see ARRETON).

KINGSTON, St. James (redundant, now a residence).

Richard Mewys, **1535**, in civil dress, inscr. (mutil.), 4 sons and 1 sh.; inscr. palimp., on rev. another inscr. to Richard Mewys, wasted work; rel., C.; now deposited with Isle of Wight Museum Service, Ryde (q.v.). *M.B.S. Bulletin,* 64, p.85 (obv. and rev.); *Palimpsests,* pl.228 (rev.); *Staines,* cover; *Stone,* II, pl.90. Style: London G.

I. Inscr. Sir Henry Bruce Meux, [3rd] Bart., of Theobald's Park, Herts., descendant of the ancient family of Meux of Meux, France, lord of the manor, 1856-**1900**, pos. by widow, [Valerie Susie], Lady Meux, maker's name H. OSBORNE ENG^R RYDE, mur., C. Recorded by Bradbury (1984).

Ref: *Brit. Lib. Add. MS. 39967,* f.165; *Haines,* II, p.76; *Heseltine, Heraldry,* p.37; *M.B.S. Bulletin,* 64, p.84; *M.B.S. Trans.,* II, p.5; *Mee, Hampshire,* p.460; *M.S.,* p.171; *Palimpsests,* L510-1, pp.xlv-xlvi; *Staines,* p.5; *Stone,* II, p.40; *Tomkins,* II, p.109; *V.C.H., Hampshire,* V, p.251.

Ch. essentially, 1872; declared redundant, 1985; converted, 1991.

LAKE, (see BRADING).

MOTTISTONE, SS. Peter and Paul.

I. Inscr. Robert Bassett, died at Calcutta, **1865**, mur., N.C.

NEWCHURCH, All Saints.

I. Inscr. with ach., **1678**, maker's name Robert Marks of London, on sundial on window splay, N.A.

II. Inscr. recording presentation of sundial in **1815** by Maurice George Bissett, John Denham and George Young, churchwardens; Rev. Welenhall Sneyd, curate, maker's name G. Nicholls Sc, on stone with no.*I*, N.A. *III.* Inscr. Maria Smith, died at Temple Place, Strood, Kent, **1874**, pos. by brother, C[harles] Roach Smith, [F.S.A.], mur., S.A. *IV.* Inscr. recording restoration of ch. (built in 11th cent. by William Fitzosborne) in **1883** by Rev. A[lfred] C[ecil] Dicker, [B.A.], vicar [1881-1893], mur., S.Tr. *V.* Inscr. Charles Roach Smith, F.S.A., died at Temple Place, Strood, Kent, **1890**, mur., S.A. *VI.* Inscr. Miss M.W. Connolly, engr. c.**1965**, on lectern, N. *VII.* Inscr. recording presentation of [south porch] doors in **1966** by Arnold Francis Webb, on door, S.Porch. *VIII.* Inscr. Arnold Francis Webb, **1975**, and [w.] Ellen Maud, 1968, on door with no.*VII*, S.Porch.

NEWCHURCH, or VENTNOR, Holy Trinity.

I. Inscr. Mary Margaret Noott, **1867**, mur., S.A. *II.* Inscr. Joseph Tanner, **1869**, mur., N.A. *III.* Inscr. Charles Caulfield Fiske, **1870**, mur., S.A. *IV.* Inscr. recording restoration to health of Prince Albert Edward, Prince of Wales, **1872**, mur., S.A. *V.* Inscr. Mary Nathison, **1874**, mur., S.A. *VI.* Inscr. Rev. James Allan Pak, **1875**, mur., N.A. *VII.* Inscr. Harriet C. Currie, **1877**, mur., N.A. *VIII.* Inscr. Henry Ingalton, **1877**, mur., N.A. *IX.* Inscr. Capt. J.B. Hennell and Lt. W.F. Heund, **1879**, mur., S.A. *X.* Inscr. with sh. John Baratty Martin, 1st [church]warden, **1890**, maker's name HART SON PEARD & Cᵒ LONDON, mur., N. *XI.* Inscr. William Guppy, **1898**, mur., N. *XII.* Inscr. Elizabeth Ann Kirtley, **1898**, mur., C. *XIII.* Inscr. Hon. Katherine Scott, **1899**, mur., N. *XIV.* Inscr. Capt. George A.F.A. Whitehead, **1908**, maker's name HART SON PEARD & Cᵒ LONDON, mur., N. *XV.* Inscr. Thomas Gibbs, churchwarden, **1909**, maker's name HART SON PEARD & Cᵒ LONDON, mur., N. *XVI.* Inscr. Ellen Olivia, w. of Rev. Arthur Lewis Babington Peile, C.M.O., M.A., [1st vicar 1862-1889, chaplain-in-ordinary to Queen Victoria 1884-1901], **1910**, mur., N. *XVII.* Inscr. Rev. Arthur Lewis Babington Peile, C.M.O., M.A., 1st vicar [1862-1889, chaplain-in-ordinary to Queen Victoria 1884-1901], **1911**, mur., C. *XVIII.* Inscr. Mary Catherine Harvey, **1913**, and Beatrice Maud Clayton, 1912, mur., N. *XIX.* Inscr. Alfred Bardie Peile, died in West Australia, 1913; Frederick Stuart Peile, died in Queensland, **1916**; and Lawrence Arthur Babington Peile, died in Ceylon, 1913, mur., N. *XX.* Inscr. [Rev.] Charles Falkingham Clayton, M.A., **1917**, mur., C. *XXI.* Inscr. 2nd Lt. Dudley Hammond Black, [20th Battn. attd.] 17th [Battn.] King's (Liverpool) Regt., [son of Thomas Fraser Black and w. Annie], **1918**, aged 28, maker's name G. MAILE & SON, LTD 367 EUSTON RD. N.W.1, mur., N. *XXII.* Inscr. 2nd Lt. Edward Harold Clayton, R.A.F., [98th Sqdn., son of Rev. Arthur Prestwood Clayton, M.A., vicar 1889-1918, and w. Mary Georgina], severely wounded and died, **1918**, buried at Valenciennes [(St. Roch) Communal Cemetery, France], mur., N. *XXIII.* Inscr. Gurney Sinclair Sutton, [30872], 6th [Battn.] Dorset[shire] Regt., [son of Robert Sutton and w. Rose Ellen, killed in action] at Flers, **1918**, aged 30, [buried at Bulls Road Cemetery, Flers, France], mur., N. *XXIV.* Inscr. James Henry Boosey, verger for 50 years, **1918**, mur., N.A. *XXV.* Inscr. May Wilson Mitchell, **1924**, maker's name J. WIPPELL & Cᵒ Lᵀᴰ, mur., N. *XXVI.* Inscr. John Liversay Whitehead, M.D., physician, **1924**, mur., N. *XXVII.* Inscr. Arthur Narnham, **1943**, mur., N.

Ch. built, 1860-2.

NEWCHURCH, or VENTNOR, Our Lady and St. Wilfrid (R.C.).

I. Inscr. Edmund Randolph, 1889, and w. Ellen Catherine, **1911**, mur., N.A.

Ch. built, 1871.

NEWCHURCH, or VENTNOR, St. Catherine.

I. Inscr. Robert Keatley Burt, **1864**, aged 3, Churchyard. *II.* Inscr. Mary Burts, **1866**, aged 4 months, Churchyard. *III.* Inscr. Irene Wilberforce Burt, **1873**, aged 1 month, Churchyard. *IV.* Inscr. H.B. Tuttrell, M.R.C.S., **1878**, mur., C. *V.* Inscr. Lucy, w. of Rev. C[harles] C[ourtney] Bluett, M.A., **1895**, on reredos, C. *VI.* Inscr. Kenneth Mackay Sinclair Coghill, killed in action at Krugersdorp, [South Africa], **1896**, mur., C. *VII.* Inscr. recording erection of organ in **1910** through [legacy] of Rev. Warneford S[eymour] T[rimmere] Gompertz, [M.A., of Hazelbrae], on organ, C. *VIII.* Inscr. with verse. Alfred Westley Faulkener, choirmaster and organist 1926-**1959**, on organ, C.

Ch. built, 1837, 1849 and 1897.

NEWCHURCH, or WROXALL, St. John the Evangelist.

I. Inscr. recording dedication of reredos by widow and children in mem. of [Rev.] Alfred Wight, M.A.(Oxon.), voluntarily gave services to the par. for 9 years [curate 1890-1898], engr. c.**1905**, mur., C. *II.* Inscr. Rev. Reginald Jolliffe Roberts, M.A., 1st vicar [1905-1908], **1911**, aged 77, [buried] at Ventnor, pos. by parishioners, maker's name H. OSBORNE FECIT RYDE, mur., N. *III.* Inscr. with regt. insignia, sword and tepee. Capt. Edward Charles Morris Layton, [11th Regt. South African Infantry, son of Charles Layton and w. Elizabeth], served in the South African War 1900-1902 and in the German South West African Campaign 1914-1915, killed in action at Kikumi, German East Africa, **1916**, [aged 48, buried at Dar Es Salaam War Cemetery, Tanzania], maker's name A&N AUX C.S.L LONDON, mur., on board, N. *IV.* Inscr. recording installation of sound system in **1989** in mem. of Olive Dove and Joyce Howell, mur., N.

Ch. built, 1875-7.

NEWPORT, or BARTON, St. Paul.

I. Inscr. John Eames, of West Cowes, **1851**, aged 78, mur., N. *II.* Inscr. John Eames, of West Cowes, 1851, aged 78, pos. in **1852** by dau., Mary Davis Parker, mur., N. See also West Cowes, St. Mary the Virgin no.*II.* *III.* Inscr. Rev. W.H. Parker, M.A., 1st incumbent and benefactor, **1853**, aged 60, buried in vault adjoining the chancel wall, mur., N.A. *IV.* Inscr. recording altar rails and tessellated pavement pos. by children in mem. of William Baron Mew, **1887**, maker's name OSBORNE ENG^R RYDE, mur., N. *V.* Inscr. recording gift of lectern in **1890** by children in mem. of Maria Bartlett, w. of William Major Cooke, of Bellecroft, on lectern, N. *VI.* Inscr. recording gift of [north aisle] window in **1890** by children in mem. of William Major Cooke, of Bellecroft, and w. Maria Bartlett, on board on window splay, N.A. *VII.* Inscr. recording dedication [of prie-dieu] in

1892 by husband in mem. of Caroline, dau. of John Cooke, of Bellecroft, w. of Charles Paget-Blake, M.D., R.N., of Torquay, Devon, 1824-1854, on prie-dieu, N. *VIII.* Inscr. recording erection of [north aisle] window in **1896** by grandchildren in mem. of William Major Cooke, of Bellecroft, and w. Maria Bartlett, on board on window splay, N.A. *IX.* Inscr. recording dedication of [west nave window] in mem. of Mary Nunn, widow of Capt. Thomas Harvey, 69th Regt., founded Broadlands Home in the par., **1897**, aged 62, mur., below window, N. *X.* Inscr. W. Russell Cooke, of Bellecroft, **1903**, mur., S.Porch. *XI.* Inscr. in raised letters. Rev. William Henry Nutter, M.A., vicar for 19 years [1890-1909], 1836-**1909**, pos. by friends and parishioners, copper, mur., S.A. *XII.* Inscr. Edward William Way, choirmaster and organist for many years, 1874-**1949**, and w. Grace, 1873-1949, on board on organ, S.A. *XIII.* Inscr. recording installation and gift of new pedal board in **1950** by dau., Winifred Tucker, in mem. of Walter William Dore, lifelong chorister, on organ, N. *XIV.* Inscr. recording refurbishment of organ in **1990** through generosity of Miss Grace Millgate and parishioners, on organ with no.*XIII*, N. *XV.* Inscr. recording gift of piano in **1997** in mem. of Rita Page and Chris Rees, choirmaster, on organ with nos.*XIII & XIV*, N.

Ch. built, 1844.

NEWPORT, St. John the Baptist.

I. Inscr. recording presentation of organ in **1890** by Miss Fanny Louisa Tull, "IN THE HOPE IT MAY BE THE MEANS OF ASSISTING THE CHOIR AND CONGREGATION IN SINGING THEIR PRAISES", on organ, Gallery/N. *II.* Inscr. on lozenge-shaped pl. recording gift of sounding board in **1893** by a family member and parishioners in mem. of Rev. Richard Hollings, B.A., vicar for 30 years, on pulpit, N. *III.* Inscr. Elizabeth Carter, [ch.] worker, **1895**; [Rev.] Henry Lewis, vicar [1892-1898]; W. Horam and John Roach, churchwardens, on altar, C. *IV.* Inscr. recording presentation of pulpit desk and communion desks in **1896** by children in mem. of James Eldridge, solicitor, twice mayor and town clerk for 27 years, "TOOK A PROMINENT PART IN THE BUILDING OF THIS CHURCH AND IN ESTABLISHING THE SUNDAY SCHOOL", and w. Maria, on pulpit, N. *V.* Inscr. recording presentation [of missal stand] by children in mem. of James Eldridge, and w. Maria, engr. c.**1896**, on missal stand, C. *VI.* Inscr. recording renovation of organ, additional stops and addition of choir organ in **1908** by Miss Fanny Louisa Tull in mem. of sister, Miss Caroline Tull, 1906, and by James Eldridge in mem. of w. Frances, 1907, on organ with no.*I*, Gallery/N. *VII.* Inscr. recording erection of communion rails by Lucy J. Mackinon in mem. of husband, Brigade-Surgeon Charles [Mackinon], A.M.D., "WORSHIPPED AND PUBLICLY PARTOOK OF HOLY COMMUNION FOR THE LAST TIME IN THIS CHURCH ON WHITSUNDAY **1914**" administered by son, Rev. W[alter] H[enry] Mackinnon, [M.A.], vicar [1913-1944], mur., C. *VIII.* Inscr. recording presentation of pulpit in **1915** by St. John's Mens Bible Class members, on pulpit, N. *IX.* Inscr. recording presentation of electric blower (used for the 1st time in **1941**) by Miss A. Dawson Horan in mem. of father, Henry William Horan, devoted to the ch. for 60 years, churchwarden for 18 years, on organ with nos.*I & VI*, Gallery/N. *X.* Inscr. recording erection of chancel oak panelling by friends and parishioners in mem. of Rev. W[alter] H[enry] Mackinnon, M.A., vicar 1913-**1944**, mur., C. *XI.* Inscr. recording gift of chancel lighting in **1949** in mem. of Rev. E[dgar] W[illiam] T[yler] Greenshield, missionary to esquimeaux of Blacklead Island, [Canada], 1904-1915, [curate 1916-1917], died at Redcar, Yorks., 1938, aged 60, mur., C. *XII.* Inscr. recording presentation of choir stalls in mem. of Harold Henry Gould, 1882-**1959**, on choir stall, N. *XIII.* Inscr. Dorothy Welby-Pryer, organist 1921-**1959**, bronze, on organ with nos.*I, VI & IX*, Gallery/N. *XIV.* Inscr. recording construction and dedication of vestries in **1964** in mem. of

Ernest Barton, churchwarden, and Charles Packham, benefactor, mur., Narthex. *XV*. Inscr. recording gift [of bookstall] by husband for 40 years devoted service to the ch. by Jessie Burt, 1898-**1970**, on bookstall, Narthex. *XVI*. Inscr. F.C. Cooper, 1976, and A.V. Cooper, **1977**, copper, on lectern, N. *XVII*. Inscr. Charles John Rose, 1924-**1991**, on missal stand, N.

Ch. built, 1837.

NEWPORT, St. Thomas of Canterbury (R.C.).

I. Inscr. Elizabeth Heneage, founder [of the ch.] and benefactress, 1800, pos. in **1961** by clergy "AND FAITHFUL", N. *II*. Inscr. recording overhaul, cleaning and decoration of organ in **1992** (par. bicentenary year) by bequest of Mrs. Ruby Eleanor Madeline Garnett in mem. of parents, John Hogan and [w.] Elizabeth, on organ, Gallery/N.

Ch. built, 1791.

NEWPORT, St. Thomas the Apostle.

I. Inscr. Elizabeth, 2nd dau. of King Charles I, 1650, aged 14, engr. **1793**; palimp., on rev. emblems of mortality and lightly engraved inscr., "HERE LYETH THE BODY OF MASTER GEORGE SHERGOLD LATE MINISTER OF NEWPORT WHO DURING SIXTEEN YEARS IN DISCHARGE OF HIS OFFICE STRICTLY OBSERVED THE TRUE DISCIPLINE OF THE CHURCH OF ENGLAND AND DISEIRING YE DEAD BODIE SHOULD BE BURIED IN GOD'S HOUSE APPOINTED TO BE INTERERED IN THIS PLACE HE DYED UNIVERSALLY LAMENTED AND ESTEEMED JANUARY XXIII 1707"; copper, mur., in reversible frame on pillar, N. *Palimpsests*, pl.195 (rev.). *II*. Inscr. on 2 pls. Thomas Sewell, 1842, aged 68, and [w.] Jane, **1848**, aged 74, mur., below window, S.A. *III*. Inscr. with island insignia recording laying of ch. foundation stone in **1854** by H.R.H. the Prince Albert; Francis Pittis, mayor; [Rev.] George Henry Connor, M.A., minister; Edward Way and Henry Loosemore, churchwardens, mur., in stone frame, N.A. *IV*. Inscr. Katharine Maude, w. of [Rev.] George Henry Connor, M.A., vicar, **1859**, aged 30, mur., on marble, S.A. *V*. Inscr. with verse. Susan Mary Mayo, died at Yarmouth, **1869**, [buried] in Newport Cemetery, pos. by sister, mur., S.A. *VI*. Inscr. recording gift of altar pavement in **1870** by children in mem. of Anne, widow of Major William Firebrace, 58th Regt. [of Foot], maker's name RICHARDSON, ELLSON & CO. LONDON, mur., C. *VII*. Inscr. on triangular-shaped pl. [Rev.] George H[enry] Connor, M.A., vicar; J. Wood and F.J. Etheridge, churchwardens, **1870**, on font cover, S.A. *VIII*. Inscr. with sh. recording laying up of colours (carried by Royal Bombay Fusiliers for 26 years) in **1871** in the presence of H.R.H. the Prince Arthur, K.G., K.T., K.P., [G.C.M.G.], His Imperial and Royal Highness Frederick William, Crown Prince of the German Empire and Her Imperial and Royal Highness Victoria, Crown Princess of the German Empire and Princess Royal of Great Britain and Ireland; Col. W.S. Furneaux, mur., on marble, C. *IX*. Inscr. with crosier and mitre. [Rt. Rev.] Samuel Wilberforce, D.D., rector of Brightstone, rural dean, [Bishop of Oxford 1845-1869], Bishop of Winchester [1869-1873], killed by a fall from his horse, [1805-]1873, pos. in **1873** "TO COMMEMORATE THE CONFIRMATION AND LAST GENERAL ORDINATION HELD BY HIS LORDSHIP IN THIS CHURCH", maker's name HART SON PEARD & C⁰ LONDON, mur., on marble, C. See also Alverstoke no.*VIII*, Alverstoke, or Gosport, Fort Brockhurst no.*XXXIII*, Hinton Ampner no.*IX*, Petersfield no.*VI*, Ryde, or Swanmore, St. Michael and All Angels no.*III* and Winchester Cathedral no.*X*. *X*. Inscr. on star-shaped pl. with regt. insignia

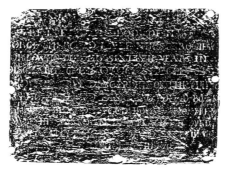

Newport, St. Thomas the Apostle *I* palimpsest reverse

Ryde, St. Mary (R.C.) *I*

recording laying up of colours (106th Bombay Light Infantry Regt., formerly 2nd Bombay European Regt.) after presentation of new colours in **1874** by Her Imperial and Royal Highness Victoria, Crown Princess of the German Empire and Princess Royal of England; Lt.-Col. R.R. Gillespie, mur., on marble, C. *XI.* Inscr. in raised letters. [Very Rev.] George Henry Connor, M.A., vicar 1852-1882, Dean of Windsor [1882-1883, 1822-**1883**], pos. by friends and parishioners, on altar rail, C. *XII.* Inscr. [Very Rev.] George Henry Connor, M.A., vicar 1852-1882, rural dean, chaplain of St. Nicholas-within-Carisbrooke Castle [1875-1882], Dean of Windsor, registrar of the Order of the Garter and domestic chaplain to Queen Victoria [1882-1883], 1822-**1883**, mur., on marble, C. *XIII.* Inscr. with verse recording probable removal of no.*I* from churchyard and pos. in 1793 over the tomb of Princess Elizabeth; restored in **1886** by Miss Mary Shergold, of Brighton, [Sussex], mur., above no.*I*, N. *XIV.* Inscr. "*Underneath in a lead coffin rest y*ᵉ *Remains of Elizabeth 2*ᵈ *Daughter of King Charles 1*ˢᵗ *Obiit Sep*ᵗ *8th 1650 cettat 14*", engr. c.**1886**, on step, C. *XV.* Inscr. Arthur Southeron Estcourt, LL.B., town and county council clerk 1853-**1892**, pos. by friends and townsmen, maker's name CAKEBREAD ROBEY & CO. STOKE NEWINGTON LONDON, mur., S.A. *XVI.* Inscr. in raised letters with bust in relief. [Ven.] Henry Haigh, M.A., vicar 1882-1890, archdeacon of Isle of Wight 1886-1906, 1837-**1906**, bronze, mur., S.A. *XVII.* Inscr. Theobald Bourke O'Fflahertie, son of Rev. T[heobald] R[ichard] O'Fflahertie, [B.A.], vicar of Capel, Surrey, [1848-1895], sacristan, died at sea en-route to South Africa, **1907**, aged 52, pos. by friends, maker's name H. OSBORNE FECIT RYDE, mur., on marble, S.A. *XVIII.* Inscr. Theobald Bourke O'Fflahertie, **1907**, aged 52, on cupboard, S.A. *XIX.* Inscr. Mondego Mary, dau. of Malcolm MacGregor and [w.] Frances, widow of Robert Gunter Wetton, 1878; also Robert Gunter Wetton, 1868, and dau. Marion, widow of Gen. J.W.A. Kennedy, R.M., **1929**, on linen and vestment press, Vestry. *XX.* Inscr. recording dedication of stained glass screen in **1935** erected with gift to the vicar and churchwardens of £300 by the will of James Henry Streynsham Gilbert Whalley Brooks in mem. of the Brooks family, on screen, N.A. *XXI.* World War II memorial; Newport Church of England Boys School, on display case, S.A. *XXII.* Inscr. Queenie Maud Witham, **1959**, on faldstool, C. *XXIII.* Inscr. Tom Carter, verger, **1960**, on chair, N.A. *XXIV.* Inscr. Reginald Thomas Brackey, **1964**, on prie-dieu, N.A. *XXV.* Inscr. recording gift of prayer desk and chair by friends in mem. of Frank Chiverton, reader, **1975**, on prie-dieu, N.A. *XXVI.* Inscr. recording installation of great mixture in **1994** in recognition of 50 years service by Kathleen E. Lower, L.R.A.M., A.R.C.M., L.T.C.L., organist, on organ console, S.A. *XXVII.* Inscr. recording presentation of [mobile bookcase] in mem. of Norman Arthur Chiverton, 1934-**2002**, on mobile bookcase, S.A.

INDENTS & LOST BRASSES. 28. Lost brass, inscr. John Skinner, 1713, aged 64, on tomb, Churchyard.

Ref: *Andrews, C., A Guide to Southampton, Netley Abbey, the Isle of Wight . . . .* , 1831, p.69; *B.A.A. Jour.*, XI, p.274; *Brit. Lib. Add. MS. 14296*, f.5, *Add MS. 18478*, f.44; *Hampshire Antiquary*, I, p.103; *Hampshire History*, III, p.45; *Palimpsests*, M446-1, p.xiv; *Soc. Antiq. MS. 943/1.*

Ch. built, 1854-5.

NEWTOWN, Holy Ghost.

I. Inscr. with crucifix on separate pl. Margaret Fleming Gibson, **1911**, Churchyard. *II.* Inscr. recording gift of altar rails by w. in mem. of Major Howard Graeme Gibson, R[oyal] A[rmy]

M[edical] C[orps, son of Arthur Stanley Gibson and w. Mary], died at Abbeville, France, **1919**, [aged 35, buried at Abbeville Communal Cemetery Extension, France], mur., on panelling, N. *III & IV.* Two inscrs. [Rev.] Edwyn Francis Heaton Thomas, [B.A.], priest 1922-**1923**, on candleholders, C. *V.* Inscr. with crucifix on separate pl. Thomas Dyer, 1926, and w. Selina, **1927**, Churchyard. *VI.* Inscr. recording gift of lectern in **1928** by friends and parishioners in mem. of Rev. Henry Rice Venn, M.A., vicar 1878-1919, 1925, mur., N. *VII.* Inscr. with crucifix on separate pl. Harry Brook, **1929**, aged 66, Churchyard. *VIII.* Inscr. with crucifix on separate pl. George Rideout Gibson, **1939**, Churchyard. *IX.* Inscr. with crucifix on separate pl. Marion Sophie Gibson, **1943**, Churchyard. *X.* Inscr. with crucifix on separate pl. Sybil Gibson, **1945**, Churchyard. *XI.* Inscr. with crucifix on separate pl. Lisa Caroline Anley, **1950**, Churchyard. *XII.* Inscr. recording presentation [of pictures] in mem. of Jane E. Chandler, died as a result of a road accident, **1959**, aged 7, mur., on board below pictures, N. *XIII.* Inscr. John Lawrence Paris, killed in an aircraft crash, **1990**, mur., on board, C. *XIV.* Inscr. George Arthur Smith, 1920-**1991**, on bench, Churchyard. *XV.* Inscr. Philip John Dennington, 1920-**2001**, on altar rail, C.

Ch. built, 1835.

NITON, St. John the Baptist.

I. Inscr. Sarah Sweet Kirkpatrick, 1874, and dau., Susan Elizabeth Ellen Daly, died at Bombay, [India], **1874**, mur., S.C. *II.* Inscr. Fanny Augusta Mitchell-Innes, **1902**, maker's name GAWTHORP S^C LONDON, mur., N. *III.* Inscr. on base of stepped cross. [Rev.] William Sells, M.A., rector 1890-**1918**, mur., C. *IV.* Inscr. [Pte.] Robson Cameron Forster, [12/2292, Auckland Regt.], died in the Military Hospital, Auckland, New Zealand, from wounds received in 1916 in France, **1919**, aged 35, [buried at Hamilton East Public Cemetery, Hamilton, New Zealand], mur., on board, N.A. *V.* Inscr. Henry Charles Haynes, A.B., **1926**, mur., S.A. *VI.* Inscr. Robert Thomas Disney Leith, 1898, and [w.] Mary Charlotte Julia, **1926**, mur., N. *VII.* Inscr. John Weston Sells, D.S.C., **1927**, maker's name K. FIRTH & CO, mur., N.A. *VIII.* Inscr. Euphemia Sells, **1929**, maker's name J. WIPPELL & C^O L^TD, mur., N.A.

NORTHWOOD, or GURNARD, All Saints.

I. Inscr. recording laying of corner stone in **1892** by Capt. Thomas Keith Hudson, R.N. and Mrs. Hudson, of The Dell; [Rev.] John Bailey, M.A., vicar [1884-1901] and rural dean of West Wight [1890-1901; Rev.] John C[ook] Ince, curate [1889-1896]; F.P. Loftus Brock, F.S.A., architect; J. Ball & Son, builders, mur., west wall outside N. *II.* World War I memorial in raised letters (48 names), **1919**, maker's name H. OSBORNE FECIT RYDE, mur., on board, N. See also Northwood no.*IV.* *III.* Inscr. Gertrude Elizabeth Hewitt, **1935**, mur., on panelling, N. *IV.* World War II memorial (8 names), mur., N. *V.* Inscr. recording planting in **1986** by Solent Flower Club, of Cowes, in mem. of Miss M. Roberton, Churchyard. *VI.* Inscr. recording restoration of [nave] windows in **1994** in mem. of Tom King and [w.] Mary, mur., on board, N.

Ch. built, 1892-3.

NORTHWOOD, St. John the Baptist.

I. Stepped cross surmounting inscr. recording renewal of tower bell in **1875** by family in mem. of [Rev.] Shadrack Seaman, curate for 22 years, mur., Tower. *II.* Inscr. John Redfern, of Woodside, 1895, and w. Harriette, 1883, pos. in **1897** by children, maker's name *J. WIPPELL & C*O *L*TD *EXETER & LONDON*, mur., Tower. *III.* Inscr. Stanley William [Redfern], died at Forest Row, Sussex, 1905, aged 55; also Frank William [Redfern], died at Bournemouth, 1887, aged 36, and John [Redfern], died at Nice, [France], 1885, aged 37, sons of no.*II*, pos. in **1907** by brother and sister, Ernest and Annie, maker's name *J. WIPPELL & C*O *L*TD *EXETER & LONDON*, mur., Tower. *IV.* World War I memorial in raised letters (48 names), **1919**, maker's name H. OSBORNE FECIT RYDE, mur., on board, N.A. See also Northwood, or Gurnard no.*II*. *V.* Inscr. A.J. Philpot, **1928**, on pew, N. *VI.* Inscr. recording gift of chancel floodlighting by Albert Ernest Long, of Palmes Farm, Wooton, in mem. of w. Hilda Ann, **1944**; also son, [Lance-Cpl.] Bernard David Long, [7901450, Royal Armoured Corps, 1st King's Dragoon Guards], killed in action in Italy, 1944, aged 25, [buried at Arezzo War Cemetery, Italy], mur., on board, C. *VII.* Inscr. recording presentation [of lectern] by parishioners in mem. of Rev. H[arold] J[ules] Nichols, rector 1947-**1952**, on lectern, N. *VIII.* Inscr. Arthur Charles Chapman, ch. councillor and sidesman for many years, **1962**, on chair, N.A. *IX.* Inscr. Kemp Day, M.B.E., 1890-**1967**, and [w.] Eva Dorothy (née Noyce), 1892-1943, of Cowes, mar. in the ch. 1916, on pew, N. *X.* Inscr. Sydney and Mabel Beasley, **1968**, on missal stand, C. *XI.* Inscr. recording gift [of reredos] in **1971** in mem. of R.M.E. Kennedy; in 2005 loose in ch. safe. *XII.* Inscr. [Rev.] Canon Herbert Thomas Cotter, [M.A.], served the ch. during retirement, 1891-**1976**, on pew, N. *XIII.* Inscr. Natasha Dawn Hailes-Furber, **1985**, aged 9, on table, N.A. *XIV.* Inscr. Kathleen Townsend, 1911-**1996**, on choir stall, C. *XV.* Inscr. Raymond George Price, [church]warden 1964-**1998**, on pulpit, N. *XVI.* Inscr. David [Emery] Gascoyne, poet, Chevalier du Legion D'Honneur, 1916-**2001**, on missal stand, S.C.

OAKFIELD, (see RYDE).

RYDE, or OAKFIELD, St. John the Baptist.

I. Inscr. in Lat. recording erection of [chancel] window in mem. of Florence Jane, dau. of Charles Brett, gent., **1868**, aged 21, maker's name HART, SON, PEARD & C° LONDON, mur., C. *II.* Inscr. Rev. Symeon Taylor Bartlett, LL.B. of Clare Coll., Camb. and University of Camb., rector of Everleigh, Wilts. 1857-1877, born at East Stoke, Notts., died at Ravenhurst, 1812-**1877**, maker's name MATTHEWS & SONS, 377 OXFORD STREET LONDON W, mur., on marble, N.Tr. *III.* Inscr. recording pulpit and prayer desk pos. by son, George Arthur Brett, in mem. of Charles Brett, J.P., of The Wood, St. John's Park, **1877**, mur., C. *IV.* Inscr. John Peter Gassiot, F.R.S., LL.D., of St. John's House and Clapham Common, Surrey, J.P. for Surrey, 1797-**1877**, mur., N.Tr. *V.* Inscr. George Arthur Brett, **1878**, on lectern, N. *VI.* Inscr. recording erection of north aisle in **1879** by children in mem. of Frances Maria, dau. of John Heard, chief justice of the Courts of Probate and Divorce of Massachussetts, widow of Grenville Temple Winthrop, 1878, maker's name HART, SON, PEARD & C° LONDON, mur., N.A. *VII.* Inscr. Edward Feben, churchwarden, **1880**, pos. by public subscription, mur., N. *VIII.* Inscr. Harry William Scott Gibb, R[oyal] A[rtillery], **1880**, ·ged 84, mur., below window, N.Tr. *IX.* Inscr. recording erection of [north aisle] window by w. ·race in mem. of Henry Sandford Pakenham Mahon, of Strokestown, Ireland and Westbrook, ·23-**1893**, on pew, N.A. *X.* Inscr. recording erection of [north aisle] window by

Grace Pakenham Mahon, of Strokestown, Ireland and Westbrook, in mem. of dau., Florence Pakenham Mahon, of Westbrook, **1900**, on pew, N.A. *XI.* Inscr. Rev. Henry Ewbank, M.A., vicar 1867-1898, **1901**, aged 73, pos. by parishioners, maker's name OSBORNE ENGRAVER RYDE, mur., C. *XII.* Inscr. recording erection of lychgate in **1902** by parishioners in mem. of Rev. Henry Ewbank, M.A., vicar 1867-1898, [1901, aged 73], maker's name OSBORNE ENG^R RYDE; in 2005 loose in C. *XIII.* Inscr. H.R., w. of Gen. Drew, **1903**, maker's name OSBORNE ENG^R RYDE, mur., N.Tr. *XIV.* Inscr. recording erection of [north aisle] window by Grace Pakenham Mahon, of Strokestown, Ireland and Westbrook, in mem. of yst. dau., Maud Pakenham Mahon, of Westbrook, **1903**, on pew, N.A. *XV.* Inscr. recording presentation [of stall] by parents, Col. and Mrs. F.D. Walters, in mem. of Capt. Hugh de Lancey Walters, South Lancashire Regt., died in India, **1906**, and Lt.-Cmdr. Francis Elliott Walters, R.N., drowned in Salonika Bay on H.M.S. Ardent, 1899, on stall, C. *XVI.* Inscr. with enamelled ach. Lt.-Gen. [Sir] Somerset John [Calthorpe], 7th Lord Calthorpe, K.C.B., served as A.D.C. to Field Marshal Lord Raglan during the Crimean War, present at the Battles of Alma, Balaclava and Inkerman and during the siege of Sebastopol, commanded the 5th Dragoon Guards 1861-1869, chairman of Isle of Wight County Council from commencement 1890-1898, 1831-**1912**, maker's name CULN GAWTHORP & SONS LONDON, mur., in marble frame, S.C. *XVII.* Inscr. recording erection of [south] chapel in **1914** by widow, [Eliza Maria, only dau. of Capt. Frederick Chamier, R.N., widow of Capt. Frederick Carew] in mem. of no.*XVI*, maker's name CULN GAWTHORP & SONS LONDON, mur., S.C. *XVIII.* Inscr. Grace Pakenham Mahon, of Strokestown, Ireland and Westbrook, 1827-**1914**, buried at Cannes, France, pos. by dau., Henrietta Foster, on pew, N.A. *XIX.* Inscr. Cmdr. Douglas Methuen Forsyth, R.N., worshipped in the ch. for 35 years, 1847-**1915**, mur., S.Tr. *XX.* Inscr. with regt. insignia. Capt. G[eorge] C[harles] S[holto] MacLeod, [2nd Battn.] Black Watch [(Royal Highlanders), killed in action] in France, **1915**, aged 37, [buried at Bethune Town Cemetery, France], maker's name OSBORNE · FECIT · RYDE, mur., S.Tr. *XXI.* Inscr. Thomas Lindall Winthrop and w. Charlotte Ann; also daus., Augusta Clinton Winthrop and Mary Winthrop Mason, engr. c.**1915**, on pew, N.A. *XXII.* Inscr. with verse and crucifix in relief. Lance-Cpl. James Ernest Tuckwell, [330144], 1st Battn. Hampshire Regt., [son of E. Tuckwell, of Grome Cottage, Elmfield], wounded at Gaza and died, **1917**, aged 22, [buried Port Said War Memorial Cemetery, Egypt], maker's name GAWTHORP & SONS LONDON, mur., on board, S.Tr. *XXIII.* Inscr. with verse and regt. insignia within border of oak leaves and acorns. Lt. Donald Howard Harrison, [C Battery, 306th Brigade], Royal Field Artillery, son of George Howard Harrison and w. Margaret Annie, of Thornton, killed in action at Sailly, France, **1918**, buried at Estaires [Communal Cemetery], France, maker's name H. OSBORNE FECIT RYDE, mur., on board, S.Tr. *XXIV.* Inscr. with verse and R.N. insignia. [Stoker 1st Class] Arthur Percy Orchard, [K/15239, son of William Orchard], husband of Alice Georgina, [of Jacinth Cottage, Bettesworth Road], lost his life on duty in H.M. Submarine G.8, "HE DIED A HERO", **1918**, aged 25, maker's name H. OSBORNE FECIT RYDE, mur., on board, S.Tr. *XXV.* Inscr. with regt. insignia. Gunner Robert Martin Wheeler, [141795, D Battery, 79th Brigade], Royal Field Artillery, [son of Robert John Wheeler and w. Eliza], chorister and server, killed in action at Hermies, France, **1918**, aged 23, mur., on board, C. *XXVI.* Inscr. [Rev.] Thomas John Puckle, [M.A.], of St. John's House, **1920**, pos. by congregation, on pew, N.A. *XXVII.* Inscr. John Yates Paterson, B.A. of Clare Coll., Camb., London and Woodlynch, St. John's Park, 1840-**1927**, maker's name A.&N. C.S.L. LONDON, mur., on pillar, N. *XXVIII.* Inscr. Frank Lyndon Tutle, chorister for over 60 years, **1931**, on choir stall, C. *XXIX.* Inscr. with verse and enamelled ach. in relief. Admiral of the Fleet the Hon. Sir Arthur Gough-Calthorpe, G.C.B., G.C.M.G., C.V.O., [2nd son of no.*XVI*], Grand Officer of the Legion of Honour, commanded 2nd Cruiser Sqdn. 1914-[1916], 2nd Sea Lord 1916, C.-in-C. Mediterranean 1917[-1919], High Commissioner of Constantinople

[1918-1919] and concluded Armistice with Turkey 1918, C.-in-C. Portsmouth, 1919[-1923], 1st and principal Naval A.D.C. to [George V] 1924-[1925], 1864-**1937**, mur., in marble frame, S.C.

Ref: *Burke's Peerage and Baronetage*, p.453.

Ch. built, 1843.

RYDE, All Saints.

I. Inscr. [Rt. Rev.] John Sutton Utterton, S.T.P., Bishop of Guildford [1874-1879], **1879**, maker's name H. OSBORNE ENG^R RYDE, mur., S.C. *II.* Inscr. on hexagonal-shaped pl. [Rt. Rev.] John Sutton Utterton, S.T.P., Bishop of Guildford [1874-1879], **1879**, C. *III.* Julia Sarah Mitchell, died at Putta Fort, Bombay, [India], **1882**, rect. pl., inscr. on base of stepped cross, maker's name JONES & WILLIS, mur., S.A. *IV.* Inscr. Joseph Wilfram Clerk, **1883**, maker's name GAWTHORP S^C LONDON, mur., N.A. *V.* Nellie Edith, eld. dau. of Nath[aniel] John Fenner, w. of H. Sweetman, "died after 10 days of extreme suffering", **1887**, aged 24, maker's name, Gaffin, Regent Street, London, rect. pl., canopy, cross, inscr., verse and sh., mur., S.A. *VI.* Inscr. with verse and sh. Edgar Ratcliffe, **1888**, maker's name JONES & WILLIS, mur., S.A. *VII.* Inscr. in Lat. [Rev.] Alexander Poole, M.A., ch. founder, vicar 1868-**1892**, maker's name H. OSBORNE ENG^R RYDE, mur., S.C. *VIII.* Inscr. Thomas White, solicitor for 35 years, **1897**, on screen, S.C. *IX.* Inscr. in raised letters. John Dudley Watkins, **1908**, maker's name H. OSBORNE ENG^R RYDE, mur., N.A. *X.* Inscr. Rev. Walter Hugh Earle Welby, M.A., [3rd son of Sir Glynne Earle Welby-Gregory, 3rd Bart., 1833-]**1912**, mur., S.A. *XI.* Inscr. Francis Harrison, **1921**, mur., on framed picture, N.A. *XII.* Inscr. Carol Patricia King, **1973**, mur., N.A. *XIII.* Inscr. Alice M. Webb, **1980**, mur., N.A.

Ref: *Burke's Peerage and Baronetage*, p.2780; *Haines*, II, p.238.

Ch. built, 1868-72.

RYDE, Holy Trinity.

I. Inscr. Catherine Elizabeth, widow of Rev. R.G. Richards, M.A., vicar of Hambledon, died at Ryde, **1870**, aged 80; also son, George John Richards, died at Buenos Aires, [Argentina], 1868, aged 37, mur., on board, N.A. *II.* Inscr. Capt. Robert Milligan, 2nd Life Guards, severely wounded at [the Battle of] Waterloo as a Lt. in the 11th Light Dragoons, 1875, aged 88; also w. Elizabeth Margaret, dau. of Matthew Baillie, M.D., **1876**, aged 82, mur., below window, S.A. *III.* Inscr. recording presentation [of lectern] in **1889** by niece, Mary, in mem. of Major-Gen. W. Nassau Lees, 1825-1889, on lectern, N. *IV.* Inscr. Augustus Alfred Waller, **1892**, aged 24, pos. by clergy and choristers, maker's name OSBORNE ENG RYDE, mur., on marble, N. *V.* Inscr. recording gift [of north aisle gates] by daus. in mem. of Emma Barry, **1899**, on gate, N.A. *VI.* Inscr. Cecil de Crespigny Pelham-Clay and w. Louisa Evelyne Selina Winton Northwick, engr. c.**1900**, mur., N. *VII.* Inscr. on sh.-shaped pl. recording erection of [north transept] window by widow in mem. of Capt. Aretas John Verlington Collins, R.N., **1901**, mur., N.Tr. *VIII.* Inscr. Louisa Frances Pilkington, **1901**, [aged 88], maker's name OSBORNE ENG^R RYDE, mur., on board, N.A. *IX.* Inscr. with 4 evang. symbols at corners in relief. Rev. Arthur John Wade, M.A., 1st vicar 1845-1893, "This church built under his care is his abiding monument", 1811-**1903**, mur., on board, C. *X*. Inscr. Anna Young, **1903**, on prie-dieu, C. *XI*. Inscr. on base of stepped cross. Samuel Witteuronge Clayton, 1803-1875, and w. Anna Maria, 1823-**1904**, [buried] in family vault at Brading, pos. by children, maker's name H. OSBORNE FECIT RYDE, mur., on board, S.A. *XII*. Cross surmounting inscr. Anna Frances Leeds, **1904**, mur., on marble, N. *XIII*. Inscr. Percy Richard Denny, **1907**, aged 40, pos. by choristers, maker's name OSBORNE ENG^R RYDE, mur., on board, N. *XIV*. Cross surmounting inscr. Maria Green, **1907**, maker's name *J. WIPPELL & C^O L^TD EXETER & LONDON*, mur., on cross-shaped board, N. *XV*. Inscr. Laura Kelly, **1907**, pos. by brother, Col. H.H. Kelly, maker's name H. OSBORNE FECIT RYDE, mur., N.A. *XVI*. Inscr. Lt. George Pilkington, R.N., [H.M. Submarine C.31], **1915**, maker's name H. OSBORNE FECIT RYDE, mur., on board, S.Tr. *XVII*. Inscr. with 4 evang. symbols at corners in relief. Emma Jane, dau. of Rev. Henry Breedon, M.A., rector of Pangbourne, Berks., widow of Rev. A[rthur] J[ohn] Wade, M.A., 1st vicar [1845-1893], worshipped in the ch. for 67 years, **1916**, aged 96, mur., on board, C. *XVIII*. Inscr. recording erection of tablet and presentation of silver communion service by congregation in mem. of James Batchelor, verger for 39 years, **1918**, aged 69, mur., on board, N. *XIX*. Inscr. Amy Delatree, widow of William Dumaresq Wright, **1921**, [aged 89], mur., on board, S.Tr. *XX*. Lt.-Cmdr. Paul Eddis, killed while in command of [H.M.] Submarine L.24 sunk by accident during manoeuvres, **1924**, rect. pl., submarine at sea in relief and inscr. in raised letters, mur., S.C. *XXI*. Inscr. Capt. John Crawford Davies, West Yorkshire Regt., died at Colombo, [Ceylon], **1927**, copper, mur., on board, N.A. *XXII*. Inscr. Major-Gen. Robert Murray, C.S.I., and w. Isabella Mary; also dau., Isabella Lucie, worshipped in the ch. 1884-**1927**, mur., on marble, S.C. *XXIII*. Inscr. Alfred Percy James, organist 1890-**1937**, mur., C. *XXIV*. Inscr. William Sylvester Hawkins, sidesman, **1940**, mur., S.C. *XXV*. Inscr. Harold Arthur Tarr, [church]warden 1979-**1986**, pos. by family, on display case, N.A.

Ch. built, 1845, 1848 and 1860.

RYDE, Isle of Wight Museum Service.

I. Richard Mewys, **1535**, in civil dress, inscr. (mutil.), 4 sons and 1 sh.; inscr. palimp., on rev. another inscr. to Richard Mewys, wasted work; from Kingston (q.v.). Accession no. IWCMS:2006.92.1-4. Eff. 462 x 121 mm, inscr. 50-81 x 349 mm, sons 155-159 x 100 mm, sh. 135 x 110 mm. Style: London G.

II. Inscr. on oval-shaped pl. Robert Bird Wilkins, **1809**, aged 55, and [1st] w. Mary, 1798, aged 32; also son, William, 1798, aged 2 years and 7 months; also [2nd] w. Elizabeth, dau. of Ja[me]s and Eliz[abeth] Sancroft, of Yarmouth, Norf., 1807, aged 42, maker's name *J. Wood Fecit*. Accession no. IWCMS:1995.LG55. *III*. Inscr. on sh.-shaped pl. Henry Lawson, **1822**, aged 73, and w. Mary, 1819, aged 70, pos. by Alex[ande]r Clarke. Accession no. IWCMS:2006.93. *IV*. Inscr. Thomas Cooke, 1792, aged 66; also Sarah, dau. of Thomas and Sarah Cooke, 1799, aged 19 months; Elizabeth Mercer, 1803, aged 25; Sarah, w. of Tho[ma]s Cooke, 1808, aged 25; Joseph Cooke, 1810, aged 23; and Sarah Cooke, **1833**, aged 74. Accession no. IWCMS:1995.LG57. *V*. Inscr. Thomas Cooke, 1835, aged 82, and Sarah Sparks, **1847**, aged 37. Accession no. IWCMS:1995.LG57.1. *VI*. Inscr. Thomas Sewell, of Newport, died at Oxford, 1842, and w. Jane Edwardes, died at Bonchurch, **1850**; also children, Ann Margaret Sewell, 1805; John George Sewell, 1822; and Thomas Sewell, 1826. Accession no. IWCMS:1999.LG53.

Ryde, Isle of Wight Museum Service *I*

Ryde, Isle of Wight Museum Service *I* palimpsest reverse

RYDE, St. James.

I. Inscr. Mrs. Mary E. Davis, **1918**, aged 82, on lectern, N.

Ch. built, 1827.

RYDE, St. Mary (R.C.).

I. Charlotte Elliot, **1861**, aged 75, rect. pl., lady, kng., under triple canopy with inscr., Lat. verse, inscribed scroll and 2 lozenges, [engr. by John Hardman & Cᵒ· Birmᵐ·], mur., on marble, N.A. Rect. pl. 830 x 455 mm. *II.* Inscr. Rev. John Telford, 1846-**1865**, mur., N.A. *III.* Inscr. Frederick de Courcy-May, benefactor of chapel, 1846-**1893**, mur., S.C. *IV.* Inscr. with crucifixion scene and scrolls. Laura Hamilton, worshipped in the ch. for 55 years, **1918**, mur., N. *V.* Inscr. Very Rev. Stephen Provost Morgan, D.D., priest 1911-**1943**, mur., N.A. *VI.* Inscr. Mrs. Mary Collyer, **1977**, mur., N.A. *VII.* Inscr. Brother Benedict Smith, **1989**, mur., N.

Ch. built, 1844-6.

RYDE, St. Thomas (redundant, now Heritage Centre and Museum).

I. Inscr. with sh. Edward Vernon, of Beldornie Tower, barrister-at-law, one of the 6 clerks of the High Court of Chancery, **1856**, aged 80, maker's name BRODERICK & CO SC; in 2005 loose. *II.* Inscr. John Turner, of Rye, Sussex, 1830, aged 42, buried in the churchyard, and widow, Elizabeth Styles, w. of James Woodrow, 1872, aged 83; also 2nd dau., Eliza, w. of Francis Carter for 35 years, **1878**, aged 57, [buried] with mother in Ryde Cemetery, maker's name H. OSBORNE RYDE, N. *III.* Inscr. Lena Houghton, **1983**, aged 86, on bench, Churchyard. *IV.* Inscr. Mrs. Maureen Sim, 1907-**1983**, on bench, Churchyard. *V.* Inscr. Mr. and Mrs. L.P. Rider, engr. c.**1985**, on bench, Churchyard. *VI.* Inscr. recording long service and work towards the ch. restoration in **2003** by Peter Snuddon, chairman of Isle of Wight Society Ryde Group, chairman and president of the Ryde Horticultural Society, on board on window splay, N.

Ch. built, 1827-8; declared redundant, 1977; converted, 2004.

RYDE, or SWANMORE, St. Michael and All Angels.

I. Inscr. Joshua Scholefield, **1864**, mur., below window, S.A. *II.* Inscr. [Ven.] Edward Wix, archdeacon of Newfoundland, 1802-**1866**, mur., below window, C. *III.* Inscr. recording erection of chancel in **1873** by Rosa C. Raine, of Haylands House, in mem. of [Rt. Rev.] Samuel Wilberforce, [D.D.], Bishop of Oxford [1845-1869], Bishop of Winchester [1869-1873, 1805-]1873, eff. of bishop in surplice with crosier, 2 shs. and marg. border with roundels at corners, mur., on marble, C. Eff. 542 x 192 mm, inscr. 90 x 425 mm, shs. 117 x 110 mm, marg. border 725 x 475 x 10 mm, roundels 20 mm dia. See also Alverstoke no.*VIII*, Alverstoke, or Gosport, Fort Brockhurst no.*XXXIII*, Hinton Ampner no.*IX*, Newport, St. Thomas the Apostle no.*IX*, Petersfield no.*VI* and Winchester Cathedral no.*X*. *IV.* Inscr. recording erection of [south aisle] window by friends in mem. of [Rev.] Richard Wilkins, assistant priest and superior of a ward of

To Gods hanour was erected by Rosa C Raine of Raylands House in this parish A·D·1873 to the Glory of God and in memory of Samuel Wilberforce for 24 years Lord Bishop of Oxford and after that for 4 years Lord Bishop of Winchester who died on the 19th day of July 1873 aged sixty—seven years

Ryde, or Swanmore *III*

REQUIESCAT IN PACE.
IN LOVING MEMORY OF
ARTHUR JOHN WHITE, B·SC· LOND·
BAPTISED AND CONFIRMED IN THIS CHURCH
AND A SERVER AT THE ALTAR.
WHO WAS DROWNED AT NIEUPORT BAINS, BELGIUM, WHILST SAVING
THE LIVES OF TWO BOY SCOUTS, ON AUGUST 3·1913 - AGED 23 YEARS -
"GREATER LOVE HATH NO MAN."
THIS TABLET WAS PLACED HERE BY HIS PARENTS AND FELLOW SCOUT MASTERS.

Ryde, or Swanmore *XIII*

479

the Confraternity of the Blessed Sacrament, **1874**, mur., S.A. *V.* Inscr. Sally Birkett, 1800-**1876**, mur., below window, C. *VI.* Inscr. "A BELOVED FATHER", **1879**, mur., N.A. *VII.* Inscr. Watson Cranston Duncan, 1826-**1881**, mur., S.A. *VIII.* Inscr. Fanny Wix, 1805-**1884**, mur., below window, C. *IX.* Inscr. Charlotte Rosa Raine, benefactress, **1894**, mur., on marble, N.A. *X.* Inscr. [Rev.] Stuart Clement Scholefield, M.A., son of no.*I*, [curate 1870-1875], died at Kamloops, B[ritish] C[olumbia, Canada], **1894**, aged 52, mur., S.A. *XI.* Inscr. Margaret Fowles, organist for 21 years and choir director 1878-1899, **1907**, maker's name H. OSBORNE ENG RYDE, mur., S.C. *XII.* Inscr. Geraldine Mary Buckley, **1912**, mur., N.A. *XIII.* Inscr. with verse on base of stepped cross and 2 separate shs. Arthur John White, B.Sc.(Lond.), baptised and confirmed in the ch., server, "DROWNED AT NIEUPORT BAINS, BELGIUM, WHILST SAVING THE LIVES OF TWO BOY SCOUTS", [1890-]**1913**, pos. by parents and scout masters, maker's name H. OSBORNE FECIT RYDE, mur., on marble, N.A. Cross and inscr. 942 x 458 mm, shs. 132 x 102 mm. *XIV.* Inscr. recording rebuilding of organ in **1913** in 50th year of ch. consecration; [Rev.] W[illiam] F[rederick] J[ames] Hanbury, M.A., vicar [1889-1923]; F.P. Mellish and C. Richards, churchwardens, maker's name H. OSBORNE ENG RYDE, mur., N.C. *XV.* Inscr. Geoffrey Nelthorpe Simeon, Imperial Forest Service, died at Calcutta, [India], 1888-**1923**, maker's name F. OSBORNE & CO LTD · London, mur., N.C. *XVI.* Inscr. recording dedication of rood in **1930** in mem. of Eleanor Maud Barry, 1929, and Agnes Mary Ferguson, 1929, mur., N. *XVII.* Inscr. Isabella Georgiana Camilla Clifford, 1895, and Augusta Susan Caroline Clifford, **1931**, worshipped in the ch., benefactresses, mur., N.C. *XVIII.* Inscr. Charles Bernard Hair, organist for 40 years, **1940**, maker's name F. OSBORNE & CO LTD LONDON W.C.1., on organ, N.C. *XIX.* Inscr. George Richards, churchwarden for 53 years, engr. c.**1980**, on pew, N.

Ch. built, 1861-3 and 1874.

ST. HELENS, St. Helen (new church).

I. Inscr. Lt. Stanley Winther Caws, R.A.F., [10th Sqdn. 1st Wing], only son of Douglas Caws [and w. Harriet, of The Lodge, Sea View Bay], grandson of Silas Harvey Caws, served throughout the Boer War, "ATTACKED BY THREE GERMAN PLANES, ONE OF WHICH HE SHOT DOWN", killed in action "AT A HEIGHT OF ELEVEN THOUSAND FEET" in France, **1915**, aged 36, mur., on board, S.Tr. *II.* Inscr. with Lat. verse and regt. insignia on sh.-shaped pl. [Pte.] Cyril C[harles] A[rnold] (Dick) Way, [16991], 2nd Regt. South African Infantry, only son of Sydney Way and [w.] Marita, served with S[outh] A[frican] M[ounted] R[iflemen] through the rebellion and German West African Campaign, killed in action in France, **1918**, aged 25, mur., on board, S.Tr. *III.* Inscr. Emily Sarah Savage, chorister for 30 years, **1924**, mur., N. *IV.* Inscr. Frederick Thomas Smith and [w.] Doris, **1972**, on door, N.

Ch. built, 1831 and 1862.

ST. HELENS, or SEAVIEW, St. Peter.

I. Inscr. recording dedication of ch. in **1859**, maker's name H. OSBORNE ENG^R RYDE, mur., N. *II.* Inscr. recording erection of screen in **1909** by 3 children in mem. of Frederick John Dawson, mur., C. *III.* Inscr. recording erection [of choir stalls] in **1909** by w. and children in mem. of

Harry Loraine Paterson, mur., C. *IV.* Inscr. Frank Godfrey, L.R.C.P., 1912; Frank Dennistoun Godfrey, L.R.C.P., **1916**; and Tom Godfrey, L.D.S., 1914, husband and sons of Eleanor Godfrey, maker's name H. OSBORNE ENG[R] RYDE, mur., N. *V.* Inscr. Lt. Norman Augustus Manders Ring, 3rd [Battn. attd. 2nd Battn.] Royal Warwickshire Regt. (Initial Reserve), of Buenos Aires, [Argentina, son of Augustus Richard Ring and w. Katharine, of Pandora Lodge], wounded at Neuve Chapelle in 1915 and killed at Boulecourt, France, **1917**, aged 27, [pos. by parents], maker's name H. OSBORNE FECIT RYDE, mur., in wooden frame, N.A. *VI.* Inscr. Mildred Winifred Grant-Davie, **1918**, aged 7, mur., N. *VII.* Inscr. Harold Gascoigne Nutt, 1918, and w. Florence May, **1921**, mur., S.C. *VIII.* Inscr. recording erection of [south] aisle in **1921** by public subscription as World War I memorial; [Rev. Thomas Sterling] O'Reilly, [A.K.C.], vicar [1914-1925]; S. Watson and T. Lander, churchwardens, mur., S.A. *IX.* Inscr. Col. Edward John Holloway, **1939**, mur., N.A. *X.* Inscr. recording gift of table in **1940** by parents in mem. of Charles Brading, lost in H.M.S. Oak, 1939, on table, S.A.

Ch. built, 1859.

ST. LAWRENCE, St. Lawrence (new church).

I. Inscr. Frances Malden, **1884**, aged 84, on lectern, N. *II.* Inscr. Rev. Clifford Malden, M.A., rector for 21 years [1865-1886], "IT WAS CHIEFLY OWING TO HIS EXERTIONS THAT THE NEW CHURCH AND PARSONAGE WERE ERECTED", **1886**, aged 53, mur., on marble, C. *III.* Inscr. Deborah Durrant, servant of Mr. and Mrs. W.E. Kilburn for 33 years, **1887**, mur., on marble, N.A. *IV.* Inscr. Hon. Evelyn Cornwallis Anderson-Pelham, J.P., D.L., [2nd son of Charles Anderson Worsley Anderson-Pelham, 2nd Earl of Yarborough], 1851-**1908**, mur., on marble, N. *V.* Inscr. Harriett Frances, [yst. dau. of Rev. George Hutton, w. of Hon. Evelyn Cornwallis] Anderson-Pelham, 1848-**1913**, copper, mur., on marble, N. *VI.* Inscr. Agnes [Elizabeth], Lady Cayzer, [dau. of William Trickey, w. of Sir Charles (William) Cayzer, 1st Bart., J.P.], **1919**, pos. by friends and parishioners, mur., on marble, N.A. *VII.* Inscr. Stephen Herbert Twining, churchwarden 1946-**1967**, mur., C. *VIII.* Inscr. recording gift [of flowerstand] in **1969** by Doreen Alldred in mem. of mother, Rose English, on flowerstand, C. *IX.* Inscr. recording installation of [nave] window by family in mem. of Donald Mills, 1904-**1972**; in 2005 loose on board in N. *X.* Inscr. Norman John Russell, 1954, and w. Winifred Emily, **1972**, Churchyard. *XI.* Inscr. recording gift of illuminated panel by family in mem. of Albert Edward Payne, 1890-1971, chorister and [par.] councillor, and Eva Elizabeth Ross, 1879-**1973**, mur., on panel, N.A. *XII.* Inscr. Col. W.M. Mackenzie, churchwarden 1965-**1975**, on bookcase, N.

Ref: *Burke's Peerage and Baronetage*, p.514, p.2893.

Ch. built, 1878.

SANDOWN, (see BRADING).

SEAVIEW, (see ST. HELENS).

SHALFLEET, St. Michael the Archangel.

I. Inscr. Rev. Thomas Cottle, M.A., vicar 1849-**1868**; also w. Louisa Georgina, maker's name
A & N AUX C.S.L. LONDON, mur., N. *II.* Inscr. Anne Pennethorne, 1883; also brother, John
Pennethorne, **1888**, mur., C. *III.* Inscr. Lt. Alistair [Thomas James] Kindersley, R.N., [808th
Sqdn.] Fleet Air Arm, of Hamstead [Grange, yst. son of Lt.-Col. A.O.L. Kindersley, C.M.G.,
D.L., and w. Edith Mary], mentioned in despatches for distinguished service, killed in action
[defending the Malta Convoy against an enemy air attack] while serving in H.M.S. Ark Royal,
[1915-]**1941**, mur., on board, C. *IV.* Inscr. recording presentation of sanctuary lamp, wafer box
and pyx by parents, [Col. T.C. Cunningham, D.S.O. and Mrs. H.J. Cunningham], sister and
brother in mem. of Lt. David Crofton Cunningham, R.N., lost in the mining of H.M.S. Neptune,
1913-**1941**, mur., on board, C. *V.* Inscr. recording presentation of flag (flown over the Allied
H.Q. at Constanza, Rumania during the British occupation in **1949**) by Lt.-Col. A.O.L.
Kindersley, C.M.G., D.L., of Hamstead [Grange], mur., on board, C. *VI.* Inscr. Prof. John
Osborne, 1911-**1984**, on screen, N.

SHANKLIN, St. Blasius (new church).

I. Inscr. Rev. Richard Walton White, rector of Wotton and Upcerne, Dorset, 1854, and w. Mary,
only surviving child of John Popham, **1856**, mur., C. *II.* Inscr. Gen. Sir William Greenshields
Power, K.C.B., K.H., commandant of 10th Battn. Royal Artillery, **1863**, [buried] in family vault at
Kensal Green Cemetery, [Middx.], maker's name HART & SON, LONDON, mur., N.Tr. *III.* Inscr.
George Payne, chief boatman in coastguards, died at Wadi Halfa on the Nile, **1870**, aged 58, mur.,
S.Tr. *IV.* Inscr. Frances Sarah Unwin, **1875**, maker's name COX & SONS, LONDON, mur., N. *V.*
Inscr. recording erection of [north transept] window in **1881** by inhabitants in mem. of Rev. George
Wrenford Southouse, [M.A., vicar] for 27 years [1854-1881], and w. Isabella; also sister, Frances,
mur., N.Tr. *VI.* Inscr. recording erection of [north transept] window by w. Margaret in mem. of
Francis White-Popham, [J.P., D.L., M.A., lord of the manor, patron of the benefice], only son of
Rev. Richard Walton White, and w. Mary, only surviving child of John Popham, **1894**, mur., N.Tr.
See also Wootton no.*III* & *VII*. *VII.* Inscr. Mary Popham Macpherson, w. of Col. John Cameron
Macpherson, 42nd (Royal Highland) [Regt. of Foot], 1899; Grace White, 1901; and Catherine
White, 1911, sisters of Francis White-Popham, [J.P., D.L., M.A., lord of the manor, patron of the
benefice], pos. in **1913** by w. Margaret, maker's name A & N AUX C.S.L. LONDON, mur., C.
VIII. Inscr. recording gift of panelling and pavement in **1914** by friends and parishioners in mem. of
Rev. William Barry Cole, B.A., rector for 32 years [1881-1913], 1913, [aged 83], mur., C.
IX. Inscr. with verse and regt. insignia. Capt. Henry Neville Le Marchant, 2nd [Battn.] Dorset[shire]
Regt., only child of Major A. Le Marchant, Dorsetshire Regt., killed in action in the Dardenells
"WHILST MOST GALLANTLY LEADING HIS MEN", **1915**, aged 33, pos. by mother, maker's name
G MAILE & SON. 367, EUSTON R^D *LONDON*, mur., N.Tr. *X.* Inscr. [Rev.] William Barry Cole, B.A.,
rector for 32 years [1881-1913], 1913, aged 83, and w. Henrietta Mary Jane, [**1916**], pos. by
children, mur., C. *XI.* Inscr. Capt. George Self, 1st rector's [church]warden 1912-**1920**, mur., S.Tr.
XII. Inscr. Edmond John Hunt, **1923**, and w. Amy, only dau. of Rev. W[illiam] B[arry] Cole, 1920,
maker's name MANNELL & C^O BOURNEMOUTH, mur., N.Tr. *XIII.* Inscr. Capt. Duncas
Macpherson, R.N., 1920, and w. Edith Julia, **1923**, pos. by 4 children, mur., C. *XIV.* Inscr. [Rev.]
Charles Butler, M.A., [of Orchardcroft, licensed preacher for the diocese of Winchester
1902-1926], **1929**, mur., S.Tr. *XV.* Inscr. James Adam Vestch, [church]warden 1920-1930, **1930**,
on pew, N.Tr. *XVI.* Inscr. William Brown [church]warden 1928-**1956**, on pew, S.Tr. *XVII.* Inscr.

Herbert Dagwell, 1903-**1971**, on table, S.Tr. *XVIII*. Inscr. George Frederick Harrison, 1898-**1971**, on hymn board, S.Tr. *XIX*. Inscr. Maud Heskey, 1883-**1972**, on bookstall, S.Tr. *XX*. Inscr. John Godsell Lusty, solicitor, benefactor, 1904-**1983**, mur., N. *XXI*. Inscr. recording refurbishment of [clergy stall], chairs and "surrounding area" in **1986** by friends in mem. of John Godsell Lusty, 1904-1983, mur., N. *XXII*. Inscr. Francis Cameron Macpherson, of Cluny, 1966, and w. Anna Elsa, **1992**, mur., C. *XXIII*. Inscr. Kenneth Heseltine, **n.d.**, on flowerstand, C.

Ch. built, 1859.

SHANKLIN, St. Paul.

I. Inscr. John W. Grare, M.A.(Oxon.), aged 55, pos. in **1876** by G.J. Karney, [Rev.] G[eorge] W[renford] Southouse, M.A., [vicar of Shanklin, St. Blasius 1854-1881], C.I. Burland and W.B. Cole, maker's name COX & SONS LONDON, mur., C. *II*. Inscr. Pte. Arthur George Harding, R[oyal] M[arine] L[ight] I[nfantry], died at sea on board H.M.S. Crescent, **1911**, pos. by shipmates, mur., S.A. *III*. Inscr. Rev. William Pettitt, M.A., vicar 1877-1907 during the building of ch., vicarage and par. hall, pos. by son, Harold, **1927**, maker's name F. OSBORNE & CO LTD London, mur., C. *IV*. Inscr. recording donation of sounding board by William Heath, **1930**, aged 76, mur., N.A. *V*. Inscr. Violet Helen Loosemoore, par. secretary 1957-**1961**, on bookstall, N.

Ch. built, 1875-6.

SHANKLIN, St. Saviour.

I. Inscr. recording presentation of east window by parents in mem. of John Peel, M.A., **1874**, and erection of reredos in mem. of Robert Smith, M.R.V.S., of Royal Sandown, mur., C. *II*. Inscr. Thomas Pridgin Teale, F.R.S., of Leeds, 1867, engr. c.**1875**, on font, S.A. *III*. Inscr. on circular-shaped pl. recording gift of font and altar rails by Frances A. Teale in mem. of Thomas Pridgin Teale, F.R.S., of Leeds, [1867]; Caroline Teale; and Charlotte Frances Teale, relatives of [Rev. Charles Isherwood Bowland, M.A.], 1st vicar [1869-1898], engr. c.**1875**, mur., C. *IV*. Inscr. recording gift of organ front in **1877** by Julia D. Scaramanga, mur., N.A. *V*. Inscr. Major Francis Henry Athererley, Rifle Brigade, of Landguard Manor, Col. of 5th (Isle of Wight, Princess Beatrice's) Volunteer Battn. Hampshire Regt., **1897**, pos. by widow, maker's name SINGER & SONS FROME & LONDON, mur., C. *VI*. Inscr. [Rev.] Charles Isherwood Bowland, M.A., of Lincoln Coll., Oxford, 1st vicar [1869-1898], **1898**, mur., C. *VII*. Inscr. recording dedication of [chancel] window by friends and parishioners in mem. of [Rev.] Charles Isherwood Bowland, M.A., of Lincoln Coll., Oxford, 1st vicar [1869-1898], **1898**, mur., C. *VIII*. Inscr. recording dedication [of prie-dieu] by w. and children in mem. of Charles Barton, **1900**, on prie-dieu, N.A. *IX*. Inscr. with verse on sh.-shaped pl. Henry Charles [Lumsden], 3rd son of Henry Lumsden, of Pitcaple, Aberdeenshire, [killed] in action as a volunteer in Lumsden's Horse at Thaba Nchu, South Africa, **1900**, aged 26, pos. by brothers and sisters, mur., C. *X*. Inscr. recording pulpit carved by Editha Chicheley Plowden and gift by Helen Molony in mem. of sister, Catherine Wheler, **1900**, on pulpit, N. *XI*. Inscr. F.H.A., 1897, pos. in **1901** by I.A. and A.H.A., on font cover, S.A. *XII & XIII*. Two inscrs. F.H.A., [1897], pos. in **1902** by I.A. and A.H.A., on stalls, S.A. *XIV*. Inscr. Alan Charles Stow, **1912**, pos. by family and friends, maker's name SINGERS, FROME, mur., C. *XV*. Inscr. with Lat. verse. Major Edward Algernon Cleader Blake, 2nd Battn.

Durham Light Infantry, yst. son of Edward Frederick Blake and [w.] Agnes, killed in action at Ennetieres, France, **1914**, aged 43, maker's name HART SON PEARD & C⁰ L⁰, mur., on board, N.A. *XVI.* Inscr. with verse. Lt.-Col. Mervyn Henry Nunn, [9th Battn.] Worcestershire Regt., [killed] at Chunuk Bair, Gallipolli, **1915**, [aged 50, buried at the Farm Cemetery, Anzac, Turkey], pos. by sister, [Ethel Mary Fryer], mur., C. *XVII.* Inscr. recording installation of electric light in mem. of Mary Margaret Veitch, **1915**, mur., N. *XVIII.* Inscr. Charles Bowland, M.D., eld. son of [Rev. Charles Isherwood Bowland, M.A.,] 1st vicar [1869-1898], **1924**, maker's name CULN GAWTHORP & SONS Lᵀᴰ·, LONDON, mur., N.A. *XIX.* Inscr. in raised letters recording gift of electric organ blower in **1929** by Ethel Mary Fryer and Charles Fryer, mur., C. *XX.* Inscr. recording gift of [north aisle] window in **1969** by Miss K.E.M. Kent in mem. of parents, mur., N.A. *XXI.* Inscr. recording restoration [of bell] in mem. of Rev. Clifford Target, priest 1980-**1986**, on bell, N.A. *XXII.* Inscr. Frances Mary Crane, **1987**, on piano, N.A.

Ch. built, 1869-87.

SHORWELL, St. Peter.

I. Richard Bethell, vicar, **1518**, in surplice with scarf, inscr., rel., C. *Brettell*, 1st edn., p.161, 2nd edn., between pp.76-7 (after Tomkins); *Brit. Lib. Add. MS. 39987,* f.49r; *Haines*, p.78 (drg. of head); *M.B.S. Trans.*, XIII, p.562; *Mee, Hampshire*, p.219 (drg. of head); *Staines*, p.9; *Stone*, II, pl.108. Eff. 516 x 148 mm, inscr. 127 x 475 mm, Unio Purbeck slab 1270 x 985 mm, approp. for John Godsall, vicar, 1732, aged 82. Style: London G.

II. Mrs. Elizabeth Bampfield, 1615, "Yᴱ MOTHER OF 15 HOPFULL CHILDREN", 10 sons and 5 daus., and Mrs. Gertrude Percevall "WHO DIED CHILDLES", **1619**, both ws. to Barnabas Leigh, esq., who pos., rect. pl. with devices, inscr. and 12 Eng. vv., curious; 2 shs. lost; mur., in Purbeck frame, covered by perspex, N.C. *Staines*, p.8; *Stone*, II, pl.107. Rect. pl. 600 x 770 mm, sh. indents 125 x 105 mm, Unio Purbeck frame 950 x 810 mm. Style: London.

III. Inscr. with 10 Eng. vv. and 2 shs. Elizabeth, dau. of Francis Helton, of Portsmouth, w. of Edward Leigh, **1621**, and her 2 sons, John, Tho[mas]; formerly mur., C., now mur., in stone frame, S.C. Inscr. 440 x 480 mm.

IV. Inscr. recording return of bible to the ch. after more than 100 years in **1891** by children, S.A. Bertram, J.D. J[olliffe], H.G. J[olliffe] and W.J. J[olliffe], in mem. of Elizabeth Mary Jolliffe, of Yafford House, on display case, S.C. *V.* Inscr. on triangular-shaped pl. recording gift [of picture] in **1899** by mother in mem. of Robert Thomas Disney Leith, died at Umballa, [India], 1898, mur., on picture, S.C. *VI.* Inscr. Frank Stileman Bostock, **1900**, pos. by C. B[ostock] and B.E. B[ostock], on prie-dieu, N.C. *VII.* Inscr. recording gift of organ by Hubert Garle, engr. c.**1900**, on organ, N.A. *VIII.* Inscr. recording gift of table by dau., Elizabeth Charlotte [Leith], in mem. of Mary Charlotte Julia Leith, [dau. and h. of Sir Henry Percy Gordon, 2nd Bart., w. of Gen. Robert William Disney Leith, C.B.], **1926**, on table, S.C. *IX.* Inscr. recording dedication of sanctuary lamp in **1929** by daus., Mary [Levina Leith], Maria [Alice, w. of Capt. Maynard Francis Colchester Wemyss, K.B.E., J.P., D.L.] and Edith, [w. of Lt.-Col. Sir Thomas Algernon Earle, 4th Bart., T.D.], in mem. of Mary Charlotte Julia Leith, [1926], mur., C. *X.* Inscr. recording gift of chancel and north aisle lighting by w. Edith, [3rd dau. of Gen. Robert William Disney Leith, C.B.], in mem. of Lt.-Col.

Of yo[ur] charite pray for the soule of S[ir] Richard
Bethell late vicar of this Churche of Shorwell
p[er] whiche decessed the xxviij day of Marche the
yer of o[ur] lord M.b.c. xbviij on whose soule Ihu haue m[er]cy

Shorwell I

TO THE REMEMBRANCE OF THE TWO MOST WORTHIE AND RELIGIOVS GENTLEWEOMEN
HIS LATE DEARE & LOYALL WIVES Mr ELIZABETH BAMPFIELD WHO DIED THE VII OF
MARCH 1615 HAVING BIN Ye MOTHER OF 15 HOPEFVLL CHILDREN AND Mrs GARTRVDE PER=
CEVALL WHO DIED CHILDLES THE XXII OF DECEMB. 1619. WAS THIS MONVMENT CONSE=
CRATED BY THEIR LOVING & SORROWFVLL HVSBAND BARNABAS LEIGH ESQ{r}

Since neither penne, nor pencill can set forth Of these two matchles wiues the matchles worth
Ware forct to couer in this silent tombe The praises of a chast and fruitfull wombe,
And with death's sable vaile in darknes hide The ritch rare virtues of a barren bride,
Sweet saintlike paire of Soule, whome did shine Such modells of perfection faminine.
Such Pietie, loue zeale. That though we sinners their liues haue lost, yet still y{em}selues are winners
For they secure heauens happines inherit, Whilst we lament their losse, admire their merit.

Shorwell II

ELIZABETH LEIGH DAVGHTER OF
FRANCIS HELTON OF PORTESMOVH,
GENT HAVING BIN 10 YEARES Ye MOST
LOVING & VERTVOVS WIFE OF ED=
WARD LEIGH OF SHORWELL GENT DEPTED THIS
LIFE Ye FIRST OF IVLY 1621 & TOGETHER W{th} HER TWO
SONNES IOHN & THO LEIGH LYETH HERE INTERRED.

IN CHRIST'S TRVE FAITH AND FEARE TO LIVE & DIE
DIRECTLIE LEADS TO IMMORTALITIE,
GLADS SAINTS AND ANGELLS GREIVES O{r} FOES INFERNAL
CONQVERS THE WORLD & WINS A CROWNE ETERNALL
THY LATE EXPERIENCE DEARE Elizabeth)
WHEN DYING THOV DIDST TRIVMPH OVER DEATH
AND WITH SOLE FAITH AND INNOCENCIE ARMED
NIMBLIE ESCAPE HIS BLOODIE HANDS VNHARMED
PROVES THIS MOST TRVE NOW LIVST THOV W{the} Ye BEST
AND LEAVST NOVGHT HERE IMPRISNED BVT THY DVST.

Shorwell III

486

[Sir] Thomas Algernon Earle, 4th Bart., T.D., of Allerton, Lancs., 1860-**1945**, mur., on pillar, N.C. *XI.* Inscr. recording gift of nave and south aisle lighting by husband, Ernest Edwin Carver, in mem. of [w.] Frances Emma, engr. c.**1950**, mur., on pillar, S.C. *XII.* Inscr. Elizabeth Winifred Stragnell, **1954**, on stall, N.A. *XIII.* Inscr. recording restoration of window mullions in mem. of [Rev.] Walter Ebenezer Grimes, vicar 1954-**1962**, mur., below window, S.A. *XIV.* Inscr. recording gift of lighting in side aisles by son, [Sir Hardman Alexander Mort Earle, 5th Bart., T.D.]; daus., [Rosemary and Myrtle Valentine, w. of Brig. Maurice Robert Lonsdale, D.S.O., O.B.E.]; and niece, M[ildred] K[atherine] L[eith], in mem. of Edith, [3rd] dau. of Gen. [Robert William] Disney Leith, [C.B. and w. Mary Charlotte Julia, dau. and h. of Sir Henry Percy Gordon, 2nd Bart.], w. of [Lt.-Col.] Sir [Thomas] Algernon Earle, [4th] Bart., [T.D.], 1871-**1963**, mur., on pillar, N.C. *XV.* Inscr. recording gift of clock in mem. of Rev. Archibald Hamlyn Wakefield, M.A., ordained 1917, vicar of Shorwell and rector of Kingston 1962-1972, 1892-**1972**, mur., Tower. *XVI.* Inscr. Eric James Harrison, churchwarden, **1978**, aged 81, mur., Tower. *XVII.* Inscr. Albert Deacon, 1916-**1990**, on lamp standard, Churchyard. *XVIII.* Inscr. Elizabeth (Bessie) Ellen Saunders, **1991**, pos. by family, friends and villagers, on lamp standard, Churchyard.

INDENTS & LOST BRASSES. 19. Indent, ?lozenge, rivets and plugs only, effaced, S.C. Purbeck slab 1730 x 740 mm.

Ref: *Brasses as Art and History*, p.166; *Brettell*, 2nd edn., p.120; *Brit. Lib. Add. MS. 39987,* f.49; *Burke's Peerage and Baronetage*, p.413, p.894; *Haines*, II, p.76; *Hants Proc.*, II, pp.231-2; *Heseltine, Heraldry*, p.38; *Jeans*, p.49; *Manning*, p.31; *M.B.S. Bulletin*, 66, p.115, 81, p.433; *M.B.S. Trans.*, II, pp.5-6, VII, p.265, XVI, p.168; *Mee, Hampshire*, p.477; *M.S.*, p.171, p.755; *Norris, Memorials*, p.168; *Pevsner, Hampshire*, p.770; *Simpson*, p.28; *Staines*, p.6; *Stone*, II, p.59; *Tomkins*, II, p.77; *V.C.H., Hampshire*, V, p.283.

SWANMORE, (see RYDE).

THORLEY, St. Swithun (old church, redundant, now a ruin).

I. Inscr. with 6 Eng. vv. and 1 sh. (another sh., now in private poss. of M.S. Urry). Thomas Urry, gent., **1631**, pos. by w. Jane, dau. of Thomas Day, S.Porch/Tower. Inscr. 395 x 545 mm, dext. sh. indent 205 x 195 mm, sin. sh. 207 x 175 mm, slab 2030 x 1025 mm.

THORLEY, St. Swithun (new church).

I. Inscr. recording gift of [nave] window by inhabitants in mem. of Capt. Reginald M. Scott Rogers, R.N., **1910**, mur., N. *II.* Inscr. Joseph Pead, **1924**, aged 82, mur., C. *III.* Inscr. Selina H.S. Pead, w. of no.*II*, **1924**, aged 81, mur., C. *IV.* Inscr. Mary Marshall, **1934**, mur., N.

Ch. built, 1871.

TOTLAND, (see FRESHWATER).

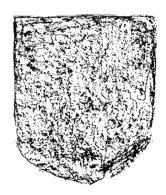

HERE LYETH THE BODY OF THOMAS
VRRY GENT WHO DEPARTED THIS
LIFE THE 25ᵗʰ DAY OF DECEMBER
ANNO DOMINI 1631.
MONVMENTVM HOC POSVERE IVNA IXOR EIVS AMANTISSIMA FILIA THOMÆ DAY
ARMIGERI FRATRIS GEORGII DAY Eᵢ CHICHESTRÆNSIS ETGVLIELMI DAY Eᵢ WINTONENS
ET THOMAS VRRY FILIVS IPSIS Ē DEFVNCTO HOC MA NATV MINIMVS

The Poore mans Comfort And ẏ Strangers Friend
A Man of godly life then Iudge his End
This Stone can tell, what Care he had to goe
Vnto his mother Earth And Fathers too
His Aged yeeres (Almoſt) were Twelue tymes Seuen
He's call'd to keepe his Christmas now in heauen

Thorley (old church) I

488

VENTNOR, (see NEWCHURCH).

WHIPPINGHAM, St. Mildred (new church).

I. Inscr. Charlotte Anby, dau. of John Stag, of Ackworth, Yorks., **1830**, aged 49, Churchyard. *II.* Inscr. Sarah Broster, of Chester, 1770-**1837**, Churchyard. *III.* Inscr. Mrs. Isabella Syme, of Millbrooke, **1840**, aged 85, Churchyard. *IV.* Inscr. Frances, w. of Rev. James Jolliffe, M.A., died at The Rectory, Stoke Charity, 1837, aged 34, buried [at Stoke Charity]; also son, James [Joliffe], died at Queen's Coll., Oxford, **1844**, aged 21, [buried at Stoke Charity], Churchyard. See also Barton Stacey no.*I.* *V.* Inscr. John Broster, F.A.S.E., [inventor] of system for removal of speech impediments at Edinburgh c.1823, 1769-**1852**, Churchyard. *VI.* Inscr. Thomas, son of [Rev.] Thomas Pittis, rector of Gatcombe, 1665, aged 11 weeks; also Henry Tomlinson, 1674, aged 63, engr **1855**, mur., C. *VII.* Inscr. John Man, benefactor to the poor of Arreton, Newport, Northwood and Whippingham, 1689, aged 56, engr **1855**, mur., C. *VIII.* Inscr. [Rev.] Benedict Ball, rector, 1713, aged 39; also eld. dau., Penelope, aged 31, and her 2 infant sons, engr **1855**, mur., C. *IX.* Inscr. Robert Blackford, 1715, aged 42, and w. Anne, 1713, aged 42; also 2nd son, Marshall, 1716, aged 15, and son, Robert [Blackford], 1729, aged 30; brother, George [Blackford], 1722, aged 41; Robert, 2nd son of Bridges Blackford, 1732, aged 5 months; and Barrington Pope Blackford, 1783-1816, engr **1855**, mur., C. *X.* Inscr. recording internal ch. fittings (including font, seats, heating apparatus and organ) were provided by voluntary contributions from Queen Victoria, H.R.H. the Prince Consort [H.R.H. the Prince Albert, K.G., K.T., K.P.], Viscountess Gort, Admiral Sir George Seymour, Henry Auldjo, Mrs. Thomas Auldjo, Robert Bell, John Green, Robert S. Holford, Rev. George Prothero, [J.P., M.A., curate 1853-1857 and] rector [1857-1894], William George Shedden, Miss Agathas, Miss Octavia Shedden, the Misses Word and Mrs. James Word; opened in **1862**; T.R. Roach and J. Drake, [church]wardens, mur., Vestry. *XI.* Inscr. Rev. James Jolliffe, M.A., of Padmore, curate "WITH SOLE CHARGE" of Barton Stacey 1818-1836, and Stoke Charity 1836-1847, 1794-**1864**, Churchyard. See also Barton Stacey no.*I.* *XII.* Inscr. [Rev. Canon] George Prothero, [J.P., M.A.], of Brasenose Coll., Oxford, canon and sub-dean of Westminster, chaplain[-in-ordinary] to Queen Victoria [1866-1894], deputy-clerk of the Closet, curate 1853-1857 and rector 1857-1894, [England cricketer 1839, born at Newport, Monmouthshire, died at Whippingham], 1818-**1894**, and w. Emma, [only dau. of Rev. William] Money Kyrle, 1822-1893, pos. by children, maker's name BARKENTIN & KRALL LONDON, mur., S.Tr. *XIII.* Inscr. "Taken from the deck of H.M.S. Blonde when broken up" and cross with inscr. and ducal crown on separate pl. [H.R.H.] Prince Henry Maurice of Battenburg, K.G., [P.C.], died at sea of fever contracted during the Ashanti Expedition, [West Africa], 1858-**1896**, mur., Battenburg Chapel/N.C. of C. *XIV.* Inscr. in raised letters recording removal from St. George's Chapel, Windsor, of insignia (which hung above stall for 10½ years) of H.R.H. Prince Henry [Maurice] of Battenburg, K.G., [P.C., 1858-1896] and pos. in **1896** by [widow], H.R.H. Princess Henry of Battenberg, [1857-1944], mur., Battenburg Chapel/N.C. of C. *XV.* Inscr. recording gift [of lectern] in **1897** by Col. Lord Edward [William] Pelham-Clinton, [G.C.V.O., K.C.B., D.L., 2nd son of Henry Pelham-Clinton, 5th Duke of Newcastle-under-Lyme, K.G., M.P.] in mem. of H.R.H. Prince Henry [Maurice] of Battenburg, [K.G., P.C., died at sea of fever contracted during the Ashanti Expedition, West Africa, 1858-1896], on lectern, N. *XVI.* Inscr. Samuel Bird, of Calcutta, [India], died at Slatwoods, **1898**, aged 75, mur., N.Tr. *XVII.* Inscr. with regt. insignia. Major E.W. Harris, 63rd Palamcottah Light Infantry, **1905**, pos. by brother officers, maker's name A. & N. AUX C.S.L. LONDON, mur., N. *XVIII.* Inscr. recording presentation [of flag] in **1907** by Flag-Capt. Mark Kerr and officers of H.M.S. Drake to Rear-Admiral Prince Louis [Alexander] of Battenburg on promotion to acting Vice-Admiral, [later Admiral of the Fleet Louis Alexander Mountbatten, 1st Marquess of Milford Haven, G.C.B.,

G.C.V.O., K.C.M.G., P.C.], on flagpole, Battenburg Chapel/N.C. of C. *XIX.* Inscr. "Taken from the deck of H.M.Y. Alberta when broken up in **1912**" and cross with inscr. and ducal crown on separate pl. [H.R.H.] Prince Henry Maurice of Battenburg, K.G., [P.C.], died at sea of fever contracted during the Ashanti Expedition, [West Africa], 1858-1896, mur., Battenburg Chapel/N.C. of C. *XX.* Inscr. in raised letters. Ethel Kate Saunders, **1913**, Churchyard. *XXI.* Inscr. with regt. insignia. Capt. Graham Percival Shedden, 35th Heavy Battery, 2nd Division, R[oyal] G[arrison] A[rtillery], son of George Shedden and w. Alice, killed] at the 1st Battle of Ypres "AT THE CHATEAU OF HOOGE WHEN H.Q. WAS SHELLED", **1914**, aged 28, [buried at Ypres Town Cemetery, Belgium], bronze, mur., N.Tr. *XXII.* Inscr. Samuel Edgar Saunders, **1933**, with no.*XX*, Churchyard. *XXIII.* Inscr. in raised letters with separate propeller. John Lovel, **1936**, aged 57, Churchyard. *XXIV.* Inscr. with musical instruments on oval-shaped pl. James William Rogerson, organist for 22 years, **1937**, aged 73, maker's name OSBORNE ENG^R RYDE, mur., N. *XXV.* Inscr. Capt. George Louis Victor Henry Serge Mountbatten, R.N., 2nd Marquess of Milford Haven, [eld. son of Admiral of the Fleet Louis Alexander Mountbatten, 1st Marquess of Milford Haven, G.C.B., G.C.V.O., K.C.M.G., P.C.], 1892-**1938**, [designed by G. Cooper], mur., Battenburg Chapel/N.C. of C. *XXVI.* Inscr. Graham Eden Shedden, **1940**, aged 80, mur., N. *XXVII.* Inscr. Edward Claude Shedden, 1885-**1967**, mur., N.Tr. *XXVIII.* Inscr. Alice Elizabeth Julia Marie, Princess of Battenburg, Princess Andrew of Greece, [eld. dau. of Admiral of the Fleet Louis Alexander Mountbatten, 1st Marquess of Milford Haven, G.C.B., G.C.V.O., K.C.M.G., P.C.], 1885-**1969**, mur., Battenburg Chapel/N.C. of C. *XXIX.* Inscr. Eden Graham Shedden, 1901-**1977**, mur., N. *XXX.* Inscr. Hiram Wheeler, verger and guide, **1984**, Churchyard.

Nos.*VI-IX* are replacements for stone slabs lost during the demolition of the old ch. in 1854.

Ref: *Burke's Peerage and Baronetage*, p.1962.

Ch. built, 1854-5 and 1861-2.

WHITWELL, SS. Mary and Radegund.

I. Inscr. with verse. George King, 1770, and w. Hester, **1776**, on gravestone, Churchyard. *II.* Inscr. Anthony Edmunds, **1839**, aged 104, mur., N. *III.* Inscr. Capt. Sir Robert Oliver, Knt., R.N., C.-in-C. of Indian Navy, died of sunstroke at Bombay, [India], 1848, buried in Bombay Cathedral, and w. Rachel May, **1867**, mur., N. *IV.* Inscr. Alexander Fraser, son of Gen. Sir John Cheape, G.C.B., died in Paris, 1861, aged 7 months; also Harry, died in Edinburgh, **1872**, aged 15, maker's name JONES & WILLIS, mur., N. *V.* David Winter, 1863, schoolmaster and clerk, and w. Marion, **1875**, pos. by son, W.P. Winter, rect. pl., canopy and inscr., maker's name F. HOLT WARWICK, mur., N. *VI.* Inscr. recording dedication of [nave] window by sister, Elizabeth, in mem. of Rev. Robert Bennett Oliver, M.A., [curate 1862-1865 and] vicar for 39 years [1867-1906], **1912**, mur., N. *VII.* Inscr. John Hardley, 1872, and w. Elizabeth, 1875; also children, Elizabeth, 1829, aged 4; William Henry, 1831, aged 3; Mary Elizabeth, 1836, aged 2 months; Walter, 1844, aged 18; John Herbert [Hardley], 1851, aged 27; Edith, 1872, aged 43; Gillingham [Hardley], died in Australia, 1877, aged 45; Frederick [Hardley], 1890, aged 55; Emily, 1902, aged 81; Frances, 1911, aged 79; and Gertrude, widow of Cornelius Cole, **1913**, aged 85, on tomb, Churchyard. *VIII.* Inscr. in raised letters with sh. [2nd-]Lt. Gurth Stephen Morse, 34th Battery, 38th Brigade, 6th Division, R[oyal] F[ield] A[rtillery], son of Amyas Morse and w. Caroline Rose], died of wounds received in action at Bailleul, [France], **1914**, [aged 20, buried at Bailleul Communal Cemetery, France], on screen, N. *IX.* Inscr. in raised letters with sh.

Capt. Stephen Ussher, 129th D[uke of] C[onnaught's] O[wn] Baluchis, [son of Rev. Richard Ussher, curate of Ventnor 1883-1889 and Godshill 1889-1894, and w. Mary, of Westbury, Northants.], killed at Givenchy, [France], **1914**, [aged 32, buried at Beuvry Communal Cemetery, France], on screen, N. *X.* Inscr. in raised letters with sh. Capt. Beverley Ussher, [attd. as Staff Capt. to 88th Brigade, 29th Division], Leinster Regt., [son of Rev. Richard Ussher, curate of Ventnor 1883-1889 and Godshill 1889-1894, and w. Mary, of Westbury, Northants.], killed at Gallipoli, [Turkey], **1915**, [aged 35, buried at Twelve Tree Copse Cemetery, Turkey], on screen, N. *XI.* Inscr. in raised letters with sh. Lt. Fothergill Rex Elderton, Royal Warwickshire Regt., [3rd Battn. attd. 2nd Battn., son of Charles Robert Elderton and w. Clara Hunton], killed at Loos, [France], **1915**, [aged 23], mur., N. *XII.* Inscr. in raised letters with sh. Capt. Norman Elliott Howell, [attd. as Staff Capt. to 35th Infantry Brigade], 82nd Punjabis, [son of Leonard Sidgwick Howell], killed in Mesopotamia, **1916**, [aged 34], on screen, N. *XIII.* Inscr. [Rev.] John Cecil, vicar, **1937**, on crucifix, N. *XIV.* Inscr. Alice Emma Hendy, organist 1933-1974, **1986**, on organ, C.

WOOTTON, St. Edmund.

I. Inscr. Rev. Robert Hilton Scott, rector for 28 years [1855-1883], **1883**, aged 93, pos. by daus., maker's name OSBORNE ENG^R RYDE, mur., C. *II.* Inscr. recording that credence table was made and given in **1890** by William Please in mem. of 3 children who died in 1863, 1866 and 1869, on credence table, N. *III.* Inscr. recording gift [of altar] in **1890** by Francis White-Popham, [J.P., D.L., M.A., lord of the manor of Shanklin, patron of the benefice], on altar, N.Tr. See also Shanklin, St. Blasius no.*VI.* *IV.* Inscr. Mary Coleman, 1887, pos. in **1891** by only son, [Rev. Dr.] W[illiam] H[obday] Coleman, [M.A.], LL.D., rector [1884-1923], maker's name OSBORNE ENG^R RYDE, mur., C. *V.* Inscr. in Lat. recording [chancel] window pos. in **1892** by pupils in mem. of Rev. [Dr.] William Hobday Coleman, M.A., LL.D., rector [1884-1923], mur., C. *VI.* Inscr. recording erection of 4 lancet windows in **1894** by William Makant in mem. of [w.] Louise Florence, 1890, maker's name H. OSBORNE ENG^R RYDE, mur., C. *VII.* Inscr. recording erection of east window in **1894** by subscription in mem. of Francis White-Popham, J.P., D.L., M.A., lord of the manor of Shanklin, patron of the benefice, 1894, maker's name H. OSBORNE ENG^R RYDE, mur., C. See also Shanklin, St. Blasius no.*VI.* *VIII.* Inscr. recording restoration of chancel in **1904** by subscription in mem. of Rear-Admiral the Hon. Albert Denison Somerville Denison, [2nd son of Albert Denison Denison, 1st Baron Londesborough, K.C.H., F.R.S., F.S.A., 1835-]1903, and Capt. Osborne Samuel Delano-Osborne, 1902, churchwardens, maker's name OSBORNE ENG^R RYDE, mur., C. *IX.* Inscr. recording restoration of pulpit in **1905** by widow Caroline in mem. of Col. Minto, on pulpit, N. *X.* Inscr. Newton Hall White, **1912**, aged 41, mur., C. *XI.* Inscr. Eva Ruth, w. of Edwin L.C. de Renzi, **1969**, mur., N. *XII.* Inscr. recording that rood eff. was carved in **1975** by Jack Whitehead in mem. of Roy Marston Cartwright, diocesan reader, mur., C. *XIII.* Inscr. recording altar rails pos. in **1985** by Peter Meech and [w.] Joyce in mem. of Thomas Hother and [w.] Lillian; Roy Meech and [w.] Irene; and Sid and [w.] Fanny, on altar rail, N.Tr.

Ref: *Burke's Peerage and Baronetage*, p.1640.

WOOTTON, St. Mark.

I. Inscr. recording gift of chair and desk in mem. of Alfred J. Reynolds, **1909**, mur., C.

Ch. built, 1910.

WROXALL, (see NEWCHURCH).

YARMOUTH, St. James.

I. Inscr. with verse recording erection of east window in **1867** in mem. of William Rivington Blackburn, B.A., died at Bournemouth, 1861, and w. Elizabeth, died at Auckland, N[ew] Z[ealand], mur., on marble, C. *II.* Inscr. with verse. Rev. [Preb.] John Blackburn, M.A., prebendary of York [Cathedral], rector for 16 years during the building of school and rectory and ch. restoration, **1870**, mur., C. *III.* Inscr. with verse recording erection of reredos by children in mem. of Ann Rebecca Blake, **1872**, maker's name COX & SONS, LONDON, mur., C. *IV.* Inscr. with verse and regt. insignia. Major Claude Burrard Lewes Dashwood, [9th Battn.] Northumberland Fusiliers, 2nd son of Rev. Robert [Vere] Lewis Dashwood, [M.A.], of The Mount, and w. Edith Theresa, died of wounds received in action at Bailleul, France, **1916**, [buried at Bailleul Communal Cemetery Extension, France], pos. by w. and children, mur., S.A. *V.* Inscr. recording presentation in **1926** by Rev. Stanley Hassall Woodin, M.A., rector [1914-1945], in mem. of parents, Alfred Woodin and [w.] Annie, mur., C.

Ch. built, 1635 and 1831.

YAVERLAND, St. John the Baptist.

I. Inscr. C.F.B., **1831**, C. *II.* Inscr. on lozenge-shaped pl. Robert Sherson, **1842**, C. *III.* Inscr. on lozenge-shaped pl. John Sherson, **1855**, aged 16, C. *IV.* Inscr. with verse. Elizabeth Bell, w. of Rev. Lee, rector, 1875; also Lt. John East Lake Lee, 55th Regt. [of Foot], died at Aden, **1876**, maker's name GAWTHORP LONDON, mur., C. *V.* Inscr. Henry Martyn Dennett White, **1887**, mur., N.A. *VI.* Inscr. with verse recording gift of [nave] window at restoration by Edward Williams Snell, **1891**, mur., N. *VII.* Inscr. Emma Maria Oldershaw, **1896**, mur., below window, N. *VIII.* Inscr. Martin White, **1897**, maker's name OSBORNE ENG^R RYDE, mur., N. *IX.* Inscr. with verse. John Henry White, **1899**, churchwarden for 40 years, and w. Emma May, 1894, maker's name OSBORNE ENG^R RYDE, mur., N. *X.* Inscr. John Percy Loveland, J.P., and w. Harriet Hannah, engr. c.**1900**, mur., N.A. *XI.* Inscr. Major A.M. Cayley, R[oyal] G[arrison] A[rtillery], commanded the 32nd Co., died at Singapore, **1910**, mur., on marble, N. *XII.* Inscr. and verse on base of stepped cross. Rev. William Day French, M.A., [rector 1897-1907], **1910**, maker's name H. OSBORNE FECIT RYDE, mur., C. *XIII.* Inscr. with regt. insignia within border of oak leaves and acorns. 2nd-Lt. Wilfrid Gladstone Holmes, 34 Co. Royal Garrison Artillery, **1913**, aged 21, maker's name H. OSBORNE RYDE, mur., N. *XIV.* Inscr. J.D.E. Loveland, **1926**, on font cover, N. *XV.* Inscr. on lozenge-shaped pl. recording candlesticks and candelabra pos. in mem. of [Ven.] Christian William Hampton Weekes, [M.A.], rector 1908-1913 and 1921-**1948**, [archdeacon of Isle of Wight 1937-1948], C. *XVI.* Inscr. recording gift of 5 light chandelier by pupils and friends in mem. of Ellen Gordon Black, organist 1923-**1970**, mur., C.

The following church has been searched but no brasses have been found:

St. Lawrence (St. Lawrence, old church).

CHRONOLOGICAL LIST OF FIGURE BRASSES WITH STYLES OF ENGRAVING

c.1365	London A	Freshwater, All Saints I
c.1380	London B	Calbourne I
c.1430	London B	Arreton I
1518	London G	Shorwell I
1535	London G	Ryde, Isle of Wight Museum Service *I*
1615	London	Shorwell II
1652	London	Calbourne III

ISLE OF WIGHT INDEX

496

Savage, Emily, 480
Scaramanga, Julia, 483
Scholefield, Joshua, 477, 480; Stuart, 480
Scott, Edward, 450; Katherine, 465; Robert, 491
Sealy, Sir Charles, Hilda, Hugh, Nigel, 447
Seaman, Shadrack, 472
Seaview, see St. Helens
Self, George, 482
Sells, Euphemia, John, William, 471
Serle, George, 435, 439; William, 435, 437
Sevenoaks, Kent, 445
Sewell, Ann, 475; Elizabeth, 441(2); Ellen, Emma,
441; Jane, 468, 475; John, 475; Thomas, 468,
475(2); William, 440
Seymour, Sir George, 489
Shalfleet, 482, vicar of, 482
Shanklin, St. Blasius, 482-3, 491, rectors of, 482(2),
vicars of, 482, 483; St. Paul, 483, vicar of, 483; St.
Saviour, 483-4, priest, 484, vicars of, 483(3), 484
Shedden, Alice, 490; Caroline, 458; Eden, Edward,
490; George, 453, 490; Graham, 490(2);
Octavia, 453, 489; William, 458, 489
Sheen, East, Surrey, 435, 441
Shergold, George, 468, 469; Mary, 470
Sherson, John, Robert, 492
Sherwood, Lord, 447
Shorwell, 484-7, vicars of, 487(2)
Shrewsbury, Salop, 445
Sim, Maureen, 477
Simeon, Geoffrey, 480; Sir John, Marjorie,
Stephen, 459
Skinner, John, 470
Smith, Benedict, 477; Charles, 465(2); Doris,
Frederick, 480; George, 471; Maria, 465;
Robert, 483; Thomas, 453
Snell, Edward, 492
Sneyd, Welenhall, 465
Snuddon, Peter, 477
Somerville, Hilda, 452
Southampton, bishop of, 450
Southouse, Frances, 482; George, 482, 483;
Isabella, 482
Sparks, Sarah, 475
Speakman, Andrew, 446
Squibb, Elsie, 444; Ralph, 444(2)
Squire, Joshua, 455
St. Albans, Duke of, 446
St. Helens, 480
St. Helens, or Seaview, 480-1, vicar of, 481
St. Lawrence, new church, 481, rector of, 481; old
church, 492
Stag, Charlotte, John, 489
Stenbury, 460
Stephens, Annie, 459
Stevenson, Kenneth, 446
Stoke Charity, 435, 489, curate of, 489
Stoke, East, Notts., 472
Stone, Margaret, 447
Stooks, Cecil, 440
Storrs, William, 444
Stow, Alan, 483
Stradbroke, Earl of, 450
Stragnell, Elizabeth, 487
Strokestown, Ireland, 472, 473

Strood, Kent, 465
Styles, Elizabeth, 477
Sumners, Edgar, 444
Surrey, J.P. for, 472
Surtees, Eleanor, Robert, 453
Sutton, Gurney, Robert, Rose, 465
Swanmore, see Ryde
Sweetman, H., Nellie, 474
Swinburne, Charles, Edith, 440
Syme, Isabella, 489
Synnot, Robert, 446

Tabuteau, Claude, Elizabeth, Ethel, Helen, Kathleen,
Madeline, Molière, Reginald, Renée, Rupert,
Winifred, 438
Tankard, Mrs., 458
Tanner, Joseph, 465
Target, Clifford, 484
Tarr, Harold, 475
Taylor, A., 460; Eleanor, 458; F., 460; Sir Henry, 458;
J., 453; Robert, 455
Teale, Caroline, Charlotte, Frances, 483;
Thomas, 483(2)
Telford, John, 477
Tennyson, Lord Alfred, 458(2)
Terrell, Thomas, 447
Thacker, Samuel, 459
Theobald's Park, Herts., 464
Thomas, Claud, 438(2); Edwyn, 471; William, 444
Thorley, old church, 487-8; new church, 487
Thunderer, H.M.S., 459
Titchfield, 454
Tomlinson, Henry, 489
Torquay, Devon, 467
Totland, see Freshwater
Towle, Charles, Eleanor, 458
Townsend, Kathleen, 472
Trickey, Agnes, William, 481
Trinder, Raymond, 444
Trotter, Agnes, Robert, 444
Trower, Gerard, 452
Tucker, Winifred, 467
Tuckwell, E., James, 473
Tudor, Elizabeth, George, 453
Tugwell, Lewen, 447
Tull, Caroline, 467; Fanny, 467(2)
Turner, Eliza, Elizabeth, John, 477
Turvey, Beds., rector of, 442
Tutle, Frank, 473
Tuttrell, H., 466
Twining, Stephen, 481

Unwin, Frances, 482
Upcerne, Dorset, rector of, 482
Upton, Alice, Richard, 460
Urry, Jane, 460, 461, 487, 488; Katherine, 460, 461;
M., 487; Penelope, 460, 461; Thomas, 460(3),
461(3), 487, 488
Ussher, Beverley, 491; Mary, 491(2); Richard, 491(2);
Stephen, 491
Utterton, John, 474(2)

Vallings, Alan, Gertrude, 452; Henry, 452(2);
Marie, 452